SCENE DESIGN AND STAGE LIGHTING

W. Oren Parker
Carnegie-Mellon University

Harvey K. Smith
Yale University

R. Craig Wolf

Holt, Rinehart and Winston, Inc.

New York   Chicago   San Francisco   Philadelphia
Montreal   Toronto   London   Sydney
Tokyo

SCENE DESIGN AND STAGE LIGHTING

Fifth Edition

Publisher **Susan Katz**
Acquisition Editor **Anne Boynton-Trigg**
Senior Project Editor **H.L. Kirk**
Art Director **Gloria Gentile**
Production Manager **Nancy J. Myers**
Interior Design **Arthur Ritter, Inc.**
Cover Design **Gloria Gentile**

Library of Congress Cataloging in Publication Data

Parker, W. Oren (Wilford Oren)
  Scene design and stage lighting.

  Bibliography: p. 581
  Includes index.
  1. Theaters—Stage-setting and scenery.   2. Stage lighting.
I. Smith, Harvey K. (Harvey Kennedy) II. Wolf, R. Craig.   III. Title.
PN2091.S8P3   1985   792.025   84-10927

ISBN 0-03-064248-5

89012   032   9 8 7 6 5 4 3 2

  Holt, Rinehart and Winston, Inc.
  The Dryden Press
  Saunders College Publishing

Composition by Waldman Graphics, Inc., Pennsauken, NJ
Color separations by Lehigh Press Lithographers, New Jersey
Printing and binding by Rand McNally

All photographs and drawings not otherwise credited by W. Oren Parker.

Cover photographs Walls of light designed by Josef Svoboda for productions of Verdi's *The Sicilian Vespers* (front cover) and Wagner's *Tristan und Isolde* (back cover). Reprinted from *The Scenography of Josef Svoboda* by permission of Wesleyan University Press. Copyright © 1971 by Jarka Burlan.

Title-page photographs (Left page) Welded structural-steel staircase with plexiglass treads. (Right page) Structural steel, plexiglass, and Mylar surfaces used in a setting for Shakespeare's *A Midsummer Night's Dream* at the Tyrone Guthrie Theatre. Designer—John Jensen. (Photos—Kewley)

To Gilbert Hemsley, Jr.

Preface

Design in the theatre has continued its gradual movement toward a refined yet innovative scenography during the few years since the fourth edition of *Scene Design and Stage Lighting* appeared. Basic principles of good design have not changed, of course, but changes of emphasis are noticeable. The integral presence of lighting in stage design today is now accepted, but there have been subtle changes of philosophy and approach in recent years. Theatre has, in general, become more theatrical. Scenic forms tend to put less emphasis on placing the stage action than on expressing theme or making a visual statement. Tangible stage objects are frequently shaped of unusual materials or by inventive structural techniques that, as functional design, create their own reality.

Stage lighting in today's scenography has similarly undergone changes of emphasis. The illumination of a scene on stage is likely to be motivated less by natural light sources than by theatrical or dramatic intentions. Light has become a directorial tool as well as a compositional force and scenic form.

This new edition of *Scene Design and Stage Lighting* reflects these trends at the same time it retains the book's basic and important aim: to bring unity and understanding to the primary areas of theatrical production—scene design, technical production, and stage lighting.

Part III, Designing the Lighting, has been extensively restructured by a reordering of sequence of the subject matter covered, updated information on instrument design and light-control systems, and expanded technical coverage.

Part I, The Design Concept, has been tightened and revised further to clarify the form and concept of design in today's theatre. Material on drafting in design has been reorganized and expanded to include technical drafting symbols, a very useful knowledge area for the stage designer.

Part II, Executing the Design, contains new and current treatment of construction materials, and the chapter on color in the theatre has been expanded to include a wider discussion of color in light.

This edition misses the valuable contributions of a longtime friend and distinguished colleague, Gilbert Hemsley, Jr., but welcomes the expertise of R. Craig Wolf, who undertook the challenge of revising Part III.

Colleagues who reviewed the revision in progress include Odia Ball (Pierce College), Allen Cornell (Adelphi University), Jeffrey Fiala (University of Massachusetts/Amherst), David Hale (Temple University), Larry Sutton (De Pauw University), and William Valle (Central Michigan University). I am grateful for their reactions and suggestions.

Like the preceding ones, this edition would not have been possible without the aid of friends. I wish especially to thank James Bakkom for generous assistance and new photographs; to record the continuing contributions of John Ezell, Steve Ross, and Cletus Anderson; and to express appreciation to William Nelson and Michael Garl for photographs from the Carnegie-Mellon University Department of Drama.

I also wish gratefully to acknowledge the aid of Howard Bay, Don Beamen, June DeCamp, Robert Dopel, Charles Elson, Ed Kook, Charles Levy, William

Matthews, Robert Melloncamp, Michael Price, Patricia Simmons, and Frederick Youens.

Special thanks, too, for help and cooperation from the staffs of the Library and Museum of the Performing Arts, Lincoln Center; the Harvard Theatre Collection; the Yale Theatre Collection; The National Theatre, London; and The English National Opera, London. I acknowledge the United Scenic Artists of America for continued generous help and the honor of life membership. And, once more as always, gratitude and appreciation to my patient wife and research colleague, Teschie.

W. O. P.

Contents

SCENE DESIGN AND STAGE LIGHTING

PART

1

THE DESIGN
CONCEPT

1

Introduction

The paths leading to a career in theatre design are numerous and varied. They may come from within the theatre itself or from the outside world. An actor or director gifted with a sense of theatre and visual ideas can contribute to design just as surely as can the more practiced visual artist equipped with a natural ability to draw and paint and a strong desire to be in the theatre. A student from the latter background standing at the threshold of training for a career in design for the theatre may puzzle over what the future holds. The flush of excitement and sense of involvement in first experiences in the theatre should not obscure the need for a long-range artistic commitment toward creative achievement and personal fulfillment. Anyone interested in working as a scene designer, however, must first thoroughly understand the complex form of the theatre as an art.

Theatre today, along with all other art forms, is undergoing rapid change. In a short interval its literary form, its physical form, and, in some cases even in the basic idea of theatre itself, its theatrical form have undergone changes. Some are natural developments or extensions of theatrical form; some are self-conscious changes for change's sake; while others, by their obscurity to present-day theatregoers, seem designed for an "audience of the future." All these changes in some measure affect designers and their position in the theatre.

The student designer is perhaps confused by the actions of numerous and diverse groups, each claiming to activities that may be called *theatre*. To set the performing arts aside from self-entertainment and group therapy, we will attempt to clarify at the outset what is meant by *theatre*, or theatrical form.

THEATRICAL FORM

Theatrical form in its simplest description is the communication of ideas between two groups: performers and audience. The assembly of audience and performers, or *performance*, is the presentation of ideas by the performers ,to the audience. These ideas may range from the very ancient to the most topical, from the profound to the absurd, and at the same time be either sentimentally obvious or intellectually obscure. The performance can exist in a number of styles and descriptions and in a variety of physical forms. Theatrical styles will be discussed in detail later; it is more important in an introduction to elaborate on the description of types of theatrical forms and the variety of physical forms, or theatre structures, that make up our sometimes controversial, frequently exciting, but always interesting, contemporary theatre.

The three types of theatrical forms that involve the designer most are the *literary form*, or drama; the *musical form*, including opera and book musicals; and, for want of a better name, the *audio-visual form*, which is nonverbal communication that places emphasis on sound and sight and not on the spoken word (for example, ballet, modern dance, and recent experiments in visual sound). All three types of theatrical form, of course, can be united into *total theatre* or joined in such combinations as dance-drama or choral readings.

Of the three forms, the literary form, or drama, has so dominated theatre historically that the word *drama* has become synonymous with *theatre*. The significance of drama to the designer is evidenced by the fact that the major portion of a designer's training for the theatre is spent in learning to interpret and expand the ideas of the playwright.

In recent years the dominance of the literary form has been challenged in the United States by musical theatre. Characterized for so long by its two extremes of either lighthearted musical comedies or the heavier fare of "grand opera," the new musical theatre has tried to unite these extremes in a concept of "total theatre." The strong book musical such as *West Side Story* becomes near-opera in its musical dimension, while its "book," or libretto, drawing a strong contem-

FIGURE 1–1a
Grand Opera

In the proscenium stage form, the Metropolitan Opera House, Lincoln Center, New York, is a dazzling example of the overwhelming scale and grandeur that is associated with grand opera and the musical theatre. Architect—Wallace K. Harrison. (Photo—Joseph W. Molitor)

FIGURE 1–1b
Light Opera

Uilheim Hall, Milwaukee's Performing Arts Center. Architect—Harry Weese. Theatre Consultant—George C. Izenour. (Photo—B. Korab)

5

porary parallel to the classic *Romeo and Juliet* theme, retains a popular appeal.

At the same time, opera has been undergoing a resurgence that in part reflects the influence of the intricate staging of musicals and the philosophy of modern scenography. Opera scenery of the past was for the most part a background of theatrical realism and painted atmosphere. In contrast, modern stage design's interpretive form, color, and light relate much more closely to the emotion of the music and the theme of the libretto. Today's stagings bring visual unity and nonverbal support to an already powerful theatrical form.

The need for the presence of the designer in the literary and musical theatre is obvious, for both place great demand on the visual background to set style and often to make a strong visual comment. The audio-visual theatre, however, is almost entirely a visual show. What the performers wear (or do not wear) and their visual surroundings become extremely important. Technical advances in the handling of lights and the electronic production of sound have opened new vistas in this type of theatrical experience. One of the most novel concepts in the audio-visual theatre is revealed in the performances of *Laterna Magika* in the Czechoslovakian theatre, where the media of dance and pantomime are combined with moving picture projections to create a new and imaginative theatrical form. The proposed theatre of sound and sight by Jacques Polieri in Paris is an audio-visual theatre form of the future. It promises either to eliminate performers altogether or to lift them to unexperienced dimensions by the use of light projections. Innovations of this type have the potential of developing into an exciting, abstract—though largely sensational—theatrical form of the future, with many opportunities for stage designers and theatre technicians.

PHYSICAL FORM

The various types of theatrical form often determine in a general way their physical form. The size of a theatre for a musical production, with its presentational style and spectacular scale, for example, is the opposite of the needs of a theatre for drama, which is more intimate in nature. Both have clung in the past to the traditional proscenium theatre arrangement of the audience facing the stage. The physical shape of new theatres, however, has undergone a variety of changes, discussed in detail in Chapter 2. Like the innovations in theatrical form, many new theatres contain either modernized improvements on the conventional proscenium shape or are completely different in form and production concept, while a few try to combine both by converting at will from a conventional to an unconventional seating arrangement.

Over the past few years, a great number of new theatres of all forms

FIGURE 1–2

Proscenium Theatre

The playhouse at Pennsylvania State University includes many of the recent improvements of the proscenium form such as an elevator system to provide a flexible apron arrangement, side stages, and a steeply graded auditorium for optimum vertical sightlines. Architect—Harry Kale of Eschbach, Pullinger, Stevens, and Bruder. Theatre Consultants—Walter H. Walters and William H. Allison. (Photo—Pennsylvania State University Photography Studio)

have sprung up all over the country. Professional resident companies have grown from coast to coast, bringing live theatre to an ever-expanding audience.

Designed primarily for drama and possibly intimate musicals, many recent theatres have taken on the new-old form of the thrust and arena stage. Prompted by the desire to bring the audience closer to the actor, these variations either partially or completely surround the acting area with seats. Although these shapes invariably reduce the "theatricality" present in the conventional proscenium theatre, they in a sense give the theatre back to the actor and playwright by minimizing the scale of a production.

Some of the unique concepts of theatre shapes are those advanced for audio-visual theatres. Although none have been "built" in a traditional sense, their projected schemes foresee a radically different audience-performer relationship. The audience, for example, may be separated into groups with widely different views of a constantly changing performance area. Aside from these audio-visual theatres of the future, dance and ballet have their own special requirements in the audio-visual theatrical form. While dance can give shape to its performance area by the pattern of its choreography, it is more fully enjoyed if viewed from a slightly steeper angle than is provided in the normal theatre seating arrangement.

The trend toward minimum-production theatres, such as the thrust and arena stages, may be disturbing to the beginning designer because of the extreme limits of the staging. Although minimized, however, the need for design is still present. The emphasis merely has changed

FIGURE 1–3

Thrust Stage

(Below) West Coast: Mark Tabor Forum, Los Angeles. (Photo courtesy Western Publishing & Novelty Co.) (Facing page, top) East Coast: Long Wharf Theatre, New Haven, Connecticut. (Photo courtesy M. Edgar Rosenblum, Executive Director.) (Bottom) The more intimate thrust stage of the Black Swan Theatre, Oregon Shakespearean Festival, Ashland. Designer—Richard L. Hay; Technical Consultant—R. Duncan. (Photo—Hank Kranzler)

9

FIGURE 1–4

Audio-visual Theatre

(Left) A sketch after Jacques Polieri's projected scheme for a *Théâtre du Mouvement Total,* a theatre in which the audience, while being carried on slowly moving platforms, is totally surrounded by an experience of sound and visual effects. Architects—Pierre and Etienne Vago.

FIGURE 1–5

Arena Theatre

(Below) A scene from the production of *Project Immortality* at the Arena Stage in Washington, D.C., a successful example of the theatre-in-the-round form. Architect—Harry Weese. (Photo—Capitol Photo Service, Inc.) (Facing page) The flexible space and interesting structure of the Pittsburgh Public Theatre was designed by Peter Wexler. Above, the dramatic entrance. (Photo—Dark Room) Below, a bird's-eye view of the acting area and audience arrangement. (Photo—Adam Weinfold) Courtesy Larry Arrick, Artistic Director, and Dennis Babcock, Managing Director.

11

FIGURE 1–6

Total Environment Theatre

The Theatre Mobile, one of the three theatres at La Maison de la Culture, Grenoble, France, surrounds the viewer with the action and environment of the production by moving both the audience and the scene. (Left) A view of the revolving seat-bank and encircling ring. The enclosing wall can be pierced at frequent intervals or remain a surface for light projections. (Below) A cutaway model of the theatre showing its egg shape. The small end of the oval functions as a conventional stage when the seat-bank is focused in that direction. Architect—André Wogenscky. (Photo—Ifert and Meyer, *Cimaise* Magazine, June–September 1968) (Facing page) The flexible space and interesting structure of the Pittsburgh Public Theatre was designed by Peter Wexler. *Above,* the dramatic entrance. (Photo—Dark Room) *Below,* a bird's-eye view of the acting area and audience arrangement. (Photo—Adam Weinfold) Courtesy Larry Arrick, Artistic Director, and Dennis Babcock, Managing Director.

FIGURE 1–7
Dance Theatre

An audio-visual theatre that involves the performer (above). This projected theatre designed especially for the dance incorporates a flexible stage and steeply banked semicircular seating to bring the pattern of the dance into the full view of everyone. Architect—Elizabeth Harris. (Photo—J. Alex Langley. Copyright © 1962, reprinted by permission of the American Federation of Arts)

FIGURE 1–8
Historic Theatre

The Goodspeed Opera House, East Haddam, Connecticut (right), a nineteenth-century opera house, faithfully reconstructed into a modern producing theatre. Courtesy Michael P. Price, Producer.

Introduction **13**

FIGURE 1–9a

Extended Apron

(Above) The greatly altered and highly mechanized forestage of the Stratford-on-Avon Shakespeare Theatre. Half of the acting area is downstage of the old proscenium line. (Photo—Joe Cooks)

FIGURE 1–9b

Modified Thrust

(Right) The Angus Bowner Theatre, Oregon Shakespearean Festival. Architects—Kirk, Wallace, McKinley; Designer—Richard L. Hay. (Photo—Hank Krauzler)

14

from the background to what the actors wear and to what they sit or stand upon. Costumes, properties, and lighting rather than elaborate scenic backgrounds become the major areas of design concentration.

In spite of the popularity of these current forms there are signs which indicate that the proscenium theatre has far from passed from the scene. Arena stage directors, feeling the strain of continually trying to top themselves on a bare stage, are beginning to use more and more traditional production devices to vary the staging. Similarly, after a number of years of staging plays on a thrust stage, the audience and director are now quietly admitting that not all plays lend themselves to thrust staging and perhaps a proscenium type theatre could *also* be used.

In an effort to find a form midway between thrust and proscenium staging, unique uses of the proscenium theatre form have evolved. In one such case, the picture-frame feeling is reduced by extending the apron of the stage and doing away with the traditional act curtain. The result gives the illusion of a thrust into the audience and at the same time provides a stage far more flexible for the limited use of scenic elements than the true thrust stage.

FIGURE 1–10
Open Staging
Two-thirds of the acting area in the Chatham College Theatre is in front of the proscenium opening and combines large forestage and side stages. Architects—Johnson and McMillin, Associates; Theatre Consultants—Oren Parker and William Nelson. (Photo—D. Meisle)

Nontheatre Form

Partly as a reaction to the theatre-building boom there has been a move toward creating theatre in nontheatre structures. The conventional audience-performer arrangement is altered to fit into an old garage, a deserted warehouse, or a gymnasium or ballroom. The unusual relationship of the seating arrangement and performance area is a part of the theatrical experience and is sometimes more exciting than the show itself. Unconventional arrangements free the audience and the performer from any preconceived notion of what will be seen or what can be done.

No matter what direction the physical form of the modern theatre may take from year to year, however, it is evident that the designer must be trained to work in all types of theatre and with all theatrical forms.

SCENE DESIGN

Theatrical form, of which scene design is a vital part, combines many related arts into the very intricate, sometimes frustrating, but always fascinating, art of the theatre. In the drama, or literary theatre, the written words of the playwright are transformed for an audience by the director and fellow artists into an audible and visible expression of the author's ideas. In the presentation of a play, scene design exists solely to bring visual substance through the stage setting to the dreams of the playwright.

In simplest terms, scene design is the designing, executing, and lighting of a stage setting. It is a very limited and specialized area of design based on a wide background of semirelated knowledge as well as specific training in modern theatre practice.

The Total Visual Effect

Scene design in the modern theatre is concerned with the total visual effect of a dramatic production. In any production the total visual effect is the sum of all the elements that depend upon being seen to make their impression on the audience. The scenic background is the largest and most obvious visual element that supports the spoken word of the dramatic form. The designing of a setting, however, is not confined to creating the color and shape of framed pieces of scenery alone. It also includes the planning of the quality and intensity of the lights

FIGURE 1–11

Nontheatre Form

(Facing page, top left) Theatre in an old railroad roundhouse: *The Round House—*outskirts of London. (Top right) Theatre in the park: *The Park Players—*Pittsburgh. (Bottom) Theatre in a garage: *The Performance Group—*New York.

The Design Concept

that reveal the scene; the selection and styling of the furniture and set-dressings; the careful consideration of the actors' costumes to blend or contrast with the background; and, because a dramatic production is not a static form, the easy movement of actors. The combination of all these visual elements represents the total visual effect.

The visual requirements of a script may be as simple as those of Wilder's play *Our Town*, which all but eliminates physical elements of scenery, or as complicated as those of Verdi's opera *Aïda*, which requires vast quantities of spectacular background. In either case the visual elements, simple or complicated, have to be designed, prepared, and lighted by someone.

Scene Designers

The esthetic responsibility of the total visual effect is normally in the hands of scene designers, although their importance and influence may vary with the extent of their talent, experience, and personality in comparison to those of fellow artists. Beginning designers are frequently dominated by more experienced directors until they develop enough ability and confidence to warrant full membership on the production team.

Qualities of Designers. Beginning designers are expected to know so many things almost at once that they may be puzzled where to begin. They will soon find that if they wish to design for the stage they must quickly develop three qualities that are directly related to the specific demands of modern theatre. Anyone who aspires to be a designer will need the vision and imagination of the creative artist, the ingenuity and skills of the stage artisan, and, above all, the knowledge and sense of theatre of the actor, director, and playwright.

To function as creative artists in the theatre, designers must be talented and articulate in line, color, and form. They must be able to bring meaning and visual significance to a stage picture through imaginative and creative qualities developed by training in the nonverbal techniques of design, drawing, and painting.

As stage artisans designers must be able, through the use of unique materials and theatrical techniques, to bring substance to their ideas with skill and dispatch and within the structural limitations of their medium. To create a design that can be wholly realized, they must know the structure of scenery, the limitations of materials, the methods of moving scenery, and lighting techniques.

As a collaborating artist the scene designer makes an important visual contribution to the dramatic form. Through the study of dramatic structure and perception of the playwright's goals the designer is better able to find the author's image and bring a visual interpretation of the theme onto the stage. Awareness of the necessary movements of the actors and directing techniques helps the designer create a proper environment to support the action of the play. This is the designer's theatrical quality. A strong sense of theatre is needed in order to bring a theatrical flair to designs while still keeping them in proportion to the dramatic import of the play and movement of the actors.

Design Collaboration

Within the realm of the total visual effect are several areas of design concentration. In this age of specialization, not all productions are designed by one designer. Frequently, the design of a large production is divided between a scene designer, a costume designer, and a lighting designer. In this case the work of the three is a collaborative effort strongly influenced by the basic ideas of the scene designer. The design of the scenery either directly controls or indirectly influences the total visual effect of any dramatic production. The scene designer, however, cannot design a setting without considering costumes and lighting, even though their design and supervision may be in the hands of someone else.

A designer also cannot design a scene without thinking of the movement of the actors, although the final action and positioning of the actors is the prerogative of the director. The floor plan of a setting influences the ease or effectiveness of the actors' movements whether the director is aware of this influence or not. The director is, perhaps, more aware of the restrictions of a poor floor plan than of the virtues of a successful one. Nevertheless a good floor plan is a highly important part of the total visual effect.

In theatre forms such as the thrust stage and arena theatre the visual effect often centers on the costume design and lighting rather than the scene design. Conventional scenery is either minimized or eliminated entirely, with greater emphasis placed on the design of properties and small fragments of scenery to help establish locale.

Costume design is an essential part of the total visual effect and, although it directly concerns the actor, it complements or highlights the scene design. But, while deeply engrossed in their own contribution, scene designers must always remember that to see and hear the actor interpret a role is the main reason the audience comes to the theatre. The costume gives meaning to the individual character, and at the same time places each character in proper relationship to the total visual effect. The major role of the scene design and of the lighting design is to supplement and emphasize the costume or actor in the ever moving stage composition. An audience may leave the theatre with a lasting impression of the costumes. But this does not mean that the scene and lighting designers have been outdone; rather the opposite: they have performed their job well.

Whether the attributes of the artist and artisan are found in one person or separate individuals, the ultimate goal of scene design is the same. Designing for the stage means working within the limitations of a given stage and with the techniques and materials common to the theatre, while at the same time satisfying the visual requirements of the script.

THE FUNCTION OF SCENE DESIGN

Scene design, like other kinds of creative design, is the creating of a form to fulfill a purpose or function. The function of scene design is obviously linked with the dramatic form it serves. Scene design, in providing a visual support to the dramatic form, is an integral part of the modern theatre. Its function, as a result, is woven into the philosophy of modern theatre practice. The basic concept of present-day theatre, as a playwriting and play-production unity, has brought scenery out of the pretty background class into full partnership in the production of a play. The scene designer brings to the production a visual expression of the author's aim. As a result, scene design becomes a fusing of the visual effect and the basic intent of the play into a single dramatic impression.

The function of scene design can be more clearly revealed by looking at the dramatic form of the play itself. The form of the play should enable the designers to understand the relationship of scenery to action, to dominant mood, to theme, and to the story in general.

Action

If scene design is supposed to bring to the play a visual expression of the author's intent, the designer must first examine the action of the play and the kind of people involved in the action. Unless completely abstract, every play (or any other theatrical form, such as ballet or pantomime) presents a conflict. Out of the conflict, whether of heroic proportions or a simple domestic problem, comes the action of the play. The action of the play is the force that moves it forward and makes it a living, breathing form. Dramatic action is a combination of physical or bodily action, visual movement, dialogue, and characterization. Characterization creates sympathy or repulsion on the part of the audience for the figures caught in the action. The characters either create the conflict or are shaped by the conflict in the ensuing action.

The Scene of Action. By incorporating all the elements of the total visual effect, scene design creates in visual terms the scene of the action. At the same time, it is more than just a place; it is an environment for the action. Sometimes the scene or elements of the scene may become a part of the action which can be seen in the frankly theatrical use of scenery in a farce or musical comedy. The scene, on the other hand, may recede into the background and become a witness to the action, to be more felt than seen.

20   *The Design Concept*

Characterization

Character development or *characterization* bears an important relationship to the environment of the scene. The people in the action react in accordance with, or in opposition to, their surroundings. The influence of the characters on scene design, sometimes subtle, sometimes symbolic, is, on occasion, more obvious. When the place is an interior, a study of the people living in the house gives the designer many important clues for details. For example, the family of Grandpa Vanderhof and his bizarre friends in Kaufman and Hart's *You Can't Take It with You* certainly contribute a wealth of detail about the kind of house and collection of curios that make up the environment of the play.

The basic function of scene design, then, is to create the appropriate surroundings and environment for the action of the play. The first function of scene design toward creating an appropriate environment is to fix the action of the play in time and place.

Time and Place

The action of the play must occur in a specific time and place, which are usually calculated, by the author, to establish the proper atmospheric surroundings for the action. Place, even though it may be in limbo, makes a visual impression on the audience. A specific time in the historical past can prepare a state of mind in the audience as much as can the absence of a specific time or place.

FIGURE 1–12

Altered Proscenium Theatre

A unique use of the proscenium theatre by the American Conservatory Theatre in San Francisco. With a firm conviction in the proscenium as an important visual frame of reference, the director and designer covered or minimized the gaudy proscenium decor of a conventional theatre, extended the stage floor forward over the orchestra pit (less than 6 feet), and then created a second temporary frame in keeping with the style of the production at a point well below the middle of the original stage. The new stage floor was ramped slightly to imporve the sightlines and the traditional act curtain was ignored. The result is an illusion of tremendous thrust into the audience and at the same time provides a stage that is far more flexible for the use of limited scenery than the thrust stage. Set Designer—Stuart Wurtzel.

FIGURE 1–13
Legend of Lovers
Designer—Eldon Elder.

Although time and place are linked with the overall atmospherics, the connection is sometimes rather loose and may merely suggest a place that carries connotations of the atmosphere inherent in the play. The first act of Anouilh's *Legend of Lovers*, for example, is set in a French provincial railroad station in the early twentieth century. A closer examination of the play shows that it is not a literal station but a point where travelers pause as they come and go between this life and the life hereafter. Specific time is thus of very little importance except that it is not contemporary.

Establishing the Mood

The second function of scene design is to establish in the visual elements of the surroundings an expression of the dominant atmosphere, or mood. Scene design aims to create in this first impression an expression of the mood and its relationship to the action and characters. Mood can be described as the quality of a play that, when properly transmitted, creates a state of mind and emotional response in the audience. It can be expressed in such words as *sparkling*, *warm*, *gloomy*, *violent*, *earthy*, *mystic*, and so forth. Some more general expressions of mood are *tragedy*, *comedy*, *farce*, and the like, that are also used to define a type of play.

The Design Concept

FIGURE 1–14

Mood

Drama. (Above) The use of light and form to establish the atmosphere of Miller's *The Crucible.* Designer—Adel A. Migid. (Right) The dramatic use of movement and light intensify the avalanche scene in Ibsen's *Brand.* Designer—Richard L. Hay. *Comedy.* (Below) Absurd decorative detail and gauche taste create a comic environment for Garson Kanin's *Born Yesterday.* Designer—Donald Oenslager; Director—Garson Kanin; Producer—Max Gordon. (Photo—Vandamm, Theatre Collection, New York Public Library.)

A play, it can be argued, is the dramatization of a mood, a theme, and a story. All three elements are always present in a play, but one may be emphasized over the other two. Hence, a play may be primarily a dramatization of mood with theme and story in a secondary position; the plays with mood dominating seem to be at the extreme ends of the emotional scale. A tragedy is usually a mood-dominated play, as is low comedy or farce. The tragedy *Legend of Lovers*, just mentioned, is an example of dramatization of mood. The Garson Kanin comedy *Born Yesterday* is another example, although it is in the opposite mood.

The relationship of mood to action is stressed, for on occasion a visual atmosphere is established in contrast to the apparent mood of a play. Comedy scenes are sometimes played in the ghostly surroundings of a haunted house, or tragedy against the raucous background of a street carnival. The contrasting moods combine into a single dramatic impression. Hence, fun in the haunted house might turn into farce, and murder at the Mardi Gras may become irony.

Tragedy, of course, frequently begins in a lighter mood which may or may not be expressed in the surroundings. A festive scene may have an air of foreboding which anticipates the approaching tragedy.

Reinforcing the Theme

Theme is, of course, closely linked with mood as well as with the storytelling part of the dramatic form. The theme of some plays is clearly apparent, especially if the author is using the dramatic form as a pulpit or soapbox to lampoon society or government. Comedy often carries a message to an unsuspecting audience as effectively as does the more direct approach of the serious play with a strong story line.

An example of an expression of theme in scenery is found in Shaw's *Heartbreak House*. The living room of Captain Shotover's house is designed like the fantail of an ancient sailing ship. The incongruity of this misplaced bit of architecture is a constant visual symbol of the lack of purpose and aimlessness of the cultured, frank, charming, unconventional people who live in it.

The expression of theme in scenery cannot always be easily achieved. More often the theme is treated with subtlety and in symbols known only to the designer and his muse. The most obvious example of a theme-oriented play is found in the documentary theatre. Removed from the fictional format of literary theatre, the documentary theatre is free to move to its objective with dramatic and theatrical directness. The most familiar documentary theatre, stemming from Germany in the 1930s, is that of Bertolt Brecht and Erwin Piscator. Their "theatre of alienation" had a sociopolitical orientation that was frankly aimed at the elimination of capitalism as a social and political way of life.

Although impact of the message has lessened as audiences have

The Design Concept

FIGURE 1–15
Heartbreak House
Designer—James Russell. (Photo—Morris Shapiro)

FIGURE 1–16
Theme, Documentary Theatre
The Clown by Bertolt Brecht. Designer—Stanford Thomas. (Photo—Nelson)

become more sophisticated and tolerant of shock, the documentary theatre remains a vital theatrical form exerting a strong influence on modern theatre practice and design. Light projections using mixed media of film and live actors to express theme have become the hallmark of documentary theatre, as have the conscious efforts to bring real-life objects and true materials to the stage in an attempt to remove scenery (and all of theatre for that matter) from the world of make-believe and playacting. The effect on the young designer is evident in the freedom of present-day stage design from the taboos of illusion and sentimentality that dominated the romantic world of make-believe.

Staging the Story

Story is the connecting thread that holds together the other elements in a complete dramatic form. It is the train of related incidents that brings continuity to the many events in a play. Story is probably more important to the theatre than to other art forms. The expression of an idea in the theatre is dependent upon having and holding the audience's attention every moment. The theatre audience, if confused, cannot turn back the pages, like a novel reader, and reread a passage for clarification. An engrossing story can hold an audience spellbound. A good storyteller, of course, uses mood to create the atmosphere for a story. The storyteller can also use the story to make a point, which is apparent in plays with strong themes. Any good play usually has a good story, but a play that is dominated by the dramatization of story is primarily dedicated to telling an interesting tale, whether it be of love, adventure, intrigue—the list is long and varied.

Because the environment of a story-dominated play is usually real, the designing problem becomes one of selection of realistic details and forms that place the action and establish the mood. This, more often than not, has already been accomplished by the author through the choice of realistic location for the scene of the action. A more important contribution of design in the story-dominated play is the staging of the action. Staging, or fitting the action on the stage, provides the areas, levels, and properties in such a way as to allow the continuous flow of action so necessary to telling a good story.

Staging can sometimes become complicated. Tad Mozel's *All the Way Home*, for example, divides the stage into the numerous areas, including exterior and interior rooms, of a late-nineteenth-century house in a small town (Figure 1–17). The various levels and areas inside and outside the house allow an easy flow of action and good audience sightlines and at the same time seem architecturally logical. The production depends heavily on light to define those areas that are only suggested, to establish time of day in both the exterior and interior, and to reinforce the changing mood and emotional ending.

The many English and French so-called bedroom farces are story-

dominated plays that depend heavily on staging. The skillful juxtaposition of hallways, doors, closets, and the ever-present bedroom, all
visible to the audience, is necessary to facilitate the fast pace and split-
second timing of the nonsensical action of the story. An unusual example of imaginative farce staging is Alan Ayckburn's *Taking Steps.*
The three floors of a house are staged on one level. Light helps to
define the change of floor levels as well as the actors when they pan-
tomine going up and down nonexistent stairs. Once the audience catches
on to the convention, its imagination separates the different levels of
the house. The cleverness of the staging adds humor to the performance and develops an interesting production style.

DESIGN AND OTHER THEATRICAL FORMS

The question may be raised whether or not the functions of scenery
for a play or any other literary form in the theatre can be applied to
other theatrical forms such as mime, ballet, audio-visual, and unstructured theatre. Unless the production is totally abstract or completely

FIGURE 1–17
Staging
The various levels and areas inside and
outside the small-town house of Tad
Mozel's *All the Way Home* are staged to
provide easy flow of action and still seem
architecturally logical. Designer—Deb
Fishman.

unstructured, the guidelines are the same. The absence of a predetermined story line may limit the planning of staging but, eventually, staging is involved even if the action is accidental or improvised.

Theme and mood are both present in any theatrical form. The psychedelic lighting of a rock show imparts a poignant theme through the atmospheric senses of sight and sound. Although classical ballet usually has a story line, its modern counterpart frequently does not. Hence the decorative background of ballet that sets the locale and mood of the dance has given way to the limited use of scenery in the form of stylized properties and arbitrary lighting more expressive of theme than anything else. Mime, both group and solo, is the most absolute of the theatrical forms. Imagination supplies the scenic background and hand props. Although the same thinking is involved, the skill of the performer, rather than the designer, creates the mood of the locale in the minds of the audience. Mime is sometimes incorporated into literary theatre. The pantomimed props and scenery in *Our Town* is an example, as well as the imagined costume in *The Emperor's New Clothes*.

In ballet the miming of dialogue by the dancers is a conscious control or theatrical convention that has little to do with the scenic background except that it establishes a performing style. (The importance of style to a designer is discussed in Chapter 4.)

Whether the play or production is story-dominated, mood-dominated, or out-and-out propaganda, it is the function of scene design to place visually the action of the play in an environment that will bring significance to the dramaturgical elements. Theatrical form is a complicated medium and a strict taskmaster. It requires of designers as well as of their fellow artists a complete understanding of theatrical organization and working methods before they can create freely and imaginatively.

2

Scene Design and the Theatre

Materials and techniques that are the bases of scene design must have a direct influence on the final design form. These materials and techniques create a medium through which design is transmitted. Each medium requires a specific handling, which gives it an individual effect. A painting, for example, may be done in an oil, watercolor, or fresco medium. Scene design, however, does not stand alone; it is a part of the overall dramatic form. As a result the scene designer is concerned not only with the media of canvas, paint, and wood, but also with theatrical materials and theatrical techniques. A scene designer may draw sketches or make models, but final designs do not reach a full state of expression until they are on stage in a theatre. If the materials and techniques of the theatre are to be used intelligently, the designer must have an awareness of the theatre as a medium of expression.

THE THEATRICAL MEDIUM

The basic communicative qualities of scene design are the same as in any other visual art—color, line, and form create the same emotional response on the stage as they do in a poster or display design. Any differences in the design form is traceable to special materials and stage techniques associated with the functions of scene design. In order to understand, at least in general terms, the extent and limitations of the materials and techniques of this medium, the beginning designer must develop an awareness of the theatre as an organization, a show, a machine.

Theatre as an Organization

The preparation of any production requires the close cooperation of many specialists. The theatrical medium brings together the writer, actor, director, designers, and audience. The ultimate success of a play often rests on the efficiency of the producing organization in: (1) selecting a play; (2) procuring financial backing and establishing a budget; (3) securing a theatre; (4) selecting and rehearsing the actors; (5) designing the scenery, lighting, and costumes; (6) building, painting, and lighting the sets; and (7) promoting an audience. Lack of cooperation or understanding, complicated by faulty planning in any phase of the organization, can weaken the production as a whole.

As in any other well-functioning organization, there must be a guiding force. The director or producer is the dean of the production group and the chief interpretive artist for the playwright. The director's basic overall concept of the production brings a unifying control to the visual elements, acting style, and literary interpretation.

The designers' contribution to the production is, of course, a vital part of the visual concept. Designers are, nevertheless, a part of the organization and its collaborative effort, which may mean subordinating personal triumph many times for the good of the whole. Great moments of unified achievement in the theatre are usually experienced when the goal of the production is placed above individual gain.

In addition to being aware of their general relationship to the overall production plans, designers need to know the specific organization of their own area of theatre—design, technical production, and lighting. A thorough knowledge of backstage and scenery-shop organization often leads to a more efficient production as well as a more faithful reproduction of design ideas. Because of its specialized nature, the personnel organization of designing and technical production is discussed in detail in Chapter 10.

Theatre as a Show

The designer's awareness of the theatre as a show emphasizes the temporal quality of scenery, the dramatic qualities of the visual elements, and above all the sense of joining with an audience to give a performance.

As a performing art the theatre has a feeling of immediacy and audience relationship that does not exist as completely in other art forms. It is true that a painting has an audience, or viewers, too, but the painting remains a painting without viewers. A theatrical performance without an audience, however, is little more than a rehearsal. The audience and its participation are a vital part of the theatrical medium. Consequently, the theatre's almost total dependence upon an audience gives it a temporal quality that becomes an intrinsic part of the medium.

The direct influence of this temporal quality brings about a specific attitude toward scene design and the structure of scenery, for although scenery may look solid for the most part, it must be lightweight and portable to move easily from scene to scene or from audience to audience. And, finally, when the production reaches its last curtain, the usefulness of the scenery ends. It is doomed to storage, rebuilding, or destruction.

The performance aspect of the theatre has a direct bearing on the attitude of designers. There is a tendency to think that the actors are the only performers, which is not the case. *All* the artists and workers in the theatre are performers. A performance is the collaborative effort of all performers. Its success is dependent on the teamwork of its members. Any sense of achievement lies in the reaction of the audience to a good performance. They are more often than not responding to an overall experience rather than to an individual performance. Visual artists working in the theatre are not their own bosses; they are collaborators in a joint venture.

The dramatic qualities of scenery are, of course, mainly achieved through the versatility of the designer's use of the visual art form. A dramatic quality more specifically related to the theatre is the use of proportion or scale. The theatre, more than other art forms, is an overstatement of life. Even a realistic play is drawn a little sharper and greater than real life. Any idea, no matter how significant, will make little impression on an audience if it is merely stated.

The size and distance of the audience in relation to the performance has an influence on the scale of any overstatement in scenery. If, for example, the theatre is large and the audience is at a great distance from the performance, the scenery has to take on an increased scale just to be in proportion to the size of the auditorium and stage. But whether a musical spectacle at a great outdoor arena or a drama of intimate proportions in a vest-pocket theatre, the theatrical medium has the capacity of offering a broad spectrum of electrifying moments.

Theatre as a Machine

The modern stage is a complex machine that promises to become even more complicated in the near future. A practical understanding of this machine is of prime importance to anyone expecting to design in the theatre. The designer's use of the physical stage and its equipment is predicated on a philosophy of scene design. To superimpose a design form without regard for theatrical techniques and the limitations of the physical stage would be as ill conceived as architecture that forces interior planning into a predetermined exterior shape.

THE PHYSICAL STAGE AND ITS AUDITORIUM

The most important step for beginning designers is to learn their new medium by becoming acquainted with the physical stage. They need to know the actual shape and physical make-up of the performance area, for each defines the space in which they must work.

Proscenium Theatre

In the contemporary theatre the stage has various forms based upon the relationship of the audience to the stage area. The most common form is the proscenium type of theatre, where the audience is arranged on one side of a raised stage area. The enclosed stage is open to the audience through the proscenium opening. Early proscenium openings were surrounded by a decorative frame to separate the audience from the play in an artificial and often unrelated manner. Modern theatre structure tries to blend the proscenium opening with the auditorium so that the stage and audience are not so obviously separated. The proscenium wall of the modern stage is merely a masking to hide stage machinery, lights, and scenery storage from view.

Teaser and Tormentors

Because the proscenium opening is a part of the architecture of the theatre, it has fixed proportions. Often the size of the opening must be changed to fit the scale of an individual production or setting. For this reason the teaser and tormentors, which are adjustable framing members, are located immediately upstage of the proscenium opening. The tormentors are the right and left vertical frames which move laterally onstage to reduce the width of the opening. The teaser is the top horizontal frame which is lowered to reduce the height of the opening. While both help shape the proportion of the frame, they also mask, or hide from view, the backstage area of the setting.

The framing of a stage opening is usually accomplished in one of three different ways. The teaser may be a neutral-colored cloth border hung in fullness or pleats accompanied by a corresponding cloth tormentor which can be pulled open or closed on a horizontal traverse track. A second variation is to frame the cloth teaser, thereby forming a continuous flat plane hanging overhead. The matching framed tormentor which sits on the floor can be easily moved on stage or off to narrow or widen the opening.

The most complicated masking arrangement furnishes the framed teaser and tormentor with a "reveal," or thickness, on the onstage edges. This gives the framing members a heavy look and at the same time provides better masking of the spotlights directly upstage of the opening. The reveal may be attached perpendicularly or beveled at about a 45-degree angle (Figure 2–1).

FIGURE 2–1

Tormentor and Teaser

The proportion of the frame for a stage setting is established by the tormentor and teaser, which may have one of several forms. The plan below shows (1) right wall of setting, (2) right return, (3) stage-right tormentor, (4) house curtain, (5) asbestos curtain.

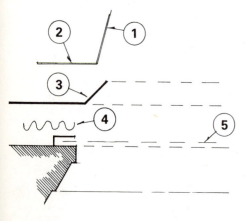

The Design Concept

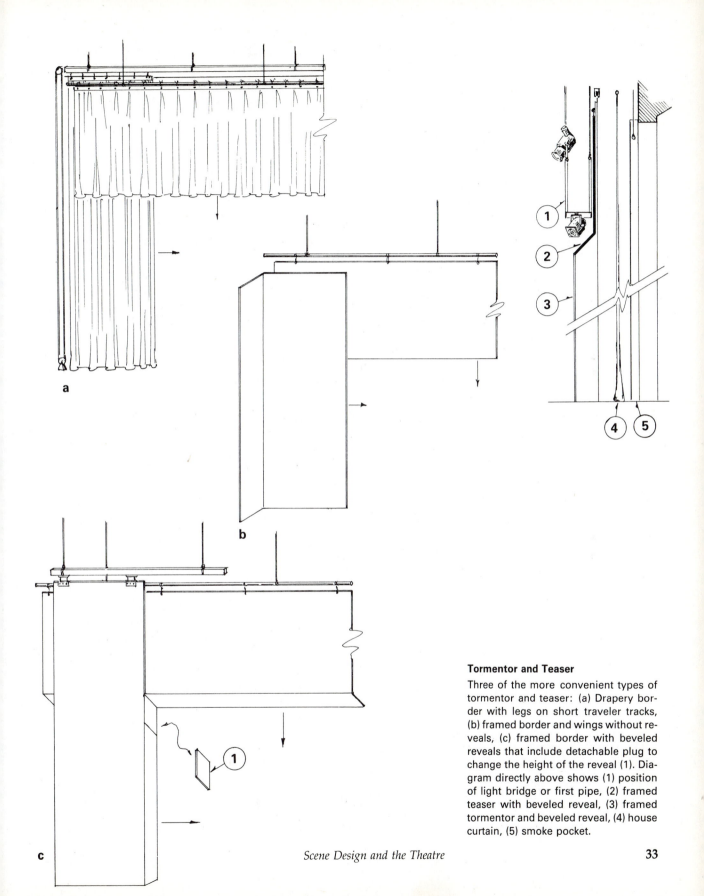

a

b

c

Tormentor and Teaser

Three of the more convenient types of tormentor and teaser: (a) Drapery border with legs on short traveler tracks, (b) framed border and wings without reveals, (c) framed border with beveled reveals that include detachable plug to change the height of the reveal (1). Diagram directly above shows (1) position of light bridge or first pipe, (2) framed teaser with beveled reveal, (3) framed tormentor and beveled reveal, (4) house curtain, (5) smoke pocket.

The downstage edge of the setting usually does not attach directly to the reveal of a framed tormentor. It is held free to allow space for lighting instruments. The free edge of the set is supported by a "return," which turns the set offstage parallel to the tormentor.

Sightlines

After learning the size and shape of the stage area, the designer is interested in the sightlines of the auditorium to determine how much of the stage is in view. The proscenium theatre has a characteristic sightline problem that varies only slightly with the different patterns of seating arrangement. If the flare of the seating arrangement is very wide, for example, people sitting on the extreme right side of the auditorium see very little of the left side of the stage and vice versa. Similarly, persons sitting in a very steep second balcony see very little of the back wall of the setting. If the auditorium floor is flat without a gradient, or if the stage floor is unusually high, the audience does not see the stage floor and sees very little even of the actors' legs as they walk upstage.

The designer must know these extreme sightline conditions in order to plan a setting that brings the most important areas into the view of all the audience. It is not necessary to find the sightline of every seat in the house but only of the extreme or critical locations.

The extreme horizontal sightlines are drawn from the seats farthest to the right and left in the audience. The horizontal sightlines are located on the plan of the stage and auditorium (Figure 2–2b).

The extreme vertical sightlines are harder to locate, for they are found on a sectional view of the auditorium and stage which frequently isn't available to the designer. The extreme vertical sightlines are drawn from the front row upward and from the last row in the balcony downward. On occasion, when a large balcony overhangs a considerable portion of the orchestra, it is necessary to consider a vertical sightline from the last row of orchestra seats (Figure 2–2a).

From the pattern of extreme sightlines, the designer can see how much of the stage is in view to each member of the audience. In Figure 2–2b, for example, the horizontal sightline (4) shows the designer how far onstage a person sitting in this seat can see and how much of the stage-right wall cannot be seen. In this manner, the designer consults the sightlines of an auditorium in order to plan efficiently the use of stage areas for staging the action of the play.

Staging

The designer uses the sightlines of a theatre in two different ways: first, when studying the staging of the play, to develop the design form, and then later, for technical reasons, to check the masking of the nearly completed setting.

When planning the staging, in collaboration with the director, the

The Design Concept

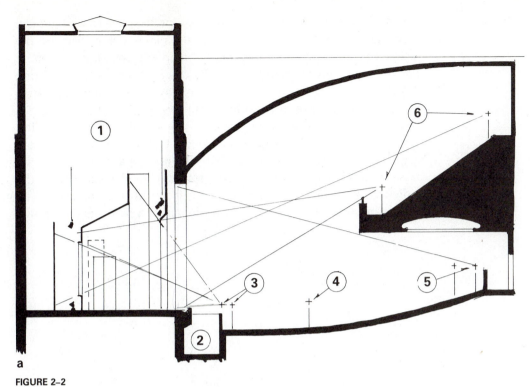

a

FIGURE 2–2
Sightlines

(a) Sectional view. (b) Plan of auditorium and stage. (1) stage area, (2) orchestra pit, (3) front row end seats, (4) widest part of the auditorium, which determines the splay of the seating arrangement, (5) back row of the orchestra, (6) balcony seats.

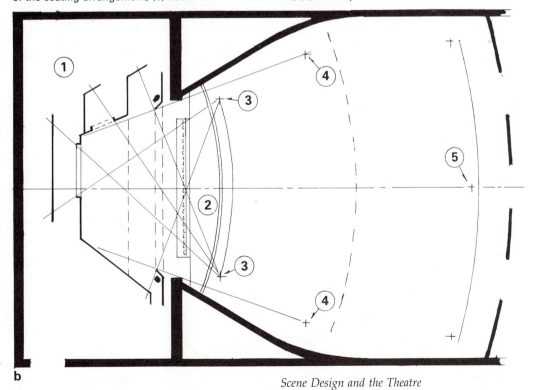

b

designer maps out the arrangement of properties, levels, and general floor plan to facilitate the easy flow of the play's action. Because the designer is thinking like a director at this point, the staging is more than a traffic pattern for the actors. Its chief concern is to help bring into focus each scene or moment in the play with the proper degree of relative importance to the other moments.

The designer, through composition of the visual elements, can alter the basic value of any stage area. Due to their position on the bare stage, certain areas are stronger than others. The very nature of the proscenium theatre makes an actor standing downstage nearer the audience more important than an actor in an upstage position. The relative importance of the various positions on a bare stage is shown

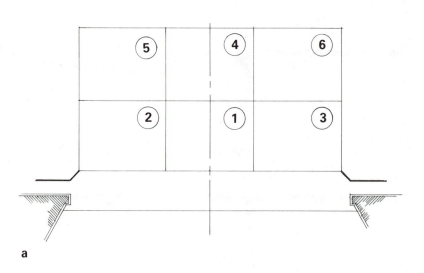

FIGURE 2–3

Stage Area

(a) The stage divided for easy identification into basic areas that are numbered in order of relative importance: (1) downstage center, (2) downstge right; (3) downstage left, (4) upstage center, (5) upstage right, (6) upstage left. (b) A second method of dividing the stage, a series of horizontal planes determined by the location of portals or wings and numbered from downstage to upstage.

a

b

in the diagram (Figure 2–3a) by first dividing the stage into six equal parts and then numbering the areas in the order of their importance.

Such devices as raking or angling the side walls of a set to force the action in the weak upstage left and right areas toward the center, placing furniture to bring important scenes into good sightlines, and using levels in the upstage areas to increase their importance are just a few examples of staging techniques in scene design.

When the stage is cut, left to right, by a series of portals made up of vertical wings and horizontal borders, as in the wing-and-backdrop type of plan, the staging becomes more two-dimensional. It falls into a series of horizontal planes related to the portals, each traditionally referred to by numbers. Beginning at the apron the downstage strip is number one, the next number two, and so on upstage. The staging can be directed by indicating whether an actor or piece of scenery is to be in "one," "two," or "three," as desired (Figure 2–3b).

Staging in Front of the Proscenium

Two variations of the proscenium theatre are the *extended apron* and the *thrust stage*. Both are outgrowths of the desire to break through the frame of the proscenium in an effort to reduce the distance between the audience and the actor. Each is a part of the contemporary trend or revolt from the romantic theatricality of the past which depended upon a certain esthetic distance to complete its illusion. Although the extended apron and thrust stage are not necessarily new forms in the theatre, they are very much a part of present-day staging and represent a space in which today's stage designer must be prepared to work.

Extended Apron

Although somewhat alike in shape, the apron and thrust stages differ in the arrangement of their respective audiences. The extended apron plays to a seating arrangement similar to that of the proscenium theatre with only slight differences in sightlines. The greatest change occurs in the vertical sightlines caused by the increased gradient. The necessity to keep an actor in full view and in a position well ahead of the proscenium results in a steeper rate of rise in each successive row of seats.

The extended apron is usually equipped with access openings or doors within each flanking wall ahead of the proscenium opening. The forestage area may be used in conjunction with proscenium staging, allowing elements of the scene to spill out onto the side stages, or in a more formalized manner, with all action originating on the apron.

The most flexible form of apron stage is illustrated in Figure 2–4, which shows how the area ahead of the proscenium opening can be modified by the use of elevators or removable platforms and seats to one of three variations: (a) full extended apron; (b) side stages with orchestra pit; (c) regular proscenium staging with additional seats.

a

b

FIGURE 2–4

Flexible Apron

A proscenium-form theatre equipped with a flexible apron that when raised or lowered can assume a number of shapes. (*a*) The apron raised to stage level, providing an extended apron ahead of the proscenium opening with entrances from the sides and through the apron floor. (*b*) The apron lowered to orchestra-pit level for a musical production. (*c*) The apron at auditorium level. This arrangement with the extra seats is for a proscenium production.

c

NONPROSCENIUM THEATRE

Thrust Stage

The thrust stage, or open stage as it is sometimes called, is as the name suggests a stage thrust out into the audience area. With seats arranged on three sides of the peninsula-shaped acting space the bulk of the audience is closer to the actor than it would be in conventional seating. Semipermanent elements of scenery or an architectural background make up the fourth side of the theatre (Figure 2–5, page 40).

Though in appearance the thrust stage is structurally related to the proscenium theatre, its chronological development stems from the arena theatre. The long-felt need in the theatre-in-the-round for greater variety of staging and a stronger axis of visual composition led to a semicircular grouping of seats around the thrust stage. At the same time, the widely diversified sightlines are an obvious improvement over the limited angle of view of the proscenium theatre. Since the upstage portion of the stage is anchored to the structural part of the theatre, a rather important axis is established in the opposite direction.

The strong visual axis, however, has its shortcomings. The people sitting in the end seats of the right and left sides have a radically different compositional view. This is even more in evidence if the seating arc is greater than a semicircle, in which case the audience in

Scene Design and the Theatre   **39**

FIGURE 2–5

Thrust-Stage Theatre

With seats on three sides of the stage area, the thrust stage and its background can assume a great variety of forms other than the conventional living-room interior in the illustration. Entrances can be made from the audience tunnels, the sides, through the stage floor, and from the back.

the extreme side seats may find themselves enjoying a vista that approaches a rear view. The ideal configuration seems to be slightly less than semicircular, thereby providing a more equitable distribution of seats without losing the sense of close contact with the actor, which is so much a part of both the thrust stage and arena theatre concept.

The features of an ideal thrust stage that influence design are the extreme conditions of both the horizontal and vertical sightlines as well as the basic aim of this theatre type to simplify the amount of scenery needed to establish the locale. The abnormally wide horizontal sightlines force the use of conventional scenery to the back wall, with properties and levels utilized on the stage to set the scene. The sharp vertical sightlines, owing to the steeper gradient, make the floor treatment an important part of the design.

Both the apron and thrust stages, because of their exposed positions, work best with one fixed setting or relatively simple modifications during act changes. Any speedy change of locale is somewhat awkward and depends upon the ingenuity of the director to stage it visually or to resort to the uncertainty of a "blackout" change.

The design limitations of both the apron and thrust stages are offset by the improved flexibility of the staging. The three-quarters facing of the thrust stage plus the presence of actors' entrances from the audience area as well as the unconventionality of the theatre itself continuously encourage a greater use of style and design detail than is called for in the proscenium theatre. Costumes and properties become the center of the visual composition with most of the environment only suggested or defined with light.

Arena Theatre

Another familiar stage form is the arena type of staging where the audience encircles the stage area. The scale of arena staging can vary from an intimate theatre-in-the-round to an arena the size of Madison Square Garden, with many sizes and variations in between (Figure 2–6).

Although the sightlines of arena staging are greatly improved over the proscenium type of theatre the stage form is very limiting to the designer in terms of conventional scenery and techniques. The visual elements have to be confined to small low units or open pieces that can be seen through. Design detail becomes more important because of the intimacy of the theatre and the lack of larger elements of scenery in the composition. This type of staging is intentionally simple, depending upon a suggestion of scenery to set the scene and stimulate the audience's imagination to fill in the rest.

FIGURE 2–6
Arena Theature

The audience surrounds the stage area, which may or may not be raised. Any use of scenic elements is limited to properties and an occasional open set piece.

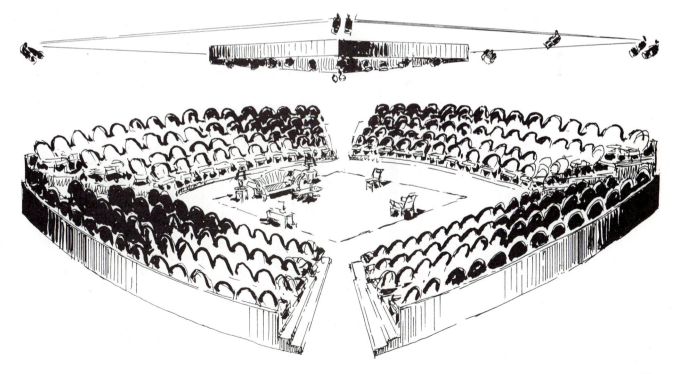

Flexible Staging

Flexible staging is an outgrowth or expansion of arena staging. It is obvious that arena staging has some advantages over proscenium staging, but on the other hand there are many plays that do not lend themselves to arena presentation.

Flexible staging provides an area for the easy changing of the stage–audience arrangement. Within this flexible space the staging can be altered from arena staging to three-quarters-round, or to proscenium-type staging (Figure 2–7). Ballroom or cabaret staging is a further variation with the audience on two sides and a small stage or bit of scenery at one end, or both. The sightlines vary, of course, depending

FIGURE 2–7

Flexible Staging

The seat platforms and stage are movable and thereby able to assume a variety of arrangements. The audience partially surrounds the stage area, which may have a limited amount of scenic background. (*a*) L-shaped arrangement. (*b*) Proscenium-type. (*c*) U-shaped, with the audience on the three sides of the stage. (*d*) The audience split to produce a number of acting areas.

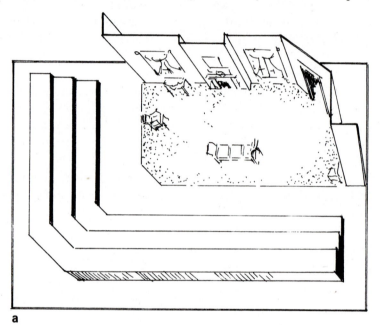

a

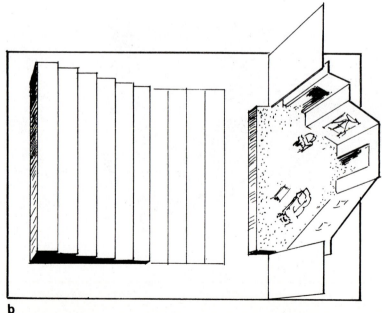

b

on the type of staging. When the seats are arranged for proscenium-type staging there is a decided improvement in the sightlines over the conventional proscenium theatre. The seating is usually arranged with a negligible flare, thereby creating good sightlines for the entire house (Figure 2–7b).

Flexible staging offers many exciting designing and directing possibilities. Its main drawback is the relatively small audience capacity, which limits its commercial use. A more serious handicap is the loss of time and energy which occurs during the changing of the theatre from one arrangement to another. It is, however, an excellent staging medium for experimentation in new dramatic forms.

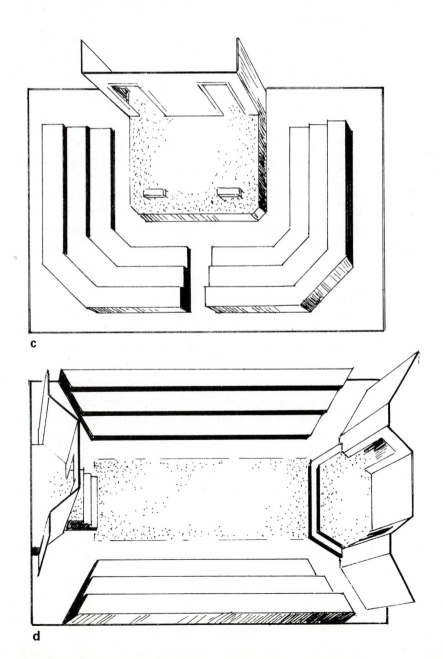

c

d

LIGHTING AND THE SCENE DESIGNER

Of all the techniques within the theatrical medium affecting scene design and the structure of scenery, lighting is the most influential. Because lighting technique will be covered in great detail later it will not be necessary here more than to point out its general influence on the materials and structure of scenery.

The use and control of lighting is strictly a theatrical technique, born and developed in the theatre. It is an additional element of design that gives the scene designer a greater flexibility in composition than occurs in any other visual art form.

Light is visible energy. Among its characteristics is the apparent ability to transmit some of its energy onto whatever surface it falls. The energy of light reveals, brightens, and adds color to an inert object, thereby increasing its vitality. By the same token, it might be argued that color also brings life to a painting, but it is not as animated as, for example, light through a stained glass window or a projected color image on the stage.

Of all the components that make up a stage composition, the two most active and vital are the *actor* and *light*. The power of light to animate form makes it a forceful design statement in a stage composition.

Aside from its design possibilities, light on the stage has an unavoidable effect on the structure and materials of scenery. The scene designer must consider in advance the relative changes in the intensity of light and the position of the light source, which may determine whether an area of scenery is to be opaque, translucent, or transparent. In the making of transparent or translucent pieces of scenery, the pattern of the framing and the location of the seams have to be carefully considered. Frequently the design is altered slightly to conceal or modify a seam or structural element. Conversely, opaque areas should not be neglected, for a strong backing light may reveal an interesting but unwanted pattern of framing.

Often the design of the lighting comes too late in the planning of a setting, almost as an afterthought. This sometimes reflects an indifference or unawareness of the theatricality and compositional value of light itself. An alarming number of young designers either cannot or do not want to be bothered with lighting their own sets. The continuation of an unfortunate disinterest of this kind can only lead to the surrender of a portion of scene design to specialists who are willing to give the thought, time, and skill necessary to design and supervise the lighting of a stage setting. Lighting is too important a part of the theatrical medium not to be considered in the beginning along with the other theatrical techniques which condition the design and structure of scenery.

3

Scene Design
as a Visual Art

The exciting interplay of line, color, and form in a vibrant stage setting or the subtle refinements of an inconspicuous scenic background do not happen by chance. The proper integration of color and style of costumes and the dramatic presence of light in the stage scene depends on an understanding on the part of all the designers of the principles of design. To create a setting the scene designer uses, either consciously or intuitively, well-established rules and fundamentals of design common to all the visual arts. The beginning designer should have a knowledge of these fundamentals to aid in the development of final design forms.

DESIGN AND THE DESIGNER

We think of design as a creation of order that is the work of the artist. Artists bring two things to their work: *emotion* and *intellect*. Both are expressed in the feeling and rationale of a work of art. The emotional aspect of creating is individual and introspective. Its intangibility is sometimes called talent. It is hard to quantify and impossible to teach.

The intellectual side of design, however, can be measured and defined in terms of composition. Within emotion or feeling lie desire, imagination, and a sense of theatre which are so necessary to creativity. Intellect, or the mind, on the other hand, cultivates the practical skills as well as the conceptual and interpretive powers of design. The merging of emotion and intellect is the beginning of the creative process which spawns the design form.

Beginning designers may wonder how this abstract definition of design applies to their special interest in the theatre. It means that during the process of designing, for example, there are two forces at work: a personal vision or feeling for the final design form and the practical realities that are tempered by thoughtful judgment and taste. Both are regulated by the dictates of the playwright, the concepts of the director, and the limits of the performance space. In other words, emotion and feeling become the *ideal*, thought and intellect the *reality*, the first being the *goal* and the second the *realization*. The greater the skill and ability to realize the ideal, the more successful the designer.

COMPOSITION AND THE ELEMENTS OF DESIGN

Composition, in general terms, is the composing or organizing of the elements of design in space into a unified *form*. The result may be a single *form* or the interaction of *several forms* acting as a whole. The elements of design are the elemental factors that make up the visual form, whether it be a two-dimensional shape or a three-dimensional sculptural object.

The elements of design can also be thought of as forces that, by manipulation, can singly dominate a composition and help give the form *meaning*. The reason or meaning of any visual form brings to a composition a unity of purpose that is particularly important when designing in the theatre. The meaning attached to the designing of a visual form may be dictated from the outside, or come from within the artist, often formulated by the simple desire for personal expression.

The major factors that make up a visual form can be listed in the order of their importance to the creative process. They are: line, dimension, movement, light, color, and texture. Of these elements, *line* and *color* are the most forceful; in terms of design, *light* and *movement* are unique to the theatre.

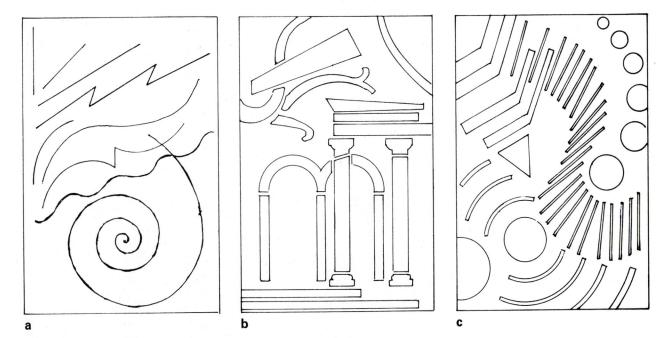

FIGURE 3–1

Real Line and Linear Shapes

(a) Examples of real line. Straight, curved, subtle and strong reverse curves, serpentine and spiral. (b) Real line can enclose space and create shape. Some shapes are linear, thereby taking on line characteristics by assuming direction and attitude. (c) Suggested line. The eye will follow a line suggested by repetition of shapes, parallel lines, concentric circles, gradation of size or color, or a shape that points.

Line

Line, as an element of design, defines *form*. It is a most important force in a composition because it is present in many different ways. Line can enclose space as *outline* and create shape (two-dimensional form), or as *contour-lines* suggest three-dimensional form. Line in a composition can appear as *real line* in many different modes (straight, curved, spiral, and so on) or as *suggested line* simulated by the eye as it follows a sequence of related shapes.

Line is a path of action and therefore cannot help but take on a sense of *direction* and become a part of *movement*. This is particularly true when the form is *linear* in shape. It soon becomes apparent that in an arrangement of several linear shapes the lines not only assume a direction but also take on an *attitude* toward each other, be it one of harmony or opposition.

The use of line and shapes with line characteristics becomes a vital force in any *form* or arrangement of forms. A composition may use *line* as a dynamic force with a sense of violent action or as a static force with a feeling of strength and stability.

FIGURE 3-2

Line and Composition

The composition is dominated by the use of curved lines. Some lines are projected, others are three-dimensional step forms, and some are bent pipe and rope. *The Atlantide* by V. Nezual. Designer—Ladislav Vychodil—Bratislava.

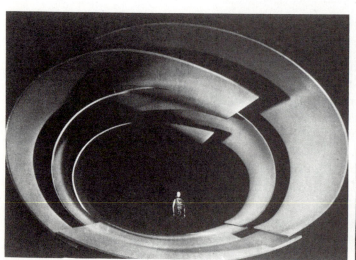 

FIGURE 3-3

Linear Form in Composition

Stage compositions dominated by the use of linear forms. (Left) *Iphigenia auf Tauris.* Designer—Ruddi Barch. (Photo—German Information Center) (Right) *Pelléas et Mélisande.* Designer—Robert Edmond Jones. (Courtesy Yale Theatre Collection)

Dimension

Dimension is the size or mass of *form*. As an element of design, dimension is not only concerned with the size of a shape or mass of a three-dimensional form, but also with the relationship of the size of one shape to another— large to small, large to large, etc. *Real dimension* is always present in a two-dimensional shape, but, of course, becomes *suggested dimension* when a three-dimensional form is represented on a two-dimensional surface.

FIGURE 3–4

Suggested Line in Composition

The eye is led by the repetition of form to the center of interest. *Lohengrin,* Metropolitan Opera, New York. Designer—Charles Elson. (Photo—Sedge Leblang)

FIGURE 3–5

Dimensional Relationships

The scale of the forms dominates the composition. Slaveship scene from *The Emperor Jones.* Designer—Donald Oenslager.

Dimension, in addition, includes the amount of space between forms in a composition. The size of the interval has a definite effect on the apparent size or mass of the form and its proportional relationship. The prominence or recession of the interval or size of mass is, of course, influenced further by the use of color, light, and texture. The proportional relationship between interval and mass also begins to establish a rhythm or sense of *movement*.

Movement

Movement is the action of *form*. It is the kinetic energy of composition. Motion in design is always present even in a static composition. The pattern of optical signals that touch the retina and then the brain is a continuous flow and hence mobile in character.

The *real movement* of form within a composition is very much a part of stage design. The movement of light, of the actors, and on occasion animated elements of scenery are commonplace in the theatre.

The movement of the eye, or *optical motion*, however, is a type of movement that is present in any fixed arrangement of forms. The use of *suggested line* (one characteristic of *line*) stimulates optical motion as the eye is led from one shape to the next.

Optical motion begins with an intuitive sense of *orientation* that everyone has or has experienced. It provides the basis for an interpretive feeling of movement frequently so subtle the viewer does not distinguish the effect as a product of optical motion. The tendency of the viewer, for example, to interpret a diagonal line extending from the lower left to upper right corner of a composition as an upward motion is a product of orientation. It is a part of the *left to rightness*

FIGURE 3–6

Movement in Composition

(Right) The kinetic energy of optical motion dominates the composition. Cabalistic scene, *The Love for Three Oranges.* Designer—Donald Oenslager. (Facing page) Transferred motion. An airplane in flight. The real movement of lights, clouds, and wind gives the fixed airplane the appearance of movement. *Flying High.* Designer—Edward Haynes.

The Design Concept

common to us all as well as the fixed association of a *top and bottom* to all compositions.

Movement also involves the fourth dimension—*time*. The interval and size of form relationship (mentioned earlier) cause a kind of movement or rhythm. The interval spacing or *tempo* may be staccato, pulsating, or ponderous in its timing. The vibration of repeated shapes, complementary colors, rapid changes of direction, and high contrasting areas are all visible examples of *optical motion.*

Although orientation brings an instinctive sense of movement to a composition, the designer has many means of controlling optical motion. Strong direction can be countered, reversed, or subtly changed by altering the *position* or *attitude* of the forms in relation to each other. The outline of the form itself can establish a direction, as can the other elements of design such as color and light.

Another interesting phenomenon of movement is its *transferability.* Both real motion and optical motion can be transferred to a static object. A simple figure or shape placed against a busy or pulsating background will appear to dance or vibrate itself. This unwanted optical motion can happen to pictures, for example, if they are hung on a background of vibrant wallpaper. Real motion can also be transferred from a moving background to a fixed object in the foreground. Most everyone, for example, has experienced the sense of motion while sitting in a stationary railroad car or bus when the adjacent vehicle begins to move. The technique of moving the background behind the actor or fixed scene to create the illusion of movement in the scene is frequently used on the stage.

It goes without saying that all movement on the stage has to be

carefully controlled and coordinated. Movement catches the eye and can detract from the scene as easily as it can enhance it. Ask any actor who has been "upstaged" by the innocent waving of a handkerchief or scarf of a fellow actor.

Light

Light reveals *form*. It is the first definition of form. Although it has not been traditionally viewed as an element of design, light is a dominant presence in all areas of stage design. As such, it must be considered a basic influence at the beginning of the creative process and not something to be studied later.

Light can be thought of in three different ways: first as *real light* capable of revealing form; second, as light having its *own* design-form; and last, as *simulated light* as it might appear in a two-dimensional representation of a three-dimensional form.

The design potential of light is inherent in its physical characteristics. The three variants of light are *intensity, color,* and *distribution.* By controlling its brightness, color, and direction, light becomes a strong factor in creating a design-form.

Intensity is the *actual* or *comparative* brightness of light. The actual brightness of the sun, for example, can be contrasted with the comparative brightness of automobile headlights at night. Spotlights in a darkened theatre offer the designer the same comparative brightness under more controlled conditions.

The ability of light to transmit and reveal *color* is one of its most dramatic qualities. The modification of local color of form by colored light is a design technique unique to the theatre. *Color modification* and the additive mixing of colored light are two basic concepts of color as a quality of light that have to be understood by all designers in the theatre.

Distribution is the energy path of light. The control of the distribution of light gives it *direction* and *texture* as a design feature. The various kinds of distribution begin with the general radiation of direct emanation, through the more specific reshaping of the light rays by reflection and optics, to the parallel rays of the laser beam. The sharp or soft-edged quality of the light beam coupled with its degree of brightness gives *texture* to light.

It is easy to see how a knowledge of the distribution of light can affect the design form by the introduction of *highlight, shade,* and *shadow* into composition. Beside the atmospheric quality that light can add to a composition there is the obvious design character of an exposed light source such as candelabra, chandeliers, or visible lighting instruments.

The final use of *real light* is as its own design form. Patterns of light can be projected over a form as a part of the composition, or the projected image can be the entire composition. Although the use of

FIGURE 3–7

Light in Composition

Use of the distribution, color, and movement of light in this production of *Prometheus Bound,* designed by Donald Oenslager, was unique for its time. Produced at Yale in 1939 and conceived much earlier, it represents the kind of innovative use of light we accept as modern practice. Within the simple "gray gauze box" sitting in space, through which light could penetrate, wash with color, project on its surfaces, or make it disappear before our eyes, we watched the anguishes of Prometheus unfold. Lighting—Stanley McCandless. Costumes—Frank Bevan.

Scene Design as a Visual Art   **53**

light as projected scenery can be thought of as a medium in itself, it is, however, still a visual art and therefore draws upon the same fundamentals of design for its realization.

The use of *simulated light* is most often present in the designer's sketch, where it represents the effect of light in the composition. Although *line* is used first to represent three dimensions, the added use of simulated light and its shades and shadows is the designer's most effective way to represent three-dimensional form in a sketch or backdrop. However, the most successful use of *simulated light* in a sketch or painting is based upon a first-hand knowledge of what *real light* can and does do.

Color

Color modifies *form*. As an element of design it is a powerful stimulus that can change the dimension of form, reverse the direction of line, alter the interval between forms, and generate optical motion. Color in the theatre comes from two basic sources: pigment or dye present on the surface of the form, or from color transmitted by light.

Color in either light or pigment has three variants: *hue, value,* and *chroma*. A specific color can be thought of in terms of its *hue,* which is the color's wavelength or position in the spectrum; its *value,* signifying the color's black-to-white relationship; and its *chroma,* indicating the color's degree of purity (saturation) or freedom of neutrality. Until it is time to go into all the aspects of color in detail (Chapter 8) only the black, white, and gray steps of value will be used to demonstrate the effects of color in design.

Texture

Texture is the tactile aspect of form. As a design feature, it adds interest by embellishing the surface and thereby giving character to the finished form. The composition takes on a temperament partially inspired by the make-up of its texture. Surfaces may vary from the extremes of highly polished to rough/natural in quality. A rough-hewn surface or decorative bas-relief, for example, stimulates different emotional responses. Each illustrates the purpose of texture as a design element.

The reason for using texture in the theatre is to catch, interrupt, and reflect light. The irregular shadows and highlights of a textured surface enrich a design form; thus the dependency of texture on light is a crucial component of design.

Texture in the theatre has two different dimensions. First, it may be seen as *real* texture: the various surface treatments just described are examples of real texture. But it may also occur as *simulated* or painted texture. The two-dimensionality of painted texture is used for the same design reasons as real texture, but the surface is mottled with paint to add interest and character.

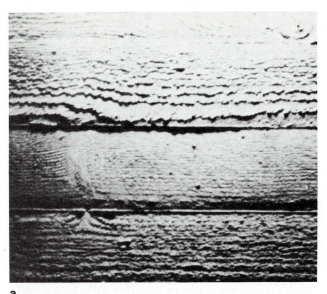

a

b

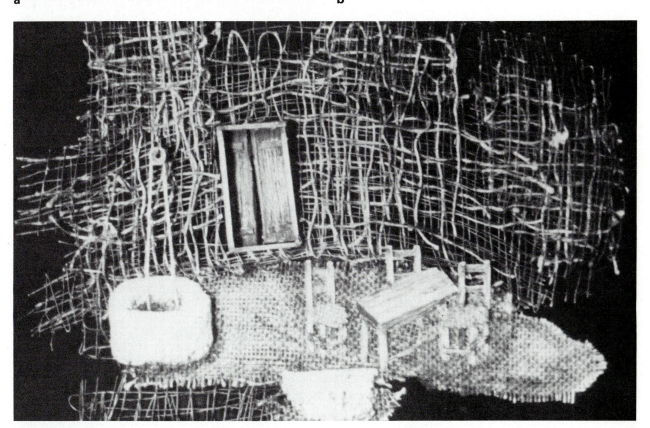

c

FIGURE 3–8

Texture and Light

(a) Rusticated surface emphasized with side lighting. (b) Decorative bas-relief. (c) This small but expressive scene design illustrates the dominance of texture in a composition. Designer—Vladimir Suchanek, Bratislava.

The earliest concept of the word *texture* was associated with weaving. The size and make-up of the warp and weft had a tactile sense that was smooth or rough to the touch. A tactile image also appeared in the woven pattern and color variation. The same textural trait can be seen in techniques of paint and in surface decoration. The enrichments of a surface with a repeated motif of wallpaper or of geometric patterns are examples of simulated or visual texture, as are mosaic, parquetry, and tiled surfaces.

Light and Texture. Real texture is best revealed by directional sidelighting, while painted texture appears more real under a wash of light without a strong sense of direction. A wash of light is shadowless and therefore does not cast telltale shadows (such as wrinkes) in a drop that may expose the simulated texture as a painted surface. Conversely, a wash of light on a textured detail such as a cornice or molding will deny its three-dimensionality and sometimes require the addition of painted shadows and highlights to create the appearance of reality.

FIGURE 3–9

Designing for Light

These two atmospheric drawings are facsimiles of the London National Theatre's production of Shakespeare's *Richard III.* Revolving forms and sliding panels cast shadows and slash the stage with shafts of light in a series of dramatic compositions. A striking example of designing for light. Scene Designer—Ralph Koltai. Lighting Designer—David Hersey. Director—Christopher Morahan.

Designing for Light. Since the function of real texture is to divide light into interesting shadows and highlights as a design feature, it is not too difficult to apply the concept of "real texture" to scenic forms as a whole. Although scenic forms are large in scale they, too, should be designed to interact with light.

The successful unity of light and scenic form results most often as a result of the close creative collaboration of the lighting and scene designers. The theatrical value of light to scenic form, first envisioned by Adolphe Appia and Edward Gordon Craig at the beginning of the twentieth century and fully realized later by the inventiveness of Josef Svoboda, is very much a part of present-day scenography. The use of abrupt surface changes, reflective covering, density variations from opaque to transparent, as well as the addition of highly textured areas on scene forms all contribute to the unity of lighting and scenic form.

Figure 3–9 is an excellent example of designing for light. The illustration shows two moments in the National Theatre of London production of *Richard III* on the open stage of the Olivier Theatre. The open stage or thrust stage shown lend themselves very well to the more dramatic use of light and scenic form.

PRINCIPLES OF COMPOSITION

The elements of design are the raw materials ready to be brought together into some order or purpose. Composition is the organization of these elements into a unified form. The principles of composition are the various ways the designer can control and use the design elements to bring unity, interest, and meaning to a stage composition. Unity brings into play two controls, *harmony* and *contrast*. The interest or appeal in a stage setting is the direct result of the manipulation of these controls.

Harmony

The simplest act of bringing order to disorder is to sort unrelated objects into groups which have some sequential relationship or continuity. The objects may have in common a similarity of shape, color, or texture. Repetition, then, is a basic control. The repetition of one or more of the elements of design shows the presence of outside control. The repeated use of line or linear forms, for example, can dominate a composition, although other elements of design may be present. In the design shown in Figure 3–2 *real line* dominates the composition in a dramatic way. The repetition of line also affects the overall mood of the design and establishes strong optical motion. Examples of set designs dominated by one or more of the other elements of design are illustrated on the following pages.

Although repetition is one of the easiest and quickest ways to bring harmonious control to a composition, it suffers the danger of becoming monotonous or gauche. The possible monotony of repetition can be relieved with a little contrast or variation.

Contrast

The designer depends upon contrast to create form. Form cannot be revealed without contrast, as is evident in the examples of the absence of contrast occasionally seen in nature. The protective coloration of an animal or bird reduces contrast to the point of making it invisible against the background. But in the theatre, such lack of contrast—an actress in a red gown sitting on a matching red sofa—would be disastrous. Between the two extremes lie infinite variations.

Variation

When the repetition of one element produces monotony, a variation of one or more of the other elements can add interest to the composition. The frenzied *motion,* for example, that dominates Donald Oenslager's design for the cabalistic scene in Prokofiev's opera *The Love for Three Oranges* is relieved by the variation of *dimension* and direction, and is enhanced, if we could see it, by the contrast of *color* (Figure 3–6a). It is also interesting to note in Oenslager's designs for Aeschy-

The Design Concept

lus' *Prometheus Bound* (Figure 3–7) that, although the design is dominated by the use of *light*, the manipulation of the direction, distribution, and intensity of light is the major variation brought to a rather simple form. *Color* of the scenic form in this production was held under strict control. The overall tonality was gray or neutral with moments of color achieved through the use of colored light.

Pattern

The injection of variation into composition to relieve repetition establishes a rhythm as the variation recurs. This is the basis of most pattern compositions, which exist in two forms: border and overall patterns. Although more obvious, the manipulation of the elements of design is the same in any composition except for *light*. The open or closed qualities of a pattern involve light, particularly if the structure is a grill or lattice designed to let light pass through. The rhythm of the variation repeat (or motif, as it is called) is known in terms of its relative positions. That is to say, the motif may be placed in relative positions of alternation, opposition, or inversion.

The motifs may be placed in alternation by alternating their position in relation to a central axis without changing the original direction of the pattern. To place motifs in opposition tends to break the rhythm into a series of static arrangements, creating a feeling of stability. To place the motifs in inversion takes the direction out of the movement, especially if used in an overall pattern. Inversion is frequently used in textile patterns permitting the material to hang either up or down without the motif appearing to be upside down.

These arrangements can be combined and compounded into numerous variations of each element of design, thereby adding interest to the border or pattern composition (Figure 3–10, page 60).

An analysis of border designs may seem unrelated to scene design. However, a border or pattern is a type of composition. It has an obvious control that is easy to see and study. The same control appears with a subtler and less restricted handling in the composition of a setting. Besides, pattern composition as found in wallpaper, paneling, and cornice decorations still occupies a large part of the scene designer's time.

Gradation

The variation of motifs within a border composition can, as has been shown, establish a rhythm or feeling of movement. The feeling of movement or change is frequently desired in composition of a stage setting where the controls will be less obvious. The sequential controls of a border composition are sometimes too obvious or abrupt. Sharp contrasts can be reduced by the use of the sequence of gradation, which by transitional steps softens contrasting elements and at the same time brings a feeling of movement into the stage picture. The

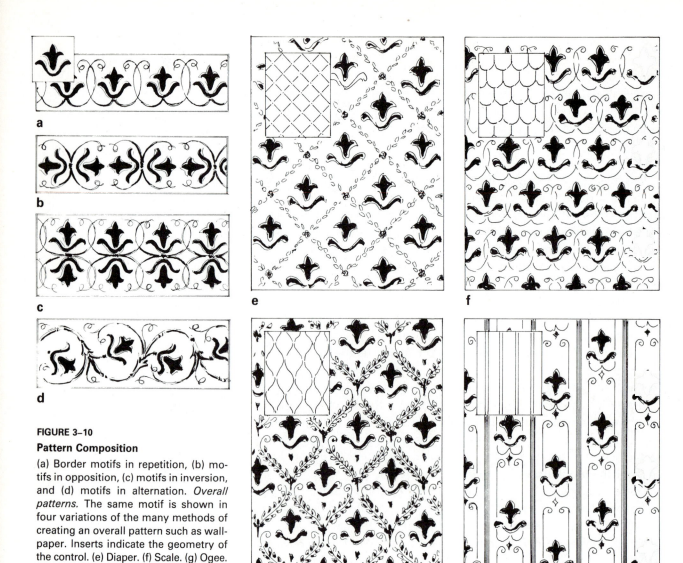

FIGURE 3–10

Pattern Composition

(a) Border motifs in repetition, (b) motifs in opposition, (c) motifs in inversion, and (d) motifs in alternation. *Overall patterns.* The same motif is shown in four variations of the many methods of creating an overall pattern such as wallpaper. Inserts indicate the geometry of the control. (e) Diaper. (f) Scale. (g) Ogee. (h) Vertical stripes.

graded wash of a skydrop as the dark blue at the top gradually becomes lighter near the bottom is an example of gradation of the value of a color. The use of gradation may occur in line, shape, or in any one or more of the elements of design. The resulting feeling of movement in the composition is free of the repetitive rhythm of the pattern composition (Figure 3–11).

COMPOSITION AND SPACE

Space is to the scene designer what a block of wood or stone is to the sculptor. The space in and around the stage becomes an area to enclose or leave open, to light or leave dark, to flatten out or to create the illusion of even greater depth.

The Design Concept

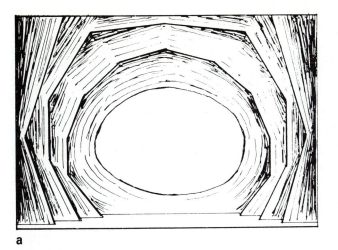

a

b

FIGURE 3–11

The Sequence of Gradation

(a) Gradation of shape from a rectangle to an oval opening. (b) Gradation of value in the sky and of direction of the steps.

Although undefined space is limitless in scope, it can be defined in two-dimensional terms. Figure 3–12 graphically illustrates the definition of two- and three-dimensional space and solid form by showing the many options a scene designer has to create a space or a form within a space. If the lines in the drawing that define a space, often referred to as a *space frame*, were considered to be outlining a plane of

FIGURE 3–12

Space and Form

(a) Undefined space. (b) Two-dimensional space frame. (c) Three-dimensional space frame. (d) Hollow solid surrounding a sculptural solid.

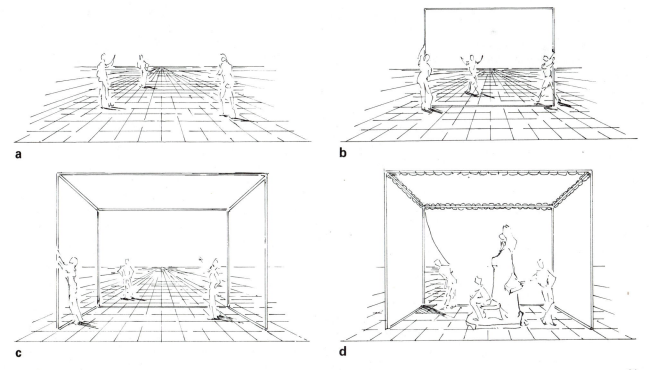

a

b

c

d

Scene Design as a Visual Art   **61**

FIGURE 3–13

Figure and Ground

(a) Ground, undefined space. (b) Single figure defining a portion of the ground. (c) Several figures. (d) The upstage figures become the ground for the downstage figures, helping to establish the planes in space. (e) Example of complicated figures against a plain ground with the reverse in the center.

solid surface, the final arrangement would be known as a *hollow solid*. The hollow solid is a familiar scenic form associated with proscenium theatre. The *sculptural solid*, designed to be viewed from all sides, is more suitable for the thrust and arena stages. The first, like scenery, defines a space which becomes the design form itself. The second creates a form within a space.

Designing within the limits of two-dimensional space begins with a perception of the relationship of *figure* and *ground*. Ground, often background, is a two-dimensional plane. In the simplest example, it can be likened to a sheet of drawing paper. The figure or shape outline has to be in contrast to the ground to be visible. An example of figure is the enclosure of a portion of the ground by an outline. For greater contrast the figure may be filled with a flat tone or color.

The space feeling of a composition made up of a single figure and ground is flat. As figures or large shapes are overlapped, one figure becomes the ground for the other and composition begins to take on depth.

The ground may be simple with a textured or patterned figure, or in reverse, with a complicated ground and simple figures (Figure 3–13).

The composition of a wing-and-backdrop type of setting is an example of the use of figure and ground in scene design. The flat plane of each wing when contrasted against the adjacent wing gives an illusion of space that belies their two-dimensionality, especially when other signs of space are used.

Up to now the figure has been thought of as an outline, or outline and flat tone. The figure can also represent a solid with not only height and width but also a depth or thickness. The representation of volume in outline or in solid areas is also an indication of space. The outline itself may be varied in thickness and the ground modeled to accentuate the three-dimensional or plastic qualities (Figure 3–14a).

The figure can be given further plasticity by chiaroscuro modeling, which is shading by means of light and dark tones without regard for a light source. Chiaroscuro modeling combined with a sequence of gradation emphasizes the structure of solids and gives stronger indication of space (Figure 3–14b).

The next step to heighten the three-dimensional quality of the form is to model it in light and shade as if coming from a definite light source. The direction of the light and the cast shadows help to describe the form and place it in space (Figure 3–14c).

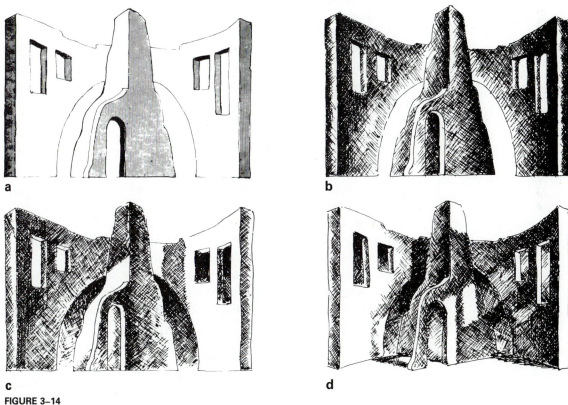

FIGURE 3–14

Composition and Space

Composition with the definition of form in space. (a) Simple outline and outline and flat tone. (b) Chiaroscuro or shading to bring out the form within the outline. (c) Cast shadows which establish a light source and increase the feeling of space. (d) Total effect combines perspective with directional lighting to create the illusion of three dimensions.

The final exploit of space perception is the illusion of literally breaking through the plane of the drawing paper with the use of perspective. Perspective and the shadows of directional lighting are combined to achieve a total effect, a feeling of space in two-dimensional form (Figure 3–14d).

COMPOSITION AND UNITY

The composition of a stage setting is expected to bring a unity to the overall arrangements of the visual forms. In addition to the unifying effect of harmony expressed in the sequence of repetition and gradation, scene design needs a greater sense of unity to bring strength to stage composition. The compositional unity of a scene design is first dependent on balance and movement and then on proportion and rhythm. At first glance, balance and movement may seem the same as proportion and rhythm; however, a closer analysis will show that they are related but not the same. Balance and movement are the outward, more obvious expressions of the subtler, more sensitive effects of proportion and rhythm.

Unity suggests balance, a balance of the forces within the composition. These forces are the forces of tension, attraction, attention, and movement that exist between the forms of a stage design. All scenery forms have mass and size (dimension), which means that their proportion must be considered. And lastly, the proportional relationship between forms cannot help but bring rhythm into the composition, whether it be static or dynamic in feeling.

Balance and Movement

Balance is described as the relationship of forces within a composition. But what is the visual expression of a force? The strong visual pull of attraction and attention are forces. The intense colors of a poster attract the eye. The attention value of the poster contains the interest and meaning that stimulate a response in the viewer.

These two forces, attraction and attention, are of significance to scene design. Many times a setting has to make a telling effect in the opening moments of a play and then have sufficient attention value to sustain interest through two hours of performance.

A visual expression of tension also exists between forms. The degree of tension is dependent upon the interval or space between forms. The space between the finger of God and Adam as God gives life to man in Michelangelo's fresco in the Sistine Chapel is an example of tension. The spark of life can almost be seen. If the fingers were touching, or moved farther apart, the tension would be absent. Tension as a force is found in the composition of a setting in the spacing of scenery masses, the grouping of furniture, or in the relationship of the actor to the scenery and furniture.

Another example of a force in composition is the force of gravity and the viewer's unconscious reaction to it. Gravity has probably the greatest effect on balance. A viewer reacts to visual signs with an organic sense of balance schooled by a lifetime of living with the pull of gravity. Because of this, an unsupported heavy object may seem to be falling, as does a leaning object, unless its center of gravity holds it in balance. Also, a recognizable shape in an unnatural position may cause a feeling of imbalance. The reverse is also true. To abstract a recognizable shape, the designer sometimes consciously uses unnatural position as pure design in an effort to deny reality.

Depth perception is also crucial in the theatre. It allows a viewer to judge whether objects are in the same plane or are receding in proper order. However, it is the same sense of depth on the part of the theatre audience that is fooled, by altering the signs of space perception through perspective foreshortening, into seeing more distance than is actually on the stage.

Movement as a contributor to unity is concerned with *change* and *time*. The harmonious and progressive change of the sequence of gradation is an example of movement as the eye is led, step by step, through the change of color, form, dimension, or direction.

A well-organized form has a firmly established plan of movement. Some arrangements of form stimulate a greater sense of movement than others. Some cause a different kind of movement, such as a precarious balance of tension. The plan of movement within a composition, in any event, is a closed plan, always staying or returning to the overall form.

In the theatre, as has been noted, the inclusion of time in actual movement is quite apparent. The actors move from area to area; the lights dim and brighten; scenery, on occasion, moves in view of the audience. All these are part of the composition of the dramatic form and involve the element of time. The element of time, however, exists in a fixed composition too.

There is an interval of time as the eye follows the pattern of movement through a composition. The interval is minute, of course, when compared to the broader movements on stage. The visual change can lead the eye, abruptly or gradually in terms of time, over the movement plan of a composition. (See "Optical motion" earlier in this chapter.)

Proportion and Rhythm

The second portion of obtaining unity in a composition is the use of proportion and rhythm. Proportional judgment is probably one of the initial signs of talent. A certain amount can be aquired by training and sharpened by analysis, but a sense of proportion is largely intuitive.

Proportion is the ratio of something to something else. On stage it is natural to relate proportion to the human figure, for the actor is a

a   b

FIGURE 3–15

Scale

The feeling of scale in a stage setting is linked to the size of the human figure. In these two examples, the design forms are identical in size. Their scale changes in relation to the size of the figure in the composition.

part of the total composition. In the theatre this is referred to as *scale*. The designer is constantly checking the size of a form in ratio to human scale (Figure 3–15). Some productions demand a greater scale or an increased ratio of the size of surrounding forms to the actor.

Proportion can also be linked to the reason or function of a visual form. The proportion of a chair as a visual form, for example, depends upon how the chair is to be used. A simple dining-room side chair is small when compared to the scale and the grandeur of a canopied throne chair. Stage settings and even entire productions can differ in scale for similar reasons. The proportions of the ballroom scene in *Romeo and Juliet*, for example, are of more significance than the scale of Friar Laurence's cell; similarly, the pageantry of *Henry VIII* demands greater scale as a production than *The Merchant of Venice*, which is of more intimate proportions.

Many forms and arrangements of forms, however, are not associated with human scale. In addition to the concept of proportion as scale a proportional relationship exists between one form and another and between the space used between forms. Perhaps more important is the proportional relationship of forms to their surrounding space. The rhythm and proportions of a sculptural arrangement of forms set in an unbound space, for example, may seem different from a similar arrangement of shapes framed or confined within a rectangular shape such as a proscenium opening.

Although scene designing, at least in its formative stages, composes within a rectangular or near-rectangular shape, it is also concerned with the freer compositions of the nonproscenium stage. Designing for nonproscenium theatre approaches the use of sculptural techniques to create a desirable proportional relationship between scenic forms in a more or less undefined space. Whereas the composition within a proscenium frame is viewed basically from a frontal direction, nonproscenium scenic forms have to be composed satisfactorily for viewers from all directions.

FIGURE 3–16

Change of Scale

Example of increased human scale. The larger-than-life actors are in the Guthrie Theatre production of *The House of Atreus,* an adaptation from Aeschylus' *Oresteia* by John Lewin. Designer— Tanya Moiseiwitsch.

As balance is linked to movement, so proportion is joined with rhythm. The space between forms and the attitude of one shape to another creates a rhythm in the composition. Rhythm is a type of movement that recurs at intervals or completes a cycle. The proportional relationship between forms establishes a rhythm, as does the subdivision of single form.

a

b

FIGURE 3–17

Rhythm and Movement in Composition

(a) A composition based on diagonal lines has a definite sense of movement. (b) A composition based on strong horizontals and verticals has a static feeling.

A conscious inner relation and rhythm is present in stage composition in many ways. It may appear in the quiet dignity of a formal arrangement or in the vigorous movement of a dynamic composition. Or it may be expressed in the rhythmic flow of harmonious forms or in a nervous, staccatolike organization of shapes.

Rhythm as a unifying factor is usually expressed in the lines or linear qualties of a stage composition. The use of actual lines or the feeling of a line caused by the position and direction of one shape to another results in a rhythmic movement that may be as strong or as subdued as the designer desires. Diagonal lines and lines parallel to the diagonals give a greater sense of movement than the use of strong horizontal and vertical lines, which tend to stop movement (Figure 3–17).

Although the rhythm of straight lines is more bold and forceful than curved lines, curved lines have infinitely greater variety. The rhythm of a curved line may have the grace of flowing lines, the turbulence of reverse curves, the whirl of a spiral, as well as the repetition and order of interlaced geometric curves such as circles and ovals.

Whether the rhythm of a stage composition is dominated by straight or curved lines, it eventually becomes a part of the basic movement plan. Likewise, the proportional relationship of forms, which determines the rhythm, forms a balance, resulting in greater feeling of unity, especially when the rhythm is visibly repetitious.

COMPOSITION AND INTEREST

In addition to maintaining unity in a stage composition, the designer tries to bring interest and meaning to the setting. Any meaning attached to the scenic forms of the composition is, of course, a part of the designer's interpretation of the scenic requirements of the play that are a result of an attempt to bring visual substance to the playwright's ideas (Chapter 1).

A stage setting, however, can fulfill all the scenic requirements of the play and still not be interesting. Just what makes one setting for a play more interesting than another?

A setting is interesting many times because of a unique and daring design interpretation which stimulates an intellectual response on the part of the audience. This is frequently possible when the play is a classic or one familiar to the audience. European scene designers constantly produce exciting and innovative design approaches to well-established classics. In university and community theatres in the United States, where people are going to see a production or interpretation of a well-known play more often than a new play, the emphasis is also often on the design idea or an exciting production scheme.

The designer, unfortunately, cannot take such great liberties with a new play. Here the audience is seeing the play for the first time and will not appreciate too "intellectual" an approach unless it is a part of the production scheme. It is more important to first stimulate the proper emotional response and not to allow a self-conscious design to overwhelm the play.

The way in which a designer achieves balance in composition also accounts for one design being more interesting than another. A mechanical balance of the design forms may bring unity to a composition but still be monotonous and uninteresting. An interesting composition varies or stretches the balance into a more exciting arrangement of forms without losing unity.

Types of Proportional Balance

Several types of arrangements of forms bring a sense of balance or equilibrium to a specific area. These arrangements are classified as axial, radial, and occult balance.

Axial balance is a symmetrical arrangement of forms of equal weight on either side of an axis. The axis may be an actual line or a central-division line. A composition based on such a symmetrical balance may seem dignified and classical in feeling though rather static and severe in effect (Figure 3–18a).

a

b

The Design Concept

c

d

FIGURE 3–18

Balance in Composition

(a) Symmetrical balance. *Fidelio.* Designer—Donald Oenslager. (Photo—Grimes) (b) Asymmetrical balance. *Up in Central Park.* Designer—Howard Bay. (Photo—Graphic) (c) Radial balance. *Les Troyens.* Designer—Peter Wexler, Metropolitan Opera. (Photo—Copyright © Beth Bergman) (d) Occult balance. *The Ancient Mariner.* Designer—Robert Edmond Jones.

The formality of symmetry can be eased somewhat by using an asymmetrical arrangement wherein the basic forms remain in symmetry but with a variation of color or detail taking place within the overall forms.

A stage setting of a formal or architectural nature frequently employs symmetrical balance, both within the composition (individual wall treatment) and as a whole. Sometimes a near-symmetrical arrangement is used to give the effect of symmetrical balance in a softer, freer manner (Figure 3–18b).

Radial balance is a symmetrical balance around a center, and the movement is always circular. It is most useful in a decorative pattern or ornamental detail, although it may occasionally be seen in the floor plan of a setting (Figure 3–18c).

Occult balance differs from axial balance in the absence of any axis or focal center. It is the balance of unlike elements, the felt balance of mass against space. There are no rules for the achievement or use of occult balance except the judgment of the designer. The result can be a feeling of greater movement and excitement which lends itself readily to dramatic uses (Figure 3–18d).

Because occult balance depends on the interrelationship of elements within the composition, the use of proportion and rhythm aid the designer to arrive at the delicate balance present in an occult arrangement.

Center of Interest

Unless the composition is an overall pattern, it is organized about a center of interest, or focal point. This is a point in the composition (not necessarily the center) to which the eye of the viewer is led by either obvious or subtle means. The leadlines which are present in the movement plan of the composition direct the eye to the center of interest. In addition to the focal center there may also be secondary areas of interest as well as intriguing bits of detail within the composition which hold attention yet do not detract from the main point of focus.

A stage setting is usually designed around a strong center of interest with important secondary areas. Although the setting as a background has its own center of interest, the true center of interest in the total visual effect is the actor. As was mentioned earlier, a stage composition is a fluid, ever-changing thing with a different center of interest for each scene.

Fortunately, stage lighting, costume colors, and the movement of actors all help to make any change of emphasis rather simple. By dimming most of the lights and brightening one area, stage lighting can easily bring focus to a specific point on the stage, as can the color of a costume in relation to the setting and to other costumes in the scene. The movement of the actor can also be used to change the center of focus, as is so effectively demonstrated in a ballet or group-dance

The Design Concept

composition. The mobility of the actor allows the director to use groups of actors as a composition tool in order to direct the interest of the audience to any portion of the stage setting. The contributions of stage lighting, costumes, and groupings of actors toward the complete stage composition all serve to emphasize the importance of the visual side of the theatre as well as to underline the function of scene design as a visual art.

FIGURE 3–19
Centers of Interest

Designer's sketch for Archibald Macleish's *JB.* The stage composition has two well-defined centers of interest. The shift of emphasis from one to the other was accomplished by varying the intensity and distribution of light. Designer— Donald Oenslager. (Courtesy Yale School of Drama)

4

The Design Idea

At this point, beginning designers should be conscious of the importance scene design has in relation to the play. They should be aware of the influences of the theatrical medium and be familiar with the intricacies of the creative process. But, they may ask, how does one get an idea for a design?

It is impossible to set down universal rules for developing a design idea; there are as many methods as designers. And an individual method is often so subjective and intuitive that it is of little value to another designer as a way of working; each must and usually does develop his or her own method of reaching the inner reservoir of creative ideas.

Still, although it is possible to make recommendations and to point to examples of good design, the actual conquest of an idea is the designer's individual struggle.

The design idea, of course, doesn't exist until the play becomes a production and the written word becomes dialogue and visible action. It is the individual expression of the artistic imagination, theatrical sense, and technical ingenuity of the designer through the visual control of line, color, and form. The design concept is often evident as a visual theme with variations that weave through a complicated setting or series of settings, bringing unity of thought to the whole. Many times the theme is so subtle that only the trained eye of another designer can see and appreciate its presence.

The design idea is aimed at stimulating an intellectual or emotional response in the audience. The control of the design elements may be broad and sensational to arouse primitive emotions, or they may be subtle and refined to stimulate an intellectual response. Good design is the result of logical yet imaginative thinking and intuitive feeling expressed through an idea or central theme.

The ideas for many an inspirational setting have been worked out on the back of an envelope during a coffee break or have been virtually completed before the author has finished the third act. Although this is frequently the pace at which a scene designer is expected to work, it is hardly a practical procedure for an inexperienced designer.

ANALYSIS OF THE PLAY

Developing a concept for a setting begins with the study of the play. Ideally, the play is analyzed from three separate readings, assuming that the designer will have the script longer than overnight or for more than two hours on a train. The three separate readings represent the logical steps toward accumulating information that shapes and inspires the design idea.

The designer's first reading of the play is for its content. The designer should react as a member of the audience, avoiding any preconceived image of the background other than the author's description. In this way a first impression will serve as an overall response that will help answer these questions: What kind of a play is it? What is the action and where is it taking place? What is the dominant mood? Is the play a comedy? Or is it a tongue-in-cheek satire with political overtones? Is it a tragedy of classical proportions or a domestic misunderstanding?

The scene of the action often suggests or sets the atmosphere of a play. A deserted house on a stormy night for a mystery or a love scene by candlelight are typical examples. The action, however, is not always in harmony with its surroundings but may be in opposition or contrast to its environment.

The mood of a play or scene often suggests *color* to the designer. Out of the mood of the environment comes the overall tonality of the play, which often can be expressed most forcefully in color or even in the absence of color.

The second reading is for the play's intent. What is the author saying? It is a more careful reading—between the lines and within parentheses. What is the theme? What is the style? Has the author expressed a point of view through allegorical symbols or in daily-life realism? Has the playwright soared into the realm of epic poetry or dropped into the lusty imagery of sidewalk prose? In the style of the play the designer finds a clue to the degree of reality or unreality of the scenic environment.

From the theme of the play the designer can usually find a visual image that leads to a design concept. And from the style of the play the designer gets an indication of the *form* of the design. Style and form interact, for style influences form. A realistic style implies realistic forms; a fantasy or dream suggests unreal forms.

STYLE, FORM, AND CONCEPT

Because style in the theatre is felt, heard, and seen in so many different ways, it is difficult to define in specific terms. Literary, acting, directing, and visual styles, as well as period styles, unite to form a single production style. Style is sometimes visually obvious, but more often it will be unnoticed by the audience unless some element of it is jarring or incorrect in terms of the whole.

Style, form, and concept are so closely interrelated that it is hard to distinguish where one begins and the other leaves off. Briefly, style can be defined as the degree of reality expressed in visual forms and the mode of performance. Style (or the degree of reality) influences form. Concept is the *idea* or manner of presenting style and form. In other words, concept is the expression of an idea in a degree of reality (or unreality) that cannot help but affect the form of the design and the manner of performance.

Production Style and Reality. The overall style of a production is expressed in the degree of reality of the performance. There are many kinds of reality in the theatre: the lifelike copy of nature (naturalism), the fantasy of dreams, the make-believe quality of storytelling, the immediacy of documentary or of improvisational style, and the performance reality of the theatrical style. The two extreme realities in a performance are the lifelike quality of naturalism and the theatrical reality of presentational theatre. It might be seen as the difference between the actor and the performer.

The theatrical reality of the performer is something that *is* happening at the moment as opposed to an actor's dramatic re-creation of something that *has* happened but in such a way as to make the audience believe that they are experiencing it for the first time. Each is a different degree of reality to which the audience reacts with contrasting emotions. Although an audience may justly appreciate an actor's convincing performance, the reality is still make-believe. If, for example, a light cue is missed or scenery falls down, the make-believe spell is broken with an unfortunate intrusion of reality. A presentational style, however, might keep technical mishaps and muffed lines in the routine to give the performance an immediate reality.

Occasionally production styles are combined. The docudrama style (documentary and literary styles) is often used to capture the emotion of an actual happening. It has the factual reality of a documentary but is actually a fictional style. The documentary format heightens the reality and holds the audience while the story unfolds.

The docudrama, as a style, is less convincing on the stage than in the more immediate media of radio and television. A classic example of the emotional impact of a docudrama style occurred in 1938. Orson Welles' famous radio adaptation of H. G. Wells' *War of the Worlds* was presented as a newscaster's report of the landing of the Martians. The docudrama was so real that many listeners were on the verge of panic.

Visual Style and Form. The effect of style on form is more easily seen in visual styles than in the performance styles just discussed, although the two are related. Visual styles can be defined in similar degrees of reality.

The representional style, for example, is lifelike. The design form is represented in a painting or sculpture rendered as near to its natural form and color as the technical skill of the artist allows.

The nonrepresentational style, the opposite reality, is ornamental. Because its goal is sensation, the interplay of sheer form and color becomes important. The designer does not attempt to create a form that bears any resemblance to natural or manmade objects.

Between these two extremes lie as many degrees of realism, symbolism, abstraction, or complete nonobjectivity as designers care to define.

The effect of style on form is more apparent as the degree of reality decreases. The form is distorted into an abstract but recognizable shape. The metamorphosis of a tree form on the stage can be used to illustrate the influence of style on form (Figure 4–1, page 78). For example, the realistic apple tree in Osborn's *Borrowed Time* contrasts with the decorative forest in Gilbert and Sullivan's *Iolanthe* and with the abstract trees in the forest scene of Dürrenmatt's *The Visit*. The trees in the latter production were reduced to pendants of gauze that were slashed with side lighting and projected patterns on the floor.

As a visual art, scenery styles conform to the same degrees of reality as do production styles. Scenery style, in fact, is the most important visual element supporting the overall production style (Figure 4–2).

FIGURE 4–1

Style and Form

The scenic tree is used to illustrate the influence of style on form. (Top) Lifelike apple tree for *On Borrowed Time*. (Center) Fanciful forest for *Iolanthe*. (Bottom) Abstract trees from the forest scene in *The Visit*.

Realism—Interior

First in Heart. Designer—William Eckart. (Photo—Shapiro)

Realism—Exterior

The Three Sisters. Designer—Alvin Schechter. (Photo—Baker)

FIGURE 4–2 (pages 79–84)
VISUAL STYLES OF SCENERY

The Design Idea

Stylization—Painted
Happy as Larry. Designer—William Bohnert. (Photo—Shapiro)

Stylization—Caricature
Tango by S. Mrozek. Designer—Travers Mercer. (Photo—Nelson)

80

Anti-Illusionary Scenery

Puntila by Bertolt Brecht. An example of Brecht's aversion to illusionary or "make-believe" scenery. Real, unconventional textures such as the straw-covered portals, unpainted old boards, and a brass sun are used. The result is of course not realism but stylization which, though denying illusion, is still theatrical. (Photo—Nelson)

Surrealism

Right You Are If You Think You Are by Luigi Pirandello. Designer—William Matthews. (Photo—Feinstein)

Fragmentary Scenery

(Above) *Beethoven.* Designer—Ariel Balif. (Photo—Shapiro) (Below) A view from the wings of a setting for the operatic version of Eugene O'Neill's *Mourning Becomes Electra* at the Metropolitan Opera, New York. The highly stylized interpretation of the stately Classic Revival style is achieved by the imaginative use of textured surfaces and exposed structural members. Designer—Boris Aronson. (Photo—Gary Renaud)

Suggested Scenery
A minimum of scenic elements suggests in a theatrical manner the elegant interior and nostalgic exterior for Turgenev's *A Month in the Country.* Scene Designer—John Conklin. Lighting Designer—Jennifer Tipton. Williamstown Theatre Festival.

Reality and Light. It is obvious that the lighting and scene designers must be aware of all styles in the theatre, for they are called upon to visually support (and occasionally contrast) the acting, literary, and directing styles and create a unified production style.

The reality of light on the stage is easily seen in its degree of conformity (or lack of comformity) to light in nature. We are so used to seeing each other under normal angles, distribution, and colors of the sun that when these angles deviate, or when colors change too much, we consider the light "unreal" or "theatrical." The low angle and rich colors of a sunset are frequently so dramatic that they seem to belong

The Design Idea

Period Theatrical Style

Not a revival but a concept in the manner of a specific period theatrical style. *The Merchants* by Plautus becomes a Roman vaudeville with an "ad-drop" oleo for a background. Designer—Donald Oenslager. Costumes—Frank Bevan. (Courtesy Yale School of Drama Library)

on the stage. For the same reason, light on an actor from a low angle seems unnatural or stylized.

Although much of stage lighting may seem naturalistic in style, there are types of theatrical productions and performances that are more dependent on a style of color, distribution, and movement of light than on general illumination or visibility. Ballet, for example, is a theatrical extension of life into a highly stylized performance technique. Realistic illumination is less important than the theatrical atmosphere, exotic colors, and arbitrary angles of light that make up this style of production.

FIGURE 4–3
Style and Light

Two versions of the same play, *Old Times*, in a flexible theatre arrangement. (Below) Abstract use of light, forms, and costumes. (Bottom) A more formal approach using light to define area.

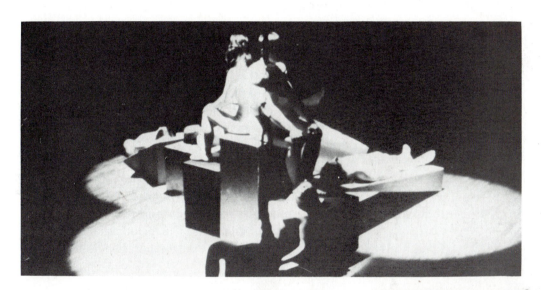

The theatrical reality of Brecht, on the other hand, strips away atmosphere and illusion. Lighting instruments are exposed and uncolored to reinforce the feeling that what we are seeing is happening *now*, on the stage in the reality of the performance.

Historical Style and Concept. Historical styles, both period and national, are significant in their own right. The effect of each period on form is quite clear. The geometric and flamboyant tracery of Gothic, for example, is distinct from the reverse curve of the baroque and the whiplash of art nouveau. The same is true of national styles. There is a difference, for example, in the forms of the rococo in France, Germany, and Austria.

When a historical style is used on the stage, however, it becomes a *concept,* for it is not *the* period that is being demonstrated but a conceptualization of the historical style. The historical scenes in Miller's *The Crucible*, for example, are conceptual versions of seventeenth-century America. It is not too difficult to see that period style can take on many degrees of reality. A historical period can be authentically reproduced, suggested, or even spoofed.

Historical moments in theatre frequently serve as a framework for a contemporary idea. The Shevelove/Gilbart/Sondheim musical *A Funny Thing Happened on the Way to the Forum,* for example, is a burlesque of Roman comedy with a present-day message. *Girl Friend* is a nostalgic spoof of life and the theatre of the 1920s. The melodramatic revival of such plays as *Under the Gaslights* is an exaggeration of period mannerism as a concept.

Finding a Concept. The search for a concept cannot help but be influenced by personal taste, background, and experience. An experienced designer falls into the habit of mentally storing ideas and then waiting for the opportunity to use them. By observing people, nature, and unusual happenings, the designer develops an eye to see and record.

Ideas in one art medium can be transposed into another. To work, for example, in the manner of a famous painter—colors from the palette of Cézanne, the light of Rembrandt, and the forms of Picasso— can suggest a compositional control of light and form within a stage production. The dramatic colors and the compositional use of light of Turner are another example of elements that are very adaptable to a stage color concept.

In Chapter 3 we mentioned that the strong emphasis of a single element such as line, color, or light in a composition becomes a design control leading to a concept. *Carmen Jones,* a black musical version of Bizet's opera *Carmen,* keyed each act to a single color. This progression of color and intensity reinforced the emotional climax.

Movement as an element of design is frequently used in a lighting concept. It can be expressed in the movement of color and the distribution of light in dance, or to interpret the rhythm of music in color and form.

Light can also dominate a composition and become a concept. Patterns of exposed sources, specific distribution, or projected images can become a visual style with light as the central force. Natural light and colors can also be an inspiration. The crushing intensity of the sun, the dampness of a forest, or the fog of a river can be lighting concepts that give the designer a control or way of thinking and creating.

A thematic image can lead to a variety of uses of symbolic form, color, or atmosphere. Symbolism in scenery and light can be extremely subtle, serving basically as a control for the director and the designers. Obvious symbolism could cause a negative response on the part of the audience and should be used with caution. Too much symbolism in scenic forms can be so overwhelming that the actor and playwright's words are anticlimactic.

FIGURE 4–4
Symbolism

The Roar of the Greasepaint and the Smell of the Crowd. Designer—Adel A. Migid.

FIGURE 4–5

Concept and Style

An interesting concept for Ben Jonson's *The Alchemist.* The Elizabethan comedy was set in the time of the California Gold Rush, when a similar preoccupation with gold prevailed. Designer—Richard L. Hay. Oregon Shakespearean Festival. (Photo—Hank Kranzler)

Style and Theatre Forms. Today's theatre is moving away from naturalism toward a more imaginative use of style. The stage, rather than trying to compete with the photographic realism of the movies and television, has turned to more abstract, stylized, and sometimes expressionistic styles in both writing and staging. However, an interesting contrast of styles has developed in the production concepts of the two nonproscenium theatre forms, the thrust and arena stage. Where the emphasis of the proscenium theatre was on *production,* we find the thrust and arena theatres concentrating on *performance.*

The lack of scenic elements on the thrust and arena stages calls on the imagination of the audience to complete the scene. Invisible walls and doors, different locales indicated by levels on the floor, hanging fragments overhead, and the color of light are common theatrical conventions on thrust and arena stages. They establish an abstract degree of reality the audience is asked to accept as a mode of production. On the other hand, furniture and hand properties are painstakingly real, and the actor's costumes are fully detailed in a contrast of styles. Be-

The Design Concept

cause the audience is physically closer to the action, it is virtually in the scene and a part of the action. There is a more subjective or intimate alliance of audience and performer when the proscenium wall is removed, although the reality is very much a theatrical reality.

The proscenium theatre, on the other hand, depends on aesthetic distance and a more objective relationship with its audience. There is, however, a great latitude of expression from bare stage to full stage productions in a variety of styles, and on occasion, a thrust through the proscenium for closer contact with the audience.

Acting and Literary Styles. Dramatic form combines the literary and acting styles. With scenery style, they all have an effect on each other and must have some degree of unity in order to create a strong dramatic form.

The literary style reveals through dialogue the degree of ideality represented in the play. The style of a play may capture a cross-section of life, such as Elmer Rice's *Street Scene,* or it may be as expressionistic as the treatment of Mr. Zero's problems in Rice's *The Adding Machine.*

The epic style of Brecht and his attempts to denude the stage of illusion or any visual make-believe obviously has had its influence on scenery style. By appealing to the intellectual side of the members of his audience, and denying them any escape into sentimentality, Brecht forces them to listen, and perhaps more important, to react. The belief that any reaction, even the shock of unconventionality, is better than having a passive, hypnotized audience is reflected in elements of scenery. Thus, a barren stage, the presence of *real* materials and textures, exposed lighting instruments, and clear unatmospheric lighting create the essence of his scenes.

Paradoxically, this opposition to the fakery of illusionary scenery and the effort to free the theatre of conventionality actually imposes a new system of theatrical hocus-pocus. The result is almost a scenic stylization that is in tune with present-day junk sculpture and pop art and which the audience responds to in vicarious recognition of its unconventional cleverness.

The acting style of today, for the most part, is believably real when compared to the highly mannered period examples of the seventeenth, eighteenth, and nineteenth centuries. Acting style, however, may vary from naturalism to conform with the style of a specific drama. It takes its cue, as does scenery, from the literary style of the play.

The theatre contains many examples of conflicting literary and acting styles: one illustration is the nineteenth-century conception of opera. A stilted literary style was combined with a presentational acting style of singing dialogue—both set against a conflicting background of painted realism. Today, the style of the scenery has been brought closer to the less realistic acting and writing styles to form a more unified and convincing art form.

FIGURE 4–6

Style and Theatre Form

The thrust and arena stage often force the designer into a theatrical convention or stylization that would be optional in the proscenium theatre. (Above) Two scenes from a thrust stage production of Miller's *A View from the Bridge.* Levels and a change of texture define the areas placed in front of an abstraction of the city. Scene Designer—Tim Jozwick. Lighting Designer—Gilbert Hemsley, Jr. Loretta Hilton Theatre, Saint Louis. (Right) An intimate staging of O'Neill's *A Moon for the Misbegotten.* Designer—Richard L. Hay, Oregon Shakespearean Festival. (Photo—Hank Kranzler)

Scene design, as a visual art, can reinforce and heighten literary and acting styles. Strangely enough, it can on occasion be a contrast to the acting style without breaking the unity of the production. The designer has always felt that stylized scenery does not necessarily call for stylized acting, as was demonstrated so expertly in Jo Mielziner's setting for Miller's *Death of a Salesman.* The reverse, however, is not true. If the acting is stylized, the scenery must be, too. The important thing is that the audience will accept any degree of departure from the real in scenery as long as it is consistent and in good taste.

90　　　　　*The Design Concept*

WORKING WITH THE DIRECTOR

During this formative stage there is only so much a designer can do alone. From the beginning there is a need for close communication with the director, especially if a strong directorial concept is considered in the design. Directorial influence on design can vary from a complete "hands-off-solve-it-yourself" attitude to a "this-is-what-I-want" directive. A more equally balanced collaboration is, naturally, ideal. One-sided domination can lead to personality clashes that abort the creative process. The most successful and unified productions are usually the result of the mutual respect and open-mindedness on the part of both the designer and the director.

The collaboration, of course, begins with talking. Preliminary discussions can lead to agreement about the nature of the play, the dramatic image, and general atmosphere (colors, style, staging, and directorial concept). Talk, however, has its limits. Words have a way of triggering a different image in each individual. At some point the designer must put visual impressions on paper. Only then can the designer and director really begin to communicate.

An understanding and agreement about *style* is probably the most important part of the designer-director collaboration, especially if other designers are involved in the production (costume and lighting). Although the impact of a style confusion appears later in the execution of the design, it is significant enough to be mentioned now at the formative stage.

The theatre, as we have seen, brings together many styles. During production, the director is the only one with an overall view and therefore must be responsible for coordinating the various styles as the show is being put together. The lack of immediate communication to the designer or designers of directorial changes or style adjustments in other areas of design can lead to conflicts at a time in the production schedule when it is too late to make changes. The best-laid plans can go astray without constant supervision and communication on the part of the director. An experienced designer soon learns to not take anything for granted and makes frequent checks with the director and other areas of design.

Final Reading

After reaching a mutual understanding with the director on theme, style, and general interpretation of the play, the designer returns to the script for a third reading.

This reading of the play is for its technique. Close attention is paid to the physical requirements of the plot structure and, if there are many scenes, to the changes of locale. The action and staging requirements are examined to determine the number of people in a scene, the types of entrances and exits, references in the dialogue to the scene, bits of action hidden from one actor but visible to the audience, and so on—all leading to the development of a basic idea and scheme of production.

Scheme of Production

The design solution of a multiscene play, which is known as a scheme of production, brings scenery-handling techniques into the design concept. The design idea is developed around a method of handling the numerous changes of scene. The kinds of changes and the methods of handling scenery, such as wagons and turntables, are discussed fully in Chapter 10 and indicate the necessity of designing a large production around at least a basic scheme for moving the scenery.

Although discussed separately, a scheme of production is, of course, closely related to *style*. Many times the designer, through a scheme of production, establishes certain conventions that the audience is expected to accept and which, consequently, create a scenery style. Conversely, a scenery style may dictate how the scenery is to be handled, thereby becoming a scheme of production.

FIGURE 4–7
The Unit Setting
The production scheme for Anouilh's *Colombe* as produced by the Yale Dramatic Association. The repetition of the theatre proscenium form brings a visual and thematic unity to the production.

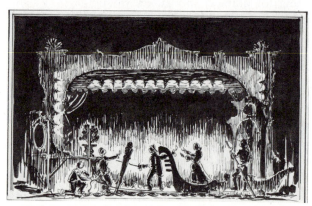

The Design Concept

Unit Setting. The movement of scenery may be reduced by the various uses of a unit setting. This form of setting is based upon the retention or reuse of certain elements of scenery to stimulate a change of scene. This is usually accomplished by repeating either the plan, design shape, or color in the various settings. The design shapes and colors, for example, may be varied in each setting although they are placed in identical floor plans, or the same shape can be moved to a variety of positions.

A unit setting can be used in two different ways, either as a cleverly camouflaged method of reusing scenery unbeknown to the audience, or as an obvious device that becomes a unifying force for the production, as well as a means of simplifying scene changes (Figure 4–7).

Simultaneous-Scene Setting. Sometimes a production scheme can eliminate all movement of scenery by placing two or more locales on the stage at the same time. The action moves from one area to the other without a break. The only movement is in the changing of lights. The areas, which retain their initial identity throughout the show, may be different rooms in a house, different houses in the same town, or remotely located scenes (Figure 4–8).

Although the simultaneous-scene setting is mentioned here as one of the many schemes of production, it was, of course, discussed earlier as a kind of production that emphasized the important design function of staging the story (Chapter 1). Even though the scenic elements and furniture in the simultaneous-scene setting may appear as extreme

FIGURE 4–8

Simultaneous Scene

(Left) The juxtaposition of several locales in *The Shadow Box.* Scene Design—Christopher Nowak. Lighting Designer—Roger Meeker. Williamstown Theatre Festival. (Right) A design by Peter Larkin for *Inherit the Wind.* Ink and wash, 1955. From *The Arts of the United States: A Survey in Color,* conducted by the University of Georgia. Reproduced by courtesy of Peter Larkin.

realism, the style of the setting is, in the final analysis, unrealistic. The audience is asked to accept theatrical conventions such as *cut-away walls* and *strange locale juxtapositions* to facilitate the staging of the story.

Formal Setting. A freer example of the simultaneous-scene setting is the use of an arrangement of abstract or architectural forms in such a way as to allow a flow of action over the set, relying on lights to change the composition. Three or four basic areas may be established, but they do not take on the connotation of a specific locale. A formal setting locates the action only in a very general way. It is contingent upon the actors, properties, and dialogue to establish the specific locale of the scene. Occasionally a formal setting is dressed with a minimum of moving set pieces to add variety (Figure 4–9).

Projected Scenery. Light projections as scenery are included with many production schemes for handling multiscene shows. The rear projection of a design onto a translucent screen makes the shifting of a scene as simple as the changing of a slide (see Chapter 18).

Because projected scenery is *light* and not *paint* it has a strong dramatic quality which tends to dominate the scene. It becomes in a sense an actor rather than scenery. Projected scenery, when used correctly

FIGURE 4–9

Formal Setting

Example of a setting based on an interesting arrangement of steps and levels, providing several acting areas for the fluid action of the play. Changes were achieved by the clever use of lighting to reveal portions of the basic setting in a variety of interesting compositions. *Divine Comedy*. Designer—Peggy Clark. (Photo—Shapiro)

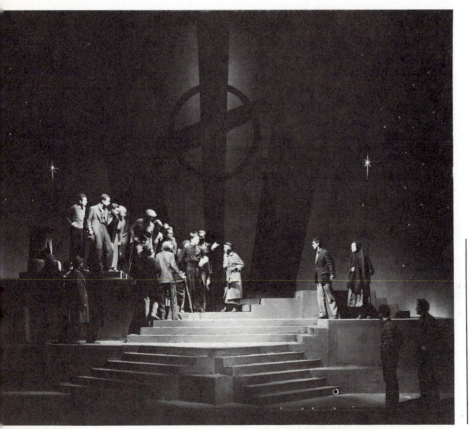

FIGURE 4–10

Projected Scenery

Page 95 shows one slide of a multiscope production of *Snows of Kilimanjaro* with a diagram of the screen, projection equipment, and setting relationships. (1) A pair of 5000-watt projection machines. (2) Translucent rear-projection screen. (3) Formal arrangement of platforms. Designer—Robert Thayer. (Photo—Shapiro)

Further examples of projected scenery appear on page 96.

The Design Concept

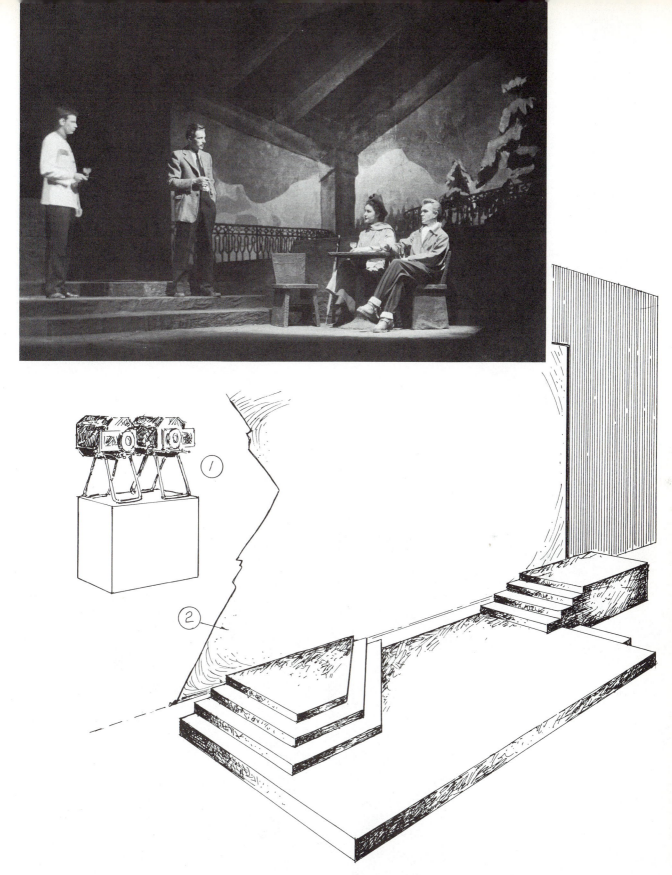

The Design Idea

A scene from Bertolt Brecht's *The Measures Taken* (above) illustrates the documentary use of projections, in which the screen is used as a visual support of a play's theme rather than to establish environment. Designer—Frederic Youens. (Photo—Nelson) (Below) In a brilliant example of the theatrical reality of projected scenery a plywood sculptural form became the icy crags of Patrick Meyers' *K2* through the joint efforts of Scene Designer Ursula Belden, Consultant Robert Westerfield, Lighting Designer Robert Jared, and Technical Director Ross Hamilton. The left photo shows one end of the Pittsburgh Public Theatre transformed into a 40-foot plywood mountain. Projected texture changed with time of day and was altered after the avalanche. Courtesy Larry Arrick, Artistic Director, and Dennis Babcock, Managing Director. (Photos—Greg Blackman)

as an integral part of the play, functions best in a nonrealistic or abstract production where the scenery is acting and not just background.

Brecht, for example, used the screen as an actor. He frequently projected instructive messages or illustrative images on the screen more as an instrument of propaganda or idea than as a visual background to set the scene. It is a classroom or documentary technique which when used in dramatic surroundings serves to heighten his epic theatre.

In spite of its limitations and dominating characteristics, projected scenery can be used as a highly dramatic and exciting production scheme. Many production designs have been based on projected scenery with successful results (Figure 4–10).

Preliminary Studies

The designer's first impression of a design concept may have been formed as early as the first reading of the play, only to be substantially revised or rejected after a closer study of the script in the second and third readings. A first impression is often correct, but sometimes it is wrong, and the designer may find it difficult to change this early impression. For this reason the beginning designer may be wise during the first reading of a new play to keep an open mind free of preconceptions until all the facts are accumulated. At that time everything usually falls into place with little or no effort.

An idea may first appear to the designer in the form of an interesting floor plan to be developed later into a related elevational drawing, or the reverse—as a decorative shape or historical form that must be adjusted to a workable floor plan.

Preliminary studies usually consist of small, freehand thumbnail sketches and rough floor plans. After consultation with the director, the tentative ideas of the designer are ready to be expanded into a more complete form of presentation.

PRESENTATION OF THE DESIGN IDEA

A designer may present ideas in two forms: as a two-dimensional sketch or as a three-dimensional model. Sometimes both a sketch and model are used. The sketch is usually used to sell the idea and the model is made later to more clearly indicate the space relationships and acting areas to the director and builder.

The Sketch

Although scene design is essentially a three-dimensional art form, the two-dimensional sketch medium is used to present the design idea. The sketch can be rendered in color and perspective to show atmosphere that would be difficult to accomplish in a model. Many

FIGURE 4–11
The Designer's Sketch

sketches can be made to show changes in lighting, scenery, and composition of the actors. The sketch is lightweight, easy to carry around, and therefore adaptable to the selling of an idea.

What is represented in the sketch depends somewhat on the working arrangement of the designer. For example, it may be an established designer working with a new producer, an established producer working with a new designer, or a producing team experienced in working together for some time.

The producer views the sketches of an established designer more with a knowledge of what the designer has done in past settings than for what is actually shown in the sketch. The producer knows that after an agreement on the general concept the experienced designer will fill in the details and create a setting to a high standard of excellence.

Because a new designer doesn't have past examples of work, his or her ideas are bought or rejected on the strength of a sketch. In addition, of course, the young designer must be able to back up all ideas with faithful execution.

Under either condition, the sketch tries to catch a significant moment in the play. The designer usually picks a moment that will best show the setting and still express the dominant mood of the play. The sketch is an idealized drawing of the total visual effect which serves as a goal

The Design Concept

for the execution and guide for the lighting. Supplementary sketches are sometimes needed to show what would happen at another dramatic moment with different lighting and actor grouping.

In the purest sense, however, the sketch is only a means of presenting an idea. It is not the final design and therefore should not be displayed or judged as a complete art form. A stage setting is not complete until it is on the stage, lighted and viewed in the context of the action of the play and the actors' movements. The judgment of the success or failure of a design in the final analysis is based on how it functions under finished performance conditions rather than as a beautiful sketch.

The sketch is not meant to be a working drawing. Although it maintains a consistent proportion to show the actor-scenery relationship, it is not necessarily drawn to an accurate scale. It is possible, however, to execute a design from a carefully proportioned sketch if large portions of the set are parallel to the footlights as in a wing-and-backdrop setting. The colors in the sketch are not intended to be the scenery colors, but represent the color as it would appear under the stage lights in the total visual effect.

If the designer is a member of an established producing group, such as summer stock or television, the sketch may take on a different character. The designer, director, builder, and painter may be so used

CONTENT
INTENT
TECHNIQUE

The Design Idea

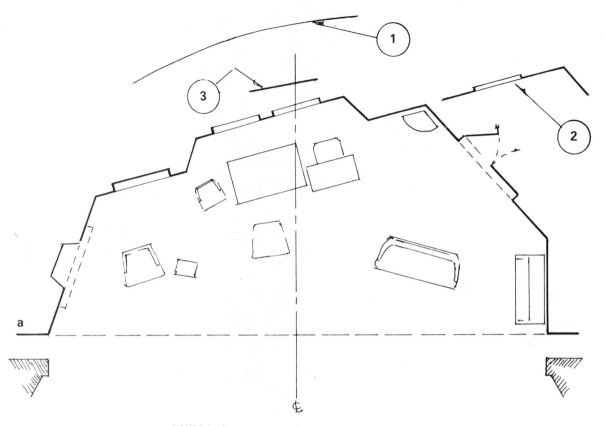

FIGURE 4–12

The Model

(a) Plan for model is the same as floor plan for the stage setting at a smaller scale, usually ¼″ = 1′0″. (b) Perspective view of assembled model. (c) Layout of set before corners have been scored or tabs cut prior to folding for assembly. (1) Sky backing. (2) Hall backing. (3) Treetop set piece. (4) Portal or tormentor–teaser proportion. (5) Block furniture to approximate space it will occupy onstage. (6) Cutout furniture. (7) Double doors.

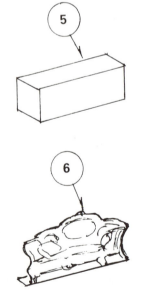

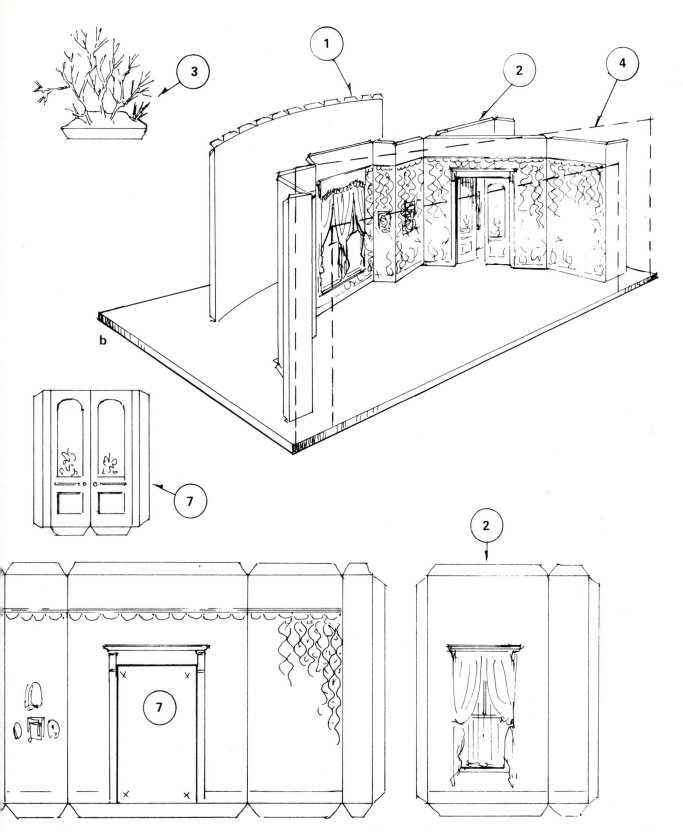

b

to working with each other that much will be understood without being set down on paper. The designer's sketch becomes schematic, with marginal notes. It is carried just as far as necessary to convey the idea and is drawn for the designer's *professional colleagues.* The designer will resort to a full sketch or model only when trying something experimental which needs careful explanation.

The sketch is always accompanied by a floor plan. If the floor plan is drawn to scale and the sketch is in good proportion, the director and others concerned with the production can form an accurate opinion as to how the actual setting will look.

The Model

Although the sketch has been pictured as the prime means of presenting an idea, it is frequently backed up by a model. Because of the three-dimensionality of scenery, some designers prefer to work directly in the model form of presentation. The model gives a true indication of the space relationships of scenery and actors and is, therefore, of interest to the director when planning the staging.

Within the model, each piece of scenery is constructed to an accurate scale, thus giving the designer a miniature preview of how the setting is going to look. Because the model is three-dimensional, composition and sightlines can be checked from all the extreme angles of view.

In addition to being a means of presentation, the model also can be used to check construction and effects before making a sketch. In this way the new designer is assured that all sketches can be reproduced in full-scale scenery without technical difficulties.

Figure 4–12 (pages 100–101) illustrates the steps in making a simple paper model. The paper used is white three-ply Bristol upon which is drawn a continuous elevation of each wall in the setting with pictures, draperies, and some furniture in place. All corners of the room are left joined so they can be scored and folded to fit the floor plans. Tabs are left on the top and bottom to stiffen the walls as well as to provide a glueing surface with which to attach the model to the floor plan and ceiling piece.

The scale of the model varies with the designer. Some like to work at the scale of one inch equal to one foot, while others prefer a smaller scale. The ¼-inch scale model is a convenient size for fast execution, which sometimes is important. The smaller scale is also convenient because it is easier to make changes and experiment with than a larger scale.

The sketch and model are the designer's means of presenting or selling a design concept. Once the director and designer have reached an area of agreement and the idea has been bought, the designer has to prepare another type of presentation; this time for the people who will build, paint, and light the design

The Design Concept

FIGURE 4–13

Designers' Sketches

(Above) The preliminary sketch: a designer's first thoughts. Sometimes in color, more often in black and white. Shown here is a preliminary ink-and-wash sketch for *Grand Hotel.* Designer—Anon Adar, Tel Aviv. (Below) A more finished sketch of the barn scene from Dürrenmatt's *The Visit.* The director insisted on a detailed, atmospheric sketch to set the tonality of the scene for everyone concerned with the production.

FIGURE 4–14

Sketch, Model, and Set

(Top to bottom) Designer's sketch, designer's model, and completed setting for *He Who Must Die,* a translation and adaptation of Nikos Kazantazakis' *The Greek Passion.* Designer—Rolf Beyer. (Photo—Street)

FIGURE 4–15

Sketch and Model

For a production of Whiting's *The Devils* the designer/director's concept was to portray the decadence and corruption of the church, government, and society of the times as a dungheap from which protruded bleached bones in Gothic shapes. Insta-foam embedded with straw and waste fragments helped convey the feeling. A less obvious influence was the unique forms of the Spanish art-nouveau architect Antonio Gaudí seen in the still-unfinished Sagrada Familia cathedral in Barcelona.

5

Drafting the Design

Although scene design is three-dimensional in final form, most of the presentation of the design idea in preparation for construction is two-dimensional in character. The graphics of presentation are the visual language or fundamental means of communication between the designer, stage technicians, and director. The planning of a show throughout all its phases relies upon a common knowledge of simple drafting techniques to communicate technical and artistic information. The designer must give simple, clear, and accurate information so that all ideas may be carried out efficiently and accurately.

DRAFTING EQUIPMENT

The young student designer will need to become acquainted with certain tools and materials. Drafting for the theatre is similar to architectural drafting and engineering drawing but is not as elaborate. For the beginner, a list of basic drafting equipment should include:

a   A drawing board or drafting table
b   Drawing board padding
c   T-square or parallel rule
d   Set of triangles or set-square
e   Small set of drafting instruments
   1   Compass
   2   Lengthening bar
   3   Inking attachments
   4   Dividers
   5   Bow compass and bow dividers
   6   Ruling pen
f   Scale rule
g   Pencils and leads
h   Tracing paper
i   Accessories
   1   Erasers
   2   Erasing shield
   3   Drafting tape
   4   Lead pointer
   5   Drawing cleaning powder
   6   Rapidograph pen

A good *drawing board* is made of clear white pine, cleated to prevent warping, and for most purposes is about 24 inches by 30 inches in size. A *drafting table*, the top of which is a drawing board, should be a little larger. A top of about 30 inches by 42 inches gives additional work space around the drawing.

Drawing boards need to be padded to prevent the pencil from following the grain of the wood. The best surface is a vinyl plastic cover that is tinted pale green on one side and an off white on the other. Although expensive, it is an excellent drafting surface and will last a lifetime.

The *T-square* guides off one side of the drawing board to establish the horizontal lines in the drawing. Its accuracy depends upon the straightness of the working edge and the squareness of the head and blade. A 30-inch T-square made of hardwood with a transparent-edge blade and fixed head is best for all-around service. A traveling parallel straight edge which serves the same function as a T-square is attached permanently to the top of a drafting table. Its length, of course, is determined by the longest dimension of the top.

Two transparent celluloid *triangles* give the customary set of angles as well as perpendicular lines when they are guided off of the

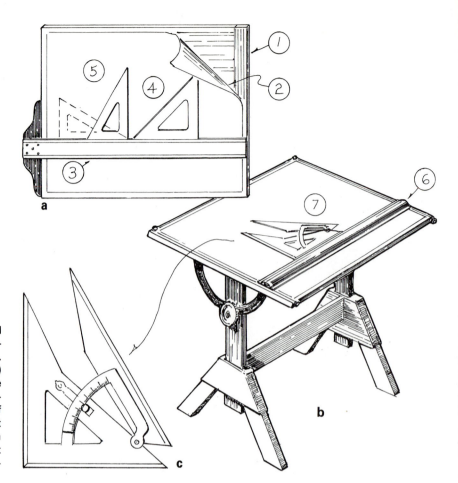

FIGURE 5–1

Drafting Equipment

(a) Drawing board and tools. (1) Cleated white-pine drawing board. (2) Tinted-vinyl padding for drawing-board surface. (3) T-square. (4) 45-degree triangle. (5) 30–60-degree triangle. (b) Drafting table with adjustable tilt and height. (6) Parallel straight edge attached to the top of the drawing table by a cable system that allows it to travel from top to bottom and remain parallel. (7) Set-triangle that is able to adjust to many different angles. (c) Detail of set-triangle.

T-square. A 6-inch 45-degree and an 8- or 10-inch 30–60-degree triangle are the most convenient sizes.

An instrument that lends itself to drawing the many odd angles so frequently found in a stage setting is the *set-square*. It is a combination triangle and protractor with an adjustable edge that allows the selection of any angle between 45 degrees and perpendicular.

When assembling drawing instruments for the first time, it is wise to invest in a good set. The accuracy and clarity of the work depends on the quality of the instruments. Buying a cheap, low-grade set is a nuisance from the beginning and will prove worthless in a short while. It is better to economize on the number or size of the set and buy good instruments.

The basic drafting instrument is the *compass*. It is necessary to draw a circle or swing an arc. Many small drafting sets consist only of a compass with lengthening bar and inking attachments. Extra points are also provided to turn the compass into dividers.

The *lengthening bar* is an attachment that increases the length of one arm of the compass, making it possible to swing a larger radius to make an arc or circle. An *inking attachment* can be fitted to the same

The Design Concept

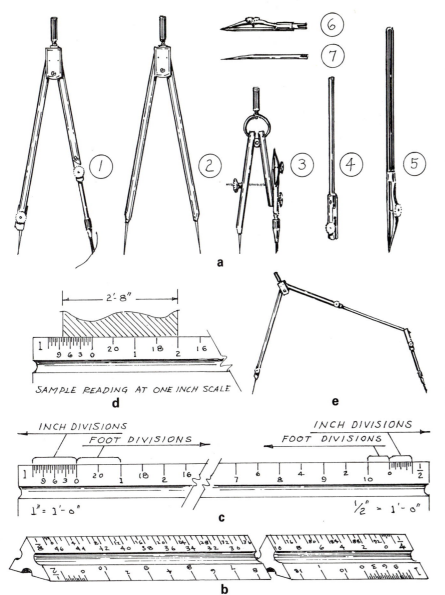

a

2'-8"

SAMPLE READING AT ONE INCH SCALE

d

e

INCH DIVISIONS
FOOT DIVISIONS

INCH DIVISIONS
FOOT DIVISIONS

1" = 1'-0"

½" = 1'-0"

c

b

FIGURE 5–2
Drafting Instruments

(a) The minimum set of drafting instruments. (1) Compass. (2) Dividers. (3) Combination bow compass and bow dividers with inking tip and divider points to replace pencil lead. (4) Extension arm for compass. (5) Ruling pen. (6) Inking tip for compass. (7) Divider point. (b) Architect's scale rule, triangular form, three edges, six faces, and twelve scales. (c) Drawing of one face to demonstrate the method of reading a scale rule. The face shown contains two scales: 1" = 1'0" to the left and ½" = 1'0" to the right. To read the 1-inch scale, for example, inches are read to the left of zero while foot divisions are read to the right. (d) Drawing showing a sample reading of a surface 2'8" in dimension at the scale of 1" = 1'0".

arm of the compass or to the end of the lengthening bar. The inking attachment, like the *ruling pen,* has a double-blade tip that holds ink and is adjustable to a thick or thin line.

Dividers are used to hold or transfer a dimension. The compass can perform the same operation but with less accuracy. Bow instruments such as the *bow compass* and *bow dividers* are better for small circles and measurements and for retaining a recurring dimension or arc.

A set of drafting instruments containing a 4-inch compass and dividers with lengthening bar and inking attachments plus a bow compass and bow dividers would fulfill the average drafting requirements.

Most scenery is too large to be represented in a drawing at actual size, so it is necessary to reduce the size in regular proportions. The *scale rule* is devised to make the change in proportion as painless as possible. The most useful scale rule is the triangular form, which provides twelve different graduations (Figure 5–2). To the beginner, a confusing factor is the discovery that there are two types of scale rules: the Architect's scale, which divides the proportional foot into twelfths or inches, and the Engineer's scale, which divides the inch into decimals or tenths, with divisions from ten to sixty. The names are trade names, not an indication of the profession using them. Engineers have as much use for the Architect's scale as do architects. Inasmuch as stage sets, like houses, are built in feet and inches, the planning of scenery is done with the Architect's scale rule.

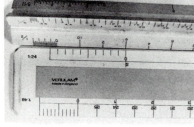

a

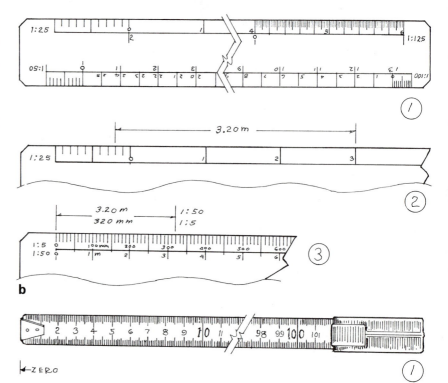

b

c

FIGURE 5–3

Metric-scale Rules and Measuring Tapes

(a) *Metric-conversion scale rule.* The metric scale 1:24 is shown in direct comparison to the scale of ½ inch equals 1 foot. (b) *Metric-scale rules.* (1) The open divided-scale rule. This example has two scales on each edge. Centimeter divisions are shown outside the zero mark, while meter divisions are indicated toward the center of the rule. Draftsmen in the theatre will find this the easiest rule to use. (2) Use of the open divided rule for dimensioning. (3) The fully divided scale rule shows centimeter and millimeter divisions the full length of the rule. (c) *Metric measuring tapes.* (1) The 3-meter tape. Numbers note centimeters; the smallest divisions are millimeters. (2) The 30-meter tape. The major divisions are at 10-centimeter intervals, with the millimeter the smallest division.

The Scale Rule and the Metric System. In the near future the United States may join the majority of nations and convert to the metric system of measurement. Until that moment the theatre draftsman may be required to know and use both systems. Plans and construction drawings for European and British imports are usually in the metric system and have to be transposed or executed according to metric rules without converting to feet and inches.

To convert into the metric system or to redimension a drawing in meters the designer can use a specially prepared conversion scale rule (Figure 5–3a). To make the conversion accurate the scales that are provided are in an unusual ratio for direct drafting in the metric system. The ratio 1:24 shown in the illustration is equal to the scale of one-half inch equals one foot ($\frac{1}{2}'' = 1'0''$). This is an odd ratio for the metric system and can lead to mistakes in the shop.

The metric drafting-scale rule (Figure 5–3b) uses two basic divisions: the millimeter (mm) and the meter (m), which is 1000mm. Although not indicated on the rule, the centimeter (cm) can be determined by noting every 100mm or by moving the decimal point of the reading. Small measurements are dimensioned in millimeters (450mm), whereas greater distances are indicated in meters and centimeters (20.52m). As a present-day point of reference it will be noted that 25mm is approximately equal to one inch, which is an easy number to remember if it is necessary to convert or refer to feet and inches. Hence the ratios: 1:12.5m is approximately one-inch scale; 1:25m = one-half-inch scale; 1:50m = one-quarter-inch scale, and so on.

Although the centimeter does not appear on the drafting scale, it is used on the measuring tape (Figure 5–3c). The tape is numbered in centimeters (cm), each being divided into tenths (mm) with, of course, 100cm equaling one meter.

Drawing pencils and leads for lead-holders have varying degrees of hardness and softness. Soft lead produces a blacker line than hard lead. The leads are graded by letters from 6B, which is very soft, through HB and H, which are medium soft to firm, to 6H, the hardest lead. The combination of H, 2H, and 4H leads gives the variety in line quality necessary for a good blueprint.

The choice of drafting paper depends, of course, on what type of drafting is planned. An ink drawing, a pencil drawing, or a preliminary study each requires different *tracing papers*. There are many kinds of paper and no standardization of the numbering system, so the beginner is wise to seek the advice of a competent dealer. The supplier can recommend the proper density of tracing paper to insure a clear, good-contrast print.

The accessories that complete the draftsman's list of equipment are made up of such items as a *lead pointer* for pointing the leads of the draftsman's mechanical pencils; a *ruby eraser* and *erasing shield* for erasing pencil-line mistakes and an art gum eraser or *drawing cleaning powder* to help keep the drawing paper clean; and *drafting tape,* which is used to fasten the tracing paper to the drawing board.

Drafting in Ink. Although most scene designers draft in pencil, some technical drawings are done in ink. The *Rapidograph,* a technical fountain pen, is excellent for this purpose. It has a long point for working against a straight edge and provides a nonclogging flow of ink. The pen uses India ink, which is opaque for clear reproduction, dries quickly, and does not smear from erasing. The most useful points for normal drafting are sizes 0 and 1.

THE GRAPHICS OF DRAFTING

Drafting practices in the theatre are so numerous and loosely defined that they cannot easily be categorized. There are as many ways to draft a show as there are designers. A close inspection, however, reveals that each designer differs only in the amount of information given and in the way the material is organized. All have in common a background of engineering drawing and its basic principle—orthographic projection.

Orthographic Projection

In spite of its academic sound, the orthographic projection is a simple drawing. Orthographic means straight line. A straight-line projection is a method of representing the exact shape of an object in a line drawing on a plane perpendicular to the lines of projection from the object. It is easier to understand when it is compared to the converging line projection inherent in the foreshortening of a perspective drawing or photograph. A perspective of a three-dimensional object is very descriptive and easy to visualize. The object, however, is not represented in true dimension because of the foreshortening of some surfaces.

For example, it is easy to recognize the familiar three-step unit from a perspective drawing (Figure 5–4a). The carpenter, however, who needs more information than a pretty sketch, wants to know height, width, and depth. An orthographic projection is a draftsman's way of drawing the three steps to give this information. It reveals the object one view at a time and from all angles. The observer is free to move around the object to view it from front to rear and from top to bottom. Each view is seen in true dimension by straight-line projection.

View Alignment

Obviously, a series of unrelated views of an object are of little value unless they are organized in a connective manner to show the position of the object in space. Hence, a conventional arrangement of views is the basis of all drafting techniques.

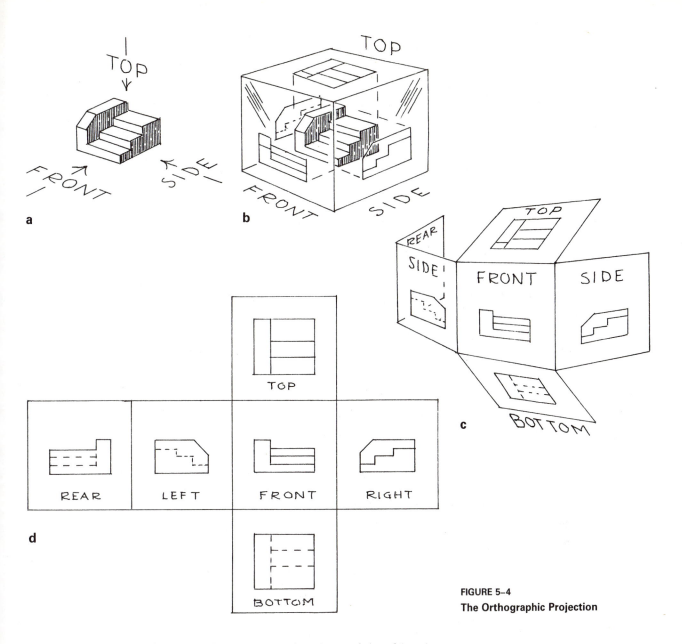

a

b

c

d

FIGURE 5–4
The Orthographic Projection

Labels within the figure: TOP, FRONT, SIDE (a); TOP, FRONT, SIDE (b); REAR SIDE, TOP, FRONT, SIDE, BOTTOM (c); TOP, REAR, LEFT, FRONT, RIGHT, BOTTOM (d)

To understand the method of transposing the views of the object in space onto the drawing board requires some visual imagination. Imagine, for example, the three-step unit in the center of a transparent cube. Projected on each side of the cube is a line drawing of the object as it appears in each view. With the side containing the front view as the center, the other faces of the cube are unfolded to either side, to the top, and to the bottom (Figure 5–4b).

The front view is always the most recognizable one, showing the main characteristics of the object. It is the key view that gives the carpenter a bearing for visualizing the three-step unit in three dimensions. The top and side views are shown above and to the side of the

Drafting the Design

113

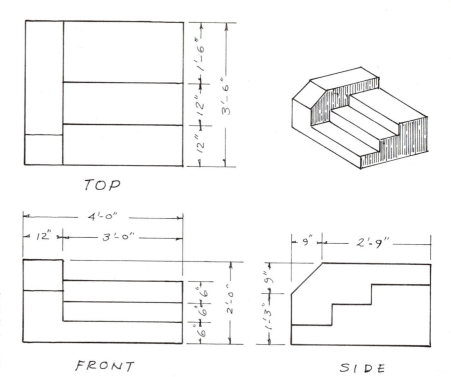

TOP

FRONT

SIDE

FIGURE 5–5

Scaled and Dimensioned Drawings

Designers' working drawings generally show three views of the object, drawn to scale and dimensioned. Occasionally one view may be omitted or an additional view (such as a section) included, depending upon the complexity of the subject.

front view, providing the three principal views of the object. Borrowing architectural terminology, some views are referred to as elevations, a term that is applied to all views seen in a horizontal direction. The horizontal views include the front elevations, side elevations, and rear elevations. An academic (and less frequently used) expression refers to the views as projections. The front, top, and side views become respectively the vertical, horizontal, and profile projections.

Of course the carpenter does not refer to the drawings as orthographic projections; they are working drawings, for with the simple addition of a few dimensions and material specifications to the orthographic projection of the three-step unit, the carpenter is ready to start building (Figure 5–5).

DESIGNER'S WORKING DRAWINGS

As the designer begins to make working drawings, which are flat and less descriptive than the original sketch, he or she soon discovers that the draftsman has a way of making the lines speak for themselves. In the draftsman's language, symbols and conventions are words. The vocabulary has lines of all types. There are thick lines, thin lines, dotted lines, dashed lines, straight lines, and curved lines. Each has a different meaning and function. The draftsman's language, like any language, depends on a mutual knowledge of the symbols to read correctly a set of working drawings.

Drafting Conventions and Line Symbols

The first and simplest convention is the drawing of lines in different weights or thickness. The scene designer drafts with three weights of line. (Occasionally for speed, or because of the simplicity of the drawing, two weights of line are used. The goal is clarity of presentation and accuracy of representation.) The three different weights—light, medium, and heavy—are relative in thickness from one drawing to another. Because the scene designer drafts in so many scales, standardization of thickness or number of weights is impossible. A floor plan may need three weights of line, a mechanical or decorative detail two weights, and a full scale pattern only one.

A line is made heavy or light depending on its eye-catching importance on the blueprint. Obviously, heavy lines are going to be seen first, medium-weight lines second, and lightweight lines last. The use of different-weight lines gives the blueprint a feeling of depth. It is a very slight third dimension, but it is enough to make the print easier to read. Beyond the slight descriptive quality of the weight of a line there is the meaning or symbol of the function implied in the use of certain lines that needs to be explained.

Medium-Weight Lines. It is easiest to begin with medium-weight lines, for they are used the most and have already been seen in the orthographic projection of the three-step unit (Figure 5–5). They are the *outline lines* that represent the shape of the object, showing visible edges of all surfaces as they appear at the angle of view. The visible outline is a solid, medium-weight line. Occasionally a view will cover or hide a surface outline. It then becomes a *hidden outline* and is drawn as a dotted line or series of small dashes.

Frequently a draftsman will want to show where an adjoining element of scenery touches a surface or show an alternate position of the same object. The *phantom line* symbolizes the removed object by outlining its position in the view. The designer has a choice of two symbols: a dashed line or the repetition of an elongated dash and two dots. Because a phantom line should always carry a label, the choice of line depends on the complexity of the outline of the removed part. Whichever symbol is chosen should be used consistently throughout the drawing.

Lightweight Lines. Lightweight lines are many and have a variety of uses. Their function is to give additional information about the object and still not detract from the overall picture created by the outlines.

Dimension lines, with arrowheads at the ends, mark the extent of the surface that is being dimensioned. Figures, set into the line, show exact distance. If dimension lines are set too close to the drawing, or within the drawing, they may become confused with outlines. To keep the dimension line away from the object, the *extension line* is used. These

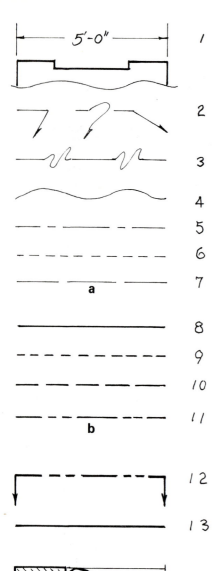

FIGURE 5–6

Line Symbols

(a) *Lightweight lines.* (1) Dimension and extension lines, (2) leaders, (3) long break line, (4) short break line, (5) center line, (6) hidden construction, (7) reference line such as setline or plaster line. (b) *Medium-weight lines.* (8) Visible outline, (9) hidden outline, (10) and (11) adjacent part or alternate position line. (c) *Heavy-weight lines.* (12) Cutting plane line, (13) section outline, (14) section outline and section lines (lightweight).

lines are solid and are drawn perpendicular to the surface of the object. As the name implies, they extend the surface to the dimension line. Although the arrowheads of the dimension line touch the extension line, the extension line itself is held clear of the object, about one-sixteenth of an inch, wherever possible (Figure 5–6).

Leaders, relatives of dimension lines, are made with one-sided arrowheads that touch the surface where a note or dimension applies. If the leader is always drawn slanted or curved, there is less chance for anyone to confuse it with the dimension line.

Break lines are space savers that denote a shortening of length or height. Occasionally, the draftsman wants to draw a unit of scenery which is too long to fit on the paper. A reduction of length is accomplished by taking a piece out of the center and using a break line to show that the piece is not represented in full length. The break line can also be used to indicate that the outer surface of an object has been cut away to show inner structure. The *long break line* is a straight line with spasmodic eruptions occurring at intervals, while the *short break line* is a more subtle curve with less regularity.

The *center line,* symbolized by an alternating long dash and dot, is used to establish the center of circles and to show the dividing line of symmetrical parts. The center line is also a familiar symbol in the floor plan of a stage setting, where it marks the center of the stage or proscenium opening. It is an important reference line for the location of scenery on the stage.

The final lightweight line is the *hidden construction* line. It is a dashed line used to indicate rear construction such as bracing, picture battens, or covered hinging not visible in the view.

Heavy-Weight Lines. Heavy-weight lines are used solely to indicate the cross section of an object or the cutting away and removing of a portion to reveal the inside. The *cutting-plane line,* drawn over an adjoining view to locate the position of the cut, consists of a repeating dash and a double dot. The arrowheads point the direction seen in the sectional view (Figure 5–7c).

The other heavy-weight line is the *section outline,* which appears in the sectional view. It is a heavy solid line that outlines the cut surface to emphasize it over the uncut surfaces. The cut surface is further set apart by the use of *section lines,* which are lightweight crosshatched lines drawn within the cut-surface outline.

Scaled Drawings

The most important part of a set of working drawings is the dimension. A carpenter cannot begin to build without some indication of size. Scaled or dimensioned drawings are crucial for such information. Most misunderstandings that occur between the drawing board and

The Design Concept

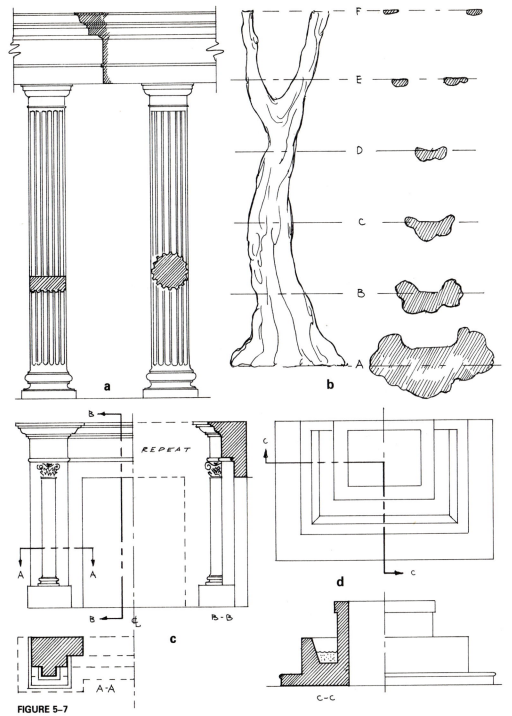

FIGURE 5–7

Sectional Views

(a) Revolved section, drawn directly on the elevation to indicate contour. (b) Removed section, a revolved section that has been removed and set to one side of the elevation. (c) Cross section B–B is a vertical section and A–A is a horizontal section, frequently called a *plan*. (d) Half section, used on a symmetrical object combining the cross-section and elevational views.

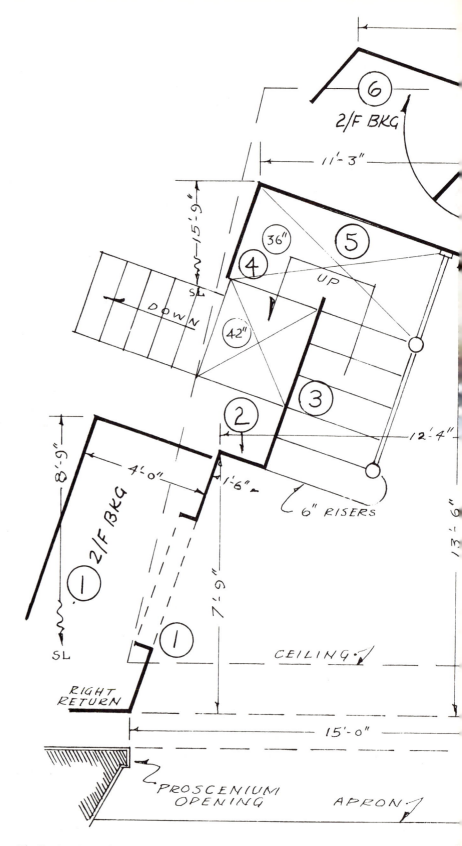

FIGURE 5–9

The Designer's Floor Plan

A horizontal section taken through all wall openings and above all steps and levels wherever it is feasible. The dark solid lines represent a cross section of the walls of the setting. The lightweight solid lines outline the steps and levels seen in a top view. The dotted lines within the wall openings indicate a header or presence of wall above the opening.

120

The Design Concept

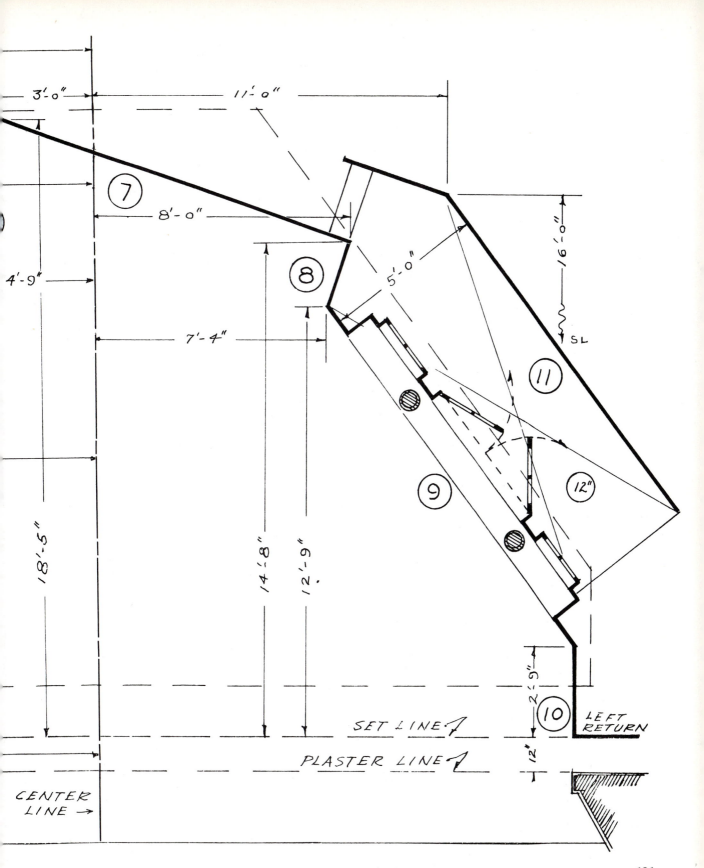

Labeling

Part of the function of an assembled view is to identify and label the parts that make up the whole. The floor plan gives this information in varying degrees of completeness depending upon the working conditions and the nature of the show. Summer stock or university and community theatres, where the bulk of the structural planning falls on the designer's shoulders, may require a more specific labeling of each piece of scenery. The label becomes an easy, accurate means of identification for a single piece of scenery or assembled units of a setting.

As in the theatre, the floor plan of a television show contains a careful notation of each piece of scenery. Television scenery is almost entirely of stock units and standard sizes. The designer's labels and notes on the plan are a catalog, or index guide, for assembling the set in the studio.

DESIGNER'S ELEVATIONS

Of almost equal importance to the floor plan, as a working drawing, are the designer's elevations. Compared to the floor plan, which is an assembled section showing the relationship of many parts, the elevational drawings are, in a sense, a disassembled or dismantled view of the individual parts. Because the elevation of an assembled set as it would appear in a normal front view has little value as a working drawing, the scene designer uses another technique. The set is taken apart, flattened out, and each piece of scenery is shown in front view at a scale of $\frac{1}{2}'' = 1'0''$. Starting with the right return, the setting is drafted to show all pieces of scenery laid out in order, piece by piece, to the left return. All pieces are represented at $\frac{1}{2}$-inch scale in true size and shape.

Each flat wall surface or unit of scenery is outlined. A solid line or space between units marks an open joint. For special reasons, it may be necessary to indicate a covered joint on the line where two or more wings are hinged together to make up a flat wall surface. The covered joint is indicated with a dotted line and a note to hinge and to dutchman, or cover, the joint. Normally, this isn't necessary because the carpenter decides just how an oversized surface will be subdivided. The decision as to how it is to be made is guided by such technical considerations as the size of the stage, the method of handling the sets, and, if the scenery has to be transported, the nature of the transportation. The standard maximum wing width of 5 feet 9 inches is based on the height of a baggage-car door through which all the scenery of a road show must be able to pass if it is traveling by train. If

The Design Concept

the scenery is moving by truck, or not traveling at all, the maximum standard width can vary accordingly. The designer will do well, however, to keep in mind these technical considerations, for they are the limiting features that often control the size and shape of the design.

Applied Detail

Designers vary in the amount of detail they show at ½-inch scale. Although the decorative trim and other details are best shown at a larger scale, it is sometimes wise to at least sketch a portion of the detail on the ½-inch elevations. It not only shows the trim in assembled view but also gives the carpenter some idea of any special construction that may be needed. Because of the light wood frame and canvas construction of scenery, pictures, valance boxes, or lighting fixtures can't be placed in the middle of a wall without providing extra structural support from behind. If the applied details are partially sketched in the elevation, or indicated with the dashed-line symbol of an adjacent part, the carpenter will know where to supply the additional construction (Figure 5–10, pages 124–125).

Obviously, the labels of the elevation must agree with the labels of the corresponding units in the floor plan. The accuracy of cross-labeling is especially important when stock scenery is being used, for unless the set is extremely simple, it is the carpenter's only guide as to how the pieces assemble. On occasion, for clarification, a portion of a floor plan may be repeated near the elevation drawings of a complicated unit of scenery. If there is still a possibility of misunderstanding, a pictorial drawing can be included.

Compositional Elevations

Borrowing a trick from the interior decorator, the scene designer sometimes uses a compositional elevation. It is most useful on an interior setting, for it is an assembled view of each wall with all the set dressings related to that wall in place. Jogs or breaks in the wall are not flattened out but are shown in position. In this manner, the scene designer can study the composition of the furniture, pictures, and window draperies at small scale.

A compositional elevation is usually drawn at ¼-inch scale or smaller. If it is drawn on graph paper, a compositional elevation does not need to show dimensions because sizes and proportions can be calculated by counting the squares (Figure 5–11b, page 126).

Compositional elevations are in no way a working drawing for the carpenter. They are of value to the designer as an aid in making decisions on furniture and picture sizes during the hectic stages of collecting properties.

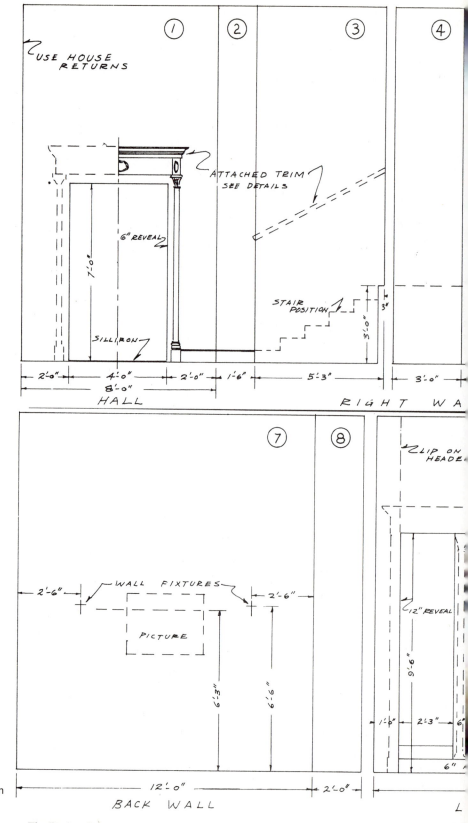

FIGURE 5–10

Designer's Elevations

Elevational drawings of the walls shown in the floor plan (Figure 5–8).

The Design Concept

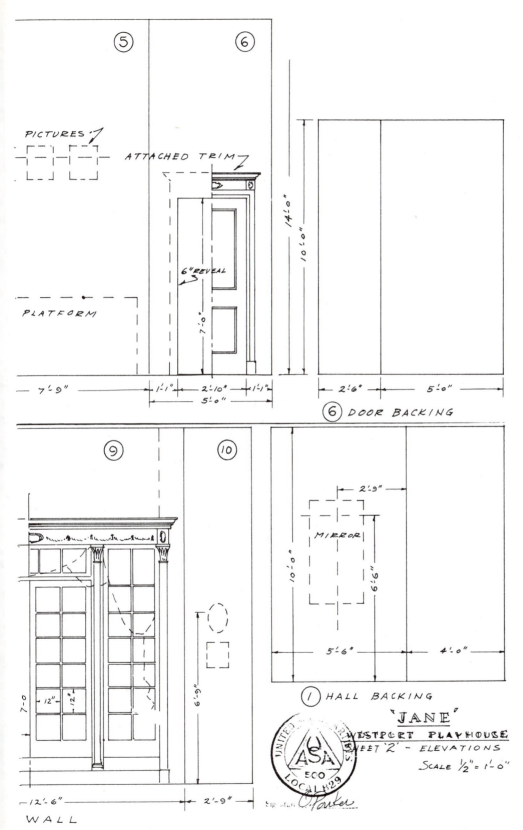

⑤ ⑥

PICTURES

ATTACHED TRIM

6" REVEAL

7'-0"

PLATFORM

14'-0"

10'-0"

7'-9"   1'-1"   2'-10"   1'-1"
              5'-0"

2'-6"   5'-0"

⑥ DOOR BACKING

⑨ ⑩

2'-9"

MIRROR

10'-0"

6'-6"

5'-6"   4'-0"

① HALL BACKING

7'-0   12"   12"

6'-9"

12'-6"   2'-9"

WALL

'JANE'
WESTPORT PLAYHOUSE
SHEET '2' - ELEVATIONS
SCALE ½" = 1'-0"

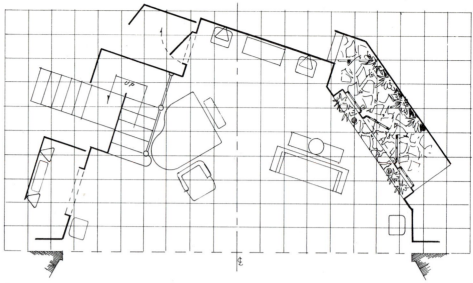

a

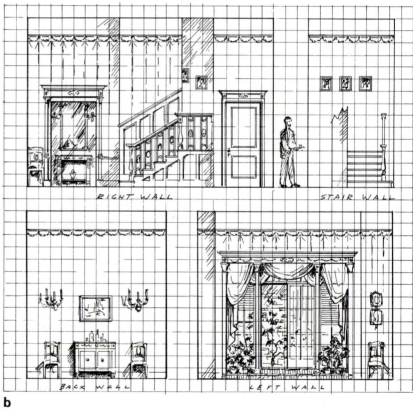

b

FIGURE 5–11

Additional Floor Plans and Elevations

(a) *Furniture plot.* An undimensioned although scaled floor plan showing the furniture in place. The grid of 2-foot squares helps to indicate the sizes of the furniture pieces and distances between units. (b) *Compositional elevations.* A perpendicular view of each important wall as it looks assembled with dress properties and related set properties in position.

The Design Concept

TECHNICAL PLANNING

For the most part, the scene designer is not concerned with technical planning unless to indicate the best place to divide an oversized element of scenery or to hinge two units. There may be occasions, however, when the scenery is built by unskilled hands, in which case the designer becomes the chief guardian of construction. To avoid being tied down by shop supervision when countless other details are pressing, the wise designer will provide construction drawings.

The simplest way to lay out the framed construction of scenery is to use rear elevations. A view from this direction looks at the scenery as it appears under construction in the shop. A rear elevation shows the framing and profiling, explains the assembly, locates the hinges, and indicates bracing and stiffening. The detail and completeness of the rear elevations must be determined by the aptitude of the shop help. An experienced carpenter might need a construction drawing for the occasional unusual piece of scenery, while inexperienced help would need every piece of scenery detailed (Figure 5–12). As can be seen,

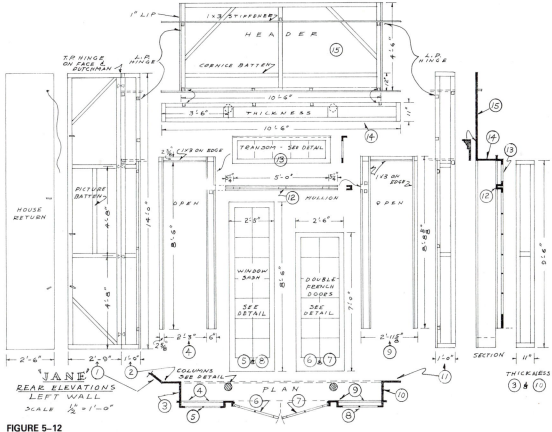

FIGURE 5–12

Rear Elevations

Detailed construction drawings show the framing of each piece of scenery and indicate how each is assembled. Note the use of vertical and horizontal sections as assembled views.

Drafting the Design

rear elevations employ many symbols to indicate joining hardware and hinging and bracing techniques, all of which are a part of technical planning. The symbols illustrated in Figure 5–13 will mean more after a study of scenery construction and tools in Chapters 6 and 7.

Three-dimensional pieces such as fireplaces, doors, steps, and rocks are not clearly explained in a rear elevation. They are built by combining sectional views with designer's front and side elevations. The sectional view not only shows the internal structure but helps to explain the contour of the object. Irregular forms, of course, may require many sections. Very special shapes or profiles are often drawn at full scale to serve as a pattern.

TECHNICAL DRAFTING SYMBOLS

Line weights and symbols used in technical drafting are slightly different from those used by the scene designer. The need for accuracy and detailed information leads to precise drafting and uniform standards. In an effort to conform more closely to ANSI* standards for engineering drafting, technical drafting for the theatre is limited to two line weights, *thin* and *thick*. These thicknesses are fixed for all drawings. USITT's† Graphic Standard Board recommends the following thicknesses:

pen thin, .010″ to .0125″
thick, .020″ to .025″
pencil thin, .3mm
thick, .5mm

A concession is made for the possible need of a heavy-weight line by supplying an *extra-thick* or double-thick line for section outline.

A comparison of line thicknesses and symbols can be seen in Figure 5–6. The thin and thick line specified for the pen are comparable to the medium and heavy line symbols in the illustration.

Other technical drafting symbols more specifically related to the planning of the construction and joining of scenery can be seen in Figure 5–13.

The Hanging Section and Plan

The hanging section is another important part of technical planning. A drawing of hanging scenery is necessary to the designer in planning a multiscene production or a heavy hanging show. The designer soon discovers that flying space is filled very quickly with lighting equipment, traveler tracks, masking curtains, and the like. To avoid a hope-

*American National Standards Institute
†United States Institute for Theatre Technology

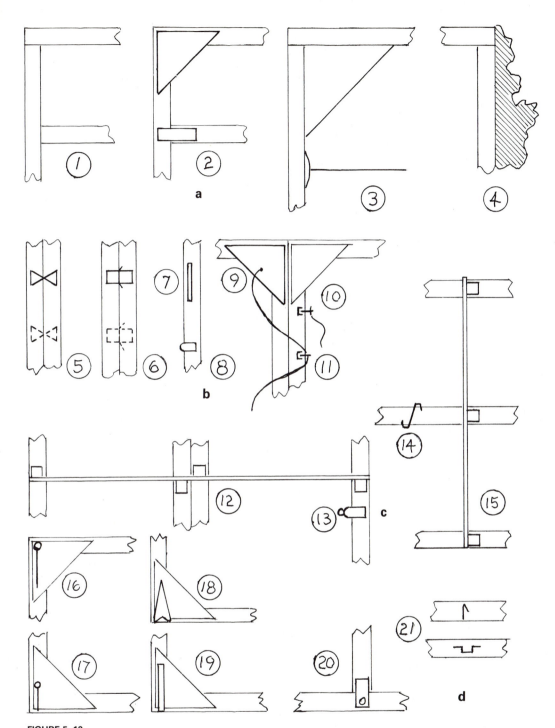

FIGURE 5–13

Technical Drafting Symbols

(a) *Framing.* (1) Layout, (2) keystone and corner blocks, (3) brace and toggle rail, (4) change of material. (b) *Joining.* (5) Tight pin hinge, (lower) opposite face, (6) loose pin hinge, (lower) opposite face, (7) stop block, (8) stop cleat, (9) lashline in corner block, (10) lashline eye, (11) lash cleat. (c) *Stiffening and bracing.* (12) LPH stiffener (horizontal), (13) brace cleat, (14) keeper hook, (15) LPH brace (vertical). (d) *Rigging.* (16) Top hanger iron, (17) bottom hanger iron, (18) hinged footiron, (19) rigid foot-iron, (20) ceiling plate, (21) picture hook and socket.

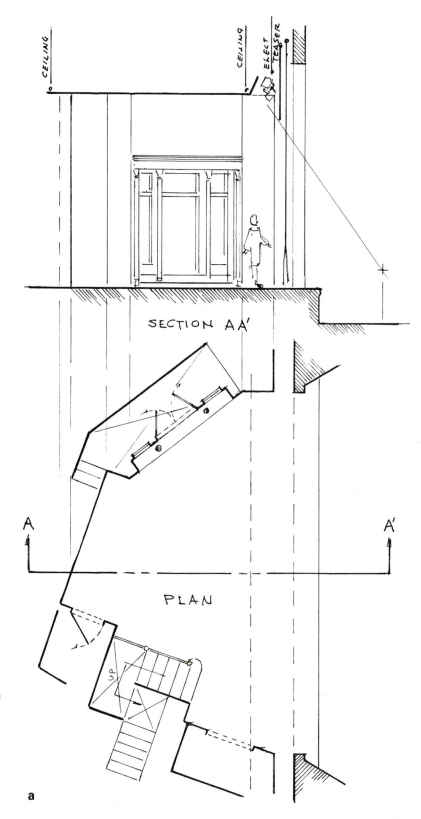

SECTION AA'

PLAN

FIGURE 5–14

Hanging Section and Plan

(a) Drawing shows the relationship of the floor plan to a section. Section cutting plane line, A–A, is taken on the center line. Sectional view is from stage right looking stage left. (b, page 131) *A typical hanging section for a musical.* The section is a necessary view for the lighting designer to establish lighting angles.

a

The Design Concept

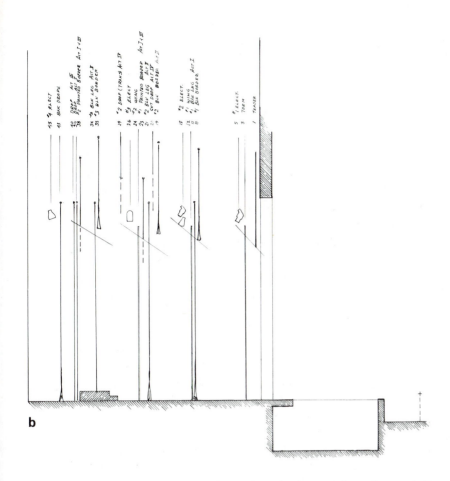

b

less tangle in the flies, the hanging plot of a heavy show is carefully studied first in plan and section.

The hanging section, which is a sectional view taken vertically through the stage on the center line, is not a working drawing in itself. It provides information that can be used in the floor plan and elevations as working drawings. In addition to taking the guesswork out of vertical masking by checking the extreme vertical sightlines, the hanging section gives an accurate picture of floor-space problems. It shows the up- and downstage space requirements more clearly than the floor plan that becomes the working drawing (Figure 5–14).

If a show is extremely heavy it may require a separate hanging plan to indicate the disposition of all scenery that is to be flown. To keep the plan from becoming confusing, most of the scenery on the floor is not shown. The hanging plan may be very general and schematic or quite detailed, depending on the proportion of the rigging, the theatre, and the type of show. For a wing-and-backdrop type of production, for example, it is little more than a listing of drops in the order they will hang and the numbering of the act and scene in which they will work. A more complicated hanging plan would indicate the exact positions of spot lines and extra rigging.

Drafting the Design   **131**

Recent engineering developments in a more flexible flying system and gridiron design than the existing pin-and-rail and counterweight methods indicate a time in the future when the hanging plan will be a required drawing for every show.

PLANNING PROPERTIES

The designer is responsible for the selection of properties, for the design of specially built pieces of furniture, and for the furniture plot or general arrangement of properties in the setting.

In planning the properties, the designer's chief concern is to coordinate design needs with those of the director. A meeting of minds can be achieved easily if the designer can show by sketches, clippings, or photographs what is planned and indicate by means of a scale furniture plot the size and position of set properties as they appear in the setting plan.

The furniture plot is a schematic plan locating the position of the set properties in each scene. It is generally drawn at one-quarter-inch scale with all furniture in position. The furniture plot is not dimensioned unless there is need to call attention to a certain measurement. It is drawn on a grid of 1-foot or 2-foot squares, so anyone can figure distances by counting squares. Such a plan is useful to the director and stage manager for laying out rehearsal space and studying the staging. It is valuable to the property person as a visual reference list of the set props. And the designer will find it useful in planning the lighting of the production (Figure 5–11a).

The floor plan of a television show is handled in essentially the same way. Drawn at one-quarter-inch scale over a grid of one-foot squares, it shows the set props in place, notes and numbers each piece of scenery.

FIGURE 5–15

Free-hand Pictorial Drawings

Dimensioned free-hand isometric drawings of simple furniture. If an object is simple in form, a pictorial drawing with dimensions can serve as a working drawing. There is enough information provided in this type of drawing to allow the carpenter to begin building immediately. A more complicated object would need additional views.

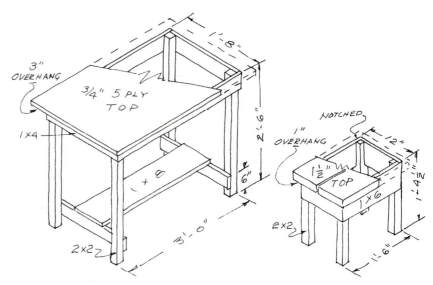

132   *The Design Concept*

The construction of a special prop, like any three-dimensional piece of scenery, would require some sort of working drawing. The usual plan, front and side views, can be used, or, if the piece is not too complicated, a dimensioned pictorial drawing will serve as a working drawing (Figure 5–15). Again, the designer will find it wise to study out all the important details at full scale.

PICTORIAL DRAWINGS

The designer's sketch is a type of pictorial drawing, but because of the foreshortening it cannot be used as a working drawing. But imagine a pictorial drawing with the edges of the receding surfaces not converging and the sides not foreshortened. Such a drawing can be drawn to scale and used as a supplementary view to the working drawings. The lack of perspective makes it possible to draw to scale, although the view may have a distorted mechanical appearance.

The two basic kinds of pictorials are the isometric and the oblique drawings. Their difference is dependent upon the angle of the view. The isometric drawing represents an object seen from one corner and slightly above (Figure 5–16a). An oblique drawing shows the object as seen opposite one face with the side angled off to the right or left (Figure 5–16c).

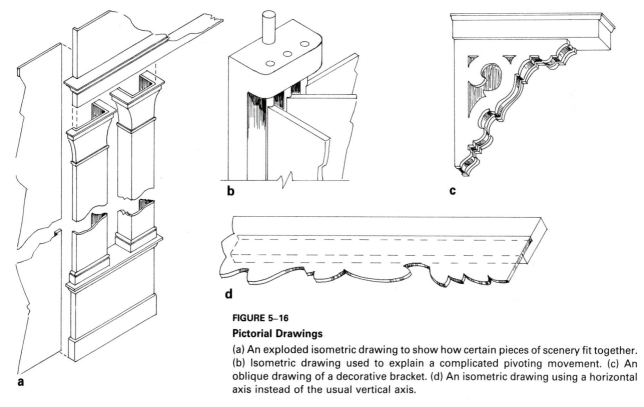

FIGURE 5–16

Pictorial Drawings

(a) An exploded isometric drawing to show how certain pieces of scenery fit together. (b) Isometric drawing used to explain a complicated pivoting movement. (c) An oblique drawing of a decorative bracket. (d) An isometric drawing using a horizontal axis instead of the usual vertical axis.

The term *isometric,* meaning equal measure (as compared to the foreshortened distances or unequal measure of perspective), accurately describes its appearance. An isometric drawing has three axes to represent the principal planes of the object. The first is a vertical line to indicate all the upright edges; second, a slanted line to the right, 30 degrees to the horizontal, for the horizontal edges of the right plane; and third, a 30-degree line slanted to the left to represent the horizontal edges of the planes to the left. These lines, and all lines parallel to them, are known as isometric lines. Conversely, lines that are not parallel to any of the three axes are nonisometric lines. Heights and distances can be measured on isometric lines but a nonisometric line cannot be drawn to scale (Figure 5–17).

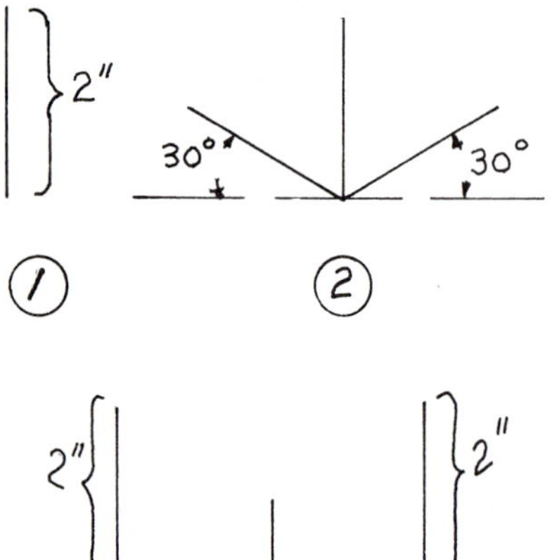

Because irregular edges, curves, and angles are distorted in an isometric view, it may be desirable to change the direction of the view to show them at a better vantage. By moving around the object until the complicated surface is parallel to the plane of the paper, or frontal position, it is possible to see the irregular edge or curve without distortion. A view from this direction is an oblique drawing.

The same general pictorial characteristics are present in the oblique drawing as in the isometric with the exception of a more pronounced distortion in appearance. Because of the frontal position of one of the principal planes, two of the oblique axes are at right angles to each other.

The angle of the third axis, representing the plane of the sides, may vary from 30 to 45 degrees to the horizontal. It can be drawn either to the right or left, and slanted either up or down (Figure 5–18). By placing the side that contains the irregular outlines, angles, or curves in the frontal position drafting time can be saved and the appearance of the view made more attractive.

To reduce the distortion and improve the looks of the oblique drawing, the draftsman sometimes uses a cabinet drawing. It is constructed with the complicated face parallel to the picture plane—like the oblique—but distances measured parallel to the angled axis are reduced in scale. A ratio of two to three or three to four between the frontal planes and the angled axis produces a pleasing proportion. By always labeling the cabinet drawing and giving the ratio of the measurements on the angled axis, the possibility of it being mistaken for an oblique drawing is avoided (Figure 5–18[4]).

Pictorial drawings may be dimensioned like a working drawing. The technique, however, is slightly different. Instead of being perpendicular to the surface, the extension lines are drawn as extensions of one of the isometric planes, and the dimension line is parallel to the object rather than perpendicular to the extension line. To help give the feeling that the dimension is in one of the isometric planes, the figures are slanted with the extension lines. If the object is not too complicated, a dimensioned pictorial drawing can be used as a working drawing.

FIGURE 5–17

Construction of the Isometric Drawing

The object is a 2-inch cube. (1) Vertical axis, the nearest corner of the cube. (2) Slanted axes, right and left. (3) Slanted lines and uprights drawn to scale. (4) The completed isometric drawing of the cube.

The Design Concept

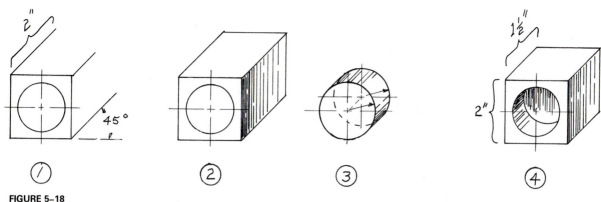

FIGURE 5–18

Construction of the Oblique Drawing

(1) The principal face with slant line drawn to right or left. All the lines are drawn to a scale. (2) The completed oblique drawing. (3) An oblique drawing of a circular disk. The center of the circle of the thickness is set to the right on an oblique line. (4) A cabinet drawing. All slanted lines are drawn at a reduced scale to minimize the distorted look of a regular oblique drawing.

Besides their use as working drawings, pictorials are frequently used as supplementary views to explain bits of complicated assembly or mechanical detail.

THE PERSPECTIVE DRAWING

A perspective drawing, as has been mentioned, is not a working drawing because of the converging of horizontal lines in the sides of the object. It is, however, a more representational view, and, in its two-dimensional concept, it is more closely related to the designer's sketch than to a working drawing.

The laws of perspective become part of the designer's drawing skill either by observation of normal foreshortening in nature or by knowing the mechanics or graphics of perspective drawing. Figure 5–19 illustrates the basic perspective views of an object in space and orientation to the horizon line (HL). Shown are a combination of views of a cube in simple perspective drawing. "A" represents the cube in a frontal position parallel to the picture plane or plane of the paper. The cube in this position has only one vanishing point (VP-C) on the horizon line. "A-1" represents the cube above HL, "A-2" on HL, and "A-3" below HL.

In "B" the position of the cube is angled to the picture plane and therefore has two vanishing points, VP-R to the right and VP-L to the left. The side walls of the cube converge to their respective vanishing points on the horizon line.

The Graphics of Perspective. The initial concept of the graphics of perspective is *foreshortening*. To understand foreshortening is the first step toward being able to visualize the graphics of perspective. Fore-

Drafting the Design

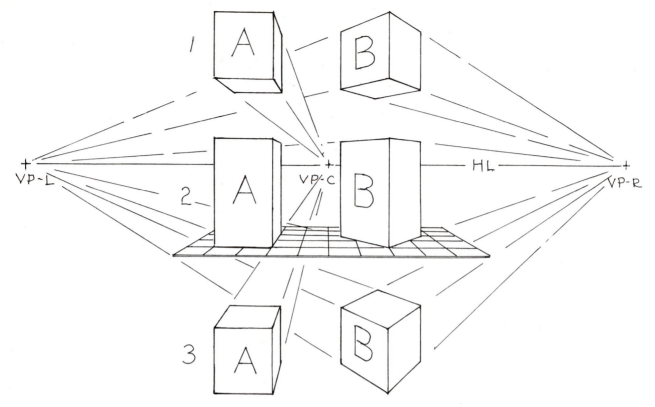

FIGURE 5–19

Graphic Perspective

The front face of box A is parallel to the picture plane. In this position the sides, top, and bottom of the box have a single vanishing point (VP-C). A-1 represents the box above the horizon line (HL), A-2 at HL, and A-3 below HL. The corner of box B is facing the picture plane. In this position the sides have corresponding right (VP-R) and left (VP-L) vanishing points. B-1 represents the box above HL, B-2 at HL, and B-3 below HL.

shortening is present, for example, in the converging lines of a fence or railroad where parallel lines appear to meet in the distance. To transpose the visual foreshortening of nature into *graphic* foreshortening on the drawing board, two assumptions have to be made.

Because the eye through peripheral vision is able to see more than is practical to draw, the first assumption is that all verticals are perpendicular to the ground. This is true in the center of the eye's vision but not true of the extreme right or left areas. The vertical lines seem to converge or diverge depending upon whether the observer is on the ground or high above the ground. The second assumption is that the horizon line is straight and parallel to the ground. This is not true of visual foreshortening, in which the horizon seems to curve around the observer in a gentle arc.

Added to these basic assumptions is the positioning of the observer at the *observation point*, which is the most desirable or ideal location. To capture an approximation or illusion of the visual foreshortening on paper the best location of the observation point (OP) would be a

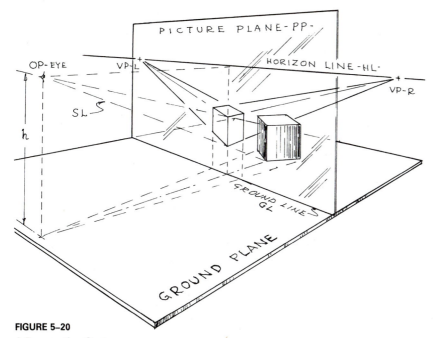

FIGURE 5–20

A Perspective System

A pictorial arrangement of the components that make up a perspective system. The picture plane (PP) intersects the ground plane forming the ground line (GL). The height (h) of the observation point (OP) determines the distance the horizon line (HL) is above GL. The object is projected into the picture plane by the use of sightlines (SL) from OP. The sides of the cube in PP converge to right and left vanishing points (VP-R and VP-L).

distance from the stage or major portion of the stage that provides a cone of vision of not greater than 30 degrees. In other words, the angle between lines drawn from the extreme right and left sides of the object to OP should approximate 30 degrees. It is possible, of course, to set up a graphic perspective system with an OP closer to the stage or with a greater cone of vision than 30 degrees, but the resulting graphic foreshortening is distorted and unnatural. The designer, however, can on occasion use this distorted foreshortening to exaggerate the perspective for design reasons.

Figure 5–20 is a pictorial representation of the components that make up a perspective system. In addition to the components already mentioned, HL and OP, the illustration also shows the picture plane (PP) and the ground plane (G), which is usually the stage floor. The picture plane is an imaginary transparent plane placed between OP and the object. It is usually perpendicular to the ground and its line of intersection with the ground plane forms the *ground line* (GL). The ability to visualize the picture plane is an important step toward understanding the process of developing the perspective drawing on this plane after it is folded into the plane of the drawing board. In the theatre, PP is normally considered to be at the proscenium opening or slightly upstage at the front edge of the setting.

Our description of the perspective system is almost complete except for designating the location of the horizon line (HL). The height of OP off the ground determines the height of HL, which is drawn parallel to GL on the picture plane. The location of OP is arbitrary. It can be placed in a position to reveal the object either in a favorable or a distorted view, whichever is desired. The normal position for a perspective sketch is a little above ground and on the center line.

It will be noted that all vanishing points fall on the horizon line. This is true of all planes parallel or perpendicular to the ground plane. The shape and vanishing points of an askew (slanted) plane can be plotted by using the floor and perpendicular walls as reference planes.

PERSPECTIVE SKETCHING TECHNIQUE

The particular perspective method a designer may choose in preparing a sketch is influenced by individual sketching techniques and personal methods of working. Individual sketching techniques vary primarily with the angle at which the setting is viewed. Whereas most designers prefer to show, for example, a little of the stage floor in their sketch, some prefer to show no floor at all while others take an elevated viewpoint showing more floor than is necessary.

There are occasions, however, when a designer may choose an extreme viewpoint in order to fit the form of the particular theatre. A high ballroom stage, for instance, with the audience seated on a flat, ungraded ballroom floor creates a situation in which no one is able to see the stage floor. The opposite might occur in an amphitheatre with a rather steep seating arrangement in which the majority of the audience sees a great expanse of the stage floor.

The three basic angles of view are illustrated in Figure 5–21. Using the conventional vanishing-point method, the perspective sketch of a simple unit of scenery is shown under three different conditions. The first is the minimum floor view (a), followed by the extreme no-floor view (b), and, finally, a sketch from a high vantage point (c). In the first condition (5–21a), OP is at a proper distance from the object, determined by keeping an angle of 30 degrees or less between sightlines (SH) drawn from the outside edges of the object to OP. The horizon line is established at a height of about five or six feet above ground or stage floor. As a result the perspective drawing shows a little stage floor and appears normal.

The vanishing point for each wall is located by drawing a line from OP parallel to the angle of the specific wall until it intersects the picture plane (PP). It is then projected downward until it crosses HL. The point of intersection with HL is the vanishing point (VP) for that wall. The vanishing point for each wall was found in this manner (some of which fall out of view in Figure 5–21b).

The Design Concept

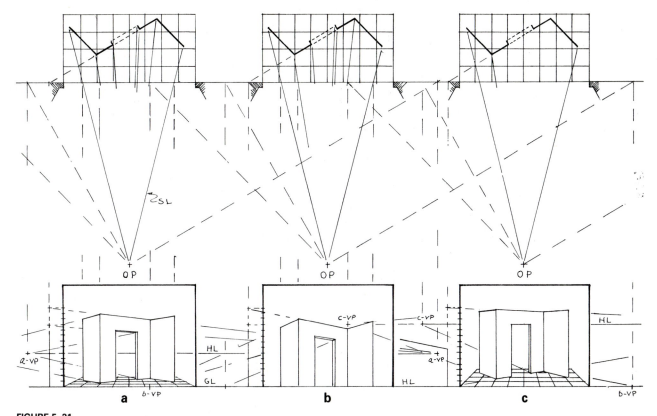

FIGURE 5–21

Perspective Viewpoints

The three basic angles of view that may appear in a perspective sketch for the theatre. (a) Minimum floor view. HL at about 6 feet above GL. (b) No floor view. HL is on the floor (GL). (c) Maximum floor view. HL is abnormally high, giving the set the look of being viewed from a high vantage point.

The conditions in Figure 5–21b and Figure 5–21c are the same except for the position of HL. The second view has located the horizon line in the floor or on GL, while the third view has raised HL above the normal view to show more of the floor.

The application of normal perspective techniques to the sketch of a stage setting does have one disadvantage. Because the walls of a setting, especially an interior, are frequently raked to bring them into better sightlines, they tend to appear more exaggerated than right angles. To a certain extent this also happens in the real set, for the raked side walls of a box set tend to make the setting look deeper than it really is. This is not so apparent until the set is placed within the two-dimensional form of a sketch. As a result, adjustments either in the sketch or floor plan are sometimes required to bring the elements of the composition into a desirable proportional arrangement. It is important to remember that if the sketch is being developed with the observation point at the conventional distance so as to form a cone of vision of 30 degrees or less, the result does give the designer some clue as to how the set is going to look before the scaled model is made.

Drafting the Design   **139**

Perspective-Grid Method. Because of the many angled walls that may occur in a setting, the designer seeks to avoid the space-consuming method of a full graphic perspective system involving the location of vanishing points from a sprawling observation point and the precisely aligned floor plan. Instead, the designer looks for an easier way or shortcut to produce an approximation of the perspective drawing. The perspective grid is an aid in simplifying the graphics of perspective.

The use of a perspective grid of the stage floor as a guide under the sketch is helpful to the beginning designer in the development of a perspective view of a setting from the floor plan. Like most shortcuts, the grid method is an approximation and therefore less than accurate. The inaccuracies, however, are not alarming and are offset by the time and space saved.

As a technique the perspective-grid method does not employ either the use of an observation point (other than the initial setup) or the cross-reference of sightline points from an aligned floor plan. It does use, however, the traditional horizon line and vanishing points in addition to measuring points.

The grid, which can be prepared in advance and reused indefinitely, is developed in one of two ways (Figure 5–22). Both begin with a scaled grid of the stage floor. The upstage and downstage lines of the grid appear in true dimension along the picture plane, or downstage, edge of the plan. All vertical lines converge to a common vanishing point at the center (VPC) because they are perpendicular to PP.

The spacing of the horizontal line parallel to PP can be located by conventional perspective methods shown to the left of the center in Figure 5–22a. Sightlines are projected from the observation point (OP) to each position on the outside edge of the grid. The corresponding positions in perspective are located by projecting downward the point of intersection of the respective sightlines and the picture plane. Once the grid has been developed in perspective the observation point is no longer needed.

Measuring-Point Method. The measuring-point method which is demonstrated in Figure 5–22b dates back to the theatre of the Renaissance. Originally known as the *distance-point method*, it was developed in 1435 by Leone Battista Alberti. The system's basic difference from the perspective-grid method is that it does not use an observation point, needing only to know the distance OP would be from the picture plane.

The formula for the method is based upon the reality that in a perspective plan the diagonal of a square, if extended, will fall upon the horizon line at a point the same distance from the center line as OP is from PP. Figure 5–22b shows how the measuring point (MP) is used to locate the position of the horizontal lines of the grid in perspective.

The Design Concept

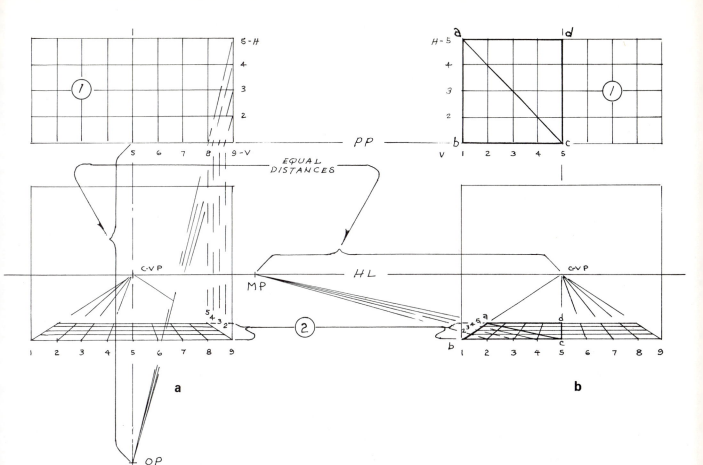

FIGURE 5–22

Developing the Perspective Grid

The two methods of developing a perspective of the stage floor are shown. (a) The observation-point method: (1) The stage floor is marked in a grid of equally spaced horizontal and vertical lines. The vertical lines are numbered from 1 to 9 and the horizontal lines are numbered on the right from 1 to 5. Because all the vertical lines are perpendicular to the picture plane (PP) they all vanish or converge to a single vanishing point in the center (cvp). The location of the depth in perspective of each horizontal line is accomplished by sighting a line from OP to the intersection point of a horizontal line and one of the vertical lines (for example, 5-H on line 9-V). The point where the sightline crosses PP (at 8-V) is projected downward until it intersects perspective line 9-V as it is converging toward cvp. As the horizontal lines are parallel to PP, it can be drawn through this point to the left, terminating at line 1-V. (2) Each of the horizontal lines is located in this manner to complete the perspective grid. (b) The measuring-point method: (1) The gridded stage floor as in (a). The measuring point (MP) is measured on HL the same distance from the center line (cvp) as OP was from PP in (a). The perspective position of each horizontal grid line is located on 1-V by sighting a line from MP to a series of points on PP representing the true distances each horizontal line is apart. As the true grid is made up of squares, vertical lines 1, 2, 3, 4, and 5 are the same distances. The points where the sightlines from MP cross line 1-V (2) locates the perspective spacing of the horizontal lines. The perspective grid is then completed in the same manner as in (a).

True dimension intervals on PP are projected back to MP, and where they cross the outside edge of the grid locates the respective spacing of each line. If accurately drawn, the right side should match the spacing to the left of the center line.

Drafting the Design   **141**

It is important to remember that to be accurate the measuring-point method is based upon the square or subdivision of the square and its diagonal. If the stage is deeper than the side of the square, the grid should be expanded offstage to make the proper double-square proportion. Although only the floor grid will be used in the perspective method of sketching, the measuring-point system can be used as a measured-perspective technique by establishing an MP to the right and left.

Perspective Floor Plan

Figure 5–23 illustrates with a simplified example of scenery the steps taken to use the perspective grid as a guide for a sketching technique. Figure 5–23a is a scaled floor plan of the set drawn over a grid of squares. For the sake of clarity in a small drawing the squares shown are 3 feet in dimension. Because their size is optional it might be desirable in a larger drawing to use two-foot squares for more dependable accuracy. If the sketch is developed on tracing paper over the perspective grid as is suggested in Figure 5–22b it can be saved for future use.

The first step toward the sketch is the transference of the floor plan onto the perspective grid by locating each element in its corresponding square (Figure 5–23c). Vertical lines representing corners and edges are extended upward, for the moment, to undetermined heights. Before individual heights can be found the vanishing points of key walls must be located. The VP of the right and left walls are the easiest to locate because of their sharp angle to PP. As their faces are parallel to each other the same VP will serve both. To locate this important vanishing point the base line of each outside wall is carefully produced from its position on the perspective grid until it intersects HL. This is the approximate VP for the base of both walls and for any line parallel to the respective base lines.

The final step to complete the drawing is to find the height of the doorway and scenic unit. One method is to use the center vanishing point (VP-C), which is the VP for the grid. Figure 5–23d shows how h–1 and h–2 are taken in true dimension from PP back along a perspective line on the grid to VP-C passing through a corner to the critical point of measurement. The point of intersection of the vertical raised from the corner in plan and perspective line h–1, for example, VP-C, determines the height. The height of the doorway and other verticals can be found by the same method.

Furniture, platforms, and set dressing can be located by using the perspective grid and approximate VP in the same manner. The ceiling or overhead area may also be gridded and constructed in perspective to the same HL and OP system to provide a more inclusive guide for the designer's sketch.

On pages 144–148 three different uses of the perspective grid as a

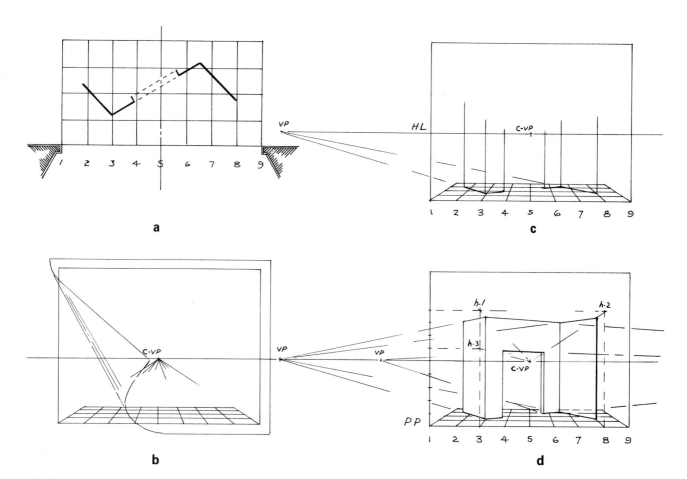

FIGURE 5–23

Using the Perspective Grid

(a) The floor plan of a simple element of scenery drawn on a gridded stage floor. (b) A perspective grid predeveloped by either the observation-point or measuring-point method is covered with tracing paper to preserve the grid for future uses. (c) By referring to the floor plan on the true grid (a), it is reconstructed, point by point, onto the perspective grid. The corners, edges, and vertical sides of openings are extended upward but not terminated. The vanishing point of the two parallel walls is located by projecting the base line in the perspective plan until it intersects HL (vp). (d) The height of the scenery is found by extending one of the corners to PP. The downstage corner resting on V-3 is projected to PP along line V-3. The height is then measured directly above and projected back to C-VP. Where it intersects the vertical of the corner from the plan (c) is the height in perspective. Other heights are located the same way: h-2 is off line V-8; h-3 is the height of the door opening. With the heights all located, the sketch is completed by drawing the tops and all lines parallel to them to their related vanishing points.

sketch technique are represented. The first is the conventional interior setting, showing the steps that were taken to develop the final sketch: (a) the scaled floor plan with a grid overlay; (b) the grid in perspective with the walls blocked in and the vanishing points located; (c) the addition of set dressings and furniture; (d) the final sketch with the grid removed.

The second example brings together some unusual conditions. The setting not only thrusts ahead or through the picture plane but also

Drafting the Design   **143**

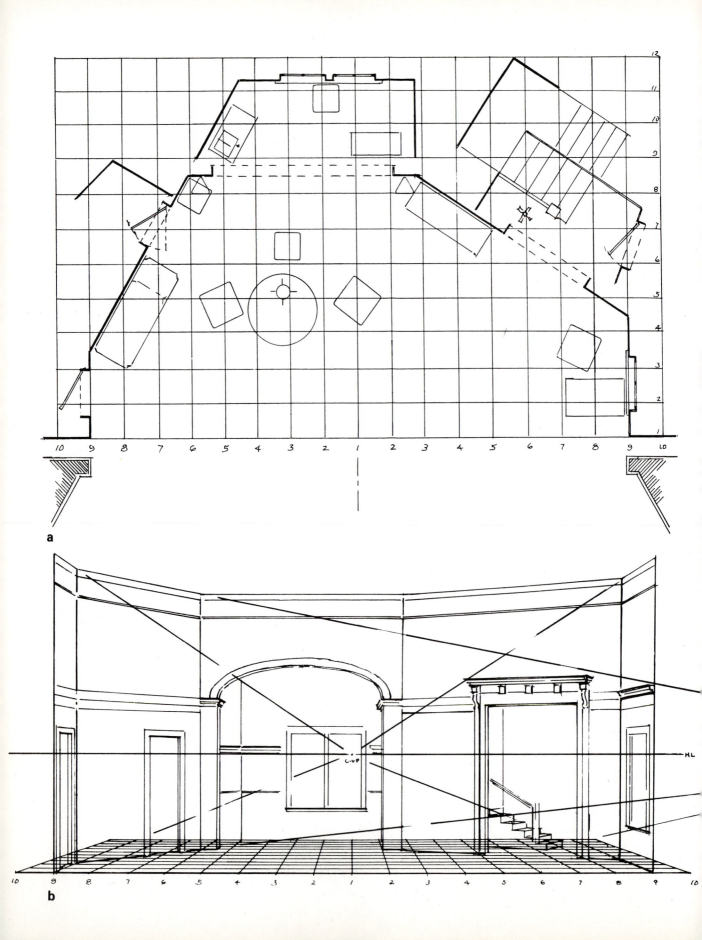

a

b

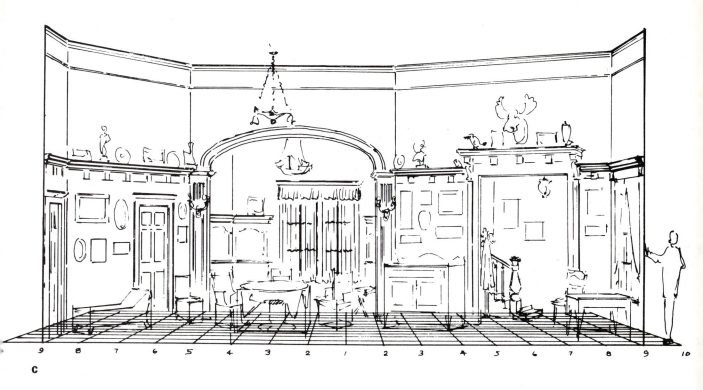

c

d

FIGURE 5–24

Perspective Sketch Technique—Conventional Interior

(a) The scaled floorplan with a grid overlay. (b) The grid in perspective with wall blocked in and the vanishing points located. (c) The addition of set dressings and furniture. (d) The final sketch, with grid and construction lines removed.

Drafting the Design   **145**

has a ramped floor and slanted ceiling. The floor plan (a) is gridded and shows the location of PP. In the split view (b) the stage left center portion shows the perspective grid and the method of determining the ramp of the floor. It will be noted that a reflected perspective grid was used overhead to plot the slant of the ceiling piece. The final sketch (c) is completed with the grid and construction lines removed.

The most difficult form to represent in perspective sketch is the thrust stage. The third illustration presents an adaptation of the perspective grid technique for a thrust-stage setting. The perspective grid is developed from an off-center view rather than on the centerline: (a) the floor plan with grid; (b) the perspective grid which, if drawn on

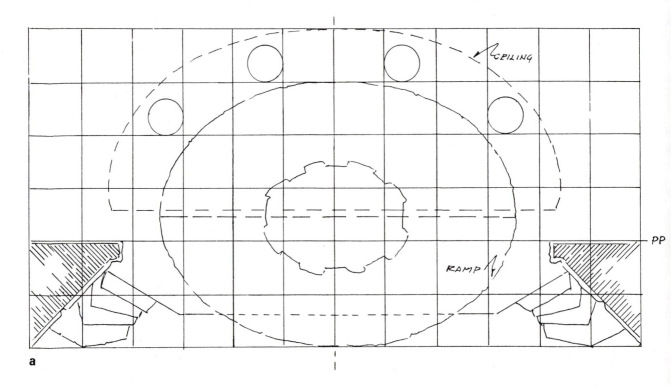

FIGURE 5–25

Perspective Sketch Technique—Angled Floor and Ceiling

(a) The scaled floor plan with grid overlay. Note the location of PP. (b) A split view showing on the stage-left side the perspective grid and the method of determining the ramp of the floor in perspective. The height of the ramp is measured on the PP at a point, h-1, on the grid. The true height of h-1 is projected upstage along a sightline to the center vanishing point (cvp) to intersect a second vertical line on the upstage edge of the ramp. A rectangle of the ramp is blocked in, within which the elliptical shape of the ramped floor can be drawn. Because the stage floor projects past PP, the height of the apron is in perspective. By extending a sightline through h-2, a vertical projected downward the height of the stage to the perpendicular at the downstage edge of the apron determines the height of the apron in perspective. The slope of ceiling is found by the same method. (1) The perspective grid. (2) A second perspective grid overhead to locate the slope of the ceiling. (3) The position of PP on the ramped floor and sloped ceiling. (4) Center line. (c) The finished sketch.

The Design Concept

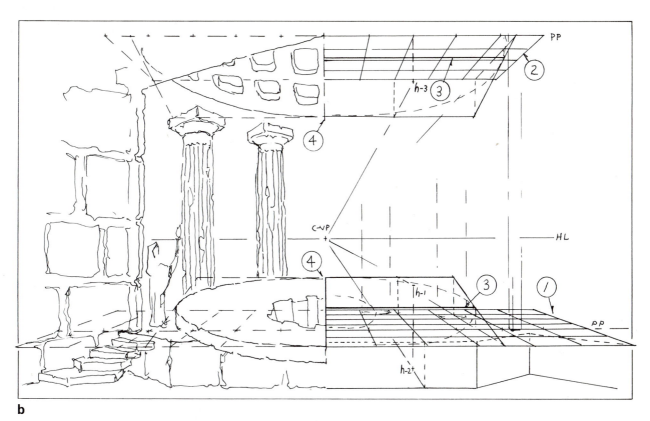

b

c

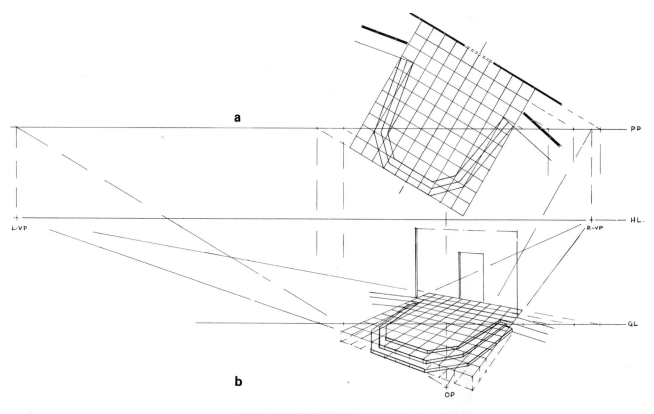

a

b

c

FIGURE 5–26

Perspective Sketch Technique—The Thrust Stage

An adaptation of the perspective grid technique to a thrust-stage setting. The perspective grid is developed from an off-center view rather than on the center line. (a) The floor plan with grid. (b) The perspective grid. (c) The final sketch.

The Design Concept

tracing paper, can be reversed to present a view from the opposite side; (c) the final sketch.

Any perspective technique in the final analysis should *guide* but not control the drawing. It should *free* rather than restrict the creative style of the designer. The mechanics of the technique should not be used as a means to the end but more as a check when, to the eye of the designer, "something doesn't look just right."

Three-dimensional Perspective

The use on the stage of three-dimensional forms, both architectural and abstract, is the sculptural use of space. It is the use of actual space and not the illusion of space. This is best dealt with in three dimensions with the use of models or real forms.

Sometimes, however, the scene designer has to produce the illusion of more space with three-dimensional forms, or combine two-dimensional with three-dimensional forms to create an illusion of space on a shallow stage. With careful study, the same techniques of space perception applicable to two-dimensional forms can be adapted to three-dimensional forms. Figure 5–27 illustrates a method of foreshortening a three-dimensional form. In this example a structure representing a garden shelter has been foreshortened in perspective into a much smaller space than it actually appears to occupy.

The technique of foreshortening a three-dimensional object is dependent upon two views, the plan and side elevation. View (1) in Figure 5–27 is the plan or view looking down on the structure. The dotted lines designated a, b, c, d represent the actual size of the plan while a', b', c', d' represent its foreshortened size. Each foreshortened point is located on a sightline drawn from the observation point (OP) to its original position on the actual plan. The position of the foreshortened points a', b', c', d' is arbitrary, depending upon how large or small a foreshortened plan is desired.

View (2) is a side view of the structure drawn next to and in alignment with view (1). The points a, b, c, d are shown in side view as well as a dotted line drawing of the rest of the elevation. The side view also shows the height of OP through which is drawn the horizon line (HL).

By projecting each point (a', b', c', d') of the foreshortened plan into the side view, being careful to relate each to its proper sightline, a foreshortened side view of the structure can be drawn. Because of the height of HL and the theatrical convention of stopping the perspective at the railing, most of the perspective appears at the top of the structure.

View (4) is a development of the four walls of the garden shelter based upon dimensions found in the two foreshortened views, plan and side elevation.

View (3) is a normal two-dimensional perspective drawing with OP

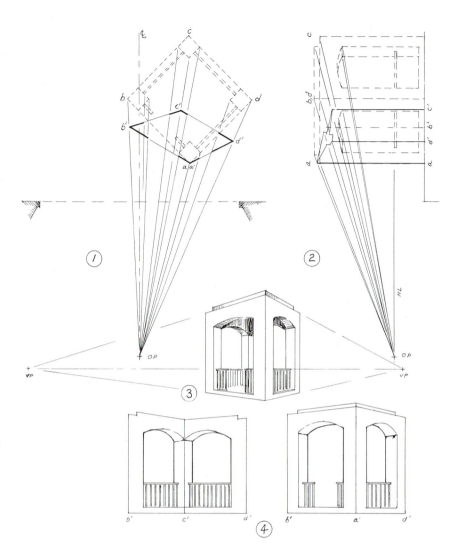

FIGURE 5–27

Three-dimensional Perspective

Illustrated are the steps necessary to foreshorten a scenic element (a gazebo or garden shelter) that in reality occupies in plan the space a, b, c, d to half the depth indicated a', b', c', d' in the drawing. (1) Using, jointly, the plan (1) and the side elevation (2) to work out the foreshortened heights of each corner, the four walls are redrawn into their new shapes (4). (3) A normal two-dimensional perspective drawing of the gazebo, which is the way it will appear if the foreshortened walls are carefully assembled on the foreshortened plan.

and HL in the same positions as in (1) and (2). To a certain extent (3) represents how the foreshortened walls of view (4) will look when they are assembled.

A second method of solving foreshortening is to work directly from the three-dimensional sketch and related floor plan. Figure 5–28 presents the two views of a perspective street scene. The plan has been located in the sketch by the perspective grid technique (Figure 5–23). The base of each house has been produced to find its vanishing point on the horizon line. (HL) house (1), for example, has a base line vanishing point on HL at the point labeled B-VP(1). All horizontal lines above HL, however, vanish to a second temporary vanishing point T-VP(1), closer to the house to force the perspective and thereby foreshorten the house. To layout house (1) in elevation for a model or designer's elevations T-VP(1) must be located in the plane of the element of scenery. This is accomplished by projecting T-VP(1) on HL directly upward until it intersects the produced base line of house (1) in plan.

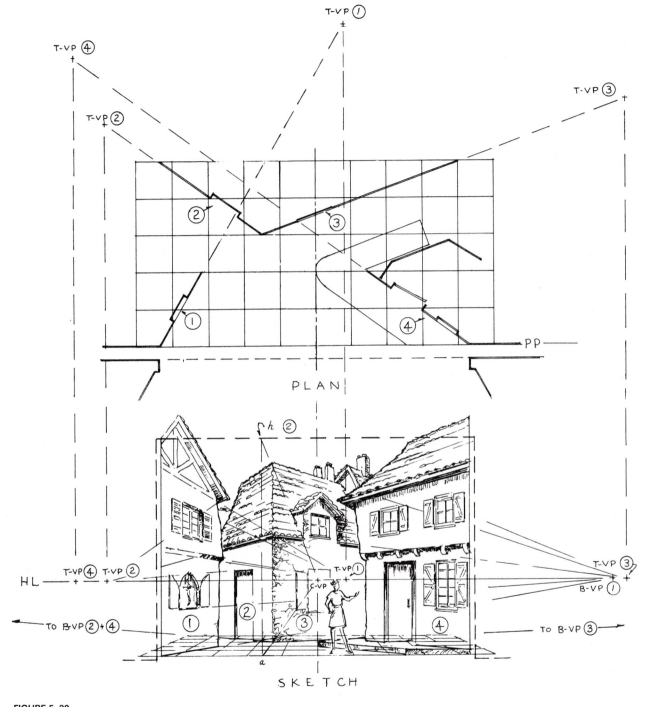

FIGURE 5–28

Foreshortened Scenery

A floor plan and sketch which has been drawn on a perspective grid. All horizontal lines *above* HL converge to a temporary vanishing point (T-VP) to heighten the normal perspective. House (1), for example, has a base line vanishing point on HL at point B-VP (1). All horizontal lines above HL, however, vanish to a second temporary vanishing point T-VP (1) to foreshorten the house.

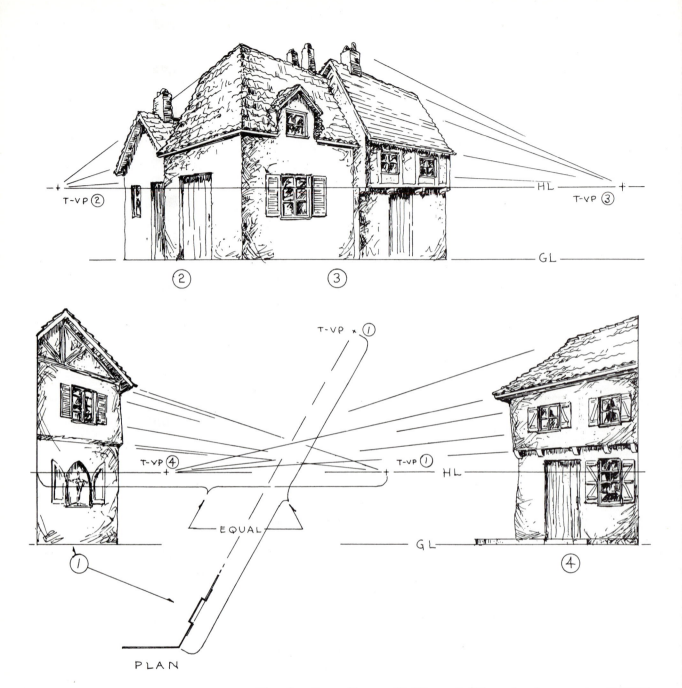

FIGURE 5–29

Foreshortening in Elevation

To resolve the elevation of the fore-shortened house (1) the distance of T-VP (1) from (1) is an important dimension. The true distance of T-VP (1) in elevation is found in the plan directly above T-VP (1) on HL. The degree of foreshortening in any of the houses is the decision of the designer.

The elevation of house (1) (Figure 5–29) can be drawn using T-VP(1) as a VP for all horizontal lines *above* HL. Note that the true distance of T-VP(1) in elevation is located in the plan view. The same procedure can be used to develop the elevation of all the foreshortened houses. Because the method is an approximation it is subject to adjustment as the designer develops the sketch.

152   *The Design Concept*

PART

2

EXECUTING THE DESIGN

6

Scene Design and Technical Production

Before the ideas of the designer can reach the stage, the designs, in the form of working drawings, have to go through a preparation or construction period. The scaled model is transformed into full-scale elements of scenery, the graded wash in the sketch becomes a carefully painted backdrop, and the insignificant spot on the elevation is fashioned into a pointed bit of detail. Step by step all the scenery is fitted together on the stage under lights and in final form.

Although the study of technical production is placed here in the logical order of the development of a stage setting, it also, paradoxically, represents knowledge a scene designer should possess *before* beginning a design. For this reason a study of technical production is a necessary part of a scene designer's training and background. As the architect is familiar with building techniques and materials, so should the scene designer be acquainted with methods of constructing and handling scenery as well as the uses of theatrical materials and techniques. A logical place to begin is with a survey of the tools and materials that are used to make scenery and an examination of the working procedures of a scenery shop.

THE SCENERY SHOP

Scenery is frequently built and painted under the adverse condition of an inadequate shop. Designers soon learn that an ill-equipped shop with sparse working space places a limit on the kind and amount of scenery that can be built and painted. Occasionally they find themselves in the enviable position of being able to plan their own shop or at least asked to specify the space requirements of the ideal scenery shop. In preparation for such an occasion, the designer should have some knowledge of the space requirements and layout of a good scenery shop.

Space Requirements

The overall area of a scenery shop depends upon four things: the size of the stage the shop is to serve, the location of the shop in relation to the stage and storage areas, the number and kinds of productions to be produced in an average season, and the nature of the shop's working procedure and personnel.

The size of the stage, or, in some cases, several stages, which the shop is to serve has a direct bearing on the size of the shop itself. A large stage requires large elements of scenery. A shop serving a large stage, of course, needs the space to execute the expansive proportions of such scenery. In a similar manner, the large amounts of scenery necessary to supply more than one stage would influence the size of the shop. The scale of the scenery may be smaller, but a shop serving several stages must be arranged to handle quantities of scenery.

FIGURE 6–1

Scenery Shop Layout

A bird's-eye view of a scenery shop for a community or university theatre. Although housed in a separate wing to isolate operational noises, it is, at the same time, attached to the left side of the stage it serves. (S) Stage—left side. (A) Assembly area—serves three functions: (a) Provides an area equal to the playing area of the stage for trial assembly of part or all of the setting. (b) Becomes space to store the offstage wagon of a transverse-wagon scheme for moving scenery. (c) Also serves as a painting area; the last stage of scenery construction before moving it onto the stage. The split paint frame (top) often can be used as two separately operated small frames or be locked together as a single large frame. The available floor space can be used for horizontal painting and full-scale lofting. Although the assembly is closed off from the stage by a pair of sound-deadening doors, the work in this area still has to be essentially quiet work, such as painting and lofting, when the stage is in use. (C) Construction area—where the cutting and working of materials as well as small-unit assembly takes place. This area is further isolated from the stage by sound-deadening doors. (T) Technician's or shop office. (B) Balcony over a portion of the shop—provides extra storage space for materials and supplies. Could also have long cutting table and sewing machine for making stage draperies. (M) Metal-working area—removes welding and metal-working tools from main shop area. (P) Property shop—area for building, rebuilding, upholstering, and finishing furniture and special properties. (D) Drafting room above metal and property shop on the same level as the balcony. (1) Space between shop building and stage house to reduce the amount of structure-borne sound. (2) Vertical painting area with movable palette table. (3) Paint supplies, sink, and burners. (4) Storage bins for scenery waiting to be painted or to be assembled after painting. (5) Drop storage racks on this wall above doors. (6) Lift—serves basement scenery and property storage rooms and balcony storage above. (7) Movable template tables which can be used together or separately. Space beneath top can serve as storage space for plywood and upson board. (8) Lumber storage racks and pullover saw tables. (9) Small tool and hardware storage. (10) Power tools in woodworking area under the balcony. (11) Canvas and muslin storage.

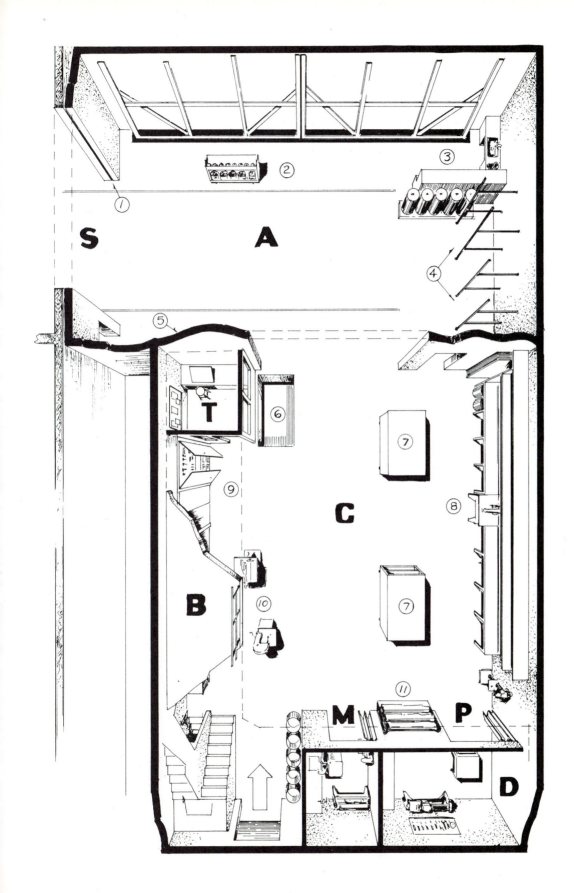

S A

B C

T

M P D

157

The location of the scenery shop also affects its size. For example, a shop near the stage could utilize stage space for the construction of scenery and thereby supplement the shop area. On the other hand, a shop in a remote location needs additional space for the storage of scenery and properties as well as the necessary construction and painting areas. Although a distant shop has the disadvantage of causing the additional handling of scenery from the shop to the stage and back again, it does have the decided advantage of being able to operate free of preperformance uses of the stage. A shop adjacent to the stage is doomed to conflict with rehearsals and performances, which will render it inoperative a major portion of the time.

The number and kinds of productions also help determine the space requirements of a scenery shop. A repertory company, for example, would require enormous storage space to retain the scenery of numerous productions intact, while perhaps only building one or two new productions a year. An opera or musical comedy production group would have a greater demand for scenery than would a company that mounts intimately scaled productions.

The final consideration that has some influence on the overall size of the shop is the shop procedure and personnel. The nature of the shop's personnel and working hours may vary from a staff of full-time professionals to scattered groups of part-time student apprentices or volunteers. A small highly skilled staff working steadily can use building space more efficiently than large sporadic groups requiring sufficient area to do many separate jobs at once. A further evaluation of the space requirements resulting from shop procedure includes an analysis of the areas of work, tools and equipment, and materials of the average scenery shop.

Work Areas

The shop is divided into areas related to the various steps in the process of building and painting. These areas are organized for: (1) storage of materials and tools; (2) the cutting and working of lumber (boring, planing, and so on); (3) the framing and covering of basic units of scenery; (4) the trial assembly of basic units into portions or all of the complete setting; (5) the painting of scenery and properties; and (6) the building of properties—which, although listed last, would be in process along with scenery construction.

1. The first necessary space in a scenery shop is for the storage of materials and tools. This means lumber racks, paint bins, and hardware cabinets located near their area of use yet convenient to the loading door. Provisions must also be made for the storage of brushes near the painting area and for small tools adjacent to the woodworking area.

2. The second area, related to the next step in building scenery, is the woodworking area. Here the lumber is cut and worked (bored, planed, jig-sawed, and so on). The lumber supply, hardware storage,

and the hand tools must be convenient to this area. Within the area there should be space for the large power tools such as table saws, band saws, drill presses, and the necessary work benches for working wood.

Careful consideration should be given to the lighting of the woodworking area and the other work areas as well as to the placement of power outlets convenient to the working position of the power tools associated with each area.

3 and 4. The third space is the assembly area, which ideally should be as large as the playing area of the stage to allow a trial assembly of the setting. The space can also be used for the framing and canvasing of basic units of scenery. Regular-shaped flats are framed and canvased on a template bench (Figure 6–2), while irregular-shaped units are laid out or "lofted" and then assembled on the floor. The assembly area can also serve as a temporary storage space for completed scenery waiting to be loaded out.

5. The painting area is another important space in the shop. It should be convenient to a sink, gas or electric burners, and the paint bins. Vertical painting, which occupies the least amount of floor space, requires overhead clearance or sufficient height to stand the scenery upright. The simplest vertical painting method is to mount the scenery on a fixed frame against a wall and paint from a rolling platform or boomerang. The most convenient method is the use of a counter-weighted vertical paint frame which lowers into a well, or raises off the floor. The painting is done from different levels or decks (see "Painting Scenery," Chapter 9).

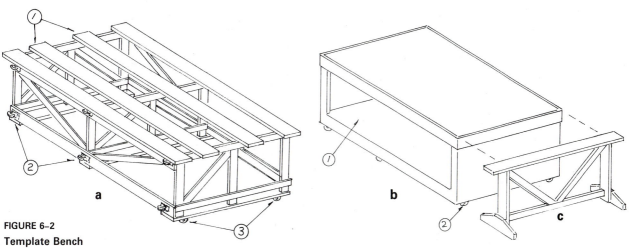

FIGURE 6–2
Template Bench

(a) The type shown is adaptable to a shop with limited working space where the same area may be needed for other operations. The template is a waist-high work bench with movable planks in the center (1) to provide support for framing the various widths of regular-shaped flats. The casters on one side (2) enable it to be tipped onto that side and pushed out of the way for storage. The casters on the base (3) provide easy movement when the bench is in working position. Although not equipped with built-in square corners and clinch plates, the template can also be used for such tasks as sabre-saw cutting and small assembly work. (b) Template bench with fixed working surface. (1) Storage space. (2) Casters for mobility. (c) Movable horse to support work longer than bench.

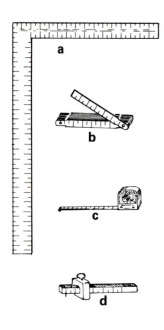

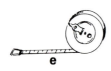

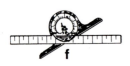

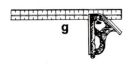

FIGURE 6–3

A more precarious method is to raise and lower a painting scaffolding in front of a fixed frame. In addition to being laborious and dangerous, the scaffolding has the added inconvenience of usually being some distance from a sink, burner, and paint supplies.

With even the best equipment for vertical painting, it is sometimes necessary to paint horizontally on the floor. Certain painting techniques require horizontal painting. The floor of the assembly area, or stage floor, often serves this purpose if stage use can be worked into the production schedule.

6. The most frequently neglected area in shop planning is a space to build properties. The altering, repairing, upholstering, and finishing of furniture is a specialized operation which requires different tools, materials, and paints from those found in the scenery shop. A property shop does not need a lot of space. It should, however, be an area near but separated from the dust and confusion of the scenery shop and the splatter of flying paint from the painting area.

TOOLS AND EQUIPMENT

The tools of a scenery shop are primarily for woodworking, with limited provisions for the working of metal. To build scenery it is necessary to cut, pare or shape, bore, and join the wood. The tools to work the wood are either hand tools for limited and special work or power tools for mass production and precision work. The working and joining of wood, however, is always preceded by careful measuring and marking.

Measuring and Marking Tools

Tools for measuring and marking are not only used with each technique of working wood but also in every step in the construction and assembly of the completed setting (Figure 6–3a-h). Almost all mistakes in building are directly traceable to wrong measurements or a misinterpreted mark. The importance of accurate measurements cannot be overstressed.

A list of the essential measuring and marking tools for a scenery shop should include:

MEASURING		MARKING	
a	Framing square	h	Bevel gauge
b	6-foot folding rule	i	Scribe
c	6-foot, 8-foot, and 12-foot steel tape	j	Tri-square
		k	Spline or spring curve
d	Marking gauge	l	Trammel points and bar
e	50-foot steel tape	m	Chalk line
f	Protractor square	n	Centering square
g	Combination square	o	Spirit level

Some of the tools are obviously for measuring only (6-foot rule and 50-foot tape) and others are made specifically for marking (tri-square, bevel gauge, scribe, spirit level, spline, and center square). A few tools are, however, designed for both measuring and marking.

The *protractor square* is able to measure an angle in degrees and provide a marking guide.

The *combination square,* with its adjustable sliding bar, is calibrated for measuring as well as establishing a marking guide for the 90-degree and 45-degree angles.

The *framing square* with calibrated edges is a useful tool in marking the angle cut of a stair carriage and for establishing a right angle for framing.

The *marking gauge* is calibrated to mark for a rip cut, an operation that can be duplicated by the combination square.

Within the group of marking tools, the *tri-square* is calibrated for limited measuring although its chief function is as a marking guide for a 90-degree angle cut. The *bar* or *beam* holding the trammel points is sometimes calibrated to measure the radius of the circle or arc it is to swing. The other tools in this group serve as marking guides only.

The *bevel gauge* is designed for transferring or saving a predetermined angle or bevel.

The *scribe* can follow an irregular surface with one point and scratch or mark the outline of the surface at a fixed distance with the other point.

The *spline* or *spring curve* is used to mark an irregular curve, or to plot a curved edge in full-scale lofting.

The *spirit level* establishes a true vertical or horizontal, and the *center square* locates the unmarked center of a circle or round stock.

The *chalk line* is for snapping an extremely long straight line that may be used as a framing guide, as a reference line for full-scale lofting, or as a guide for painting.

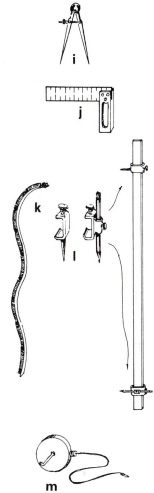

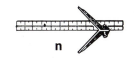

Cutting Tools

The chief cutting tool is the saw (Figure 6–4a-m, page 162). A list of saws for a scenery shop includes:

HAND SAWS		POWER SAWS	
a	Ripsaw	g	Saber saw
b	Crosscut saw	h	Pullover saw
c	Keyhole saw	i	Cut-awl
d	Scroll saw	j	Jigsaw
e	Miter box and backsaw	k	Skilsaw
f	Hack saw	l	Table saw
		m	Band saw

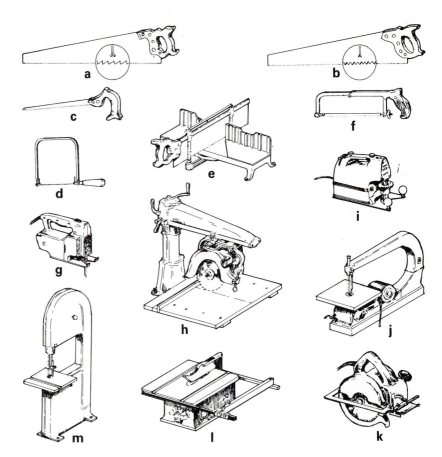

FIGURE 6–4

The specific work a saw can do depends upon the shape of the tooth (pointed or chisel), the set of the tooth (flare of every other tooth in the opposite direction), and the tooth count (number of teeth per inch). Because wood has a grain, which is the alternating density of the fibers within its structure, it requires a different kind of saw to cut across the grain than to cut with the grain. The teeth of a crosscut saw are sharp and straight to cut through the wood fibers, while the teeth of the ripsaw are angled and flat-edged like a chisel to chip the wood with the grain. The ripsaw has the widest set and the lowest tooth count (6 to 8 teeth per inch). The crosscut saw has a tooth count of 8, 10, to as many as 12 teeth per inch.

The *ripsaw* and *crosscut saw* are for straight-line cutting, as is the *hack saw*, which is used to cut metal. A hack saw, with a tempered-steel blade of l8 tooth count, will cut the strap iron, bolts, and pipe that are frequently used in scenery construction.

An angled cut or miter can be cut freehand with a crosscut saw, or it can be accurately cut in a miter box with a backsaw. The *backsaw*, with a high tooth count (10 to 12 teeth per inch) is a stiff-bladed saw with a straight back which serves as a guide in the miter box (Figure 6–4e). It is extremely useful in mitering moldings for a cornice, picture frame, or panel.

Executing the Design

Power Saws. Power tools made for straight-line cutting are the table saw, pullover saw, and Skilsaw. Each may be fitted with a rip, cross-cut, or combination blade for specific work.

A 10-inch, tilting-arbor, 1-horsepower *table saw* with miter gauge and rip fence is a basic piece of equipment. It is a heavy enough tool to do precision work in quantity. It miters and rips with ease and accuracy.

A 10- to 12-inch 1-horsepower *pullover saw* provides the necessary power for cutting heavy lumber. Its pullover action above the wood and long table make it an accurate crosscut and limited mitering tool. Because the guide fence becomes inaccurate from repeated cross-cutting, it is not a very accurate ripping tool.

The *Skilsaw*, which is a portable circular saw, is designed to be brought to the work rather than for bringing the work to the saw. It can be used to advantage as a rip or crosscut saw on partially completed units of scenery. Because of its light weight and small blade it is limited as to depth of cut and accuracy. It is, however, a useful tool to have in a busy shop.

Irregular Cutting. Not all cutting in the making of scenery is straight-line cutting. As a matter of fact, a high percentage of the cutting is irregular or scroll work. Cutouts and profile edges require the greatest amount of scroll work.

A hand saw to cut on an irregular line must necessarily have a small blade to be able to turn and follow the irregular line. The *scroll saw* has a high tooth count of 12 per inch to produce a smoothly cut edge. It also has a removable blade for inside cuts. The deep throat of the frame that holds the blade allows the saw to reach well into the work.

The *keyhole saw* with a tooth count of 8 to 10 is made for heavy, coarse, and fast work. The small blade, although not as small as the scroll saw, allows irregular cutting beyond the limits a scroll saw can reach.

Power Tools for Irregular Cutting. Power tools that speed up the production of scroll work are the band saw, jigsaw, saber saw, and cut-awl. The *band saw* with its continuous blade is limited to outside cutting and to work as large as the depth of its throat. A band saw with a 20-inch throat will serve the average need of a scenery shop if it is supplemented with other equipment to do inside cutting.

The *jigsaw* with its removable straight blade and deep throat is made for both inside and outside scroll cutting. The *saber saw,* which is a portable jigsaw, does not limit the size of the work. It is a very versatile tool for scroll cutting at any stage of assembly.

The *cut-awl*, which is designed for light, detailed cutting, works best on profile and composition board. It also requires a padded bench or table for satisfactory results.

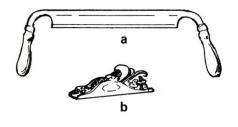

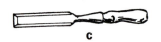

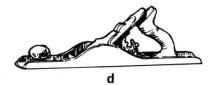

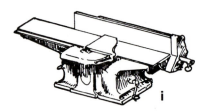

Paring Tools

Chisel or knifelike tools to smooth or shape wood are known as paring tools (Figure 6–5a-k). A list of the most useful:

HAND TOOLS

a   Drawknife
b   Block plane
c   Chisel
d   Smoothing plane
e   Rasp
f   Rasp blade in holder
g   Triangular metal file
h   Flat metal file

POWER TOOLS

i   Rotary planer (joiner)
j   Disk and belt sander
k   Router
l   Mortise machine
m   Rotary shaper
n   Emery wheel
o   Lathe

The simplest tool for freehand shaping of wood is the *chisel*. Although the hand chisel cannot compare in speed and accuracy to power tools,

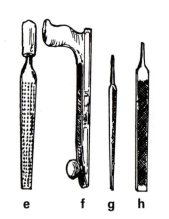

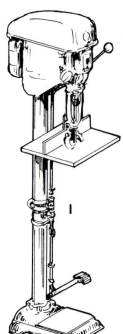

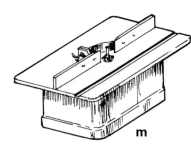

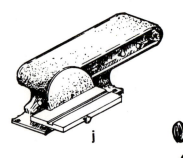

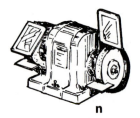

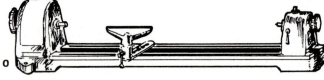

FIGURE 6–5

Executing the Design

it can be used to do a limited amount of shaping and notching of wood. It is an excellent tool to clean up a power-cut dado, rabbet, mortise, or routed area. With skilled handling it can, if necessary, make any of these cuts itself. A set of chisels would include a variety of widths from ¼ inch to 1¼ inches.

The *drawknife* is not a precision tool. It is useful to pare away waste or roughly shape a surface before planing.

The *smoothing plane* can pare a surface to an accurate dimension. It is made to smooth with the grain of the wood while the small *block plane* is designed to work across the grain and to smooth or shape the end of a board.

The *rasp* is also used for cross-grain smoothing or shaping. Its sharp teeth tear the fibers so that unless a rough finish is desired the surface has to be smoothed with a fine rasp or sandpaper.

Power tools designed to do various shaping and smoothing operations are limited mostly to special cuts. The *rotary planer* or *joiner,* for example, can smooth a board, size a board by changing the depth of cut, bevel the edge by angling the fence, as well as cutting a rabbet on one side of the board.

Likewise the *rotary shaper* is designed especially to cut moldings. It can cut a variety of molding by changing or combining different blades.

The *mortising machine,* or mortising attachment for a drill press, with its square chisel, is limited to cutting the deep square hole of a mortise. It is a time-saving tool in a professional scenery shop where there is a lot of mortise-and-tenon joining.

Probably the most useful small power tool for shaping is the *router.* In addition to routing to countersink hinges, it can cut tenons, dados, and rabbets. With special bits it can also do a limited amount of molding cutting.

Some of these shaping operations can be performed on the table and pullover saw. The circular table saw can be equipped with a dado head, which is a set of special blades to cut a groove. Molding cutters can also be attached to the circular saw for simple molding cutting. The pullover saw can also be rigged to dado, shape, and rout. Any change-over, of course, takes time and ties up the saw for other uses.

For finished smoothing, a power *sander,* both belt and disk, quickly and accurately smooths the end, edge, or face of a board. In this same category, the *emery wheel* is used to smooth and shape metal as well as sharpen hand tools.

Boring Tools

Tools with a cutting edge that revolves about a central axis to cut a circular hole are called boring tools (Figure 6–6a-m, page 166). The tool consists of two basic parts: the bit, which is the cutting part of the tool, and the brace or some similar mechanism to rotate the bit.

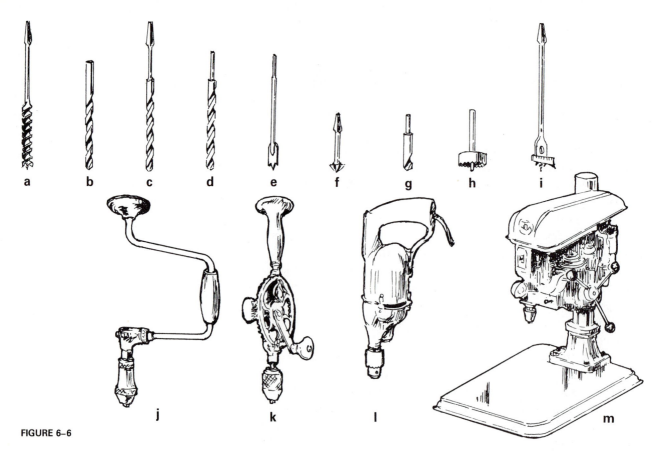

FIGURE 6–6

There is, of course, great variation in the types of bit, depending upon the size and depth of the hole, kind of hole (clean bore, taper, ream), and the nature of the material (hardness, thickness). Likewise the power-providing part of the tool will vary with type of bit used and the speed of rotation necessary to do the work. The types of bit and means of rotation found in the average scenery shop are:

BITS		ROTATING TOOLS	
a	Auger bit (square shank)	j	Brace
b	Twist drill (round shank)	k	Hand drill
c	Twist drill (square shank)	l	Power hand drill
d	Twist drill (¼-inch round shank)	m	Drill press
e	Power bit (¼-inch round shank)		
f	Countersink, wood		
g	Countersink, metal		
h	Hole-cutter		
i	Expanding bit		

The *auger bit* has a screw lead which, when rotated, pulls the cutting edges of the bit into contact with the wood. The auger bit does not need to rotate at a high speed. It is usually driven with the brace made to receive its square shank. The *brace* is a cranklike form designed to give the carpenter a mechanical advantage rather than to increase the speed of rotation. Augers are manufactured in size differences of ¹⁄₁₆ inch. They are numbered by sixteenths; thus a ½-inch auger would be a No. 8 bit.

Twist drills have no screw lead and depend upon speed of rotation and pressure to advance into the material. The *hand drill* is designed to increase the speed of rotation as well as provide some mechanical advantage. The high-speed portable *power hand drill* is excellent for this type of work.

The *power bit* is a wood-cutting bit made for high-speed rotation with a small round shank (¼-inch) for the small power drill.

Also in the auger-bit class are the gimlet and expanding bit. The gimlet is made to bore a small hole in an inaccessible place; the *expanding bit,* which is adjustable, can bore a hole as large as 1¼ inches to 2½ inches in diameter.

The *countersink bit* is used on either wood or metal after the hole has been bored. It enlarges the top of the opening with a beveled cut of sufficient depth to set a flathead screw or bolt flush with the outer surface of the material.

The *hole-cutter* is to cut oversized holes (1½ inches and up) at high speed. Although faster and cleaner than the expanding bit, it is limited in its depth of cut.

The *drill press,* which is a stationary power drill, has added advantages of such controls as depth of bore and speed variation for precision work. The drill press with a mortising attachment makes a very useful tool in the scenery shop.

Wood-Joining Tools

The joining of wood is the last stage of carpentry. The tools that are used are designed to drive or set the joining hardware (nails, screws, or staples) in such manner as to hold the pieces of wood together (Figure 6–7a-x, page 168). The hammer and hammerlike tools (staple gun) drive a nail or staple; the screwdriver sets a screw into wood; the wrench and pliers tighten a bolted joint; and the clamps hold a glued joint together until the glue has set. A list of the most frequently used tools follows:

a	Claw hammer	i	Crescent wrench
b	Straight claw hammer	j	Pliers
c	Blacksmith's hand hammer	k	Mat knife
d	Ball peen hammer	l	Staple gun
e	Mallet	m	Staple hammer
f	Magnetic tack hammer	n	Scissors
g	Ratchet screwdriver	o	Tin shears
h	Screwdriver	p	Stillson wrench

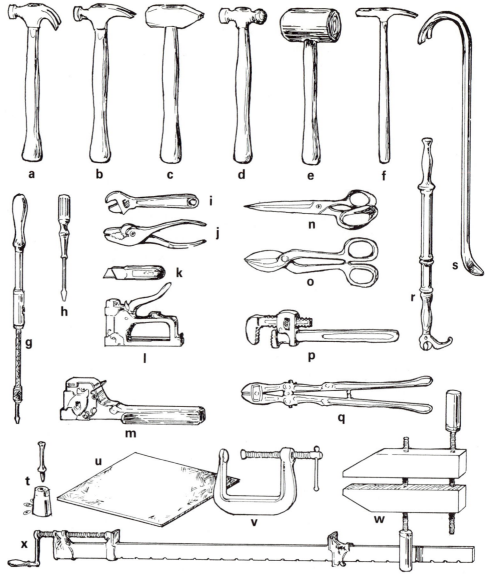

FIGURE 6–7

q	Bolt-cutter	u	Clinch plate
r	Nail-puller	v	C-clamp
s	Pinch bar	w	Jorgensen hand screw clamp
t	Grommet-setting die	x	Bar clamp

The bolt-cutter, tin shears, scissors, and mat knife are cutting tools that are used in the covering and assembly process of scenery construction.

Pneumatic Tools

No well-equipped scenery shop is without the speed and efficiency of the pneumatic hammer or staple gun (Figure 6–8). Because these

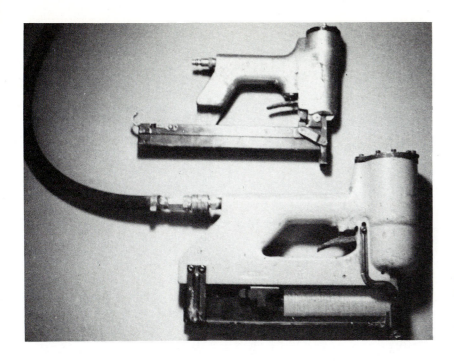

FIGURE 6–8
Pneumatic Tools
Two useful pneumatic staplers suitable for attaching corner blocks and light-weight nailing.

tools require about 90 pounds per square inch of air pressure to operate, the shop must have a heavy-duty compressor or compressed-air service at convenient positions in the shop. In addition to the air-hammer the shop should have a pneumatic reversible drill with socket wrench and screwdriver attachments.

Metal-Working Tools

The ever-increasing use of structural steel, pipe, and tubing in scenery as either framing or decorative materials makes it advisable to include a few necessary metal-working tools in the well-equipped scenery shop (Figure 6–9a-g, page 170). Many of the basic hand tools for cutting and working metal have already been mentioned, including the hack saw and metal file as well as such power tools as the drill press for the drilling and countersinking of metal. Additional hand tools for the cutting and working of pipe not mentioned are the pipe-cutter, threader, bender, and vise stand.

The *pipe-cutter*, when rotated around the pipe, applies an even pressure to the cutting wheel, thereby insuring a square, clean cut. A *pipe-threader* set should include *die heads* to thread at least ¾-inch, 1-inch, and 1½-inch pipe. Both the cutting and threading of pipe require a *pipe vise*. Rather than attaching a pipe vise to a fixed bench position, it is easier to use a *portable vise stand* which can be brought to the work on the stage or in the shop to minimize the handling of material. The vise stand shown in Figure 6–9d is also equipped with slots for limited pipe bending. For larger-scale bending of heavier pipe it is best to use a regular *pipe-bending tool* (Figure 6–9e).

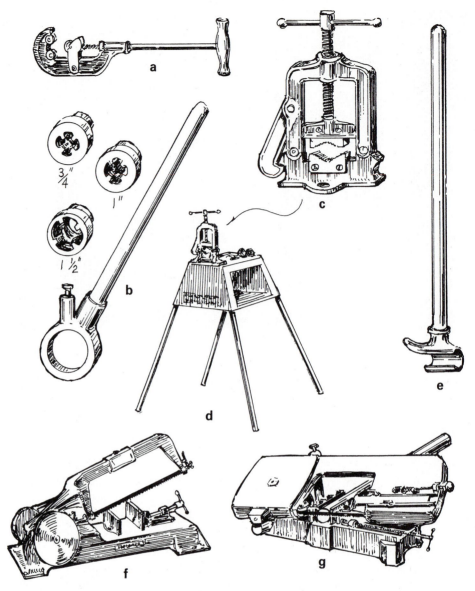

FIGURE 6–9

HAND TOOLS	POWER TOOLS
a Pipe-cutter	f Power hack saw
b Pipe-threader with ¾-inch, 1-inch, and 1½-inch die heads	g Power band saw
c Pipe vise	
d Portable vise stand	
e Pipe-bender	

The cutting of pipe or structural steel by hand can be time-consuming and inaccurate. Two power tools, the *power hack saw* and *band saw,* are designed to cut up to 2-inch stock pipe, structural steel, or cold-rolled steel bar at an adjustable angle cut of 45 to 90 degrees. Both tools are adaptable to mass producing or multiple cutting, with the band saw being the more accurate and of course the most expensive.

The occasional need to cut light-weight sheet metal or aluminum can be accomplished by using a metal-cutting blade in either the saber saw or regular band saw.

WELDING

The joining of metal structural or decorative members is obviously more complicated than the joining of wood. Structural steel may be joined by drilling and bolting; pipe may be joined by a coupling or union fitting, and so on. A faster method, which at the same time produces a rigid permanent joint, is welding. The two most useful welding processes adaptable to the construction and designing of scenery are *gas-welding* and *arc-welding*.

Gas-Welding Equipment

Oxy-acetylene welding (OAW) ignites an oxygen and acetylene mixture to produce one of the hottest flames known. Welding is possible with or without a filler metal. Gas-welding can perform a wide range of work. In addition to joining or fusing the metals together it can be used for low-temperature welding or *brazing*, to cut metal with a cutting attachment, and to preheat metal for reshaping on the anvil. The chief disadvantage to gas-welding is heat warpage.

Unless handled very carefully, gas-welding can cause warping of the metal near the welded point. The choice of a welding rod which will melt at the same temperature as (or slightly lower than) the melting point of the steel will minimize the amount of distortion.

The relative harmlessness of the flame is another advantage of gas-welding when used in the scenery shop or on the stage. The only exception is when the cutting tip is being used. To cut metal with a torch, a tiny jet of oxygen is directed onto the white-hot metal, producing a rather spectacular shower of sparks. The operator should wear goggles and gloves, more for protection from flying sparks than from the intensity of the flame itself. Because there are no ultraviolet rays generated in the flame by gas-welding, it does not have to be isolated or shielded from other shop activity. Precautions should be taken, however, to guard flammable materials from the sparks by using sheetrock pads under and around the work.

The most cumbersome parts of a gas-welding outfit are the heavy tanks containing the two welding gases, oxygen and acetylene. A tank truck is essential to make their movement easier. The methods of acquiring oxygen and acetylene vary with the suppliers. Some gas suppliers charge a fixed deposit on the tank which is refunded when the empty tank is returned, while others rent the container on a per diem basis. If a supplier insists on the tank-rental arrangement, it pays in the long run to purchase a set of empty tanks to exchange for each tank of gas and thereby eliminate the per diem rental charge which, though small, can mount up during idle times between productions.

A listing of the parts and attachments of a gas-welding outfit including the gas tanks is as follows (Figure 6–10a-p):

a   Oxygen tank
b   Acetylene tank
c   Tank truck
d   Gauges: oxygen regulator and acetylene regulator
e   25-foot twin ³⁄₁₆-inch hose with connectors
f   Welding butt
g   Cutting attachment
h   Welding nozzles, sizes 00, 1, 3, and 5

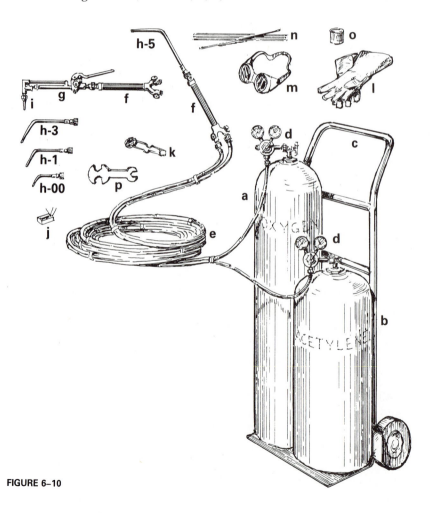

FIGURE 6–10

Executing the Design

i   Cutting tip size 2
j   Tip cleaner set
k   Flint lighter
l   Welding gloves
m   Goggles
n   Rods: ⅛-inch fluxcoated brazing rod (for thin-walled conduit)
        ⅛-inch mild steel rod (for structural steel)
o   Flux
p   Wrench

Arc-Welding Equipment

The heat of arc-welding comes, as the name implies, from the arc of a high-amperage short between the metal and the rod or electrode. The work has to be grounded to complete the circuit from the rod to the holder through the electrode cable to the transformer. *Shielded metal arc-welding* (SMAW) is the most adaptable arc-welding technique for the theatre workshop. Upon striking, the arc is enveloped in a shield

of inert gas as the coating of the rod burns. This shield of inert gas keeps the oxygen in the air out of the critical metallurgical change of the welding process.

Of the two welding methods, arc-welding requires more skill. It takes practice to develop a steady hand to strike an arc and draw a good bead. Arc-welding's chief advantage is in the speed of the welding operation. Because a welding temperature is reached almost instantaneously and in such a small area, the amount of heat warpage is negligible. This is important in the welding of a preassembled part when its fit is critical to the final shape of the completed structure.

A transformer of at least 40 to 230 amperes capacity with multiheat selection is an ideal welder for stage and scenery application. With the proper rod it will solder; weld bronze, steel, or cast iron; and, with special attachments, heat metal for reshaping.

The most obvious disadvantage of arc-welding is the harmful intensity of the flash. Because of the presence of ultraviolet rays, it is very injurious to the eyes to look directly at the flash for any length of time. Hence it becomes necessary to shield the eyes of the operator with ray-absorbing glass and a protective hood. As bare arms and hands are also subject to ray burns, gloves and protective long sleeves are an added precaution for the operator.

The flash can also affect the casual observer or fellow worker in the shop. If arc-welding cannot be isolated in a special area away from other shop activities, it is possible to shield the flash from others with a folding screen.

The parts of an arc-welding outfit are as follows (Figure 6–11a–j, page 175):

a   Transformer: 40–230 amperes
                 16–20 heats
    Supply cable (20 feet for greater mobility)
b   18-foot electrode cable
c   18-foot ground cable
d   Electrode rod holder
e   Ground clamps
f   Helmet, fiberglass with ray-absorbing viewing glass
g   Gloves
h   Apron or smock
i   Rods: ⅛-inch mild steel rods (structural steel and pipe)
           ⅛-inch hard-surface rods (chrome carbon steel)
j   Folding screen

Gas-Metal Arc-Welding

A third welding process which is rapidly becoming adaptable to theatre shop use is the gas-metal arc-welding method commonly re-

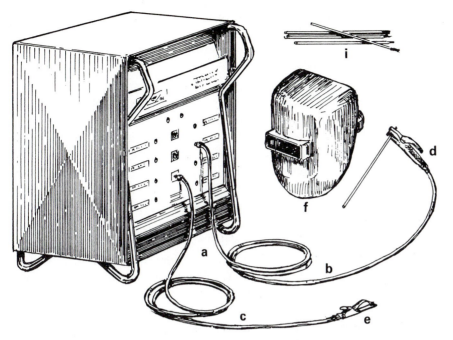

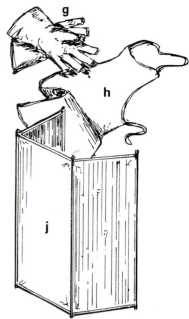

FIGURE 6–11

ferred to as *metal inert gas* or MIG. MIG uses a wire-fed electrode through a gas hose and gun nozzle to the work. The arc is surrounded with an inert gas shield and is automatically fed with a wire electrode in the center of the nozzle. MIG welding is a simple one-handed operation that is easy to learn. The heat of the arc and gauge of the wire can be altered to weld various metals including aluminum. A special

Scene Design and Technical Production

spot-welding fitting can be attached to the end of the nozzle for temporarily tacking or permanently joining adjacent surfaces. Some MIG units can also switch to stick-welding (regular arc-welding with rod) without the use of gas.

As welding equipment MIG is more expensive than arc or gas but is easier to operate and provides a variety of uses. Its chief disadvantages are its weight and bulk. It is not very mobile for other than metal-shop use.

Tungsten inert gas or TIG is also a gas-metal arc-welding system. TIG uses a tungsten electrode in the gun nozzle rather than a wire feed. The tungsten electrode has the advantage of eroding more slowly than other refractory metals and can withstand higher currents. The electrode, however, does not act as a filler metal as in MIG and therefore requires the two-handed skill of the gas-welding method to operate.

Because an arc is involved in gas-metal arc-welding it is subject to all the safety precautions of arc-welding mentioned earlier. The components of MIG equipment are as follows (Figure 6–12a-o):

a   Power unit MIG—160 amperes DC at 22 volts

(60% duty cycle)

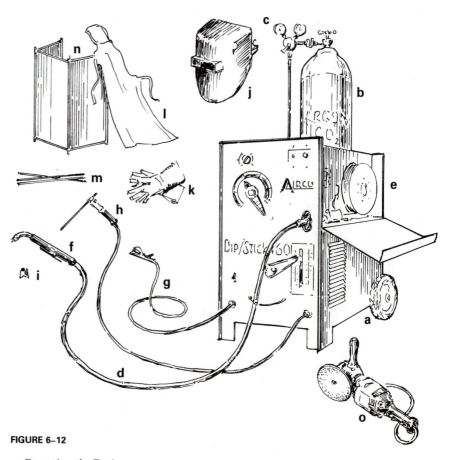

FIGURE 6–12

Executing the Design

STICK—160 amperes DC at 28 volts

(35% duty cycle)

Supply cable

b Gas cylinder—mixture of argon and CO_2 or helium

c Gauges—tank pressure

work pressure

d Gas hose-cable

e Automatic wire-feeder

built-in wire-feeder is a feature of this
particular unit (AIRCO, DIP/STICK 160)

f Gun and nozzle

g Ground cable

h Electrode cable for stick-welding

i Spot-welding attachment

j Helmet, fiberglass with ray-absorbing viewing window

k Gloves

l Apron or smock

m Rods for stick-welding

n Folding screen

o Angled grinder to smooth-weld

MATERIALS AND SUPPLIES

Although some materials will be mentioned in relation to the construction of certain types of scenery, it may be wise to consider briefly all the materials that are used for making scenery. To compile a comprehensive list is, of course, next to impossible, for designers and technicians are constantly bringing new materials into the theatre every day as well as discovering new uses for old materials.

Materials can be divided and classified into four groups of similar functions: (1) structural (lumber and metal), (2) cover stock (fabric and hard surfaces), (3) hardware (joining and stage hardware), (4) rigging (rope, cable, and chain), (5) paints and related supplies (Chapter 9).

Structural Materials

Lumber is the principal framing and structural material, supplemented and reinforced on occasion by structural steel, pipe, and aluminum. As supplies and prices change, aluminum may become the framing material and wood the supplementary or decorative material. Until this is an actuality, lumber remains the chief structural element.

Lumber. To fill the needs of scenic construction, lumber must be lightweight, strong, straight, and inexpensive. The best combination of weight and strength is found in white pine. Although woods such as redwood and spruce are lighter, they do not have the strength and tend to splinter and split. The hardwoods are stronger, of course, but weigh and cost too much.

Lumber is classified at the yard into quality groups. The straightness of grain and freedom from knots determine the quality. Hence, clear white pine is of the highest quality. It is further classified as to its expected use. A board that is to become trim or a finished surface is of a higher quality than a structural member hidden from view.

The finishing lumber or "select" grades are designated by the letters A, B, C, and D. Hence B-select or better is a high-grade pine. C-select is the usual quality of lumber used in professional scenery.

The common grades are numbered 1 to 5. They are not intended for a finished surface although many times 1- and 2-common are used as knotty-pine paneling. No. 2-common is the usual framing material for amateur scenery unless the theatre is in an area of the country where the better grades of pine are available at reasonable prices.

The stock sizes of lumber refer to the rough-cut size and not to the finished dimension after the wood has been dressed (planed or smooth on all sides). Thus 1 by 3 is really ¾-inch by 2½-inch. The longest stock length is 16 feet, although longer lengths can be obtained on special order.

Because lumber is cut in a variety of widths and thicknesses, it has a unit of measurement, the board-foot, common to all sizes. A board-

Executing the Design

foot is a 1-foot-square unit measuring 1 inch in thickness. A piece of lumber of any size can be reduced from its linear dimensions into board-feet. A 16-foot length of 1 by 3, for example, contains 4 board-feet. All lumber prices are based on the board-foot measurement.

Special shapes like "rounds" are stocked in diameter from ¾-inch to 1½-inch and sometimes as large as 3 inches in diameter. Dowel is available in ⅛- to 1-inch diameter and 3-foot lengths made of maple and birch.

Other special shapes are stock moldings which are made in a great variety of sizes and contours. A few of the most frequently used moldings are illustrated in Figure 6–13 along with the stock lumber sizes.

Metal. Structural steel has many special uses in scenery construction. The sizes and shapes in relation to their uses are illustrated in Figure 6–14 (page 180).

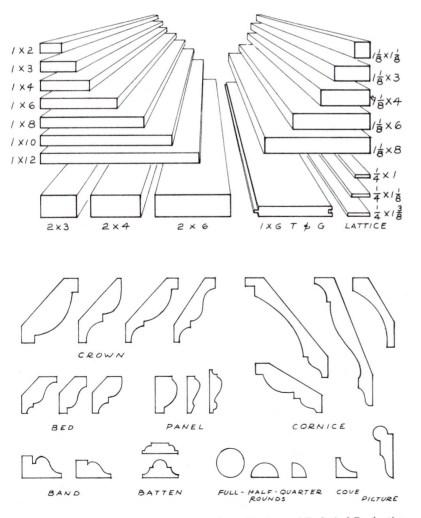

FIGURE 6–13
Stock Lumber Sizes and Molding Shapes

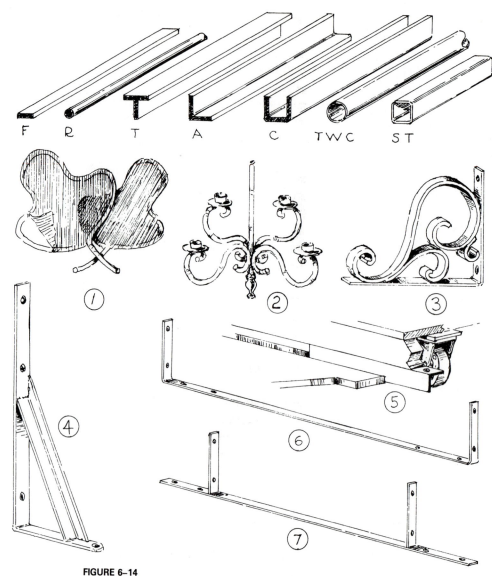

FIGURE 6–14

Some Structural Steel Shapes

Shown are a few of the basic lightweight structural steel shapes and their uses in scenery construction: (F) Flat or strap iron. (R) Round or rod. (T) Tee. (A) Angle. (C) Channel. (TWC) Thin-wall conduit. (ST) Square tube. *Decorative Uses of Rod and Strap Iron:* (1) Stylized leaf forms. (2) Chandelier or candelabra shapes. (3) Decorative bracket. *A Few Familiar Uses of Steel in Scenery Construction:* (4) Special jack or oversized footiron. (5) "Knife" guide in the track of a guided wagon. (6) Sill iron used under door opening in a flat. (7) Saddle-shaped sill iron.

Uni-strut with its fittings is a method of knockdown framing in special channel-shaped steel that is adaptable to platforming and trussing in the theatre. It eliminates the necessity of welding and cutting and is available in different forms.

Thin-wall galvanized-steel *conduit* pipe has become a very popular structural and decorative material in the theatre. With walls too thin to thread and therefore easy to bend, it has many uses in scenery construction (Figure 6–14). It comes in three diameters, ½-inch, ¾-inch, 1¼-inch, in 10-foot lengths. It is lightweight, inexpensive, and easy to gas-weld with fluxcoated brazing rod.

Malleable *iron pipe* is used for battens to support hanging scenery, as a weight or bottom batten for a drop, for lighting booms, and as structural elements. Pipe-fitting and pipe-bending increase the number of uses pipe can perform in the theatre. Figure 6–15 shows the stock sizes and fittings, and some of the uses.

Galvanized iron, aluminum, tin, and zinc are the most frequently used *sheet metals*. Light pans, shadow boxes, and special effects are a few of the uses of sheet metal in scenery construction.

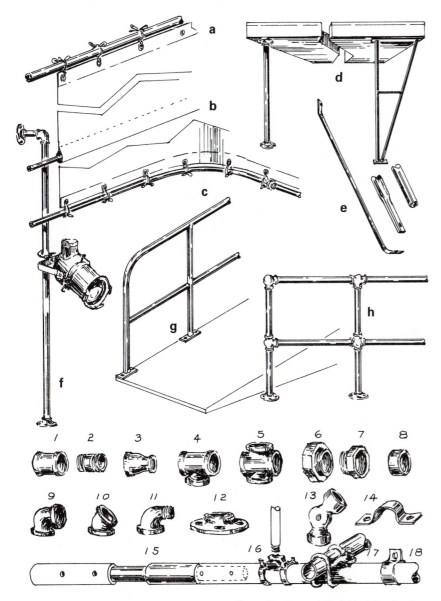

FIGURE 6–15

Various Uses of Iron Pipe

(a) Top batten for drop, cyclorama, or stage drapery. (b) Bottom batten for a drop-in pipe sleeve. (c) Curved bottom batten using tielines. (d) Free-standing platform legs. (e) Special bracing. (f) Lighting booms and battens. (g) Bent pipe and welded railing. (h) Cut pipe and fitted railing. *Some of the Screw Fittings Used to Join Section of Pipe:* (1) coupling, (2) nipple, (3) reducing coupling, (4) tee, (5) cross, (6) union, ring end, (7) union, screw end, (8) cap, (9) 90-degree elbow, (10) 45-degree elbow, (11) street ells, (12) floor flange, (13) adjustable elbow (railing fitting), (14) pipe strap, (15) batten inside sleeve splice, (16) saddle tee, double strap, (17) rotolock, (18) pipe hanger.

The *metal screening* such as hardware cloth (¼-inch mesh), galvanized screen (¹⁄₁₆-inch mesh), and chicken wire (1-inch mesh) are primarily used as structural materials. Occasionally, galvanized screening is used to simulate window glass.

Cover Stock

The material used to cover the structural frame of scenery, thereby providing a surface for painting, is known as cover stock. The frame can be covered with a fabric or hard surface depending upon the use and handling of the particular piece of scenery. A translucent backing, for example, is framed and covered differently from a section of wall that must support the weight of an actor.

Covering Fabrics. The usual covering fabrics for framed scenery are 8-ounce canvas duck and 5- to 6-ounce unbleached muslin. Muslin is more frequently used as a drop material than as cover stock for framed scenery. However, almost any fabric can become a covering material to serve as a special effect or as an unusual painting surface. Burlap, velour, scrim, terry cloth, and even string rugs have been used as covering fabrics. The thin, translucent materials are backed with canvas, of course, if the surface is supposed to be opaque.

Hard Surfaces. If the surface has to withstand active handling during the action of a play, the frame is covered with a harder surface than canvas. The most frequently used hard-surface material is ⅛-inch plywood board called EZ curve or profile board. It is lightweight but still strong enough to supply a hard surface with a minimum of framing. Tek board, ⅛-inch laminated wood and paper, is a close substitute for profile board although not quite as stong.

Other hard-surface materials include ⅛-inch and ³⁄₁₆-inch Upson board, an inexpensive but weaker substitute for profile board made of laminated paper; ¼-inch fir three ply, a very sturdy but heavy board (also used for keystone and corner blocks); ½-inch Homosote, a paper-pulp board with very little strength but thick enough to be carved or textured; and ³⁄₁₆-inch Masonite, a very heavy, hard surface of compressed wood pulp. The tempered Masonite is an extremely hard surface that is occasionally used as a floor covering. Double-faced corrugated cardboard is an inexpensive hard surface for limited profiling and covering providing the scenery is not subjected to excessive handling. Some shops also include ¾-inch and 1-inch five ply as cover stock, although its chief use is for platform tops.

Most of the cover-stock materials are available at the local lumber yard in stock 4-by-8-foot sheets. Occasionally, oversized sheets, such as 5 feet by 9 feet, 4 feet by 10 feet, and 4 feet by 12 feet are stocked.

Plastic Surfaces. Because the use of modern plastic as a scenery surface is usually related to a textured or relief-sculptured surface, it is reserved for discussion in Chapter 7, where the techniques of working plastics such as Styrofoam, urethane foam, and thermoplastics are treated.

Hardware

In the scenery shop, hardware is divided into two categories: joining hardware and stage hardware.

Joining Hardware. This is an important part of normal scenery construction. It includes all the necessary nails, screws, and bolts for joining wood or metal. Stage hardware is a part of knockdown construction methods, stage assembly, and handling techniques peculiar to scenery.

A list of joining hardware most frequently used in the construction of scenery would include:

Nails	Common—8d, 10d
	Box—3d, 6d
	Finish—4d, 6d, 8d
	Clout—1¼-inch (or 3d box nail)
Screws	Flat-head bright steel:
	No. 8—¾-inch, ⅞-inch, 1¼-inch
	No.10—2-inch, 3-inch
Tacks and Staples	Carpet—No. 6, No. 10
	Gimp—½-inch
	Staples—⅜-inch, ½-inch
Bolts	³⁄₁₆-inch stove—2-inch, 3-inch
	⅜-inch carriage—3-inch, 4-inch, 6-inch
Washers	¼-inch ID (inside diameter)
	⁷⁄₁₆-inch ID

Supplementary to this list are many special items which might or might not be stocked, depending upon the personal style of the shop carpenter's construction techniques. Such items as lag screws and machine bolts are sometimes used under special conditions. Corrugated fasteners, wire brads and nails, screw eyes, eye bolts, and decorative-headed tacks are often needed.

Stage Hardware. The necessary portability of scenery leads to the use of many pieces of hardware made especially for the stage. Most of it is designed to brace, stiffen, and temporarily join units of scenery as well as provide rigging hardware for the flying of scenery (Figure 6–16, page 184). A list of essential stage hardware would be:

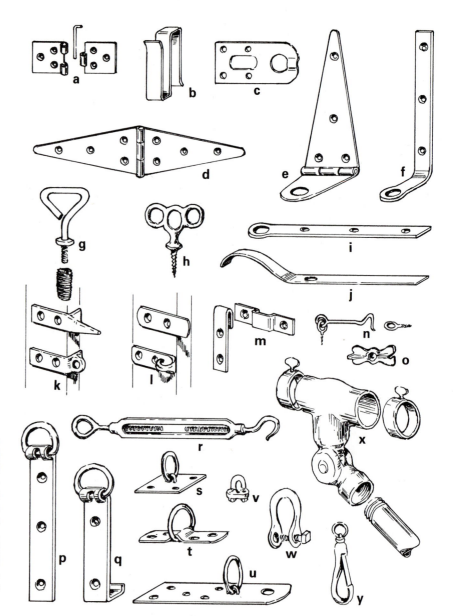

FIGURE 6–16

Stage Hardware

(a) Loose-pin back-flap hinge. (b) Batten hook. (c) Brace cleat. (d) Strap hinge. (e) Hinged footiron. (f) Bent footiron. (g) Stage scew and plug. (h) Stage screw. (i) Straight footiron. (j) Floor stay. (k) Lash cleat and lash eye. (l) Stop cleat and lash hook. (m) Picture-frame hanger. (n) Hook and eye. (o) Turn button. (p) Hanger iron, straight. (q) Hanger iron, hooked. (r) Turnbuckle. (s) Square plate and ring. (t) Oblong plate and D-ring. (u) Ceiling plate. (v) Cable clamp. (w) Shackle bolt. (x) Cyc knuckle. (y) Swivel-eye snap hook.

Stiffening	Batten hooks
	Loose-pin hinge (back flap)
Bracing	Footirons (straight, bent, and hinged)
	Stage brace
	Stage peg
	Stage screw and plug
	Brace cleat
Joining	Lash cleat and eye
	Stop cleat
	Loose-pin hinge (strap, butt, and back flap)
	Hook and eye

Rigging
Rigging   Hanger irons (straight and hooked)
Ceiling plate
Wire clamps
Rope clamps
Shackle bolts
Turnbuckles

Rope, Cable, and Chains

A number of specific types of rope, chain, and cable are important in the rigging and joining of scenery. A listing of their specification and uses on the stage follows. Rope used in the theatre is of two general types: cotton braid and stranded manila. The cotton braided rope is softer, easier to handle, more flexible, but of course not as strong as the stranded manila rope.

FIGURE 6–17

Metal Scenery

(Above) Sheet metal (16 to 18 gauge) over square tube structural framing. (Right) Rear view of welded frame. The Tyrone Guthrie Theatre production of *Oedipus the King* by Sophocles. Designer—Desmond Heeley. (Photo—Kewley.)

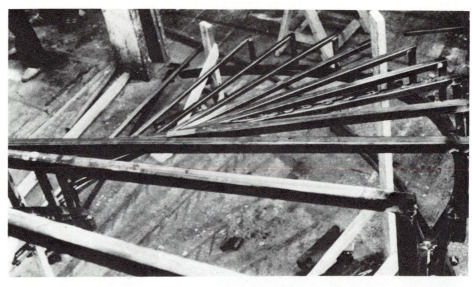

FIGURE 6–18

Steel Staircase

Spiral staircase for a production of Molière's *Tartuffe* framed with 1-inch square steel tube. (Bottom left) Full assembly. (Top) Framing of tread supports. (Bottom right) Bending the sweep of the helix. Designer—Douglas Maddox. Construction—Eric Harriz and Roger Segalla. (Photo—Mark Baird)

Executing the Design

Cotton braid rope

> No. 8 sash cord—used as lash line, lightweight rigging, and as an occasional draw line on a lightweight traveler.
>
> No. 10 braided rope—draw line for heavy traveler track.
>
> ⅛-inch awning cord—lightweight curtain rigging and trick line to trigger a mechanical effect from an offstage position.

Manila rope

> ¾-inch three-strand manilas—purchase line of counterweight system (see Chapter 7) and heavy rigging line.
>
> ½-inch, ⅜-inch manila—lightweight rigging, breasting, and bridling.

Wire rope or cable is used to hang scenery when the supporting wires will be in view. The wire rope is very strong for its small diameter and can inconspicuously support a fairly large unit of scenery. The types of wire rope used most frequently in the theatre are aircraft cable, tiller rope, and hoisting rope.

Aircraft cable

> 1/32-, 1/16-, ⅛-inch—nearly invisible at a distance, very strong for size, flexible but expensive.

FIGURE 6–19
Decorative Use of Thin-wall Conduit
Forest scene from Shakespeare's *As You Like It.* Designer—John Kavelin. Carnegie-Mellon University. (Photo—Nelson)

Tiller rope (6 by 42)

⅛-inch (smallest diameter)—strong, flexible, and less expensive.

Hoisting rope (6 by 19)

¼-inch (smallest diameter)—extremely strong, less flexible, and not too expensive for its weight.

Chain, outside of instances of special rigging, is used primarily as weight for stage draperies.

Jack chain

½-, ¾-inch (single or double)—curtain weight.

7

Constructing Scenery

Scene designers are interested in the construction of scenery not only to become familiar with building techniques but also to become aware of the uses and limitations of various materials. The more they know about present-day theatrical materials and techniques the better they are able to introduce new materials and original methods into designs as well as to develop a knowledgeable use of contemporary types of scenery.

TYPES OF SCENERY

Scenery construction may seem at first glance to be unduly flimsy and unnecessarily complicated. This is due, chiefly, to the unique demands placed upon scenery by the theatre. First, it must be portable and lightweight in structure so as to move easily on the stage and from theatre to theatre. Second, scenery has to be able to assume large-scale proportions for either decorative or masking reasons. Therefore, large areas of scenery must be furnished with the minimum of structure and the maximum of portability. And last, because scenery is here today and gone tomorrow, its construction must be economical. To be economical does not necessarily mean to buy the cheapest materials. It means to balance costs against the weight and structural demands of a material. It also implies the economical use of scenery. Higher material costs can be afforded if a scenic element has more than one use or can be reused at a later date.

For the purpose of discussing construction techniques, the various types of scenery are divided into groups which are similar in construction and alike in function as well as related in handling methods. Scenery is broadly divided first into two general classifications: two-dimensional and three-dimensional.

Two-dimensional scenery, under this broad division, is meant to include all flat scenery with reference to its basic shape rather than to the way it is used on the stage. Although units of flat scenery, for example, may be assembled together to make a three-dimensional form on the stage, the individual pieces are still classified as two-dimensional scenery.

Two-dimensional scenery is further subdivided into two groups: framed and unframed, or soft, scenery. Within these two groupings falls the bulk of the scenery that is used on the stage either in the form of stage draperies and drops or wings and flats.

Three-dimensional scenery obviously refers to the pieces that are built in three dimensions to be handled and used as solid forms. Some three-dimensional units, particularly platforms, knock down into smaller, nearly flat, pieces for ease of handling, but, because of their weight and use, they are still classified as three-dimensional scenery.

Three-dimensional scenery is also separated into two basic groups: weight-bearing solids, meaning the weight of the actor, and non-weight-bearing forms. Steps and platforms are examples of weight-bearing scenery as compared to such nonweight-bearing examples as tree trunks, logs, and the like.

SOFT-SCENERY CONSTRUCTION

Such large unframed pieces as stage draperies, the drop, and the cyclorama, or "cyc," are counted as soft scenery. They all have the same function, to provide a large area of scenery with a minimum of construction and a maximum of portability. Being soft, they are dependent upon hanging from a batten or pipe for support. As a result they can be easily folded or rolled for transportation or storage.

Stage Draperies

The large panels of stage draperies are made by sewing small widths of materials together with vertical seams. There are three sound reasons for using vertical seams. First, because the direction of the weave or decoration is with the length of the fabric, it hangs and looks better in a vertical position. Second, a vertical seam is less conspicuous because it is lost in the folds of the drapery. Third, there is less strain on a vertical than on a horizontal seam, which carries the cumulative weight of each width of material from the bottom seam to the top.

The seams are face to face to present a smooth front surface. The top is reinforced with a 3- to 4-inch webbing through which are set the grommet rings at 1-foot intervals for the tielines. The bottom has a generous hem containing a chain which functions as a weight for the curtain. Occasionally, the chain is encased in a separate sound-deadening pocket which is sewn on the backside of the drapery instead of being enclosed directly in the hem.

Drapery fabrics may be sewn on the top webbing or may be gathered or pleated onto the webbing to give a fixed fullness to the curtain. Fixed fullness is an advantage for a front curtain or traveler curtain. However, it is not as flexible as a flat curtain panel, because the latter can be hung either flat or with varying degrees of fullness in a greater variety of uses (Figure 7–1).

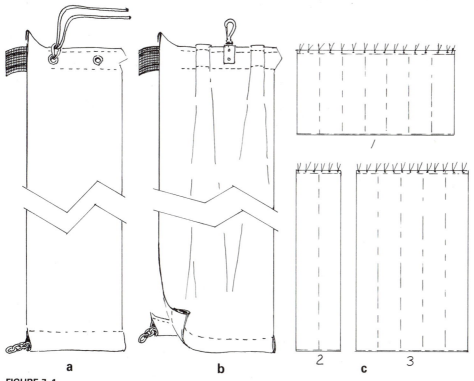

FIGURE 7–1

Stage Draperies

(a) Flat drapery construction. Webbing with grommets and tie-lines at top; hem enclosing chain weight at bottom. (b) Gathered drapery. Fullness gathered on top webbing; chain pocket attached above hem at the bottom. (c) Types of stage draperies: (1) border, (2) leg, (3) panel.

Constructing Scenery

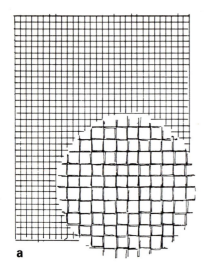 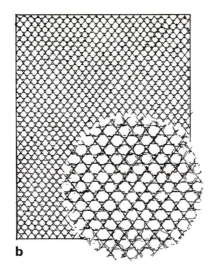 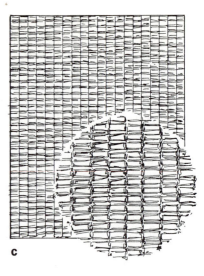

a   b   c

FIGURE 7–2

Gauzes

The three basic gauze materials: net, bobinette, and scrim are illustrated to show their difference in weave. (a) Net, square weave. A larger mesh (1 inch) is knotted like a fish net. Loose, tabby-weave materials are sometimes called gauze. The fabric, which looks like surgical gauze, has very little strength. (b) Bobinette, hexagonal weave. Very transparent and strong, but stretches out of shape easily. (c) Shark's-tooth scrim, ladder weave. Strong, not as sheer as bobinette; best for dye painting.

Drapery Materials. Stage draperies can be made of a variety of fabrics, depending upon the specific use they are to serve and the limitations of the budget. Are the draperies to be opaque, translucent, or transparent? Are they to be pictorial, decorative, or just masking? Are they to be stock draperies or a one-shot special effect? Answering such questions helps decide the kind of material to choose and its relationship to cost and use.

Velour, although expensive, is the favored drapery material. Its pile weave has a rich texture under the stage lights that cannot be duplicated with cheaper substitutes. It hangs and drapes beautifully and is also easy to maintain, handle, and store. Among the more economical velour substitutes which bear mentioning are duvetyn and flannel.

Duvetyn is almost as opaque as velour but drapes poorly and lacks as rich a surface quality. Flannel drapes a little better than duvetyn, and it has almost the same opacity. Its woolly nap surface has a fair texture under stage lights.

Stage draperies are made of other materials not with the intention of imitating velour but to create their own effect. Cotton rep and monk's cloth have enough texture to make an interesting inexpensive curtain when hung in fullness. Wide-ribbed corduroy is another drapery texture which, though semi-opaque, drapes and hangs well.

Sometimes draperies are expected to be translucent or, on occasion, transparent. Dyed muslin is the least expensive translucent fabric. It has a further advantage of coming in wider widths than such materials as satin or nylon crepe in the translucent class.

Gauze, the general term applied to all transparent materials, is available in a variety of fabrics such as cotton or nylon net, chiffon, and organdy, to name a few familiar commercial textiles. Although these fabrics are available at the local dry-goods store, their chief disadvantage is their narrow width, which increases the number of seams in a curtain. The seams become visible when the transparent curtain is back-lighted. There are gauzes, as well as muslins, that are woven on wide looms especially for theatre use. Bobbinet and shark's-tooth scrim, two transparent materials, are made in 30-foot widths. Bobbinet is a hexagonal net that is more sheer but weaker than shark's-tooth scrim, which has a rectangular or ladder pattern. The shark's-tooth, in addition to draping well, is dense enough to provide a dye-painting surface and still become transparent when back-lighted.

Drops

Another large-area piece of scenery is the drop, taking its name from the fact that it hangs on a batten and is dropped in, as opposed to the older method of the shutter that slid on stage from opposite sides. The drop is made with horizontal face-to-face seams to create a smooth surface. The horizontal seams, when the drop is hanging, are under enough tension from the weight of the material and bottom batten to stretch into a smooth surface. A drop can be made to fold or roll depending upon whether it is to be translucent or opaque.

A translucent drop is dye-painted and can be equipped with tielines at the top and tielines or a pipe pocket at the bottom. The position of the seams of a translucent drop are important, because if they are not carefully hidden in the design they produce a distracting shadow line. For this reason, translucent drops are sometimes made with vertical seams and with irregular spacing, or, if the budget permits, they are made seamless by using 30-foot-width muslin.

Since opaque scene paint is used on a regular opaque drop or a drop with opaque areas, it cannot be folded and therefore is rolled on the bottom batten. The opaque drop has a top and a bottom batten. Its construction and shape variations are shown in Figure 7–3 (page 194).

Drops are commonly made of muslin because it is available in wide widths and is an excellent inexpensive translucent material. Drops are sometimes made of other materials, frequently for an unusual textural quality, such as burlap, velour, and terry cloth. And, of course, drops can be made of the gauze materials. Shark's-tooth and bobbinet are used more often than other sheer fabrics because they come in wider widths.

The cut-drop in Figure 7–3c is often backed with bobbinet or scrim more for a lighting effect than for strength. The cut edges of a drop or border are better supported with a special lightweight net which has a 1-inch-square mesh. When the net is dyed to match the background it becomes nearly invisible.

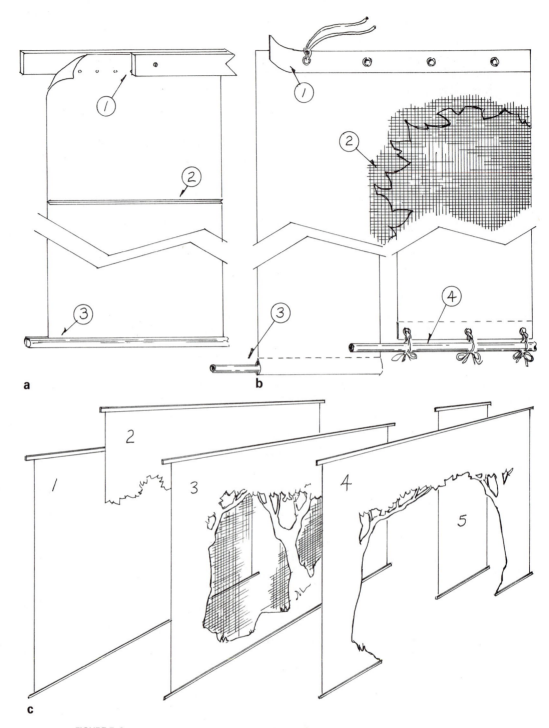

FIGURE 7–3

Drop Construction

(a) Rear view of a roll drop. (1) Top batten, double 1 × 4. (2) Face-to-face horizontal seam. (3) Bottom batten, doubles 2 inches half round. (b) Rear view of a folding drop. (1) Top webbing with grommets and tie-lines. (2) Netting glued over openings or cut edges to support loose ends. (3) Drop bottom with pipe sleeve for the removal of bottom batten. (4) Drop bottom made with grommets and tie-lines. (c) Types of drops: (1) Plain back drop. (2) Cut border. (3) Cut drop, netted. (4) Leg drop. (5) Also referred to as leg drop or leg.

The Cyclorama

The largest single piece of scenery in the theatre is the cyclorama or "cyc." As the name implies, it encircles or partially encloses the scene to form the background. The cyclorama's most familiar use is as a sky or void backing a setting or elements of scenery placed in the foreground. Because the flat center of the cyclorama blends into the sides in a gentle arc, it cannot be made on rigid battens like the drop can. It is kept soft by using dyed material which is fastened by the tielines to a curved top-and-bottom batten of pipe.

A cyclorama is not always a sky or void. Occasionally it is painted with a decorative or pictorial scene to fit a specific show. Sometimes, stage draperies are hung in the same position to form a drapery cyclorama.

The sky cyclorama presents the greatest problem in its necessity to create a large, uninterrupted, smooth surface. Because the "cyc" material, dyed or dye-painted canvas, is hung flat without fullness from a curved batten, the direction of the seams becomes important. If the seams are horizontal the tension on the seams draws the surface smooth, but the resulting strain distorts the shape of the curve as the seams turn the corner.

Vertical seams round the corners better than the horizontal seams, but they do not present as smooth a finished surface. In both cases the seams are sure to show under a high level of illumination. This can be corrected by hanging a large flat panel of dyed (very light blue) shark's-tooth scrim directly in front of the canvas cyclorama, using the same batten. Because it is a wide material the number of vertical seams can be reduced to two on the normal cyclorama. The scrim becomes the reflecting surface and the canvas acts as a backing (Figure 7–4).

FRAMED SCENERY

The structure of framed scenery is planned to support itself in a standing position. Although a framed piece may be aided by hanging support, or may be flown altogether, the basic framing principle remains the same. Framed scenery, as a construction technique, does not lend itself easily to the framing of a large area. It is possible to develop the framing for a large area, but to do this, it has to be hinged to fold into a smaller size or be dismantled into smaller parts to move in and out of the theatre. Most framing, then, deals with relatively small modules when compared to the large sizes of unframed scenery.

Wood Joints

Scenery construction, although special in its framing techniques, employs the normal methods of joining wood. The various wood joints

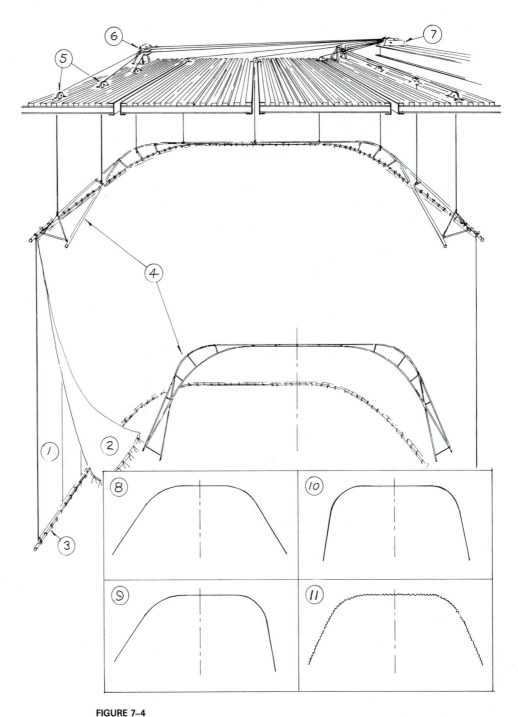

FIGURE 7–4

The Cyclorama

(1) Cyc backing, white vertical-seamed canvas. (2) Cyc face, shark's-tooth scrim dyed pale blue. (3) Bottom pipe, made of various curved sections that can be joined to match the contour of the top. (4) Top batten, a combination of shallow and deep curves to provide a variety of contours. (5) Spot-sheaves, spotted on gridiron over the general shape of the top batten. (6) Mulling blocks, a change-of-direction pulley to direct the lifelines towards the headblock. (7) Headblocks. (8), (9), (10) Some of the cyc contours achieved by selecting various curve combinations in the top batten. (11) A drapery cyc hung from the same top batten.

are derived from the many ways of combining lumber surfaces. The surfaces of lumber are described as its face (flat surface), edge, and end. The surface-joining combinations are classified as end to end, face to face, end to face, edge to end, edge to face, and edge to edge.

The making of a joint has two steps: first, the cutting and fitting of the joint, and second, the securing of the joint with hardware or glue. In scenery construction the joint is not always fixed but is many times temporarily secured or hinged. The fixed or permanent joint is used on standard-sized units of scenery, or smaller. The knockdown or temporary joints are used on oversized pieces that must be dismantled to get in and out of the theatre.

Figure 7–5 illustrates the numerous joints used in scenery construction classified in groups that combine the same surfaces. Fixed joints are secured with nails, clout nails (soft nails that clinch on the opposite side of the joint), screws, and glue. Knockdown or temporary joints are held with bolts, loose-pin hinges, keeper hooks, pegs, and turn buttons.

The framing of a simple flat illustrates the basic technique that is applied to any size or irregular shape (Figure 7–6). The area is enclosed with a lightweight frame of 1 by 3 white-pine lumber. The face of the lumber is kept flat in one plane, causing end-to-edge butt joints at the corners. In this way, the wide surfaces of the framing boards are in

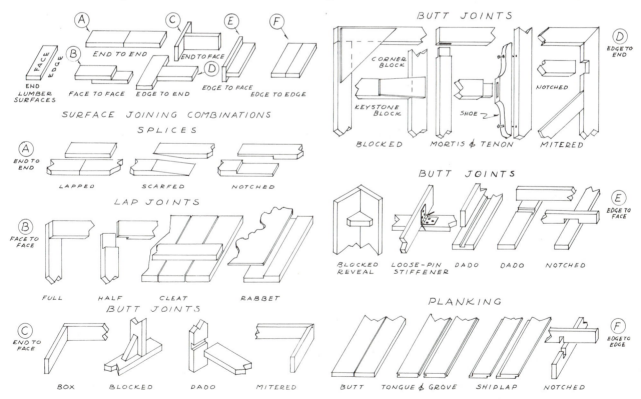

FIGURE 7–5

Typical Wood Joints Used in Scenery Construction

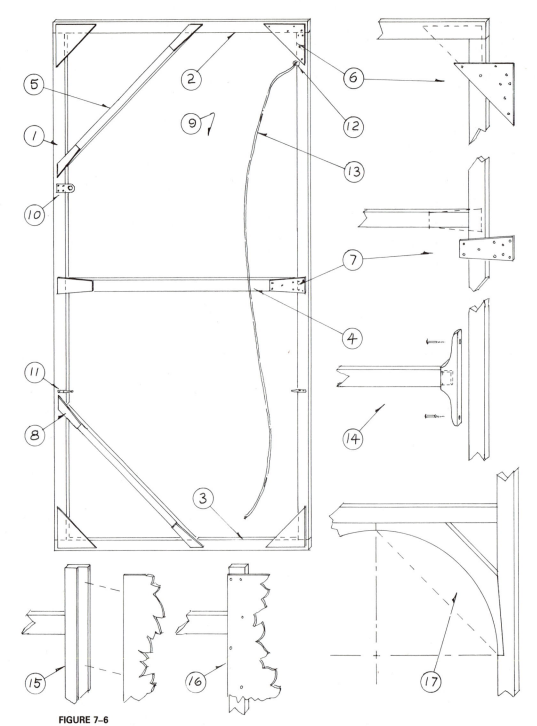

FIGURE 7–6

Framed Scenery

Basic framing techniques for the single unit of framed scenery, the flat. (1) Style, vertical member. (2) Top rail. (3) Bottom rail. (4) Toggle rail. (5) Brace. (6) Corner block. Note nailing pattern. (7) Keystone block. (8) Split-keystone block. (9) Canvas 8-ounce duck. (10) Brace cleat. (11) Lash cleat. (12) Lash-line eye. (13) Lash line. (14) Toggle rail and shoe. (15) Profile edge. Style rabbeted for profile board. (16) Profile edge. Cut profile board attached over style. (17) Method of setting curved sweep into flat. Note that the sweep butts to the toggle and is notched into the style. Sweep can be cut into any shaped curve.

position to support the canvas which is tacked to the inside edge of the outer frame and then pasted down. The end-to-edge joint is strengthened by one of two methods, or both. The joint can be mortised and tenoned with glue or a simple butt joint reinforced with a ¼-inch three-ply plate or corner block. The mortise and tenon, although a stronger joint, takes longer to cut because it requires special power machinery or special attachments. It also reduces the amount of lumber that can be salvaged if the scenery undergoes remodeling. Unless the scenery is going to be subjected to excessive handling, the butt-joint keystone and corner-block method provides a simple, sturdy joint.

Toggle rails and diagonal braces are the internal members which function to strengthen and hold square the shape of the outside framing. If the flat has an opening, they also help to frame the opening. Any irregular shape involving profile edges or elaborate openings is framed in fundamentally the same manner (Figure 7–7).

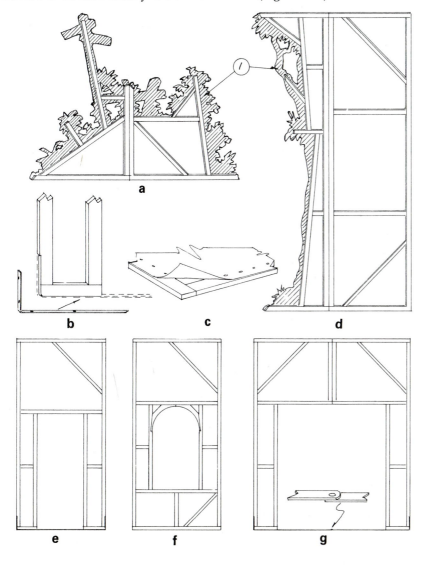

FIGURE 7–7

Types of Framed Scenery

(a) The framing of a set-piece with profile edges of three ply (1). (b) Detail of sill iron used across the bottom of a door opening in a flat. (c) Detail of canvas-covering technique. Note that tacks or staples are set on the inside edge of the external framework. The loose outside edge of canvas is then pasted to the flat surface of the frame. (d) Flat with profile edge. (1) Three ply. (e) Door flat. (f) Window flat. (g) Two-fold flat with double-door opening. Note hinged sill iron.

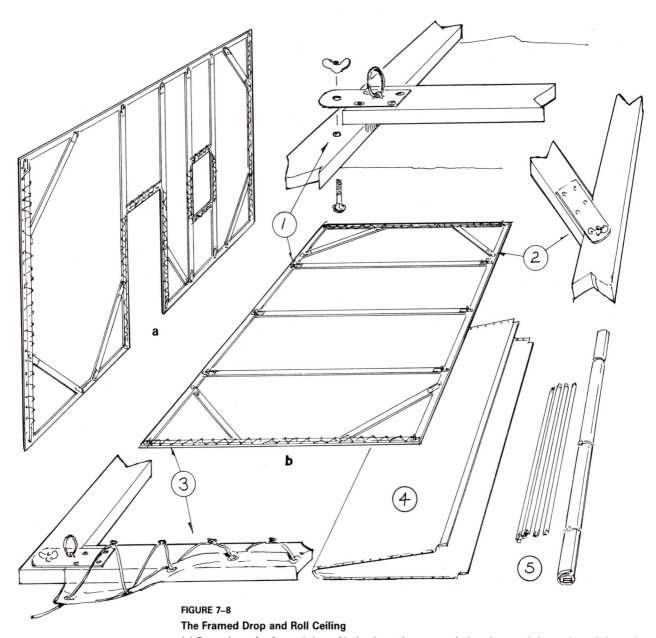

FIGURE 7–8

The Framed Drop and Roll Ceiling

(a) Rear view of a framed drop. Notice how the canvas is laced around the ends and through the openings. The canvas is permanently attached to the top and bottom battens. The vertical stretchers and braces are removable. (b) Rear view of a roll ceiling which is very similar to the framed drop in construction. (1) Detail of ceiling plate on the end of the stretcher. The stretcher is bolted to the two battens. (2) Same technique used on the diagonal brace. (3) Detail of lacing. (4) To roll, stretchers are removed and battens are brought together, face to face. (5) Ceiling rolled on battens.

The Framed Drop

As mentioned earlier, it is possible to frame a large area of scenery. The framed drop and ceiling piece are examples of this technique. They

Executing the Design

use a droplike construction except that the battens are single instead of double and therefore are made of heavier lumber stock (1 by 4 or 1⅛ by 4). The top and bottom battens are held apart by stretcher bars at about 6- to 8-foot intervals. They are bolted by means of ceiling plates to the battens. The loose ends of the drop are laced around the two end stretchers (Figure 7–8). A ceiling piece is made in the same manner, but will of course hang flat instead of vertically like the drop. Both the drop and ceiling fold and roll on their battens when the stretchers are removed.

Doors

Doors and windows are those important details that are often neglected in the haste of preparing a set. A door, in a sense, is a moving piece of scenery that is used by the actor. In a split second, its malfunction can not only give away the scenic illusion but can also break up the carefully built-up mood of a scene.

The building and hanging of a door is a skilled and time-consuming job. For these reasons, the average amateur group is better off to make or have made a set of good stock door casings that can be used in a variety of ways.

In the making of a door the normal scenery-framing techniques are often too lightweight. There was a time when the audience would accept a canvas door painted to look like oak planking but sounding and handling like a screen door. The modern audience, schooled by years of movie and television realism, is jarred by this obvious theatricality. There is a limit, however, to the weight of a door that can be supported in framed scenery which doesn't have the solidity of the stud framing or masonry it is simulating. Hence it is necessary to reach a compromise in a construction technique that will keep the door portable and lightweight enough to shift while at the same time achieving a degree of solidity and sturdiness for the action.

A door unit is made up of three basic parts: (1) the actual door, sometimes called "shutter"; (2) the reveal, comprised of the jambs (vertical members), header (top), and sill (bottom); (3) the trim, which forms the decorative frame around the door opening. The door is always hinged to the reveal. The trim, however, is constructed in one of two ways: it may be attached to the reveal, or it may be kept as a separate member and applied to the face of the flat. The first method, called a "cased door," is a complete unit. With the trim permanently attached to the reveal, the reveal of the cased door assembly slides through a prepared opening in the flat which is considerably larger than the size of the door itself (Figure 7–9a, page 202).

In the second method, referred to as a "scene door," the trim is not attached to the reveal, which is built to the exact size of the flat opening. The reveal, containing the shutter, "butt fits" to the opening from behind (Figure 7–9b). The scene door provides a great deal more flex-

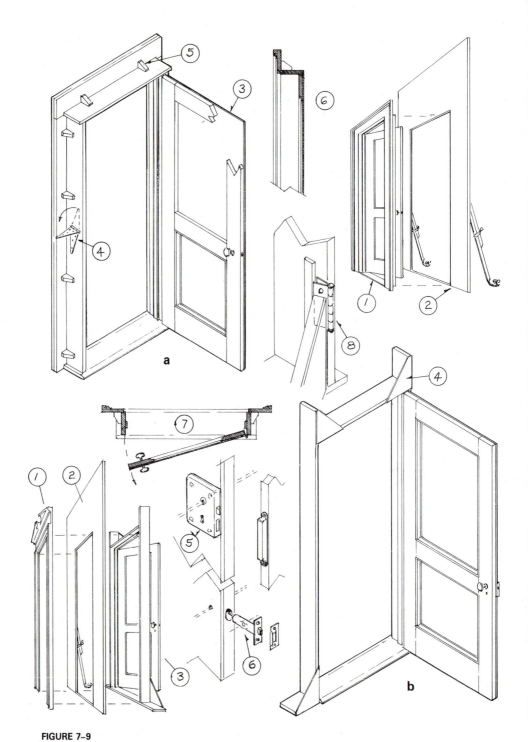

FIGURE 7–9

Stock Door Construction

(a) Cased-door unit. (1) Door reveal and trim built as one unit. (2) Flat with a standard door opening. (3) Detail of door construction. (4) Angled strap hinge on jamb to hold door unit in the opening. (5) Blocks to hold trim in place. (6) Cross section of door unit through the header. (7) Plan of the cased-door unit showing the hinging. (8) Butt hinge on door. (b) Scene-door unit. (1) Separate trim. (2) Flat with a standard door opening. (3) Door and reveal. (4) Corner blocks to hold reveal frame square. (5) Rim lock. Attached on back side of door. (6) Tubular latch. Sets into edge of door.

ibility in the ways the trim can be handled. It can, for example, be completely painted or attached and set away from the opening to increase the apparent size of the doorway (Figure 7–10a).

The action of a door affects its construction. For example, a door that swings onstage requires double facing; a double-action door (kitchen door) takes special hinging as does a Dutch door; sliding doors involve tracking; and additional rigging becomes necessary for the trick door that, as if by magic, opens and closes by itself.

FIGURE 7–10

Variations in Door Trim and Paneling

(a) Various methods of handling the trim around the same-size door opening, possible with a scene-door unit. (1) Wide-set trim. (2) Close-set and high trim with transom. (3) Painted trim. (b) Door paneling. The paneling for (2), (3), and (4) are all constructed within the basic paneling of a stock door (1). (5) The flush side of a stock door painted and cleated to look like a planked door.

Windows

Similar to the door, a window has a reveal and trim, but the window sash takes the place of the door. The arrangements of panes within the sash varies with the style of the window. Because the window sash is more open than a door, it is difficult to build. The pattern of the thin mullions often becomes too fragile for normal stage framing unless the window is far enough upstage to fake them in profile board. Delicate tracery is frequently reinforced by a backing of galvanized screening that passes for glass and strengthens the mullions at the same time. To simulate glass, panes are sometimes left clear or backed with netting. The net, although nearly invisible, has enough density to give the feeling of glass. It is more apparent by contrast if the window is opened during the action of the play.

Window action, like that of the door, involves sliding or swinging on hinges. A window may have the vertical sliding action of a double-hung window, or slide horizontally. It may have the vertical hinging of a casement window or the horizontal hinging of the awning-type window.

It is a little more difficult to plan a set of stock windows than doors because of the greater variation in sash styles. Certain often-used conventionally styled windows can be standardized and put into stock. Also the casing (reveal and trim) may be kept in stock to be used with interchangeable or new sashes for each show (Figure 7–11).

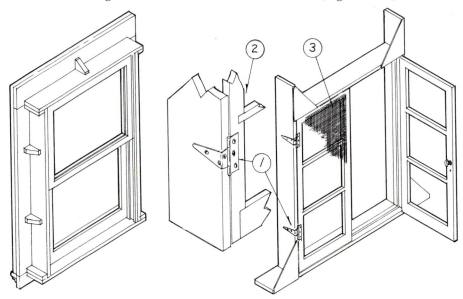

FIGURE 7–11

Window Construction

(a) Double-hung window. Trim is attached to reveal in the same manner as the cased door. (b) Casement window. The reveal is constructed in the same way as the scene door with hinged sashes. (1) A bent T-strap hinge in place of the butt hinge. (2) Notched mullions. (3) Galvanized screening to strengthen the sash and simulate glass.

Executing the Design

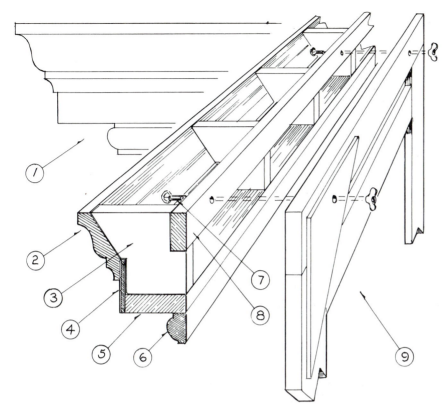

FIGURE 7–12
Cornice Construction
A cornice is a lightly framed three-dimensional element of trim designed to attach along the length of a wall. The perspective view shows the block-framing technique and a method of attaching the cornice to the scenery. (1) An elevation of the cornice showing the amount of overhang. (2) Stock crown molding. (3) Nailing block. (4) Three-ply face. (5) Linear support for blocks. (6) Bed molding, stock. (7) Carriage bolt. (8) 1 × 2 stiffener along the back of the blocks. (9) Added support at the top of the flats.

Trim

Decorative trim appears in a set in places other than around door and window openings. Some additional areas of trim, painted or practical, are baseboards, chair rails, wainscoting, cornices, and overmantel decoration. Trim that is attached in these areas must be removable so the flat scenery will fold easily.

The attached trim requires additional framing within the flat for support. Chair rails and baseboards are easy to attach but the construction and hanging of a cornice is more complicated. Although trim details are slightly oversized for the stage, the average cornice can be made up of stock moldings. To keep the framing lightweight, the molding is nailed to blocks set at about 2-foot intervals and backed with 3-ply or longitudinal framing strips. The whole assembly is attached to the wall flats with bolts or turnbuttons (Figure 7–12).

THREE-DIMENSIONAL SCENERY

Weight-Bearing Structures

Certain elements of scenery cannot be reduced to flat planes. Others, because they are so small, are more practically built as three-dimensional forms. This is especially important if the form is to bear the

Constructing Scenery

weight of a sitting or standing actor. Weight-bearing structures are present in such architectural forms as steps, ramps, and raised levels; in the irregular forms of rocks; and in the free form of an abstract design. The raising of a large portion of the stage floor and the use of steps and ramps brings excitement to the design composition, variation to the staging, and headaches to the stage technician. In the absence of any mechanical means of raising sections of the stage floor, the problem becomes one of creating a second floor at a specific distance above the stage floor. The level must be structurally sound enough to support actors and furniture with a minimum of deflection and, at the same time, be portable and economical. A large expanse of platforming is subdivided into smaller units for ease of handling. A single unit is made to knock down into even smaller parts.

The Parallel. The familiar way of providing a raised level for the stage is the parallel method. The parallel is a hinged trestle structure that opens to support a top and folds into a flat pack when not in use (Figure 7–13).

As a stock platforming method, the parallel has the advantage of being lightweight, easy to assemble and transport, and fairly sturdy. It also can be adapted to irregular shapes as well as to the conventional rectangle. Its chief disadvantage is a storage problem. To maintain any variation in levels, duplicate sets of parallels of different heights have to be kept in storage.

A convenient stock size for regular-shaped parallels depends first upon general handling and storage conditions; second, the construction of the top; and last, the riser heights of stock steps which work with the platforms.

If the top is to be made of ¾-inch 5 ply, a 4-by-8-foot top is the most economical size. Planked tops, however, can be made smaller or larger without material waste if space permits the storage of larger parallels.

Stock parallel heights, obviously, should be at intervals related to riser heights of the steps, 6- or 7-inch intervals being normal. Parallel heights usually vary at double-riser intervals such as 12-, 24-, and 36-inch, or 14-, 28-, and 42-inch intervals.

There have been various attempts to standardize platforming construction with the aim to cut down the size of stored parts, to reduce the amount of internal framing (by using material other than wood), and at the same time to provide a sound structure. The post-and-rail and scaffolding methods (Figure 7–14) are ventures in this direction. Both succeed in reducing the storage space of spare parts and each provides a very sturdy platform with a minimum of framing. The techniques, although very practicable for regular shapes, do not lend themselves readily to irregular shapes. The limits placed upon design, however, are minor when compared to the stage-space and sightline limitations imposed by some theatre buildings.

Executing the Design

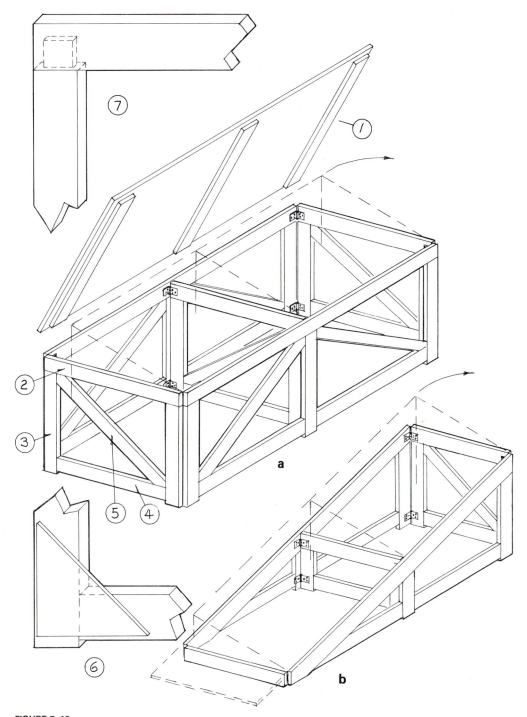

FIGURE 7–13

The Parallel Platform

(a) Basic parallel construction with open-corner hinging. (1) Top ¾-inch 5-ply with cleats. Typical trestle framing includes (2) top rail bearing on (3) the post, tied by (4) the bottom rail, and strengthened by (5) the diagonal brace. The framing may be joined either by (6) corner blocks or (7) by mortise-and-tenon joints. (b) The parallel technique used on a slanted platform or ramp.

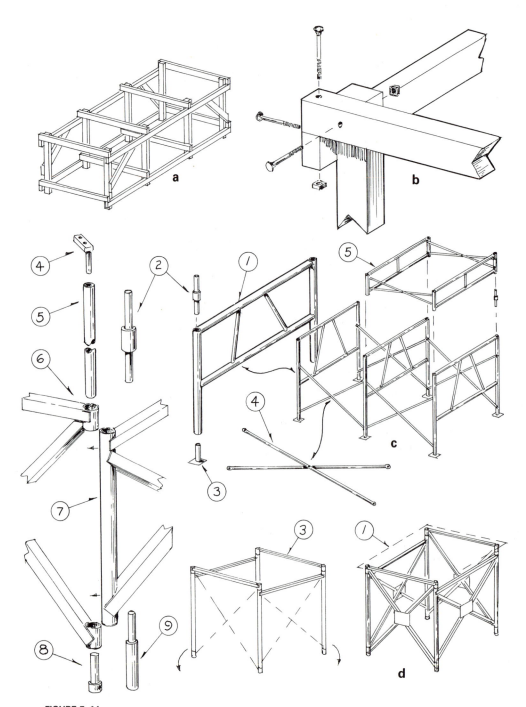

FIGURE 7–14

Other Platforming Techniques

(a) Post-and-rail method which knocks down into individual 2 × 3 units. (b) Detail of post-and-rail corner bolting. (c) Scaffold method. (1) Tubular steel or aluminum scaffold unit. (2) Spacer to interlock units. (3) Foot. (4) Cross braces to space and stabilize scaffold units. (5) The stacking of one scaffold unit upon another to gain height. (d) Steel parallel method. A smaller moduled tubular steel and angle iron-framed parallel. (1) Top overhangs unit to allow for facing flat. (2) Spacer to interlock and stack units. (3) Corners become hinges. (4) Pin attached to top to lock it in place. (5) Internal pin of hinge corner made up of (6) and (7). (6) Opened-end trestle. (7) Closed-end trestle. (8) Foot. (9) Extended foot.

Steel pipe and aluminum tubing have been used as platforming materials in two different methods. The first method involves the adaptation of construction scaffolding for stage uses. Each scaffold unit is made out of aluminum tubing and at heights of 1 to 3 feet at 1-foot intervals. Figure 7–14c illustrates how the various heights of scaffolds interlock, or stack, one on top of the other. Each set has its own system of cross bracing.

A more recent use of pipe for platforming is in the parallel method (Figure 7–14d). The unique feature of the design is the making of the corner into its own hinge. The unit takes a 4-foot-square top which is overhung 1 inch for a facing flat.

Other examples of steel in platform framing involves the use of manufactured shapes of structural steel. The shapes are designed to interlock and bolt together. Figure 7–15 illustrates the use of the Unistrut channel, and the Telspar and Dexion slotted angles as platform. Dexion, with its slotted flat angles, offers ample surfaces for combining wood with steel in platform construction.

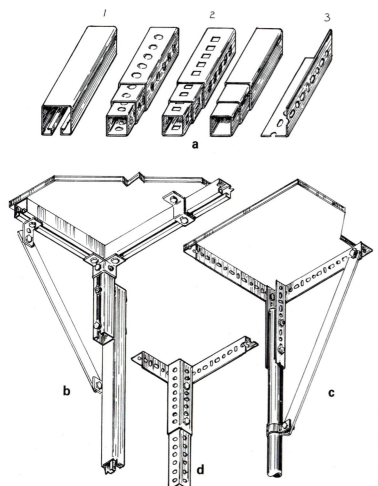

FIGURE 7–15

Platforming Techniques Using Preformed Steel

(a) Commercial preformed steel shapes. (1) Unistrut channel. (2) Three types of Telspar, a telescoping square pipe shape manufactured by Unistrut Corporation. (3) Dexion, a slotted angle iron also made in bar and channel shapes. (b) A corner view of a platforming technique using Unistrut channel as the basic corner post. Longer extensions of optional lengths are attached with stock Unistrut fittings and cross bracing. (c) Slotted angle framing with a basic post of slotted channel. Iron pipe is used as the extension. (d) Slotted angle framing with a slotted channel or Telspar basic post. The extension is Telspar. (Drawing after designs by Philip Eck and Ned Bowman.)

Constructing Scenery   **209**

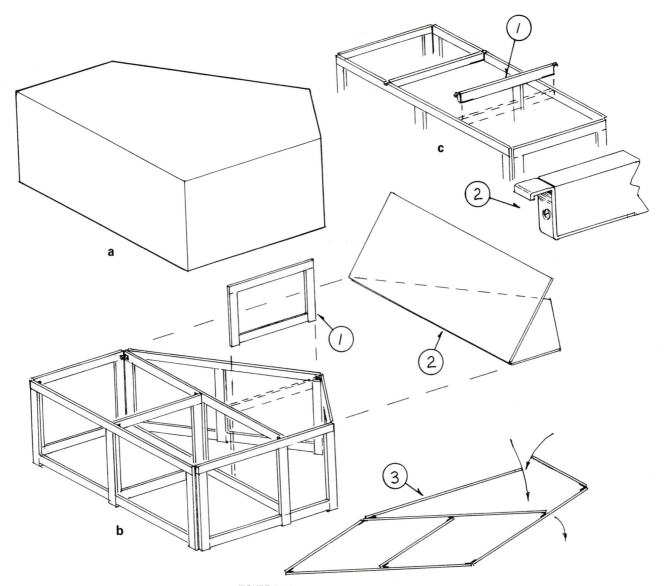

FIGURE 7–16

The Irregular-shaped Platform

(a) The hinging and assembly of an irregular-shaped platform are solved individually. (b) To fold: (1) Loose-pin-hinged internal trestle is detached after top (2) has been removed. (3) By unpinning the hinges of one corner, the parallel will fold into a flat pack. (c) The use of a "spanner" allows the removal of internal trestles in cases where it is necessary to keep the area under the top clear. (1) Spanner is of heavy enough stock, usually 2 × 4 or 2 × 6, to make strong span. (2) Detail of keeper-hook on end of spanner.

Regardless of whichever type of platforming is favored, the parallel method is, like the framing of a plane flat, an example of basic structural framing. With this basic knowledge the carpenter can modify or embellish the technique to fit all special needs.

Executing the Design

Platform Construction. Any platforming technique can be resolved into the three structural members which are always present in some form or other: they are the top, rail, and post. The top, which is the actual bearing surface, is directly supported by the rails. Crossrails run parallel to the shortest dimension of the level. Their interval is linked to the material and thickness of the top. The average top, made of 1 by 6 tongue-and-groove planking or ¾-inch 5-ply board, should be supported at 30-inch intervals. The span, however, can be increased by use of cleats or stiffeners on the underside and thereby, in effect, increase the thickness of the top material.

The rail is, in turn, supported by the post. The interval of posting is dependent upon the size of the rail. A 1 by 3 rail (on edge) should be posted at not more than 3-foot intervals and at 4-foot intervals for a 1 by 4 rail.

The framing of a single trestle or "gate" of a parallel employs the post-and-rail technique. In Figure 7–13a note that the top rail is borne by the two vertical members, or posts, which carry through to the floor. The bottom rail is merely a tie-rail that completes the rectangle. The diagonals are necessary to hold the gate square and eliminate side sway or "rack" in the finished platform. The single gate, though light-weight, gathers strength when it is hinged to the other members of the parallel. The parallel to fold flat must hinge as shown.

Any irregular shape that can be reduced to flat planes may be constructed by the parallel method. The gates can be loose-pin-hinged together rather than folding, for many times the pattern of the supports is so irregular the parallel cannot fold flat (Figure 7–16).

Free Forms. The irregular surfaces that cannot be reduced to a series of flat planes have to be constructed as a three-dimensional unit. Rock pieces and abstract forms that have to bear weight are examples of this type of irregular surface.

The framing of an irregular surface is, of course, more or less extemporaneous and dependent upon some final sculptural touches by the designer to complete the form. For this reason the design drawings of a free form should be accompanied by a scaled model. The form usually suggests the manner of construction; nevertheless there is a basic method that can be adapted to most irregular shapes.

The method of construction of a rock piece demonstrated in Figure 7–17 goes through the following steps: (1) The exact shape of the base of the rock is framed in the conventional flat-scenery technique. (2) Across the shortest dimension of the base is set a series of contour pieces that follow the contour of a section taken at that point (see "Sections," Chapter 5). (3) The contour pieces are stiffened with cross bracing and all bearing surfaces are reinforced. (4) Over the contour pieces is placed 1-inch chicken wire or ½-inch screen wire, which is

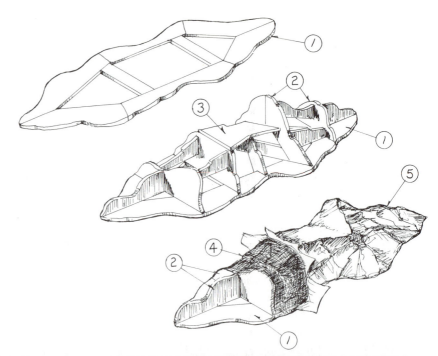

FIGURE 7–17

Construction of Rock Forms

(Right) (1) Shape of form on floor. Conventional framing. (2) Contour pieces. (3) Cross bracing. (4) Wire screening. (5) Burlap. (Photo, left) Three-dimensional shape before covering with burlap. (Right) Same shape covered.

a

b

Executing the Design

pinched or stretched in the desired shape. (5) The final surface is applied to the screen wire. The kind of covering material depends upon the nature of the texture that is desired. The best results are usually obtained with burlap. It is applied by first dipping it into a mixture of strong glue size and base color. The burlap is then draped over and tacked to the framework and allowed to harden. A form made in this manner is lightweight, inexpensive, and surprisingly sturdy.

Ramps. The parallel as a platforming technique can also be adapted to a ramped surface (Figure 7–13b). The side trestles are built to the angle of the incline. Gates of varying heights connect the outside trestles and are hinged to fold like a regular parallel.

Steps. Whereas the ramp is a gradual change of level, the step is more direct, dividing the change into a series of intermediate levels. A flight of steps is made up of risers and treads. The tread is the bearing surface and the riser is the interval of change in level. The rule of thumb guiding the size relationship of the tread to the riser is based upon the ease of movement up and down the steps. The sum of the riser and tread in a continuous flight of steps is kept about 18 inches. Hence a 6-inch riser would require a 12-inch tread; an 8-inch riser a 10-inch tread, and so forth. Obviously the low-riser and wide-tread combination is more desirable for the onstage steps, permitting the actor to move easily and gracefully up and down.

A flight of steps can be built for the stage in one of two ways. One method is a modified platform trestle construction with each tread

Constructing Scenery   213

supported by a complicated post-and-rail framework (Figure 7–16a). This way the steps are a part of a bulky three-dimensional platform which is difficult to store and move.

Steps can be made to knock down into more easily handled parts by the use of the cut-carriage method of construction (Figure 7–19b). The pattern of the riser and tread is cut from a wide board running parallel to a line drawn through the nosing of each step. The nosing is at the intersection of the top of the riser and the outside edge of the tread.

A carriage is cut from a wide enough board to retain at least 3 inches of uncut board along the bottom edge. The thickness of a carriage depends somewhat on its unsupported length. Frequently 1⅛-inch pine stock is used, chiefly for its lightness as well as strength. Sometimes 1-inch pine stock is substituted for lightweight construction while 2-inch stock is used for a heavier structure.

The choice of carriage stock is also affected by the nature of the riser material. Is the riser made of 1-inch pine or ¼-inch 3-ply or is it left open? As the riser material becomes lighter, the carriage stock should increase in thickness.

A flight of steps would have, of course, two carriages. Additional carriages would depend upon the thickness of the tread and the width of the steps. For example, a ¾-inch-thick tread would need a carriage every 30 inches of width.

The lower step of the carriage sits on the floor and the top step rests on a prepared cleat fastened on the front of a platform, thus eliminating the need of a post underneath. The steps, or carriage unit, can be lifted off the cleat to be handled and stored separately.

The facing of stairs (also levels) is a separate piece of scenery attached to the downstage edge of the step or platform. The facing of a stair is a more complicated unit because it includes the stair rail, balusters, stringer, and newel post (Figure 7–19e). The stringer, which parallels the carriage, supports the bottom ends of the balusters. It can be an "open stringer," revealing the tread and risers, or it may be a "closed stringer," masking the ends of the steps with an uncut surface.

The railing completes the stair facing. It spaces the top ends of the balusters while being supported by them. The whole assembly of the stair-facing flat and steps must be kept to a practical size or it can become too large to handle.

Nonweight-Bearing Structures

Columns, tree trunks, and any other objects that have to have dimension but do not bear weight form the last type of scenery. Since these kinds of structure need only be strong enough to hold their shape, framing is lightweight in comparison to weight-bearing structures.

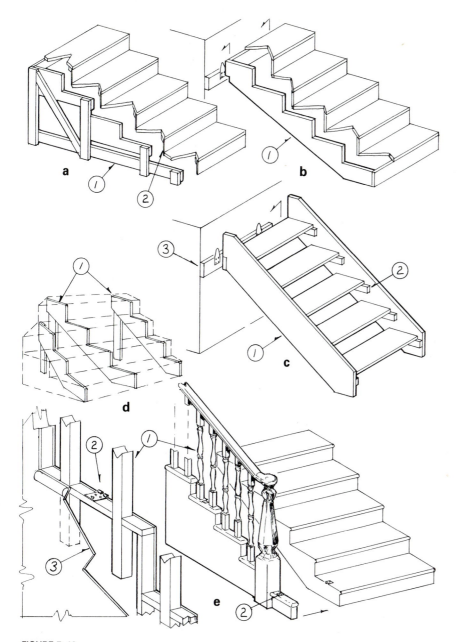

FIGURE 7–19

Stair Construction Techniques

(a) Trestle method. (1) Trestle with the top edge framed to riser-tread pattern. (2) Three ply used as riser stock. (b) Cut-carriage method. (1) Carriage cut to riser tread pattern. Step unit leans on platform for support. (c) Closed-carriage method. (1) Closed carriage can only be used on the outside of stair unit, hence this type of construction limits the width of the stairs. (2) Cleat to hold tread. Note that no riser is used. (d) Cut-carriage method used on an irregular-shaped flight of steps. (1) Carriages with same riser height but varying tread dimensions. (e) Stair facing, framed out of 1⅛-inch baluster stock (1) which is pin-hinged to steps (2). If both faces are covered with 3 ply (3), the facing unit becomes reversible with minimum alterations.

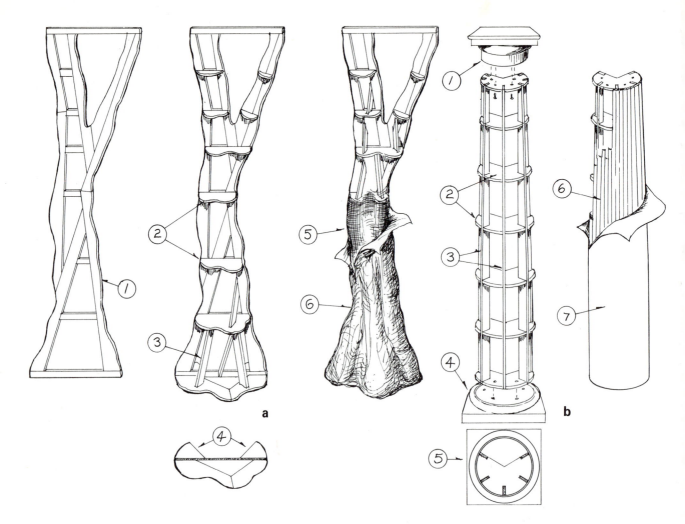

a

b

FIGURE 7–20

Columns and Tree Trunks

(a) Construction of a tree trunk. (1) Framing of basic silhouette. (2) Contour pieces set at intervals. (3) Cross bracing. (4) Pie-shaped contours to fill out base of tree where it meets the floor. (5) Wire-screening or chicken wire. (6) Burlap. (b) Stock-column construction. (1) Removable cap. (2) Contour pieces. (3) Vertical stiffeners. (4) Removable base. (5) Top view showing stiffener spacing. (6) Lattice slats. (7) Canvas cover.

An irregular shape is built in three dimensions by the use of two structural elements: the basic silhouette of the object and numerous contour pieces. In a tree trunk, for example, the basic silhouette is the vertical outline of the trunk and branches. The contour pieces are spaced at intervals perpendicular to the silhouette frame. After sufficient bracing and stiffening, the form of the trunk is rounded into shape by attaching chicken wire or wire screening over the contour pieces (Figure 7–20a). The chicken wire is covered with burlap or canvas for the finished surface.

In a rock, the basic silhouette is horizontal and the contour pieces are vertical, which, as has been mentioned, can become structural if the rock has to bear weight.

Columns have regular shapes and lend themselves to a slightly different construction method. It is not necessary to use a silhouette piece. The circular or semicircular contour pieces can be attached to a central core or be held at intervals by slats on the outer surface (Figure 7–20b).

The exterior surface of the column can be handled in two different ways. The surface can be made up of thin vertical slats (best for a column with a taper or entasis) that are covered with canvas after all of the slats have been rounded with a plane or rasp.

The column can also be covered with a flexible paperlike ⅛-inch EZ curve, or for a temporary column, heavy building paper can be used. When a light exterior covering is used, the amount of bracing between contour pieces has to be increased to stiffen the column.

TEXTURED AND SCULPTURED SURFACES

Designers are always fascinated by a deeply textured surface. It reacts well under stage lights and gives the scenery a feeling of authenticity and stability. A deeply textured surface like the stone wall in Figure 7–21 (page 218) is usually accomplished by using the laborious technique of applied papier-mâché. New plastic foams and forming techniques have made it easier to texture a surface or to create sculptural relief, architectural details, and many three-dimensional forms.

Rigid Foams

The demand for greater perfection in the design and construction of decorative details on both properties and small elements of scenery, which grew out of the intimacy of the thrust and arena theatres, has led to easier methods of simulating a sculpture form. The closeness to the audience, the increased amount of handling, and the change of design focus from scenic background to set properties are the basic influences on new theatre forms.

Styrofoam, the trade name of Dow Chemical's low-density rigid polystyrene foam (RPF), has been used successfully as a lightweight material that is easy to carve into three-dimensional details or textured surfaces. Blocks of Styrofoam can be glued together or to a scenery surface for convenient carving.

Regular Styrofoam is low-density and therefore very porous. This limits detailed carving and reduces its strength. *Urethane* is a high-density, rigid foam (RUF) that, because of its high density, is easier to carve in detail or turn on a lathe. It also has greater strength than a low-density foam.

Sections of rigid or flexible foams can be glued to reinforcing wood or adjacent surfaces with Illbruck Adhesive PA–02. Hyde glue is a good second choice.

Sculpture surfaces can be primed with casein paint or flexible glue and then finished with scenery paint. For an extremely hard finish the surface can be coated with a mixture of fiberglass resin and hardener in about five-to-one proportions. Further uses and techniques can be seen in Chapter 11.

Both foams, of course, are very lightweight and many times have to be counterweighted or attached to heavier units of scenery to maintain

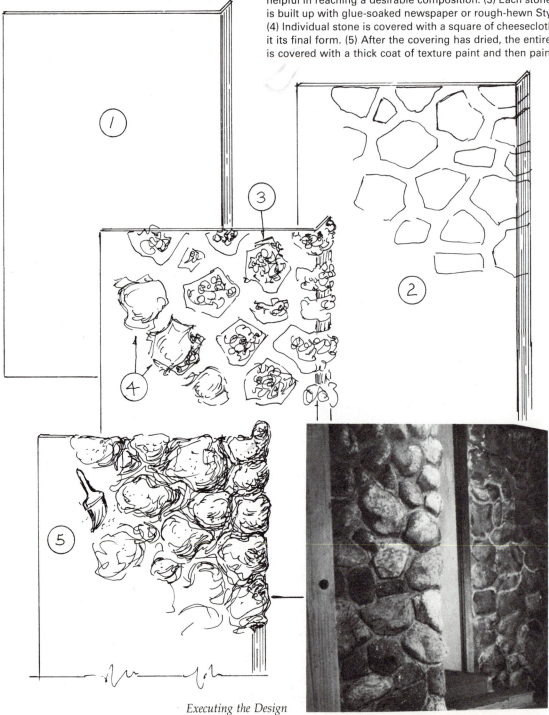

FIGURE 7–21

Three-dimensional Surface

Shown are the steps in the construction of a highly textured surface such as a stone wall. (1) Hard undersurface, either ⅛ plywood, upson board, or double-faced corrugated cardboard, shellacked to reduce warpage. (2) Surface is diagramed into areas representing the shape of each stone. Cutout appliqués of corrugated board are helpful in reaching a desirable composition. (3) Each stone surface is built up with glue-soaked newspaper or rough-hewn Styrofoam. (4) Individual stone is covered with a square of cheesecloth to give it its final form. (5) After the covering has dried, the entire surface is covered with a thick coat of texture paint and then painted.

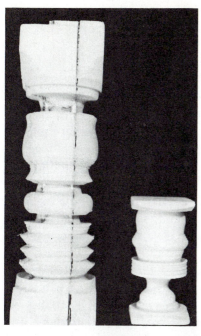

FIGURE 7–22

Carved and Turned Rigid Foam

(Far left) Turned rigid urethane foam: left, baluster with wooden core; right, turned finial. (Left) Relief carving, Styrofoam, sealed with flexible glue, finished with casein paint. (Below) Sculptured Styrofoam and mulched wood embedded in polyurethane foam with welded iron cyclone fencing. *Oedipus Rex* by Stravinsky/Cocteau. Final ritual masks were each 9 to 12 feet high. The set measured 54 feet at the highest point. Designer—John Ezell.

the proper esthetics. Nothing is more disconcerting than to see a supposedly quarter-ton Greek statue bounce like a ping-pong ball if accidentally knocked over.

Foam Casting

If a sculptural element or decorative detail recurs several times on a set it is often better to prepare a mold and cast the detail to insure a matching likeness. The mixing and casting of a polyether or urethane foam into a negative mold is the easiest method. It brings together two chemicals that produce a rigid foam of considerable strength and stability.

The chemicals are described by the supplier, IASCO (Industrial Arts Supply Co.), as, first, a Prepolymer A and, second, a Resin-Catalyst B. When mixed in equal parts they provide a rigid polyether foam.

Flexible Foam. The application of relief detail on a curved or flexible surface requires a flexible foam. IASCO's Isofoam F is a flexible urethane foam that serves this function. There is, however, a new flexible foam known as *Hydrofoam*, which is a hydrophilic polyurethane prepolymer that has the unique property of being formed with the addition of *water*. Different densities of foam are obtained by varying the amount of water.

All foams should be mixed in a disposable container such as a No. 10 can, beaten with a high-speed mixer for about thirty seconds. The creamy mixture is then poured into a hollow mold, the surface of which has been sealed with shellac and coated with paraffin or a prepared parting agent. If it is necessary to delay the action, Acetone is a solvent before the foam sets-up. The foam can be demolded in about thirty minutes (Figure 7–23).

A Word of Caution. Because the chemical action in all foam systems is highly toxic, precaution should be taken to ensure proper ventilation and protection of the hands. The use of a respirator mask and disposable surgical gloves is strongly recommended. Any contact of the foam chemicals with skin should be washed with soap and water immediately.

Foam Texture

Polyurethane foam applied under pressure hardens into an interesting deep-textured surface. Two chemicals are brought together under pressure inside a spray gun and mixed in the air as they are shot onto a surface, where the mixture foams into a bubbly texture in a matter of seconds. To control the chemical proportions that establish the denisty of the foam requires a high-compression tank, specific spray gun and nozzles (two hoses), and the necessary valves and gauges to vary the quantity of chemical from each tank. If all of the above

Executing the Design

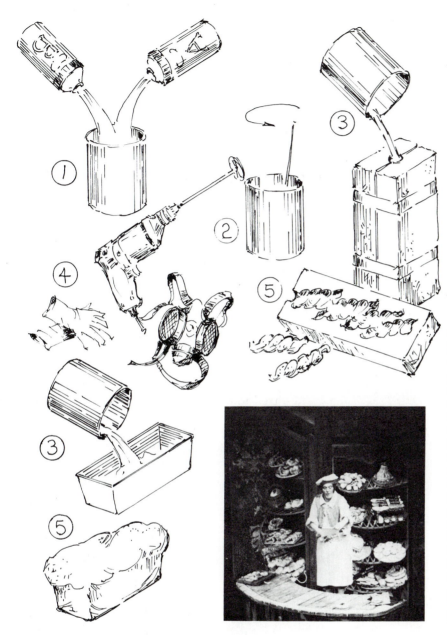

FIGURE 7–23
Foam Casting
Demonstrating one of the many forms plastic foam casting can take. Drawings show the steps taken to duplicate various forms of bakery goods. (1) Mixing IASCO's Prepolymer (A) with a Resin-Catalyst (B) in equal parts. (2) Mixture is stirred vigorously for about 30 seconds. (3) Mixture poured into hollow mold prepared with parting agent. (4) Mixing tool and a visual reminder of mixing precautions, disposable surgical gloves and respirator mask. (5) After liquid foam expands into the mold (about 20 minutes) the casting is removed from the mold. With the excess foam cut away, the form is ready for painting. Photo: bakery shop full of foam cast bakery goods, *Cyrano de Bergerac,* Guthrie Theatre. Designer—John Jensen. (Photo—Kewley)

equipment is not available, it is easier to use *Insta-Foam,* a trade name for aerosol urethane foam in a disposable kit form.

Although developed for the building trades, Insta-Foam is adaptable for stage use. Insta-Foam, manufactured by Insta-Foam Products, Inc., is sold in a variety of mixtures for specific commercial uses and construction techniques. The Insta-Foam *Froth-Pak* in the Standard Foam mixture is ideal for the textured surface just described. The kit consists of two aerosol tanks of chemicals, two hoses to a mixing spray gun, and a variety of nozzles. The several nozzles not only give a selection

Constructing Scenery

of distribution (fan to round), but are also expendable. The nozzles clog with hardened foam very quickly if work is stopped for any length of time and have to be replaced. The chemical content of the two tanks is Polymeric Isocyanates in the first and Polyops with Amines and Fluorocarbons in the second.

The mixture is toxic and thus the mixing process should be performed only in a well-ventilated room. Prolonged breathing of the vapors or spray mist should be avoided. The empty tanks should be vented, the valves removed with caution, and the chemicals drained. An unvented aerosol tank can be dangerous if handled carelessly or if stored near heat (over 120° F). Safe storage for full tanks is 60° to 80° F.

Insta-Foam will adhere firmly to any surface except polyethylene (a transparent filmlike plastic called Vis-queen, which, incidentally, can be used as a parting agent or separator between units of scenery). After is has hardened, the foam can be painted with dye or scene paint. For added texture, materials or objects can be imbedded and held by the foam. The hardened foam is quite durable and compares in density and hardness to high-density rigid urethane foam. It will withstand normal handling on the stage but would have to be handled with care were it to go on tour.

FIGURE 7–24

Foam Texture

The Insta-Foam texturing process. (Below left) Froth-Pak tanks and surface ready for spraying; articles to be embedded are in place on the scenery surface. (Right) Mixing nozzles and foam spray in action. (Opposite page, top left) Detail of texture. (Top right) Finished unit ready for painting. (Bottom) Foam texture and welded metal sculpture, *The Song of the Lusitanian Bogey* by Peter Weiss. Designer—Dennis McCarthy.

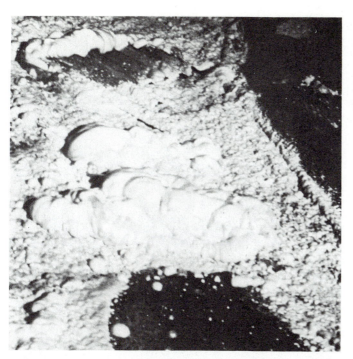

FIGURE 7–25
Foam Textured Scenery
Except for some architectural fragments the entire set was covered with a foam texture with bits of mirror, straw, and other bits of rubbish embedded in the surface. *The Devils* by Whiting. (Photo—Nelson)

Thermoplastics

Another method for the shaping of three-dimensional details such as arabesques, props, masks, armorplate, or the duplication of real objects is the vacuum forming of sheet plastic. Formerly a manufacturing technique that was out of reach of the average scenery shop, it is fast becoming an important construction method for those hard-to-execute details. Thanks to detailed research by Nicholas L. Bryson on thermoplastic scenery (see "Additional Reading on Technical Production") the trial-and-error approach has been taken out of the process.

The chemical structure of a thermoplastic is such that when heated it loses its rigid state and becomes ductile. While it is in this pliant condition it can be reshaped or stretched over a positive (or negative) mold, then allowed to cool and return to a hardened state. The fact that a true thermoplastic can be reheated and reshaped without a discernible change in its physical properties makes it economically feasible for theatre use.

Executing the Design

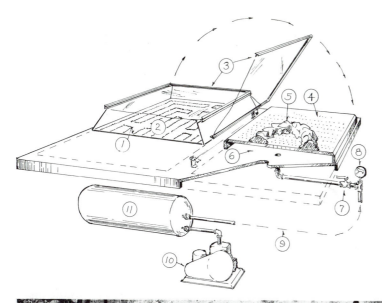

FIGURE 7–26

Thermoplastics

The cut-away drawing is of a vacuum-forming machine suitable for a scenery shop. (1) The oven has slanted metal sides with asbestos lining. The floor of the oven is covered with a pattern of coiled resistor wire forming a heating element. (2) Plastic sheet in angle-iron frame. (3) Frame is hinged to swing off of the oven and onto the mold and forming table when the plastic sheet is ductile. (4) Forming table. Floor is pierced with ⅛-inch holes spaced at 1-inch intervals to vent the vacuum chamber underneath. (5) Mold. (6) Vacuum chamber. (7) Bleed valve; can be rigged for pedal action. (8) Gauge reading inches of mercury. (9) Air hose or pipe to reservoir tank. (10) Vacuum pump. (11) Reservoir tank. The photograph is of a vacuum-forming machine suitable for piecework and original designing but not mass production. Note that the reservoir tank is made of wood. It is reinforced internally to resist pressure or sealed on the outside with canvas, flexible glue, polyethelene, mastic, and enamel paint. (Constructed, after designs by N. L. Bryson, by Les Zellan)

Of the many thermoplastics available there are three that seem best suited for use in the theatre. They must be opaque, translucent, or transparent, have a selection of color or take paint and dyes, be non-combustible, and be strong enough to withstand normal handling on-stage and the mechanics of fastening (nailing, stapling, and so on). The three thermoplastics meeting these requirements are high-impact polystyrene, low-density polyethylene, and cellulose acetate. The working thickness need not be greater than .0040″ (40 thousandths of an inch); it depends on how rigid or flexible the final form is meant to be.

High-impact polystyrene, as the name implies, has a high impact strength, great flexibility for intricate forming, a wide range of colors, and is obtainable in opaque or translucent sheets.

Low-density polyethylene is also tough and flexible. It is normally milky white (no colors) and opaque, but turns translucent when heated and formed.

Cellulose acetate is a well-known plastic with excellent forming characteristics. It is also very sturdy with the distinct difference of being completely transparent.

Vacuum Forming

The heated thermoplastic sheet, in order to take an accurate impression copy of the mold, must be tightly drawn or sucked by a vacuum around the form. The process is called vacuum forming. The basic steps of vacuum forming are: (1) Heat the plastic sheet uniformly to the temperature that renders it flexible (750–1000° F). (2) Transfer it quickly to a forming table where it is stretched over the mold and its edges clamped to the table in an airtight seal. (3) The air is removed through the forming table by a vacuum tank and pump, thereby sucking the heated plastic sheet over the mold. (4) Allow the plastic to cool and harden into its new shape. (5) Break seal and remove the plastic form for trimming, painting, and attaching to scenery, costume, or any other formed unit.

The use of a reservoir tank permits a rather rapid vacuuming action that is necessary or the plastic will cool and return to a rigid state. The pump then recovers the vacuum in the tank while the next sheet of plastic is being heated. Figure 7–26 illustrates the various components that make up a vacuum-forming machine.

Heat Gun. There are some additional tools that are useful accessories to the thermoplastic-forming process. The heat gun, which is capable of delivering a blast of hot air (750–1000° F) from an enclosed heating element and turbo fan, is used at close range to soften portions of the plastic sheet that may not have taken to the mold accurately.

FIGURE 7–27

Thermoplastic Forms

A few of the many architectural and decorative details that can be vacuum formed for use on the stage setting. (Above left) A cornice section. In this category, column capitals and bases, pilasters and panel molding can be included. (Above right) Open grill work, split baluster, and decorative details. (Left) Low relief panel decoration. Additional thermoplastic forms can be seen in Figure 11–10.

FIGURE 7–28

Fabrication of Rigid Foam

Armor has fiberglass under form. A one-to-one mix of 16-pound density IASCO rigid foam to build pea-pod form, caskets, gauntlets, and details. Latex and graphite surface with paper-doily appliqué as decorative detail. Armor and photo—Jim Bakkom.

Welding Gun. Similar to the heat gun, the hot-air welding gun produces a fine jet of hot air (400–700° F) which, when directed at a seam or thermoplastic welding rod, can weld plastic sheets or plastic forms together. Because the welding gun needs a jet flow of air it has to operate from an air compressor.

Hot-Wire Cutter. Although not used in the thermoplastic process, the hot-wire cutter is a handy tool for cutting and shaping rigid foam. Both the table hot-wire cutter and the hand cutter using the flexible wire loop (Figure 7–30) are useful to cut large blocks and to carve small forms. The wire loop is made of a high-resistance wire conductor (Chromel or Nichrome resistor wire). The wire's resistance generates enough heat to melt the rigid foam, thus enabling it to cut the block cleanly and quickly.

Executing the Design

FIGURE 7–29
Cast Plastics

This altar for *Oedipus the King* was designed to look like an oversized, polished half of a geode. The top surface is made of layers of tinted Clear-cast, a clear polyester available at local craft shops, supported on a hollow frame of wooden ribs with a Celastic covering. The crusty edge is modeled fiberglass resin and Cab-o-sil (formed silica), an inert powder that gives the mixture body for modeling. (Photo—Bakkom)

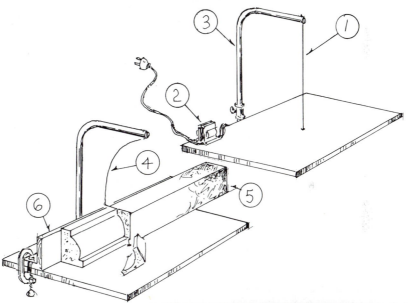

FIGURE 7–30
Hot Wire Cutters

Table and hand hot wire cutters for sculpting rigid foams. (Right drawing) (1) Nichrome resistance wire. (2) Low-voltage, high-amperage transformer (about 16 amperes). (3) Adjustable arm to facilitate the cutting of large blocks of foam. (Left drawing) Table hot wire cutter rigged to shape molding. (4) Hichrome wire bent into the shape of the molding. (5) Strip of styrene foam or rigid urethane foam. (6) Fence guide clamped to table top. Photo: hand hot wire cutter.

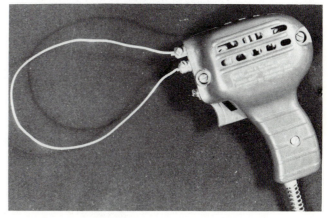

Constructing Scenery

Other three-dimensional forming techniques such as fiberglass, Celastic, and the like are discussed in Chapter 11, because they relate to properties, furniture, and costume accessories.

MIRROR SURFACES

Highly reflective surfaces and optical mirror surfaces have always fascinated the scene designer as a theatrical effect. Until the mylar surface entered the theatre, large mirrors were heavy and awkward to handle. A mylar mirror surface, when rigidly mounted or tightly stretched, provides the reflection optics of a real mirror that is lightweight and easy to handle.

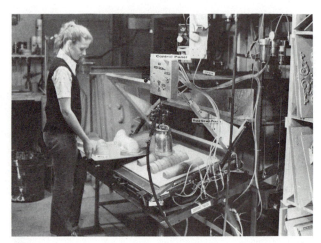

a

FIGURE 7–31

Commercial Vacuum Forming of Stage Products

Shown are process pictures of the more sophisticated vacuum-forming equipment developed in the Tobins Lake Studios for the mass production of stage properties, armor, and architectural elements. Although this special equipment is capable of producing more than the average scenery shop, the studio's output is still far short of commercial manufacturing production. (a) View of forming table. Note overhead oven. (b) Plastic sheet in place over molds. (c) After the "pull" with the oven raised. (d) The making of a permanent mold to withstand the heat and pressure of numerous pulls. A fresh pull from the prototype is used as a negative mold. It is backed with sand for stability. (e) The negative mold is filled with epoxy resin sometimes loaded with aluminum to save weight. The final mold is drilled with a pattern of small holes to improve the suction of the pull. (f) Storage shelves of permanent molds.

d

Silver Shrink Mirror. This technique utilizes a vinyl-backed reflective surface designed to be tacked to a frame and then shrunk with heat to a smooth mirrorlike surface. The heat source can be a normal portable electric heater or a heat gun. The 54-inch width of the material, however, limits the size of the individual frame. A full stage mirror, for example, would have to be made of several frames. However, if the planes of the frames are parallel, the divisions are not noticeable.

Scrim-Backed Mirror. This form of stage mirror is backed with a scrim instead of vinyl and thus has the added advantage of being transparent when lighted from behind. When stretched and heat-shrunk, it serves as a mirror surface, transparent scrim, or a rear projection screen.

Both mirror surfaces in silver or gold are available at Rosco Laboratories.

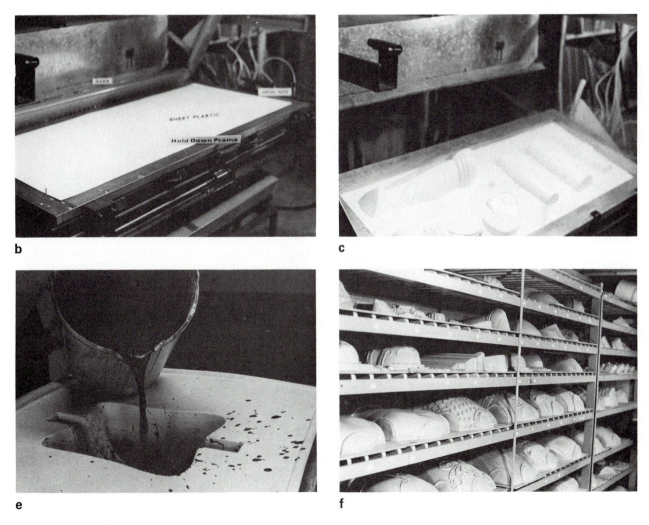

b

c

e

f

8

Color in the Theatre

The final step in the execution of the design, the painting of scenery, is yet to be discussed, but it is imperative to examine first the use of color in the theatre as it relates to painting, lighting, and the designing of scenery and costumes. This might be begun by asking the question "What is color?"

"Color is *light*," says the physicist when referring to the small visible portion of the electromagnetic spectrum. "Color is *paint*," replies the artist, "light merely reveals it." "Color is in the *eye*," says the physiologist, "for no two people see color in the same way and some are color-blind." "Color is in the *mind*," the psychologist insists, to explain why some experience color with their eyes closed or in their dreams. All these attributes, of course, are present in any color experience. To these the artist in the theatre might add, as a part of its creative use, critical analysis and emotional response—the *philosophy* of color.

Although scenery, costume, and lighting designers desire knowledge of color to the same degree, they have slightly divergent interests in its use. The lighting designer, for example, is more involved with the physics of color, while the scene and costume designers are interested in the painting and dyeing of color as well as the manipulation of colored materials. Whatever the final use of color may be, each designer has need of the same knowledge of color, for eventually all areas of design must come together onstage to form the total visual effect. The beginning designer in the theatre must be aware of the separate uses of color and seek a color explanation that satisfies both the use of color as light and as paint.

It can be seen that any explanation of color in the theatre must, therefore, involve not only the separate study of color in light and color in pigment but also the integration of the two in an inclusive definition.

The Language of Color. It is always difficult to talk or write about color, for words trigger individual images and do not convey accurate information. There are, however, a few terms that are so much a part of the description of a color that it is impractical to converse without knowing their meanings.

The three variants of color, *hue, value,* and *chroma,* are the most familiar terms used to describe a specific color. All will be discussed and illustrated in detail later, but briefly one can describe a color by hue identification (red, yellow, and so on); value level, or the black to white relationship of a color; and the degree of chroma or freedom from neutralization by mixture with another hue.

Within the framework of these variants an elusive color can be described in simple semiscientific terms by referring to its hue, degree of chroma, and value level. In normal communication their use brings to mind a more consistent image of a specific color than would the use of such emotionally charged labels as ''blushing pink'' or ''passionate purple.'' Because descriptive labels are so firmly a part of the advertising and merchandising of color in fabric, paint, and the light-color medium, a designer soon learns to translate them into more communicative terms. A ''chocolate'' shade, for example, might be described more precisely as a spectrum orange neutralized to one-half chroma but retaining its normal low-light value position.

COLOR IN LIGHT

A basic knowledge of color begins with its presence in light. Without light there would be no color. Everyone has seen in some form or other the breaking-up or refraction of sunlight into a spectrum of color. The refraction of sunlight through a bevel-edged window or in a rainbow are simple examples. The physicist with more precise laboratory prisms can produce an accurate spectrum with wavelength values for each hue and can explain the existence of these hues, from infrared to ultra-violet, as a visible part of the electromagnetic spectrum. This is the beginning of *hue,* the first variant of color (Figure 8–1).

Hue. The position of a color in the spectrum determines its hue. The number of hues that can be separated or identified as principal hues in the spectrum is arbitrary. Six easily identified hues are red, orange, yellow, green, blue, and violet. The expanding of the number of discernible hues depends upon their ultimate use or application in a color theory or system of color notation. The use of color by the artist, for example, is linked to a medium such as paint or dye. Light, on the other hand, is colored by passing it through stained glass or colored plastic. Because of the purity of the color mediums in light, it is possible to establish *light* primary hues.

A primary is a basic hue that is suitably located in the spectrum to mix secondary colors (see "Additive Mixing"). Red, green, and blue are light primary hues. The intermediate hues, or secondaries, are produced by mixing any pair of primary hues (Figure 8–2b).

It is important to mention at this point that mixing of paint as a color medium is not as accurate as the mixing of colors in light. It involves a different physical process, hence the painter requires a finer separation of spectrum hues to creatively mix and use color (see "Color in Paint").

Value. The light-to-dark relationship of a hue or mixed color is its value. The lighter values, nearer white, are known as *tints* and the darker values, approaching black, are referred to as *shades*. Both represent a variation from the true hue.

The use of value as a color variant or control is more the tool of the painter than of the lighting designer because of the necessarily greater range in pigment mixing. Subtle value differences are easier to accomplish in paint, particularly in the darker ranges, because in the use of colored light there is no black.

The number of steps in a value scale is arbitrary. The limiting factor is usually the ability of the eye to distinguish the difference between adjacent steps. Seven steps between black and white seem to be a comfortable number (Figure 8–2).

Some hues come from the spectrum with a natural value difference. The light-to-dark difference of yellow and violet is the most extreme example. Other hues have less value difference and some, of course, are about equal. Hues that have little value difference contrast each other with another force. They are usually hue opposites. When certain hue opposites are placed side by side the color contrast is so high that it produces an apparent vibration in the eye. This phenomenon involves both the physics and optics of color and will be discussed later, after all the aspects of color have been examined.

Hue opposites, however, do perform another function. When mixed in equal parts they tend to neutralize each other. Hue opposites in light produce white, while their mixture in paint results in neutral tones. This change in the purity of a hue is the third variant of color, *chroma*.

Chroma. The instant the purity of a principal hue is modified, the change is referred to as a change of its chroma. The degree of pureness, or freedom from neutrality, like the value scale, can be measured in steps. The number of steps from pure hue to complete gray varies according to color theories. A very precise measuring and mixing method can produce a great number of steps. The artist, however, can see and work easily in quarter portions, moving from a fully saturated hue to one-quarter neutral through one half, then three-quarters to full neutrality. This serves merely as an explanation of chroma, and the artist is free to use more steps for a more subtle change.

It is interesting to note in Figure 8–3, which shows the value and chroma changes produced by the mixing of orange and blue hues, that when the value of either orange or blue is raised or lowered its chroma is also changed as the tint or shade becomes more neutral. On the other hand, the quarter steps on the direct horizontal line to the value scale represent a chroma change without a value drop. This is accomplished on the orange side by the proportional mixing of blue (the hue opposite or complement of orange) after it has been raised to the matching value of orange. In other words, it is possible to change the chroma of a hue without affecting its value, but it is impossible to change the value of a hue without modifying its chroma.

All neutralization can be accomplished, theoretically, by the use of black or white paint. It is possible under scientifically controlled conditions of paint manufacturing, but the scenic artist knows that certain opaque colors do not respond to mixing with black. The use of a complementary color to neutralize a hue gives the painter a chromatic neutral that has a little more life under the stage lights. The neutralization of a pigment hue or its modification by another color is due to the particular method of mixing colors in paint. When painters mix colors on the palette or in the bucket they are using *subtractive mixing*.

COLOR MIXING

Although hue, value, and chroma are theoretical variables of color, a designer must understand them also as means to describe a color and use them to create new shades and match old ones. Color is varied by mixing. The two methods are *additive mixing* and *subtractive mixing*. While both methods affect hue changes, additive mixing also noticeably alters value, and subtractive mixing modifies chroma.

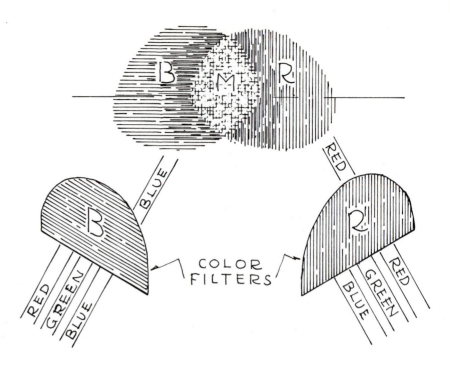

Additive Mixing (see also Figure 8–4)

Light represented in its primaries—red, green, and blue—is passed through a blue filter (B). Red and green are filtered out, resulting in a blue-colored light (drawing, lower left). Red filter (R) absorbs green and blue, passing red (drawing, lower right). The fields of red and blue light overlap and additively mix a third, magenta (M), shown in the top diagram. Magenta is red-violet raised in value. That additive mixing raises the value of a mixed color can be seen clearly in the mixing of light primaries (Figure 8–4b).

Additive Mixing. The mixing of colored *light* from two or more sources is additive mixing. It can be demonstrated by the overlapping of the sharply defined fields of two or more spotlights, each with a separate color medium. A single red color filter, for example, absorbs all other hues from the spectrum and transmits only red. When red rays overlap with light from a blue filter (see diagram) the colors are "added," resulting in a red-violet or magenta hue. The most spectacular example of additive mixing is the combination of two contrasting colors, for example, red and green. Their mixing produces a yellow or amber. (Note that the yellow and orange hues fall between red and green in the color spectrum.) The additive mixing of a secondary and primary hue, or of all three primary hues, results in a synthetic white. Remember that all colors resolve into white before being refracted into the color spectrum.

Primary and secondary hues are frequently used to light the actor. The favorite combination of Lavender and Bastard Amber, for example, are tints of primary blue and secondary amber. Medium Straw and Steel Blue, for example, are tints of complementary hues blue and orange. The additive mixing of the two colors models the actor's face in a flattering white light than can be warmed (more red) or cooled (more blue) by changing the intensity of one of the spotlights (Figure 8–4b).

Subtractive Mixing. The opposite of additive mixing is subtractive mixing—the crossing or combining of color mediums in front of a single source of light. Figure 8–5 illustrates the effect of combining two color mediums, blue-green and yellow, in front of a light source containing all the spectrum hues. The green color that is transmitted is the only hue not subtracted or filtered out of the light by the combined color mediums. It is not as visually apparent, but the same subtractive results are present when the artist mixes blue-green and yellow in paint.

Subtractive mixing in paint and light is characterized by a move toward neutrality and darker shades. This is particularly evident when the hues are complementary colors. It is understandable that the closer the color mediums are to hue opposites the less light can be transmitted until a block or point of negative transmission is reached. The mixing of complementary colors in paint results in a nearly black neutral for the same reason. Because painters use subtractive mixing most of the time, they have a slightly different attitude toward color than the lighting designer.

COLOR IN PAINT

Color in paint, of course, depends upon light to realize its physical properties. The color of a surface reaches the eye by the reflection of the light that is illuminating it. Just as a light color medium transmits a color by absorbing some spectrum hues and letting through others, so a colored surface absorbs and reflects only the colors of the paint (Figure 8–6). These are the physical properties of a paint surface that begins with its coloring agent, pigment.

Pigment. The term *pigment* is an inclusive term that refers to the coloring agent in paints, dyes, and nature. It can be best explained as the chemical properties of color that create hue. At first, pigments came from natural sources; the indigo and madder plants are familiar examples. Minerals and semiprecious stones were also pulverized and made into pigments. The crude chemistry of the past established many of the traditional names of colors still used today, such as madder lake and indigo blue.

Colors, other than those found directly in nature, were often made synthetically from known minerals and their compounds. In the mid-nineteenth century, organic colors made their first appearance as organic dyes. Most present-day colors are a product of organic chemistry, which essentially deals with the carbon compounds. The names of organic colors often signify their chemical origin, such as chrome green, alizarin crimson, and calcium red.

Modern chemistry has given artists many new colors, which have allowed them to increase their palette. Because of the subtractive result of most paint mixing the painter cannot begin with a palette of primary hues to develop a full range of colors. The intermediate colors of combined primaries are not pure and do not relate to the spectrum hues. Hence, the painter prefers to begin with a larger palette that might include all the principal hues of the spectrum. While a small palette made up of the six principal colors already mentioned is usable, the scenic artist favors a palette of twelve principal colors for reasons of flexibility and economy.

Twelve Principal Hues. Beginning with the six original hues (red, orange, yellow, green, blue, and violet) six additional hues may be created through intermediate steps. The new hue thus formed takes its name from the two original hues on either side. The hue between yellow and orange, for example, would be *yellow-orange* and so on around the color wheel (Figure 8–7).

The new intermediate color is not thought of as a paint mixture of the two adjacent colors but as a full chroma hue from the spectrum. The result is a working palette of twelve full-intensity hues which will reduce the degree of neutralization from subtractive mixing that might have occurred with a smaller palette. Some scenic artists even prefer a palette with more than twelve hues. Also, in certain situations, such as the commercial or industrial use of color, the number of principal colors may be expanded to twenty-four or more. In any event, the expansion is based on the twelve principal hues that become a basis of reference for individual use.

The Color Wheel

To better show the physical relationship of spectrum hues most color notation systems use a color wheel. The circular arrangement of colors brings into view the diametric and adjacent correlation of the twelve spectral hues and thus provides designers a schematic view of primary and secondary hue relationships as well as pairs of complementary colors that appear diametrically opposite each other around the wheel. A knowledge of complementary hues is not only necessary for mixing both light and pigment, but it also is important in composition. This is apparent in the choice of tints and shades in a production color scheme. Because color in light and pigment are constantly brought together in the theatre, they must be aligned in a compatible arrangement so that both have the same complementary colors.

Intergrating Light and Pigment. The attempt to bring color in light and pigment into one system of notation is best illustrated in the color wheel. The steps taken toward the merger are shown in the diagram. The light primaries and secondaries are represented in diagram a and the pigment primaries in b. Note that the complementary colors within each circle are different. The complement of blue in light, for example, is yellow, while its opposite in pigments is orange. To intergrate light and pigment into one wheel, c, the light primaries have been moved

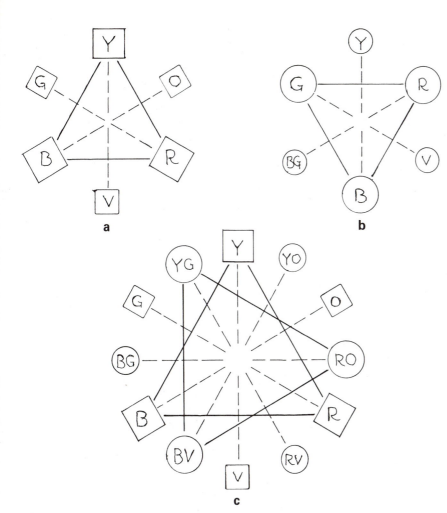

a

b

c

Intergrating Light and Color (see also Figures 8–7 and 8–8)

(a) Pigment primaries with complementary hues. (b) Light primaries and complementary hues. True light primaries are described as red-orange, blue-violet, and yellow-green. Light and pigment are intergrated in a single color wheel accounting for the twelve principal hues. Light and pigments now have the same complements (c).

slightly to fit into the pigment wheel. Light primary red becomes red-orange (RO), green a yellow-green (YG), and blue a blue-violet (BV). The maneuver also more accurately represents the light primary hues.

The Pigment Color Wheel. In addition to showing a contiguous relationship of the twelve principal colors, the pigment color wheel (Figure 8–7) also emphasizes hue opposites of complementary colors. The hues are full chroma and represent the basic pigment colors of the painter's palette.

Because most pigment mixing is subtractive, the gray tone in the center indicates the neutralizing effect of any pair of complementary colors. The many tints and shades resulting from the mixing of one pair of complementary hues, orange and blue, has been shown in Figure 8–3, where the flexible relationship between *chroma* and *value* was demonstrated. The subtlety of neutral shades and almost unlimited combinations of hues is the major advantage of subtractive mixing in pigments.

The Light Color Wheel. Although the conception is different, the arrangement of the twelve principal colors in the light color wheel is the same as the pigment wheel. The primary, secondary, and intermediate colors are developed from the additive mixing of the light primaries (Figure 8–8). As the additive mixing of colored light tends to move toward white the secondary and intermediate colors are therefore lighter in value than their companion colors in the pigment wheel.

The light color wheel in Figure 8–8 is shown more to represent the interrelation of colors in light with the twelve principal hues than to indicate a complete range of colors in light. A full range of saturated color mediums of all spectrum hues is available for selective use.

Lighting designers vary their choice of color filters used as primaries depending on need. There is a great difference, for example, between primaries selected to light a sky cyclorama, a painted drop, or acting areas.

With some latitude light primaries can be described in terms of Roscolux color mediums (Rosco Laboratories, Inc.) as (1) a red with some orange content (Roscolux No. 26, light red) designated as Ro (small orange). (2) A blue containing some red (Rv) Roscolux No. 47, light rose purple plus No. 65, daylight blue, is very close to primary blue. (3) The remaining primary, green, is obtainable by combining No. 89, moss green, and No. 12, straw. These primary hues are close enough to be thought of as red-orange (RO), blue-violet (BV), and yellow-green (YG) as they appear in the pigment color wheel (Figure 8–7).

The light secondaries are the result of the additive mixing of the primaries. They are complementary colors and are located directly opposite each primary in the pigment color wheel. Yellow-orange (YO) is opposite light-primary blue-violet (BV) and can be produced in light by doubling Roscolux No. 03, dark amber. Blue-green (BG), across from primary (RO), is near Roscolux No. 71, sea blue; and red-violet (RV), the complement of primary (YG), is almost the same as Roscolux No. 48, rose purple. Note that the light secondaries are lighter in value than their corresponding pigment hues because of the additive mixing that formulated them.

COLOR VISION

The source of color can be scientifically explained; the mixture of color can be diagrammed; and all the variants of color can be arranged in a system of notation. However, what the eye sees and the brain interprets is an individual and personal color experience. Although the eye functions very much like a camera, it is not a scientific instrument. It receives light through its lens, which focuses the image or impression onto the layers of the retina in the inner eye. The innumerable nerve endings (rods and cones) of the retina culminate in the optic nerve, which carries the impression signal to the brain for interpretation. The impression is registered in terms of color and intensity (brightness), which in a sense is another way of saying hue and value. The eye sees value differences because of the variation of reflected intensities. Lighter pigment tints, for example, reflect more light (intensity) than do lower value shades. A few people can only distinguish value differences and not variations of hue. Because the greatest differences in hue fall in the middle of the value scale, most color-blind individuals cannot see the difference between reds and greens.

Intensity and Color. The hue of the painter's pigments and colors in light are influenced by the intensity of the light that is reflected by, or transmitted through, the respective surfaces. A saturated hue (full chroma) has an inherent brightness or intensity level that corresponds to the hue-value relationship established in pigments (Figure 8–3). Any change in the relative intensities would change the comparative value of the color. If, for example, the fields of two clear spotlights side by side on a blue wall were of different intensities, the brighter spot would appear to be a lighter value of blue. The opposite is true of a *blue* spot of light on a blue surface. Under blue light a blue surface is more brilliant in hue because, within the lighted area, more blue wavelengths are being reflected in comparison to the rest of the surface (Figure 8–9).

Any change in intensity of a light by dimming affects color not only by the drop in brightness but also through a reduction in the warmth thrown off by the lamp. Many intensity differences on the stage are achieved by higher or lower wattage or by the *distance of throw*. Remember that light falls off in intensity at the rate of the square of the distance between the source and the object being illuminated (the inverse square law). If a light is moved twice the distance away from a surface, four times the intensity will be needed to achieve the same brightness. This can be a critical factor when the designer is trying, for example, to balance color and brightness from two different slide projectors.

Color Perception. Knowledge of *how* we see color is perhaps of greater interest to the lighting designer than to other designers in the theatre. An understanding of the physiology of the eye as it relates to color vision gives the designer some indication of how the audience reacts to both intensity and color.

The eye's sensitivity to high or low levels of light affects the color we see. Since the rods of the retina, for example, produce most of the low-level or night vision, their sensitivity to green-blue would tend to add a greenish-blue cast to all hues seen under a low level of light. Moonlight, for example, though it is the reflection of the sun greatly reduced in intensity, appears to have a blue tint. However, blue tint, as far as the brain is concerned, is a *color impression* a designer has to consider within a stage composition. The high-intensity vision of the cones in the retina are more sensitive to yellow; the sun at noon, although a brilliant white, appears to have a yellowish tint. In a stage composition, however, there is a less apparent shift of color under high intensities.

Intensity and Color Overload. The retina of the eye assimilates light energy. When it is saturated (isomerized) it is said to be *bleached*. Hence after any sudden change of intensity or color, the retina has to regenerate itself. This process takes place over a noticeable period of time. Since the rods are sensitive to both intensity and color, and the cones are sensitive *only* to intensity, there is a difference in the time it takes the eye to readjust from a sudden intensity change than to a color change. It takes the eye about 1 to 1½ minutes to adjust in a blackout, for example (cone regeneration), while a color change (rod regeneration) may take as long as 5 minutes.

The time lag the eye experiences after a sudden change of color explains *after-image,* a phenomenon of color vision. Until the eye has recovered, it retains an image of the object and a color impression long after the object has been removed or changed. The after-image, however, is in the *complementary hue* of the original image color.

A theatrical demonstration of after-image was present in the production of Diaghilev's Ballet Russe *Le Coq d'Or* with décor by Natalya Goncharova. The first scene, a garden, is dominated by a brilliant red-orange tree. During twenty minutes of dancing the eye was saturated with an unbalanced color scheme; upon changing to the next scene the audience was plagued by a blue-green after-image of the first-scene tree floating ethereally about the stage. The impression was in the eye, of course; the tree was not on stage.

The phenomenon of after-image or the color-balancing tendency of the eye is present in other forms. The shadow cast from a colored light source, for example, appears to the observer to be in a complementary color. Figure 8–10 illustrates the pale red-orange shadow cast from a blue-green light which is not there in reality but is an optical illusion or color impression within the eye. It should be mentioned that the shadow has to be faintly illuminated with a colorless light to accomplish the demonstration accurately.

Modern abstract art has taken optical color demonstrations out of the laboratory and turned them into exciting examples of so-called op art. This and other phenomena of intercolor action, however, are not new. It was first referred to in 1886 as the *simultaneous contrast of color* by M. E. Chevreul, an early color theorist. In 1960, Joseph Albers referred to the same effects more correctly as the *interaction of color.*

The Interaction of Color. How a color reacts to an adjacent hue or to its background is known as the interaction of color. Certain reactions are painfully obvious while others are extremely subtle. The degree of color interplay is a critical element in the use of color by all stage designers. Aside from the mixing and creating of colors itself, the designer's choice and arrangement of colors become one of the most forceful elements in stimulating an emotional or intellectual response on the part of the audience.

The interaction of colors affects all variants of color. The *value* of a color can seem to change by juxtaposition; a neutral can be influenced by a surrounding color and appear to take on a *hue;* and the *chroma* of a color can be sharpened or deadened by its background. Figures 8–11, 12, 13, and 14 are a few classic examples of obvious color interactions that have an influence on the designer's use of color or choice of a color scheme.

COLOR SENSATION

The experience of color includes elements of sensation or emotion as well. Designers in the theatre must be aware of the scope of this emotional response on the part of the audience (which is often sub-conscious) when they choose colors to establish a mood or specific atmosphere on the stage. The psychological affect of color, however, is difficult to measure. To some extent the designer must depend on a measurable individual response and hope it will multiply.

Most emotional response to color is conditioned by a lifetime of reaction to colors in nature and under natural light. We are repulsed, for example, by strong colors in light that produce unnatural flesh tones or discolor our food. We are also influenced by centuries of social and religious conventions that are buried deeply in the subconscious. Finally, we react to symbolism in color, some primal and others more contemporary (such as traffic lights and color-coded road signs).

With these psychological influences in mind—the natural, tradi-tional, and symbolic sensations of color—we will attempt to describe the general emotional connotations attached to the six basic spectrum hues.

Yellow   Radiant, light-giving, golden, saintly; in light values near white, virginal.

Orange   Festive, earthy, peasant colors, neutral shades, nature in the fall.

Red   Active, passionate, full of inner warmth, fiery, strong, forceful.

Violet	Royal, piety, deeper shades, shadows, terror, chaos, a reddening color.
Blue	Passive, receding, deep, cool, purity, icy tints.
Green	Tranquility, compassion, nature in the spring and summer.

The psychological description of a hue is, at best, very general. The emotional response to a color can be countered or modified by adjacent colors, as well as the color of the background. The intercolor experience, which involves both the psychological response and the physiological limitation of the eye, can also be tricked by an optical illusion. This phenomenon of fooling both the eye and the mind is dependable enough to be considered an important part of the impact of color on a theatre audience.

COLOR MANIPULATION

Some designers have an intuitive sense of color. The colors they put together seem right for the specific dramatic moment or atmospheric scene. A designer in the theatre, however, frequently has to suppress personal preferences to bring a color scheme into harmony or contrast with the colors in the show. To ensure the chances of a unified color solution, all designers—scenery, costume, and lighting—rely on advance color schemes to coordinate the final color impression.

The Color Scheme. The development of a production color scheme may be as simple as deciding on the overall tonality of a single hue, or it may involve selecting a number of related or contrasting colors. The *harmony* or *contrast* of hues becomes the basic control of a production color scheme. The mood of the production is often expressed in the interrelationship of the colors in the scheme. Although the basic control is established in full chroma on the color wheel, all the variants of color (hue, value, and chroma) are called upon to provide interest and flexibility to the final colors in the composition. The complementary color scheme of orange and blue, for example, can be expressed in a variety of values and chromas as is seen in Figure 8–17.

Aside from the obvious harmony of a *monochromatic* color scheme, which relies on the manipulation of the value and chroma of a single hue, various schemes can be created in terms of *chords* on the color wheel.

The Geometry of a Color Scheme. One way to develop a color scheme is to draw chords from color to color on the circumference of the wheel. A short chord system, of course, furnishes a closer interval between

FIGURE 8–1

Spectrum Hues

The breakdown of sunlight through prism refraction into first six and then twelve spectrum hues.

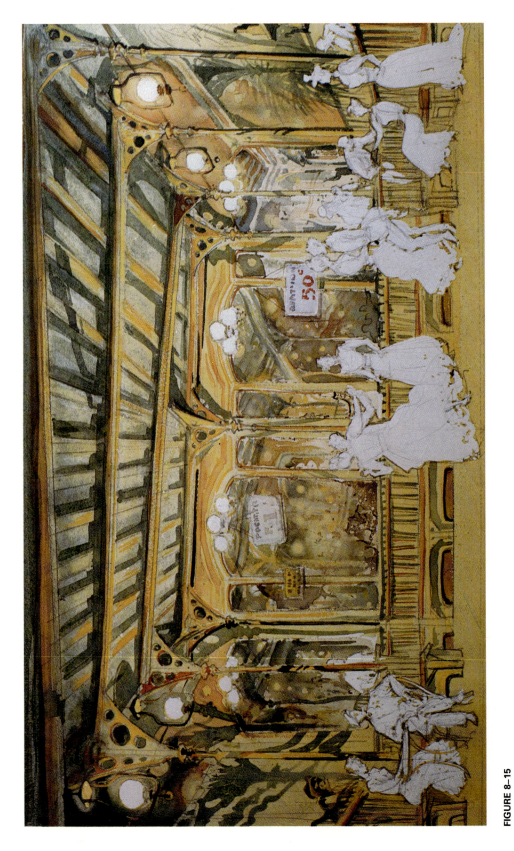

FIGURE 8–15
Third Interval Triad Color Scheme

This vibrant designer's sketch by Jo Mielziner for the dance hall scene in *Can Can* is in a third interval triad: green, yellow, and orange. Courtesy Jo Mielziner estate.

FIGURE 8-16
Monochrome Color Scheme
Sketch for a velour dye-painted traveler curtain in shades and tints of one color, blue.

FIGURE 8–17

Complementary Color Scheme

Sketch for a setting using orange and blue as a color control.

FIGURE 8–18
Color Plot to Costume Sketch
From the simplified colors in a color chart of Molière's *The Misanthrope* the costumes of two characters have been developed in final individual color schemes. Designer—June DeCamp.

FIGURE 8–19
Color Modification

A demonstration of the subtractive mixing effect when a colored surface is modified by a colored light. (a) Yellow surface under red light. (b) Green surface under red light.

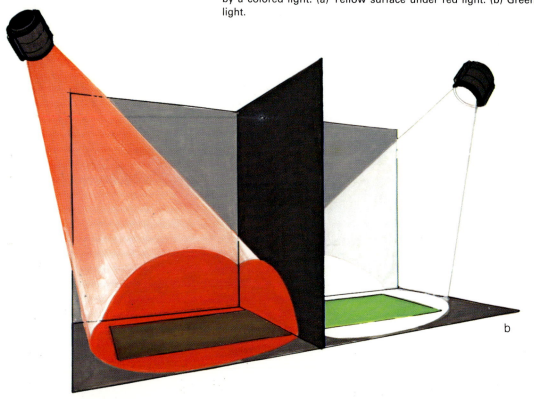

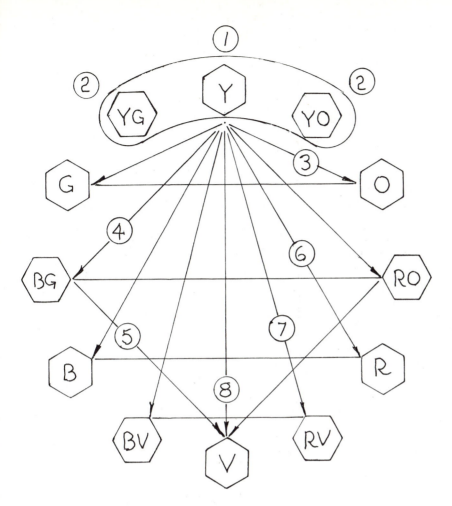

Color Chords (see also Figure 8–15)

Various color schemes related to color wheel. Shown is one of the six complementary areas, yellow to violet. The various schemes are: (1) monochromatic; (2) analogous or neighboring colors; (3) third interval triad; (4) fourth interval traid; one pair of complementaries; (5) fourth interval quadrate; two pairs of complementaries; (6) fifth interval triad, primaries or secondaries; (7) split-complement triad; and (8) complementary.

hues than a scheme of longer chords. As the interval grows longer hue contrasts will increase until hue opposites or a complementary scheme is reached.

To show a few of the unlimited color combinations enclosed in the geometry of the chords, the diagram above demonstrates all of the possibilities on a single axis (yellow and violet). They vary from the close *harmony* of one hue to the vibrant *contrast* of a pair of complementary colors.

1 A *monochromatic* scheme. The natural high value of yellow limits its range. It can be neutralized into ochres, warmed with orange, and cooled with green to add variety to a one-color control.

2 An *analogous* scheme combines neighboring hues with the shortest chord into a harmonious scheme. The three hues in this example are yellow-orange, yellow, and yellow-green.

3 A *third interval* triad of hues derives from a triangle including yellow, orange, and green. The chord has lengthened, thereby

Color in the Theatre

increasing the interval between colors and providing slightly more contrast to the scheme.

4   The *fourth interval* scheme is first illustrated as a three-color combination—yellow, red-orange, and blue-green. A fourth interval chord always involves one pair of complementary colors, which increases the contrast of the scheme.

5   A *fourth interval* scheme is shown involving four colors. The quadrate of chords includes two pairs of complements when violet is added to the triad of yellow, red-orange, and blue-green. The designer can soften the contrast of the scheme by varying the value and chroma of one or all of the hues.

6   A *fifth interval* triad. The equilateral triangle of chords takes in the pigment primaries red, yellow, and blue as a scheme. The fifth interval scheme is not as obvious when the axis is between intermediate colors such as yellow-orange, red-violet, and blue-green.

7   *Split-complement* is a rather arbitrary selection of chords. It is usually used to soften the high contrast of a complementary scheme. In this example, yellow is in combination with red-violet and blue-violet, which flank the complementary hue, violet.

8   *Complementary* hues offer the highest contrast as a color scheme. The two-color scheme, yellow and violet, also have a high value contrast. The most vibrant pair of complementaries is red-orange and blue-green.

The Color Plot. The control of color within a composition is only a portion of the color planning that occurs in designing for the theatre. The color scheme for each setting of a multiscene play must also be considered in the content of the *whole* production.

Most scene designers use some form of a *color plot* to make preliminary studies of the entire production. Although it is a view of the show the audience will never see, it does serve as a color guide for the lighting and costume designers. Through the color plot the overall development of color can be studied. The functional relationship of connecting colors and hue accents is clearly visible. The progressive unfolding of color change within a scene or throughout a production, as well as moments of high contrast or subdued uniformity, can be demonstrated in the color plot.

The color plot is very important to the costume designer. It shows the overall relationship of all costumes in the production and enables the costume designer to plot small scenes and families of color that may help to visually define sympathetic characters and rival groups or individuals. The focus or center of attention in a large group scene can be planned as well as the control of the overall emotional impact or mood within the scene. The color plot also establishes the progression of colors from scene to scene and act to act.

Executing the Design

A character's age and position in society (deacon, servant, master, and so on) can enter the color plot in the broad, symbolic statement of a single color note. The costume designer, however, frequently uses more than one color to note a single costume as a means of studying color accents and harmonies between characters. The costume color plot in Figure 8–18 illustrates in particolor swatches the color interaction and character relationship within Molière's *The Misanthrope*.

Color Modification. We have seen how color can be changed by mixing, influenced by interaction with other colors, and created by optical illusion. Surface color can also be modified by colored light. The constant use of colored light on a colored surface is unique to the theatre. Designers in the theatre not only have to consider the colors of a painted background, costumes, and other materials of a set, but also the colors of the lights that will reveal them. This is especially true if the lighting for the scene is unusual, such as a romantic moonlit scene or the flooding of the stage with red or green hues to provide an unnatural effect.

Fortunately, color modification is not quite as complicated as it seems. The effect of colored light on a colored surface is a result of subtractive mixing. In other words, if a red light is thrown on a yellow surface, the yellow is modified into orange tones (Figure 8–19).

The modification of a color in a costume or on scenery by colored light is a theatrical example of the joining of two color media, pigment and light. Designers in the theatre are constantly aware of how colored light and pigment influence each other. They are always prepared to compensate in either medium to create a natural effect or to deliberately cause dramatic reversals of color.

Color modification charts can be prepared for the reference of all designers in the theatre by systematically matching the shade of the modified color chit on the white-light side of the dividing shield of a testing apparatus similar to the setup indicated in Figure 8–19. If each of the twelve principal colors is subjected to the influence of at least the light primaries, a rather informative set of colors notes is collected. It will be noted that when like hues are brought together, blue light on blue pigment, for example, the modified pigment hue is raised in value. This slight alteration of value is true of all alike color combinations. The degree of value change in a given situation depends upon the relative value of the background surrounding the color chit and the comparative intensity of the two light sources.

The chart will indicate the many possibilities under light primaries; however, unusual color combinations should be checked under the exact lighting conditions. Some designers prefer to use a miniature duplication of the planned stage lighting setup to check their color schemes and plan color effects. The consideration of the color of the stage lights is, of course, most important to the scene designer when preparing to paint the scenery.

9

Painting Scenery

Scenery painting is a highly skilled and specialized portion of creating a setting. It is also a very interesting and fascinating part of scene design and technical production. Most of the methods and techniques of handling scene paint are familiar to anyone with visual-arts training. The main difference between scenery painting and easel painting is one of scale. Instead of painting at a small drawing board, the scenic artist paints at life size or larger.

Because the scale of scene painting is so large, the scenic artist uses a broad technique, sometimes so broad that what appears to be slaps and dashes up close does not take form until viewed from a distance. Learning to paint on a large scale and in broad technique is an easy adjustment for the visual artist. The uninitiated, however, should first become accomplished in handling watercolors in sketch form before attempting large-scale painting. Sketching and painting from still life or landscape not only improve student designers' drawing and painting ability but also increase their perception of light and color in nature. These processes also serve to underscore the significance of color as an element of design.

PAINT AND COLOR

The design of a setting can succeed or fail on the strength of the painting. Hence, the designer should carefully plan how the scenery is to be painted. The most important consideration is the use of color. A scene designer must be familiar not only with the mixing and use of pigments but also with the use of colored lights.

The prominence and forcefulness of color as an element of design was mentioned in Chapter 3. The attributes of the color experience and the philosophy of the use of color in the theatre were discussed in Chapter 8. The scenic artist or scene designer employs the same philosophy, terminology, and mixing procedures in the use of color for scenery as would any other visual artist.

SCENE-PAINTING PALETTE

The scenic artist's first act is to create a working palette of scene paint that will relate to the twelve principal hues of the spectrum. The size of the palette will vary from at least twelve to many additional pigments depending on the individual artist's tastes and working methods; on pureness of hue and mixing behavior of the available pigments; and finally, on the relative cost of individual colors.

When designers choose their paint they must judge how the pigment color compares to the corresponding spectrum hue. If the paint sample does not match favorably in hue, value, and chroma, they may have to compensate by choosing colors on either side of the spectrum hue and stock two pigments instead of one. The pigment yellow is a good example. Because a true spectrum yellow may not be obtainable, two yellows are usually stocked, one that will mix with blue or green and the other with orange.

There are two types of scene paint: the unmixed dry pigments and ready-mixed paints. Mixture in this case refers to the presence of all or part of the properties of paint as a medium, which will be discussed separately under mixing procedures. The choice of a palette in either type of paint is related to the mixing of colors or of one pigment with another.

Dry Pigment Palette. Dry pigments are ground for theatrical use and, therefore, the spectral hues at least are available only at supply houses specializing in scenic paints and supplies. Earth colors (ochre, sienna, umber, and the like) can be found in local paint shops, although many times they are of inferior quality for painting scenery.

In preparing a list of stock scenic colors it is natural to compare the quality of the pigment's hue to the twelve principal colors of the color wheel. A good scene-painting palette would include them as well as some special colors and the earth colors.

The following hues have been selected from Gothic Scenic Paints (Gothic Color Company, Inc.) and Iddings Dry Pigments (Rosco Products).

Yellow

Light Chrome Yellow — A straight yellow, close to a primary hue. It is important to have a yellow with a sharp cut-off (minimum green or orange content).

Yellow Orange

Medium Chrome Yellow — Excellent yellow-orange hue. Not necessary to stock with light chrome yellow. Some painters, however, prefer stocking two yellows, warm (slight red content), and cool (slight blue content).

Orange

French Orange Mineral — Excellent spectrum hue. Heavy, therefore a little expensive.

Red Orange

American Vermilion — Brilliant red orange.
Bright Red — Also a brilliant red orange.

Red

Turkey Red Lake — Good red, slight yellow content.
Red — Close to spectrum red.
Dark Red — Deep red with blue content.

Red Violet

Magenta Lake — A brilliant bluish red, makes rich violets with blue. Expensive but goes a long way.

Violet and Blue Violet

Purple Lake — A rich, brilliant violet. Very expensive. Special, not necessary to stock with magenta lake at hand.

Blue

Cobalt Blue — A pure primary blue although a little high in value.
Ultramarine Blue — A rich blue with a touch of red content. Mixes well to make purples, but poorly for greens.

Blue Green

Italian Blue	A brilliant turquoise, although not a true blue green (high in value), it is a very useful color. Mixed with primrose yellow, it makes vibrant yellow greens and greens.
Celestial Blue	Dark turquoise.
Prussian Blue	Dark, rich blue green. Difficult mixer, good for near-black tones.

Green

Emerald Green	Intense green, slight yellow content.
Medium Chrome Green	A straight green but a little low in value.

Yellow Green

Primrose Yellow	A cold yellow. Not necessary to stock with light chrome yellow, except as a special color.
Primrose Yellow and Emerald Green	A cold yellow mixed with an intense green makes an excellent yellow green.

Earth Colors

The earth colors are inexpensive neutral shades that can be used in place of the expensive method of neutralizing the more intense colors.

French Yellow Ochre	Rich ochre or neutral yellow shade, extends into good cream shades.
Raw Italian Sienna	Warmer and richer than ochre.
Burnt Italian Sienna	Terra cotta and brick color
Raw Turkey	A cold brown, has greenish cast. Not too useful by itself. It is used to neutralize other colors.
Burnt Turkey Umber	Rich brown, good wood-graining color.
Van Dyke Brown	Very rich brown, but hard mixer. Excellent wood color.
Ivory Drop Black	A bone black (avoid using lampblack, which is commonly mistaken for bone black. Lampblack is greasy and therefore a hard mixer).
Zinc White	A white pigment, not whiting. Sometimes called permanent white.
Danish Whiting	Pure whiting, doesn't settle out. Excellent filler.

Ready-Mixed Paints. The color range of ready-mixed paints is not as extensive as that of dry pigments. Although their colors are brilliant there are not as many intermediate tones. The following paint colors are from three major sources, Gothic Fresco Paints, Iddings Deep Colors, and Roscopaint. They are fairly representative of the range of colors found in all premixed paints.

Yellow

Lemon Yellow   A good straight yellow close to spectrum hue.

Yellow-Orange

Golden Yellow   Not quite a full yellow-orange in hue. Closer to an orange-yellow.

Orange

Orange   Has more red than a spectrum orange.

Red-Orange

Bright Red   Excellent spectrum hue.

Red

Red   Good spectrum hue. Just a shade off in chroma.

Dark Red   A step lower in value than red and has a little blue content.

Red-Violet

Magenta   The hue is right but it is about three steps too high in value.

Violet and Blue-Violet

Purple   Excellent spectrum hue. When mixed with ultramarine blue it produces fine blue-violet.

Blue

Ultramarine Blue   A blue with a red content. Too deep in value to be a true spectrum blue.

Blue-Green

Turquoise Blue   Excellent spectrum hue.

Cerulean Blue   A brilliant blue-green but high in value. Makes vibrant yellow-greens when mixed with lemon yellow.

Green

Emerald Green   Excellent spectrum hue.

Yellow-Green

Cerulean Blue and Lemon Yellow   No prepared yellow-green available.

Earth colors

Yellow Ochre   Rich neutral yellow.

Raw Sienna   Neutral yellow. Warmer and richer than ochre.

Burnt Sienna	Darker and less red than traditional burnt sienna.
Raw Umber	Cold brown. More blue than green, the cast of traditional raw umber.
Burnt Umber	Good rich brown.
Black	Deep flat black. Covers and mixes well.
White	Opaque. Good tinting white.

MIXING PROCEDURES

Components of Scene Paint

The three basic components of scene paint are pigment (color), binder, and vehicle. The pigment and binder are suspended in a liquid which allows the paint to be brushed or sprayed onto a surface. The vehicle then evaporates and the binder holds the pigment to the surface.

The dry colors used for scene paint are the pigments suspended in a water vehicle with a water-soluble glue as a binder. A filler is frequently added to scene paint: whiting, which is an inexpensive chalk and not a pigment, is often added to the mixture to give the paint body and opacity. Because whiting affects the intensity of the color, it is not used in pure or full-intensity colors.

The mixing of scene paint begins with the preparation of the binder and vehicle which the scenic artist calls "size." The mixing proportions of a working size depend upon the kind of glue that is being used. Ordinary flake or ground glues are strong and usually have to be cut about 16 to 1 to make a size. Rubber and gelatine glues, although more flexible and easier to handle (they dry slower), make into about a 10-to-1 size. Both types require advance preparation. They have to be soaked and cooked in a double broiler to soften them into a liquid state. Once the glue has been made into size, it stays in a liquid state. The size will deteriorate, however, if it is allowed to stand for too long a period. A small quantity of carbolic acid or Lysol added to the size acts as a preservative.

Because scene paint dries about two to three values lighter than it appears when wet, it is easier to mix the dry colors together first to acquire the desired tone. The size is then added to the premixed pigment, thereby saving repeated testings and sometimes the mixing of twice as much paint as is needed in the attempt to match an elusive shade. The size is added slowly, first making a pulp or paste. If the paste is vigorously stirred to make sure all the dry color is thoroughly moistened before thinning it to painting consistency, there is no need to break up the unmixed lumps by hand. If the dry paint refuses to go into suspension (some colors such as Van Dyke brown and Prussian blue are poor mixers), a little alcohol added to the paste helps to wet the troublesome color.

Ready-Mixed Paints

The pigment color, binder, and vehicle are premixed in proper proportions into a creamy paste. Since most scenery paints are suspended in water, ready-mixed paints are identified by their binder. Casein, acrylic, and latex-based paints are those most often used in the theatre. Although casein, a milk derivative, has given way to other protein binders such as soybean, the term is still used to identify this type of ready-mixed paint. Gothic Casein Fresco Paints and Iddings Deep Colors are two brands of protein-based premixed paints that have already been mentioned.

Roscopaint, a product of Rosco Laboratories, is an acrylic-based paint. Although most premixed paints are somewhat concentrated, Roscopaint is supersaturated and is made to extend to a dye consistency without losing brilliance. For easier mixing with other colors, the basic paste can be thinned with equal parts of water. It can then be further extended with up to three parts of water, depending upon the degree of opacity that is desired. The acrylic binder is compatible with any water-extended paint.

Latex-based paints are also adaptable to scenic painting. Vivid-Deep Color (Long Island Paint & Chemical Co.) produces a complete range of colors. Although most Vivid colors are in full chroma and concentrated, they are liquid in consistency and therefore do not go as far as a pulp mixture. Because latex and casein paints are compatible, the painter is free to select favored hues from each system as stock colors.

PAINTER'S ELEVATIONS

Designers must prepare for scene painting even if they do their own painting. Painting ideas are expressed in painter's elevations, which, unlike sketches, remove all the atmosphere of stage lighting to show true colors and exact form. The painter's elevation is a scaled drawing showing in detail the cartooning, or line drawing, a notation of actual color, and a clear indication of the painting technique. The scale of the drawing varies with the designer. The larger the scale, however, the more accurately it can be interpreted. The painter's elevations for most settings can be done at ½-inch scale, with details shown at a larger scale.

If a designer is doing the painting, the preparation of painter's elevations is the point at which to think through the appropriate painting technique and procedure. If lights are to play an important part of the design, the designer can check the painter's elevations under colored lights to foresee the effect of the stage lights on the setting colors.

Working from the painter's elevation, the scene painter can proportionally enlarge the drawing to full scale. A grid of horizontal and vertical lines is placed over the drawing, spaced, in the scale of the drawing, at 2-foot intervals. A similar grid, at full scale, is drawn on the priming coat of the surface to be painted.

Ways of numbering or lettering the grid vary. In Europe, for example, the artists prefer to number the spaces (Figure 9–1), while in the United States the numbering of the lines is favored. Proceeding square by square, the painter transposes the small-scale elevation into a full-scale layout of the design.

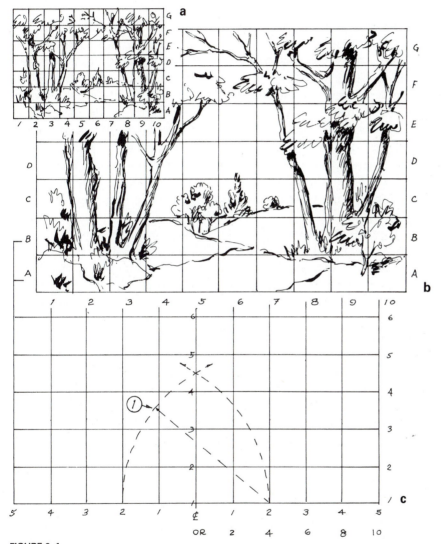

FIGURE 9–1

Methods of Proportional Enlarging

(a) The designer's elevation with a grid of two- or three-foot squares. Spaces are numbered from right to left and lettered from bottom to top. (b) Full-scale layout of the drawing with the same labeling method. (c) Full-scale grid with the lines numbered from the center line in opposite directions and from the bottom to top. The base line and center line are established first. (1) A perpendicular center line is constructed off the base line through the intersection of two arcs swung from centers equidistant from the center point.

PAINTING PROCEDURE

The three steps toward preparing a surface for decorative painting are the size, prime, and base coats of paint. Their individual use or omission varies in accordance with the complexity of the design, the nature of the surface, and the painting technique.

Size Coats

The first step toward preparing new canvas or muslin is the size coat, which shrinks the canvas and glazes the surface without filling it. There are several uses and ways to mix size coats that bear mentioning. The starch size is used to prepare canvas or muslin for dye painting or very thin opaque paints. It can also serve as a surface for opaque paints, especially if the opaque coat is not completely covering the surface but is applied to leave large areas of unpainted background. A starch size is made by adding a cup of cooked Argo glossy starch to a 16-quart bucket of hot working size of about 20-to-1 proportion. A touch of dye or scenic color is added to make it more visible for brushing on the canvas. The resulting coat is a taut, slightly glazed surface that is excellent for dye painting.

The alum size is used over old painted canvas to stop an old coat of paint from picking up or bleeding through succeeding coats. A small quantity of powdered alum (½ cup to a 16-quart bucket) is mixed into working size of about 10- or 16-to-1 proportion.

A third use of a size coat is as a glaze. A glaze is a thin, transparent coat that is more of a painting technique than a preparation step. It gives the surface a slight gloss without covering up the undercoat. A glaze mix is prepared by weakening or strengthening the working size, depending upon the degree of gloss that is desired. The stronger the size, the higher the gloss. The technique can vary from a filmy, transparent wash to a fairly glossy finish. A glaze technique is tricky and difficult for a beginner. It has to be applied quickly and lightly to avoid moving the painted detail underneath.

Prime Coat

The second step in preparing new canvas is the prime coat, which has the function of filling the canvas. When painting on new canvas it is necessary to have it filled or the colors will "strike in" and lose brilliance. This phenomenon is very noticeable when old canvas is used beside new canvas on a flat.

A prime coat is made of working size and whiting with a touch of color to facilitate the application. It is kept thin in order not to overload the canvas. Because the prime coat fills the canvas, it tends to be an opaque coat and therefore cannot be used over areas of canvas that are to be translucent or dye-painted. If there are no translucent areas

FIGURE 9–2

Scenery Painting Procedure: Painter's elevations to finished scenery

(Left) Painter's elevation of an oleo drop prepared by the designer. The drawing has been gridded with 2-foot squares in preparation for enlarging. (Below) Proportional enlarging. The muslin has been sized and the drop has been gridded with charcoal and snap line to full-scale dimensions. The design is sketched in with charcoal so that mistakes and construction lines can easily be "flogged" or dusted off. [Illustration of procedures continues on the next two pages.]

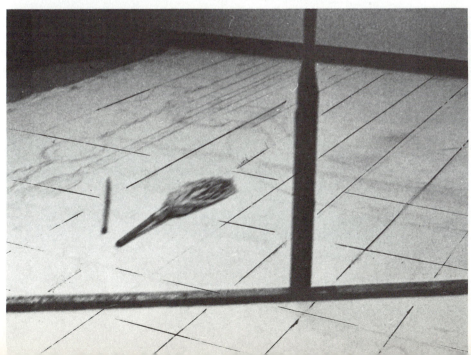

Executing the Design

Scenery Painting Procedure, continued
(Page 258, top) Inking the cartoon. The charcoal drawing or cartoon of the design is fixed to the muslin with a thin dye outline. (Page 258, bottom) Painting into the cartoon. Wash backgrounds and detail painting can proceed without fear of losing the cartoon since the dye will bleed through the paint and be visible as guide lines. (This page) Finished drop. An oleo drop for *Under the Gas Lights* by Augustin Daly. Designer—Glenn Gauer. (Photo—Nelson)

on the flats, the size and prime coats are sometimes combined into one operation, shrinking and filling the canvas at the same time.

All cartooning or layout drawing is done in charcoal on the prime coat. After the drawing is completed, key points or portions of the cartoons are "inked" in a fine line of dye or indelible pencil. The rest of the charcoal is "flogged" or dusted off the surface in preparation for the base coat. The inked-in portions of the design will bleed through the base coat and serve as a guide for later detailed painting.

Base Coat

The base coat is the under-painting for the final decorative painting and texturing. The application and color of the base coat depends on what is to follow. For example, a base coat may be one tone as a basis for a slick, modern paneled wall; it may be a scumbling of two or three tones in preparation for an antiqued, weather-beaten surface, or it may become a graded wash under a stenciled wallpaper design.

As a mixture, the base coat is kept thin in order not to overload the canvas. Because it is more intense in color than the prime coat, it will have less whiting and more pigment.

Painting Scenery   **259**

Detail and Decorative Painting

The final step in scene painting is the definition of form or the illusion of form through the various painting techniques of lining, texturing, and stenciling. We will also discuss the designing and painting of trees and the technique of pouncing.

Lining. The technique of lining, with straight edge or free hand, is to represent in two dimensions the complicated surfaces of the moldings in a cornice, chair rail, panel, or door trim.

Careful lining, in addition to local color, is done with a minimum of three tones: high light, shade, and shadow. Sometimes in showing a large cast shadow two shadow tones are used consisting of a light and dark shadow. The high light is cooler and, of course, lighter in value than the local color, while the shade and shadow are in warmer and darker tones.

The order of lining for a panel or cornice is determined after first studying a cross section of the molding and the direction of the light that would reveal the molding if it were real. The position of a window or artificial-light sources are clues for fixing the general direction of light for each wall in the set. If the paneling is for a stock set that will be used in many positions, the light source is standardized as if it were coming from above and left of the surface (Figure 9–3).

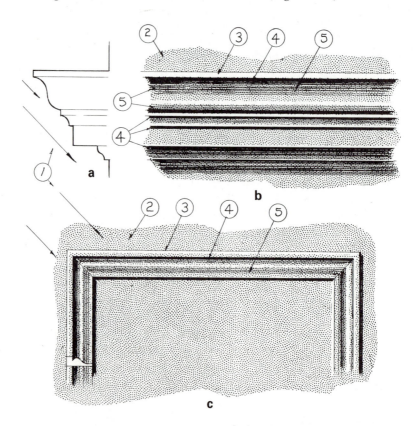

FIGURE 9–3

Lining Techniques

(a) Profile of cornice to be painted. (1) Assumed direction of light. (b) Lining of cornice molding. (2) Local color. (3) Highlight. (4) Shadow, darkest tone. (5) Shade. (c) Lining of a raised panel molding.

Executing the Design

Texturing. To avoid the starkness of a single tone and to bring more depth to a flat surface, the painter uses various texturing techniques. Because stage lighting is from many sources most natural shadows and reflected-light tonalities are eliminated. Much of this natural variation of tonality has to be painted into the set through the use of texturing techniques.

One of the simplest texturing techniques is to wet-blend or scumble three or more tones of a color on a surface. Using three brushes, one in each bucket, the three tones are brushed or blended together on the canvas while the paints are still wet. The result is an impression of one color with more depth and quality than is found in a single flat tone. This technique is usually handled on a broad scale with subtlety or obviousness depending upon the contrast or harmony of the tones.

A scumbling technique can also be done over a dry surface by blending the tones together with a dry-brushing or feathering. Dry-brushing, as the name implies, is done with the tip of a relatively dry brush in order to cover the under surface only partially and thus let it show through. Feathering refers to the direction of the brush stroke. The brush is drawn from the wet surface toward the dry so that the stroke ends in a featherlike pattern.

Other texturing techniques on a smaller scale include sponging, stippling, spattering, combing, use of a paint roller, and spraying. Each technique creates an individual feeling of texture as well as blending the tones into a vibrant surface (Figure 9–4, pages 262–263).

All these techniques can be used to simulate the textural qualities of a specific material such as stone, plaster, wallpaper, and the like. Some materials, however, require texturing techniques that border on decorative painting; wood and wood graining are a prime example (Figure 9–5, page 264).

The painting of wood graining employs the same movement of color found in the other techniques. The grain pattern, of course, will vary with the type and use of the make-believe wood. Is it to be matched-grain walnut veneer on a late Empire breakfront secretary, or knotty-pine vertical paneling? Any attempt at realistic representation of wood graining on the stage should be preceded by a careful study of the real wood's color and grain characteristic.

If the wood is a door or door trim and should appear as a varnished finish, the graining can be glazed. Glazing, however, not only reduces the contrast between colors but also lowers their value. This must be taken into consideration in the preparation of the grain colors.

The glazing of grain that has a varnished finish can be accomplished in two different ways. The first method is to grain the surface first, then apply a glue, shellac, clear latex, or flat-varnish glaze. Of the three glazes, clear latex is the easiest to handle and gives the best results. The results, however, are hard to predict especially if there is a change of surface materials, as from wood to canvas or vice versa.

1   **2**   **3** ✳

4   **5**   **6**

FIGURE 9–4

Texturing Techniques

(1) Wet blending or scumble. (2) Dry scumble. (3) Spattering. (4) Combing or dry brushing. (5) Rag rolling. (6) Spraying. (7) Feather duster. (8) Paint roller. (9) Taped paint roller to add a pattern to texture.

A safer and easier approach is to put something with the paint (dry color) that will give a gloss and eliminate the necessity of glazing the surface at all. Scene paint can be mixed directly with a flat varnish, which serves as a binder as well as giving the paint a slight sheen. Liquid wax mixed with scene paint produces the same effect as does clear acrylic. Both are easier to mix than varnish or shellac. Either method can be brought into a higher luster by polishing with paste wax later. Glazed surfaces must be handled with caution, however,

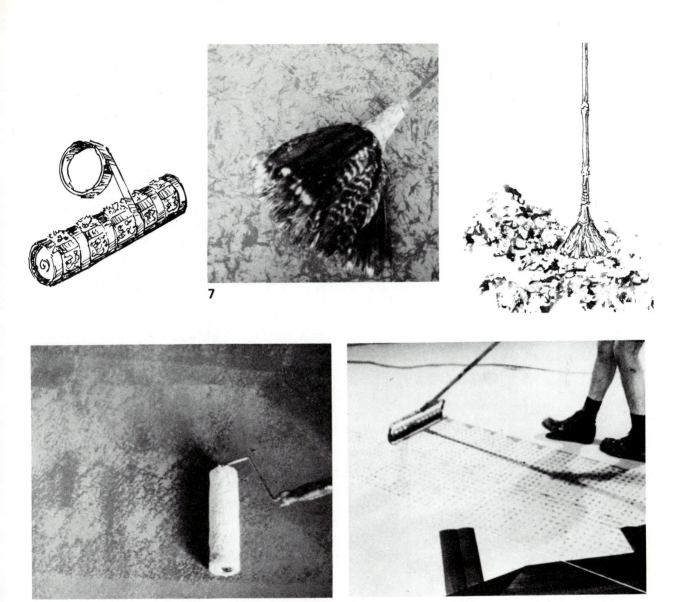

7

8

9

for there is always the danger of creating a surface that is too reflective; it then becomes annoying to actors and audience.

Foliage. The designing and painting of trees and foliage requires practice and a study of natural forms. The designer should first study trees in their natural state, perhaps painting them in watercolors. A designer will soon learn to see the overall mass of foliage, then the subdivisions of smaller units relating to the branches of the tree's structure, and finally, the detail of a single leaf. It is interesting to see how light reveals the forms, passing through translucent areas. Some branches catch light while others are silhouetted.

The conceptual treatment of a tree on stage can assume many forms. Stage foliage can be translucent, opaque, or textured. The tree style

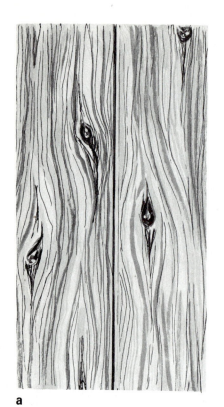

a

b

c

FIGURE 9–5
Wood-grain and Marble Texturing
(a) Pine grain. (b) Oak grain. (c) Marble.

may be real or stylized, or it may even be suggested with light patterns. Foliage can be carefully painted leaf by leaf or boldly painted in block areas loosely suggesting the organic form.

A landscape artist often starts with the darkest tones. Leaf masses in the shadow or silhouette are blocked in first. The lighter shades and highlights are painted last in opaque paint. If the foliage of the tree is to be translucent and painted with dyes, the technique is reversed: the lighter tones are painted first and the darker shades last.

Stenciling. The chief use of stenciling is for a painted wallpaper (or something similar) in which a design motif is repeated in an interlocking overall pattern. The cutting and printing of a stenciled design is the fastest and most effective method of repeating a small motif. After the means of interlocking the motif has been carefully figured out in relation to the size of the wall area, the motif is traced upon a sheet of stencil paper. Stencil paper is a tough, oil-impregnated paper especially for stencils. It is readily available in art shops or paint and wallpaper stores or can be made by applying a half-and-half mixture of linseed oil and turpentine to a heavy wrapping paper.

A well-planned stencil has at least one full motif with portions of adjacent motifs to key the stencil into an interlocking scheme. The size of the motif and the amount needed for interlocking the design more or less determines the size of the stencil sheet. Care should be taken

264

Executing the Design

not to create too large a stencil that might become awkward to handle. The motif is cut out of the paper with a sharp knife, razor blade, or Exacto knife. Be sure to leave some tabs within the open parts to support the loose ends and strengthen the stencil as a whole. Two or more stencils can be cut at one time, for it is wise to have more than one stencil, especially if there is a large area to cover. They can be alternated in use so as to minimize the tendency of a stencil to become damp and misshapen from hard use.

After the stencil is cut, it is framed at the outside edges with 1 by 2 on edge to further strengthen it and at the same time provide a shield to the spray if the paint is being applied with a spray gun. The stencil is coated with clear shellac or any water-repellent plastic spray as an additional protection from the water-soaking effect of scene paint.

The stencil print can be made by three different methods: by spray gun, by brush, or by sponge. The spray gun is fast but sometimes messy. Stenciling with a brush is slower. The brush should be kept fairly dry and stroked toward the center of the openings to avoid dribbles. The use of a sponge or soft cloth to apply the paint works best on an open stencil, for the print is purposely textured and not clean cut (Figure 9–6, pages 266–267).

Pouncing. Pouncing is another method of transferring and repeating a design motif. It is generally used when the motif is either too large for a stencil, doesn't repeat enough times for one to bother cutting a stencil, or is repeated in reverse. Pouncing differs from stenciling in that only the outline or cartoon of the motif instead of a painted print is transferred.

The pounce pattern is made by first drawing the design on a piece of wrapping paper and then perforating the outline with a pounce wheel. The best type of pounce wheel (Figure 9–6c) has a small swivel-mounted perforating wheel. It works better on a padded surface, such as a blanket or fold of canvas, than on a hard table top or floor.

After the design is perforated and the back-side rough edges are lightly sanded, the paper is laid on the canvas in the desired position. The pattern is rubbed with a pounce bag made of a thin material such as cheesecloth filled with a dry color or charcoal dust. The outline is strengthened after the pouncing with charcoal, paint, or dye, depending upon the painting technique to follow.

TEXTURED SURFACES

Although their value on the stage is debatable, textured surfaces are sometimes desirable. Important points to consider before texturing a surface are: (1) a textured surface cannot be reclaimed for a different use without re-covering the piece of scenery; (2) deeply textured sur-

a

b

c

① ② ③ ④

Executing the Design

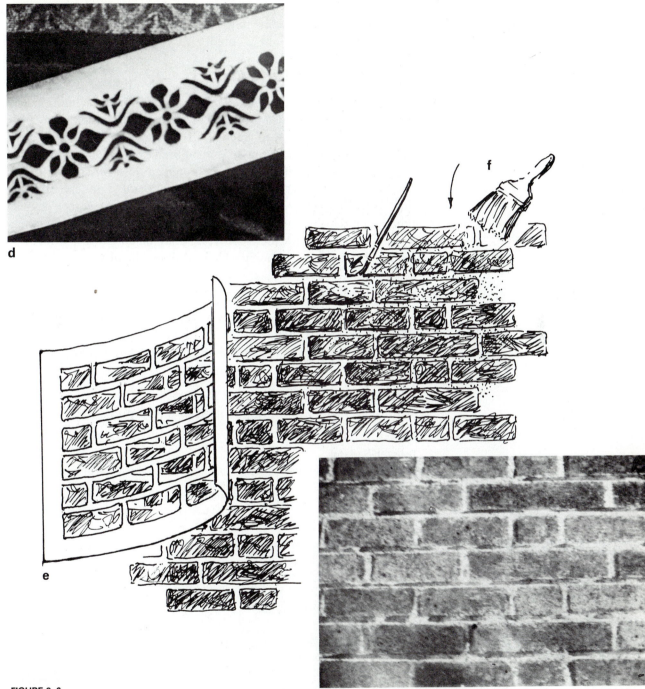

FIGURE 9–6

Stenciling Techniques

(a) Unframed stencil for dry-brush application. (b) Framed stencil for spray-gun application. Note how the stencil is keyed at the top and bottom. Because this stencil follows a vertical line it is not necessary to key it horizontally. (c) Pouncing: (1) Pounce, or perforated design. (2) Pounce wheel. (3) Pounce bag. (4) The pounced design transferred onto the canvas. (d) Border stencil. (e) Brick stencil. (f) Lining and spattering the stencil pattern. (g) Finished brick pattern.

faces will not stand excessive handling or wear; (3) unless the texturing is in a position on the stage to get the proper lighting (preferably side lighting), it may as well be painted.

TEXTURE COMPOUNDS

Spackle. The use of a prepared mixture of plaster and whiting called Spackle is the most familiar method of texturing. Because of the tendency of any texture coat to crack and flake off, Spackle is applied on a base of the same color unless, as an aging technique, some areas are purposely knocked off to reveal an undercoat of a contrasting color. The Spackle, which can be obtained at local paint shops, is mixed in cold water, colored with dye, and applied in about ¼-inch layers. While it is damp it may be roughed, combed, or grained for more texture. Sawdust, cork, or wood chips may be added to the mixture for extra texture. After the Spackle coat dries (about 24 hours), it can be shellacked and detail painted.

Sawdust Coat. Sawdust or wood chips can be mixed directly with scenic paint and applied as a texture coat. The size should be stiffened a little to bind the sawdust firmly. A sawdust coat requires less preparation and dries more quickly than Spackle but does not have as deep a texture.

Water Putty. Durham's Water Putty, a commercial surface repair mixture in powder form, can be used as a texture coat. It works best

FIGURE 9–7

Textured Surfaces

(a) Preparation for textured surface. Burlap, muslin, and random shapes of upson board glued to the surface of scenery units. (b) Appliquéd surface is covered with a mixture of joint cement and sawdust. After it is dry, the surface is painted in dark tones and then higher surfaces are dry brushed with lighter tones. For a deeper textured surface see Figure 7–21.

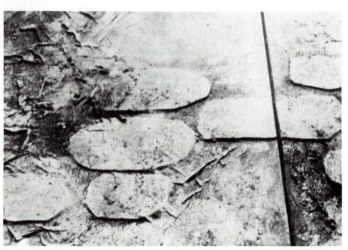

a

b

Executing the Design

on a hard surface (3-ply or wood) and can be combed or stippled into a deep texture. Although it dries off-white it can be colored either with dye during the mixing or with paint after it has dried. When hardened it is tougher than Spackle but still subject to chipping.

Joint Cement. A compound developed commercially to cement tape over dry-wall joints in house construction; it will hold a deep texture if a little white glue is added to the compound before application.

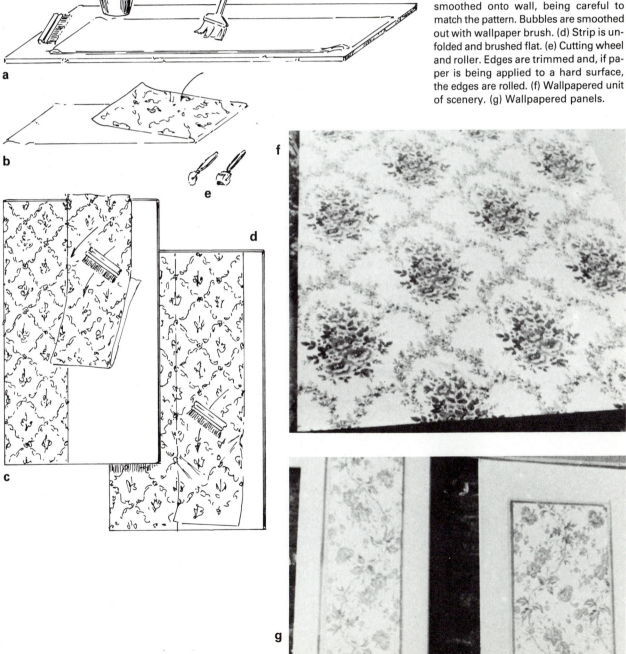

a

b

c

d

e

f

g

FIGURE 9–8
Wallpapering

Occasionally the scenic artist is expected to hang wallpaper. The surface, if canvas, should be sized and based with casein or latex paint. If the wall surface is hard a size coat is sufficient. (a) Wallpaper strips of approximate length face down on pasting board. Wheat paste is used for regular wallpaper, or vinyl paste on vinyl wallpaper. (b) Paste-covered strip is folded one third as shown. (c) Exposed portion of pasted strip is smoothed onto wall, being careful to match the pattern. Bubbles are smoothed out with wallpaper brush. (d) Strip is unfolded and brushed flat. (e) Cutting wheel and roller. Edges are trimmed and, if paper is being applied to a hard surface, the edges are rolled. (f) Wallpapered unit of scenery. (g) Wallpapered panels.

TEXTURE PAINTS

J.C. Penney Texture Paint. A prepared texture paint that is easy to apply. It holds a deep texture on a hard surface and is flexible enough to hold a medium texture on canvas.

Marble Coat. A texture paint made of marble dust that sets up extremely hard. It takes a deep texture, can be colored when mixing, and when hardened it can be handled with the minimum of chipping. It is the hardest of the prepared texture coats.

SURFACE MATERIALS

Surface materials used mainly for textural purposes exist in a variety of forms. Each has its special handling and individual effect.

Irish linen has, of course, long since disappeared from the American theatre as the standard covering for framed scenery. Its durability and excellent texture have not quite been replaced by the scene canvas now in common use.

Canvas, which is 8-ounce cotton duck, has been discussed (see "Size Coats") as a painting surface. It is the standard and most frequently used painting surface for all types of scenery. All other surfaces are limited in use to a special effect.

Muslin (unbleached) is the next most frequently used covering material. Although it lacks the texture and durability of canvas, its lightweight weave is useful for other purposes. As was mentioned, muslin in an excellent dye-painting surface for translucencies.

Scrim can be used as a painting surface in addition to its general use as a dye-painted transparency. It can also be used as a covering material if backed by canvas or some other opaque fabric.

Unbacked scrim can also be painted (dry brushed) with thin scenic colors. They are not as good as dyes, for they tend to stiffen the scrim, which is a disadvantage if it has to fold or roll. If large areas of scrim must be painted, it is best to use a spray gun to avoid stretching the scrim out of shape.

Filling Scrim. The open mesh of a scrim can be filled to create opaque areas. One means of doing so is to squeeze pure undiluted clear latex mixed with a casein color in a paste consistency onto the scrim to fill the mesh. A table mustard squeeze bottle is a good applicator. If the scrim is to be filled while it is on the floor in a horizontal position, steps should be taken to prevent the latex from sticking to the floor. Vis-Queen, a clear transparent plastic, is a good separator. More expensive premixed fillers are also available (for example, Roscofiller).

Burlap is frequently used as a covering material chiefly for its texture. Burlap should be backed or fastened to a firm surface, for it is made

a

b

c

FIGURE 9–9
Textured Details
Decorative details such as this rinceau pattern
are often in slight relief. (a) A cut-out of the border pattern is prepared in upson board. Thick
texture paint (J. C. Penney) is applied with a
cake decorator to the cutout, which is then glued
to the architrave position of the entablature. (b)
When dry, all recessed surfaces are stained dark
and later brushed with metallic gold paint. (c)
Final assembly.

of jute and may stretch or sag under a heavy coat of paint. Sometimes it helps to paint and dry burlap horizontally.

Burlap needs to be heavily sized to keep the color from "striking in." However, this may be a desirable effect if it is to be an old tapestry or wall hanging.

METHODS OF PAINTING

Scenery is painted in two different positions, horizontally and vertically. The various methods of painting are devised to facilitate either way of painting.

Horizontal Painting

Painting on the floor is the oldest and simplest method and requires the least mechanical assistance. Long handles on the brushes, charcoal-holders, and straight edges help to take the backache out of horizontal painting. The most essential requirement is lots of smooth floor space (preferably wood) and good overhead illumination (Figure 9–10).

Although some painting techniques are best employed horizontally, others are accomplished more easily in a vertical position.

FIGURE 9–10

Painting on the Floor

Extensive floor painting is made easier with the use of proper tools and the right type of brushes. (a) Individual paint-bucket carrier. (b) Long handles for the brushes. (c) Paint cart with palette area for mixing paint. (d) Straight edge with handle.

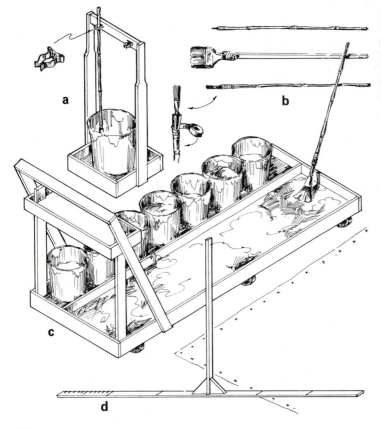

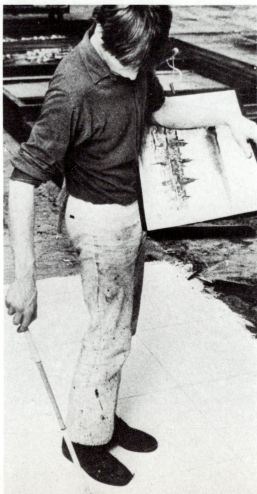

Stationary Frame and Boomerang

It is easy to fasten scenery against a wall or on a stationary frame along a wall, but it is not so easy to paint all areas without using a ladder. A rolling platform, or *boomerang*, as it is called, provides the painter with two or three painting levels (Figure 9–11).

Moving Frame

The moving paint frame which raises or lowers past the working level brings the greatest flexibility to vertical painting (Figure 9–11). The frame lowers into a well or to a second painting level. Some unusually high frames many times have two or three decks so that the painters can work at different levels at the same time.

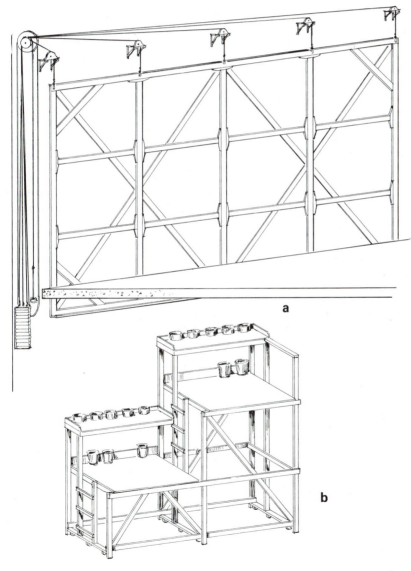

a

b

FIGURE 9–11

Vertical Painting Methods

(a) The moving paint frame raises and lowers into a well extending below the main working-deck level. Scenery is attached to the frame and is painted in a vertical position by raising and lowering the frame. (b) The boomerang, a stepped-level platform on casters, provides a variety of working levels for the painter.

TOOLS AND EQUIPMENT

The painter's most important tool is, of course, the brush. A good brush should have long bristles and a full shape. (Avoid hollow centers.) Pure bristles are so expensive, especially in the larger sizes, that many painters have turned to nylon brushes. A nylon brush with sandblasted tips is about half the price of the pure-bristle brush of the same size. The difference in price is offset by the slight disadvantage of nylon, for watercolor tends to run off nylon, causing it to hold less paint than a pure-bristle brush.

Because scene-painting brushes are used predominately in watercolors, the bristles should be rubber set. Some brushes set in glue are suitable for oil paint but will break down with the continued use in watercolor.

Types of Brushes

The types of brushes for scene painting are classified by the work they do, such as priming, base-coating or "lay-in," decorating, and lining (Figure 9–12).

The priming brush is the widest brush (6 to 8 inches). It holds a large quantity of paint, which makes it good for spreading size and prime coats quickly and efficiently.

The lay-in brush, about 4 inches wide, is used for the more careful painting of a base coat, blending, spattering, and similar techniques.

A decorating brush is from 1½ to 3 inches wide with a long handle. Sometimes called a foliage brush, it is used for most decorative painting, including tree leaves. The foliage brush is a pure-bristle brush made especially for scene-painting and is quite expensive. A sash tool, which is a long-handled brush for painting window sashes, is an inexpensive decorating brush.

Liners are also long-handled brushes varying in width from ¼ to 1 inch. Liners should have long pure bristles to perform well. A 1-inch sash tool can do limited lining, but there is no substitute for the smaller brushes.

Painting Tools

In addition to brushes and paints, the painter uses other implements to prepare, lay out, and paint scenery. Other necessary painting tools are:

1 Beveled straight edge (6 feet)
2 Rule or steel tape
3 Snap line (50 feet)
4 Charcoal stick and holder
5 Large compass (36 inches)
6 Tank sprays

Executing the Design

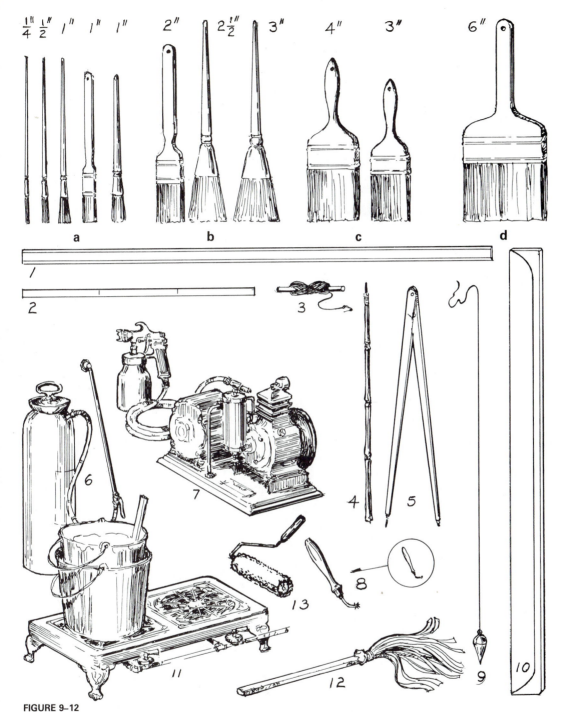

FIGURE 9–12

Brushes and Tools

Scene-painting brushes: (a) Lining brushes, flat and oval. (b) Decorating brushes. (c) Lay-in brushes. (d) Priming brushes. *Painting tools and accessories:* (1) Beveled straight edge. (2) Yard stick. (3) Snap line. (4) Charcoal and holder. (5) Large compass. (6) Tank spray. (7) Spray gun and compressor. (8) Pounce wheel. (9) Plumb bob. (10) Bow snap line. (11) Burner and double boiler for glue. (12) Flogger. (13) Paint roller.

7 Spray gun and compressor
8 Pounce wheel
9 Plumb bob
   Buckets (14 and 16 quarts)
   Small pots or cans (No. 10 cans)
10 Bow snap line (6 to 8 feet)
11 Burner and double boiler for glue
12 Flogger
13 Paint roller

RELATED MATERIALS

Aniline Dyes

Aniline dyes are available in almost all the standard colors. They are used for inking in outlines, thin wash glazes, translucencies, and for dip-dyeing fabrics.

Dyeing or painting with dyes is a different process than painting with scene paints. Scene paint changes the color of a surface by covering it with a pigment which is held in place by a binder. Dyeing, on the other hand, is a chemical process. The dye color becomes a part of the material it is dyeing. It is important that the dye and material have an affinity for each other, or a complete chemical action will not take place.

To dye cotton duck or muslin it is sometimes necessary to add a small amount of acetic acid or vinegar to the dye solution. The acetic acid increases the affinity of the cotton for the dye, causing the fabric to absorb more color from the dye bath. The addition of a small quantity of salt also helps to increase the amount of absorption. Salt counteracts the tendency of dyestuffs to go into solution, making it easier for the dye color to be absorbed by the material.

However, the presence of too much salt in the mixture, possibly from salted dyes or flameproofing compounds frequently mixed with the dye bath, can keep the dye from going into solution. All crystals must dissolve, or streaks of concentrated color will appear on the surface of the canvas. If the dye separates, the addition of some alcohol will insure a complete solution. Normally, the crystals go into solution in hot water without any trouble.

For extensive *dye-painting*—when painting a translucent drop, for example—the muslin is prepared with a starch size (see "Size Coats"). If the painting is being done on a fabric that cannot be starch-sized, such as velour or silk, a small amount of starch can be added to the dye mixture to keep it from spreading on the fabric.

Dip-dyeing is used mostly on small pieces of fabric, such as window drapes or tablecloths. Occasionally, large gauze pieces are dipped with excellent results.

The preparation of the dye for dip-dyeing is the same as for dye-painting except, of course, larger in quantity. It is important to be sure that enough dye has been mixed, for to run out of dye mix in the middle of a dipping is disastrous. The color of the mix should be checked by dipping a sample of the fabric before preparing it for dipping.

In preparation for dip-dyeing, the fabric is first dipped in water. If it is new material, it should be washed to remove the size. After wringing, the still-damp fabric is dipped into the dye mix. If it is a stage gauze, after squeezing or wringing out the excess dye, it should be stretched to dry, or hung in place and stretched back into shape as it dries.

An important thing to remember is that dip-dyeing will take out any flameproofing that might have been in the material. It has to be re-flameproofed later, or better still, flameproofed directly by a mixture added to the dye. The regular sal ammoniac and borax mixture can be cut to half strength by adding water and still give a satisfactory result. It is best, however, to run some test experiments under dipping conditions before taking a chance with a large piece.

Flameproofing

Canvas and muslin can be purchased already flameproofed, but if the scenery has been washed for reuse the canvas will have to be flameproofed again. A mixture of one pound of sal ammoniac, one pound of borax, and three quarts of water is an inexpensive flameproofing formula. It is brushed or sprayed onto previously dampened material for the best results. Sheer materials, such as scrim or bobbinet, should be dipped to ensure successful flameproofing.

Because flameproofing mixture is highly corrosive to metals, brushes and spray cans should, after use, be washed thoroughly in cold water. A small amount of acetic acid in the water helps to counteract the corrosive action.

Additional Supplies

There are some additional supplies that supplement dry colors, glue, and dyes which are directly associated with scene painting. Some have already been mentioned in relation to a particular painting technique. These supplies and their uses are:

White shellac	For glazes, water-repellent finishes, binder and hardener.
Alcohol	Solvent for shellac and speeds the dissolving of colors that are poor mixers.
Flat varnish	Glaze finish and paint binder.
Turpentine	Solvent for varnish and oil paints.

Liquid wax	Glaze finish and paint binder.
Metallic paints	Powder mixed with strong size or clear acrylic for metallic surfaces. All right for scenery, but not for props. Spray cans (Krylon) have harder finish, good for props, more expensive.
Glycerin	Added to paints for slow drying.
Lysol	Preservative.
Alum	For alum-size preparation.
Sal ammoniac	Flameproofing chemical.
Borax	Formula—1 lb borax, 1 lb sal ammoniac to 3 qts of water.

10

Handling Scenery

Confronted with a multiscene play, a designer has to consider, early in the planning, a method of handling the settings. A production scheme is developed from the numerous ways of moving scenery, and this scheme frequently influences the design concept. Consequently, the more designers know of the mechanics of the modern stage and of theatrical techniques for moving scenery, the closer they can come to fully realizing their design concept. This is especially true of some theatre outside New York, where the designer has to be clever to overcome limited funds and poorly equipped stages. Thus, technical knowledge can help a designer solve scenery-shifting problems with an ingenuity that often becomes inventively original.

METHODS OF HANDLING SCENERY

The four basic methods of handling scenery, in the order of their increasing complexity and additional construction are: (1) the moving or running of scenery on the floor; (2) the flying of scenery; (3) the moving of scenery on casters, including such large units as wagons and revolving stages; and (4) the handling of scenery through the stage floor by elevators.

How scenery is to be handled is influenced by four major factors: the play, the theatre and its stage, the design of the production, and the budget.

Play Structure

The form of the play and its plot structure are the primary influences on the handling of scenery. A play, for instance, may have many unrelated episodic scenes, a flash-back technique, several simultaneous scenes with continuous action, or the conventional three-act form. The structure of the play, in addition to determining the number of scenes or locale changes in their order of appearance or reappearance, also establishes the *kind* of change.

The most common interval for a change of scene is between acts. The act change, which can be as short as three minutes or longer than fifteen minutes, presents no great problem under optimum conditions, assuming the stage has adequate flying and offstage space. Even under limited stage conditions, an act change usually allows enough time to maneuver the scenery, although it may require more ingenuity and hard work.

A change within the act, or a scene change, can be as short as thirty seconds to as long as a minute and a half. A scene change, by necessity a fast change, can be handled in several different ways. It may be a hidden change, taking place behind a curtain, or without a curtain but hidden by a blackout. It may be a *visible* change (avista) made in full view of the audience with a display of theatrical magic, or by actor-stagehands openly moving elements of scenery as a part of the action.

In contrast to the other kinds of changes, the avista, or visible change, becomes a part of the play by calling attention to the movement of scenery. As a theatrical technique, it obviously fits only certain types of plays and production schemes.

Theatre and Stage

The shape of the theatre and the size of the stage, of course, have an important influence on the movement of scenery. The amount of flying space and equipment, the extent of offstage and wing space, the size of the proscenium opening, and sightline conditions obviously help determine the way scenery can be handled.

Some stages have more elaborate mechanical aids or stage machinery for shifting scenery, such as a built-in revolving stage, tracking and offstage space for full-stage wagons, or elevator stages. The existence of one or more of these mechanical aids in a theatre cannot help but influence scenery-handling techniques.

Traveling productions have other scenery-shifting considerations. Instead of one theatre and stage the designer has to consider the size and sightline conditions of many stages and auditoriums as well as the physical limitations and extreme portability expected of scenery for a road show.

Elaborate scenery-moving devices such as turntables and treadmills are sometimes duplicated in order to reduce the setup time in each theatre. Two crews are used. The first specializes in assembling shifting machinery, for example a turntable. They work in advance of the second crew, who run the show. When the run is finished, the second crew moves the show from theatre A to theatre B and onto preassembled turntable No. 2, leaving behind turntable No. 1. The first crew then returns to theatre A and moves turntable No. 1 in leap-frog fashion to theatre C, and so on.

Design and Scheme of Production

The scene designer reconciles the needs of the play and the stage and adds a third control, the scheme of production. The designer's production scheme stems from the kind of scene or locale change inherent in the play, the physical limitations of the stage, and a concept of the play's setting (Chapter 4). A designer cannot design a large production without thinking through, at least in basic terms, a method or scheme for handling the changes.

Budget

The influence of budget on the handling of scenery is felt directly through the control of the scale of the set designs and general size of the productions. Although the operational budget has little direct effect on the form of the physical stage, it does influence its operation through the provision of funds for an adequate production staff. A large stage with a small technical staff, for example, would limit the amount of scenery that could be efficiently handled.

An operational budget also is tied in with the estimated length of a run. A Broadway show with a prolonged run, for example, can reduce its operational costs by spending more money on costly mechanical aids to shift the scenery, thereby cutting down the number of stagehands on the weekly payroll.

The operational budget of a university or community theatre influences scenery handling in a slightly different way. The decision to use an extensive mechanical aid is based upon its reuse value for other productions. Cost is thus spread throughout the season's operational budget.

BACKSTAGE ORGANIZATION

Anyone who has seen a fast change from a backstage vantage point has been amazed by the teamwork and precision with which the large pieces of scenery, properties, lights, and actors seem to move. This is due, to some extent, to careful rehearsing, but largely it is the result of normal backstage organization and its division of responsibility. Under the coordinating management of the stage manager a production has two major divisions: acting and technical. The technical responsibilities are divided between the scenery, electrical, property, and costume departments.

Stage Manager

Once the production is on the stage, the stage manager becomes its field commander, fully responsible for the performance. The stage manager starts each performance, gives all cues, calls the actors, posts all daily calls, and is charged with maintaining both the production standards set by the director and company discipline onstage.

Stage Carpenter

Although taking cues from the stage manager, the master carpenter is in charge of the shifts, the rigging, and the general condition of the scenery. The crew, which is made up of assistant carpenters, grips (stagehands), and flymen, report to the master carpenter.

Master Electrician

The responsibilities of the master electrician include the hanging and focusing of lighting instruments, the maintenance of all electrical equipment, and operation of the switchboard for the lighting cues. Any movement of lighting equipment during a shift comes under the supervision of the stage carpenter but may be done by grips assigned to the electrical department.

Property Master

The property person's duties include the care and maintenance of the set and hand props, rugs, ground cloth, mechanical sound effects, and any trick device handled by the actors that is too small to be classified as scenery. The property master supervises handling of props during a shift, helped by grips assigned to the property department.

Sometimes electrified props cause what may seem to be double handling. A living room lamp, for example, is placed on the set by a member of the prop crew, but it is connected and lighted by the light crew. The offstage storage and visual appearance of the lamp is the responsibility of property people, while all electrical maintenance is done by the electrician. The division of responsibility is clearly and logically defined.

Executing the Design

Sound Technician

Although traditionally a member of the electrical department, the sound technician is established in many theatre organizations as a separate function. The increasing use of high-fidelity recording for a major portion of sound effects and incidental music warrants in many cases the creation of a sound department.

The sound technician is responsible for the recording and editing of each show tape as well as the operation of sound equipment for sound cues. He or she supervises the placement and installation of speakers and microphones, maintains all sound equipment, the stage manager's inner-communication, and, for a permanent producing group, might organize and service a sound-recording library.

FIGURE 10–1

Running Scenery

The running or "gripping" of scenery is the simplest handling method although, occasionally, the awkward shape or extreme size of a piece may require experience to handle it successfully. (a) "Walking-up" a stiffened two-fold. (b) "Edging-up" a single flat. (c) Running or "gripping" a single flat. (d) Making a lash. (e) Running a two-fold. (f) Three men running a top-heavy piece. (g) "Floating" down a single flat.

Handling Scenery

Wardrober

The care and maintenance of all costumes is the responsibility of the wardrobe supervisor (and, during a fast costume change, of the actors as well). The backstage organization of community and university theatres often places the supervision of make-up in the costume department.

RUNNING SCENERY ON THE FLOOR

Running or "gripping" of scenery is the simplest handling method and requires the least additional construction. If the units are strong enough to support themselves, usually the only additional support that is needed is horizontal stiffening, the vertical bracing of the piece in an upright position, and a quick and easy method of joining together the various parts of the set. Occasionally the extreme height of scenery combined with its traditional thinness makes it difficult to move for anyone not experienced in handling scenery.

The designer frequently must decide how scenery is to be handled before choosing the scale and relative weight of the design. Some of the many ways of handling single flats, twofolds, and partially assembled units of scenery on the floor are illustrated in Figure 10–1.

Stiffening, Bracing, and Joining

Because scenery has to travel in units of relatively small, lightweight sizes to get in and out of theatres, the joining or unfolding of these smaller units into larger shapes is crucial. The new larger shape requires stiffening to be safely handled in a shift.

A stiffener is usually a horizontal stiffening member (1 by 3 or 1 by 4 on edge) that is loose-pin-hinged into place as the set is assembled. A vertical stiffener is often called a "brace," especially if it is in the form of a "jack." Bracing and stiffening can take a variety of forms depending upon the shape and size of the scenery they are reinforcing (Figure 10–2).

The three different categories of joining are related to the portable nature of scenery and the degree of permanence of the joint. Elements of scenery may be joined together by fixed or permanent joining, by assembly joining, or by temporary joining. The kind of joint and its location are often important to the design, for the designer will seek ways to avoid a crack or open joint in a conspicuous area of the setting.

Fixed joining occurs as the scenery is being built (with use of nails, screws, and so on). A fixed hinged joint is made with tight-pin hinges so that larger units composed of several small pieces may unfold into larger sizes. The smaller pieces remain fixed together and travel or

Executing the Design

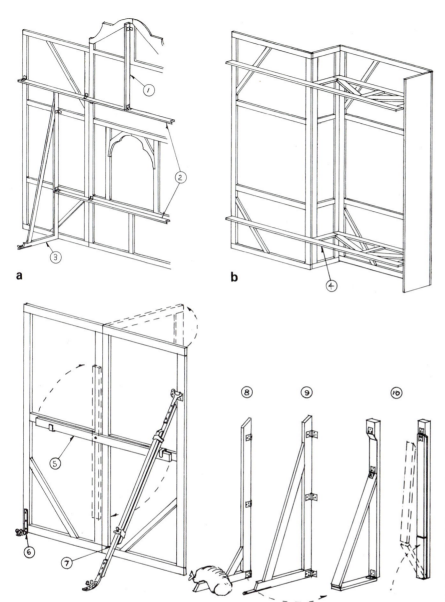

a

b

c

FIGURE 10–2
Bracing and Stiffening

(a) Stiffening a flat wall: (1) Vertical stiffener. (2) Horizontal stiffener. (3) Bracing or "jack." (b) Stiffening a jogged wall: (4) A framed stiffener which conforms to the shape of the wall. (c) Other bracing and stiffening techniques: (5) A swivel keeper bar and keeper hooks. (6) Bent footiron and stage screw. (7) Adjustable stage brace. (8) L-jack and sandbag (no stage screw). (9) Hinged jack. (10) Folding jack.

move folded from shop to stage, to be unfolded and stiffened into their final shape in the theatre (Figure 10–3a–d, page 304).

On the other hand, large areas of scenery may be made in separate small pieces to be assembled in the theatre. Loose-pin hinges, bolts and wing nuts, and turn buttons are some of the most frequently used methods of assembly joining pieces of scenery together into a larger unit. After a larger unit is stiffened and braced, it can be handled in its assembled form until time to leave the theatre (Figure 10–3e,f,m).

The temporary joining of scenery occurs at the time of the striking and making of a set during an act or scene change. The lashed joint

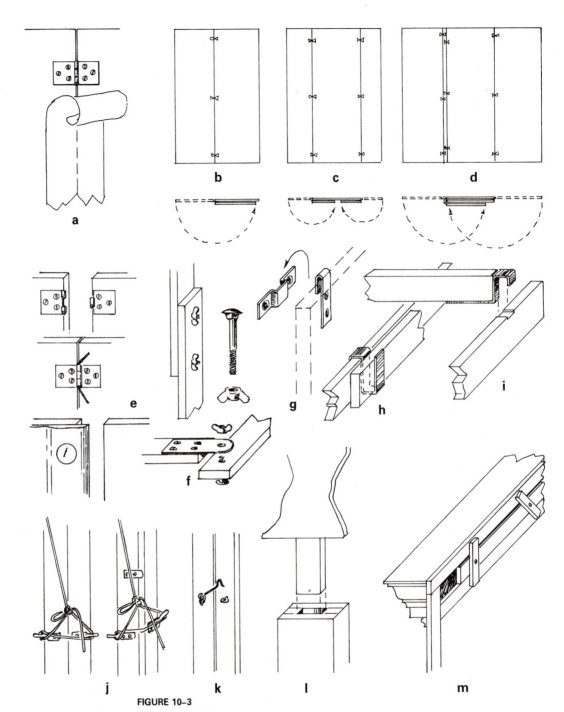

FIGURE 10–3

The Joining of Scenery

Fixed joining: (a) Tight-pin hinge and dutchman. (b) Two-fold, two flats tight pin-hinged together. (c) Three-fold, two jogs, and a flat hinged together. (d) Three-fold and "tumbler" to hinge three full-width flats together. *Assembly joining:* (e) Loose-pin hinge. (1) Front view of a lip as it is used to cover a flush joint. (f) Bolting. (g) Picture hanger. (h) S-batten hook. (i) Keeper hook on end of a spanner. *Temporary joining:* (j) Lashing, flush and around corner. Note stop cleat. (k) Hook and eye. (l) Tongue and socket. (m) Turn buttons.

Executing the Design

is the most common means of temporarily joining units of scenery. Loose-pin hinges, turn buttons, and hooks and eyes are some additional ways that scenery may be temporarily joined (Figure 10–3e,j,k).

A lip is often used to cover a flush temporary joint between two flats. The lip, which is made of a 4-inch strip of ¼-inch plywood with both edges beveled, is secured to an edge on the face of one of the joining flats. It is attached under the canvas with about an inch overhang (Figure 10–3a).

FLYING SCENERY

The designer is always interested in the size of the stage house and type of flying system, if any, over the stage. A good stage house that is designed to handle scenery in the air will have an adequate flying system and a generous amount of hanging space, which means a high and wide loft. The two common methods of flying scenery are the pin-and-rail and counterweight systems. Both are based on the presence of a gridiron over the stage to support the sheaves or pulley blocks and the extended control of the line-sets to one of the side walls. They differ in the complexity of the rigging, cost of installation, and the flexibility of use.

Gridiron

As the name implies, the gridiron is a grid or open floor of iron high over the stage. The average gridiron has at least three and sometimes four or five channels which run up and down stage and are spaced at approximately ten-foot intervals across stage. Across each channel opening, which is about six to eight inches wide, sit the sheaves that make up the line-sets. Each line, as it runs over the sheave, drops through the channel to the stage floor.

The space between the channels is floored with strips of 3-inch channel iron running parallel to the main channels. The channel-iron strips are set far enough apart to allow the spotting of additional sheaves for special spotlines (Figure 10–4c-1 and 2, page 288).

Recent gridiron designs employ the use of many more channels at about four-foot intervals. Swivel loft blocks are suspended above the gridiron floor from beams over each channel. The multichanneled gridiron is discussed in more detail later in this chapter and is illustrated in Figure 10–5 (page 289).

Line-Sets

A line-set refers to the grouping of three or more lines into a set to be handled as one line. The sheaves of a line-set are usually placed over each channel opening and are all at the same distance from the proscenium, thus forming a line parallel to the footlights.

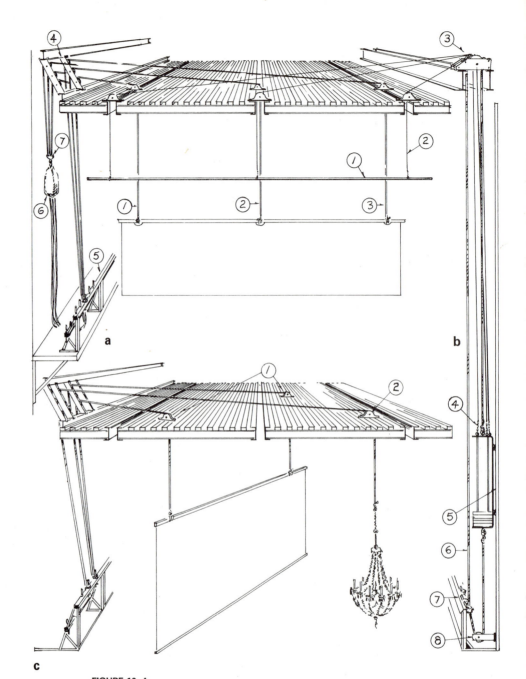

FIGURE 10–4

Flying Systems

(a) Pin-and-rail or "hemp" system: (1) Short line. (2) Center line. (3) Long line. (4) Tandem head block. (5) Double pinrail on fly door. (6) Sandbag counterweight. (7) Clew or "sunday" on a line-set. (b) Counterweight system: (1) Pipe batten, a fixed line set. (2) Hoisting cable for liftlines. (3) Head block, multi-grooved. (4) Trim chains at top of arbor. (5) "T" track. (6) Purchase line. (7) Lock and safety line on lock rail which may be on a fly floor or the stage deck. (8) Idler pulley. (c) A demonstration of the flexibility of the pin-and-rail system: (1) Spot sheaves used to fly a drop at an askew angle. The spotlines use the same or adjacent head blocks. (2) The separation of a single line from a line-set to use in a spot-sheave.

Executing the Design

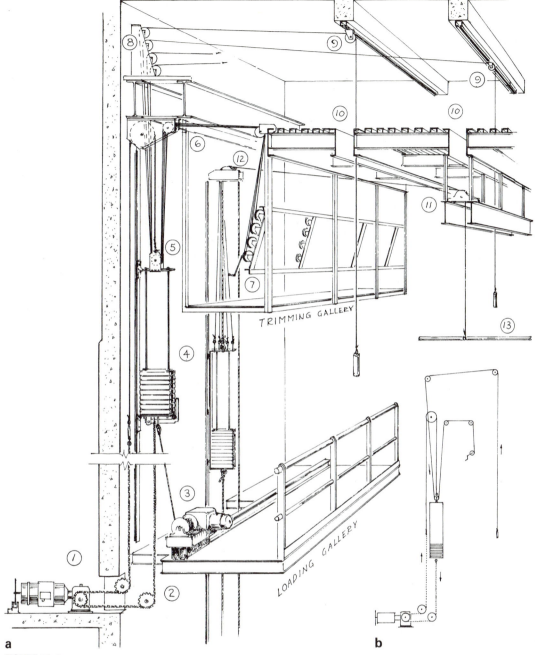

a

b

FIGURE 10–5

Motor-driven Spotline System

(a) A pictorial drawing of the rigging for one line-set: (1) Driver motor, a ¾ horse-power, variable speed d-c motor. (2) Sprocket and roller chain drive. (3) Movable bull-winch to retrieve empty arbor for loading. (4) Arbor. (5) Grooved pulleys to return the four liftlines to (6) Grooved muling pulley, the normal dead-tie position on the regular double-purchase counterweight system. (7) Trimming winches to adjust the length of each liftline. (8) Swivel head blocks in tandem mount. (9) Swivel loft blocks. (10) Channel openings at about 4-foot intervals. (11) Underslung channel supporting loft blocks for rigid line sets. (12) Head block for rigid line-set. (13) Pipe batten. (b) Schematic diagram of the motor-driven spotline system.

Handling Scenery   **289**

The number of lines in a line-set depends upon the number of channels in the individual gridiron. A stage with a wide proscenium opening might have as many as five lines in a set, while a small stage usually has only three lines to a set.

The lines are named by their length and position on the stage. The line nearest the control side (pinrail or lock rail) of the stage is called the short line and the line to the far side of the stage is the long line. The line in between is, of course, the center line. A four–line-set would have two center lines, a long center, a short center, and so on.

Pin-and-Rail

The pin-and-rail system is the older though more flexible of the two flying systems. It is a less costly installation but does require more skill and more people to operate. The hemp system, as it is sometimes called, uses ¾-inch manila rope for liftlines. As illustrated in Figure 10–4a, the individual line in a line-set (1), (2), (3) comes up from the stage, passes through the loft block, and travels horizontally to one pulley in the head block (4) located on the left or right stage wall. From the head block, in which the pulleys are mounted in tandem, the lines are brought together as a set and tied off at the pinrail (5). The lower rail of the pinrail is usually the trim tie for the drop in its "in" or working position, and the top rail receives the tie for the "out" or stored position. A line-set can be "clewed," or bound together (7), and sandbagged (6) to counterweight a heavy piece for easy handling.

As can be seen, the pin-and-rail system has great flexibility in its ability to use only part of a line-set, add a spotline to a line-set, or, in some instances, cross line-sets. The adding of a spotline employs a single rope and loft sheave occasionally placed in a remote position on the gridiron to fly a raked, or angled, piece of scenery (Figure 10–4c-1).

The chief disadvantage of a "hemp house" is in the number of hands required to run a show, as well as in the professional skill necessary to rig and safely counterweight heavy pieces of scenery. To the designer, this disadvantage is far outweighed by the greater design possibilities inherent in the flexibility of the pin-and-rail system.

The Counterweight System

Unlike the pin-and-rail system, which can separate lines or add a single line to the line-sets, the counterweight system uses fixed line-sets. Although the counterweight system was born in an era of box settings and raked scenery as theatrical styles, it is, paradoxically, rigidly based upon wing-and-backdrop staging. It keeps the lines in sets fixed to a pipe batten parallel to the footlights.

The system, as illustrated in Figure 10–4b, begins at the pipe batten (1) and the permanently attached wire-cable liftlines (2). Lifting the batten, the lines pass through the individual loft blocks at each channel, over a multigrooved, single-pulley headblock (3) and attach to the top of the counterweight arbor (4). The arbor is guided by a "T" track (5), or guy wire, and controlled by a separate purchase line. The purchase line (6) is also attached to the top of the counterweight arbor and passes through the large groove in the head block. It then turns toward the floor and after going through the lock (7) on the lock rail and around the idler pulley (8) fastens to the bottom of the arbor.

Pulling down on the outside purchase line lifts the arbor and lowers the scenery hanging on the batten. A corresponding amount of weight placed on the arbor balances the weight of the scenery. Although the counterweight system is easy to run with parallel scenery, it is less flexible because of the fixed line-sets. Most of the rigging time used to hang an angled or raked piece is spent in overcoming rather than using the system.

Winch Systems

There have been attempts in the past to electrify a flying system, for example, by using a single electric-motor-driven winch to lift a battened line-set. In this system, all the lines in the set are wound upon a single drum which turns in only one direction to lift the batten. A mechanical clutching and braking device disengages the drum from the motor, allowing the weight of the attached scenery to bring the batten back down to the stage floor. Its only advantage over the counterweight system is that it requires only one person to run the remote-control operation. The slow fixed speed and insensitivity of the system combined with the rather hazardous braking operation has caused the "electric batten," as it was once called, to fall into disuse.

A new but short-lived method of flying scenery was the synchronous-winch system designed by George Izenour. It was based on a radically different approach to the control and placement of the winches and on a unique gridiron concept. Although the synchronous-winch system promised to give the theatre both the flexibility of the pin-and-rail and the weight-lifting capacity of the counterweight system (plus the added feature of a centralized electronic control), it failed in its initial obligation—synchronization. Repeated attempts to improve the design only proved that the system could never provide a dependable trim over a group of winches. While the synchronous winch has fallen short of being the ultimate method for flying scenery, it proved moderately successful in installations where it was combined with both the pin-and-rail and counterweight systems. It functions best when limited to scenery loads involving a scattered pattern of liftlines and conditions where accurate trim is not critical.

Perhaps the most important by-product of the synchronous-winch venture is the new look of the gridiron. The two features that have improved the gridiron for any flying system are, first, the increased number of channel openings positioned to extend from wall to wall of the stage, and second, the use of swivel loft blocks suspended at head height over each channel.

More channel openings at closer spacing (about 4- to 5-foot intervals) make it easier to spot lines away from the playing area to positions offstage. This gridiron can provide a spotline in any area of the stage without involving a major rigging problem to overcome rather than extend a flying system.

The overhead swivel loft block allows a cleaner gridiron floor, which is normally filled with sheaves and fixed line sets. A single bolt or pin holds the swivel block in the overhead channel beam, making it a simple operation to loosen and slide up or down stage or move to another channel. An additional feature contributing to an uncluttered gridiron floor is the mounting of all fixed line-sets under the gridiron floor in a lower set of channels at the conventional spacing of a counterweight system.

An equally important outgrowth which, perhaps, made the new gridiron possible was the increasingly widespread use of ⅛-inch aircraft cable as liftlines in place of hoisting cable or hemp rope. The use of the smaller, more flexible steel cable resulted in smaller sheaves and working parts.

Motor-Driven Spotline System. In an attempt to bring to the counterweight system the flexibility of the pin-and-rail, Izenour and associates developed the motor-driven spotline system (Figure 10–5). It is apparent from the drawing that the basic concept of the system is to use an individual driver motor on a specially designed double-purchase counterweight line-set. The theory is that after the weight of the scenery on the individual arbor has been counterweighted, the work load on each motor would be more or less the same, thus keeping the horsepower of the drive small and eliminating the need for line-to-line synchronization within the working set. The electronic read-out of the exact position of the arbor has been retained from the synchronous-winch system, but the operational accuracy is greatly improved.

The driver, which is a variable-speed ¾-horsepower d-c electric motor, is placed either under the stage floor or behind the stage wall to minimize noise. It is attached through a quadrature reduction gear to the lower portion of the purchase line by a sprocket and roller chain drive and utilizes both dynamic and electromechanical braking.

The top of the arbor is not connected to the conventional fixed line-set arrangement but utilizes new spotline and trim adjustment features. The head block, although in tandem mounted position, is made up of individual caster-mounted swivel pulleys, which increase the "fleet angle" or spread of the lines in the set. The swivel head block, while allowing a wide spread to the pattern of the loft blocks in the line-set, is dependent upon the adjustable length of each line in the set to be completely flexible. The length adjustment of an individual

Executing the Design

line is accomplished by taking up each line on a trimming winch at the trimming gallery position. This small hand winch is located at what would normally be the end or "dead tie" of a single liftline in a double-purchase system.

To base the motor-driven arbor on a double-purchase counterweight system, however, gives the flyman cause for concern because of the tremendous demand for counterweights. The nature of the rigging produces a mechanical disadvantage of two to one, thereby creating a counterweight load twice the weight of the scenery it is lifting. The storing of counterweights and the endless job of loading and unloading an arbor are tasks that are not eliminated but are *doubled* when the double-purchase system is employed.

The advantages of the new motor-driven spotline system over the synchronous-winch are threefold. First, the number of lines to each motor is quadrupled; second, the synchronizing problem within a line-set is eliminated and improved between line-sets; and last, by using the double-purchase rigging, the top speed is doubled from 2 feet per second to 4 feet per second.

The motor-driven spotline system in its present form is not intended to be the sole method of flying scenery. An installation including twelve to twenty-four motor-driven arbors interspersed with several counter-weighted rigid line-sets, as well as the always flexible pin-and-rail line-sets, would be considered ideal.

RIGGING

Whether a stage is equipped with a pin-and-rail, counterweight, or synchronous-winch system, there are several flying and rigging techniques common to all systems. While many of the routine problems inherent in the older systems are eliminated in a winch system, certain specific problems pertaining to the movement of scenery in relationship to its hanging position and loft height will be forever present.

Stage rigging begins with the relatively simple process of hanging scenery and includes the more complicated maneuvers of breasting and tripping scenery elements. The handling of stage curtains (such as the traveler, tableau, and contour curtains) and the unframed drop are also a part of stage rigging.

Hanging Scenery. An early step in rigging is the preparation of scenery to hang by providing hardware or some other means of attaching the liftlines. Hanger irons or D-rings, which are used on framed scenery, should be bolted to a vertical member of the framing for greater strength. On extremely tall or heavy pieces two rings are used, the one at the top serving as a guide for the liftline which is attached to the bottom. To lift the load from the bottom is not only a safer

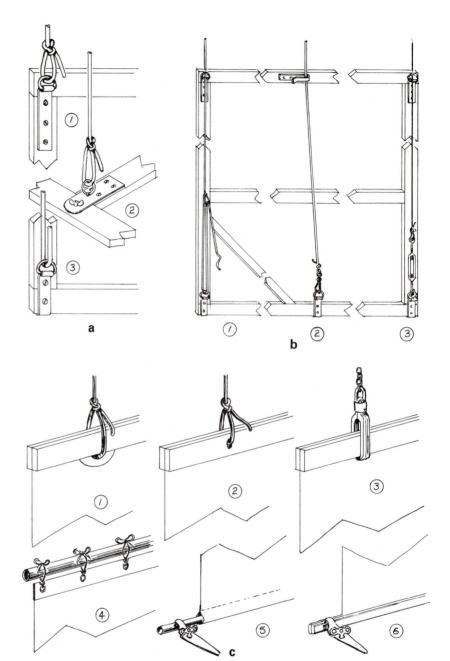

FIGURE 10–6

The Hanging of Scenery

(a) Hanging hardware: (1) Top hanger iron, straight. (2) Ceiling plate and ring. (3) Bottom hanger iron, hooked. (b) Trim adjustments: (1) Trimming hitch using hemp rope of sash cord. (2) A snatch line. The snap hook on the end of the liftline makes it possible to unhook a flown piece of scenery. (3) Turnbuckle on wire cable, another way to adjust the trim of a flown piece of scenery. (c) Various methods of hanging a drop: (1) Tie around top batten. (2) Tie through batten. (3) Drop holder. (4) Tie-lines to pipe batten. (5 and 6) Floor stays.

procedure, but it also provides a convenient position to trim each line (Figure 10–6a,b). The use of the turnbuckle or trimming hitch as illustrated is, of course, not necessary on the pin-and-rail system, for each line can be brought into trim from the flyfloor. The same is true of the winch system, which can "inch" an individual line into exact trim.

Unframed pieces of scenery, such as drops and borders, are hung from their top battens and can be fastened to a pipe batten or can be picked up by a set of lines in many ways (Figure 10–7c). The long thin

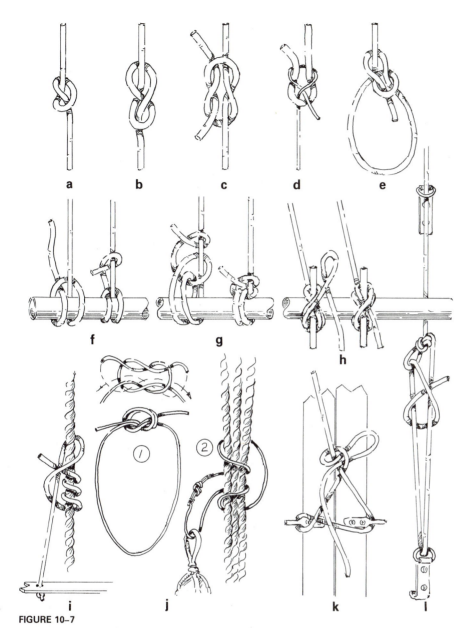

FIGURE 10–7

Knots Used in Stage Rigging

(a) Half hitch or overhand knot. (b) Figure eight, used to put a knot in the end of a line to keep it from running through a pulley or eye. (c) Square knot, for joining ropes of the same size. (d) Sheetbend, for joining ropes of different sizes. (e) Bowline. A fixed loop used on end of liftline through ring. (f) Clove hitch on a batten, finished with a half hitch. It grips firmly under tension, but is easy to adjust or untie. (g) Fisherman's bend. Excellent for a tie onto a batten. Not as easy to adjust as the clove hitch. (h) Half hitch over a belaying pin. Used as tie-off on pinrail. (i) Stopper hitch, made with a smaller line in the middle of a larger rope. The safety line on the counterweight lock rail uses a stopper hitch on the purchase line. (j) Sunday: (1) A method of joining the ends of a small loop of wire cable without putting a sharp kink in the cable. (2) The loop is then used to clew a set of rope lines together so as to counterweight them with a sandbag. (k) Lashline tie-off. (l) Trimming hitch, to adjust the trim of a hanging piece of scenery.

Handling Scenery   295

batten requires numerous pickup points, about every six feet (see "Bridling"), to keep it from sagging and thereby spoiling the trim of the drop.

Knots. Safe stage rigging requires the use of many familiar knots. The stage technician and the designer who has to supervise rigging should both be skilled in the use of at least a few of the knots and hitches that appear in stage rigging. Some of the most frequently used knots are illustrated in Figure 10–7 along with notations of their uses for stage rigging. A more detailed and comprehensive manual of knots and splices can be found in the catalogues of cordage companies (see bibliography at the back of the book).

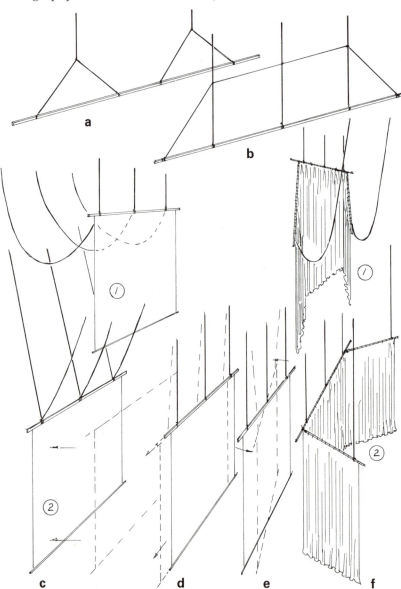

FIGURE 10–8

Bridling and Breasting Techniques

(a) A simple bridle. (b) A bridle of a set of lines to support the overhang of an extra-long batten. (c) Breasting a drop up- and downstage: (1) Stored position. (2) Working position. (d) Breasting across stage. (e) Twisting a batten into an angled position. (f) Breast lines on the side-tab arms of a drape cyc.: (1) Stored position, arms hanging down. (2) Working position, arms pulled by breast lines into spread position.

Executing the Design

Breasting Scenery. Regardless of which flying system is being used, two pieces of scenery cannot occupy the same space at the same time, although the designer may wish they could. Consequently, it sometimes becomes necessary to hang a unit away from its working position and rely on breasting lines to bring it to its proper location. A breasting line (sometimes called a checkline or restraining line) is usually dead-tied at one end to the gridiron or side-stage position and fastened to the scenery at the opposite end. When the piece is in its flown position the breasting line is slack, but as the piece comes into its working position the breasting line becomes taut and breasts the unit off dead-center hanging. (Several breasting maneuvers are illustrated in Figure 10–8c–f).

Bridling. The bridle is a simple rigging used to spread the load picked up on one line (Figure 10–9a,b, page 298). The number of lines in a set can be reduced, or the number of pickup points increased by the bridling technique.

Tripping Scenery. Many rigging problems result from too low a loft or the complete absence of one. Tripping, which can only be used on soft or semisoft scenery, is one way of flying scenery in a limited space (Figure 10–9d–f). By picking up the bottom of a drop as well as the top, it can be flown in half the height necessary to clear a full drop. The height can be further reduced by picking up the drop a third of the height off the floor and thereby tripping it in thirds.

An extreme variation of tripping is to roll a drop on its bottom batten or drum at the bottom edge (Figure 10–10a–c, page 299). The old opera house "oleo" drop was rigged in this manner, and it still is a good way of flying a drop on a stage with reduced flying space.

Levitation. The flying of objects or persons, as if in defiance of gravity, requires special rigging. To create a workable setting for flying actors or objects, a designer should be familiar with the special rigging that is required for a flying effect. The right kind of background, properly planned exits and entrances, and atmospheric lighting can serve to mask or camouflage any exposed support wires and highlight the illusion.

To create the illusion of floating in space, an object must be supported on as fine a wire as possible so that the support will disappear from view at a distance. Lightweight objects, such as a bat or bird, can be supported on fishing line (20-pound test), which becomes invisible at a very short distance. The size and strength of the support wire to fly an actor, however, is more critical. The kind of wire used depends upon whether or not it has to go over a pulley. Wire rope, such as airplane strand, is extremely flexible and strong for its size—$\frac{1}{16}$-inch aircraft cable tests at 500 pounds and has a recommended safe load of

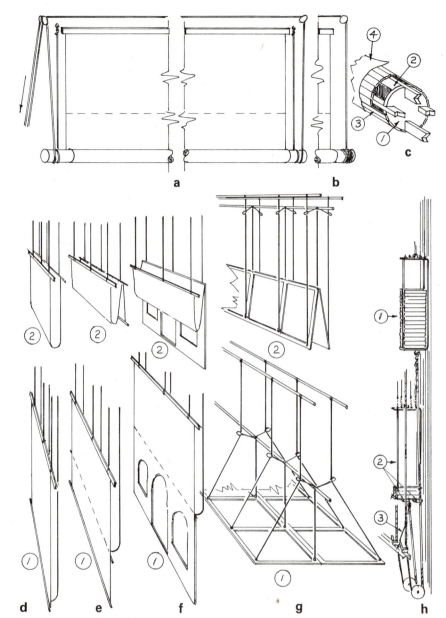

FIGURE 10–9

Tripping Techniques

(a) The "oleo" drop, which rolls on the bottom batten or drum. Note: the rigging of the rope gives operator a mechanical advantage of two. Drop is made with horizontal seams to make roll flat. (b) An alternate rigging. Liftline has equal turns on the end of drum, in reverse direction of drop. When liftline is pulled, it unwinds as the drop winds onto the drum and thus rises. (c) Detail of drum construction: (1) Contour pieces. (2) Linear stiffeners. (3) Lattice slats. (4) Padding and final cover. (d) Tripping a drop; back set of lines is attached to bottom batten: (1) Working position. (2) Stored or tripped position. (e) Tripping in thirds. Upstage batten is attached at one-third height of the drop off the floor: (1) Working position. (2) Tripped position. (f) Tripping a drop which has the lower portion framed: (1) Working position. (2) Tripped position. (g) Book ceiling rigging: (1) Working position. (2) Booked position. (h) Carpet hoist, handling a variable load: (1) Free arbor (no batten attached) carrying counterweights. (2) Working arbor with batten that handles the variable load. (3) Free arbor is locked off at top position allowing working arbor to run free of counterweight after load has been removed from batten (rigging is only usable on light loads of 100–150 pounds).

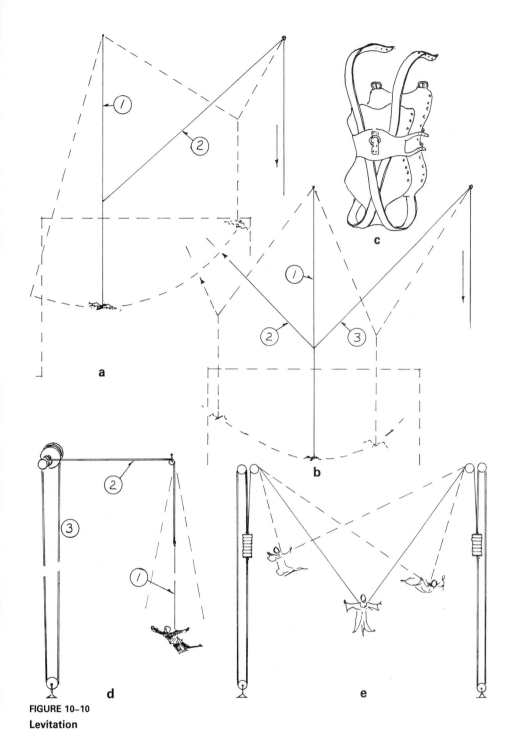

FIGURE 10–10

Levitation

Types of rigging for flying objects or persons: (a) Pendulum and breast line: (1) Pendulum line, placed off center, has long arc when it is swinging free of breast line. (2) Breast line shortens arc and lifts object up and out of sight. (b) Pendulum and double breast line: (1) Pendulum line. (2) First breast line. (3) Second breast line. (c) Harness for actor. (d) Schematic diagram of Joseph Kerby's flying rig for Peter Pan: (1) Piano wire lead. (2) ⅛-inch wire cable feeds through swivel sheave at gridiron to a drum off stage. (3) Operating line turns large drum, thereby achieving a mechanical advantage and avoiding the use of counterweights. (e) Double-line counterweighted rigging provides a very flexible lateral movement although the actor has to remain attached to rig.

100 pounds; 20-gauge (.045-inch) piano wire has great tensile strength (500 pounds) for its size but is a single strand and cannot be run through a pulley. Any sharp bend or kink quickly weakens piano wire to the point of breaking.

Flying Apparatus. A flying apparatus begins with a harness for the actor. It is made of strong webbing and is fitted about the legs and chest like a parachute harness. The ring, to which the wire is attached, is placed approximately in the middle of the back, a little above the actor's center of gravity. The harness, of course, is worn under the costume with only the ring protruding.

Variable Load. Of the many rigging problems experienced with conventional flying systems, the most annoying is the variable load or unbalanced condition resulting from the removal of part or all of the scenery load from a set of lines. The deus ex machina, descending with a live cargo of gods or goddesses and then ascending to the heavens empty, is an example of a variable load.

If the weight variation is not too great (100–150 pounds), the carpet hoist is one way of compensating. The counterbalancing weight to the variable load is not directly attached to the load-bearing batten but is handled on a separate purchase line. Figure 9–10h shows a carpet hoist rigging on a counterweight system. The counterbalancing weight is on the first arbor (1), which is a "free arbor," meaning that it is not attached to a batten or line-set.

The second arbor (2), which carries only enough weight to bring the arbor down, is attached to the batten handling the variable load. The extending hooks on the bottom of this arbor pass under and engage the first arbor to utilize its weights. Note that when the first arbor is locked or tied off in an up position at the moment the variable load is being removed, the second arbor is free to disengage and return to a down position. The counterbalancing weight can be returned to the second arbor by reversing the procedure and unlocking the first arbor.

Any larger weight variation has to be handled by an electric floor winch or a hand winch which provides a mechanical advantage to offset the unbalanced load condition. The synchronous-winch system, of course, eliminates any variable load problem because it is based upon a direct, not a counterbalance lift.

The type of rigging for levitation depends upon the movement of the actor both in the air and on the floor. For instance, the Rhine Maidens in Wagner's *Das Rheingold* keep flying in a lateral pattern back and forth across the stage. On the other hand, Peter Pan, in addition to flying in all directions, also lands and walks about on the floor.

Most flying apparatus is based on a pendulum action whether the pattern of movement is lateral or in all directions. The pendulum is usually placed off center for a lateral movement and center stage for a free-movement pattern. Figure 10–10 illustrates, schematically, the various pendulum riggings as well as other methods of flying actors, some of which require two wires and more complicated apparatus.

Curtain Rigging

The actions or movements of a stage curtain, other than raising or lowering on a batten, are classified into three groups. A curtain can be drawn horizontally from the sides, tripped diagonally into a tableau shape, or tripped vertically into the varied patterns of a contour curtain.

Traveler or Draw Curtain. The conventional action of a traveler curtain is the drawing together of two curtain halves on two overlapping sections of track. The track guides the carriers, which are attached to the top edge of the curtain at about one-foot intervals. The draw line is fastened to the first or lead carrier, which pushes or pulls the rest of the carriers to open or close the curtain. The many track and carrier designs and the rigging of the drawline are illustrated in Figure 10–11.

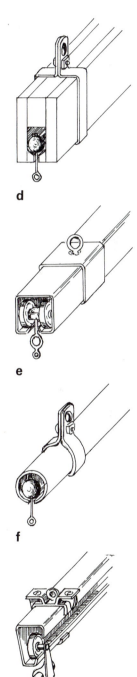

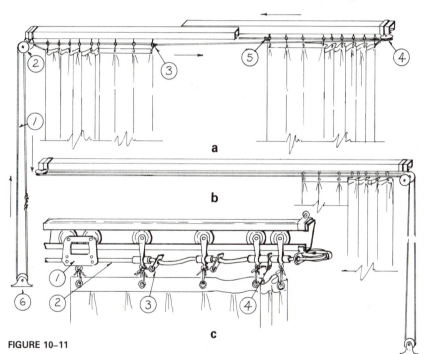

FIGURE 10–11

Traveler Curtains and Tracks

(a) Rigging of a draw curtain or two-way traveler: (1) Draw line. (2) Head block. (3) Lead carrier on downstage curtain, fastened to drawline. (4) Change-of-direction pulley. (5) Lead carrier on upstage curtain also fastened to drawline. (6) Floor block. (b) One-way traveler curtain. (c) Detail of rear-fold attachment. All carriers move at once with drawline and curtain folds offstage rather than bunching onstage. (1) Lead carrier. (2) Drawline. (3) Rear-fold attachment grips drawline until it is straightened up by bumping into the next carrier. (4) Drawline now passes through the rear-fold attachment. Various Types of Traveler Tracks and Carriers (right): (d) Wooden track with ball carriers. (e) Square steel track with double-wheel carrier. (f) Round steel track with ball carriers. (g) Triangular steel track with side opening and single-wheel carriers. (Vallen, Inc.)

Sometimes a one-way traveler is needed, which means that instead of coming from opposite sides of the stage the curtain is drawn on stage from one side on a single long track (Figure 10–12b). Also illustrated is a rear-fold device which causes all carriers to move at once rather than being pushed or pulled by the lead carrier (Figure 10–12c).

Tableau Curtain. Like the traveler, the tableau curtain is made up of two curtain panels hung, with a center overlap, from a single batten. Each panel is lifted or tripped by a diagonal drawline attached to the central edge, about a third of its height off the floor, that runs through rings on the back of the curtain to a pulley on the batten (Figure 10–12a). The tableau has a quicker action than a traveler, but doesn't lift completely out of sight unless the batten is also raised at the final

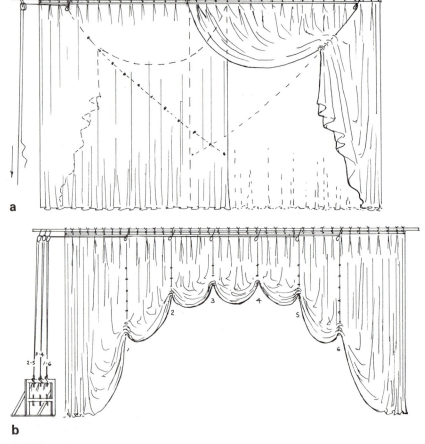

a

b

FIGURE 10–12

Front Curtain Riggings

(a) Tableau curtain. (b) Contour curtain. (c) Brail curtain. (d) Detail of the liftline rigging for a brail curtain. The same technique can be applied to the contour curtain and, when placed on the diagonal, to the tableau curtain. (1) Pierced wooden or fiber balls to keep rings from fouling. (2) D-ring sewn at regular intervals to (3), a vertical strip of webbing usually attached to the curtain seams. (4) ⅛-inch aircraft cable lift line. (5) Curtain weight to bring the curtain back to its down position.

Executing the Design

moment. Because of its picturesque quality, the tableau curtain drape is frequently left in view as a decorative frame for the scene.

Contour Curtain. The contour curtain is made in a single panel with great fullness, usually about 200 percent of the curtain width. The curtain, which is made of thin or soft material to drape well, is tripped by a series of vertical drawlines attached to the bottom edge of the curtain and running through rings on the back to pulleys attached to the batten. By varying the lift on certain lines the bottom edge of the curtain takes on many different contours (Figure 10–12b).

Brail Curtain. The front curtain in a no-loft stage is sometimes rigged as a Brail curtain to achieve a faster and more desirable lifting action

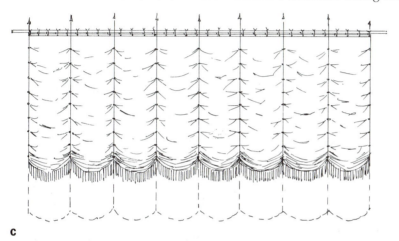

c

d

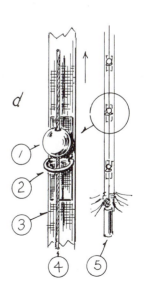

than the slower side motion of a traveler curtain. In this case the amount of lift on each drawline is equal, eliminating the need for the abnormal fullness of a regular contour curtain. To add a decorative quality the curtain may have the horizontal fullness which is obtained by gathering material on the vertical seams, thereby producing a series of soft swags (Figure 10–12c).

SCENERY ON CASTERS

Moving a three-dimensional piece of scenery on the floor is made easier and faster if it is mounted on casters. Such mounting can vary from a single caster on the edge of a hinged wing to the large castered platform or wagon to move an entire set. In between are such techniques as castered tip and lift jacks and outrigger wagons for rolling.

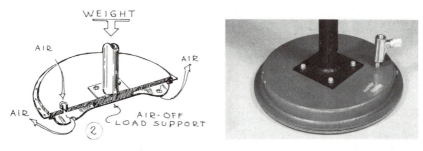

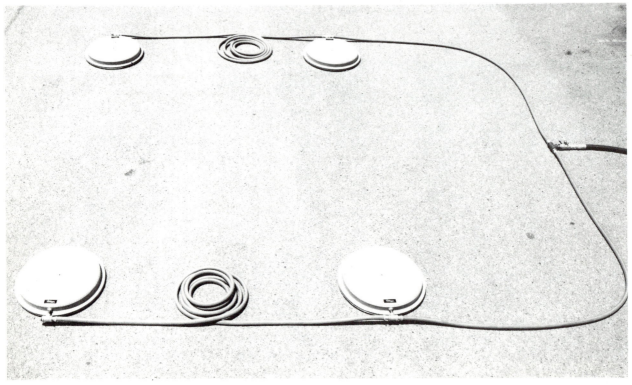

Executing the Design

Casters

The stage places special demands on casters. A good stage caster should first of all run quietly, which requires a rubber wheel or a rubber-tired wheel. The rubber-tired wheel is a better long-time investment because the tires can be replaced as they wear.

Secondly, the caster wheel should have as large a diameter as possible (3½ to 4 inches). A wagon on 4-inch diameter caster wheels rolls with little effort and is not as easily stopped by small obstructions such as rugs, padding, ground cloth, or lighting cables.

Casters are of two general types: those made to move freely in any direction and those made to move in a fixed direction. The swivel caster has a free action that allows it to move in any direction, while the fixed caster is limited to one direction in a guided or tracked movement. It is more economical to invest in swivel casters which, when necessary, can be blocked into a fixed position for a tracked movement

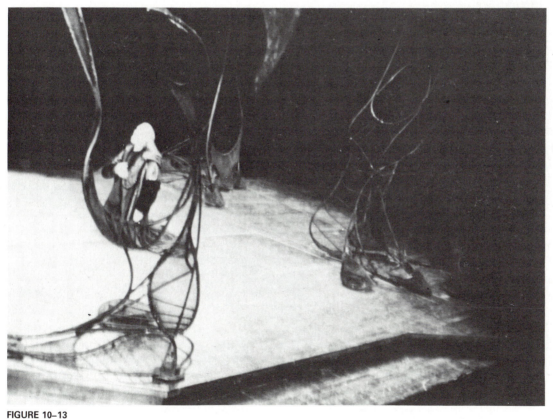

FIGURE 10–13

The Air Bearing Caster

(Photos, page 304) Basic air bearing unit. (Sketch) Cross section of the unit showing the flow of the compressed air into the flexible inner tube and out through the vent holes, thereby lifting the object on a film of air for a frictionless movement. (Above) Theatrical use of the air-bearing caster for a production of *The Tempest* at the Tyrone Guthrie Theatre. The upstage supports function as a pivot. (Caster photos courtesy of Rolair System, Inc., Santa Barbara, Calif.; Guthrie production photo—Bakkom)

Handling Scenery

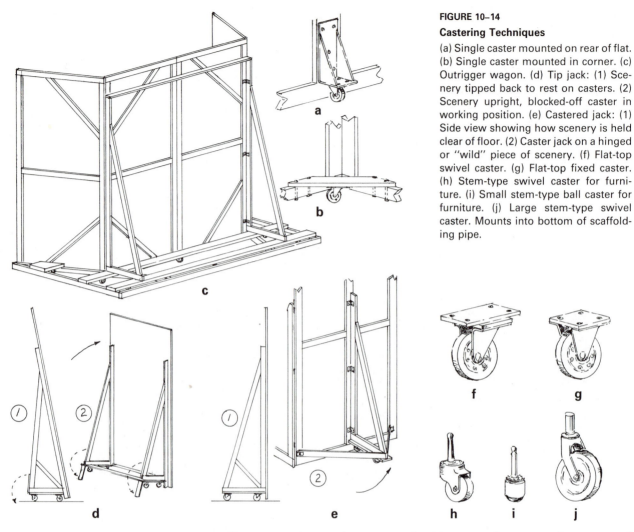

FIGURE 10–14

Castering Techniques

(a) Single caster mounted on rear of flat. (b) Single caster mounted in corner. (c) Outrigger wagon. (d) Tip jack: (1) Scenery tipped back to rest on casters. (2) Scenery upright, blocked-off caster in working position. (e) Castered jack: (1) Side view showing how scenery is held clear of floor. (2) Caster jack on a hinged or "wild" piece of scenery. (f) Flat-top swivel caster. (g) Flat-top fixed caster. (h) Stem-type swivel caster for furniture. (i) Small stem-type ball caster for furniture. (j) Large stem-type swivel caster. Mounts into bottom of scaffolding pipe.

(Figure 10–14). An alternate method is to purchase swivel casters and a matching set of fixed forks without the wheels. The wheels of the swivel casters may be removed and inserted into the forks to create a fixed caster that is easier to mount.

Lift and Tip Jacks

Mounting scenery on casters in order to make it move easily creates a paradoxical problem of anchoring: preventing the unit from moving at an undesirable moment. Lift and tip jacks are methods of lifting or tipping a piece of scenery from a standing position onto casters to move (Figures 10–14d, 15e,f). The scenery, however, sits firmly on the floor when it is in its working position.

Another way to anchor a castered platform or a bulky three-dimensional piece of scenery is to attach it to units that are sitting on the floor or by tipping the piece onto casters mounted on its offstage or upstage edge (Figure 10–15d).

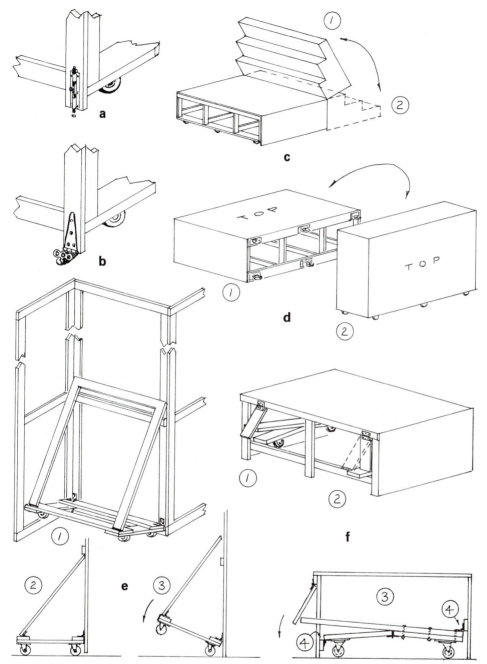

FIGURE 10–15

Methods of Stabilizing Castered Units

(a) Barrel bolt fits into hole in stage floor. (b) Hinged footiron and stage screw. (c) Portion of platform not on casters: (1) Steps hinged to castered platform folds on top for easy movement. (2) Unfolded and resting on the stage floor, the steps stabilize the platform unit. (d) Casters on offstage edge of platform: (1) Platform in working position, casters on back edge. (2) Platform is tipped onto casters to move. (e) Lift jack: (1) Pictorial view of lift jack. (2) Side view showing jack lifting scenery. (3) Jack released, scenery rests on floor. (f) Lift jack under a platform: (1) Jack released. (2) Jack depressed to lift platform on casters. (3) Sectional view. (4) Note eccentric hinging.

Outrigger Wagons

An outrigger wagon is essentially a pattern of castered jacks or braces around the outside of a set or portion of a set. The scenery remains on casters. It is a skeleton wagon intended to brace and caster the scenery. The action of the scene is played not on a wagon but on the stage floor (Figure 10–14c).

Wagons

The low-level platform (6 to 8 inches) on casters or wagon can carry a large portion of a setting including the set props. Large wagons often carry an entire setting, which can swiftly and easily move into place for a scene change. Although requiring ample floor space, the wagon is a flexible and efficient method of handling scenery.

Wagon Construction

Wagon construction is basically the same as platform construction. The caster in a sense becomes the post of the platform. If the casters are mounted on caster planks (2 by 6 feet or 1⅛ by 6 feet) the minimum span between supports can be increased. The caster plank, in addition to providing a sturdy mount for the caster, serves as a cleat for the top to increase the overall strength of the wagon. Normally, unless the wagon is to carry an extremely heavy load, such as a piano, the spacing of casters at 3-foot intervals is sufficient to remove any noticeable deflection.

Stock wagon units made in a convenient size (3-by-6-foot or 4-by-8-foot modules) for handling are pin-hinged together to make larger units (Figure 10–16). Although stock wagons use more casters than are necessary for the total area, the flexibility of arrangements and handling and ease of storage justify the module system.

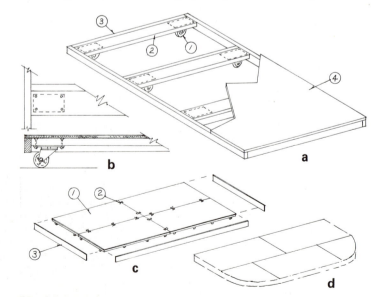

FIGURE 10–16

The Wagon Unit

(a) Construction of a stock wagon: (1) 4-inch swivel casters. (2) 2 x 6 caster planks. (3) 2 x 3 frame. (4) 4 x 8-foot, ¾-inch 5-ply top. (b) Cross section. (c) Large wagon made up of stock units: (1) Stock unit. (2) Units pin-hinged together. (3) Facing boards. (d) A different shape made of three stock wagons and two special corner pieces.

Executing the Design

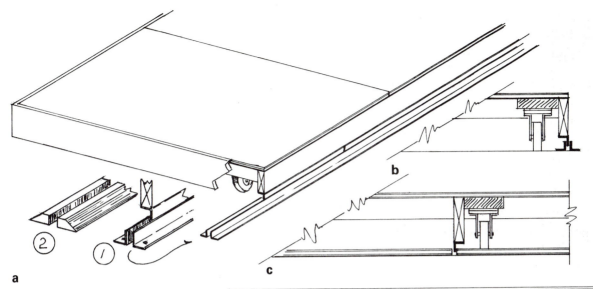

a

b

c

FIGURE 10–17

Tracked Wagon Movement

(a) Tracks on top of the stage floor. (1) Steel angle irons. (2) Beveled wood which though subject to wear is quieter than steel on steel. (b) Section detail. (c) Section showing track cut into the stage floor. In an elaborate tracked-wagon scheme such as those diagramed in d, e, and f, a temporary stage floor is installed with space beneath the track groove for cables to drive the wagon unit by hand winch from an offstage position. Types of Tracked Wagon Movements: (d) Transverse movement. (e) Split transverse wagons and a large single wagon moving up- and downstage. (f) Multimovements: transverse, diagonal, as well as up- and downstage.

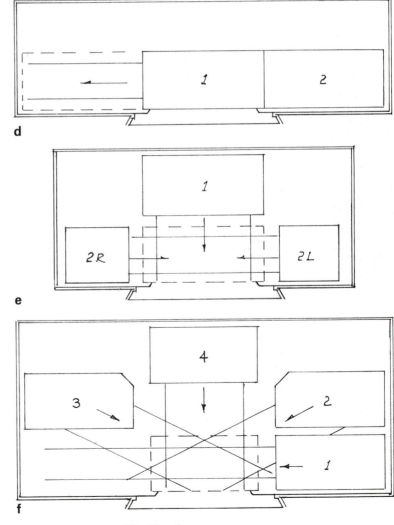

d

e

f

Handling Scenery   **309**

Wagon Movements

Aside from the free movement of a wagon carrying a full or partial set, there are several controlled or tracked movements that can become a scheme of production for handling scenery entirely on casters. The scheme may be based upon a pair of alternating wagons that allow the scenery and props to be changed on the offstage wagon while the alternate wagon is in the playing position. The transverse, jackknife, and split-wagon movements operate on this principle (Figures 10–17, 10–18).

When there are small sets in a production it is sometimes desirable to keep each set intact on separate wagons. The stage then becomes packed with wagon sets and the shifting is accomplished by shuttling each wagon into position. The pattern of movement varies with the size and shape of the sets and their order of appearance in the play.

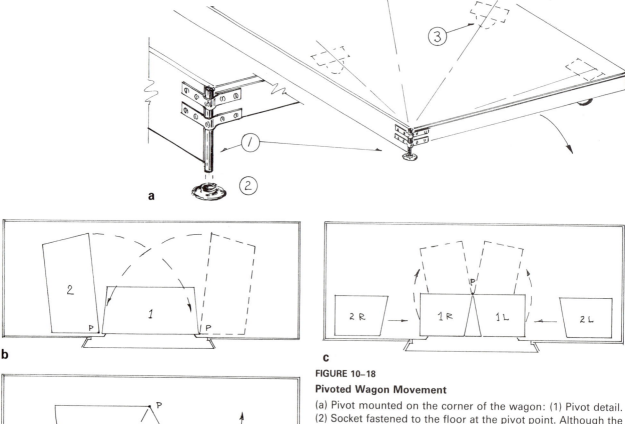

FIGURE 10–18

Pivoted Wagon Movement

(a) Pivot mounted on the corner of the wagon: (1) Pivot detail. (2) Socket fastened to the floor at the pivot point. Although the pivot and socket positions are often reversed in a turntable installation, it is best under the illustrated conditions to place the socket on the floor. A corner pivot, besides being an awkward mounting position, may also have to bear weight because the nearest caster is usually about four feet away. (3) Fixed caster set perpendicular to radius. (b) Jackknife wagons. (c) Type of jackknife in combination with split wagons. (d) Pivoting a segment of a circle, semirevolving.

Executing the Design

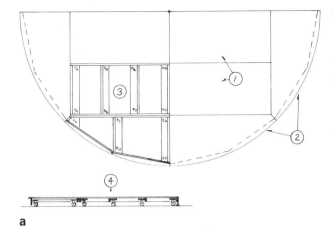

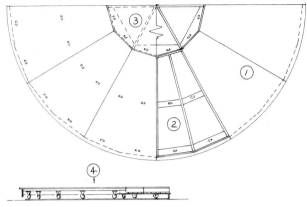

a

b

FIGURE 10–19

The Revolving Stage

A portable revolving stage or turntable can be built many ways. Shown here are two methods. (a) Turntable made up of stock wagon units with special-shaped wagons to form the curve of the outside edge: (1) Stock wagon. (2) Special wagon to complete circle. (3) Casters blocked perpendicular to radius. (4) Section. (b) Turntable made of wedge-shaped units around central core. Fewer casters are used, creating less noise: (1) Basic wedge-shaped unit. (2) Top removed showing the position of casters. (3) Central core. (4) Section.

Turntable Construction, Reverse Castering (c)

(1) Basic wedge-shaped unit. (2) Central core, ball-bearing pivot. (3) Single unit viewed from underneath to show framing. (4) Bearing surface in path of casters, ¾-inch 5-ply or particle board. (5) Casters mounted on the stage floor in patterns that are the same circumference as the caster-bearing surface on the underside of the turntable. (6) Spirit level and rotating bar to check the level of each caster mount to insure a steady, level rotation. Although the reverse caster turntable takes longer to assemble, it is quieter and easier to turn than the conventionally castered unit.

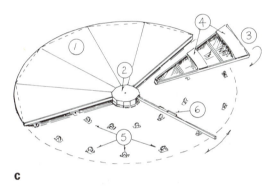

c

The Revolving Stage

Another controlled movement is that of a castered unit around a fixed center: a revolving stage. Such a stage that is not permanently built into the stage floor is similar to the wagon in structure. To remain portable, a turntable is made in small pie-shaped sections which are bolted or pin-hinged together (Figure 10–19). The casters are mounted in a pattern to properly support each unit and are fixed in a position perpendicular to a radius line drawn through the point of attachment. If the casters are carefully mounted, the turntable will revolve about its pivot point with very little effort.

Another method of assembling a portable turntable is to reverse the normal position of the casters under the table and place them upside down on the stage floor (Figure 10–20). The casters are placed in concentric circles as bearing points on a prepared rolling surface on the under side of the table. Each caster is shimmed to the same height to

Handling Scenery   **311**

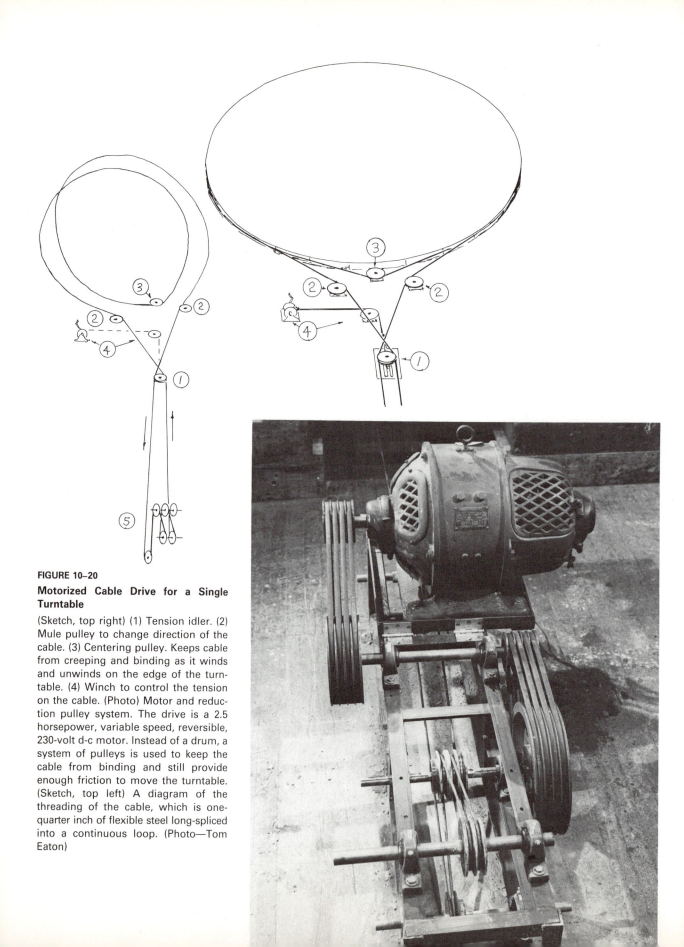

FIGURE 10–20

Motorized Cable Drive for a Single Turntable

(Sketch, top right) (1) Tension idler. (2) Mule pulley to change direction of the cable. (3) Centering pulley. Keeps cable from creeping and binding as it winds and unwinds on the edge of the turntable. (4) Winch to control the tension on the cable. (Photo) Motor and reduction pulley system. The drive is a 2.5 horsepower, variable speed, reversible, 230-volt d-c motor. Instead of a drum, a system of pulleys is used to keep the cable from binding and still provide enough friction to move the turntable. (Sketch, top left) A diagram of the threading of the cable, which is one-quarter inch of flexible steel long-spliced into a continuous loop. (Photo—Tom Eaton)

insure a level turntable floor. Although the assembly time is longer and the table is a little higher off the stage floor, the result is a smooth-running, quiet turntable. Figure 10–20 illustrates the assembly steps as well as the cable-drive and motor method of powering a revolving stage.

Single Turntable. The revolving stage as a basic device can have a variety of sizes and uses. The most familiar is the large single turntable. Unless the stage is especially designed for a large turntable, its diameter is limited by the depth of the stage. If the stage happens to be shallow in proportion to the proscenium opening, a single turntable will leave an awkward corner in the downstage right and left positions. Attempts to fill the area with a show portal or with hinged pieces on the turntable which unfold and mask the corner more or less negate the basic function of the single revolving stage (Figure 10–22a, page 316).

Two Turntables. A shallow stage is adaptable to the use of two turntables that either touch in the center or are held slightly apart. This method removes the awkward corners of the single turntable, but it creates a design problem—that of joining all the sets in the center (Figure 10–22b).

Three Turntables. Occasionally, a large turntable is combined with two small disks in the downstage right and left positions. The small disks either carry scenery related to the large set in the center or are small independent sets. The production scheme for *I Remember Mama* designed by George Jenkins used this technique (Figure 10–22e).

Ring and Turntable. A great deal more variety of movement is achieved by using a ring and turntable combination. The ring and turntable are individually powered so that they can turn in the same direction at identical or different speeds, or they may revolve in opposite directions. The possible combinations of fixed units on the ring and turntable are almost endless. If the changes are made avista it becomes a delightful scheme of production. The settings for *Protective Custody* designed by Peter Larkin were handled in this manner (Figure 10–22f).

Two Rings and Two Turntables. Although less adaptable to revolving fixed units than the single ring and turntable, two rings around two turntables are a very flexible method of changing elements of scenery and properties. This was demonstrated in the production of *Lady in the Dark* designed by Harry Horner. With the help of flown pieces of scenery, the settings were able to blend from one scene to the next in full view of the audience (Figure 10–22c).

Semirevolves and Combinations. The remaining variations of the revolving technique are the semirevolving stage and combination of a turntable and a wagon.

The semirevolving stage is a portion of a ring or turntable tracked to swing in half an arc and then return to its original position (Figure 10–22g). The semirevolving stage may be large or small, used singly or in pairs, or, in some cases, combined with a turntable.

A combination of revolving and lateral movements can be accomplished by building a turntable into a full-stage transverse wagon (Figure 10–22d). This combination works best when a portion of one set is reused many times during the show. The lobby of *Grand Hotel,* for

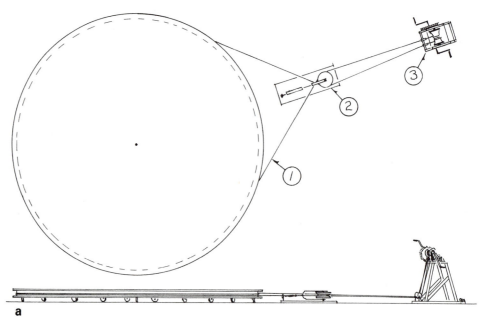

a

FIGURE 10–21

Methods of Powering a Single Turntable

(a) Cable and winch: (1) A spliced cable with one turn around the outside edge of the turntable is held taut by (2) a tension idler and powered by (3) a hand winch. (b) Motor-driven turntable: A reversible and variable-speed electric motor underneath a highly mounted turntable. (1) Motor. (2) Reduction gear box. (3) Spring loaded friction drive wheels, or bevel gears. (4) Drive ring for friction drive, or gear ring for bevel gear drive. (5) Raised, fiber-padded track for fixed casters. (6) Steel channel-beam framework. (7) Roller-bearing pivot. It should be noted that both a and b turntables are usually surrounded by a raised temporary stage floor flush with the top of the turntable. (c) Drive wheel power unit. An example of a turntable on top of the stage floor with an eccentric pivot position making the use of the ring drive or cable drive impracticable: (1) Basic platform structure on fixed casters perpendicular to radius. (2) Pivot located off the center of the platform. (3) Wheel drive power unit hidden by (4) superstructure of the setting. (5) The path of rotation. (6) Components of the power unit: 5-horsepower, reversible d-c motor linked to (7) gear reduction box. (8) Drive wheel which turns the platform by friction drive off of the stage floor. It is connected to the gear box by a sprocket and roller-chain drive. (9) Ball-bearing socket fixed to the platform. (10) Turn indicator. A self-synchronizing motor (SELSYN) mounted on the wagon with its shaft fixed to the pivot and wired to a companion motor mounted offstage. An arrow attached to the shaft of the second "selsyn" becomes a pointer to indicate the exact position of the turntable. (11) Dial face of the turn indicator. (Original installation designed and constructed by George B. Honcher and Pat Mitchell).

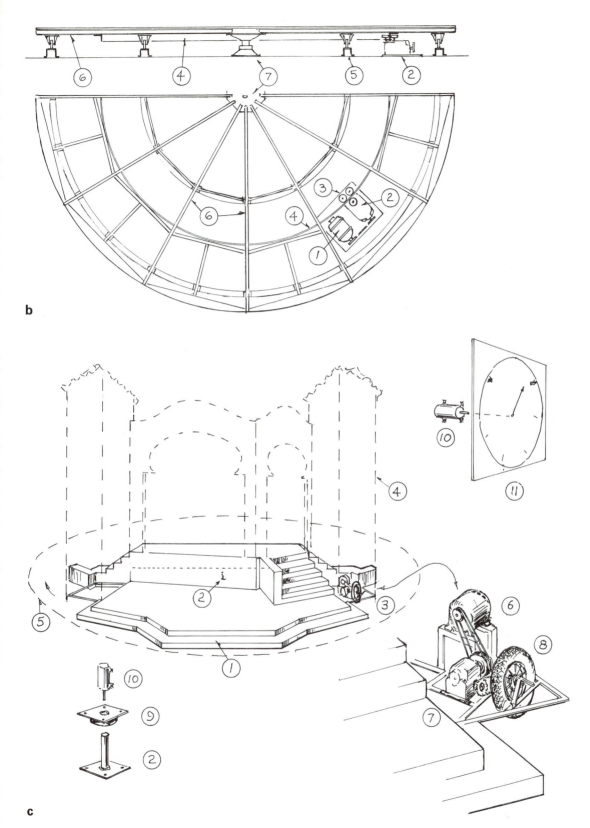

b

c

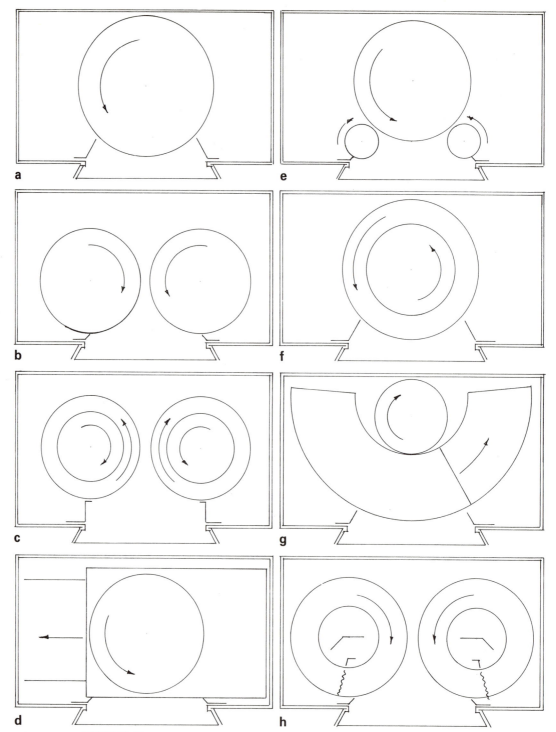

FIGURE 10–22

Turntable and Ring Combinations

(a) Single large turntable. (b) Two small turntables. (c) Two small turntables with rings. (d) Single turntable in a transverse wagon. (e) Large turntable with two small disks. (f) Large turntable with ring. (g) Semi-revolving ring-segment and small turntable. (h) A pair of rings.

Executing the Design

FIGURE 10–23
Elevator Stage
A backstage view of the elaborate elevator installation at the Metropolitan Opera House, New York.

example, was saved in this manner. Most of the lobby settings remained on the left side of the wagon while a portion moved on the turntable. The smaller rooms and other scenes in the hotel occupied by the remainder of the turntable and were moved into better sightlines by sliding the wagon to the left.

The scheme can be varied by setting the turntable into the center of the wagon and having elements of scenery on both sides instead of one side.

Handling Scenery   317

ELEVATOR STAGES

As a means of moving scenery, the elevator stage requires the maximum amount of stage machinery. Unless the theatre is in the position to make constant use of the equipment, or the elevators have a second function such as a scenery and property lift to remote storage areas, the installation is extravagant. With few exceptions (The Metropolitan Opera, Radio City Music Hall, and similar presentation houses), the normal legitimate theatre in the United States has little use for the elevator stage as a method of changing scenery (Figure 10–23).

The financial organization and scale of production of numerous state theatres in Europe make the elaborate elevator stage a more feasible method of handling scenery than could be supported by the unsubsidized theatres of the United States.

Small Elevators and Traps

Although the average stage may not have an elevator system, it usually has a portion of the floor area made in sections or "traps" that may be used to raise small elements of scenery through the stage floor. The traps can be removed to give access through the stage floor into the trap room below. Entrances by stairs or ladder can be made from below through such an opening. Trap openings are made between transverse beams that run parallel to the footlights. As a result, the designer has great freedom in planning the size and position of an opening running across stage. Openings running up and downstage, however, are limited by the transverse beams.

The construction of a temporary lift which can be used for scenery or actors is shown in Figure 10–24a. Although the elevator platform can be as large as a single trap opening, the example illustrated is smaller. A larger elevator would require more guides and liftlines. Figure 10–24b is an example of an elevatorlike mechanism under the stage floor designed to raise a small curved batten supporting a curtain. The technique is probably very similar to the methods used to raise a curtain out of the front pit of the Roman theatre.

The Elevator Floor

The elevators designed to move scenery should not be confused with the short-run elevators used to shape the stage floor in some of the more recent theatres. In this instance, sections of the stage floor can be raised or lowered by elevators to make levels or pits but are not used to move scenery. They can, however, be considered as a means of changing the appearance or form of the stage floor, thus creating a new scene without moving scenery.

Executing the Design

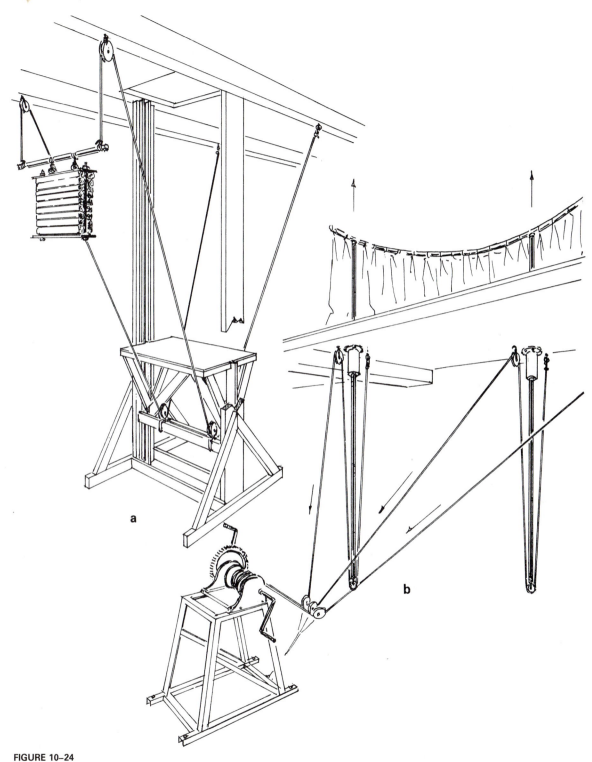

FIGURE 10–24

Beneath the Stage

(a) Counterbalanced disappearance elevator. (b) A highly specialized example of rigging through the stage floor to raise a curtain batten up from the floor.

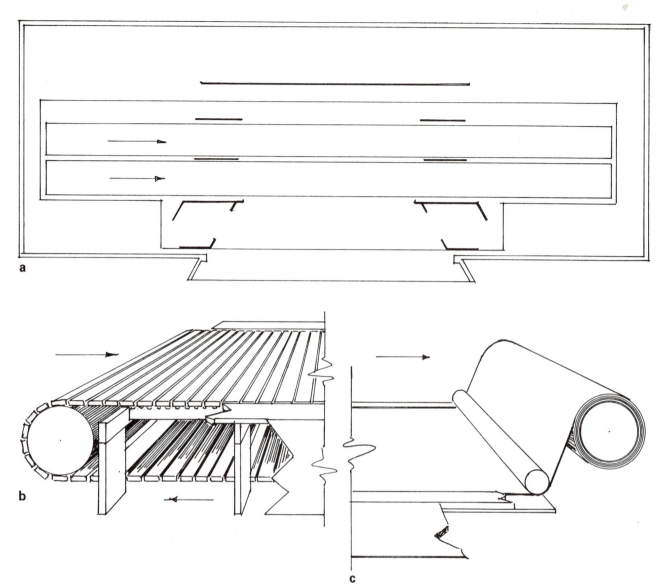

FIGURE 10–25

The Treadmill

(a) Plan of a pair of treadmills showing the amount of offstage space needed to use treadmills effectively. (b) Construction diagram of a treadmill with continuous action. (c) A simpler treadmill design; however, action is not continuous. The belt moves first to the left and then to the right as it winds or unwinds off the drums.

The Treadmill

Like transverse wagons, the treadmill moves laterally. A conveyor-belt method of moving light scenery and properties to the right or left, it consists of an endless horizontal belt or flexible surface made of narrow wooden slats held apart by two drums on opposite sides of the stage. Like a conveyor belt which is taut around the drums, the treadmill surface will move to the right or left when the drum is being

Executing the Design

turned. Because the belt has to return underneath itself, the space has to be kept clear of obstructions. This limits the width or height of the platform, for the wider the belt the higher the platform to allow for the framing of the span over the returning belt. The usual belt is about four feet wide, which keeps the platform about a foot in height (Figure 10–25b).

A unique variation of the treadmill, developed by the Tobin Lake Studios in South Lyon, Michigan, allows a vinyl plastic belt to rest on the floor. The belt is rolled onto motor-driven drums at opposite sides of the stage. The action is limited in one direction by the length of the belt, which is not endless but rolls up on one drum or the other. In addition to not requiring extensive platforming, this type of treadmill has the added advantage of being extremely simple to install (Figure 10–25c).

11

Stage Properties and Effects

In addition to large scenic background elements of the stage setting, the designer is responsible for the design and selection of stage properties and smaller bits of scenery used by the actors. This may vary from finding a marble-topped Louis XV console table to making an exotic sofa for a Turkish Cosy Corner, or from borrowing a Victorian tea set to fashioning tree leaves. Whether borrowed or constructed, each property must be carefully coordinated into the design composition and adjusted to the production scheme and must also be checked for size and ease of use by the actors.

Stage properties are in essence the design details of the overall visual composition. Although the visual significance of properties applies more specifically to a realistic interior setting than to an exterior or abstract scene, their contribution cannot be overemphasized. Stage properties are, many times, the accent or artistic touch that makes or breaks the effectiveness of a stage setting.

Perhaps a more significant use of properties occurs on the thrust and arena stages, both of which are almost entirely dependent on properties to set the scene visually. Because of the close audience-stage relationship in both cases, the finished detail and quality of all properties are subject to closer inspection than they are on the proscenium stage.

Another important visual consideration of a stage property is its "rightness" for the play. The designer has to continually ask such questions as: Is this chair in the right historical period and nationality? Is the sideboard the kind Mama would choose? And so on. The selection and designing of furniture and properties is done in close collaboration with the director in order to insure their appropriateness for the play and to check how they fit into the staging of the action. For example, large furniture may hinder movement, or a high-backed chair may block off a view of upstage action.

Real furniture is, of course, used in the modern theatre, although it is often altered to become stageworthy. Scale and color are sometimes changed to improve its relationship to the stage composition. Because of these alterations even real furniture may take on a theatrical look. It becomes a stage property suggesting, sometimes faintly, sometimes openly, that it is no longer real. The name, property or "prop," is often synonymous with the unreal or theatrical.

Properties of a setting should be planned and built simultaneously with the rest of the scenic elements. Their importance to the design and production scheme is sometimes overlooked in the planning period. The construction of built properties is often started too late, or too many decisions in the selection of furniture or decorative features are postponed until the final hectic rehearsals. This often occurs when the designer, overworked and pressed for time, places the responsibility of organizing the properties on the shoulders of a willing but not-too-able apprentice.

To make better use of their time, designers should have a competent background in historical furniture styles and period decorations and should be thoroughly acquainted with the traditional uses of properties in the theatre. They must also be able to evaluate a property in terms of its importance to the action of the play and its sheer decorative qualities.

PROPERTIES VERSUS SCENERY

What is a prop? When does a small piece of scenery become a property or a large property become scenery?

Stage properties are traditionally defined as: (1) all objects carried or handled by the actor; (2) separate portions of the set on which the actor may stand or sit, such as rocks, stumps, or logs; (3) decorative features not permanently built or painted on the scenery (pictures, draperies, and so on); (4) the ground cloth and rugs; and (5) all sound and visual effects that are not electrically powered.

In the average show, the categorical division of properties is based for the most part upon these traditional definitions of a property. An occasional exception or collaboration is made with the agreement of all concerned. Hence, a tree trunk may be scenery and foliage a property; a pair of glasses discovered on the stage is a property while those brought on stage by the actors are considered costumes. Heavy properties often become scenery because of their size or necessity to be fastened to the scenery for movement.

Properties may also be classified according to their size and use. Properties can be designated as either hand, set, or dress properties, or as visual or sound-effect properties.

Hand Properties

The small objects handled by the actor on the stage are hand props. They include such items as teacups, books, fans, letters, and many more similar articles.

Set Properties

As the name implies, set properties are the larger elements more closely related to the scenery but still used by the actor. This group includes furniture, stoves, sinks, rugs, ground cloth, and any domestic object. Exterior set props consist of small rocks, stumps, bushes, foliage, real dirt (*Tobacco Road*), grass mats, and so on.

Set properties are in the care of the property person, who supervises the placing of the set prop on the stage and its removal to a stored position offstage.

Dress Properties

Dress properties are more closely related to the setting. Their chief function is decorative. Dress properties consist of all the elements not specifically used by the actor which serve to fill in and complete or dress the set. Window curtains, pictures, wall hangings, flower groupings are a few typical dress properties.

As a class, dress properties are not necessarily superficial. They can become a strong decorative feature in a setting. Becasue they are not used by the actor they can often be faked in order to be handled more easily or in a different way from the normal set property. Bookcases, for example, may have faked books and be attached to the scenery. A saloon back bar is often dressed with fake plastic or papier-mâché bottles to cut down the weight. A period piano or spinet, which is hard to find and harder to borrow, can be easily built and faked as a dress prop (Figure 11–1). These are, of course, just a few of the many, many types of faked dress properties.

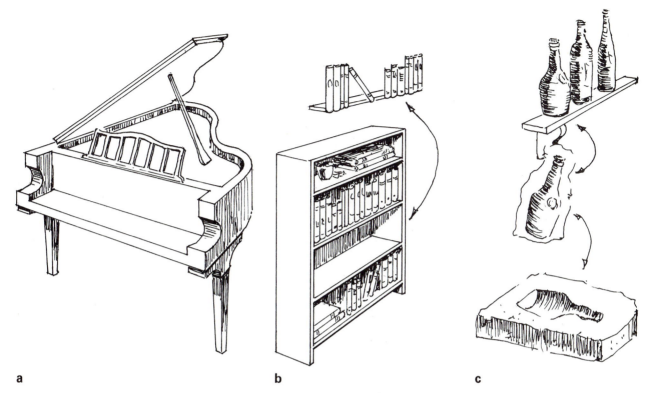

a   b   c

FIGURE 11–1
Dress Properties

(a) Fake spinet piano. (b) Dummy books in book case. (c) Papier-mâché bar bottles.

SELECTING SET AND DRESS PROPERTIES

The designer is responsible for the compositional unity, period continuity, and color relationships of the set and dress properties. Their first notation appears in the designer's sketch, which may or may not be clear as to the indication of the real form. Once the general idea of the design has been accepted the designer can turn to a more careful study of period line and availability of each piece.

The final decision on each piece of furniture is made by the designer with the director's approval. To help reach this decision at an early stage in the planning, the designer uses individual sketches or illustrational clippings. The selection of set properties can be further facilitated by the use of a furniture plot and compositional elevations as suggested in Chapter 5, which give exact references to the size of an individual piece in relation to its surroundings.

Period Styles and Ornamentation

Needless to say, scene designers must be well grounded not only in furniture styles but also in period interior decoration and architecture. The more familiar designers are with the historical background of a period style, the easier it will be to design, select, and make up set and dress properties which bring a feeling of authenticity to the setting.

Throughout the period of selecting or designing the properties and setting designers draw heavily on a knowledge of period style. They cannot hope to recall at an instant the details of a certain period, but they should have a general sense of period style at the tip of their pencils. For detail and enrichment of the general form designers must depend on research. Research doesn't always mean leafing through reference books or old periodicals. It frequently involves study of the real thing in a museum or in actual surroundings. Designers frequently resort to sketches or photographs to collect this information. Although these are not presentation drawings they can become important to the designer as personal reference material.

Designers soon learn to conserve energy and legwork when doing research by avoiding duplication. Generally much more material is gathered than is finally used. If all the research examples are filed and catalogued, they may come in handy at a later date on another show. Designers in this way soon find themselves in possession of an efficient reference library. They should also have several inexpensive illustrated books (such as those listed in the bibliography) containing collections of furniture styles and ornamentation. More extensive research, of course, may be needed to back any one style, depending upon the needs of the play.

Draperies

Of all the dress properties used onstage, draperies are the decorative detail that brings character to an interior setting. Their elegance or cheapness, style or lack of style or even their complete absence contributes immeasurably to the visual expression of the kind of place and people in the play.

From historical references, the designer can plan to use draperies which, depending upon the period, may include window, door, fireplace mantel, picture, and mirror draperies. The designing of draperies is based upon a knowledge of the way the material drapes or hangs and the methods of cutting and assembling the material into the desired effect.

A New York designer needs only to prepare a carefully scaled or dimensioned drawing of the assembled drapery, specifying the material and the action, if any. Window curtains, for example, may have to be drawn for a tableau during the action of the play.

For university and community theatre production, the designer is expected to guide the execution of the draperies and therefore needs to know something about drapery patterns and assembly techniques.

Window Drapery. Although draperies may occur in many positions other than at the windows of a setting, the fundamental parts making up the decorative portion are the same. The basic parts of the window drapery, which may or may not be used all at the same time, are: glass curtains, shade, overdrapery, and valance. The overdrapery and the valance are the frame, so to speak, while the glass curtains and shade diffuse the light or cut off the view into the room from the outside. Each is made of a different type of material.

Drapery Materials. The materials for window draperies are divided into three groups: the transparent or sheer fabrics for glass curtains and some types of draped shades; the translucent materials for the shade, unless it is opaque; and the opaque materials of the overdrapery and valance. The sheer materials may be chiffon, organdy, net, or theatrical gauze, to name a few. Muslin, silk, and handkerchief linen are samples of translucent fabrics. Though the opaque materials for overdraperies are numerous, they usually are made of a fabric that will drape well such as velour, velveteen, corduroy, or monk's cloth.

Types of Draperies. Because most of the decorative emphasis of a drapery is in the valance, it requires the greatest variety of draping techniques. A valance may be made up of plaits, swags, tails, or wing pieces, or even festoons. The festoon, which is one continuous piece of material, is the basis for the more exaggerated shape found in the swag and tails. Although the swags and tails are cut separately, they are frequently sewn together to look like a continuous piece of drapery. Examples of the types of draperies and their patterns are shown in Figure 11–2 (page 328).

The side draperies, which are vertical members of the overdraperies, are usually a simple rectangular piece of material hung in fullness and drawn into a gentle or deep swag with a "tie-back" or decorative loop. Side draperies are sometimes shaped by cutting the bottoms on the diagonal similar to the festoon pattern (Figure 11–2e). Side draperies, although frequently draped symmetrically, can take on an eccentric draping depending upon the the design and period style.

Shades

A shade normally is not included in a stage window unless there is action in raising or lowering it. Roll shades are fairly easy to make and install. A dye-painted shade of muslin or handkerchief linen can be attached to a commercial spring-loaded roller that has been cut to fit any special size of window.

A more special type of shade for a very grand window is the festoon-draped shade, sometimes called a French drape or Brail curtain. It is pulled up from the bottom by a series of vertical liftlines, which have been threaded through rings on the back of the curtain like the rigging

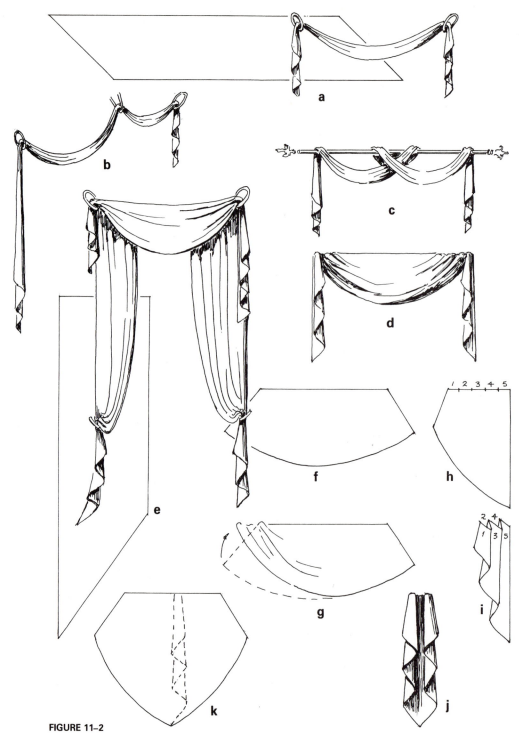

FIGURE 11–2

Types of Draperies and Valances

(a) Festoon valance and pattern. (b) Eccentrically draped festoon valance. (c) Crossed festoons as valance. (d) Valance of swag and wing pieces. (e) Festoon valance and side draperies showing pattern for side drapery. (f) Swag pattern. (g) Draping swag. (h) Pattern of wing piece or tail. (i) Draping or folding a wing piece. (j) A double or central tail. (k) Pattern of a central tail.

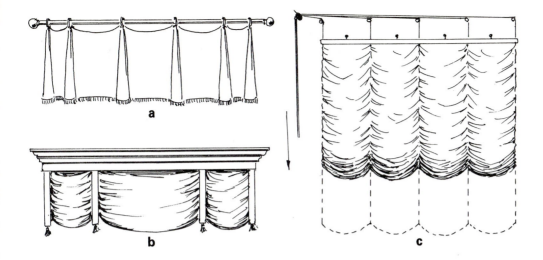

a

b

c

of a contour curtain (Figure 11–3). The bottom of the festoon-draped shade is shaped so that its top position becomes part of the valance design. The shade may work in front of or behind the side draperies.

Borrowing or Renting Properties

Nonprofessional producing groups must rely on renting and borrowing furniture or maintain in storage a collection of stock period furniture for continuous use. Storing select period pieces is by far the most satisfactory method of securing properties for a repertory or stock company. Stock furniture can be varied with new upholstering and painted for reuse in future productions.

A producing group which depends upon borrowing furniture and other articles must make an effort to maintain good will with the community. It pays to be businesslike when borrowing properties. Unfortunately, many a property room has been furnished with unreturned props, which is obviously not the way to build good will. A few simple rules for borrowing will help create a friendly, businesslike way of handling a loan.

1 Make a list of each borrowed article that includes the name and address of the owner, date borrowed and date to be returned, estimated value, description noting condition (scratches, cracks, or parts missing), remuneration (cash, complimentary tickets, or program credit), and request a signed receipt from the owner upon return of the article.

2 Centralize all borrowing in one person rather than in different people for each production.

3 Never borrow priceless heirlooms or irreplaceable antiques.

4 Take special care of all borrowed properties on the stage, using dust covers and padding to prevent damage from movement of the scenery.

FIGURE 11–3
Shades and Valances
(a) Café-curtain valance. (b) Boxed-festoon drapery valance. (c) Festoon drapery shade.

Stage Properties and Effects

5 Return borrowed pieces promptly and on the date promised.
6 Secure and file a receipt. Records become an excellent source for quickly locating and reborrowing for another production.

FLOOR COVERING

Traditionally, all floor covering (such as rugs and ground cloth) was handled by the property department. In present-day theatre, however, with its greater emphasis on floor design, floor covering has become more and more a part of scenery. Many modern proscenium theatres have an increased seating gradient that allows the audience to see more of the floor; on the thrust and arena stage, the floor is an important part of the overall design. As a result, the modern designer must be conscious of the floor covering as a means of unifying the stage composition.

A floor-cover design might involve painting the ground cloth to simulate wood or mosaic or creating a related hue to help anchor the design to the floor. Any stage setting on an unrelated or contrasting floor seems to float in space. If it does, it should be an intentional effect and not an accident of design.

A built-up or sloped stage floor will often be made of real materials, such as a planked floor that has the look and sound of wood. Such a floor can also be marbleized by using paint on a tempered masonite or particle board to create the highly polished surface of marble.

Latex and acrylic-based paints are durable enough to use on rigid surfaces, especially when they are later glazed with clear latex or acrylic. Such a surface can be damp-mopped and polished to perfection for each performance.

There are many examples of unusual floor coverings that go beyond conventional ground cloth or painted floor: the real dirt in *Tabacco Road,* for example, and the artificial snow in *Ethan Frome.* An unusual Spanish production of Aristophanes' *Lysistrata* comes to mind. The entire stage floor and scenery were covered with free-form overstuffed canvas, which obviously encouraged very unconventional movement.

Functional Floor Covering. A stage floor may have to be covered for purely technical reasons. An entire stage, for example, may be built up to surround a turntable or to provide slots to guide wagon movements. Stage floors are also notorious for their poor condition, a situation which bothers dancers the most. To correct this, most ballet companies and dance groups prefer to cover an imperfect floor with a vinyl covering. Some dance companies even carry their own portable floor. D'Anser, the trademark name of a portable modular floor, is transported in 4-by-8-foot units. This floor is 3 inches thick with offset wooden supports and gives the "bounce" dancers want. The units connect with interlocking hardware and can cover the entire stage area. D'Anser was designed by Ronald Bates and Perry Silvey of the New York City Ballet.

MAKING AND REMAKING FURNITURE

Cabinetmaker styles of furniture are often too difficult to produce in the average scenery shop, which is not equipped to finish or work hard woods. There are, however, several carpenter styles and rustic pieces of furniture that may be easier to make than to find or borrow. Some of the unupholstered, carpenter-style pieces shown in Figure 11–4 can be made without too much trouble.

Furniture can also be altered easily, especially if the alteration involves reducing rather than adding to the original structure. The practiced eye of the designer will be able to see in an otherwise hideous late Victorian "masterpiece," after a little painting, reupholstering, and trimming away excess parts, a Louis XIV side chair that would fool

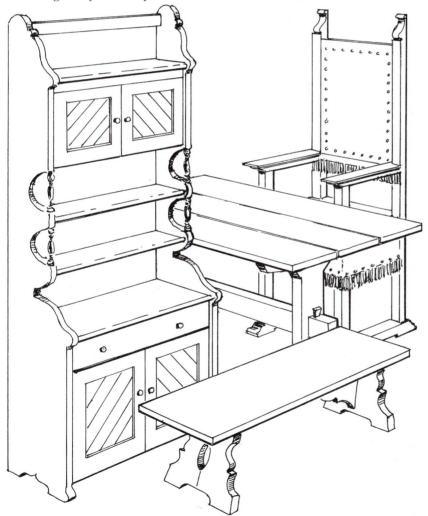

FIGURE 11–4
Examples of Carpenter-style Furniture That Are Easy to Make

Stage Properties and Effects

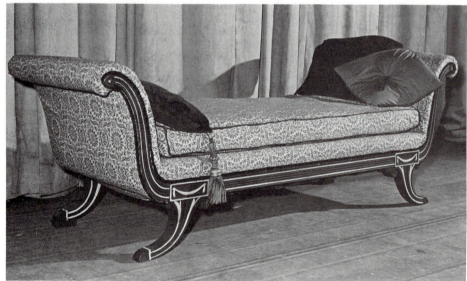

FIGURE 11–5

Remaking Furniture

Remodeling a sofa: (Top) The original sofa before alterations. (Above) Back removed, re-upholstered, and freshly painted. Reupholstering, tufting (page 333): (Top) Tufting a sofa. (Bottom) Rear view of ties used to form tufts (Photos—Gene Diskey)

Molière. Armed with a knowledge of period style, the designer frequently can turn a second-hand furniture store into a treasure house of antiques (Figure 11–5).

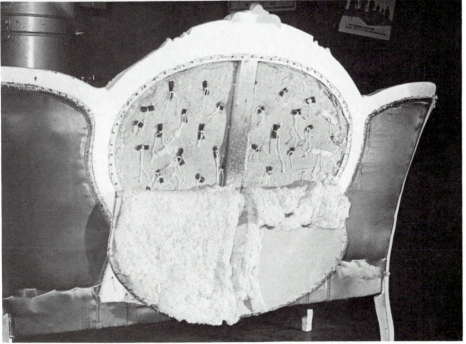

Upholstering

When sundry set properties are brought together on the stage for the first time, some or all may have to be upholstered for either color or compositional reasons. Extensive reupholstering is not recommended on borrowed pieces, although it is possible to cover the existing surface with a new material by catching it lightly with a needle and thread. This should not be attempted on antiques, however, which might have weak upholstering. Bright colors or shiny materials on a borrowed piece can be dulled by covering them with a black net.

To reupholster furniture that belongs to the theatre, it is best to follow the same method of covering used originally. If the old covering is removed carefully, the pieces can serve as a pattern for cutting the new material. While the upholstering is off, repairs can be made to

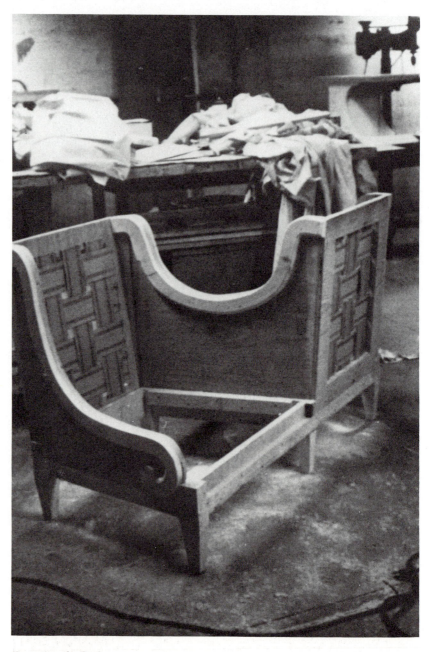

Executing the Design

the springs, webbing, and padding (Figure 11–5b). If the furniture is going to be kept in stock, the padding can be covered first with muslin, which serves as a base for any future changes in upholstering.

Expert upholstering will hide or cover the tacking. This may be accomplished in many ways. The material can be tacked on a hidden edge in back or underneath or tacked to a surface that is later hidden by a covered panel. Exposed tacks can be covered with a decorative gimp braid or fringe. Sometimes tacks may be studded and left exposed as a decorative feature in themselves (Figure 11–7, page 336).

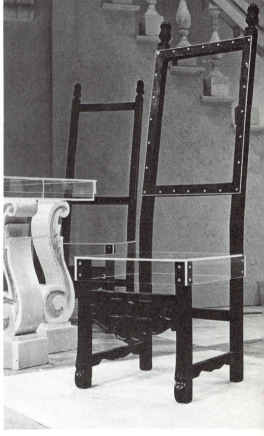

FIGURE 11–6

Making New Furniture

(Left) A hard-to-find tête-à-tête is constructed in the property shop. Frame and webbing ready for padding and upholstering. (Above) Finished settee. (Right) Plexiglass seat and back give a side chair a new look. On the left, rigid urethane foam with wooden core carved into legs for a console table. In the right background, turned rigid foam baluster.

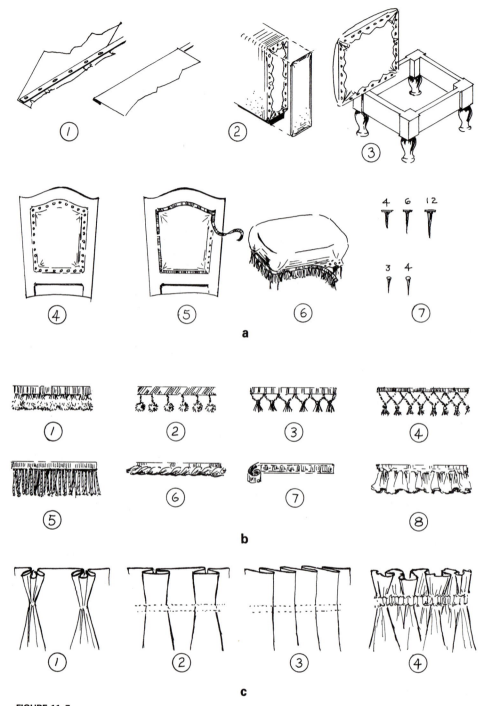

FIGURE 11–7

Upholstering Techniques

(a) Tacking: (1) Hidden tacking. (2) Tacking covered by a panel. (3) Tacking kept on an unexposed surface. (4) Decorative tacking. (5) Tacking covered with gimp braid. (6) Tacking covered with fringe. (7) Upholstering tacks, 4, 6, 12, and gimp tacks, 3, 4. (b) Fringes and braid: (1) and (2) Ball fringes. (3) and (4) Tassel fringes. (5) Bullion fringe. (6) Braid. (7) Gimp braid. (8) Ruffle. (c) Plaits: (1) Pinch plait. (2) Box plait. (3) Accordion plaits. (4) Gathering.

Executing the Design

FABRICATING AND CASTING TECHNIQUES

Properties often require decorative details or bold relief at an exaggerated scale beyond that of conventional furniture. These and other forms (such as architectural details, costume armor plate, small properties, and various free forms) are often made in the shop to obtain the exact shape and dimension the designer seeks. The forms may be fabricated or cast from a real object or the prepared mold of a three-dimensional shape.

Papier-Mâché

The term *mâché work* has grown to include all techniques and materials used to mold or fake carved relief detail on furniture or scenery. The original papier-mâché technique used paper or paper pulp, which was either modeled directly on the surface, or, in order to duplicate a large number, was fashioned from a plaster mold.

When modeling directly with papier-mâché, a porous paper is used, such as tissue, paper toweling, or newsprint. The paper, after being torn into convenient strips and dampened in water, is dipped into binder consisting of wheat paste and strong glue size. Any excessive binder is lightly squeezed out of the now near-pulp mass, and then is applied to the furniture surface to be modeled into the desired shape. If the relief is high, some preliminary modeling can be done with wire screening, to which the mâché is applied as the final surface. The technique is very similar to that described in Chapter 5 for construction of irregular shapes.

To duplicate identical forms, the same process can be applied to a greased positive or negative mold. In molding mâché there is a noticeable amount of shrinkage in the size of the final shape that has to be taken into consideration.

Celastic. Because papier-mâché is fragile, a sturdier substance may often be needed. Although more expensive, Celastic, or Sculpt-o-fab, can be used for small relief details and irregular forms that need to be resistant to the effects of excessive handling.

Celastic or Sculpt-o-fab is a cheesecloth impregnated with cellulose nitrate and a fire retardant. This rather stiff fabric, when softened in a special solvent, becomes pliable and can be shaped or molded in a negative or positive mold. As the very volatile solvent evaporates, the cellulose nitrate hardens into the new shape. The Celastic form will separate easily from a mold that has been covered first with aluminum foil. There is very little shrinkage and the resulting shape is extremely sturdy (Figure 11–8).

A word of caution: Because of the volatile nature of the solvent, the softening and shaping process should be done in a well-ventilated area.

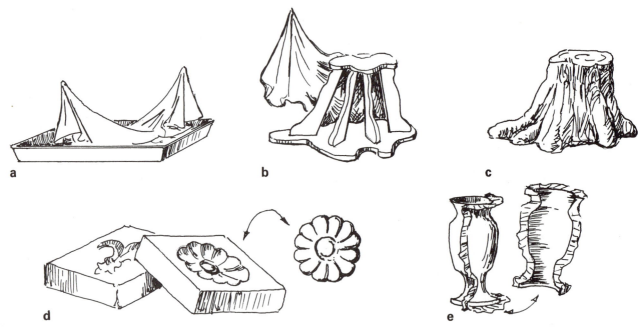

a

b

c

d

e

f

FIGURE 11–8

Celastic

(a) Fabric is softened in special solvent. (b) Softened fabric is draped over prepared understructure. (c) Final form after Celastic has hardened. (d) Celastic used in negative mold. (e) Over a positive mold. (f) Greek statuary. Celastic No. 411 (lightweight) over an armature, spray-enameled white, then antiqued. Statue and photo—Jim Bakkom.

Styrofoam. Architectural details, sculptural pieces, and out-of-the-way dress props may often be fashioned out of Styrofoam. However, unprotected Styrofoam is fragile and its surface has to be hardened. For an extremely hard finish, the foam surface must first be sealed with flexible vinyl glue. It is then coated with a mixture of catalyzed fiberglass resin and Cab-o-sil, a silica glass filler. (The use of Styrofoam and other foams adaptable to scenic use is discussed in Chapter 7.)

Fiberglass. Fiberglass is easily adaptable to three-dimensional details on scenery or properties. The technique, like the papier-mâché and Celastic procedures, shapes a fiberglass cloth over a positive form or into a negative mold after first coating the mold with a releasing agent. The pieces of fiberglass cloth are saturated and cemented together with a solution composed of a fabricating resin and a hardener. Because the hardener is the catalytic agent of the mixture, the amount present controls the degree of hardness of the final form. The proportion of resin to hardener is usually about five to one, but, because the strength of these plastics may vary from dealer to dealer, any mixture should be tested for its finished hardness before beginning extensive fabrication. Acetone, which is the solvent for the plastics, is used to clean brushes and hands.

Executing the Design

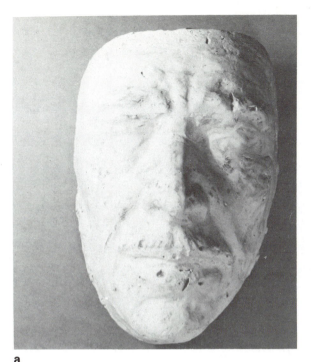

a

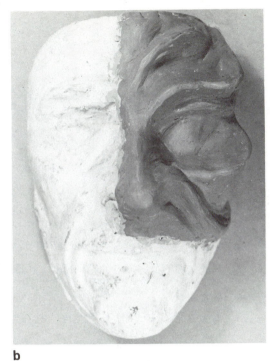

b

FIGURE 11–9

Mask-making Techniques

(a) A simple half mask is used to demonstrate the steps taken to design and fit any mask to the actor's face. A life mold cast from a surgical gauze (plaster impregnated gauze) impression of the actor's face. (b) The new form and dimension of the mask is modeled directly on the mold in plasticine clay. The completed design form is cast in plaster to create a negative mold of the mask. (c) Raw latex mask cast from the negative mold. At this stage, any one of several processes can be used such as Celastic, Polysar, liquid rubber, or papier-mâché. (d) The finished mask, painted and decorated. (Techniques continue on pages 340–341.)

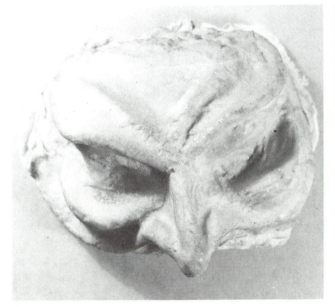

c

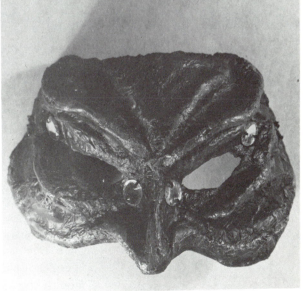

d

Mask-making Techniques

An example of a full-face mask and its negative mold. Ritual or larger decorative masks can be reproduced in number by using the vacuum forming technique if water clay is used in place of plasticine to make the mold. Designer—Pat Moser.

There are many types and weights of fiberglass cloth. Woven glass cloth is available in light, medium, and heavy weights. The woven glass cloth is not suitable for making objects with opaque surfaces that are to be painted. The medium and heavyweight cloth works very well for making costume armor plate and helmets. The matted glass cloth is generally lightweight and quite translucent and is often used for fabricating shapes like lamp globes or similar translucent forms.

An easy way to experiment with the technique is to purchase a fiberglass boat-repair kit and follow the directions in the manual. Although the kit may not supply a releasing agent, that may be purchased separately.

Executing the Design

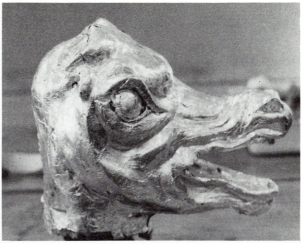

Fantasy Mask
Positive mold technique using Celastic. (Top left) Plasticine clay original. (Top right) Foil covering the clay mold as a parting agent. (Bottom left) Softened Celastic strips applied to the mold. The hardened form is then cut off the mold and sealed together to complete the raw mask. (Bottom right) Finished mask with a velour covering and applied hair. Designer—Louise Krozek.

Body Armor and Mask Making. Some of the mâché techniques can be applied to the making of full or partial masks, or, in some cases, to appear as decorative details on scenery. Figure 11–9 illustrates the designing and making of masks in the three basic forming techniques: papier-mâché, Celastic, and rubber latex. Fiber glass and thermal plastics lend themselves to the forming of body armor, such as breast plates and helmets (Figure 11–10).

Laminated Felt. Another method for constructing small set or dress properties is the laminated-felt technique. It is a process that works best for hollow forms, such as vases, goblets, and body armor. It can also be used to make open filigree or oversized costume jewelry.

Working over a position form covered with aluminum foil to ensure its "parting," the shape is built up with laminated strips of felt coated with Elmer's or Poly-vinyl glue. Decorative detail is appliquéd in the same manner. Once the shape is hardened it is painted with a glaze made up of shellac cut one half with thinner. The glaze is applied in

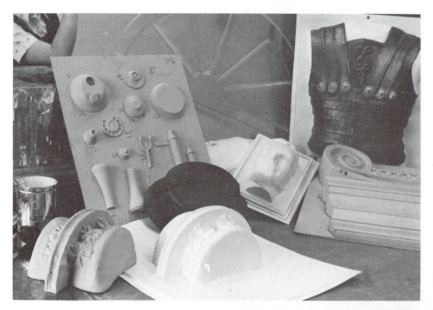

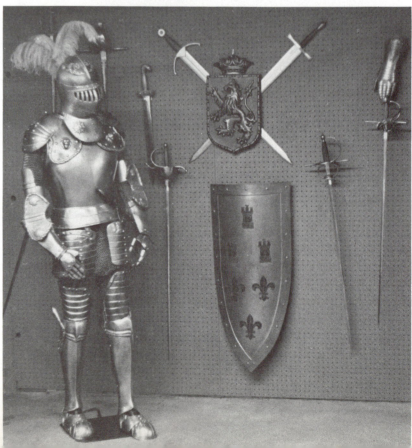

FIGURE 11–10

Properties and Armor

A few of the innumerable vacuum-formed articles for theatre use from Tobin Lake Studios. (Left) Prop telephone, architectural details, armor breastplate, and other articles are shown in various stages of assembly and surface finish. (Below) Full armor and shields vacuum-formed from vinyl plastic sheets. The swords in the display are made of tempered steel.

successive coats to build up a hard surface. Aniline dye may be added to the glaze to serve as an undercolor or as an antique effect if it is the final coat.

If the surface is metallic (to simulate silver, gold, or bronze) the dry metallic powder is brushed into one of the glaze coats as highlights. A metallic surface developed in this manner has a very authentic look on the stage.

Felt can be kept flexible by using a flexible glue rather than Elmer's. A flexible glue made by Swift and Company, Adhesive Division, is a transparent polyvinyl which can, with dye staining, make felt look and feel like leather. The same flexible glue is also an excellent sealer for Styrofoam and Artfoam prior to painting.

EFFECT PROPERTIES

There was a time in theatre history when visual and sound effects were the major concern of the property department. Before the advent of high-fidelity recording many sound effects were created mechanically by the property person. Most of these old machines are now gathering dust in the property room. An adequate sound system can bring any effect to the audience with a truer quality and a more sensitive control than any mechanical sound effect. There is one possible exception: the effect of offstage gunfire. The recordings of distant battle scenes are fairly convincing, but close rifle or revolver shots are better when a gun with blank cartridges is fired backstage.

More as historical record than as modern practice, Figure 11–11 (page 344) shows some of the mechanical sound effects that are a part of the property department. Directors, on occasion, have requested old mechanical sound effects for their theatrical quality rather than having the movielike realism of electronic sound.

Although some visual effects have become electrified, most are still produced mechanically. Smoke, fire, and flash explosions are usually electrically controlled; however, smoke also can be made nonelectrically (Figure 11–12, page 345).

Some familiar visual effects that are mechanical are the snow cradle and rain pipes, which are shown in Figure 11–13 (page 345) along with other special effects that call upon the ingenuity of the stage technician and property person to rig and trigger on cue.

Breakaways

Many times pieces of furniture, dishes, or other objects have to break on stage. The chairs that collapse and the flagpole that falls down in *Cockadoodle Dandy*, the bullet fired through the windowpane in *The Front Page*, or a railing that breaks during a fight scene are a few examples of properties or scenery breaking on cue and in a predetermined manner.

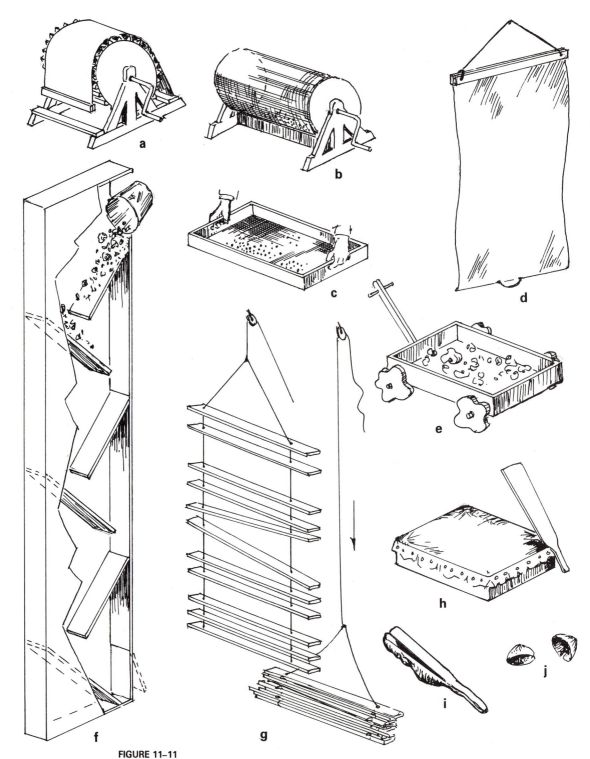

FIGURE 11–11

Mechanical Sound Effects

(a) Wind machine. (b) Rain, shot in rotating drum. (c) Rain, shot in tray with wire-screen bottom. (d) Thunder sheet. (e) Rumble cart. (f) Falling rubble after an explosion. (g) Wood crash. (h) Gun shots. (i) Slap stick. (j) Horses' hoofs.

FIGURE 11–12

Smoke Effects

(a) Smoke bomb. (b) Dry ice and water. (c) Heated sal ammoniac. (d) Heated mineral oil. (e) Squib, means of electrically firing a flash or firecracker. (f) Flash box containing flash powder over low-amperage fuse wire for electrically firing flash and smoke.

FIGURE 11–13

Visual Effects

(a) Snow cradle. (b) Rain pipe. (c) Water reflection.

In Figure 11–14, a railing breakaway is prebroken and lightly glued together. Thin strips of orange crate are tacked to the back of the repair to give a convincing splintering sound as the railing breaks again. The pattern of the break is carefully planned in order to control the fall of the pieces in the same manner for each performance.

Breakaway Windowpanes and Mirrors. Breaking real glass on stage is somewhat dangerous. Flying glass and broken glass left on the floor can be a hazard. If an actor must be close to breaking glass it is sometimes desirable to use other materials. One familiar substitute used often in the motion picture industry is candy glass. Candy glass, or hardened sugar and water, is prepared like old-fashioned rock candy. After a supersaturated solution of sugar and water is brought to about 260 degrees Fahrenheit it is poured on a smooth surface into a thin sheet. The sheet hardens into a clear, transparent solid. Candy glass, however, has a low melting point and may soften under stage lights or excessive handling.

Pottery Breakaways. Opaque shapes, such as teacups, dishes, or small objects of art are much easier to make into breakaways. Because they are not transparent, inexpensive pottery or china pieces may be prebroken and lightly glued together again to insure their breaking on stage. As the second breaking usually shatters the piece beyond reclaiming, a breakaway should be prepared for each preformance.

Special opaque breakaway shapes can be prepared by casting a mixture of plaster and Styrofoam into a mold of the shape. To keep the casting hollow for easy breaking requires a core mold, which makes the whole casting process very complicated and time-consuming.

If the authenticity, both in sound and looks, of the breakaway object is extremely important to the play a replica can be made in clay bisque. A clay slip or solution of powdered water clay and water is poured

FIGURE 11–14

Breakaway Railing

(a) Railing prepared for breaking: (1) Prebroken spots, lightly glued. (2) Loose spindles, lightly glued. (b) Railing after breaking: (1) prepared hinge points.

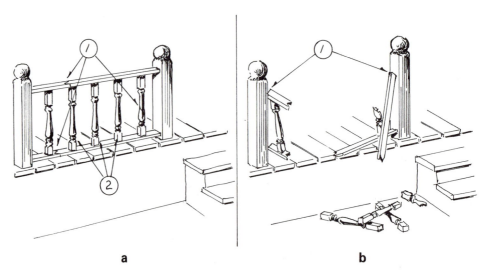

a   b

Executing the Design

into a mold of the object and after setting a few minutes is poured out. A thin shell of clay adheres to the mold, making a hollow casting of the object. After drying thoroughly (48 hours) the raw-clay casting is fired in a ceramic kiln to bisque hardness. A great number can be prepared this way.

Electrically Triggered Breakaways. To cue a breakaway in a remote position it is frequently easier to use an electrial trigger rather than a manual operation. A chandelier shattered by gunfire, a picture falling off the wall, or the decapitation of the weathervane cock in *Annie Get Your Gun* are a few examples of remote breakaways.

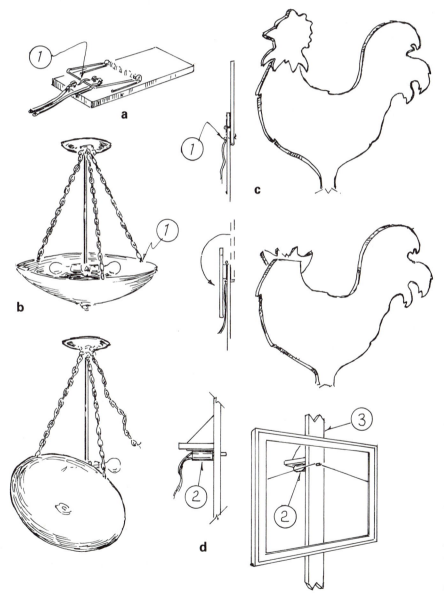

FIGURE 11–15

Electrically Triggered Breakaways

(a) The mousetrap is a simple mechanism that can be used to trigger a breakaway: (1) Fuse wire holding trap in "set" position. An electrical short melts fuse wire and the trap is sprung. This action can be used to break glass or spring load a hinge as in c. (b) Breakaway chandelier: (1) Fuse wire link which can be located anywhere on chain. The effect is helped if there is a little sand or dust in bowl to spill after the break. (c) Decapitating a weathervane cock: (1) Fuse wire holds spring-loaded hinge in upright position. Head folds behind body when fuse wire melts. 3- to 5-ampere fuse wire usually works best. If spring is too strong fuse wire can be doubled for strength. (d) Falling picture. (2) Solenoid coil mounted on rear of (3) picture batten. In off position the spring-loaded pin is extended through the batten to hold picture frame in place. When current is sent into the coil the pin withdraws and picture falls.

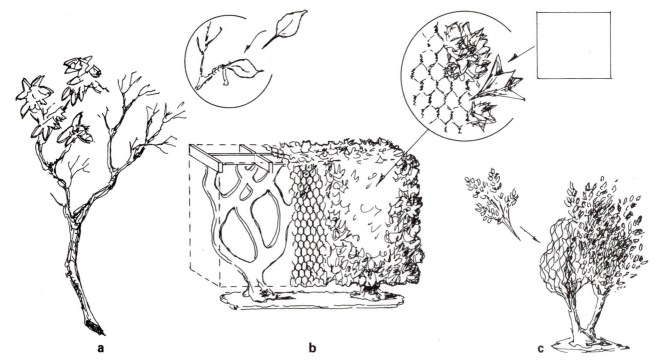

a   b   c

FIGURE 11–16

Foliage

(a) Artificial leaves wired or taped to real tree branches or section. (b) Trimmed boxwood hedge made of frame covered with inch-mesh chicken wire. Crepe-paper or fabric squares are pushed into openings (color is more convincing if two or three shades of green are used). (c) Untrimmed box or ilex bush; checken wire shaped over basic frame and filled with sprays of artificial boxwood or ilex.

A mousetrap spring can be released by shorting out the low-amperage fuse wire that is rigged to hold the spring under tension. Melted fuse wire can also be used to break a support chain of a chandelier (Figure 11–15, page 348).

The magnetic power of the solenoid coil can be used to withdraw the support of a picture on the wall or as a trigger for any other breakaway. When a current is passed through the coil of the solenoid it becomes an electromagnet which draws the spring-loaded center pin into the coil. Upon breaking the circuit the pin is released with considerable force. Either action can be used to trigger a breakaway.

Foliage

Artificial flowers and the foliage of hedges, bush pieces, and small trees are considered properties, as are live flowers, potted plants, and sprays of real leaves used to dress the setting. The expression "prop bush" means that the bush is not real but also implies that it is shaped in three dimensions, as opposed to a flat, painted set piece.

Lifelike artificial flowers can be obtained easily from display houses, local variety stores, or the home-decoration section of a department store. (Although they are more expensive than real flowers, with proper care they can be used over again.)

Stylized or caricatured blossoms have to be specially made. Their scale and design determine the material used. Exotic tropical flowers in a musical comedy, for example, have been made of velveteen or satin with leaves made of wire loops covered with sheer chiffon.

Banks of blossoms and box hedges can be made of shaped 1-inch mesh chicken wire with ruffle-edged colored crepe paper or silk pushed into the openings. A more realistic box hedge can be made of chicken wire holding sprays of artificial boxwood or ilex leaves (Figure 11–16). Large-mesh chicken wire can be used to support clumps of leaves on a tree branch, or as a hanging border related to a tree trunk. The leaf material, which can be either paper or fabric, should have sufficient stiffness to hold a leaflike shape, or it will have to be stiffened with wire. Window-shade stock, which comes in several shades of green, makes a good leaf fabric to staple onto a branch or chicken-wire frame.

PART

3

DESIGNING
THE LIGHTING

12

Introduction to Stage-Lighting Design

Scene design, unlike the other visual arts, is deeply dependent on the use of light as a part of the final composition—the dramatic picture. Stage lighting holds such importance in contributing to the total visual effect that every designer should be familiar with its techniques.

The design of lighting often begins with the scene designer's sketch which presents a suggestion of the light that will illuminate the scene. It may appear to be coming from such natural sources as the sun, the moon, or a fire, or from artificial sources as table lamps or ceiling fixtures. In contrast, the sources may be frankly arbitrary and depend on the position and color of the instruments used to build the composition. If the sketch is carefully done, the direction and color of the light will be apparent. If necessary, the designer will have prepared several sketches to show major changes in composition or color (Figure 12–1, page 354).

Such sketches, however, are only a start in the planning of stage lighting. Although a sketch represents an artistic concept, it must be technically sound to be properly realized. The floor plan and section that accompany the sketch give the first clues as to the credibility of

FIGURE 12–1

The Scene Designer's Sketch

The planning of stage lighting usually begins with the scene designer's sketch where the kind of illumination, its distribution, color, and general atmosphere are indicated. The sketch is for the opening scene of *Don Juan, or the Love of Geometry* by Max Frisch.

the designer's lighting ideas. Many a beautiful sketch has been based on a floor plan that revealed, on closer study, impossible lighting angles and insufficient space for the lighting instruments.

Ideally, a single person should design the entire production—scenery, costumes, and lighting—thus assuring a unified concept. But more often today we see a production design team made up of three designers and the director. Diverse ideas and views must be brought together into a single outlook or concept by active and open communication among all designers as well as strong leadership from the director. A study of stage lighting will certainly broaden design concepts and even more surely allow a designer to escape the pitfalls that await the uninformed.

Designing the Lighting

STAGE LIGHTING

What is the magic of stage lighting? The demands on it are many. The costume designer, while considering period, silhouette, color, and character in choosing the fabric for a costume, also wonders how it will look *under the lights*. The scene designer, in selecting the colors of draperies and upholstery or deciding the scale of detail on the scenery, hopes they will show *under the lights*. The actor in the dressing room ponders if makeup will look right *under the lights*.

Good lighting—and there is much that is not good—should tie together visual aspects of the stage. The primary concern of stage lighting is, and will always remain, *visibility* (a rule that the designer must never forget). Yet, we will see that visibility is much more than simple intensity or brightness of light. The lighting designer must also be concerned with revelation of form, with the mood of the scene, and with the overall composition of the stage picture.

Scripts often call for startling effects such as an explosion, a fog, a flashing sign, lightning, or a hearth fire. Effects usually occur either to advance the plot or establish the mood for a scene and are most often the responsibility of the lighting designer.

Recent trends in stage design have given lighting such a conspicuous share of the total visual effect that it often is the basic element of scenery. The new scenic role of light can vary from the conventional use of a projected scenic background or shadow patterns (see Chapter 22) to extreme abstract forms.

The Lighting Designer

In contemporary theatre, the lighting designer is the newest member to join the design team. Except for a few scene designers who enjoyed lighting their own scenery, the lighting of most Broadway productions in the first half of this century was neglected and became, by default, one of the innumerable duties of the stage manager or stage electrician. It was inevitable that lighting specialists would eventually move into this neglected field and demonstrate with startling results what could be done if one person devoted his or her sole attention to the planning of lighting. This trend continued as lighting designers, inspired by the work of people like Jean Rosenthal, Stanley McCandless, and Abe Feder developed their art and craft.

Contemporary theatre training and awareness of total theatre on the part of the lighting designer have brought greater unity to the visual side of today's theatre. The lighting designer must have compassion for and understanding of the total design effort since he or she is the only design member who does not make an advance statement in visual terms of what is intended. The costume and scene designers submit a multitude of sketches, material samples, and models as visual examples of their intent. The lighting designer, on the other hand, simply submits a light plot and a verbal description. Fortunately, the lighting designer will most often have the advantage of seeing and discussing the work of the other designers and the director before the final plot is completed.

Training. Of course, there is no formula which outlines exactly what makes a good lighting designer—or, for that matter, a good lighting design. It is clear though that the student of lighting must seek, before all else, a well-rounded background in the art of the theatre. Ideally, he or she should know what it is like to be on stage before an audience, understand how a flat is constructed and why it is done that way, be aware of the choices the costume designer goes through in creating a design and in choosing fabric, and understand why an audience enjoys Shaw, how to feel the poetry of Shakespeare, and why O'Neill captivates an audience with hours of dialogue. The lighting designer should know what it is to back-paint a flat every bit as well as how to wire a pin connector. Only then can the young lighting person begin to learn what it is to design lights.

The mechanics of lighting design are fairly simple. The script is read (many times), conferences are attended, rehearsals are viewed, a light plot is drafted, instruments are hung and focused, levels are set and cues adjusted, and another production opens. While a more detailed examination of process will be found in later chapters, it must be understood at this point that the first thing the young lighting designer must concentrate on is learning to *see*. There is not a practicing lighting designer worth his or her salt who doesn't possess a strong visual memory. In order to develop a mental file of visual experiences, one must first learn to notice, to observe, and to analyze light and shadow. Light is a constant part of our lives. The lighting designer must enjoy neon for its uniqueness, realize the effect of mercury vapor, feel the qualities of fluorescence, and see the color of the noonday sun. Learning to see is an ongoing process, not one to be learned in a month or even several years. We are constantly seeing anew.

STAGE LIGHTING AND THEATRICAL FORM

Several factors have a great effect upon the development of a lighting design and the subsequent plot. The production concept and resulting scene and costume design will influence color palette as well as style. Scenery will affect specific placement of lighting instruments. The style of the production as well as the script itself guides the lighting designer toward an approach. Finally, the physical form of the theatre will have significant impact upon the lighting design.

Designing the Lighting

Production and Lighting Style

While the term *style* is subject to overuse and misunderstanding (see Chapter 3), we use it here in its broadest sense. At the most basic level, there are two styles of lighting: motivational and nonmotivational. Motivational lighting will attempt to reinforce a specific source or sources (the sun, a candle, a window, and so on) as well as be concerned with actual environmental conditions such as time of day, weather, time of year, and locale (Figure 12–2). Nonmotivational lighting will ignore the above rationale as a basis for color selection, instrument choice, and lighting angle. Instead, the lighting designer will make these choices as a result of the desired mood, compositional requirements, or simple "feeling" about a scene.

The young lighting designer should concentrate on motivational lighting but must realize that a nonmotivational approach can be quite as valid and sometimes more expressive and exciting. The production style will help the designer select an approach which will employ one or perhaps both of these two basic lighting styles (Figure 12–3, page 358).

Physical Plant

The shape of modern theatre has had an influence on the development of stage lighting. Beginning with the *proscenium theatre* and its

FIGURE 12–2
Motivational Lighting
This designer's sketch for a ballet version of Maxwell Anderson's *Winterset* indicates a motivational approach to the lighting.

Introduction to Stage-Lighting Design   357

FIGURE 12–3

Lighting Styles: Motivational and Nonmotivational

(*Top*) The documentary style of Brecht's *The Measures Taken* illustrates a highly motivational approach to the lighting. Designer—Frederic Youens. (Photo—Nelson) (*Above*) The symbolic style of *Owner of the Keys* lends itself well to a nonmotivational lighting approach. Designer—Josef Svoboda—Prague. (Photo reprinted from *The Scenography of Josef Svoboda* by permission of the Wesleyan University Press. Copyright 1971 by Jarka Burian.)

Designing the Lighting

traditional audience and stage arrangement, lighting, for the most part, is essentially shadowbox illumination catering to theatrical realism or the illusory theatre. Lighting instruments are traditionally concealed behind masking on stage and in "ports" or "beams" front-of-house. Positions are often limited front-of-house, possibly to only a balcony rail. Worth noting is the fact that, scenery permitting, the proscenium stage is the most versatile form for side lighting positions.

The *thrust stage*, with its audience on three sides, minimizes the use of scenery and makes illusion a greater responsibility of the lighting designer. This new-old form of theatricality (popular in the sixteenth century) relies chiefly on lighting, costumes, and properties for its visual composition. Thrust staging requires full coverage (360°) lighting and is an exciting and challenging theatre form. The modern thrust theatre provides great flexibility in lighting positions both front-of-house as well as over-stage.

Arena staging surrounds the stage area with audience. The arena-theatre form increases the demands on stage lighting and virtually eliminates scenery. Like thrust, the arena requires 360° coverage but is usually a bit more restrictive in terms of lighting possibilities. A good arena theatre will be equipped with a lighting grid which covers the entire space and allows total flexibility in hanging position.

Theatre of total environment, the most recent form, not only brings back scenery elements but also expands the use of lighting to even greater dimensions by surrounding or immersing the audience in the atmosphere or environment of the play. The circle has been completed by returning to a proscenium form. The production, however, is not contained behind the frame, but is allowed to spill out and surround the audience.

Flexible or *black box staging* should not be neglected, for it is capable of achieving, on a small scale, any of the aforementioned audience-stage arrangements and even more. It is, by its sheer flexibility, a frankly impromptu form with its exposed lighting instruments and temporary seating arrangement.

It can be seen by now that, between the rapid expansion of imaginative theatrical forms and the numerous physical forms in the explosion of new theatres, lighting designers are facing demands on their skills that are totally different in taste and technical capabilities of only a generation or so ago. The opportunities are challenging. You by now may be asking, "Where does the study of stage lighting begin?"

Setting aside the technical aspects of electricity, instrument and control design, and the nitty-gritty of plotting, scheduling, and handling of equipment, the lighting designer is concerned first with the esthetics of light. To develop a sense of composition and taste in color, a lighting designer must start with qualities and limitations of the medium, light, itself.

QUALITIES OF LIGHT

Once light is created, whether it be from the sun or an artificial source, it has certain inherent qualities that become characteristic of the light medium. Just as paint has traits particular to its medium, so light conforms to its own set of attributes. The physical characteristics of light as a design potential are discussed in Chapter 3, where light is presented as a very important element of design in context with the development of scene design as a visual art. The separate study of light in its application to stage lighting involves these same qualities: intensity, distribution, and color.

Intensity

The first and most obvious quality of light is its intensity or brightness, which may be actual or comparative brightness. The actual brightness of the sun, for example, can be contrasted to the comparative brightness of automobile headlights at night. Spotlights in a darkened theatre offer the designer the same comparative brightness under more controlled conditions.

Varying intensity of a light source is achieved by means of a dimmer. Groups of dimmers working together can direct audience focus as well as alter the stage composition.

Distribution

Light rays follow an energy path which is known as distribution. The control of the distribution of light gives it direction and texture as a design feature. The various kinds of distribution begin with the general radiation of direct emanation through the more specific reshaping of the light rays by reflection or optics to the parallel rays of the laser beam. The sharp or soft-edged quality of the light beam coupled with its degree of brightness give texture to the light itself (Figure 12–4).

It is easy to see how the distribution of light can affect the ultimate design of a scenic form. The considered use of the direction and texture of light can introduce highlight, shade, and shadow into the composition. The angle or direction of the light that is illuminating the actor, for example, becomes very important in giving the actor a natural look as might occur under sunlight. Unnatural angles such as illumination from below distort the face with unusual shadows and misplaced highlights.

Color

The third property of light is its ability to transmit and reveal color. Color, in addition to being a forceful element of design in all phases of the visual side of the theatre, is often considered the most effective and dramatic quality of light. Setting aside the physics of color and its origin in the electromagnetic spectrum (see Chapters 8 and 18) and

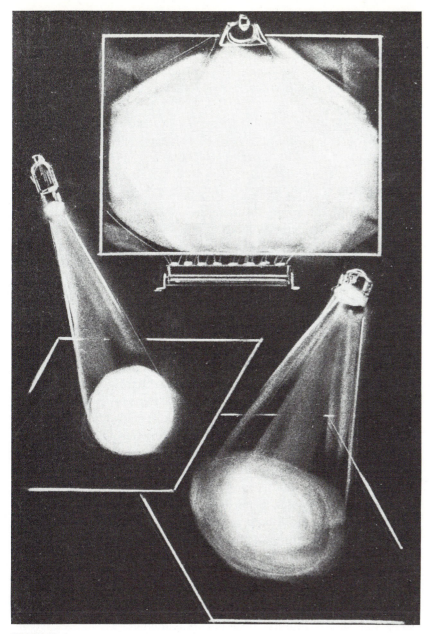

FIGURE 12–4
Distribution
Both specific and general distribution are illustrated from four different theatrical light sources.

turning to the design aspect of color in light, we find that its chief contribution is the transmitting of color or colored light. The modification of the local color of a scenic form by colored light is a design technique unique to the theatre. Color modification and the additive mixing of colored light are two rather basic concepts of color as a quality of light that has to be understood by all designers in the theatre. Both are discussed in detail later.

Movement. Movement cannot be categorized as a quality of light, yet its effect upon the theatrical use of color, distribution, and intensity is enormous. While movement implies change, it does not necessarily mean a change in focus or composition; it might be as subtle as the slow color shift from pre-dawn to daybreak.

STAGE LIGHTING AND THE FUNDAMENTALS OF DESIGN

Composition

The principles of composition are the same for the lighting designer as they are for the scene designer or any visual artist (see Chapter 3). Composition is the organizing of the visual elements of design into a unified form or arrangement of forms. The meaning attached to forms in a stage composition is, for the most part, a visual interpretation of the playwright's ideas. Lighting is the final unifying force of the stage composition.

Unlike a painting, a stage composition is not static but is an ever-changing arrangement of forms with a moving center of interest. More than any other design element, light is able to direct the audience's eye and control what is and isn't seen. Since light possesses the additional quality of incredible fluidity, stage composition can be altered with relative ease. Although light can have composition of its own (projected patterns, for example) its chief function is to reveal stage forms in the proper relationship to other forms and to the background. And here the complexity of compositional lighting begins.

Compositional lighting means lighting one form and not another; lighting two-dimensional forms to make them look three-dimensional; keeping shadows off the background; lighting three-dimensional forms to make them look three-dimensional (not as easy as it seems); and many other similar problems, the most important of which is the compositional lighting of the actor (Figure 12–5).

The Elements of Design

The role of the lighting designer as a member of a design team demands that he or she be acutely aware of the elements of design that affect the creative process of the scenery and costume designers.

The fundamentals of design as applied to scene design are discussed in detail in Chapter 3, where the basic elements of design are presented and their contribution to the stage composition is explained. The elemental factors that make up any visual form can be listed in the order of their importance to the creative process. They are: line, dimension, movement, light, color, and texture.

Line as an element of design defines form. Its force is present in a composition in many ways. Line can enclose spaces as outline creating shape (two-dimensional form), or as contour-line suggesting three-

FIGURE 12–5

Composition

Two photographs from *Summer Tree* by Ron Cowen illustrate the use of compositional light in a simultaneous setting. Set Designer—Richard Churchill. Lighting—Bertrand Cottine. (Photo—Nelson)

dimensional form. Strong backlighting, for example, would emphasize the silhouette or outline of a form while directional side lighting reveals its contour. Light has the power to deny, alter, or accentuate line (Figure 12–6).

Line can appear in a composition as real line in many different modes (straight, curved, spiral, and so on) or as suggested line simulated by the eye as it follows a sequence of related shapes.

Line as a path of action frequently assumes direction. A strong beam of light cannot help but establish direction. The linear shape of the beam coupled with a concentration of brightness creates a strong focus in the composition.

Dimension is the size of form. As an element of design, it is not only

FIGURE 12–6

Textured and Low-relief Surfaces

Demonstrating the effects of angle and distribution of light on a highly textured surface or low-relief carving. (Top) A low-relief sculptural form lighted with a single source from the front. (Right) The same form lighted with two side-angle sources of different intensity or color.

Designing the Lighting

concerned with the *size* of a shape or mass, but also with the relationship of the size of one shape to another—large to small, large to large, and so on. Hence the size of the interval has a definite effect on the apparent size or mass of a form and to its proportional relationship to other forms in the composition.

Control of light on either the form or the interval influences the dimension of one or the other. Light can reverse the feeling of dimension by making a two-dimensional shape look three-dimensional and vice versa.

Movement is the action of form. It is the kinetic energy of composition. Motion can exist in a stage design as real movement and as the movement of the eye or optical motion within a static composition.

The real movement of lights, of the actor, and on occasion, animated elements of scenery, are all very much part of a theatrical production. Any change of intensity, distribution, or color is the movement of light. The movement of a follow-spot beam, the change of a color on the cyclorama, and the raising or lowering of lights on different areas of the stage are a few examples of real movement.

Optical motion is the movement of the eye over a composition. When a form or arrangement of forms is static optical motion is dependent on the sequential arrangement of forms or elements of design. The movement of the eye can easily be altered through a shift in light intensity or composition. Strong directional light rays or the sequential arrangement of light sources are examples of the use of light as optical motion. The subtle gradation of one color and the vibration of two hue opposites are the extreme uses of color as optical motion.

Light reveals form. The dominant presence of light in all areas of stage design makes it imperative that light be considered as a basic influence in the beginning of the creative process and not something to be studied later. The early awareness of light as a design element is as important to the scenery and costume designer as the appreciation of all the elements of design is to the lighting expert to whom this section of the book is devoted.

Color modifies form. As an element of design it is a powerful stimulus within the composition. It can change the dimension of form, reverse the direction of line, alter the interval between forms, and generate optical motion. Color in the theatre comes from two basic sources: pigment or dye colors present on the surface of the form, or colored light that modifies the color of the form.

Texture is the tactile aspect of form. It is the treatment of surfaces which is of interest to the lighting designer. Surfaces may be highly polished, rough-hewn, or rusticated, to name a few that may reflect light or cast interesting shadows. Real texture is best revealed by directional side light (distribution), while painted or simulated texture appears more real under a wash of light without a strong sense of direction (Figure 12–6).

In its simplest form, the texture of light is the product of a specific type of lighting instrument (Figure 12–4). Certainly one of the considerations in choosing the type of instrument to use involves the textural quality of its light. In addition, the designer can alter texture in light by adjusting focus or breaking up the light with specially designed patterns or frost media.

THE FUNCTIONS OF STAGE LIGHTING

Although visibility is the primary concern of stage lighting, the basic obligation of light on the stage is to give the actor or performer *meaning* in his or her surroundings and to provide an atmosphere in which the role may be logically interpreted. At the same time, stage lighting, like scene designing, has to bring to the audience the full meaning and emotions of the playwright's concept.

The lighting designer does not begin work until the setting has been designed but is guided by the same fundamentals of dramatic form as the set designer. Through the use of light in all its aspects—intensity, color, distribution and movement—the lighting designer assists in creating the proper environment for the play by helping to place the

FIGURE 12–7

Visibility

Illustrating the effect of four different kinds of visibility. (a) An object visible in silhouette only. (b) With front light added, the object is visible as a three-dimensional form. (c) With the addition of another angle of light, the object's detail becomes visible. (d) An example of detail and form becoming less visible as a result of too much light.

a   b

Designing the Lighting

action, establish the mood, reinforce the theme, and stage the story of the play or related theatrical form.

Placing the Action

In some plays the designer may find that mood and theme are so much a part of the story line that it is hard to separate their functional differences. On the other hand, the action of a play is usually easy to isolate. Action, the designer soon discovers, can vary from a static, wordy, psychological study to a fast-moving farce or to the violent contact of a murder mystery. The physical action of a play or any theatrical performance is of prime importance to the lighting designer. We must know where the action has to be clearly seen, half seen, or not seen at all. For this reason and others, the process of viewing rehearsals is of utmost importance. In following the action, the designer frequently manipulates the intensity and distribution of light.

The placing of the action usually happens in the opening moments of the performance and can set the tone of the show. Whether it be a specific room in a house, a street in a village, a cabaret, or just action in limbo, it is still the place of the action that will set the proper environment for the rest of the scene.

Visibility. We cannot define visibility as a fixed degree of brightness or an established angle of distribution. It is the amount of light needed for a moment of recognition deemed appropriate for that point in the action of the play. "To see what should be seen" may mean the revealing of only the silhouette of a three-dimensional form, the solidity of its mass, or the full detail of all surfaces with decoration and texture. Each degree of visibility cannot help but take on an atmosphere or mood that will affect the action (Figure 12–7).

c

d

Establishing the Mood

The overall mood of a play or scene is the next important clue to the lighting designer. A color impression comes from the mood as well as a suggestion of the intensity and distribution of light. The word *mood* tends to suggest dark and gloomy surroundings, but bright comedy or nonsensical farce also indicates a type of mood.

Although an abstract or dramatic mood is more impressive and eye-catching than the realistic visibility of a conventional interior setting, it is also far easier to accomplish with light. How many times have the dancing shadows of an actor sitting in front of the single source of a hearth fire won more acclaim for the lighting designer than the hours of careful lighting of a realistic interior.

Reinforcing the Theme

The key word here is *reinforcing.* Because the visual expression of theme depends on the scene designer's interpretation of the playwright's message, the lighting designer is concerned with compositional revelation of the thematic forms of the setting. The theme-dominated play (Tennessee Williams' *A Streetcar Named Desire,* for example) asks the lighting designer to reveal the fragmented setting first as a

FIGURE 12–8

Theme

Tennessee Williams' *A Streetcar Named Desire* is an example of a theme-dominated play. The lighting designer is asked to support the theme with a distribution of light that follows the action in all areas within the apartment (below) as well as revealing the outside through transparent walls (page 369). Set Designer—Edward Pisoni. (Photo—Nelson)

structure having solid walls, then as a transparent, see-through skeleton; finally the designer is asked to illuminate the constantly moving center of attention from room to room, interior to exterior (Figure 12–8).

In the more extreme theme-oriented or documentary plays of Bertolt Brecht the theme is stressed by eliminating the theatricality of stage lighting and playing the show under a clear, uncolored wash of light. Lighting, however, is used to reinforce the theme visually through the use of projections. These take the form of propanganda pictures or subtitles and are used in place of scenic background.

Staging the Story

The story line of a play may be developed very simply as in a one-set, seven-character, domestic comedy or as in an extremely difficult, episodic marathon with a cast of hundreds. The narrative may require the cross section of a house or the establishment of many unrelated locales in a single-setting arrangement. The movement from scene to scene or from area to area requires logistical planning for the scene designer, while for the lighting designer it is an exercise in control of precise distribution and the delicate intensities of light. Movement or transitions within a scene or from scene to scene by lighting become a connecting or unifying factor in the production.

FIGURE 12–9

Lighting Style

Highly stylized motivational lighting is shown here from a production of *You Can't Take It With You.* Set Design— R. Craig Wolf. Lighting Design—Doug Grekin. (Photo—Mountain Mist)

DEVELOPMENT OF A LIGHTING DESIGNER

Designing for the theatre requires a great deal from an individual. Not only must one have artistic talent and technical knowhow, but the designer must also be able to communicate. The next few chapters will instruct the young designer in the nuts and bolts of lighting, but it must never be forgotten along the way that a *designer* is being nurtured. The importance of "learning to see"—of establishing visual memory—must always be in the forethought of the reader. Experimentation is essential: lighting instruments should be examined, dimmer systems operated, and colors mixed. The lighting designer can learn only so much from theory and example; he or she must have opportunities to put theory into practice. Since production space is always in great demand, a lighting laboratory becomes a tremendous aid to practical training.

But always remember, while wandering through the maze of technical information, pause now and then—and *look.*

Designing the Lighting

13

Stage Lighting and Electricity

An understanding of electricity may seem nothing more than a bother to the lighting designer/*artist;* but such information is essential for the lighting designer/*practitioner.* At the very least, we must understand electricity and basic electronics well enough to make intelligent choices concerning usage and safety. Unfortunately, too many people believe that electricity is solely an electrician's concern and, as a result, a curious mystique surrounds electrical practice and theory. The fact is that electrical theory and basic electrical practice are simple and quite unmysterious.

ATOMIC THEORY

According to presently accepted theories, all matter consists of molecules, which are made up of atoms. Each atom is composed of a positively charged center called the nucleus around which are distributed a number of negatively charged bodies called electrons. The nucleus of an atom consists of protons and neutrons. Neutrons have no electric charge, but each proton has a positive charge exactly equal to the negative charge of an electron.

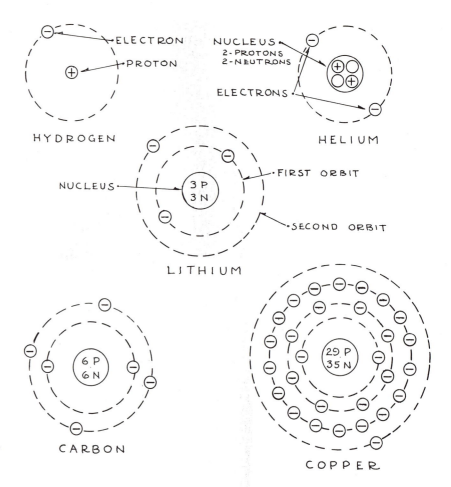

FIGURE 13–1

Schematic Diagram of the Structure of Certain Atoms

Every normal atom has as many electrons surrounding the nucleus as it has protons within the nucleus, and thus has an equal quantity of positive and negative charges. Thus hydrogen has one proton in its nucleus and one electron outside it; helium has two protons and two electrons; lithium has three of each, carbon has six, copper has twenty-nine, and so on up to uranium, which has the most: ninety-two protons and ninety-two electrons. It is thought that the electrons are in constant motion, revolving around the nucleus in orbits much the same as the planets revolve around the sun. Figure 13–1 shows a few examples.

In the atom of lithium, the lightest of all metals, the three protons are balanced by two electrons in the inner orbit plus one in the outer orbit. Carbon also has two electrons in the inner orbit, plus four in the outer orbit, to balance the six protons. Copper requires four orbits to take care of its twenty-nine electrons.

The various orbits are not all in the same flat plane, like a plate, but rather they are at angles to each other, somewhat like a number of rubber bands stretched haphazardly about a baseball.

The importance of all this is that the electron in the fourth and outer orbit of copper may be easily dislodged, providing a free electron, the basis of the flow of electrical current. The same is true of the outer electron in the lithium atom. In fact, all metals have electrons that can be readily dislodged and, therefore, are good electrical conductors.

CONDUCTORS AND INSULATORS

To allow electric current to move through circuits (established paths for electricity) of any kind it is necessary to provide a path through which the electrons may move as easily as possible. Materials made up of atoms that release free electrons readily also permit the movement of electrons through them and are known as conductors. Actually all materials will offer some resistance to such movement, but all metals are relatively good conductors, and silver is the best of any substance known.

Because of cost, the use of silver for extensive wiring is not very practical, and some less expensive material must be used. Copper is this material: its conductivity is almost as good as silver's, it is relatively inexpensive, and it is easy to work—to form into wires and other parts. Aluminum is coming more and more into use in some applications, and brass is valuable for large, permanent parts that need to be especially rugged. Other materials are also used for special purposes, but by and large when we think of electric wires, switch parts, and the like, we think of copper.

An important rule to remember is that electricity will always follow the path of least resistance. Some sort of insulation is necessary to prevent the electrons that are flowing in a conductor from short-circuiting—that is, escaping into other channels. This "short" may result in severe shock to anyone chancing to come in contact with the new and unprotected channel of flow. And because it may offer little resistance, this new channel may allow a higher current than the legitimate circuit was designed to carry, thereby causing damage to it.

Just as there is no material that is 100 percent conductive, so there is nothing that has 100 percent insulative properties, but there are many materials that can serve various practical purposes. Glass and ceramics are excellent for small permanent parts such as sockets and switches, slate for larger switch and fuse panels, and asbestos where heat is involved. For wires and cables, rubber and fiber are used, while plastics are becoming increasingly common. The most useful insulator of all is dry air. If this were not so, every open socket or wall outlet would drain off current!

Permanent wiring such as stage circuits, which should be laid by a licensed electrician only, may have a solid copper core through which the current flows, but the temporary wiring cable used on the stage always has a core made up of a number of small strands of wire. This is to provide proper flexibility in handling and laying. Standard stage cable consists of two or three such cores, each surrounded by a strong rubber insulation. For physical strength, tough fiber cords are laid alongside, and the whole surrounded by either a rubber or a fiber sheathing.

National electrical codes now specify that all new electrical installations be grounded. Grounding requires that a circuit or cable have three rather than two wires. The third, the ground wire, is designed to offer an emergency path through which the current can flow in case of a short circuit. The wires of a stage cable or circuit are always covered with rubber insulation color coded as follows:

> black or red = "hot" line
> white = "neutral" or "common" line
> green = ground

Care must be taken in wiring plugs onto cable that the ground wire in particular is attached to the proper pin of the connector (see "Types of Connector").

Stage cable comes in different sizes, or gages, each of which is designed to carry a specific maximum current or amperage. These limits should never be exceeded. The most useful sizes are:

Size (gage number):	18	16	14	12	10	8	6
Capacity (amperes):	3	6	15	20	25	35	50

The most common (nearly standard) stage circuit will carry 20 amps. As a result, the most common cable will be #12, Type SO (rubber coated). Occasionally, for a very small load and a very short run, ordinary lamp cord (or zip cord), which has an 18-gage core, may be used, but this should be kept to a minimum and carefully guarded against abuse.

A final category of stage cable must be mentioned here because of its inevitable importance to a successful "put-in." The first members of this category are cables which allow the electrician to plug several lighting instruments into a single circuit. These cables may be called "two-fers," "Y-connectors," "spiders," or "three-fers"; all of them allow the electrician to plug two or three instruments into one circuit. One must remember that 20 amps is circuit capacity. Adaptors are the other type of special category cable. Simple adaptors are seldom more than 2 feet long, with one of various connectors on each end. Applications are endless, but an example of the use of an adaptor would be plugging a backstage work light equipped with a pin connector into an "Edison" or parallel blade socket.

Designing the Lighting

SOURCES OF ELECTRIC CURRENT

Just as you cannot get water to flow out of one end of a pipe unless there is water being poured into the other end, so free electrons will not move through a conductor unless there is a supply of free electrons being introduced into it. Such a supply of electrons is known as voltage or as an electrical force (EMF). It can be established in a number of ways.

Battery

A common device for supplying an EMF is a battery, such as one consisting of a glass container filled with a dilute sulphuric acid solution into which are placed a strip of copper and a strip of zinc. If a meter is connected between these two strips, it will show a small electric current passing from one to the other through this connection (Figure 13–2). This is caused by the acid attacking the zinc, which dissolves into the solution and releases two electrons from each of its atoms. These electrons are left on the zinc strip, and because the acid will not permit them to return to their atoms, they flow through the wire to the copper strip.

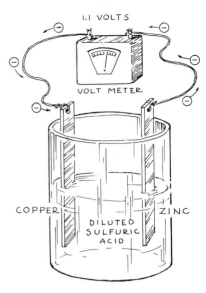

FIGURE 13–2
A Simple Copper-zinc-acid Battery

Other Sources

An EMF may be built up in a number of ways other than the battery. *Electrostatics* produces electricity by rubbing two dissimilar substances together. *Photoelectricity* is the action of sunlight on certain photosensitive materials. *Thermoelectricity* is the application of heat to the junction of two dissimilar metals that have been welded together. *Piezoelectricity* is the mechanical compression of certain crystals. New techniques to produce electricity are being developed, but the method most important to the stage electrician is that of *electromagnetism*: the creation of an EMF through a generator, powered by water, steam, or other means.

Generator

The principle of the generator is the relative movement of a conductor within a magnetic field. The conductor may be moved while the field is stationary, or the field may be moved and the conductor remain stationary. The latter is usual in very large installations, but it is somewhat easier to comprehend the operation by considering a moving conductor in a stationary magnetic field.

The two diagrams in Figure 13–3 show a highly simplified a-c generator, usually called an alternator. We see an armature in the shape of a single coil of wire being rotated through the magnetic field between the two poles of a magnet. This induces an EMF in the coil causing negative electrons to accumulate at slip ring 5 and flow off the

Stage Lighting and Electricity

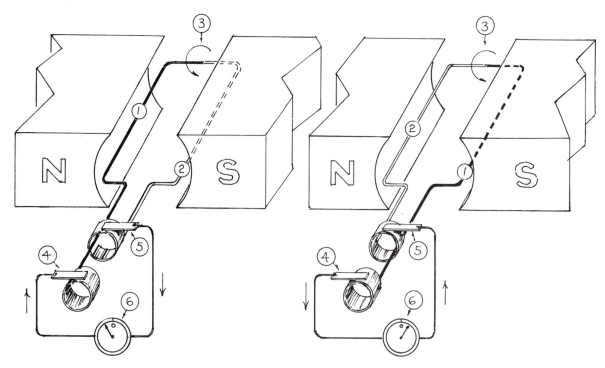

FIGURE 13–3

Simple A-C Generator (or Alternator)

(1) Side 1 of coil (2) Side 2 of coil (3) Direction of rotation of coil (4) Slip ring A (5) Slip ring B (6) Volt meter.

slip ring through the brush and thence along the connecting wire and through a voltmeter to slip ring 4, whence they reenter the coil. In the second diagram the sides of the coil have reversed positions and directions, so now the electrons will accumulate at slip ring 4, pass through the connecting wire and meter and reenter the coil at slip ring 5. Each complete revolution of the coil is called a cycle, so for one half of each cycle the electrons move in one direction and for the other half in the opposite direction. Thus the current is said to alternating (a-c).

In Figure 13–4 we see the construction of the sine curve that represents the variation of the induced EMF for any portion of the complete cycle of the armature through the magnetic field. At the exact instant that the armature is passing the 0-degree point in its rotation it is moving parallel to the magnetic field, not through it, and hence is producing no EMF at all.

As it reaches the 30-degree mark it is cutting into the magnetic field somewhat and hence is generating a small EMF as depicted by extending a line from the 30-degree point to a somewhat later point than the 0-degree reading of 0. At the 60-degree position, an EMF of greater magnitude is produced and at 90 degrees the maximum EMF. After this the EMF drops back to 0; then in an a-c generator it starts to build up in the opposite direction as depicted below the time line.

Designing the Lighting

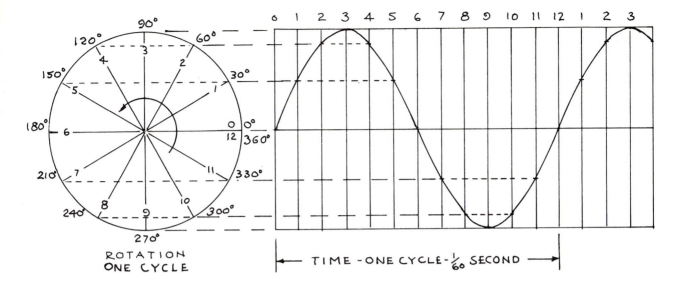

ROTATION
ONE CYCLE

|← ── TIME - ONE CYCLE - 1/60 SECOND ──→|

For the sake of economy it is practical to build not a single armature into a generator, but several of them. Because they must be at angles to each other, it is obvious that their respective EMFs will not reach any one point at the same instant, but rather they will produce sine curves as indicated in Figure 13–5. Here we see the very common arrangement of three armatures each producing its own curve. This is known as three-phase current and will be discussed later.

FIGURE 13–4

The Construction of an A-C Sine Curve

ELECTRIC UNITS OF MEASUREMENT

Four basic measurements can be made in any electric circuit. Their definitions and relationships are below.

Volt

The volt is the difference in electrical potential between two points in a circuit. Another way of putting it is to ask how many more free electrons are there at point A than at point B, to which they will flow if a path is opened for them. Voltage is also called electromotive force (EMF), and its symbol is E.

Voltage can be thought of as the pressure behind electrical flow, although this definition is not completely accurate.

Ampere

The ampere is the rate of flow of current through a conductor: how many electrons pass a given point in one second? The symbol for the ampere in mathematics is I (for intensity of current flow). Amperage is used to describe a stage circuit's electrical capacity. For instance, most theatrical circuits will carry 20 amps.

Stage Lighting and Electricity

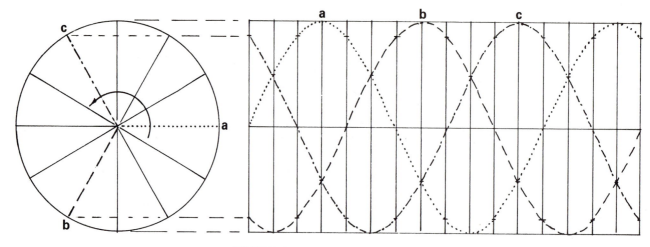

FIGURE 13–5

Overlapping Sine Curves Produced by an A-C Generator with Three Armatures at 120 Degrees to One Another

Ohm

Every substance offers some resistance to the flow of current; some, such as copper, offer very little while others, such as rubber, offer a great deal. The ohm is the measurement of such resistance and its symbol is R.

Watt

The watt is the rate of doing work, whether it is turning an electric motor, heating an electric iron, or causing a lamp to glow. Its symbol is P, for power. Wattage can be thought of as "consumption" of electricity, although one must be aware of the fact that flowing electrons are never actually consumed.

The Power Formula

The power formula is important to remember because it expresses the relationship between wattage (P), amperage (I), and voltage (E). It states that the rate of doing work (wattage) is equal to the product of current flow (amperage) and potential (voltage):

$$P = I \cdot E \text{ (Called the "pie" formula)}$$

or

$$W = V \cdot A \text{ (Using first letters of unit names—called the "West Virginia" formula)}$$

An application of the power formula might be to determine how many 750-watt lamps one could plug into a single 20-amp circuit.

378   *Designing the Lighting*

$$W = 750 \text{ per lamp}$$
$$V = 120 \text{ (U.S. Standard)}$$
$$A = 20 \text{ (given)}$$

$$X \cdot 750 = 120 \cdot 20$$

$$X = \frac{2400}{750}$$

$$X = 3$$

A 20-amp circuit thus will carry three 750-watt lamps.

Ohm's Law

Ohm's law introduces resistance (R) into a useful formula. It states that amperage (I) will equal voltage (E) divided by ohms:

$$I = \frac{E}{R}$$

DIRECT AND ALTERNATING CURRENT

Before the recent development of new techniques, direct current was not an efficient way to transport electricity over long distances. However, it was the only way known in the early days of electricity, and for that reason was installed in the downtown areas of many cities, where it can still occasionally be found. Elsewhere it has almost entirely been replaced by the more versatile alternating current.

Alternating current has the great advantage of being easily changed from low voltage to high and from high voltage to low by means of transformers. A transformer consists of an iron core, frequently doughnut shape, about which is coiled two wires, the primary and the secondary. When an alternating current is sent through the primary coil, it sets up a magnetic flux in the iron core, and in turn this flux induces a new current in the secondary coil. It must be understood that there is no electrical connection whatever between the two coils, and that the voltage transformation is solely the result of fluctuating magnetic fields which surround any electrical conductor through which power is flowing.

If the primary has few turns about the core and the secondary has more, the voltage induced in the secondary will be higher than that in the primary, but if the primary has more turns than the secondary, then the induced voltage will be lower. These are known as "step-up" and "step-down" transformers, respectively.

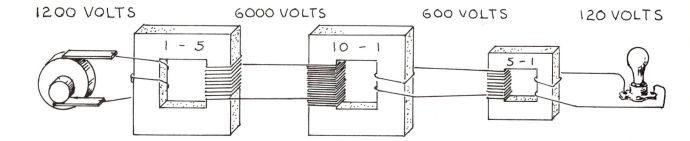

1200 VOLTS   6000 VOLTS   600 VOLTS   120 VOLTS

1 - 5   10 - 1   5 - 1

FIGURE 13–6

Schematic of A-C Transportation from the Generating Station to the Home

Figure 13–6 depicts a portion of a typical arrangement for a modest alternating-current service. At the left side we see the a-c generator station producing an EMF of 1200 volts. This is fed to the substation where a transformer boosts it to 6000 volts, because the higher the voltage the less loss there will be in transit (some high-power transit lines carry as much as 500,000 volts!). As the current nears the neighborhood in which it will be consumed, it passes through another substation where the EMF is reduced to 600 volts. This is sent out over a local wiring system until it reaches a house, where a small transformer on a pole by the highway reduces it still further to 120 volts for use in the home.

In this country the most common household service is 120 volts a-c at 60 cycles. Many foreign countries use quite different voltages, ranging from 105 to as much as 240, and these are usually at 50 cycles or even fewer.

ELECTRIC SERVICES

It is essential for the stage electrician to know which of several possible wiring systems (referred to as "service power") is carrying electricity to the theatre. This is especially true when a touring company moves into an unfamiliar building and must connect up its portable control board and other equipment. Let us glance briefly at the three forms of service in common use (Figure 13–7).

The first is the two-wire system, in which one line is said to be "hot" and the other "neutral." The potential between them is 120 volts.

It should be noted at this point that 120-volt service is often, in fact, closer to 115 volts and may drop as low as 110 volts. But today's portable lighting equipment will operate well on any of these voltages.

The second form of service is the three-wire system, in which the two outside (hot) wires usually have a potential of 240 volts between them. However, each hot wire has a potential of only 120 volts between it and the third wire, the common neutral. A familiar domestic application of this service is found in many homes, where the electric lights are on two or more circuits of 120 volts each, while the electric range operates on 240 volts. Great care must be taken when working

Designing the Lighting

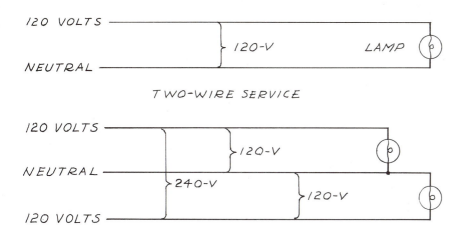

TWO-WIRE SERVICE

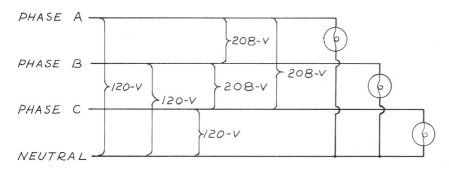

THREE-WIRE SERVICE

FOUR-WIRE (THREE-PHASE) SERVICE

FIGURE 13–7
The Three Kinds of Electrical Distribution Service

with such a system to avoid connecting any apparatus designed for 120 volts across the two hot lines. The 240 volts will blow lamps at once, ruin other equipment promptly, and provide grave danger of fatal shock. The British, who use 240 volts for all their home lighting, must take precautions that would seem very irksome to us, who are used to our comparatively mild 120-volt service.

The third type of service, and one that is popular because of its efficiency in distribution, is the a-c 120–208-volt, four-wire system, also known as the three-phase system. The generation of these three phases is illustrated in Figure 13–5. The EMF produced by each phase is said to be at 120 degrees to the others. If the EMF in relation to a common neutral conductor is 120 volts, then any two phases will be 208 volts from each other, this being the product of 240 volts times the sine value of angle 120 degrees, or .8660. Many motors are built to run on this 208 voltage, but this is of little concern to us, except that we must be sure never to connect standard-voltage equipment between two hot lines of a three-phase system. This type of service is quite commonly found in theatres.

Stage Lighting and Electricity

SERIES AND PARALLEL CIRCUITS

Once the current has been received from the supplying mains in any location, regardless of how it reaches the building (by two-, three-, or four-wire systems), it is distributed in two-wire systems, similar to the one diagrammed in Figure 13–7. The various elements that work in these circuits—lamps, switches, dimmers, fuses, and the like—may be connected in either of two ways.

One is the series circuit, in which the flow of current passes through the various elements successively. In the top diagram of Figure 13–8 we see that the current must pass through each of the four lamps, one after the other, before returning by the neutral wire. But in the center of the diagram the same four lamps are connected "in parallel," and it is apparent that a portion of the total current can flow simultaneously through each lamp.

Almost all practical lighting circuits are a combination of these two. The bottom diagram of Figure 13–8 shows a typical example. The switch and fuse are in series, and they are also in series with each of the lamps. But the four lamps are in parallel with one another. Let the switch be opened or the fuse blown and all the lamps will be extinguised. One of the lamps may be removed, however, and the remaining three will not be affected. In other words, the series portion is used to control the circuit as a whole, while the parallel portion is valuable as a distributor of the current.

In stage lighting we find that switches and fuses are most often replaced by circuit breakers and that these breakers and the dimmers

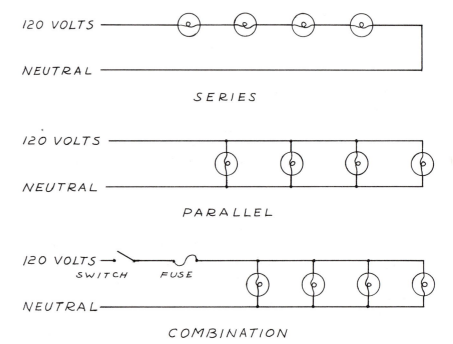

FIGURE 13–8
Types of Electric Circuits

Designing the Lighting

are put in series with the stage lights for the sake of control. The circuit breaker can act as a switch, but its primary function is to protect the entire circuit against a short circuit or an overload that would result in a harmfully high flow of current.

The lights themselves are always in parallel, as several spotlights ganged on one dimmer or the lamps in one color circuit of a striplight. In each case they are simultaneously under the control of the dimmer and the circuit breaker, but each is independent of the other. If they were connected in series, none would burn at full brightness; and, like strands of old Christmas tree lights, if one lamp fails, no lamps can burn (the broken filament will act like a switch). One or more lamps in a parallel circuit may be removed, or, providing no overload is involved, one or more may be added in parallel, without affecting those already in the circuit.

A calculation of the utmost importance in parallel circuitry is to ascertain quickly the ampere flow in a circuit. This is usually necessary when several stage instruments are ganged together or several striplights are fed through each other.

Suppose we have four spotlights ganged on one circuit, each one burning a 500-watt lamp. We may invert the power formula $(P = I \cdot E)$ to read $I = \dfrac{P}{E}$. Then:

$$I = \frac{4 \times 500}{120} = 16.67 \text{ amperes.}$$

If our circuit is fused at 20 amperes we are safe. But if we wish to change the lamps to the more powerful 750-watt variety, then:

$$I = \frac{4 \times 750}{120} = 25 \text{ amperes.}$$

This is too much for our 20-ampere circuit, so we must go back to the 500-watt lamps or put one or two of the spotlights on a different circuit.

STAGE CONNECTORS

Types of Connector

Lights on stage are temporary. They are moved after each production and even between scenes of a play. Thus, it is not wise to make permanent connections of the cables to the various lighting instruments. Devices that can be easily connected and disconnected are needed. Ordinary household plugs with parallel blades are used on some small stages, but because they are easily disconnected in error

FIGURE 13–9

Connectors

(a) Female and male heavy duty parallel-blade plugs. (b) Female and male twist-lock connectors. (c) Female and male three-wire twist-lock connectors. (d) Male and female pin connectors. (e) Male and female three-wire pin connectors. (f) Full stage plug.

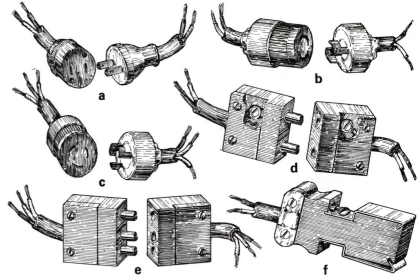

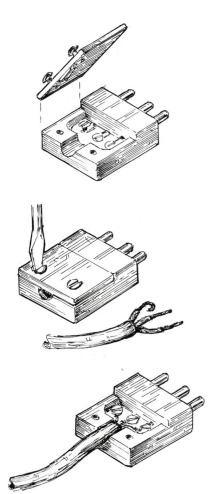

FIGURE 13–10

Steps in Wiring a Pin Connector

(a) Remove cover plate. (b) Wrap wire around screw terminal clockwise, making sure that the green or ground wire is attached to the center screw terminal. (c) Tighten screws and replace cover plate, making sure that the strain release is effective.

and have limited capacities, they are not advisable. A departure from this style that is in popular use is the twist lock, roughly similar in appearance to a heavy-duty parallel blade plug but with a design that permits the male and female caps to be locked together quite easily yet firmly (see Figure 13–9).

Beware!

Unfortunately, the electrical industry has seen fit to manufacture an amazingly large number of twist lock blade configurations. The most common stage twist lock is the 20-amp, three-prong variety, which, however, comes in several styles. The most significant difference among these styles is in the third or grounding blade, which will often have a part of the blade bent either toward the center of the plug or toward the outside. These two variations are commonly called "pin-in" or "pin-out," respectively, and cannot be used interchangeably.

When wiring a three-prong twist lock, always be sure that the grounding (green) wire is connected to the grounding prong (marked "G" or having a green screw head).

Pin connectors, heavy-duty fiber blocks with sturdy brass pins and sockets, are probably used as much as any other devices. They have the disadvantage of not always giving a firm electrical connection, and they can be easily pulled apart by mistake unless the two cables or connectors are tied together. Pin connectors have a "split" down the center of each brass male pin (hence the name split-pin connector). If a pin is not making a good connection, electrical arcing will occur and the connector will overheat. To avoid this, the individual pins can be "split" or slightly separated with a small knife blade.

Note that in pin connectors with three pins, the grounding pin is *always* the center pin.

Designing the Lighting

As in the case with cables, all such connectors come in different sizes, each rated to carry specific maximum amperages. For the stage it is wise to settle on one size and one type of connector to avoid confusion and save time. The 15-ampere pin connector or the 20-ampere twist lock is the usual choice.

The connectors described above can all be used to join a lighting instrument to a cable, or two cables to each other, or a cable to a switchboard or cross-connect panel. There is also a nearly obsolete device, known as a stage plug, which is used solely to connect a cable to a switchboard or a plugging box designed to accept it. The stage plug is a block of hard wood with a strip of brass down each of its edges that fits into a porcelain receptacle of rectangular shape. The standard plug is about 1 inch thick and is rated to carry 50 amperes.

Wiring Connectors

Proper wiring of stage connectors is important to insure against short circuiting or loose connections which can result in arcing within the plug. Stage cable and "leads" from lighting instruments will consist of small strands of copper wire. The easiest method of wiring a pin connector is to twist the small strands together (forming a more cohesive single strand) and then wrap the exposed wire around the screw terminal (Figure 13–10). Be sure to take the following precautions: (1) Expose only as much bare wire as is necessary. (2) Always wrap the wire in the direction the screw will turn when being tightened down (clockwise). (3) Be sure that the connector's strain relief is effective. The strain relief feature of a stage connector will insure that any pulling tension is placed on the cable rather than on the connecting terminals.

Pin connectors are available for two different types of stage cable: rubber cable (Type SO) and asbestos leads from instruments. The rubber cable type will have a single hole in the back of the connector while the asbestos type will have two or three smaller holes. These two connector types should not be used interchangeably.

A better and safer technique of wiring a connector involves "tinning" the exposed copper wire. The tinning process simply requires soldering all the small copper strands together to form one stiffer strand. This tinned lead will then be connected to the terminal as explained.

A third technique involves the use of a small connecting device commonly called a "Sta-kon" (Figure 13–11). The "Sta-kon" is pinched onto the exposed wire with a crimping tool. The ring is then placed around the screw terminal of the connector. Make sure that the "Sta-kon" is the proper size for the wire and that the two or three "Sta-kons" cannot make contact with each other.

Perhaps it is obvious, but one should realize that a male connector must never be "hot" or "live." For example, leads from a lighting instrument will always terminate in a male connector so that the "live" shielded female connector will plug into it.

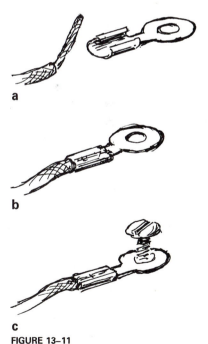

a

b

c

FIGURE 13–11

The "Sta-kon" Solderless Terminal

A special crimping tool is required to securely attach the copper wire to the "Sta-kon" terminal.

SWITCHES

A switch is a device put into a circuit to interrupt and restore the flow of current as desired, or, in more familiar terminology, to open and close the circuit. There are many types of mechanical switches, from the familiar domestic wall type to great knife-blade arrangements that handle many hundreds of amperes. Like everything else electrical, the type and size to use depends on the duty the switch is expected to perform and the load it is intended to carry.

The "disconnect" box is a heavy-duty switch housed in a metal box which may also contain fuses (Figure 13–12). A disconnect may be permanently mounted in the theatre to receive temporary lighting-control equipment, thus allowing quick and easy access to a power supply. In addition, a disconnect box, fused to the proper amperage for a traveling control system or other electrical apparatus, might also be carried by a touring production. In this case, the disconnect (fused at 100 amps, for example) would be connected to a larger amperage power supply (perhaps another disconnect) in order to protect the touring equipment from a power overload.

A contactor is an electrically operated device in which a small switch, located at some convenient place on-stage, controls a magnet which operates a large-capacity switch in a remote spot. This has the double

FIGURE 13–12
Disconnect Box
Shown is a 300-amp three-phase disconnect. Power in at the top goes through knife switches (shown in off position) and fuses to copper buss bars. Touring "road boards" and auxiliary equipment are connected to the buss bars by means of lugs or bolts.

386   *Designing the Lighting*

advantage of keeping the dangerously high current at a distance from the operator and allowing the heavy-duty portion, which is very noisy, to be placed where it cannot distract the audience.

CIRCUIT PROTECTION

No chain is stronger than its weakest link, and should an electric circuit suffer damage that causes a short circuit somewhere along the line, the ampere flow will increase to a point where *something* must burn out. The same thing will happen in the case of an overload—that is, if too many lamps are connected to the circuit. By using the power formula, we see that if six 500-watt lamps are connected to a 120-volt circuit, 25 amperes will flow through it. If 14-gage wire, which has a capacity for only 15 amperes, is used in the circuit, its limit will be greatly exceeded and again something must burn out.

To protect against such occurrences, fuses of suitable capacities are inserted to form the weakest link in the electrical chain. Then, should the current flow increase to dangerous levels, it will be the fuse that gives way, thus breaking the circuit and preventing more serious damage. The trouble is then located and corrected, and a new fuse is inserted with a minimum of trouble.

FIGURE 13–13

Fuses and a Circuit Breaker

a, b, and c are knife-blade cartridge fuses, capacities as indicated; d, e, and f are ferrule-tipped cartridge fuses; g is a typical circuit breaker; h and i are standard plug fuses; j and k are type-S plug fuses (note the difference in the threads as shown in the inserts).

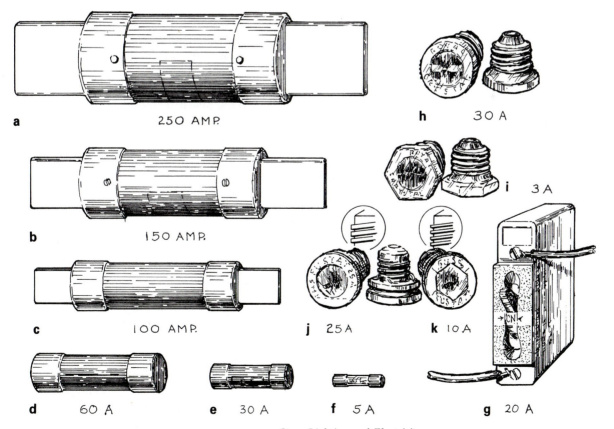

a   250 AMP.   h   30 A

b   150 AMP.   i   3 A

c   100 AMP.   j   25 A   k   10 A

d   60 A   e   30 A   f   5 A   g   20 A

Figure 13–13 shows various forms of fuses in common use at the voltages usually encountered in stage-lighting circuitry. Everyone is familiar with the plug fuse which screws into a socket like a lamp. There is a special and very useful variation of the plug fuse known as nontamperable or "Type S," which has one thickness of threading for ratings up to 15 amperes and a different threading for those rated 16 to 30 amperes. The socket is designed to take either one threading or the other but not both. When wiring up a switchboard, for example, the electrician will install a socket that takes only the proper-capacity fuse, depending on the other elements in that circuit. Thus no one can change to a higher-capacity fuse, and the circuit is always protected.

A different shaped fuse is the cartridge, which is available in contact types, sizes, and ratings as listed below.

CONTACTS	LENGTHS	CAPACITIES
Ferrule	2 inches	up to 30 amperes
	3 inches	31 to 60 amperes
Knifeblade	5⅞ inches	61 to 100 amperes
	7⅛ inches	101 to 200 amperes
	8⅝ inches	201 to 400 amperes
	10⅜ inches	401 to 600 amperes

If fuses continue to blow whenever replaced, it is a sign that there is either an overload or a short circuit, and immediate steps should be taken to eliminate the hazard. Overfusing, or bypassing a fuse, is a dangerous and foolish practice that can cause a fire.

Circuit Breakers

Today, in many installations, the fuse is being replaced by the circuit breaker. This, briefly, is a form of switch that automatically opens when the current flow becomes higher than it should. For most installations the circuit breaker is a great convenience: it saves the trouble of keeping a supply of fuses on hand, it cannot be carelessly replaced by one of the wrong capacity, and it can also serve as a switch for the circuit.

TESTING EQUIPMENT

A stage electrician must have ready access to various testing tools in order to "troubleshoot" electrical problems which invariably arise precisely when time is most critical. These tools range from the simplest test lights to rather sophisticated meters. A test light such as the one shown in Figure 13–14 will indicate whether an electrical circuit is "live" simply by either lighting or refusing to light. Test lights should be inexpensive, easy to carry, and hard to break. The neon tester shown in the figure should prove most satisfactory.

Designing the Lighting

FIGURE 13–14
Neon Test Light

A fairly recent addition to the line of stage testing equipment is the compact continuity tester (manufactured by Frontal Lobe, Ann Arbor, MI). This simple female pin connector contains a small battery which passes a low-voltage electrical current through a connected circuit. If the circuit is complete (lamp good, connector good, cable good, and so forth), a small indicator lamp in the tester will light. This simple device eliminates the necessity of a circuit being live to test for a break. A continuity test, as its name indicates, will simply determine whether a circuit is complete.

More sophisticated testing equipment in the form of meters can read voltage, amperage, and resistance (ohms) in a circuit. Most meters will combine functions (such as the V.O.M.—volt-ohm meter), are fairly delicate, and are also fairly expensive.

ELECTRICAL SAFETY

Electrical safety, like most everything else, is a matter of common sense. If you don't know what you're doing, don't do it! Attention to the following points will be helpful:

1 Always remember that electrical current will follow the path of least resistance and that your body could be that path.
2 Insulation is a good thing. Tools should be insulated with plastic or rubber handles. Soles of shoes should provide good insulation.
3 Electrical fires are most commonly caused by heat buildup caused by arcing or a short circuit.
4 Know the locations of electrical (red) fire extinguishers.
5 Fuses and circuit breakers protect equipment and insure circuit safety. Never attempt to bypass them.
6 Never use a metal ladder for electrical work unless it is insulated with rubber foot pads on all legs. Wooden ladders are always safest.
7 Be particularly wary of damp or wet conditions. Water is a fairly good electrical conductor.
8 Strain relief in electrical connectors is important.
9 Green is ground.
10 Voltage kills.

14

Light Sources

The development of even an adequate lighting design depends on a strong working knowledge of light sources and instrumentation: quality of light, distribution of light, intensity of light, color of light, and shaping or control of light. Obviously, much of this depends on the actual source of illumination. The theatre uses three basic types of light sources:

1 *Incandescence* Light given off by a glowing metal filament.
2 *Arc Light* Electrical arc that gives off intense illumination.
3 *Gaseous Discharge* Light production that depends on reaction of gases within an enclosure, but also requires an electrical arc.

INCANDESCENT LAMP

The most common source of light used on the stage today is the incandescent filament lamp: a gas-filled glass bulb containing a tungsten filament which emits light when an electrical current is passed through it. Tungsten is a metal which is relatively resistant to electrical flow. As a result, it will heat up and glow when a current is passed through it. The three important parts (Figure 14–1) of an incandescent lamp are the bulb (the glass envelope that encloses the inert gas), the base (to hold the lamp in position and to make electrical contact), and the filament (to pass the current, yet offer enough resistance to effect the transfer of electrical energy into light energy).

There are two basic categories of incandescent lamps: the standard incandescent lamp and the tungsten-halogen lamp. Thomas Edison developed the standard incandescent lamp in 1879, and it really hasn't changed much over the years. The tungsten-halogen lamp (also called the "quartz lamp," the "quartz-iodine lamp," and abbreviated "T-H") was developed in the 1950s and has become a popular theatrical lamp for reasons that will be discussed throughout the chapter.

Lamp Filaments

A passing acquaintance with optics (not a bad thing for lighting designers) tells us that a reflector of light wants to see as tiny a source as possible. The smaller the source, the more efficiently the reflector will carry out its job of gathering and precisely redirecting the light rays. Since almost all stage-lighting equipment uses reflectors of various types, the ideal lamp filament would be what we refer to as a "point source" (the size of a pinhead would do nicely). We have a long way to go toward achieving such a source, but attempts have been made to make tungsten filaments as compact as possible. The tungsten wire is often coiled (designated "C") and sometimes double-coiled (designated "CC" and called a coiled coil) in order to maintain as small a size as possible.

Among the standard incandescent filament forms used in stage-lighting equipment are the barrel (C–5) and the corona (C–7). These are designed to throw out their light equally in all directions. On the other hand, the monoplane (C–13) and the biplane (C–13D) emit most of their light in two opposite directions only, thereby permitting a larger proportion to be picked up and made useful by a reflector or a lens. The tungsten-halogen lamp uses a filament which is double coiled and tends to be a bit longer and narrower than the standard incandescent filament (Figure 14–2, page 392).

The LCL (light-center length) of a lamp is the distance from the center of the filament to some definite place in the base. With a screw-base lamp, the measurement is to the contact button at the end of the base (Figure 14–1). With a prefocus base it is to the fins, and with the

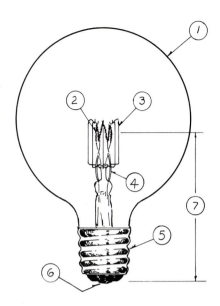

1. GAS-FILLED G-SHAPED BULB

2. BARREL FILAMENT

3. FILAMENT SUPPORTS

4. LEAD-IN WIRE

5. SCREW BASE

6. BOTTOM CONTACT BUTTON

7. L.C.L. (LIGHT CENTER LENGTH)

FIGURE 14–1
A Typical Standard Incandescent Lamp

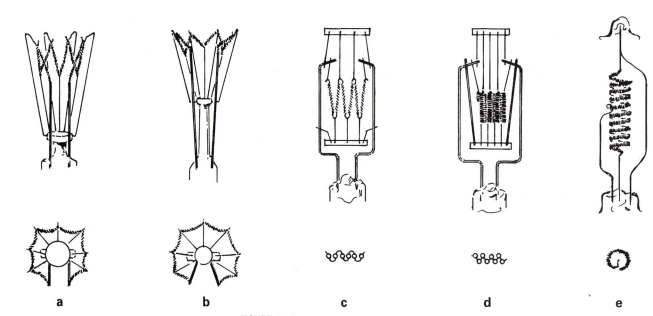

FIGURE 14–2

Filaments Frequently Used in Stage-lighting Instruments

The upper row shows a side view, the bottom row an end view of each. (a) The barrel. (b) The corona. (c) The monoplane. (d) The biplane. (e) The coiled coil.

bipost to the shoulder of the pins. It is particularly important to know the LCL when a lamp is to be used in conjunction with a reflector or a lens, for the center of the filament must be exactly aligned with the centers of such optical devices.

One important characteristic of the incandescent filament to remember is that when voltage to a lamp is reduced by using a dimmer, the color of light emitted is altered. This can be extremely important on the stage and also in color television, for the appearance of colored materials such as costumes and scenery, and even the faces of the actors, may be changed. This color shift will be discussed in greater detail later in this chapter.

Lamp Bulbs

The bulbs of standard incandescent lamps are made of ordinary glass, while the bulbs of tungsten-halogen lamps are made of the more heat- and pressure-resistant quartz glass. As a result, the standard incandescent bulb needs to be larger in order to dissipate the heat given off by the filament. The smaller envelope of the tungsten-halogen lamp has an important advantage over the standard incandescent lamp, for the size of a stage-lighting instrument is often dictated by lamp size.

Bulbs come in a variety of shapes, sizes, and finishes. The shape of a bulb is designated by a letter. The A (for arbitrary) and PS (for pearshape with straight sides) are common forms seen in the general line of household lamps (Figure 14–3). Lamps used in stage-lighting in-

Designing the Lighting

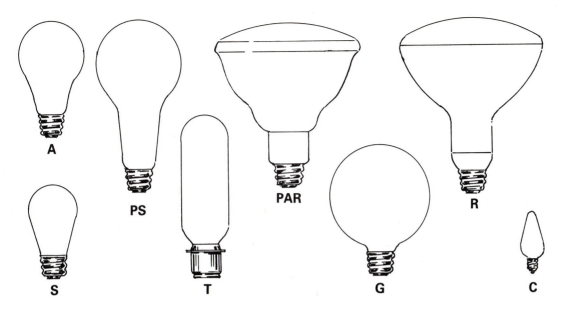

FIGURE 14–3

Typical Bulb Shapes

(A) Arbitrary designation. (S) Straight side. (PS) Pear shape, straight neck. (T) Tubular. (PAR) Parabolic aluminized reflector. (G) Globular. (R) Reflector. (C) Cone shape.

struments are usually either globe-shaped (G) to permit the even dissipation of heat or tubular (T) to allow the filament to be brought closer to some optical feature. There are a number of other shapes, some of which are purely decorative. Reflector lamps (R and PAR) will be discussed separately.

The size of a bulb is designated by a numbering system which may seem unnecessarily complex but which is, at least, standardized. The diameter of the bulb at its largest point is expressed in eighths of an inch, and this number is used to designate size. Therefore, a T–12 lamp (common in ellipsoidal reflector spotlights) means that the bulb is tubular in shape and $^{12}/_8$ of an inch (or 1½ inches) in diameter.

Bulb Finishes and Color. Lamps used on the stage usually are made of clear glass, which is essential for any source used in an instrument with reflector or lens. But the smaller wattage A and PS lamps are more readily obtained with an inner finish (called "frosting") that is intended to diffuse the light. If desired, these sizes can be ordered in the clear-glass style, but this is seldom necessary because they are rarely used in stage-lighting instruments of any precision. There are many kinds of finishes available, some purely decorative and others for some special application. The side-silvered showcase lamp that can be tucked away behind very little cover is often handy on the stage for throwing a little light in difficult corners. Colored-glass lamps are obtainable in the smaller wattages only and are not very useful on the stage except in the smallest installations.

BAYONET

SCREW

MINI-CAN

PREFOCUS

BI-PIN

BIPOST

FIGURE 14–4
Common Base Types

Lamp Bases

The electrical contact part of the base of a lamp is generally made of copper, though aluminum is now being used for many of the smaller wattages. The base may be any of several sizes, but the medium size (as in common household lamps) with a 1-inch diameter and the mogul with 1½-inch diameter are the ones most commonly used in stardard incandescent theatre lamps. The tungsten-halogen lamp, because of its smaller size, will almost always have a smaller base.

Bases also vary in type, with the common screw base (which comes in all sizes) being the simplest (Figure 14–4). Occasionally this type is sufficient, but it is often necessary to provide some sort of locking device in the base so that the lamp and particularly its filament may be held in a precise relationship with optical features of the instruments in which it is designed to burn. This relationship is referred to as "lamp alignment." Standard incandescent lamps requiring specific alignment will usually have medium or mogul prefocus bases or medium or mogul bi-post bases. Smaller lamps such as the 100-150-watt, 3-inch Fresnel lamp may use the bayonet base illustrated in Figure 14–4. The prefocus bases and the medium bi-post base slip into the socket and require slight pressure downward and a turn before the lamp "clicks" into alignment.

Tungsten-halogen lamps will normally have special bases, although quartz lamps called "retrofits" are manufactured with standard incandescent bases so that the newer T-H lamps can be used in lighting instruments designed for standard incandescent lamps. Most T-H lamps have one of two types of bases: The bi-pin base or the double-ended recessed single-contact base (Figure 14–6). The bi-pin lamp slides straight into its socket and is held in place by a pressure plate. Excessive handling or jarring may cause this lamp to dislodge from its base, so care must be taken with instruments requiring the bi-pin lamp. The double-ended lamp is held in place by two metal contacts mounted so that they protrude through the reflector of an instrument. Depending on the design of the lighting instrument, these lamps can be difficult to get properly seated. Care must therefore be taken not to damage either the contacts or the seal of the lamp base, which is most often porcelain or glass. A fairly recent addition to T-H lamp bases is the small-size screw base called a "mini-can" (short for miniature candelabra) base. This base is extremely easy to use and seems to hold up quite well under the high heat conditions of the T-H lamp.

R AND PAR LAMPS

The R (reflector type) and PAR (parabolic aluminized reflector) lamps are discussed separately here because each is essentially a self-contained lighting instrument. Both the R- and PAR-type contain a par-

Designing the Lighting

abolic-shaped reflector, either a standard incandescent filament or a small quartz lamp and a sort of lens. Because much of the light emitted by the filament is reflected out of the lamps in a useful direction, and because the reflector is sealed into the bulb itself, R and PAR lamps are extremely efficient.

PAR lamps are made out of molded, heat-resistant glass and can be used outdoors without danger of cracking if snow or rain strike them while they are hot. They are a good deal heavier and sturdier than the Rs, which are made of blown glass and are light in weight and more fragile.

A PAR lamp costs more than an equivalent wattage R-type, but it will deliver a more powerful beam of light. However, the R-type lamps have a smoother pattern of light. Both lamps are available in spot and flood beam spreads from 75 to 500 watts; higher wattage PAR lamps are available in wide flood and in medium, narrow, and very narrow beams. The lower wattage R-type and PAR lamps have medium screw bases (up to 500 watts); R-type lamps above 500 watts have mogul screw bases; and the larger (300–1500 watt) PAR lamps have either side or end-prong bases (Figure 14–5).

Automobile headlights have used PAR lamps for years, but it took rock-concert lighting to introduce these high wattage lamps to the theatre. Quartz PAR-64 lamps are mounted in a very simple housing

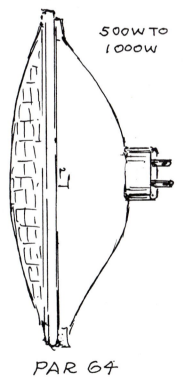

500W TO 1000W

PAR 64

FIGURE 14–5
PAR-64 Lamp
Shown with extended mogul end prong base.

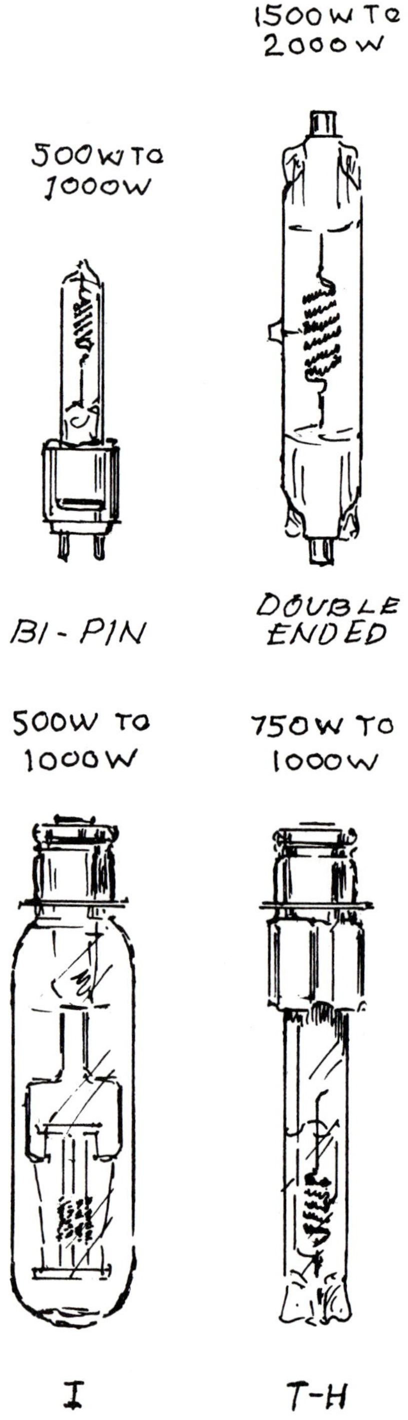

1500W TO
2000W

500W TO
1000W

BI - PIN

DOUBLE
ENDED

500W TO
1000W

750W TO
1000W

I

T-H

FIGURE 14–6

Tungsten-halogen Lamps

Top: Two common types. Bottom: Incandescent and tungsten-halogen lamp,
both with medium prefocus bases.

(aptly named PAR cans) and have the ability to throw a highly concentrated beam of light over a considerable distance. The light has a
very distinctive quality because of its nearly parallel rays and its sheer
intensity. The beam from quartz PAR lamps is more oval than round
because of the filament shape and has a very soft and fuzzy edge,
making it easy to blend one beam with another. The direction of the
oval beam is altered simply by rotating the lamp within the PAR can
housing. The PAR lamp has one distinct disadvantage over more conventional stage-lighting instruments: It is nearly impossible to control
and shape the beam. Therefore, the application of PAR lamps to theatrical lighting, although significant, has been limited.

Because of the great breadth of beam typical of R and PAR lamps,
they can be very useful in striplights, where it is necessary to blend
the light from different color circuits smoothly and at short range.
Since the reflectors are sealed into the bulbs, there is no worry about
dirt or corrosion affecting their surfaces. If the same type and size of
base is used, it is a simple matter to change from type to type depending on the precise effect desired. For example, PAR spots may be
used for a long, very intense throw and R floods for a short throw
where smoothness is more important than brightness. It should be
emphasized that the beam pattern from the R-type lamp is quite superior to that of the PAR, and, as a result, the R-type is a better general
purpose striplight lamp.

Small wattage (30–75 watts) R-20 and R-30 lamps, often used in
showcase lighting applications, are frequently useful in lighting tight
spaces where a standard stage lighting instrument would be too large,
heavy, or clumsy.

TUNGSTEN-HALOGEN LAMPS

The development of the tungsten-halogen lamp has led to significant
changes in the lighting industry. The most important, perhaps, has
been the creation of smaller and more powerful lighting instruments
designed specifically for these new lamps, a development that has
freed the lighting designer from the restrictions of relatively archaic
equipment. Not only are the T-H lamps much more compact than
standard incandescent lamps (see Figure 14–6), but they also have a
much longer life and maintain initial intensity throughout their life-
span.

The secret of this significant innovation is the halogen-family gas
introduced into the bulb. As a tungsten filament burns, particles evap-
orate from the filament and deposit themselves on the cooler glass
envelope. The result of this process is a gradual darkening of the bulb
and, consequently, a lessening of light output from the lamp. In the
T-H lamps, however, the halogen gas gobbles up the elusive tungsten

Designing the Lighting

particles and redeposits them at the hottest point within the bulb—the filament. (The lamp ultimately fails only because the halogen gas does not redeposit the particles evenly.) Because the desired reaction between the tungsten particles and halogen gas requires a great deal of heat, the glass envelope is made smaller and constructed out of strong quartz glass.

Naturally, the T-H lamp costs about twice as much as a standard incandescent lamp of comparable wattage; but its life is nearly two times longer and it is more efficient.

A significant disadvantage of the T-H lamp is that the quartz glass envelope cannot be touched by fingers. No matter how clean your hands happen to be, oil from your skin is deposited on the glass and will react with the quartz when it is heated. The result of this reaction not only weakens the envelope (possibly causing explosion) but also produces a frosted effect on the glass (if we had wanted frosted, we would have ordered frosted).

The tungsten filament found in most stage T-H lamps is probably more fragile than the standard incandescent filament. The only real explanation for this is poorer filament support within the envelope. As a result, many rental houses continue to use the older standard incandescent lamp, although they are now being forced to change over to quartz because of new instrumentation requirements. This unfortunate weakness in T-H lamps must be recognized, and all instruments equipped with them should be treated with great care. *Never* jar an instrument with the lamp burning, for the supple tungsten filament will almost surely break.

LAMP LIFE

The rated-average life for the common household lamp is usually 750 burning hours, but for many standard incandescent stage lamps it is only 200 hours. Rated-average life is determined by the manufacturer, who takes a number of lamps at random and leaves them burning under normal conditions until (1) they burn out completely or (2) their light output drops to 80 percent of what it was originally.

Rated-average life is presumed to apply under usual operating conditions. But a lamp's life may be shortened in a number of ways. It will give out more quickly if burned while enclosed in an excessively hot place such as one from which its own heat cannot escape (lighting instruments are specifically ventilated for this purpose). Rough handling may break some interior part, even though the outer appearance has not changed. If connected to a higher voltage than it was designed for, a lamp will burn out rapidly, even abruptly. And in the case of many standard incandescent lamps used in stage instruments, burning in the wrong position results in rapid failure. The correct burning position, if important, will always be marked on the end of the bulb and should be consulted if any doubt exists.

Standard incandescent T-12 and T-14 lamps are particularly susceptible to failure if they are burned in the wrong position. A nonquartz T lamp designed to be used in an ellipsoidal spotlight should be burned base up, or nearly so, for the filament is close to the end of the bulb, which would be melted by the heat if it accumulated there. On the other hand, the T-20 lamp intended to be used in a Fresnel spotlight should be burned base down or no more than 90 degrees from the perpendicular, for the filament is close to the base and if the heat should concentrate there it would crack the cement seal between bulb and base (Figure 14–7). All T-H lamps (except retrofits) are designed to burn in any position.

If a lamp designed to be used on 120-volt service is fed with only 110 volts, the lamp will last almost four times as long as it would on 120 volts, but there will be only about 74 percent as much light.

On the other hand, if this same lamp is fed 130 volts, there will be 31 percent more light, but the lamp will last only a third as long.

This relationship of voltage, intensity, and life must be kept in mind, especially when bargains in "lamps that burn twice as long" or the like are offered. It also explains why stage lamps often last far longer than anticipated: they have been burned at low dimmer readings.

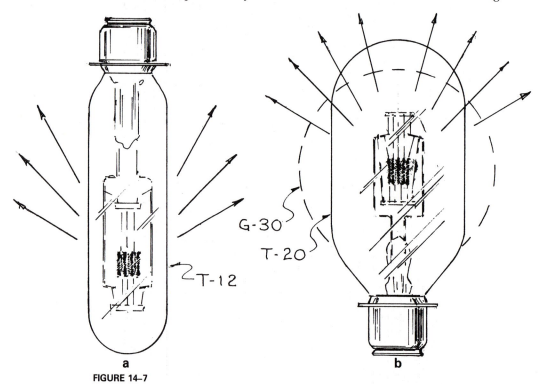

FIGURE 14–7

Dissipation of Heat from Incandescent Lamps

(a) A lamp designed to be burned base up. (b) Lamps designed to be burned base down.

Designing the Lighting

Watts	GE Ordering Code	ANSI Code	National Stock No. 6240-00-	Std. Pkg. Qty.	Approx. Color Temp. °K	Approx. Hours Life	Approx. Initial Lumens	Lighted Length— Inches	Bulb Finish
1000	Q1000T6/CL	DWT	917-6915	6	3000	2,000	23,400	1	Clear
	FER-Q1000T6/4CL	FER	—	6	3200	500	27,500	3/4	Clear
1500	DVV-Q1500T8/4CL	DVV (11)	—	6	3200	500	42,700	1 1/4	Clear
2000	FEY-Q2000T8/4CL	FEY	231-0761	6	3200	300	59,000	1	Clear

FIGURE 14–8

Comparison of Wattage, Color Temperature, Life, and Lumen Output

(Table courtesy General Electric Company. Publication SS-123: *Stage Studio Lamps.*)

Wattage and Lumen Output

The general public has been taught by lamp manufacturers to equate the wattage of a lamp with its brightness. If our 75-watt reading lamp is too dim, we simply replace it with a 100-watt lamp. But, as we learned in Chapter 13, wattage is the rate of doing work and, therefore, is not necessarily an accurate measure of lamp intensity. Lamp manufacturers use a measure of intensity called the lumen to measure the light output of a lamp. Figure 14–8 shows how two lamps with identical physical specifications can be very different in brightness (compare DWT and FER). Note that as lumen output is increased, lamp life is significantly decreased.

IDENTIFYING AND PURCHASING LAMPS

The American National Standards Institute (ANSI) has established a system for identifying lamps by a three-letter code called the "ANSI Code." If one lamp differs in any way from another, it will be assigned a separate ANSI code (Figure 14–8). Although the three-letter codes are totally nondescript by themselves, they have greatly simplified the process of specifying lamps. One may now simply order a lamp by giving the supplier the ANSI code.

Of course, the wise electrician will also be familiar with all possible variations in lamp manufacture and will have access to up-to-date lamp catalogs. Not only are these catalogs useful when ordering spare lamps, but they also offer quick access to special application lamps such as flashbulbs, low-voltage lamps, and photo-floods. The two major lamp manufacturers in the United States are willing to supply you with their current catalogs. Write to either their regional sales offices or to the following addresses:

SYLVANIA

GTE Products Corp.
Lighting Center
Danvers, MA 01923

GENERAL ELECTRIC

General Electric Company
Lighting Business Group
Nela Park
Cleveland, OH 44112

In addition to its lamp catalogs, Sylvania publishes a short and easy-to-use book called *Sylvania Lighting Handbook* (currently in its seventh edition), which will be sent to you upon request.

COLOR TEMPERATURE

We tend to think of the light emitted from an ordinary lamp as being "white," but the fact is that so-called "white" light is relative, and the actual color of light given off by sources can vary greatly. The method we have to identify the color makeup of any light source is called color temperature and its measurement is in Kelvin (K) degrees. To standardize color notation, a light-emitting device called a blackbody was developed; when heated it emits light consisting of various color wavelengths. The blackbody responds to heat in much the same way that a tungsten filament does; it begins to glow a very warm red-yellow, moves toward "white" as more heat is applied, and will finally appear to approach blue when a great deal of heat is applied. The color wavelengths of light emitted by the blackbody are identified by a sophisticated meter called a spectrophotometer. Any color can thus be equated with the temperature of heat being applied to the blackbody, resulting in a meaningful Kelvin figure.

This is fairly important for a lighting designer to understand because theatre sources will typically range from standard incandescence, which is around 3000° K, to the much cooler arc lamps which can be as high as 6000° K. Obviously, the same color filter placed in front of two such different sources will project very different colors. For all practical purposes, no one will notice a source color difference of less than 200° K; but any more of a difference will be noticeable. The color temperature of stage lamps is often printed on their containers and is always noted in catalogs. A general rule to go by is the higher the color temperature, the cooler the light. And always realize that dimming a source decreases color temperature significantly.

LOW-VOLTAGE LAMPS

Low-voltage light sources are lamps designed to operate with less than 120 applied volts. Sealed-beam automobile headlights operate to full potential with only 12 volts, while aircraft lamps operate with 24 volts. The advantage of low-voltage lamps for theatre application is in the intensity and quality of the light they emit. The lower the voltage applied to a lamp filament, the smaller the filament can be. Therefore, low-voltage sources have filaments which really do begin to approach the much-desired point source of light. The more closely we approximate a point source, the better we can control the light through the use of reflectors and lenses.

Low-voltage lamps such as aircraft landing lamps (ACLs) deliver an incredibly coherent light that is intense and harsh in quality. To use such lamps on the stage, however, a low-voltage power source is necessary. A variable voltage transformer is a good equipment investment for an active theatre, but it can be fairly expensive. Two substitutes come to mind. The first is the continuous duty car battery charger, which is actually a step-down transformer from 120 to 12 volts. The second is the auto transformer, which functions as a dimmer by reducing the voltage to a lamp (not true of the modern SCR and other electronic dimmers). One can put a meter on the output of an auto transformer dimmer and set the reading to any desired voltage.

When using low-voltage sources, care must be taken not to overload a circuit or the transformer. The power formula tells us that, given the same-wattage lamp, as the voltage is lowered, the amperage is subsequently raised.

ARC LIGHT

The first electric light source to be used in the theatre was an arc light in the form of limelight. Blocks of calcium oxide (lime) were used in place of the more modern carbon rods in spotlights each requiring an operator. In fact, there are reports that the quality of limelight was so flattering that patrons bemoaned the installation of more modern incandescent light sources in many theatres. Arc light is impressive because of its brilliance—a streak of lightning during a thunderstorm is an example of arc light on a grand scale. The brief off-stage striking of an arc is a theatrical technique used to simulate lightning on stage.

Carbon-Arc

The carbon-arc light source became popular in the theatre because of its intense and high color temperature light. American taste in follow spotting, especially for Broadway-type musical productions, calls for a strong frontal source; and, because of physical restrictions on where one could place such a lighting instrument and operator in the typical Broadway house, an instrument with the potential of delivering a whole lot of light was developed. This instrument was the carbon-arc follow spot.

Two copper-coated carbon rods, about the size of pencils, are mounted within a housing along with a reflector and lenses. Electricity is conducted to the tips of the rods via the copper coating. The two rods are brought together to begin the flow of electricity (called "striking" the arc) and then backed off, forcing the electricity to jump the ¼ - ½ inch gap. This gap, which is air filled with a few flying carbon particles, offers a good deal of resistance to the electrical flow and, as a result, quite a bit of heat and light is generated. The arc is fairly small, so it works well with the instrument's optical system. As the carbons burn down (the life of a carbon should be at least 45 minutes), they are slowly fed into each other, thereby maintaining a constant gap.

A byproduct of carbon-arc combustion is carbon monoxide gas, a lethal substance. Never operate a carbon-arc follow spot or projector without proper ventilation.

The major manufacturer of carbon-arc follow spots in the United States is Strong Electric, a company well known for its Trouper and Super Trouper series of follow spots. While carbon-arc sources had a stronghold on follow spotting and projection for many years, recent developments in arc lamps will ultimately make carbon-arc as antique a light source as limelight.

Short-Arc Lamps

Two tungsten electrodes in a strong glass enclosure of gas under high pressure produce an intense light source when the current arcs between the electrodes. The result is a brilliant point source. Because the arc is shielded from the oxygen in the air, the tungsten electrodes do not burn up as do the carbons in the arc light.

Of the short-arc lamps currently available the xenon lamp is the oldest. The xenon lamp, which is filled with high-pressure xenon gas, burns with a brilliant, cool light. Its high efficiency and long life help to compensate for its high cost. Because of its efficiency and long life

FIGURE 14–9
Short-arc Lamp
The HMI lamp, 2500 watts.

Designing the Lighting

it has been standard installation in motion picture projectors and long-range follow spots.

The problem with the xenon lamp is that it has a tendency to explode because of the high pressure of the gas within the glass envelope. Several xenon lamp accidents (with small fragments of glass being propelled through the air at startling velocities) have prompted the enactment of safety regulations for the use of xenon sources. Among others, these include explosion-proof lamp housings that further increase the user's cost.

The more recent HMI lamp is constructed like the xenon lamp but with the gas under a much lower pressure. It is a good projector lamp, although the light has such a high Kelvin temperature that it needs a warm filter to correctly project the colors of the film or slide (Figure 14–9). HMI follow spots are becoming more common, and this trend will probably continue unless an even more acceptable high-intensity source is developed.

A final note: The major disadvantage of any arc source for theatrical applications is that it cannot be electronically dimmed.

GASEOUS DISCHARGE LAMPS

The most familiar form of gaseous discharge lamps is the fluorescent tube, which never achieved its promises of becoming a major light source in the theatre. Current passing through a pressurized mercury vapor causes a gaseous discharge, predominantly in the ultraviolet zone, which is absorbed by the phosphorous coating on the inside walls of the tube. The coating reemits the energy, becoming the light source itself.

Because the fluorescent tube is a line of light and not a point source, its uses in the theatre are limited to producing a wash of light on a cyclorama or backdrop. The shape of the lamp makes it difficult to achieve smooth color blending. The fluorescent hoods, however, can be installed with black light flourescent tubes to flood the stage with ultraviolet light for a black light effect.

A black light effect is the illuminating of a surface treated with fluorescent paint or dye with ultraviolet light (UV). The fluorescent surface becomes, in effect, the light source as it reemits the energy of the ultraviolet light.

The mercury vapor lamp with a UV filter is another effective instrument to produce black light. Both the black light fluorescent tube and the mercury vapor lamp require a ballast and warmup time and cannot be dimmed.

It should be also be mentioned that the arc-light follow spot can be equipped with a UV filter and be used for a black light effect.

SAFETY AND LIGHT SOURCES

A good electrician follows several simple rules when working with the various light sources found in the theatre:

1 Always unplug a lighting instrument before replacing a bad lamp.
2 Lamps are expensive, so be sure to treat them with care.
3 Unshielded arc light is bright enough to blind anyone looking directly at the source. A warning to contact lens wearers: An unshielded arc flash has been known to weld the lens (plastic type) to the cornea, resulting in blindness. (From the latest report of the Union [USA] Safety Study.)
4 Keep your fingers off quartz bulbs.
5 The envelope of a burning lamp gets too hot to handle even with the best of gloves.

15

Reflection and Refraction

When a beam of light passing through air encounters anything in its path, three things can happen. The light may be absorbed (for example, by a sheet of black material), it may be refracted (through a lens), or it may be reflected (by any opaque substance it strikes). Actually, none of these things will happen completely: a mirror or a lens will absorb a small portion of light, the blackest of materials will still reflect some light, a piece of colored glass will absorb certain light rays and allow others to pass through. All stage-lighting instruments use reflectors to increase the efficiency of a light source, and some use lenses to gather and redirect light from the source. By understanding the laws by which reflection and refraction operate, we can better understand how stage-lighting instruments work and why light behaves as it does when it strikes the stage and actors.

REFLECTION OF LIGHT

The law of specular reflection explains what happens to a light beam when it strikes a smooth, shiny surface, such as a mirror. It is reflected at an angle equal to the angle at which it struck, but in the opposite direction. (The angle of incidence is equal to the angle of reflection.) A moment's contemplation of a mirror will make this clear. Of course, if the beam strikes the surface head on, it will reflect directly back over the same path (Figure 15–1).

If the beam strikes a surface with slight irregularities, for example etched aluminum or foil paper that has been crumpled and smoothed out again, the same law applies. However, because there are now innumerable small surfaces rather than a single, perfectly flat one, the reflected rays will tend to be scattered but will not diverge too greatly from one basic direction. This phenomenon is known as spread reflection.

A piece of blotting paper or soft cotton cloth will produce a diffuse reflection because of the vast number and varied angles of the surface. In the case of these surfaces, there will be no single direction to the reflected light. Rather the whole surface will appear much the same from whatever angle it is viewed.

A combination of specular and diffuse reflection is known as mixed reflection. A piece of crockery with a high glaze will produce this: the rough surface of the ceramic will create diffusion, while the shiny glaze will act like a mirrored surface to give specular reflection. Furthermore, the diffused light will show the color of the material itself, while the other reflected light (or highlight) will have the color of the source.

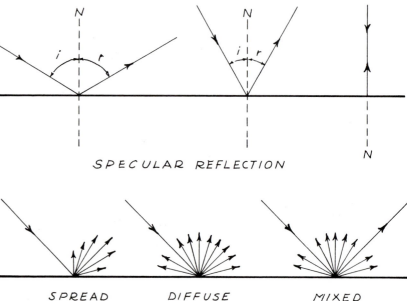

SPECULAR REFLECTION

FIGURE 15–1
Types of Reflection

SPREAD REFLECTION   DIFFUSE REFLECTION   MIXED REFLECTION

Designing the Lighting

REFLECTORS

Early stage-lighting instruments used reflectors which were molded glass mirrors, but modern reflectors are constructed of a lightweight spun metal. After fabrication, this metal shell is given a highly reflective and durable surface treatment called the Alzak process. The Alzak reflector has become an industry standard.

Stage-lighting instruments use one of three reflector types or shapes:

1 *spherical:* found in the Fresnel-type spotlight.
2 *parabolic:* found in beam projectors and PAR- and R-type lamps.
3 *ellipsoidal:* found in ellipsoidal reflector spotlights (ERS).

As one would expect, the shape of the reflector determines exactly how it redirects light from a source.

Spherical Reflectors

If polished metal is made into a reflector in the form of a part of a sphere, and a source of light is placed at the center of the curvature of this form, each ray of light that strikes the reflecting surface will do so squarely. It will be returned through the source, thereby increasing the amount of light emanating from the source in the opposite direction (Figure 15–2, page 408).

Naturally, it is necessary for the source, say the filament of a lamp, to be located precisely in relation to the reflector, or its rays will not strike the reflector straight on but at various angles. Although not doubled, the efficiency of a light source in combination with a spherical reflector is increased significantly.

Parabolic Reflectors

The nature of a parabolic reflector is such that if a light source is placed at its focal center, or focal point, all rays that strike the reflective surface will emerge parallel to one another (Figure 15–3, page 408). This will naturally give a great concentration of light in a tight beam, rather than the spread effusion from a spherical reflector.

Moving the source from the focal point toward the reflector will spread the light, while moving it away from the reflector causes light rays to converge.

The only problem with the parabolic reflector in stage-lighting instruments is that in addition to the valuable parallel rays being reflected, the source also emits nonparallel rays out the front of the instrument. When we study the beam projector we will look at attempted solutions to this problem.

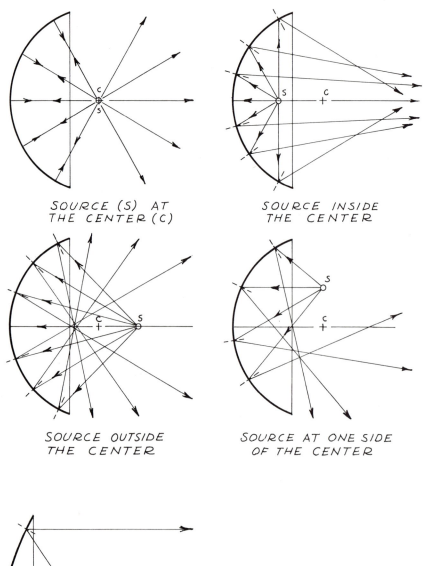

SOURCE (S) AT
THE CENTER (C)

SOURCE INSIDE
THE CENTER

FIGURE 15–2

**Reflection from a Spherical Reflector
Under Different Conditions**

SOURCE OUTSIDE
THE CENTER

SOURCE AT ONE SIDE
OF THE CENTER

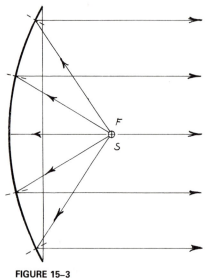

PARABOLIC
REFLECTOR

SOURCE (S) AT THE
FOCAL POINT (F)

FIGURE 15–3

Reflection from a Parabolic Reflector

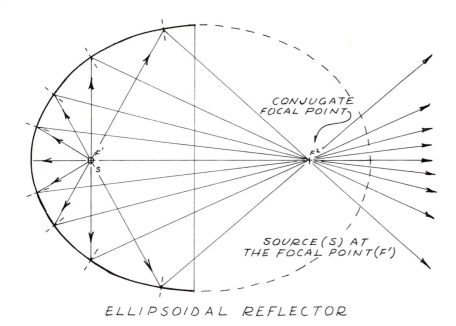

ELLIPSOIDAL REFLECTOR

FIGURE 15–4
Reflection from an Ellipsoidal Reflector

Ellipsoidal Reflectors

The ellipsoidal reflector is more efficient than either the spherical or parabolic reflectors. By mathematical definition an ellipsoid has two focal points. When a reflector is constructed in the form of half of an ellipsoid and a source is placed at the focal point at that end, all rays of light that strike the reflector will be diverted through the second or conjugate focal point (Figure 15–4). The result is that an enormous percentage of the light from the source is directed in a manner that makes it easily usable, as we shall examine in Chapter 16 in the section on spotlights.

As we saw earlier, the ideal source of light is a point source; stage lamps only approximate such a source. Because of this, some ellipsoidal reflectors are not a continuous smooth surface, as expected, but are regularly broken up into small rectangles or facets. These facets tend to more precisely direct the light to the conjugate focal point of the ellipsoidal reflector. Such a reflector is called a flatted reflector (Figure 15–5).

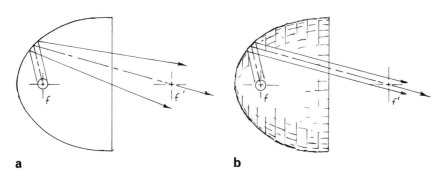

a   b

FIGURE 15–5
Double-plated Ellipsoidal Reflector

(a) The interaction of an area light source with a nonflatted reflector. (b) How the same light source reacts to a flatted reflector.

Reflection and Refraction

Other Reflectors

Two other reflectors should also be mentioned: the combination reflector and the dichroic reflector.

The combination reflector unites the properties of all three reflectors discussed above and is more efficient. Light quality from this reflector is nearly identical to that from a normal ellipsoidal reflector but lamp efficiency is greater.

The most common example of a dichroic reflector can be found in the lamp and reflector assembly used in the Kodak Carousel slide projector (ANSI code: ELH). The term *dichroic* does not refer to a particular reflector shape but to the special properties of selective reflection. Put simply, the dichroic reflector will allow a great deal of heat to pass through it while still reflecting nearly 100 percent of the visible light. This is especially significant in projection equipment, where major efforts are taken to protect the slide or film from overheating.

REFRACTION OF LIGHT

Refraction is a phenomenon observed by anyone who looks into a pool of water and notices how a straight stick will seem to bend sharply as it passes beneath the surface. The law of refraction states that when a ray of light passes into a denser medium (for example from air into water), it is bent toward a perpendicular drawn to the surface at the point of entry; when it reemerges into the less dense medium, it is bent away from the perpendicular drawn at that point.

Plano-Convex Lens

If the two surfaces of a sheet of glass are parallel, the path of an emerging ray will be parallel to its entering path but slightly offset (Figure 15–6). But if the two surfaces are not parallel, then the emerging ray will take a different course depending on the angle at which it strikes each surface. This is the principle of all lenses, of which there

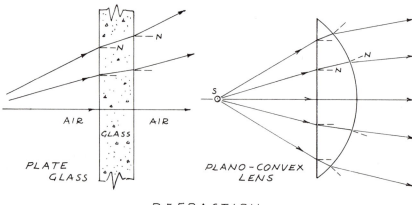

FIGURE 15–6

Refraction of Light

(Left) Refraction of rays of light passing through a sheet of glass. (Right) Refraction of rays of light passing through a plano-convex lens.

are many forms, but the plano-convex lens, with one flat side and one curved surface (or modifications of this) is the only one of importance to us. It is the simplest and least expensive lens for concentrating spreading rays into a compact beam of great brightness.

Focal Point and Focal Length

Every lens has a focal point. If parallel light rays (such as those from the sun) strike a lens, they will converge at the focal point. Conversely, if a source of light is placed at the focal point of a lens, all the rays of light that emerge from the lens will be parallel one to another.

Lenses are identified by two numbers. The first gives the diameter in inches, while the second gives the focal length (the distance from the focal point to the approximate center of the lens). Thus, a 6-by-9-inch lens (6 × 9) will have a diameter of 6 inches and a focal length of 9 inches. The greater the curve of the convex face, the greater the refracting power of a lens. Therefore, a thick lens will have a shorter focal length than a thin one.

It is usually desirable to know the focal length of a lens. However, because this information is rarely marked on lenses, a quick method of determining focal length is valuable. If the sun is shining, the lens may be carried outdoors and held, plano side down, so that the sun's rays are concentrated on the ground. Then, using a ruler, measure the distance from the ground to the focal plane. For lenses used in stage-lighting equipment the focal lengths are measured in even inches.

When indoor light is used, stand as far away as possible from the light source. The resulting measurement will be, in this case, somewhat longer than the true focal length but by less than an inch. So by simply eliminating the fraction, we can calculate the exact focal length quite accurately. For example, if the measurement is 11½ inches, we know the focal length is 11 inches; if we measure 9¼ inches, we know the focal length is 9 inches.

Figure 15–7 (page 412) illustrates how emerging rays diverge if a source of light is placed between the focal point and the lens. If the source is placed farther from the lens than the focal point, the rays will converge and eventually cross one another. Since the light from a stage-lighting instrument should spread in the shape of a cone, the lenses of the ellipsoidal reflector spotlight will cause the light to converge and cross at some point beyond the lens barrel.

Fresnel and Step Lenses

The thick glass of a lens with a short focal length has a tendency to crack because of excessive heat from the source. Ellipsoidal reflector spotlights often compensate for this deficiency by using a combination of two lenses rather than one. In this way, each lens is thinner and therefore less likely to crack from heat build-up.

Two other solutions have been developed, both using the technique

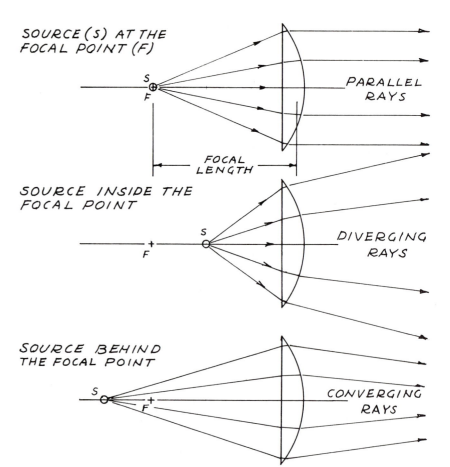

SOURCE(S) AT THE FOCAL POINT (F)

PARALLEL RAYS

FOCAL LENGTH

SOURCE INSIDE THE FOCAL POINT

DIVERGING RAYS

SOURCE BEHIND THE FOCAL POINT

CONVERGING RAYS

FIGURE 15–7

Refraction

Refraction of light passing through a plano-convex lens under different conditions.

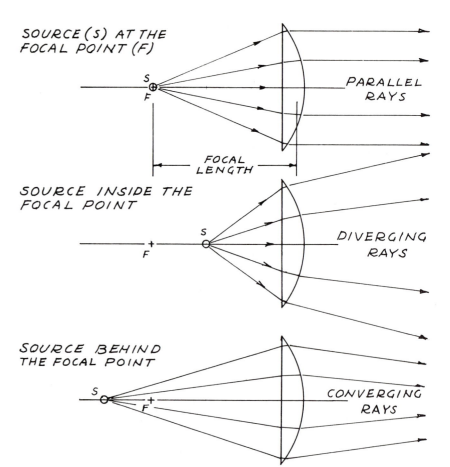

"CUTAWAY" PORTIONS

FRESNEL LENS   STEP LENS

FIGURE 15–8

Simplified Diagrams Showing How Fresnel and Step Lenses are Derived from the Plano-convex Lens

of cutting away part of the thick glass yet retaining the basic relationships between the curved and the plano surfaces. The first of these is the Fresnel (pronounced Fre'nel) lens, in which the plano face is retained, but the curved face is cut back in steps. More recent is the step lens, in which the convex side retains its shape while the plano face is cut back (Figure 15–8).

The Fresnel spotlight derives its name from its lens. The plano surface of the lens is broken up by either a light frosting technique or by a series of dimples molded into the glass. This breaking up of the light results in the very smooth and soft illumination distinctive of the Fresnel spotlight.

The step lens was put to use in ellipsoidal reflector spotlights and became fairly popular because of its low cost and light weight. Yet, the light from a step lens simply is not of the same quality as that from a plano-convex lens. Disturbing ring patterns from the step risers are commonly projected by a step-lens instrument, and the light is never as clean or crisp in quality. As a result, instrument manufacturers have returned to the plano-convex lenses, using them in adjustable relationships to allow variable beam spreads.

412

Designing the Lighting

Lenses in the Theatre

An ellipsoidal reflector spotlight will be designated either by its lens diameter and focal length (6 × 12, for instance) or by the spread of its light beam in degrees. Both designations are accurate, but the labeling by degrees is probably the most helpful. A general rule to follow is that the shorter the focal length, the wider the beam spread (given identical lens diameters). The following table illustrates some standard instrument designations and their respective field* spreads in degrees:

INSTRUMENT	FIELD SPREAD
6 × 9 ERS	40°
6 × 12 ERS	28°
6 × 16 ERS	20°
8 × 9 ERS	15°
10 × 12 ERS	10°

Always consult the specifications published by instrument manufacturers to determine the exact light-beam spread for a specific instrument.

The quality of light from a stage-lighting instrument greatly depends on its optical system. This not only involves the type of reflector and lens but also their condition. Mistreated or dirty lenses and reflectors can turn a very fine spotlight into little more than a lamp in a can. Keep lenses and reflectors clean; replace cracked or chipped lenses; and treat your spotlights with the care they deserve. You'll have a happier bunch of luminaries, and your work as a designer will be much more gratifying.

---

*The definition of, and distinction between, field and beam spread will be discussed in following chapters.

16

Distribution Control

Distribution is the first of the controllable properties of light we will discuss in depth. Recall that the term *distribution* refers not only to direction or angle of illumination but also to quality of light. Will the light be soft or harsh; will it be textured and broken up or coherent and smooth; will it have sharp, linear edges or a soft, rounded shape? The lighting designer must always go through a specific (although often subconscious) process of matching known instrument capabilities with specific requirements of a production. Assuming the designer has an image of the quality of light desired, the next step is to determine what lighting instrument will be most capable of delivering that specific feeling. Several factors will affect this determination:

1 Instrumentation available.
2 Physical (theatre) restrictions.
3 Quality of light.
4 Beam shaping and control.

Instrumentation Available

Choices of lighting instruments would be unlimited with a large budget; but the lighting designer is seldom in such an enviable position. Most often, the designer will be working with a limited and specific equipment list and with a restricted budget. It is always wise to confirm the accuracy of an equipment list before completing the design work.

Physical Restrictions

Physical restrictions invariably affect lighting possibilities. They include the throw distance (distance from lighting instrument to target), the amount (if any!) of offstage space for sidelighting positions, the adequacy of hanging positions both front-of-house as well as overstage, and the degree of restricted space to make a lighting "shot."

Quality of Light

The designer must now consider the quality of light possible. Perhaps an 8-inch Fresnel would be a better choice than a 6 × 12 ERS because of the softer quality of its beam. Perhaps an ERS is the only answer because we want to break up the light with a template. Perhaps a PAR can will best deliver the strong yet soft-edged illumination sought by the designer.

Beam Shaping and Control

The final consideration is a simple one: will the chosen instrument provide the desired beam shaping and control?

The following information on stage-lighting instruments will give the reader a basis for making intelligent decisions. Because stage workers have a habit of referring to whole classes of instruments by trade names or other slang terminology, there seems to be a bewildering complexity of such instruments. Actually, there are just a few basic types.

SPOTLIGHTS

The spotlight is by far the most important lighting instrument on the modern stage. Broadly defined, the spotlight is a metal hood containing a high-powered source of light which is made more effective by use of a lens and usually a reflector as well. The resulting beam of high-intensity light can be shaped by various means to forms that may be significant in the stage picture.

The Plano-convex Spotlight

The first incandescent spotlight, and for many years the only kind, was the plano-convex spot. In a simple hood a G-shaped lamp is mounted on a sliding carriage to which is attached a small spherical

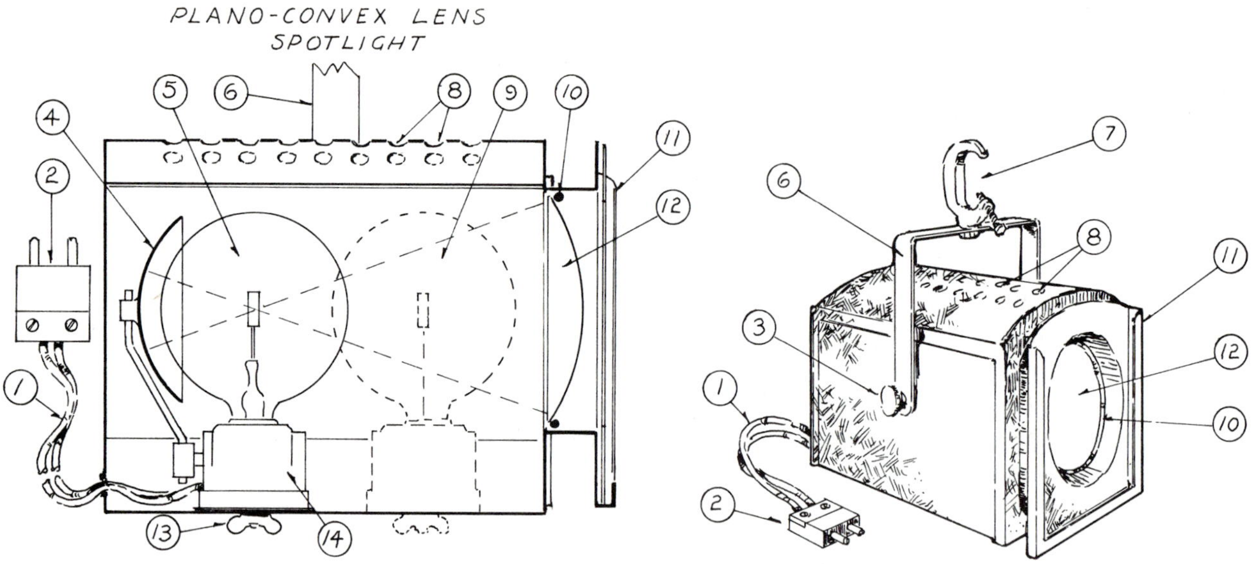

FIGURE 16–1

The Plano-convex Spotlight

(1) Asbestos-covered lead wires. (2) Pin connector. (3) Vertical adjustment knob. (4) Spherical reflector. (5) G-shape lamp. (6) Yoke. (7) Pipe clamp. (8) Ventilation holes. (9) Lamp in flood focus position. (10) Spring ring to hold lens in position. (11) Color-frame holder. (12) Plano-convex lens. (13) Focus-adjustment knob. (14) Movable lamp socket.

reflector that rides behind the lamp and is always in correct relationship to it (Figure 16–1). As was explained in Chapter 15, such a reflector sends all rays that strike it back through the original source, thus increasing output.

In front of the lamp and carefully aligned with its filament is placed a plano-convex lens which refracts all the rays that strike it and bends them into a comparatively narrow beam. When the lamp is close to the lens in flood position the percentage of total light that strikes the lens is quite high, but because this spreads into a wide angle after leaving the lens, there is no great intensity to the beam at any distance from the instrument. When the lamp is moved back toward the focal point of the lens, the angle of acceptance of the lens is less and the beam much narrower. So, although a smaller percentage of the light is utilized, the beam then has greater intensity because all the light is concentrated in the narrower shaft. The inside of the hood is painted a flat black to absorb all rays of light that do not strike the lens directly.

Spotlight Accessories. The lens of a plano-convex spotlight is held in place by a strong metal spring ring. Above and below the lens opening in the hood there are small troughs to hold color media frames. Every spotlight has some means of mounting, usually a yoke held in place on side studs by large nuts or set wheels and a C-clamp for attaching the instrument securely to a pipe. Ventilation must be supplied—above to allow hot air to escape and below to let cool air in. The ventilation holes or slots are fitted with baffles to prevent light spill. Some means of access permits the electrician to inspect the hood's interior and change the lamp without otherwise disturbing instrument or focus.

Plano-convex Spot Sizes. The P-C, as the plano-convex spot is frequently called, was manufactured in three sizes, the smallest and least powerful of which had a 5-inch lens and burned G-shaped lamps of 250 and 400 watts. It was useful for short throws, as on a very small stage and could be hidden in nooks where other instruments would prove too large. This small spotlight was usually referred to as a "baby."

Larger "brothers" were those with 6-inch and 8-inch plano-convex lenses. In general it may be said that the 8-inch type burned 2000-watt lamps while the 6-inch models ranged from 500 to 1500 watts, all of the G type.

While important in the minds and hearts of stage-lighting practitioners, the fact is that today the P-C is almost never found in everyday use. Because of their greater efficiency, the Fresnel and ellipsoidal reflector spotlights have replaced the P-C in nearly every application.

Fresnel Spotlight

The Fresnel is actually very close to the P-C in design and operation. The main difference between the hoods of the plano-convex and the Fresnel spots is that the latter are considerably shorter, because the short focal length of the Fresnel lens makes a long movement of the lamp unnecessary. The lamp and the spherical reflector move together from spot focus (narrow beam, source farthest from lens) to flood focus (wide beam, source closest to lens) by means of a worm screw or a thumb screw similar to that found on a P-C spotlight (Figure 16–2).

While internal beam shaping is not possible, accessories called "barn doors" can be placed in the color frame holder to effectively shape the beam by cutting it in a linear manner from either of four sides (Figure 16–3, page 418). It is wise to "safety" a barn door to the pipe or yoke of the instrument by means of a small chain or wire rope. This is particularly important for the larger Fresnels, whose barn doors tend to be heavy and are easily dislodged by scenery flying on an adjacent batten.

Another spotlight accessory which is particularly useful with a Fresnel is the "top hat" or "snoot." A top hat is nothing more than a tin can open on both ends, attached to a rectangular metal frame which fits into the color holder and is painted flat black inside and out. The top hat controls lens flare by absorbing stray light refracted by the risers of the Fresnel lens. If the lens is in audience sight, lens flare can be quite distracting.

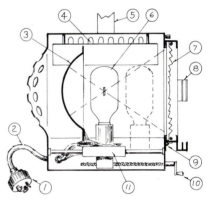

FIGURE 16–2

The Fresnel Spotlight

(Top) An 8-inch Fresnel that uses the tungsten-halogen lamp. (Above) Section. (1) Three-wire twist-lock connector. (2) Asbestos-covered lead wires. (3) Spherical reflector. (4) Ventilation holes. (5) Yoke. (6) T-shaped lamp, base down (tungsten-halogen or incandescent). (7) Fresnel lens. (8) Color-frame holder. (9) Hinged lens front for interior access. (10) Lead-screw drive for movable lamp socket and reflector. (11) Movable lamp socket. (Photo—Kliegl Bros.)

FIGURE 16–3
A Fresnel with Barn Doors

Fresnel Sizes. Fresnel spotlights come in a number of sizes, the smallest of which has a 3-inch lens and burns a 150-watt G-shaped standard incandescent or T-shaped quartz lamp. Fondly called an "inky," this little instrument, although not possessing much punch, is very handy for tucking into small corners.

The most common Fresnel is the 6-inch, burning 500- and 750-watt T-shaped lamps. This spotlight is a true workhorse, being invaluable for the upstage acting areas, where its soft-edged beam fades away on the scenery without leaving obvious and distracting lines and patterns. It throws a good punch with a typically smooth beam pattern. For the larger stage the 8-inch Fresnel can be almost as valuable and with its 1000- to 2000-watt lamps has a powerful beam that can be put to many uses.

The Fresnel spotlight is also sold with lenses from 10 to 20 inches in diameter. These have little importance for the conventional stage, being primarily designed for television and motion-picture studios. They might be useful in outdoor productions, where exceptionally long throws are often the rule. Another feature that has been introduced for television purposes is the Fresnel lens that throws an oval beam. This can be very useful on the stage as well, to spread the light laterally, making cross-stage blending easier.

Designing the Lighting

Fresnel Beam Characteristics. The beam of light from a Fresnel is soft in quality, with a smooth, even field. The light will appear to "wrap around" a figure and shadows will be soft edged and not very harsh. Being a spotlight, the light from a Fresnel exhibits a good sense of direction, but it can also be used for wall washes or blending. In a proscenium theatre the Fresnel is limited, however, to use over-stage because of its scattered beam characteristics. Also, throw distance of even the 8-inch Fresnel is restricted for the same reason. The following table lists beam spreads for typical 6- and 8-inch Fresnels at both flood and spot focus:

	SPOT FIELD ANGLE	FLOOD FIELD ANGLE
6-inch Fresnel	16°	60°
8-inch Fresnel	14°	50°

While the Fresnel is an ideal instrument for some spaces and certainly a practical instrument for almost all spaces, the ellipsoidal reflector spotlight is a more versatile lighting instrument.

The Ellipsoidal Reflector Spotlight (ERS)

This is, unquestionably, the most important, useful, and common stage-lighting instrument today. In Chapter 15 we saw that if a source of light is placed at one of the focal points of a reflector built in the shape of half an ellipsoid, all the light rays that strike this reflector are diverted through the conjugate focal point. By placing a lens just in front of this secondary focal point a spotlight of great efficiency and power can be constructed. Such an instrument, properly called an ellipsoidal reflector spotlight (ERS) is also commonly referred to as a Leko or a Klieglight, the trade names of Strand-Century and Kliegl Brothers, respectively.

Most ellipsoidal reflector spotlights manufactured before 1980 will burn either a standard incandescent T-12 or T-14 base-up lamp or a quartz lamp designed to replace them (Figure 16–4, page 420). Nearly all newer ellipsoidals are designed to take only quartz lamps, usually in an axial-mount configuration (Figure 16–5, page 420).

Beyond the conjugate focal point, where the rays of light are starting to spread again, a lens (or lenses) is mounted to refract these rays into a comparatively narrow beam. In most ellipsoidal spotlights two thinner lenses are employed to get the effect of the one thick one, although a single step lens may also be used.

ERS Beam Shaping. Just before the conjugate focal point, where the various rays are still converging, is a metal baffle known as the "gate." This cuts off stray rays of light that are not useful in forming a well-controlled beam. It is an image of the opening in this gate, called the aperture, which appears as a round and reasonably smooth pattern

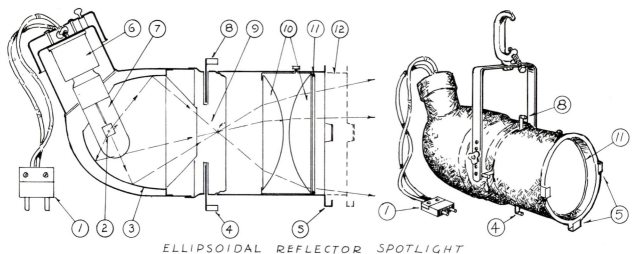

ELLIPSOIDAL REFLECTOR SPOTLIGHT

FIGURE 16–4

The Ellipsoidal Reflector Spotlight

(1) Pin connector. (2) Monoplane (or biplane) filament, with its center at the focal point, "f." (3) Ellipsoidal-shaped reflector. (4) Bottom shutter, which shapes the top of beam. (5) Color-frame holder. (6) Prefocus base socket. (7) T-shaped lamp, to burn base-up. (8) Top shutter, which shapes the bottom of the beam. (9) The "gate," with typical reflected rays crossing at the conjugate focal point, "f¹." (10) Two plano-convex lenses. (11) Spring ring, to hold lens. (12) Alternate position of lens system.

when the ellipsoidal spotlight is focused on a plain surface. Various other features to shape the beam may be placed at the gate, a standard device being four shutters which, by proper manipulation, can change the beam pattern into almost any simple linear shape. An iris is sometimes inserted here, allowing the circular form of the beam to be made smaller or larger at will, though this is most significant when the instrument is to be used as a follow spot.

A well-equipped ERS will also have a pattern or template holder located just in front of the four shutters. A template, commonly called a "gobo," is a metal plate with a pattern cut in it. When equipped

FIGURE 16–5

Axial Mount Ellipsoidal Reflector Spotlight

(1) Three-wire pin connector. (2) Coiled-coil filament. (3) Ellipsoidal reflector. (4) Bottom shutter which shapes the top of the beam. (5) Color-frame holder. (6) Axially mounted socket. (7) Tungsten-halogen lamp. (8) The "gate" with typical reflected rays crossing at the conjugate focal point. (9) Top shutter. (10) Double plano-convex lenses. (11) The lens barrel in alternate positions.

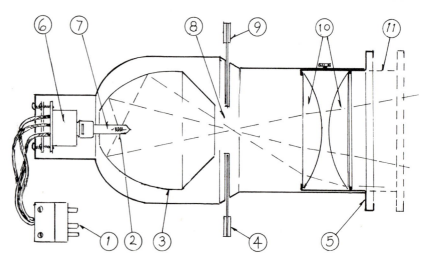

420   *Designing the Lighting*

with a gobo an ERS can serve as a shadow projector. Light can simply be textured, or specific patterns can be projected on scenery, actors, or the stage floor. Stainless steel templates available in a large variety of patterns can be purchased, or homemade gobos can be cut out of pie tins or aluminum lithoplates. (You can probably get lithoplates free from a local printer.) In using a gobo, remember that the pattern image will be inverted because of the crossing of the light rays. Consequently, the gobo should be placed in its holder in an upside-down position.

ERS Beam Characteristics. The ellipsoidal reflector spotlight throws an extremely powerful beam of light capable of creating harsh and sharp shadows. An "edging" of light can best be achieved with an ERS, whose light is much more controllable than that of other theatrical lighting instruments. Because the lamp, reflector, and lens are in static relationship, there is no flood and spot focus as in plano-convex and Fresnel spotlights. But the lenses may be moved a few inches, allowing the beam pattern to be thrown out of focus and thus softening the hard, sharp edge of the field.

Because of the delicate relationship between filament and reflector, it is easy for the instrument to get out of adjustment, particularly if an inexperienced electrician tampers with the adjusting devices on the socket cap of older ellipsoidals. Sometimes the lamp base has not been properly seated in the socket. At other times it is necessary to focus the spotlight on a plain surface and manipulate the adjusting devices until a firm, circular field is found again. The better of the new axial-mount ellipsoidals will have the lamp socket (normally a bi-pin) mounted on a ball-and-socket type joint and attached to a "joy stick" handle or knob. This arrangement allows for rapid and simple lamp alignment.

ERS Sizes. The ellipsoidal reflector spotlight comes in several sizes, from one with a 3½-inch lens that burns 400- and 650-watt lamps and throws a wide beam, suitable for small stages and auxiliary use on large stages, up to a 12-inch model that uses a 2000-watt lamp for a very narrow and extremely powerful beam intended for long throws.

The workhorse of the ellipsoidal line is the 6-inch, which is available in a variety of focal lengths (see table on page 422). Older 6-inch units will accept either a 500- or 750-watt lamp, while the newer quartz units can be lamped to 1000 watts. The 8-inch and 10-inch ERS will provide a narrower beam as well as allow for higher wattage lamps, usually up to 2000 watts.

Beam and Field Angle. The table on page 422 lists typical beam and field angles for various sizes of ellipsoidal reflector spotlights. Note that these figures are approximate and may not correspond exactly to the performance of any specific unit. Consult manufacturer specifications before using.

When an ERS is properly aligned, its cone-shaped beam of light will

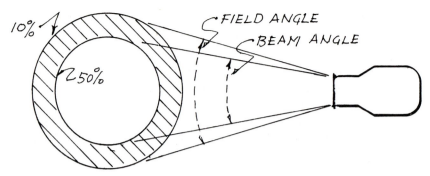

FIGURE 16–6
Beam and Field Angles

be most intense along the center line of the cone and drop off evenly toward the edge of the beam (Figure 16–6). If the intensity of light from an ellipsoidal is considered in terms of percentages, and the beam center line illumination is 100 percent, the beam and field angles are defined as follows:

Beam angle is the point where the illumination falls off to 50 percent.

Field angle is the point where illumination falls off to 10 percent.

ERS TYPE	BEAM ANGLE	FIELD ANGLE
3½ × 6	25°	32°
3½ × 8	18°	24°
3½ × 10	16°	20°
6 × 9	24°	40°
6 × 12	16°	28°
6 × 16	15°	20°
8 × 9	7°	15°
10 × 12	7°	10°

It is important to note, however, that many of the newer axial-mount ellipsoidals allow an additional adjustment of the lamp in respect to the focal point of the reflector. By moving the entire lamp housing either in or out, an electrician is able to change the field of light from an extremely "hot center" to a "flat" field. The hot center concentrates a greater percentage of the light into a small beam, while the flat field evens out the intensity through the beam. This adjustment does not alter the effective field angle but obviously changes beam angle considerably. Because of this new design feature, manufacturers have begun exclusively to use field angle degree designations for their ERS instruments.

New Silhouettes. The development of the tungsten-halogen lamp triggered new instrument design, particularly in the ellipsoidal reflector spotlight. The near point source, reduced size, and greater intensity of the lamp has increased the efficiency of the reflector and changed

422

Designing the Lighting

the hood design. The forerunners in new instrument design were Colortran and Electro Controls with its Parellipsphere, but Strand-Century and Kliegl have rapidly followed suit.

In addition to an improved hood design, the new ellipsoidals provide a variable focal length adjustment of the front lens system which increases the number of uses of an individual instrument. The Parellipsphere has a mechanism to change focal length (almost a zoom lens) as well as a new reflector design. As the name implies, it involves three surfaces. The basic shape of the reflector is ellipsoidal with a parabolic apex at the lamp position and an off-axis spherical reflector in front facing the lamp to redirect outside rays back into the ellipsoidal portion of the reflector (Figure 16–7).

The introduction of Colortran's mini-ellipse has made a significant contribution to the line of short-throw ellipsoidals. Like its bigger 6-inch counterpart, the mini has a three-position lens adjustment allowing beam spreads of 30°, 40°, and 50°. Its 500-watt compact quartz lamp delivers a great deal of intensity and is relatively inexpensive (Figure 16–8, page 424).

The new quartz ellipsoidals are already having a positive effect upon theatrical lighting design. The greater flexibility and higher intensity of these instruments has proved a tremendous aid to the lighting de-

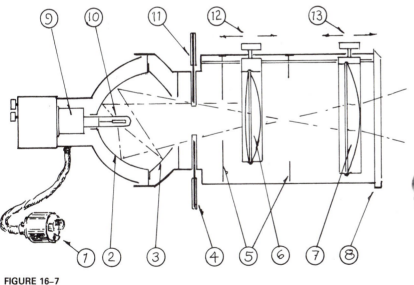

FIGURE 16–7

The Parellipsphere

Although basically an ellipsoidal reflector spotlight, the Parellipsphere has a more sophisticated reflector design and greater flexibility in the lens system. (Photo courtesy Electro Controls, Inc.) (1) Three-wire twist-lock connector. (2) Parellipse part of reflector. Apex of reflector is parabolic in action. (3) Kickback reflector with slight spherical configuration. (4) Bottom shutter. (5) Baffles. (6) Nonsymmetric biconvex lens. (7) Plano-convex lens. (8) Color-frame holder. (9) Prefocus medium base socket axially mounted. (10) T-H lamp. (11) Top shutter. (12) Lens adjustment knob to change focal length of objective system. (13) Knob to change beam spread.

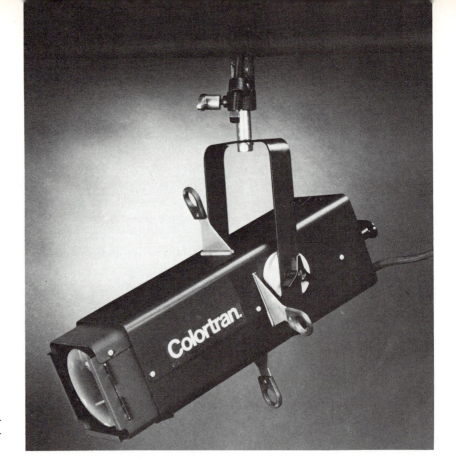

FIGURE 15–8
The Mini-ellipse
An efficient short-throw ellipsoidal reflector spotlight developed by Colortran. (Photo courtesy Colortran, Inc.)

signer in the transfer of a visual image in the mind's eye to reality on the stage.

BEAM PROJECTOR

Despite its narrow beam and intense output, the beam projector is not a true spotlight. It has no lens, and, more important, its beam pattern cannot be greatly altered from the small and very bright circle that is its characteristic. The lamp can be moved slightly in relation to the reflector, which results in a somewhat larger pattern but one which has a "hole" or dark spot in its center. In no case is the beam projector's pattern very smooth, and masking will not alter the shape in any way but instead dims it in an erratic fashion.

This instrument makes use of a parabolic reflector which sends all the rays that strike it forward and parallel one to the other. In order to eliminate diverging rays of light that would not contribute to the tight beam pattern, but would prove undesirable and distracting, a spherical reflector is often placed in front of the lamp to redirect such rays back to the parabolic reflector, from which they may augment the other parallel rays (Figure 16–9). In some styles of beam projector baffles or louvers serve to intercept and absorb such diverging rays. The beam projector is basically a searchlight adapted to the theatre.

Designing the Lighting

FIGURE 16–9

The Beam Projector

(1) G-shaped lamp. (2) Parabolic reflector. (3) Concentrated filament. (4) Lamp socket, adjustable. (5) Pin connector and lead wires. (6) Spherical reflector. (7) Color-frame holders. Photo of 11-inch Kliegsun Beam Projector, 500–1000 watts. Also available in 15-inch, 1000–1500 watts. (Photo—Kliegl Bros.)

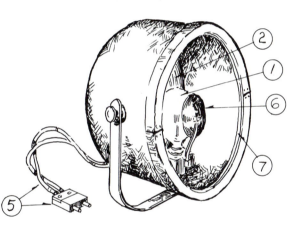

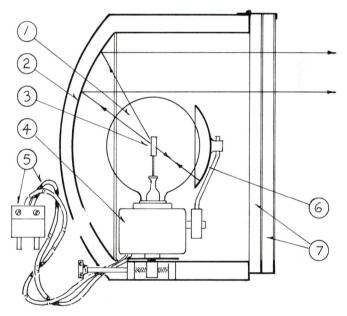

BEAM PROJECTOR

Its stage uses are largely limited to strong shafts of light of great intensity but confined to small areas, for example sunlight through a window. For musical comedy and the like, great banks of beam projectors may be employed, but for the modest stage this instrument has limited uses.

The beam projector comes in various sizes, from 10 to 30 inches in diameter. The 10-inch style may take a 250- to a 750-watt T-lamp, while the larger types use 1000- to 2000-watt lamps, either quartz or standard incandescent. Anything larger than 16 inches would scarcely be required for even a sizable stage. Because of the tremendous punch of the light, the beam projector is very hard on non-Mylar color media, burning the color out of some shades within minutes after replacement.

Distribution Control

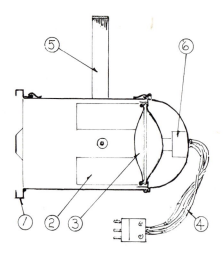

FIGURE 16–10
The PAR-64

(1) Color-frame holder. (2) Light baffle over air vent holes. (3) PAR-64 lamp. (4) Three-wire cord and pin connector. (5) Yoke. (6) Lamp socket.

PAR CAN

The parabolic aluminized reflector (PAR) lamp was mentioned earlier in the chapter on light sources. Its housing, the PAR can or PAR head, and its applications for stage lighting will be discussed here. The extruded-metal PAR can housing simply secures its PAR-64 lamp in place by means of a large spring ring and absorbs immediate flare created by the built-in lens of the lamp (Figure 16–10). The butt of the housing hinges opens to allow access to the lamp and socket, and color frame holders are fixed to the front of the unit. The PAR-64 lamp is rated at 1000 watts and is available in the following beam spreads:

	ANSI CODE	BEAM ANGLE	FIELD ANGLE
Very Narrow	FFN	6° × 12°	10° × 24°
Narrow	FFP	7° × 14°	14° × 26°
Medium	FFR	12° × 28°	21° × 44°
Wide	FFS	24° × 48°	45° × 71°

The oval-shaped beam of light cannot be effectively altered or adequately controlled, but the quality of light is uniquely harsh, and the beam edge is fairly soft. Relative to other stage instruments, the PAR can is nearly indestructible, and the lamp life is long. Although not an ideal stage-lighting unit because of its lack of beam-shaping capabilities, the PAR can is economical and may be perfect in certain applications.

FLOODLIGHT

A floodlight is, as its name suggests, a device for throwing a broad wash of light over a wide area. For many years the so-called Olivette was the standard instrument for such a purpose. Large and unwieldy, burning a 1000-watt G-lamp, the Olivette reflected a smooth wash of light from its boxlike hood and white-painted interior.

The most common floodlight today is the ellipsoidal reflector floodlight (ERF), or "scoop." It has a matte finish that distributes the light smoothly and without a sharp edge to the beam. A single such instrument can be valuable for lighting a fair-sized window backing, while a bank of them may be used to illuminate a drop. They are especially useful for washing any curved surface, such as a cyclorama.

Most of these floodlights are about 15 or 16 inches in diameter and burn general-service PS lamps or quartz lamps of up to 2000 watts. There is also a small 10-inch model that uses 250- and 400-watt G-lamps, or, occasionally, gives good service with a 100-watt A-lamp when only a very low illumination is required.

STRIPLIGHT

One form of stage-lighting instrument that predates the invention of the incandescent lamp is the striplight, which produces the effect of a line of light by means of a number of sources—formerly candle or gas, but now electric—adjacent to each other. In its crudest form, the striplight can be found as footlights, a row of bare bulbs, sometimes as far apart as 12 inches, extending the entire width of the proscenium opening.

While permanently installed footlights are still fairly common, the more general approach today is to have striplights prepared in sections between 3 and 9 feet in length. These sections may then be placed about the stage, including the usual footlight position on the apron's edge or hung from overhead. This system allows far greater flexibility in the use of equipment than do permanently installed striplights.

Certain basic principles in striplight design must be understood. The lamps should be wired in several color circuits, three or four being the most common. Then, by using different colors in each circuit and properly controlling their respective intensities, practically any color or tint of light may be attained. Obviously, the lamps should be closely spaced, so that their various beams will blend together more readily.

Types of Striplight

For small and most medium stages, only one style of striplight is needed: that with PAR or R lamps on 6-inch centers (Figure 16–12, page 428). Color frames that will accept both color media and glass should be employed. Because the lamps have built-in reflectors, these strips do not need any of their own—a saving in money and time. The strips should be wired in three- or four-color circuits, depending on the preference of the producers; probably three is sufficient in the great majority of cases.

The 150-watt R and PAR lamps prove adequate for many stages, though occasionally the 300- or 500-watt R spots may be needed for extra punch, for example, in lighting a large cyclorama. The 150-watt PAR spots are also effective but throw too narrow a beam for anything but a sheet of light focused up or down a flat surface. For a very broad, smooth field of medium intensity the flood types of either R or PAR lamps are the most useful. Larger stages use striplights specially designed to take the 200-watt PAR-46, the 300-watt PAR-56, or the 500-watt PAR-64 lamps.

With the advent of the quartz lamp came a new design in striplights. Although each manufacturer uses a different trade name for its particular unit, they all use 1000- to 2000-watt double-ended quartz lamps and are available with one to four lamp compartments per section (Figure 16–13). Because of the reflector design, each color compartment

a

b

FIGURE 16–11
Floodlights

(a) Soft Lite, 2000 watts, double-ended, linear filament T-H lamp. Also available, 4000 watts. (Photo—Kliegl Bros.) (b) Ellipsoidal Reflector Floodlight. Often called ERF's or "scoops," 300–500 watts. T-H lamp. (Photo—Kliegl Bros.)

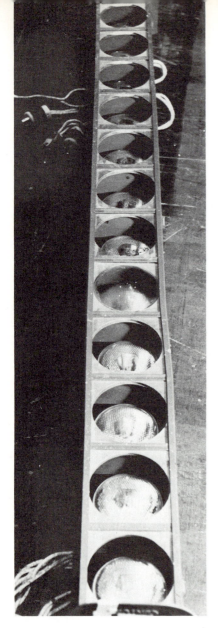

FIGURE 16–12
Striplight with R-type Lamps

FIGURE 16–13

The "Far Cyc" Striplight

An example of new-generation striplights manufactured by Colortran. (Photo courtesy Colortran, Inc.)

can be spaced as far as 8 feet apart and still maintain a smooth wash of light on a cyclorama or a drop. Quality of light as well as output is far superior to the older R and PAR strips for general wash applications. Roundels (glass color filters) are not made for the newer quartz strips, but the use of Mylar color media is perfectly satisfactory.

FOLLOW SPOTS

Carbon-arc light, discussed in Chapter 14, has been the traditional high intensity source for follow spots for many years. Although newer

Designing the Lighting

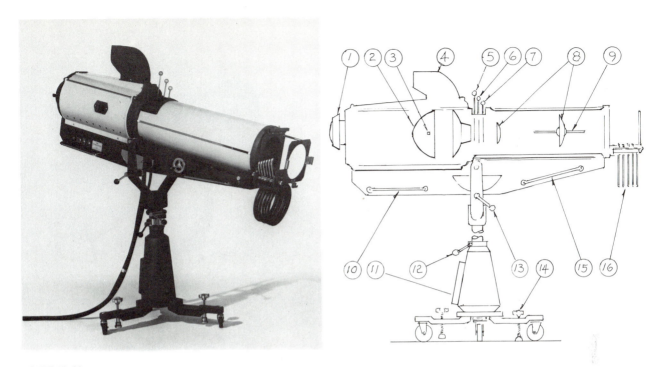

FIGURE 16–14

The Carbon Arc Follow Spot

(1) Lamp adjustment and changing assembly (arc lamp only). (2) Spherical reflector. (3) Light source: carbon arc or arc lamp. (4) Cooling and exhaust vent (carbon arc only). (5) Dimming control (Douser). (6) Horizontal shutter control (Damper). (7) Iris control. (8) Lens system. (9) Zoom track. (10) Rear pan/tilt handle. (11) Compact solid state switching regulator. (12) Pan lock. (13) Tilt lock. (14) Lock-down stabilizer. (15) Front pan/tilt handle. (16) Six-color boomerang. (Photo courtesy Colortran, Inc.)

and more effective sources are replacing carbon arc, the principle of the follow spot instrument remains the same (Figure 16–14). A spherical reflector is used to help direct the light to an aperture similar to that of the ERS. Mounted at the aperture will be an iris, a mechanism called a "damper" or curtain shutters which chops the beam of light horizontally, and possibly a mechanical dimmer called a "douser." Mounted in a long barrel in front of the aperture will be a lens or lenses which can be moved to adjust beam size and sharpness as well as a color boomerang which allows for rapid color changes.

In the carbon-arc follow spot, adjustments for the reflector and the arc source itself are found at the rear of the instrument. These adjustments move the carbon rods forward or back in relationship to the fixed reflector for better source alignment. They also tilt the reflector itself for more accurate focus. An arc source is desirable for throw distances of 75 feet or more, while one of the various quartz-lamp follow spots is sufficient for shorter throws.

The newer xenon and HMI sources (see Chapter 14) have stimulated change in the design of follow spots. More compact units which are generally easier to operate are currently available (Figure 16–15).

Distribution Control   **429**

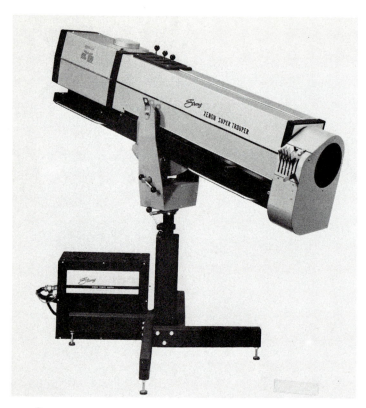

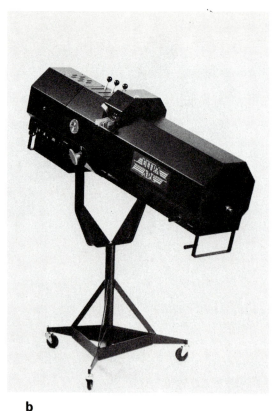

a

b

FIGURE 16–15

High Intensity Arc Lamp Follow Spots

(a) The Strong Xenon Super Trouper uses a xenon arc lamp for high intensity over long throws. (Photo courtesy Strong Electric) (b) The Long Throw Ultra Arc Followspot uses a G.E. Marc 350 projector lamp for high intensity and is one of the lightest followspots available. (Photo courtesy Phoebus Manufacturing)

SAFETY AND CARE OF LIGHTING EQUIPMENT

Some houses require that lighting equipment mounted above the audience be secured to a pipe with a safety chain or wire in addition to the C clamp. While the likelihood of an instrument falling during a performance is slim, nothing could be more unnerving for a theatre patron than to have a 10-inch Leko fall from 30 feet and land nearby. To prevent accidents, the "safety" should ideally be attached to the instrument itself (not to the yoke) and then clipped around the pipe. Other theatres may require that a wire mesh separate all instrumentation from the auditorium.

The best way to prevent accidents from happening is to keep your equipment in good condition. Sticking shutters, bent bolts, and missing knobs or handles all frustrate an electrician and encourage mistreatment. A stock of commonly needed spare parts should be kept on hand. Most instrument manufacturers require a fairly large minimum charge for parts orders and, to add insult to injury, take forever to fill the orders.

Keep your instruments clean. Lenses can be washed in mild soap and water or with a good glass cleaner. Reflectors should be wiped with a soft cloth or washed with vinegar and water. A clean spotlight will dissipate heat better, thereby increasing lamp life, and will also deliver more intensity.

Designing the Lighting

17

Intensity Control

Another one of the controllable properties of light is intensity, which refers to the brightness of a source. Intensity is controlled by the use of dimmers. To dim a tungsten-filament lamp, the voltage to the lamp is reduced and the metal will glow less brightly as well as give off a warmer light. The minimum requirement of any dimming apparatus is the capability of dimming a lamp completely to black in a smooth and even manner. When this is possible, dimmers can be used to alter the composition of the stage picture by dimming (up or down) one or a whole series of lighting instruments. Such movement of light can suggest time change, alter the mood or feeling of a scene, or shift emphasis from one area of the stage to another.

Huge advances in lighting control have taken place over the past ten years thanks to the electronic revolution and to the theatre's insatiable demand for better equipment. New control systems have been springing up so quickly that it is difficult to keep track of them all; but it is clear that electronic dimming (using the SCR) is here to stay, tape or disc memory storage systems will replace preset systems in nearly every application, and dimmer-per-circuit has become an economically viable system.

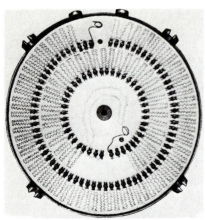

a

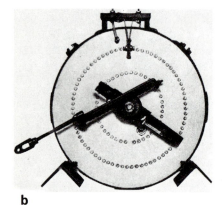

b

ARCHAIC FORMS OF DIMMING

The history of the use of dimming is a long one. On seventeenth-century stages cans on cords were lowered over the candles to vary the light; and in the eighteenth century candles in the wings were frequently mounted on vertical boards that could be revolved to turn the light away from the stage or back toward it. In the nineteenth century the gas table—a complex of pipes, rubber tubes, and valves—adjusted the flow of gas to the various jets about the stage and provided quite a complete control over intensities.

With the advent of the incandescent lamp, crude forms of dimming control were introduced almost from the start. These all utilized the principle of placing in series with the lamp some sort of resistance that could be varied at will. The carbonpile and salt-water dimmers were among these. But the most popular of all and one that only recently has been retired is the resistance-wire dimmer, often called a rheostat.

Types of Resistance Dimmers

The resistance dimmer is found in two standard forms. The less complex contains two coils of resistance wire placed parallel to each other and a short distance apart. The circuit enters at the top end of one coil and leaves at the top end of the other. A conducting shoe slides up and down between the two coils, making contact with each. When this shoe is at the top it bridges the gap in the circuit without introducing any resistance whatever. But when it has been moved to the bottom the full lengths of both coils have become part of the circuit. This so-called slider dimmer is quite simple in its operation but is so difficult to maneuver smoothly that the light tends to jump when its intensity is being changed. Further, it is impossible for one operator to manipulate more than two of these contraptions simultaneously.

The other form of resistance dimmer (called a resistance plate) has its wire in the shape of a multi-pointed star, or as two stars, one within the other. The wire is fastened to a circular vitreous plate and is sometimes baked into it with only taps showing at the surface. The shoe is on the end of a pivoted sweep (when two coils are involved there is a shoe at each end of the sweep) and the sweep is moved by means of a projecting handle. Various refinements such as a cutoff switch at the low end, provision for interlocking all the handles in a bank of them, and the like, were supplied with this type of rotary dimmer.

Disadvantages of the Resistance Dimmer

Because the resistance dimmer consumes full current as soon as it is switched on—whether the lamp burns full up or otherwise—it is extremely wasteful of electric power. And the heat generated by the coils can be quite overwhelming unless adequate ventilation is provided. But these are less important from the artistic point of view than

Designing the Lighting

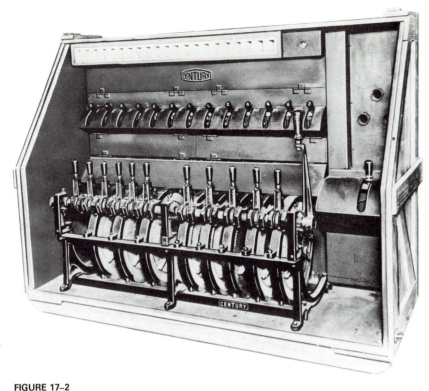

FIGURE 17–2

A Resistance Board

Example of an early switchboard, built into a box for travel. At the right end of the row of dimmer handles is the long interlock handle and beyond it the master switch, above which can be seen holes for a three-wire service. (Photo—Century-Strand)

is the problem of fixed capacity. The length of wire in each dimmer is determined by the exact wattage of the lamp it is expected to control. If a lamp of a smaller wattage is used instead, the dimmer will not put it out completely, and what dimming it does accomplish will be at a different rate from those lamps of proper size on adjacent dimmers. This must be corrected by the expedient of connecting, in parallel with the stage light, a second lamp or "ghost load" hidden offstage and of sufficient wattage to make the total load on the dimmer approximate what it was designed to control.

AUTOTRANSFORMER DIMMERS

Many complaints about resistance control were solved by the auto-transformer dimmer. This device consists of lots of copper wire wound around an iron core. The wire is wound in such a manner that the magnetic fields created anytime electricity flows through a conductor are made to work against each other, causing a phenomenon called back-electro-motive force (back-EMF) or back-voltage. If the wire is arranged properly, a variable voltage will be available along the coil.

Intensity Control   **433**

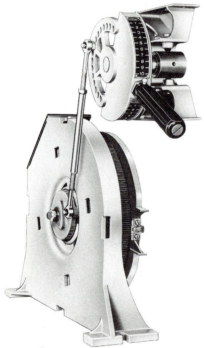

FIGURE 17–3

Autotransformer Dimmers

(Top) A 1000-watt capacity rotary auto-transformer dimmer. At the top is the handle which revolves the contact within the coil below. Note the provision for two-, three-, or four-wire service and two- or three-wire output. (Above) A large capacity dimmer built in this shape to save space in a switchboard and to provide handle control and interlock possibility. (Photo—Superior Electric)

By means of a sliding contact shoe called the "brush" moving over the bared turns of the coil, the exact voltage required is drawn off. Because this tapped-off voltage does not depend on a resistance relationship between the coil and the lamp, it will be the same regardless of what load is placed on it. Thus any lamp from the smallest to the highest allowable can be dimmed smoothly and effectively between full out and full up.

Because the only current drawn is that actually used by the load, the autotransformer is not wasteful of power nor does it create any appreciable amount of heat. Autotransformers were built in two styles. One of these has a rotating knob control and therefore is not suitable for stage use; the most skillful operator can handle only two at the same time and it is doubtful if even then they can be brought smoothly and correctly to exact readings (Figure 17–3). The more useful kind is somewhat akin to the rotary resistance dimmer in that it can be mounted with others in a bank and has a protruding handle that makes manipulation simple; this handle can be mechanically interlocked with those of its neighbors.

Mechanical Mastering

The simplest method of mastering autotransformer dimmers is by interlocking. A number of dimmers mounted side by side may have their handles locked to a shaft that runs the length of the dimmer bank. This is usually done by twisting the end of the handle and thus releasing a spring-loaded plunger which drops into a spline, or groove, cut into the shaft. By means of a long master handle (for leverage), the shaft is turned and all dimmers locked to it will simultaneously turn to the same reading. When a handle is twisted in the opposite direction, the plunger is withdrawn from the spline and the dimmer may be worked independently of the others (Figure 17–4).

The drawback is obvious. If we want one dimmer to stop at a reading different from the others, it will take some fast and dexterous work on the part of the operator to disengage the proper handle at the proper place. If several dimmers must be dropped off at different readings during a fairly rapid dim, the whole process becomes impossible. Further, those that are dropped off correctly will have reached their desired readings while the other lights are only part of the way to theirs.

Of course, the same thing happens in reverse when dimmers are set at different readings and the attempt is made to use the interlocking mechanism to take them to "out" simultaneously. Those dimmers that are set at the higher readings will start down first, and their lights will be partially out before dimmers set at lower readings are picked up by the revolving shaft. Although preferable to no master whatever, interlocking is an awkward, inartistic makeshift.

Designing the Lighting

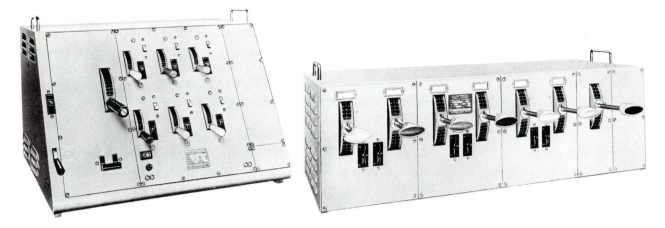

FIGURE 17–4

Autotransformer Package Boards

(Left) A package containing six 1300-watt autotransformer dimmers and one of 6000-watt capacity. By means of the white switches one or more of the small dimmers may be put under control of the large one, thus providing proportional dimming for up to a total of 6000 watts. Or the large dimmer may operate independently with its own big load and each small dimmer with its lesser one. Note the different color for each handle for easy identification, and the circuit breaker adjacent to each. (Right) A package with six 2500-watt autotransformer dimmers and an interlock handle to which several or all the others may be connected. Proportional dimming is not provided. This model was manufactured with three, four, five, or six dimmers. The interlock handle is optional, but even without it several handles may still be locked to the shaft and the handle of any one of them used as the master. In both models the plugging is on the rear face. (Photo—Superior Electric)

Electrical Mastering

In order to get truly proportional dimming, a master dimmer of large capacity may be employed to control a number of smaller ones and their respective loads. Obviously such a master must have a capacity equal to the total capacities of the lesser dimmers combined. And if these are resistance dimmers, all including the master must be loaded to full capacities for proper performance.

Autotransformer Package Boards

A "package board" is a relatively compact unit containing several dimmers, circuit breakers, and often a plugging panel (Figure 17–4). Although heavy, these boards were transportable and a popular means of control for a number of years. Figure 17–4 shows two styles of the package board, both manufactured by Superior Electric and called Luxtrol control boards. Several years ago the final Luxtrol package board rolled (or lumbered) its way off Superior Electric's assembly line—the electronic dimmer had finally and rightfully taken over the entire market of intensity control.

ELEMENTS OF ELECTRONIC CONTROL

The basic thing to understand about electronic control systems is that the operational or control part of the system can be (and in larger systems almost always is) separate from the actual dimmers. The way this works is quite simple: a low-voltage current (somewhere between 11 and 20 volts, depending on the system) is sent to the remotely located dimmers telling them what to do. This signal is either generated by a small fader called a controller or potentiometer in the "preset" system, or by a computer-stored intensity level in the memory system. Of course, the actual electronic dimmer handles full-voltage current (120 volts) and alters the flow of this current to the lighting instrument per instructions from the low-voltage control signal.

Aims of Electronic Control

Before taking a look at the various types of apparatus, let us consider briefly the advantages of electronic control over the older systems. It must be emphasized that the object of electronic devices is not mere gadgetry and certainly not complexity for the glorification of the technician. Rather their purpose is to free the artist from the tyranny of earlier crude mechanisms. Under the older methods a simple shift of emphasis in the stage lights required the designer to instruct (either directly or through a boss electrician) several operators, who probably could not even see the results, in what they were expected to do and coach them repeatedly and carefully on timing. If what was desired was executed correctly once out of five times, the designer would probably be considered fortunate.

With the low-voltage miniaturized control systems provided by electronics all facets of stage lighting, or any portion of it (sub-mastering or group mastering), can be mastered. Readings for future changes (presetting) can also be set up and can be brought into effect on cue and at whatever rate of speed is desired. The dimming devices are multicapacity: each dimmer will successfully control any lamp load from the top capacity of the dimmer down to the smallest load desired. And because the current is low in both amperes and volts, and the controls are miniature, the control panel is compact and may be located anywhere in the theatre that is practical rather than being pushed into a corner backstage. This allows the operator to follow the action on stage with ease and to make changes with accuracy.

Early Types of Electronic Dimmers

All electronic systems share basic elements. In most systems the same set of controllers, masters, and memories can be used, with slight modification, to control any of the dimmers used in the various systems.

Saturable-Core Reactors. Although not strictly a fully electronic device, the saturable-core reactor was the first attempt along these lines. It consists of a transformer built on a core shaped like the figure eight. The primary and secondary coils are wound around the opposite ends of the eight, and a low-voltage d-c control current coil around the common central bar. By varying the control voltage, the current flow in the secondary is affected, thereby furnishing the lamps with greater or lesser voltage.

There are a number of disadvantages connected with the saturable-core reactor which prevented it from receiving wide acceptance. First, the load current and the control current are related, so the reactor can operate effectively only in a comparatively small range close to its rated load. Secondly, the reactor itself is a ponderous piece of apparatus, and it dims ponderously, with a noticeable time lag between the giving of a control command and the resulting change of the light. However, saturable-core reactors were installed in a number of large houses during the 1920s.

Thyratron Tubes. The first truly electronic system was put into operation by George Izenour in 1947 at Yale University. The dimming device is a pair of thyratron tubes which are controlled by varying their grid voltages from the control panel. This results in a rapid switching on and off of the supply voltage which modifies the familiar a-c sine-wave form, thus feeding more or less voltage to the lamps.

The tubes are multicapacity, dimming any loads up to their top rating; the reaction time is instantaneous, and only current that is actually consumed by the load is drawn.

But thyratron tubes also have their disadvantages. They require a certain warmup time before loads may be placed on them, and they give off a good deal of heat that must be disposed of to prevent their early failure. The tubes have a tendency to ''drift''—that is, to get out of adjustment—and therefore demand frequent and careful attention. And they do need replacement now and again, making maintenance a time-consuming and costly affair.

The Magnetic Amplifier. During the 1950s the magnetic amplifier seemed to be the answer to the electronic dimming problem. A refinement of the saturable-core reactor, the magnetic amplifier is multicapacity, has a fast reaction time, needs no warm-up, gives off little heat, and has an unlimited, maintenance-free life. Its only disadvantages seemed to be its bulk, its weight, and its cost. But, soon after the magnetic amplifier became a reality, a new breakthrough in electronic dimmers was made: the silicon controlled rectifier. This little wonder quickly made all other dimmers obsolete.

Silicon Controlled Rectifiers

Usually referred to as the SCR dimmer, its name means "a silicon rectifier under control" and not "a rectifier controlled by silicon." A kind of large-capacity transistor, this device presents all the advantages of the magnetic amplifier but it is quite small and light in weight and is a good deal less expensive. The early SCRs were sensitive both to overcurrents and to high ambient heat, but special fusing and fans took care of these drawbacks. Another problem was that its rapid switching action often caused a distinct and annoying hum in the lamp filaments, requiring the addition of a special filter called a "choke" to correct it.

As indicated above, the SCR performs its dimming task by very rapidly switching on and off, thereby "chopping" the a-c sine wave. Two SCRs are required for a single dimmer, but the actual SCR is only the diameter of a nickel and is ¾-inch thick. These little "buttons" are mounted in metal finlike devices called "heat sinks" which dissipate the heat generated by the rapid switching. An entire SCR dimmer (never larger than a shoe box) will also include a circuit breaker and a printed circuit card which contains the other necessary electronic components (Figure 17–5).

A welcome result of the SCRs' gain in popularity was the steady decrease in cost to the point where today we are experiencing patch or interconnect panels being replaced by dimmer-per-circuit systems.

The Interconnect System

Figure 17–6 illustrates the flow of power from the service entrance of a theatre to a lighting instrument in a typical electronic system using

FIGURE 17–5

SCR Dimmer Plug-in

A modern SCR dimmer plug-in which contains two 2400-watt capacity SCR dimmers, circuit breakers, and printed circuit cards. The small jacks designated TP1 and TP2 are for testing purposes. (Photo courtesy Kliegl Brothers)

Designing the Lighting

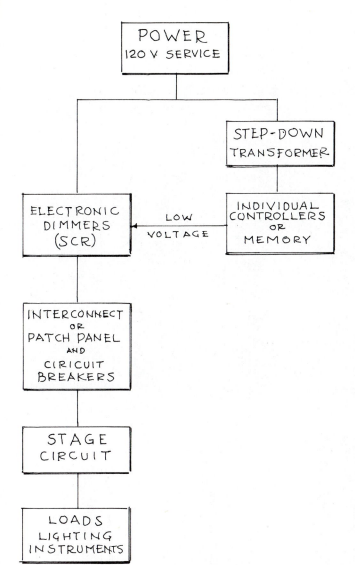

FIGURE 17-6

Typical Theatrical Power Flow

A block diagram illustrates the flow of power from the service entrance through control and to a lighting instrument.

an interconnect or patch panel. In all but the smallest theatres it is normal to have many more stage circuits than dimmers. In order to make possible the connection of any circuit to any dimmer, or indeed to place several lights under the control of a single dimmer of suitable capacity, flexible systems, variously referred to as interconnecting, cross-connecting, or patching, have been devised.

Possibly the simplest and most common form of cross-connecting panel is the type that has all the stage circuits terminating in plugs at the end of retractable cables, much like the old-fashioned telephone switch boards (Figure 17–7, page 440). The dimmer circuits end in jacks mounted in the panel. Any plug may be pushed into any jack; therefore any instrument may be under the control of any dimmer. Usually there are several jacks for each dimmer circuit, thus providing a simple way to gang several instruments on the same control if desired.

Intensity Control   **439**

FIGURE 17–7

Telephone-type Interconnect or Patch Panel

Single jacks representing each circuit in the theatre are plugged into one of several receptacles assigned to each dimmer. Circuit breakers for each individual circuit are located on the face of the panel below the jacks. Repatching during a show is often done by throwing the proper circuit breakers.

The "slider" patch is a full-voltage sliding contact system arranged on a grid. Stage circuits are normally represented by vertically sliding clips while each dimmer is assigned a horizontal buss bar. One need only align the slider (circuit) with the dimmer in order to complete the patch. This system eliminates the "spaghetti" of cable too often found in the telephone-type patch board, but several problems have surfaced with the slider patch:

1   The circuit-to-dimmer connection is not a sure one, and it is easy to make a poor contact.

2 Often the sliders are not built to take the rugged treatment and frequent use given nearly every patch panel.
3 It is quite simple to overload a dimmer by placing too many circuits on it.

A recent development in patch systems is the miniaturized low-voltage matrix patch, which looks much like a cribbage board and employs metal pins to make the low-voltage connection. This low-voltage patch in turn remotely activates a standard voltage connection. Have a good supply of pins on hand and keep dirt out of the holes.

The Dimmer-per-Circuit System

Although patch systems are still very common, new installations are frequently opting for the dimmer-per-circuit system. The dimmer-per-circuit concept has been with us for many years, but only recently with the introduction of high-density dimmers, computer control, and lower dimmer cost has this system been considered a truly competitive alternative to the interconnect system. Dimmer-per-circuit is exactly what its name implies: a system with an individual 2000- or 2400-watt dimmer assigned to every circuit in the house. Patching still exists, but it is of a different kind. Instead of patching a circuit into a dimmer, circuit and dimmer are patched electronically to a control channel at the console. This patch is totally flexible, allowing as many circuits and dimmers to be controlled by an individual channel as is desired. Note that a slight change in commonly used terminology is necessary with this system: no longer can a control channel be referred to as a dimmer, for the relationship between the two is no longer constant.

This system is an exciting one for the lighting designer because of its great flexibility—provided, however, that the number of stage circuits has not been compromised in the initial installation. Where this has occurred the theater would be better off with an interconnect system.

TYPES OF ELECTRONIC CONTROL

For all practical purposes, only two types of electronic control exist: the manual system and the memory system. The manual system always consists of at least one controller or potentiometer per dimmer as well as a master controller. It may be quite sophisticated, with a great number of possible presets, masters, submasters, and group masters.

FIGURE 17–8

Six-dimmer SCR Controller

A six-dimmer controller with master and circuit breakers; manufactured by Electronics Diversified. Each dimmer has a capacity of 2400 watts. Circuit plug-ins are located on the rear panel. A remote control unit is also shown. (Photo courtesy Electronics Diversified, Inc.)

Manual and Preset Systems

The simplest and least expensive of the manual electronic control systems provides one controller per dimmer and might very well be contained in a single housing (Figure 17–8). Although these systems are inexpensive and quite portable, they are also inflexible and can be poorly built. When considering purchasing such a control system, pay close attention to the following considerations:

1   Are the dimmers themselves easily accessible for repair?
2   Have the dimmers been properly protected from power surges?
3   Is proper dimmer ventilation provided?
4   Are chokes installed to prevent excessive lamp-filament vibration?
5   Is a master controller provided?
6   Do the controllers work smoothly and seem sturdy?
7   Finally, can the system be expanded?

The only advantage these systems provide over the older autotransformer package boards are in compactness, lightness of weight, and electronic mastering.

FIGURE 17–9

Two-scene-preset Console

The transparent disks with the white handles are the controllers for the thirty dimmers, one apiece for each preset. Below them is a row of off–on switches for each circuit. At the right end of the white plate may be seen the fader handle. The six switches to the left are for the non-dim circuits. At the extreme left is the master dimmer for houselights and a lock for the board. (Photo—George Izenour)

Presetting. Preset systems provide, in addition to the direct, manual control of each dimmer from the console, one or more additional sets of controllers. When only one duplication of controls is provided, it is usually identical to the manual control and located in the same panel. This is referred to as a two-scene preset board (Figure 17–9). The set of controllers energized at a given moment also acts as the manual control, while the readings on the other set of controllers are being adjusted as a preset that will shortly be used.

When there are several duplicate controls, usually five or ten, they are placed in a panel adjacent to the console, and an assistant sets the readings on them. In running the show with, let us say, ten presets already set up, the operator need only cross-fade back and forth from one preset to another at the speed dictated by the cues and the action. If a set of readings is not required again once it has been used, it may be erased and a new preset set up in its place. Thus as many as sixty or more complex readings may be utilized in desired sequence for a single performance. This is certainly a simple enough procedure and one not likely to cause confusion in the mind of the operator. Figure 17–10 (page 444) shows a multipreset board and its console.

FIGURE 17–10

A Ten-scene-preset Console

To the left is the preset panel with ten rows of forty-five controllers each, for the forty-five dimmers. The upper portion of the console desk contains the forty-five manual units, each with its reading indicator at the top, below which is the controller handle, and beneath this the transfer switch, which allows the circuit to be placed under either manual or preset control. At the left end of the desk are the selector buttons for the ten presets, plus blackout. There are two rows, one for the "up" and one for the "down" position of the fader, which is adjacent. When the fader is "down" (as in the picture) the preset "selected" in the bottom row is energized. As the fader moves toward "up," the preset "selected" in the upper row fades into prominence, cross-fading the former selection, until the handle reaches its top limit. When the "down" preset has been eliminated a new preset may be selected on the bottom row. At the right end of the desk is the master dimmer handle, which dims all circuits on manual control proportionately down or up. (Photo—George Izenour)

The presetting approach does create certain problems, however. A completely new preset is required for most lighting changes. It is sometimes possible to make a minor change in the preset panel itself, but this is frequently awkward and, in some models, impossible.

Further, all fades between presets must be linear; that is, if it is desirable to dim spotlight A from 10 (full up) to 0 (full out) while spotlight B is moving from 0 to 10, then when A reads 8, B will read 2, when A is at 5, so is B, and when A reaches 3, B will be at 7.

Split-faders (two cross-faders rather than one) help to solve this problem. One cross-fader is assigned to the preset first in use, while the second is ready to activate the next preset in order. The fade can then be nonlinear and two presets can even be active at the same time (a phenomenon called "pile-on").

Group Mastering. Another method of designing a control board does not depend exclusively on separate preset panels but divides the manual board into various groups and subgroups, each with its own master control. This system is known as group mastering. The groups may be used as presets independent of each other, operated together, or used to pile on new readings on top of the old ones, as well as other combinations.

Unfortunately, the operation of such a console can become extremely complex if a great many changes are needed in rapid succession. There are just too many things for an operator to keep track of in a swiftly moving play. But for fewer cues and with a tempo that permits careful checking and preparation for the next change, this type of system has much to offer.

A very distinct advantage of the group system is that the console may be run effectively with little rehearsal, a great boon for multipurpose auditoriums, while the preset system demands considerable preparation time to record the readings.

Combination Systems. The most desirable manual system obviously will combine the virtues of presetting with those of group mastering and sub-mastering. An incredible variety of such control systems exist today, each with its own idiosyncrasies. Although computerized memory systems have almost eliminated large preset systems from the market, smaller systems such as Strand Century's Mantrix and Colortran's Patchman have a great deal to offer (Figure 17–11). These manual control systems are equipped with a two- or four-scene preset, sub- and group mastering, matrix patching, and timed split cross-faders. They are economical, portable, and offer a good alternative to small computer memory control.

FIGURE 17–11

Two-scene-preset Control System with Sub-mastering

The "Mantrix" control system, manufactured by Strand Century. This system has twenty-four channels, eight submasters, split cross-faders, and a grand master. Also included is an electronic dimmer to channel patch (left side of board). (Photo courtesy Strand Century)

Computerized Memory Systems

The combination of the SCR dimmer, low-voltage control circuits, and miniaturized parts has led inevitably to computerized control of lighting. The ability of the computer to store information enables it to hold preset or cue information in whatever quantities a production situation might desire. A computer can be programmed with the digital information of a cue that is randomly recalled with push-button speed. The only limit to capacity is the size or number of storage elements in the memory bank.

Types of Memory Systems. Compared to those being manufactured today, early memory systems were generally large and bulky. They would often have a single set of controllers or potentiometers as well as a keyboard, and cue information could be stored in the memory by either means. A split-fader, often a timed-fader, and possible group and/or sub-masters were also standard equipment. The main memory storage was either disc or core, and only later was disc or magnetic tape "library storage" added as a standard feature. Q-File, developed by Thorne Electric of Great Britain and by Kliegl Brothers, was one of the first systems to eliminate a full set of controllers and add library storage (Figure 17–12). Autocue, manufactured by the now-defunct

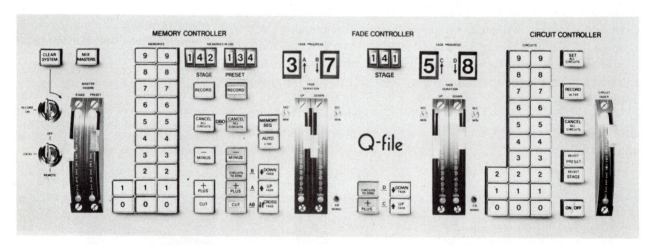

FIGURE 17–12

Q-file Memory System

The first successful preset memory system designed and manufactured by Thorn Electrical Industries, Ltd. Originally developed for television lighting control, it revolutionized theatre lighting control. The console has fingertip control of a keyboard of close to 400 lighting-control circuits with a Servo Fader to control levels of one or a group of dimmers prior to memory storage; for faders grouped in inverted pairs with time-controlled cross-fading capabilities; a keyboard for the selection of nearly 200 memory positions; a status display panel to tell the operator at a glance (1) the control channels that are energized in the stage mode and (2) the channels being held in the next preset mode, and a peg matrix or patch panel. Extra features include an auxiliary control panel, a portable remote-control panel, and a library device in which an entire show can be stored on standard tape cassettes for recall at a later date. (Photo Kliegl Bros.)

Skirpan Lighting Control Corporation, introduced the video monitor (a standard TV screen) to their control system. Although more complex than necessary, Autocue led the way to the development of current state-of-the-art equipment.

Kliegl took Q-File off the market and replaced it with their more sophisticated and less complex Performance system. Colortran introduced Channel Track, which has since been updated; and Strand Century developed Multi-Q and Micro-Q.

State-of-the-Art Control. Today's memory systems can be fairly easily categorized into two classes: the small, portable systems such as Strand Century's Mini-Palette, Kliegl's Performer series, and Colortran's Color Track (Figure 17–13), and the larger, more sophisticated

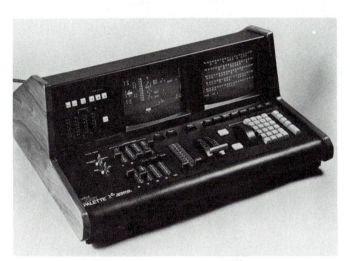

a

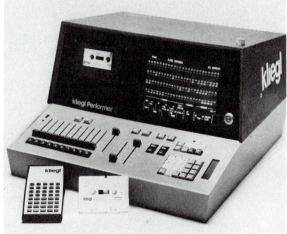

b

c

FIGURE 17–13
Small Memory Systems

(a) The Mini Light Palette has two video screens (one for dimmer levels and the other for cue sheet), rate wheel, group and sub-masters, and a split cross-fader. The slot at the lower left of the console is for disc memory. (Photo courtesy Strand Century) (b) The Performer II is a popular control system for touring productions. As indicated, its memory is provided by tape. Also shown is the hand-held remote control unit. (Photo courtesy Kliegl Bros.) (c) The EDI Mini-Memory Control Console (Photo courtesy Electronics Diversified, Inc.) Most of these units have similar features.

Intensity Control   **447**

console systems such as Kliegl's Command Performance, Colortran's Dimension Five, and Strand Century's Light Palette (Figure 17–14).

The smaller systems are all similar in that each will contain the following features or functions:

1 Library storage (either disc or tape).
2 A single video display able to inform the operator of various memory functions.

FIGURE 17–14

Large Memory Control Systems

(a) The Strand Century Light Palette has several specialized features not available on the Mini Light Palette. (Photo courtesy Strand Century) (b) Colortran's Dimension Five control system uses rate wheels and is equipped with color CRTs. (Photo courtesy Colortran) (c) Kliegl's Command Performance is another state-of-the-art control system. (Photo courtesy Kliegl Bros.)

Designing the Lighting

3 Timed split cross-faders.
4 Group or sub-masters.
5 Key pad access to memory.

These units will typically have limited memory and are ideal for small to medium facilities as well as touring.

The larger console systems generally have greater memory capacity, are more flexible, and offer more features:

1 Remote control console and keypads.
2 Hard-copy printers.
3 Greater number of group and sub-masters.
4 Two video displays.
5 More sophisticated memory backup systems.
6 A greater variety of control functions.

Designing with Memory Systems. When Tharon Musser, one of America's most outstanding lighting designers, insisted on a Light Palette control system for her Broadway production of *Chorus Line*, it became obvious that even New York was going to have to accept memory lighting control. There is no doubt that lighting designers can achieve a higher level of artistry with the help of the computer. Cue writing is simplified, the potential for more complex and sophisticated cues is greatly expanded, and changes are made quickly and accurately—every time. The systems offer the designer a choice of manual or automatic operation with manual override (the operator simply presses a "go" button), simultaneous fades, channel tracking, electronic patching, and a variety of more specialized functions. In effect, these memory systems have passed the artistic "buck" back to the designer. No longer does a control system place severe limitations on what can be achieved. New levels of creative lighting design are being reached every day with the help of computerized control.

THE OPERATOR AND REMOTE CONTROL

As we have pointed out, the low amperage and low voltage used by the control system permit the operator to be placed at any distance from the stage and in any location that seems appropriate. Of the practical places, the rear of the main floor of the auditorium is unquestionably the best. It is a good place from which to run the show, the view of the stage is satisfactory, and the operator and light designer are, during rehearsals, in easy and direct communication with director, scene designer, and others. It is inexcusable to place the control panels backstage, although the cross-connecting system should be there, while the actual dimming apparatus can be tucked away in the basement or other convenient location. This applies equally to a permanent installation consisting of console and preset panels and to the controller units of a portable board.

It would not be wise to leave the subject of electronic dimming without speaking of the person who will operate the controls. This is a very different task from that presented to an electrician standing backstage and manipulating several large handles, heavy with friction, under the direct supervision of a stage manager or a chief electrician.

A console operator is usually in a booth out in the house. Cues may be taken from the stage manager, but if the show is being called from backstage, the operator should take sight and sound cues from the stage action itself. Often the control apparatus is delicate and complex, not at all like a bank of simple and rugged resistance or autotransformer dimmers. An error could very well result in every light on the stage assuming the wrong reading. Nothing is more agonizing than watching an operator fade to a blank or totally incorrect preset in the middle of a subtle stage moment. While a good memory control system will lessen the chances of operational error, a highly competent operator is still essential.

A good operator will have confidence, a cool head, and enough understanding of the control system to rectify an error before it gets out of hand. In addition, the operator must know the show and fully understand the lighting designer's intentions. He or she *must watch the stage*.

Perhaps, most of all, the operator requires a sensitivity and sense of timing akin to that of an actor's. In a very real sense, the operator is also an actor. An operator does not merely snap lights on, but dims in gently, with feeling, perhaps at a varying pace to suit best the action on the stage. If the actors are fast in their pace one night, an adjustment must be made to the new tempo. Many highly competent electricians cannot adjust to this sensitivity. They may understand, but the delicacy of feeling isn't there: their lights are always a trifle off cue, a bit jerky on the fade-up, a little slow on the dim, a trifle rushed on the cross-fade sequence. A lot of sensitivity and a little know-how is a good formula for a successful operator of today's control systems.

18

Color in Light

The relationship of color in light to other uses of color in the theatre was discussed and illustrated in Chapter 8, "Color in the Theatre." The beginning of color in the refraction of light, the chemistry of color in paint, and a system of color notation are exemplified there in detail, as is an overall philosophy regarding the use of color in costume, scenery, and lighting design.

At this point, however, we will focus on color in light. Like color in paint, it has to be studied in greater detail in order to fully understand the differences and similarities of the two media.

THE ELECTROMAGNETIC SPECTRUM

Light is caused by certain waves of radiant energy. The electromagnetic spectrum (see Figure 18–1, page 452) contains waves as long as 3100 miles, those of electric current produced by standard 60-cycle generators. It contains waves as short as one ten-thousandth of an angstrom unit (and 254,000,000 angstrom units make up only one inch!).

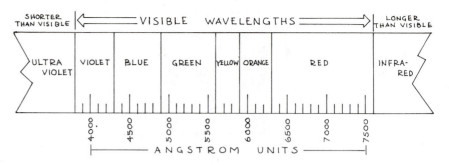

FIGURE 18-1
The Electromagnetic Spectrum

These very short waves are cosmic rays which come to the earth from outer space. The waves which produce the sensation our eyes recognize as light range from 3800 to 7600 angstroms. Radiant energy in waves between these two limits makes up the visible spectrum.

The shortest of such waves, 3800 to 4300 angstroms, produce what we call violet light. The next longer waves make blue light, followed by green, yellow, orange, and finally (between 6300 and 7600 angstroms), red light. All these together make white light.

Waves somewhat shorter than 3800 angstroms are called ultraviolet (*ultra* being Latin for "beyond"). Their effects are not visible to the human eye, but they have many uses, such as killing germs and creating photochemical, photoelectric, and fluorescent effects. They also give a beautiful summer tan, or for those exposed too long to them, a painful sunburn. Waves longer than 7600 angstroms, also invisible, and called infrared (or "below red"), are useful for heat therapy and commercial drying processes.

PRIMARY COLORS IN LIGHT

All waves in the visible spectrum together form white light. But it is not necessary to use every single wave length to create this result. White light can be produced quite effectively by mixing, in the proper proportions, red, blue, and green light. Red, blue, and green are, therefore, considered the primary colors in light, for no mixtures of other colors will produce these at full purity; but together, in varying proportions, they can produce any color. Thus, primary colors in light differ from the pigment colors in which red, blue, and yellow are the primaries; it is sometimes difficult for painters to convince themselves that in light, green takes the place of the familiar yellow as a primary.

Color Mixing

If we mix red and blue light together, we get the color called magenta; if green and blue are mixed the result is a blue-green that is referred to as cyan; red and green mixed will form a yellow light called amber. These are the secondary colors in light, and just as red, blue, and green can be mixed to form white light, so, too, can magenta,

Designing the Lighting

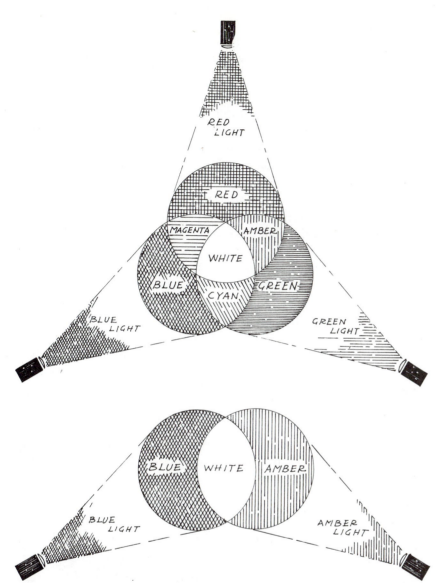

FIGURE 18–2
Additive Color Mixing

(Top) The three primary colors which, by overlapping, produce the secondaries (any two) and white (all three). (Below) A primary and its complementary secondary produce white.

amber, and cyan produce white (Figure 18–2). This should be obvious, for the secondaries are nothing but combinations of the primaries. In fact, by mixing the secondaries in varying proportions, we can achieve almost any color of the spectrum except those very close to the purest primaries themselves.

Likewise if we mix any secondary with the primary that has not gone into its making—say amber and blue—we again get white, for the amber already contains the red and green waves.

In using the word "mix" above we mean it in the sense that various beams of colored light are focused, one on the other, against a neutral surface and the resulting effect is what we see on this surface. This is additive mixing, and it is one of the two ways of producing and changing color in light and light effects.

Color Filtering

The second way of altering the color of light is known as color filtering (or sometimes called subtractive mixing). It is best explained by examples. Suppose we have a beam of white light falling on a neutral surface. That surface will reflect white. If we place a sheet of pure red glass in the path of this beam, the red sheet will absorb all the blue and green waves of the white light and allow only the red waves to pass through to the neutral surface, which will now appear red. Or, if we put a sheet of pure blue in the beam, the red and green waves will be removed, the blue waves will pass through, and the neutral surface will appear blue. But if we put both the red and the blue sheets before the beam, no light whatever will come through, for the red sheet will filter out the blue waves, the blue sheet will absorb the red waves, and both will remove the green waves—leaving nothing to strike the neutral surface! (Figure 18–3)

If we put a piece of magenta glass and a piece of amber glass in the same beam, the magenta will filter out the green in the amber while the amber will stop the blue in the magenta. Result: red, which is common to each. Notice that this red is produced by the negative approach of filtering out the other colors, not the positive approach of adding or mixing colors to achieve it, so our statement that a primary cannot be produced by mixing other colors still holds.

Absorption

Absorption takes place to some degree whenever light strikes any object, no matter how mirrorlike or crystal clear that object may seem. But absorption is particularly important to us in connection with solid objects.

FIGURE 18–3
Color Filtering

(Top) White light, when filtered through two secondaries, produces a tint of their common primary. (Bottom) Light, when filtered by two primaries, is completely absorbed so that no light whatever emerges.

White Light. If a beam of ordinary white light strikes a white surface, most of it will be turned back by reflection, but 10 percent or more will be absorbed, regardless of how purely white the surface appears. If the same light is directed at a black object, it may reflect 5 percent or so, but the greater part of the light will be absorbed. In each case, of course, the reflected light will be white light, and the reflecting surface will appear the same: the white one white, the black one black, for nothing has happened to change their colors.

On the other hand, if this white light were to strike a pure red surface, over 80 percent of the light would be absorbed but the balance would be reflected as red light. That is how we identify the surface as red. The only way we can tell the color of any object is by the color of the light that is reflected from it to our eyes.

Colored Light. If we direct a pure blue light at this red surface, we will see it as black, for the red will reflect only red waves and no red waves were directed on it. This is similar, of course, to what we learned about white light and color media. Because pigments used to paint walls and dye cloth are seldom completely pure, we cannot count on a perfect demonstration of this phenomenon on every occasion, but the principle holds true and should be constantly kept in mind.

On the other hand, if we shine a red light on a neutral surface, whether white, gray, or black, we will find that the object will appear red, for that is the only light available for reflection. Further, if a red light is directed on two surfaces, one the same red and the other white, both these surfaces will seem to be almost exactly the same color to the viewer. This is a most important phenomenon to be kept in mind by the designer, for the use of strong tints may make large portions of the scenery or costumes appear to be exactly the same.

Before we leave the subject of absorption, other warnings must be issued. White, or extremely pale colors, will always reflect a large portion of light and are, therefore, inclined to be very obvious on stage. A white costume can draw attention away from more important action no matter how the stage is arranged. The best-lighted actors will appear as silhouettes before a very bright backdrop, and this effect can trouble the audience greatly. On the other hand, no matter how black the scenery and whatever the material, it will reflect a certain amount of light, even that which has been already once reflected from the stage floor. The "living darkness of the theatre" is one of its most difficult concepts to attain if, indeed, it can be achieved at all, except with charcoal on the scene designer's sketch pad.

Uses of Mixing and Filtering

Both color mixing and color filtering are extremely important in stage lighting, and it seems that the use of color is one of the areas in which the young designer feels most insecure. Of course, we all make numerous color choices in the course of our everyday lives, but the average human being will make many or most of them on a subconscious level. The interior designer, fashion designer, and theatre designer must force such choices to the conscious level and begin to analyze how and why specific color determinations are made.

First of all, the term "white light" is heard a great deal in the theatre when talk turns to color. The fact is that so-called white light is relative, and our eye will accept an astonishing range of colored light as "white," depending on the circumstances. For this reason, the term "no color" (abbreviated N/C) is preferable to "white" when one discusses color and filtering. The concept of color temperature (measured in degrees Kelvin, or K) is also valuable to a discussion of color. (Refer to Chapter 14, "Light Sources.")

Most stage-lighting instruments deliver a light which we consider "white" rated at approximately 3200° K. Unfortunately, the only practical means of significantly altering this color is by interrupting the beam of light with a filter. Clear glass vessels containing red wine and other colored liquids were once employed as filters, but we have advanced into the age of modern technology and now use colored plastic. This method of altering the color of light, however, is really quite inefficient, for any filtering will decrease light transmission; in fact, highly saturated filters, such as primaries, may allow as little as 5 percent light transmission.

Mixing occurs anytime two colors of light are used on the same area. The resultant color depends on colors and angles of the two light sources as well as the surface on which they fall. If two light sources strike a surface from different angles, and if the surface is three-dimensional and sculpted (an actor's face, for example), many interesting things happen. First of all, one source will cast shadows which will be filled or partially filled by the other source's light and color. Second, an overall even color mix won't be achieved because the sources are coming from different directions. What will be seen, instead, is a heavy coloration from one source that merges gradually to an even mix with the second color and finally moves into the color of the second source. Such coloration adds to the three-dimensionality of a figure on stage and can help establish a direction of light.

Another form of color mixing involves the placement of two or more light sources very close to one another so that they effectively act as a single source. The most common example of such mixing in the theatre is the use of striplights on a cyclorama or backdrop. But this technique is also employed for area lighting using spotlights placed very close to one another. The point of this is to give the designer a large range of color options through mixing while only using two lighting instruments. Of course, this type of mixing depends on dimming, and therefore each instrument must have separate control.

The designer chooses colored light for one of four reasons:

1 The light is motivated by a specific source (the sun, a lamp, the fireplace), and colored light will help convey that motivation.
2 The mood of a scene is reinforced by the light, and color will heighten the effect.
3 A visual contrast between light sources is desirable, and color will increase that contrast.
4 Change or dramatic effect for its own sake is desired.

DESIGNING WITH COLOR

As indicated earlier, successful designing with color depends on taste, knowledge, and experience. Let us begin with a technique developed by Stanley McCandless, a man who more than any other might be considered the founder of lighting design in the United States. McCandless suggested that one way to achieve the most *natural* look when lighting the actor on stage is to position lighting instruments to each side of the actor at an angle of approximately 45 degrees (Figure 18–4). Two complementary colors will then be placed in the instruments—say a light blue in one and a warm amber in the other. The amber will act as a "key" or primary source light while the blue will read as a "fill" or reflected light. The colors will mix with each other on the actor's face and body front to a shade which will be read as white. This technique is a basis of modern lighting design.

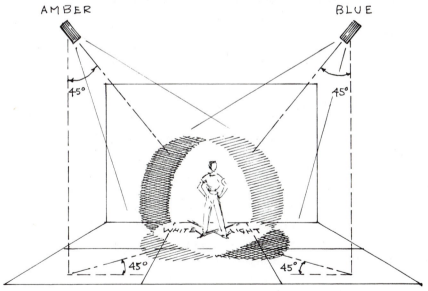

FIGURE 18–4
45°–45° Color Mixing
A stage-left blue and a stage-right amber will mix toward white light at the center of the actor's body.

Warm and Cool Colors

In general, most people will consider the color red as bloodlike, typifying anger and war. Amber is likely to be perceived as sunlight, warm and comfortable. Blue will typify restraint and coolness, while green may be seen as restful. These and similar identifications must always be taken into consideration when a designer selects stage colors. But for us there is no advantage in going deeply into the psychology of color, about which there are many (often contradictory) theories.

There is one psychological aspect, however, that cannot well be ignored: the matter of the relative warmth and coolness of colors. Few people would deny that a bright red-orange suggests warmth; most would agree that a brittle blue-white gives an impression of coolness.

Given samples of twenty different tints and shades, rarely will two people list them in exactly the same order from most warm to most cool. But in general we can say that the reds, oranges, and ambers are considered in the warm group, while the blues, violets, and greens fall within the cool range. Some mixtures of hues from the opposing groups seem on the border line, and the particular effect they give at any moment is in contrast to whatever other color is seen in relation to them.

As a matter of fact, the precise feeling given by most tints is purely a matter of contrast. A pale blue that seems positively icy in contrast to a strong amber will appear quite warm when placed next to a stronger shade of blue. Pink and lavender are frequently used on the stage as freewheeling tints whose effects we can reverse merely by changing the hues used in association with them.

Two other factors in the use of colored light, one psychological and the other physiological, are important to note. The first has to do with colors which appear to recede or move away from the viewer and those which seem to accede or move toward the viewer. The cool colors (blues and greens) fit into the former category of those that recede, while the warmer colors (reds and ambers) tend to accede. This phenomenon may be put to use by the lighting designer only in specific instances but is one that should always be kept in mind.

Our eyes tire of a constant color, especially if it is at all saturated and tending toward one of the primaries (blue is a good example). A stage picture washed only in blue light will soon lose its color quality because of this fatigue effect. Color contrast or variation will counter fatigue and maintain the intended look.

Unfiltered light may also seem to have warm or cool characteristics. Opposite a cool color, such as the palest of blues or greens, uncolored light will appear quite warm. But when it is opposite a pink or pale amber, white light will definitely be on the cool side in contrast.

Remember that as dimmer readings are changed the color of light produced by a source changes. A low dimmer level will generate a very warm light compared to a reading at full intensity.

Designing the Lighting

Colored Light and the Actor

In a later chapter, we will suggest specific colors to use in different situations, but here we will consider general effects desired in various portions of the stage picture. For acting area front light, for example, it is best to stay clear of saturated and unnatural shades that will adversely affect the faces and costumes of the actors.

Preserving color integrity of costumes can be a difficult task. Often the acting areas are lighted with tints of pinks and ambers, flattering enough to the human face, but deadly to green materials. Because the scene may definitely call for such colors in the light, the lighting designer should be in contact with the costume designer sufficiently ahead of time to prevent later distress.

Knowing what will happen to a given costume under colored light is simplified by breaking down the colors into primaries. For example, let us assume a yellow dress will be lit by a cool blue light from one angle and a straw or cool amber from another. The cool blue contains some mix of green and blue, the cool amber is made up of both red and green, and the yellow dress is going to reflect red and green. The conclusion, reached by simply noting the preponderance of green, is that we are probably going to be in trouble. A warmer blue or a lavender and a warmer amber light might be a better choice.

Beware of Green! Green light has limited use on the acting areas of the stage. Green on the human face is extremely unbecoming, muddying the natural healthy colors of cheeks and lips, deadening blonde and reddish hair, and exaggerating to the point of grotesqueness the slightest blemish in the complexion.

This does not mean that green should never be used. It is an extremely useful color, especially for the enrichment of costumes and scenery. But it should be handled with considerable care, unless, of course, a distorted effect is actually desired.

Colored Light and the Scenery

Always operate on the assumption that the scene designer has painted the settings the way they should appear. Thus, for a lighting designer to attempt to improve on the scene designer's artistry would be impertinent. Enhance it, yes, but strictly in accordance with the scene designer's wishes. Ideally, of course, the scene designer should light settings, and many of the finest do just that. At other times, close collaboration between scene and lighting designers is crucial. The result will usually be that nearby scenery, such as the walls of an interior setting, will, like the acting areas, receive tints of light only. Strong colors, as we have made clear, will tire the audience and will alter the appearance of the painting. Furthermore, being so close to the acting areas, it is almost impossible to separate light on such scenery from other portions of the stage.

A good rule of thumb for a lighting designer to begin with is "If you are debating whether or not to light the scenery—don't." Generally, light on scenery such as flats and drops will cast unwanted shadows and possibly create a situation where the walls and the actors are competing for focus. On the other hand, color washing the scenery can help to create some very nice and useful effects. Nearly any scenic or costume color can be made to appear warmer or cooler—more or less inviting—through the use of colored light. A scene designer may, in addition, actually paint the set in several different colors which can be selectively accentuated or deemphasized by colored light. But remember: Only a foolish lighting designer would keep such treatment a "surprise" for the scene designer.

Color on the Sky

At some point a lighting designer will be called on to use color on a sky drop or cyclorama. Specific lighting techniques are discussed later, but the use of color deserves some comment here. Careful consideration and experimentation must be given before choosing a color to light a backdrop. The color of the drop itself will affect the lighting choice, for sky drops can vary from numerous shades of white to blue.

Is it better to select a single color medium that gives the exact hue desired or is a blending of several colors preferable? Of course, if there

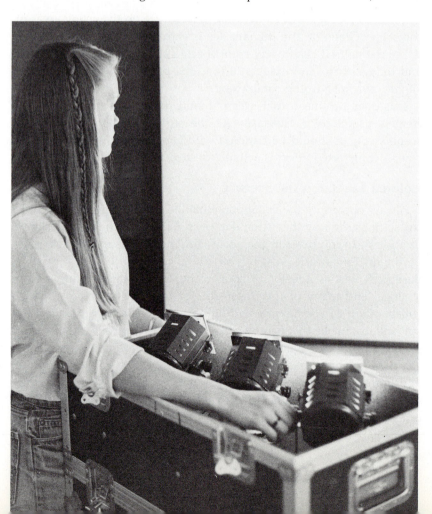

FIGURE 18–5

The Color Mix-Box

Three Fresnels on dimmers allow the designer freedom to mix colors in a space other than the theatre.

is to be a color change during the scene, then more than one color must be provided. More delicate and precise shadings can also be achieved if several different colors are blended into one.

Mixing of the three primaries is a traditional method of achieving variable color on a sky drop, and striplights will commonly be supplied with glass color filters (roundels) in the three primary colors. Remember, however, that light transmission from primary colors is extremely low, and pale tints usually are too pale for a sky drop. Therefore, colors closer to the secondaries are often the best solution.

Selecting Color

Experimenting with color mixing is especially important for the young lighting designer. Colors projected by stage-lighting instruments can be seen in the theatre or in a lighting laboratory—in fact, any place that has dimmers. However, a useful tool for experimentation outside the theatre is the color mix-box (Figure 18–5). Three-inch Fresnels and three common household dimmers are used in the mix-box shown. The box is portable and can be plugged into any household circuit. With the mix-box, the task of color selection is made easier and more convenient.

COLOR MEDIA

In order to use a mix-box, a lighting designer must have available a file box of color media that contains a frame-size cut of every color the designer may need. There are three kinds of color media in use today.

Gelatin

The least expensive of the color media, gelatin comes in the form of very thin sheets and in a considerable range of colors. But its disadvantages are numerous. It has to be cut with care to prevent tearing, it dries out and becomes brittle with age, and it loses all form when dampened, drooping like a wet dishrag in folds that adhere to each other and can never be separated. Some of its shades, particularly the blues and pinks, fade quite easily and must be replaced in the instruments frequently—sometimes after a single performance. The only remaining manufacturer of gelatin in this country is Rosco Laboratories, and their product is called "Roscogel."

Plastic Media

Two types of plastic color media are available: acetate and Mylar. While acetate is less expensive than Mylar, it too will fade and even change color over a period of time. Both plastics are waterproof and considerably more durable than gelatin and come in a wide range of colors.

Acetate. Two acetate colors are in common use in the United States: "Roscolene," manufactured by Rosco Laboratories, and "Cinemoid," manufactured by Rank Strand in Great Britain. Unfortunately, the high cost and unreliable availability of Cinemoid is forcing it out of the American market. The colors in most Cinemoid color reference (or "swatch") books will be numbered from 1 on into the 70s, but for identification it is a good idea to use the 500 series which is common to Great Britain. This practice eliminates any confusion with other brands of color which also begin their numbering with 1.

Mylar. Mylar was marketed several years ago for use with the hotter quartz stage-lighting instruments. Like acetate, Mylar is available in sheets (approximately 21" × 24") but also comes in rolls. It is extremely durable and may be reused. Three companies supply Mylar filters in the United States: Lee ("Lee Filters"), Colortran ("Geletran"), and Rosco ("Roscolux"). Lee Filters are numbered in the 100 series and spill over into the 200 numbers. Both Roscolux and Geletran begin their numbering at 1. Use an *R* prefix before Roscolux numbers and a *G* prefix before Geletran numbers for clarity.

Most often the choice between acetate and Mylar is simply a matter of durability. Mylar is now available in a wider range of colors than acetate, but its higher cost can be prohibitive. However, the use of Mylar is recommended in the following situations:

1 In sky drop or cyclorama lighting, particularly if the lighting instruments are placed on the floor shooting up.
2 When using high-intensity lighting instruments with lamp ratings of over 1000 watts.
3 In scenic projection or follow spotting.

Handling Plastic Media. A new piece of plastic may, when placed in the heat of a light beam, give off considerable steam for a period. This effect, which appears to be smoke, can be quite distracting, if not alarming, to the audience. It is wise, therefore, to test new plastic well before curtain time and, if it smokes, leave the instrument switched on to dry it out before the show starts.

To allow the heat of an instrument to escape when acetate is used as its color medium, it is a good idea to perforate it with numerous small holes. These will not affect the performance of the plastic in any way, except to prolong its life, nor will the holes appear in the beam pattern. An ice pick, nail, or awl may be used for this purpose, but the neatest and easiest method is to run a pounce wheel several times over the full sheet before cutting it to size.

Colored Glass

The most expensive medium of all is glass. While gelatin and plastic may be cut to any size or shape desired, glass must be ordered for exactly the purpose required. It comes in few colors, is heavy and bulky to store, and although it never fades, is rarely affected by heat, and stands up well under ordinary usage, it can be smashed. Glass has two great advantages: it is heat resistant, and it can be molded into markings and prismatic lines that will spread light.

Roundels can be obtained with the following features:

Plain For color filtering only.

Stippled For color and also to diffuse the beam.

Spread For color and also to spread the beam laterally, so that the various colors will blend more readily.

Stripped Very thin glass in narrow strips to color the light from extremely hot-beamed instruments.

Diffusion Material

Diffusion material, often called "frost," diffuses light from an instrument and softens or even eliminates a shutter cut or beam edge. Although not a color medium, it is manufactured by the companies that produce color media, is listed in their swatch books, and is commercially available in sheets. Frosts have been with us for a long time, but recently Rosco Laboratories has greatly increased its selection of such media (in part due to the efforts of lighting designer Gilbert Hemsley).

Color Manufacturers

It is good practice to replace swatch books every two or three years to avoid faded color samples and keep aware of newly added colors. For a variety of reasons, a manufacturer may not be able to match exactly the color of a filter from one batch to another. Rosco has taken to adding a letter suffix to the number of a color filter that was not able to be adequately matched (R35A).

Finally, never trust the color names which the various manufacturers assign to each color. Names are assigned to aid in communication and to make a particular color easier to remember, but one need only compare Cinemoid's "Steel Blue" (517) with Roscolene's "Steel Blue" (854) to fully understand why such labels are meaningless.

To obtain color swatch books contact your local color media supplier or write the following manufacturers:

ROSCO: Rosco Laboratories, Inc.
36 Bush Avenue
Port Chester, NY 10573

LEE: Belden Communications, Inc.
534 West 25th Street
New York, NY 10001

GELATRAN: Colortran
1015 Chestnut Street
Burbank, CA 91502

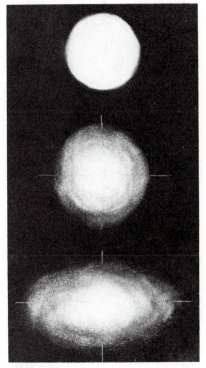

FIGURE 18–6
Diffusion Material
The effects of three different diffusion materials. (Top) A light frost. (Middle) A heavy frost which keeps a hot center. (Bottom) A spread frost such as Roscolux R104.

Color in Light

463

19

Stage Lighting Practice

The young lighting designer should first study motivational lighting. Accordingly, the early part of this chapter will lean toward a discussion of the types of light from those sources with which we are all familiar: daylight, night light, and light from artificial sources.

LIGHTING THE ACTOR

Actors must be seen in proper relationship to their backgrounds. This relationship, of course, is different for each play or dramatic situation. In general, the designer must vary the intensity, distribution, and color of light to solve the problem. Distribution is of primary importance because it involves the angle and direction of light that reveals the actors, especially their faces, in natural form.

The expression "in natural form" is the clue. It means the actor's face should be seen as it appears under natural lighting. Our eyes have been schooled by a lifetime of seeing one another under sunlight or interior lighting coming from above. We are so accustomed to seeing the features of a face disclosed by light from an overhead direction that to light it from below, for example, produces for us an unnatural look.

Anyone who has done outdoor photography knows how to maneuver a subject into a position where the sun will reveal the face most favorably. Overly bright sunlight from a single direction will cast such deep shadows that visibility of the face will be reduced. In the diffused light of shade or of an overcast sky the face appears in full visibility, although it is missing the dramatic accent of the brilliant sunlight.

Through the elaborate control of intensity and distribution possible in stage lighting, the face of the actor can be lighted to appear the way it does in nature.

It has long been a practice of artists and architects to render their drawings as though light were falling on the subject from over the artist's shoulder at an angle of about 45 degrees. The lighting designer adopts the same concept. Using spotlights, the beams may be directed on the actor at a 45-degree angle above and at 45 degrees from the right and left. To give the face an accent of brightness or color difference on one side, the intensity or color of the right or left spotlight may be varied. The face is then disclosed by a *fill-light* on one side and an accent or *key-light* on the opposite side. This slight difference in color and intensity not only improves the visibility of the face but also adds interest to the composition.

Back Lighting. A third angle also can be employed to further define the actor: lighting from overhead and behind. Back lighting is a stratagem borrowed from movie and television lighting. Because of the need to separate an actor from the background, back light is necessary in television lighting. (The tendency of the TV camera is to flatten or shorten distances appearing on the reception screen.) The use of back lighting on the stage to separate an actor from the background adds another dimension to the stage composition. It allows the lighting designer to put a brighter light on the background than would otherwise be possible, and it permits the scene designer to use colors without fear of failure to bring the actor's face into relief. Back lighting produces highlights on the head and shoulders of the actor that give a halo effect if the light is too intense. When it is kept in proper balance with the front lights the actor is etched clearly against the background.

Because back light tends to "rim" an actor, stronger colors than those used in front lighting may be employed. Such creative use of color can help to establish an overhead motivational source or simply color and texture the stage floor for a specific mood or effect. Back light will normally require a more intense source than front light. Care must be taken to keep back light from shining into the first row of audience seating. This often presents a problem, and the lighting designer may be tempted to compromise the back angle, making it more of a top or down light. Top light is not at all the same as back light, for it tends to "squash" rather than rim an actor.

Side Lighting. Side lighting gives the designer additional flexibility. Both color and angle add variety as side lighting is used in combination with frontal sources. Side lighting comes from the wings or tormentor positions and is best when directed parallel to the apron. A great variety of vertical angles, however, are available to the designer—from the low, straight-side angle of dance lighting to a high side that rims an actor from the side (Figure 19–1).

FIGURE 19–1
Sidelight

Designing the Lighting

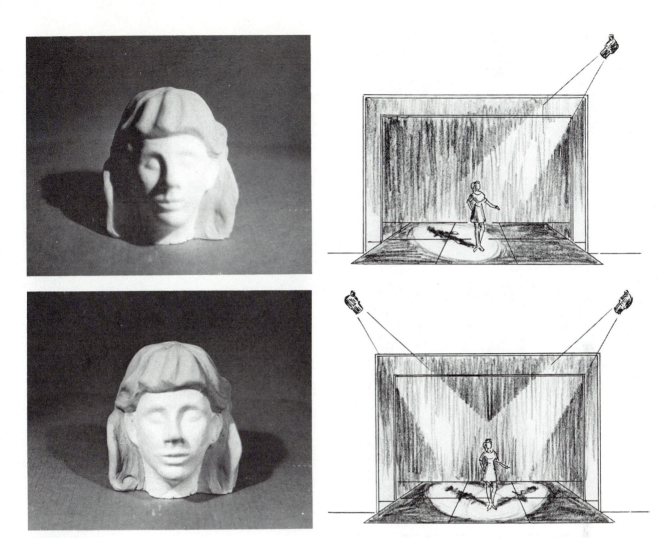

FIGURE 19–2

Lighting the Actor

The photographs through page 470 illustrate the effect of the angles of light on the composition of the face. (Top) Front light from stage-left, 45-degree angle. Lack of visibility on the dark side of the face. (Above) Front light from the left and right, 45-degree angle. The right side of the face has a higher-intensity light suggesting the direction of the motivating or "key" light.

Because side lights hit the actor from the extreme right and left, their color need not be as unsaturated as the front lights. They may be used with more chromatic colors to accent costumes or to add colored highlights to white or neutral costumes. Strong side lighting is frequently used for musical production as a part of this more presentational style of theatre.

Like back light, side light also can be used to establish a motivational source through color, angle, and intensity. In addition, such light is more apparent to the audience simply because it will "read" side light more readily than back light. Thus, dramatic lighting effects can be established through the creative use of strong side light.

Lighting the Actor

(Top) Side light from the right, 45-degree angle. (Center) Side light from the right, 30-degree angle. (Bottom) Side light from the right and left, 30-degree angle. Note the shadow in the center of the face.

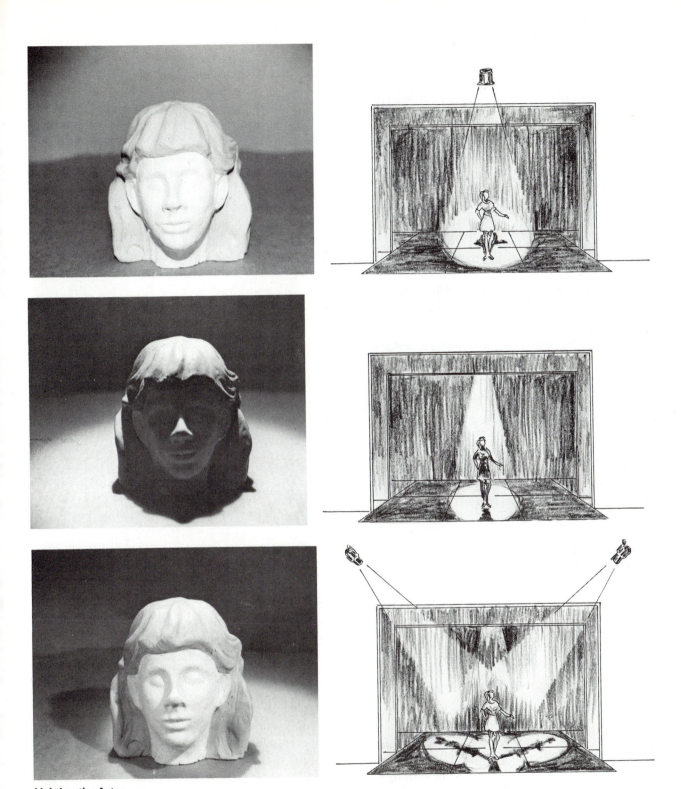

Lighting the Actor

(Top) Full front light. Note lack of definition. (Center) Backlight producing a halo or "rim" effect. (Bottom) Three angles: right and left front light and back light. The key light is from the left from a 45-degree angle, fill light from the right front and rim light from the overhead rear.

Stage Lighting Practice

469

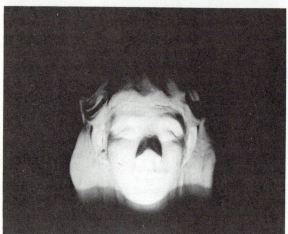

Lighting the Actor

(Top) Downlight or "pool," 90-degree angle. (Bottom) Upward angle from the foot-lights or apron. An unnatural, though dramatic, angle.

Lighting the Acting Area

Lighting an actor from various positions and angles is, of course, easy if the subject is posed or remains in a fixed position on stage. The actor, however, usually moves. Therefore, to produce the same uniformity of coverage as on a stationary figure, the lighting designer must constantly duplicate the focus of spotlights on many similar areas over the entire playing area.

By dividing the playing portion of the setting into convenient areas and then lighting each area with the same number of spotlights, the acting area is covered with a balanced illumination. The area method of lighting the actor, which was first developed by Stanley McCandless in the 1930s, has proved a very efficient and systematic technique. As scenery style has changed and lighting instrument design has improved, the method has been modified and expanded. The original

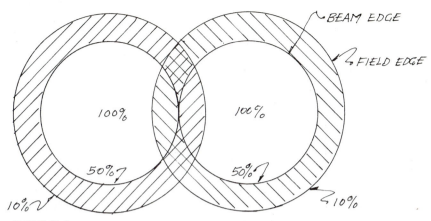

FIGURE 19–3
ERS Beam Alignment for a Smooth Field

concept of providing a smooth coverage through the use of a minimum of instruments has given way to double and triple hanging in the name of greater flexibility in color control and distribution. The resulting number of lighting instruments used in some shows is staggering. Although the area method was first developed for the proscenium theatre it has been readily adapted to other theatre forms such as thrust and arena (see Chapter 21).

In using the area system, one of the first things a designer learns is that areas must overlap considerably or the actor will pass through dark spots ("dips") in lighting when moving from one area to another. A general rule of thumb for this overlap is to align adjacent instruments beam edge to beam edge, thus producing 100 percent light throughout (Figure 19–3). Ideal lighting angles often must be compromised. An example particular to lighting the proscenium stage is illustrated by the placement of instruments 1-L and 3-R in Figure 19–5, page 473. Since the desired 45-degree angle is impossible to maintain because of the proscenium arch, these instruments must be shifted toward center until they adequately cover the area.

The placement and choice of the number of areas are the lighting designer's decision and, of course, vary with the size and shape of the setting (Figure 19–4, page 472). However, in general, areas will vary from 6 to 10 feet in diameter, with 8-foot areas being a good average. Of course, area size is determined by beam spread along with throw distance of a given lighting instrument. The young designer should consider making up a beam and field spread template for each of the instruments in common use. Such a template, drawn to scale on drafting or tracing paper, can be used as an overlay on a sectional view of the theatre and will quickly show approximate area coverage.

The action of the play or the staging of the production also helps to determine the number of areas and the distribution of the coverage.

Stage Lighting Practice

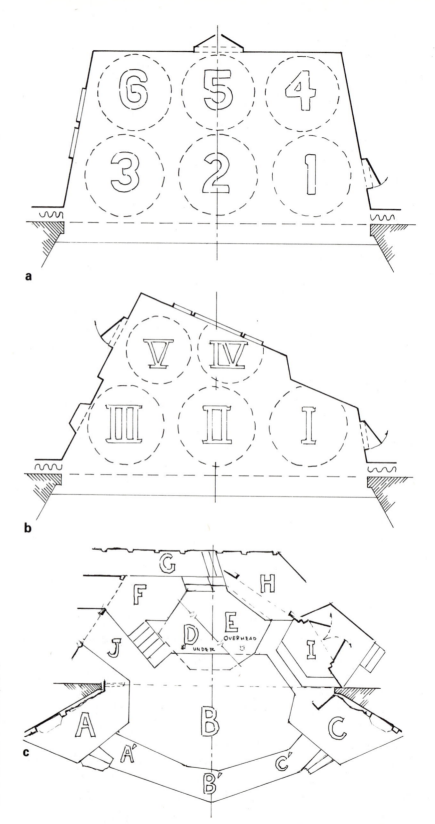

FIGURE 19–4

The Acting Areas

(a) A conventional box setting. Note the numbering of the areas from down-stage left to up-stage right. The total number of areas will vary with the shape and number of settings in the production. (b) An irregularly shaped interior setting. Some designers prefer to designate the areas with Roman numerals to avoid confusion. (c) A complicated set. For ease of communication, the director may establish areas and labels and the lighting designer may use the same system.

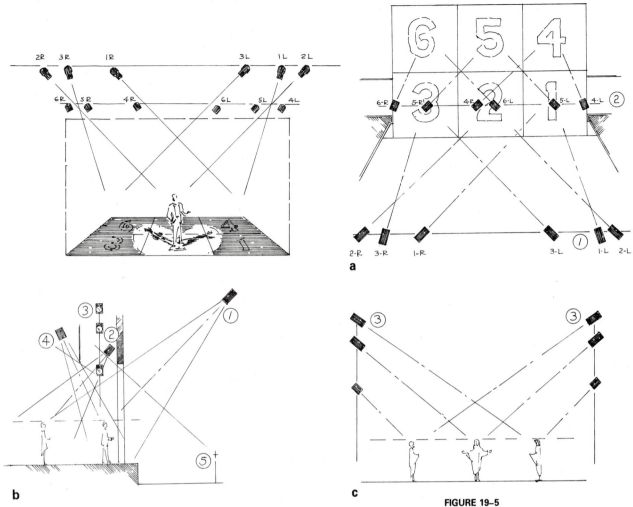

a

b

c

FIGURE 19–5

Lighting the Acting Areas

(a) The area system with a minimum of spotlights for each area. (1) Beam or ceiling position in front of the proscenium covering the downstage areas, 1, 2, and 3. (2) Teaser position. Spotlights on the first pipe batten upstage of teaser or proscenium opening are focused on the upstage areas, 4, 5, and 6. (b) A sectional view of the area system. (1) Beam spots. (2) Teaser spots. (3) Side lights and (4) back lights are additional angles that can be added into each area. (5) Extreme vertical sightline. (c) Front view showing the angle of side lighting for areas 1, 2, and 3.

In a multiscene production some of the areas can be planned for use in more than one set, providing the floor plans are close to the same configuration.

One bit of advice: Most directors and actors have a tendency to love center stage (actors have been known to be attracted to center stage much like moths to a flame), so the prudent lighting designer should be sure to have a controllable center area.

Area Flexibility

The demand for greater and greater flexibility in area lighting stems from the trend toward increasingly complex staging, more frequent repertory organizations (where several shows are kept in rotation), and high labor costs that force the elimination of unnecessary handling or manual operation of equipment. It is cheaper, for example, to hang a few extra instruments than to pay an electrician to be present at each performance to change a color medium.

Double Hanging. To improve the limited flexibility of simple cross lighting the designer can hang two more instruments, right and left, as additional lights for each area (Figure 19–6a). By duplicating the area coverage on each side, several possibilities for color control are created. The designer can (1) change the warm-cool accent from left to right; (2) change the area color by independently mixing the colors from either the right or left; or (3) flood the stage with only one of the two area colors. If the setting is open enough to permit it, the back lights can also be double hung, providing even further flexibility.

Triple Hanging. A third spotlight may be added to each position lighting an area (Figure 19–6b). The extra light can give further dimension to color control, increase the intensity of the area, and provide greater flexibility of distribution for the area. An area, for example, can have both tight and wide coverage. To achieve tight coverage, the two extra spots are focused onto a smaller portion of the stage so that the focus on the scene is more concentrated.

Distribution Flexibility. Double and triple hanging offer the designer excellent color control, but an additional degree of flexibility can be achieved by varying the angle and direction of light. If side lighting (either from the wings or from a more frontal side position such as the traditional box booms) is added to area lights, the designer can then alter color as well as direction. For example, front-of-house right instruments can work with the stage-right side lights.

High side can be hung in addition to low side to create a different quality and color tonality for a given scene. Low-angle front-of-house sources called "washes" are often hung on a balcony rail and can be subtly used to change color tonality as well as the texture of a scene. However, care must be taken in using this rather flat angle in order not to lose dimensionality and lighting quality.

The possibilities are endless, and the more a lighting designer ex-

FIGURE 19–6

Double and Triple Hanging

(a) Double hanging on the stage left side. Only the downstage areas, 1, 2, and 3, are shown. The stage-right beam spots are cool in color while the spots on the left are both warm and cool to allow a color selection in the acting areas. (b) Triple hanging on area 2, double hanging on areas 1 and 3. The center area has a tight and open focus as well as a selection of color and direction of key light in each area.

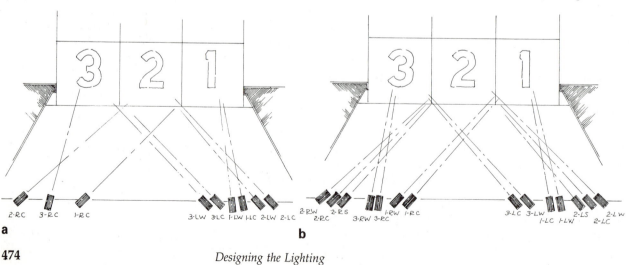

a   b

periments with area flexibility, the more diverse and exciting the product can be.

Area Specials and Special Visibility

Area specials are a variation of regular area lighting that uses instruments to specifically define or emphasize a part of the setting or draw attention to an actor at a given moment and in a certain position on the stage. Examples include a door special, an extra spot carefully framed to catch an actor in the doorway; a couch special, extra punch on the couch or settee where an important scene takes place; or a pin spot, a narrow beam of light on an actor's face that is held a moment longer than the rest of the stage lights on a final dim-out. Area specials influence composition by pulling the eye to the center of action.

Special visibility deals with the moving actor under more arbitrary or abstract conditions. The movement of light can be achieved in one of two ways. The actor can be covered by a series of carefully focused spotlights on the path of movement that dim up and down at the proper moments. The more traditional method is to use a follow spot. The movement of the actor is followed by a single freely mounted spotlight. The follow spot has long been in use in musical comedies, revues, and other presentational productions, where realism is of minor importance. It usually appears as a sharply defined, brilliant circle of light outshining all the stage lights.

Another form of follow spotting, often referred to as "European follow spotting" after the practice of placing follow spots and operators on a first light bridge, has become fairly popular for more dramatic productions. Unlike American Broadway musical follow spotting, the goal of European follow spotting is subtlety. A soft-edged incandescent follow spot is used to highlight the action unobtrusively. A vertical angle closer to 60 degrees than 45 degrees is preferable in order to mininize shadows around the actor. With good operation European follow spotting can be an extremely effective lighting technique.

Area Control

We now must touch on the tricky problem of control. Unless fortunate enough to be working in a situation offering unlimited dimmer control (such as that provided by dimmer-per-circuit installations), the designer must soon face the task of assigning instruments to dimmers. Color control is normally a high priority; seldom will it be desirable to have two sets of instruments of differing colors on the same dimmer. Area control is the next priority; which stage areas should be controlled individually and which "ganged" or grouped together? The latter is a critical decision, for the designer must work with the chosen control flexibility throughout the production. Before a choice is made, the designer should view rehearsals and discuss questions of control with the director.

Although there will never be absolute rules of control priorities, the following is suggested as a beginning:

1 Control of the front-of-house "visibility" area lighting is most important.
2 Area control of side-lighting sources, although of secondary importance, is still important.
3 Area control of back or top light is of least importance unless the stage floor and its composition are visible to the majority of the audience.

Of course, most specials require their own control channel but can be re-patched at an intermission in many instances. Don't forget to assign control for practicals, house lights if necessary, and curtain warmers or stage toners. Also, it is always good practice to save a couple of dimmers as spares in case of dimmer failure or additional control requirements are made during final rehearsals.

LIGHTING THE BACKGROUND

The mood of the environment surrounding the action of the scene is often so fully expressed in the intensity, color, and distribution of the area lighting that, except for special occasions, the area lights provide the major portion of the illumination of the setting.

In the case of a conventional interior or box setting, the area light will usually suffice to light the walls of the set. However, several precautions are necessary to make such wall illumination successful. Too often we see a box set with the stage-right wall a totally different color from that of the stage-left wall. This appallingly common mistake, a result of poor color mixing from the frontal-area instruments, can be corrected by making sure that all frontal colors hit the walls with relatively equal intensity. Instruments lighting the walls of a box set should be put into soft focus if they are ellipsoidals in a front-of-house position. Over-stage instruments should be Fresnels or frosted ellipsoidals.

Shadows from actors or furniture are a problem that may be difficult to solve. The best solution is to change the angle of light causing the shadow, but at times this may not be possible. Instead, a wall wash, using 6-inch Fresnels, or even strip lights, will help (but not solve the problem completely).

Background areas and backings, however, are a different matter. Many times the lighting problem may be small, for example the backing behind a doorway, rarely seen for more than a moment at a time, and then not directly by most of the audience. Not very elaborate equipment is needed to give these backings enough illumination so that an actor, when leaving the stage, does not seem to be retiring into a dark closet.

Backings can assume greater proportions, for example a section of exterior seen through a large window which might contain ground-rows of distant hills or hedges and a section of sky. Rooftops or the exterior walls of an adjoining building may also be seen in a more detailed backing. Such backings usually demand greater attention to distribution and color control (to perhaps simulate different times of day) than would the simple doorway backing.

For the most complicated backgrounds, such as vast areas of sky sometimes with a painted scenic vista, large backdrops or cycloramas are usually used. These require rows of high-wattage instruments, both from above and below, in order to give the proper amount of light as well as even distribution and blending of color over the entire surface. Greater control of color is required if the mood of the background is expected to change with the time of day. Changes in distribution can also occur, especially if the backdrop is partly translucent, allowing a cross-fading from front lighting to back lighting furnished by an additional bank of lights behind the drop.

Scrim is a particularly useful material because of its capability to appear either opaque or transparent. Scrim in front of a backdrop or cyclorama will add the somewhat hazy quality of distance to the backing. The scrim itself can be lit, or, better yet, the drop behind the scrim may be illuminated (Figure 19–7c). Scrim may also be used alone as a drop, in which case the designer will most certainly need to pay close attention to the light that falls directly on as well as behind the scrim. A high-angle top light is the best means to create an opaque scrim. To

FIGURE 19–7

Lighting the Background

Various methods of lighting the backdrop and background arrangements. (a) Painted backdrop (1) lit from above and below. (5) Floor striplights behind a groundrow. (6) Overhead strip behind a border. (b) Painted backdrop (1) lit only from above. (c) Translucent drop (3) is illuminated by backlight reflected off a reflecting drop (2) lit by floor strips (7) and overhead strips (8). Frontlight comes from a second overhead strip (9). (d) A translucent drop upstage of a scrim. The drop has front and back lighting to change its quality or time of day. The scrim has front lighting to add depth and atmosphere. (10) Floor strip. (11) Overhead strips for backlighting. (3) Translucent drop. (12) Floor strip. (13) Overhead strip for front lighting. (4) Scrim. (14) Overhead strip for frontlighting scrim.

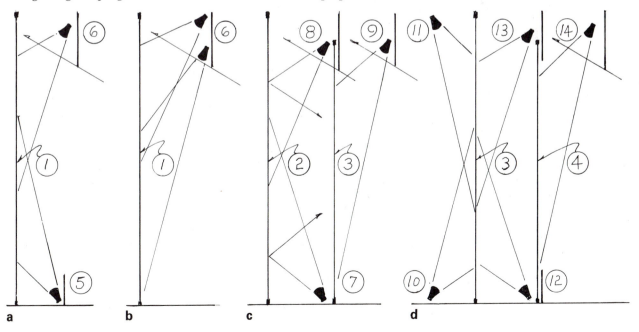

a   b   c   d

make a scrim transparent, keep as much light as possible off the scrim itself while illuminating objects behind it.

Successful background lighting depends on the close cooperation of the lighting and scene designers. All too often the scene designer does not leave enough space between groundrows and the backdrop or between borders and the cyclorama to allow sufficient distance for proper distribution of the striplights. Backgrounds representing distant fields are sometimes so close to a window or door that it is impossible to keep the area lights from casting shadows on the background, thereby destroying any illusion of distance.

DESIGN DECISIONS

The designer is constantly making decisions concerning type and position of instruments, color filtering, and dimmer readings. We have discussed many of the technical considerations in making decisions about lighting design and now will look at the aesthetics of such decisions. The lighting designer must be equipped to make choices involving instrumentation, angle, color, and finally, dimmer readings.

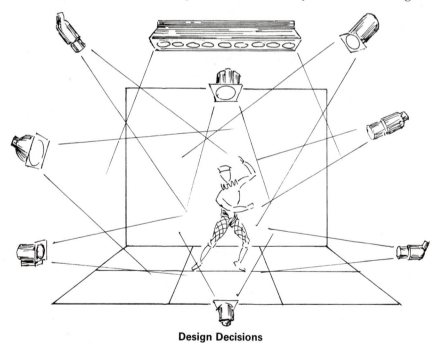

Design Decisions

Choice of Instrument Does it support an incandescent or fluorescent; practical, daylight, sunlight, moonlight, etc.?
Choice of Angle What is best position for the actor, director, costume, or set designer? View from balcony
Choice of Dimmer Reading(s) Intensity, movement, focus, nonverbal communication.
Choice of Color Motivation, nature, or optional. Brilliance, atmosphere, style.

FIGURE 19–8
Design Decisions

478   *Designing the Lighting*

Choice of Instrument

As previously noted, a particular stage-lighting instrument will be chosen because it comes closest to satisfying requirements of intensity, coverage, and quality of light. Adjustability of beam spread and field quality of most of the new ellipsoidal reflector spotlights (ERS) along with increased light output certainly make this instrument the most valuable for the lighting designer (Figure 19–9). While the ERS is the logical choice for front-of-house, this workhorse of a unit also serves well backstage and should be considered along with the Fresnel, beam projector, and PAR can.

The Fresnel delivers a soft light whose beam blends very easily and therefore is ideal for upstage areas of a box set (Figure 19–10). Fresnels, having a tremendously variable beam spread, can be used over a wide range of throw distances: the 6-inch Fresnel lamped at 500 or 750 watts is effective to somewhat more than 20 feet, and the 8-inch Fresnel with lamps up to 2000 watts can be useful up to 40 feet. The soft light of a candle, the quality of dusk or an overcast sky, or the scattered, almost shadowless light from fluorescent tubes will all be most closely reproduced by using the Fresnel.

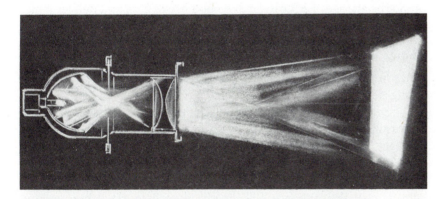

FIGURE 19–9
Ellipsoidal Reflector Spotlight

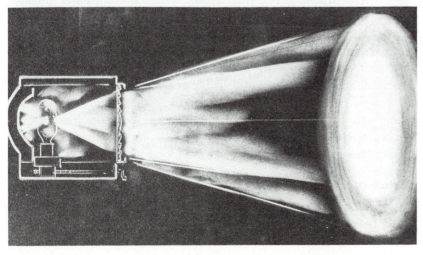

FIGURE 19–10
Fresnel Spotlight

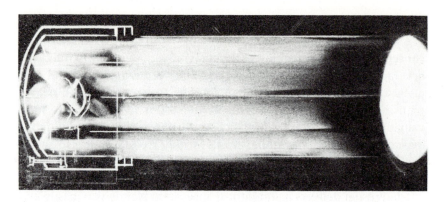

FIGURE 19–11
Beam Projector

The light from a beam projector cannot be shaped, but its near-parallel rays come closest to those of the sun (Figure 19–11). This quality can serve as a motivational source, whereas Fresnel and even ERS light will act as fill or bounce. Banks of beam projectors have been employed as "walls" of light shooting from an over-stage batten.

The PAR can, like the beam projector, has a parabolic reflector, but the lens of its lamp breaks up the light enough to cause a softer-edged beam than that of a beam projector. Yet, the PAR still delivers a sharp and intense light, harsh in quality. Remember, its beam is oval and cannot be shaped. PAR cans make good back lights and deliver a nice quality of light for dance.

Choice of Angle

Angle and color are probably the two most difficult choices for the young designer to make.

The purpose of two front lights at angles of 45 degrees each, rather than a single unit straightaway, is to add dimension to the actor's body and face. As the angle of front light is lowered, it tends to flatten features more and more. As the angle is raised, features become sharper and sharper, with deeper and deeper shadows. Remember that front light is what the audience will "read" more than any other angle of light.

Whether it be a bit frontal or straight out of the wings, side light is an exciting angle for both variety and revelation of form. A low angle side, such as that commonly used in dance lighting, will light the entire height of the body fairly evenly. The problem is that it is quite difficult to control. Therefore, a slightly higher angle side (from 30 degrees to 60 degrees) is often used in the theatre. Here is where the designer can begin to use richer and more expressive colors in order to establish a motivational source or simply set the mood for a scene.

Choice of Color

Color selection requires experience—experience in observing traditional theatrical usage (blue = night), experience in color mixing, as well as experience in knowing how a given color will act on stage. The lighting laboratory and color mix-box will help, but the lighting designer ultimately has to do some experimenting with the real thing. A masterful use of color can be one of the most exciting elements of stage lighting, but it takes time and taste.

Try to analyze color by feeling as well as seeing—how does sunlight feel? Then translate the feeling into color. This is why a visual memory is so important, for we tend to store feelings more than angstrom units. Why does the warmth of sunlight *feel* different than the warmth of a fireplace fire? It has something to do with color.

Throw distance tends to affect the intensity or saturation of a color—colors appear more saturated over shorter throw distances.

Choice of Dimmer Readings

Setting dimmer levels for the first time will probably be a painful and time-consuming experience, but be assured that it gets easier. Force yourself to write your dimmer levels "blind" several days before actually seeing them on stage. Take the time to think through each preset or stage picture: Which sets of instruments should be reading highest and which control areas should take focus? Write the levels on your "cheat sheets" (more information to come) and have your board operator transfer them to standard preset sheets or directly into the memory of a computer system. You will find that this process of writing blind takes a good deal of time, but it ultimately results in a better-looking product and can cut hours off a technical rehearsal.

In general, it is best to write and design for the highest dimmer levels to be between 80 and 90 percent. Then, if more light is required, you have room to maneuver. Depending on the curve of your dimmers, a reading of 10 percent will barely warm the filament, and a reading of 20 percent will just begin to deliver light. Keep in mind the saturation of color filters, for the more saturated filters will cut down light transmission significantly. Finally, always remember that the perceived intensity of light is relative.

THE LIGHT PLOT

The light plot and its accompanying paperwork (the instrument schedule, hookup, and section) forms the link between the designer's ideas and the reality of theatrical production. The importance of this piece of paper cannot be overstated. It must be 100 percent accurate and complete so that the "put-in" (hang, circuit, focus) can proceed in an orderly and rapid fashion. The simple process of executing a plot enables the designer to discover and eliminate many artistic as well as technical problems well before ever setting foot in the theatre.

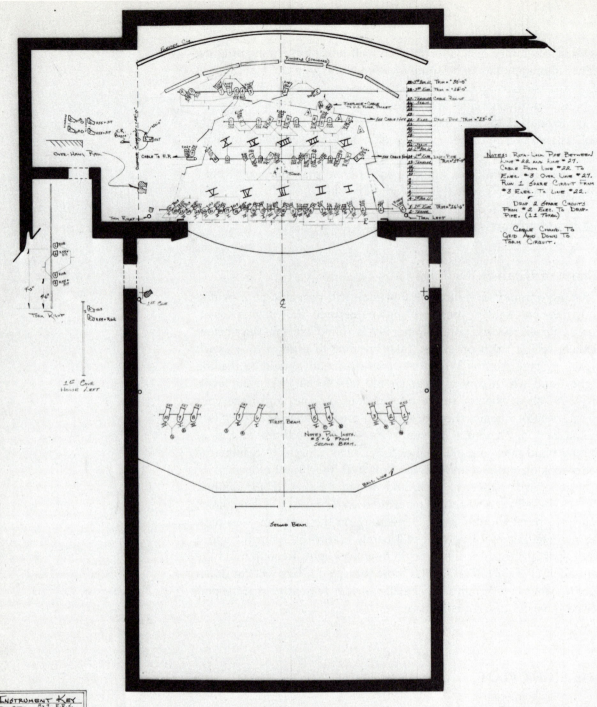

Notes: Rota-Lock Pipe Between Line #22 and Line #27. Cable From Line #22 To Elec. #3 Over Line #27. Run 1 Spare Circuit From #3 Elec. To Line #22.

Drop 2 Spare Circuits From #2 Elec. To Drop-Pipe. (11 Total)

Cable Chand. To Grid And Down To Turn Circuit.

First Beam

Note: Pull Insts. #5 & 6 From Second Beam.

Second Beam

Instrument Key

- 8×9 E.R.S. 750 w.
- 6×12 E.R.S. 750 w. — Players
- 6×6 Step E.R.S. 500 or 750 w.
- 6×9 E.R.S. 750 w. — Players
- 6×9 E.R.S. 750 w. — House
- Mini-Eclipse 500 w.
- 8" Fresnel 1 K
- 6" Fresnel 500 w.
- 3" Fresnel 150 w.
- Practical
- Fresnel With Barn Door
- C-S Strips 3 Circuit 2,000 w./Circuit

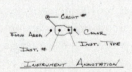

Color Key

- 500 Series = Cinemoid
- "R" Series = Roscolux
- 800 Series = Roscolene
- 200 Series = Lee
- N/C = No Color

Instrument Annotation

Circuit #
Focus Area
Color
Inst. #
Inst. Type

M.E.T. Production of **A Doll House** Lighting Plot Design By: R. Craig Wolf

Drawn By: RCW — Scale: 1/4" = 1'-0" — Dates: 1-83 — Plate # 1 of 3

Working on the premise that some standardization is desirable for any communicative tool, the light plot should include the following:

1 A plan of the theatre drawn to scale (preferably ½ inch—*never* ⅛ inch) showing and labeling all lighting positions.
2 A plan of the stage setting drawn to scale in light weight lines.
3 The lighting areas indicated by Roman numerals in heavy weight lines beginning down-stage left, working stage right and then up-stage.
4 Exact instrument placement, type and size, color and number.
5 Title block in lower right-hand corner, instrument key, instrument annotation key, and color key.

The Theatre Plan. This plan should show all rigging for the production, including masking, flying scenery and drops, as well as electric pipes. Critical audience sight points must be included. It is permissible to show distance to front-of-house lighting positions in a smaller scale, but this deviation should be noted. A lighting position is indicated by a single, solid line of medium weight. All positions must be clearly labeled.

Some designers prefer to include a plaster line scale and sometimes an up- to down-stage scale in order to facilitate hanging and placement of instruments. Refer to Figure 19–12 for examples.

The Stage Setting. The lighting designer's set plan need not be as complete as the scene designer's floor plan, but it should include elements of importance to lighting such as walls, doors, major levels, large pieces of furniture, and so forth. Plaster line and center line should be included. If the production requires several sets, the lighting designer may use transparent overlays of each set.

Instrument Annotation. One of the several available lighting instrument templates should be used to trace outlines of the various instruments (Figure 19–13, page 484). Templates can be ordered in either ¼- or ½-inch scale as well as in plan or sectional view. These outlines must be bold enough to stand out from all the other information on the plot. While the lighting instrument should intersect the lighting pipe, the pipe should never be drawn through the instrument. In most situations, instruments are numbered by position beginning house-

FIGURE 19–12

The Light Plot

A light plot for Michigan Ensemble Theatre's production of Ibsen's *A Doll House*. The theatre is a fairly typical proscenium with limited front-of-house lighting positions. Visibility instrumentation front-of-house is colored in R55 and 547. Double-hung back light is 504 and 552. Double-hung high side motivational sources from stage right are colored with R55 and R62 in one instrument and 503 in the second. A ½-inch-scale hanging plot was developed in addition to the ¼-inch-scale plot shown to clarify circuiting and distribution. Scene design by W. Oren Parker; lighting design by R. Craig Wolf.

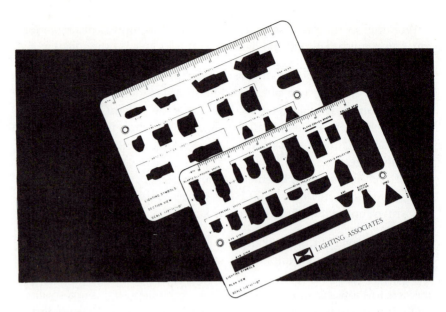

FIGURE 19–13
A Standard Lighting Template

right at the rear and working on-stage. Numbering by position means that all instruments in each position are numbered consecutively beginning with one (Figure 19–12). Some situations, however, may make numbering by position rather confusing (for example, a flexible theatre with a full overhead lighting grid). In such cases, *all* instruments should be numbered consecutively.

The instrument annotation shown in Figure 19–14 is recommended, although some designers might prefer not to include circuits, dimmers, or focus area on the plot itself.

The accepted method of indicating *type* of instrument is to cross-mark the barrel, as illustrated in Figure 19–15.

Of course, all notation is explained in the instrument key.

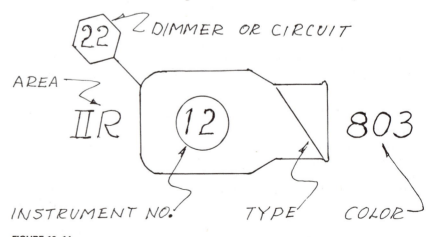

FIGURE 19–14
Instrument Annotation

Designing the Lighting

Instrument and Color Keys. The instrument key indicates exactly which symbol the designer is using for a specific instrument. This key, which should include the wattage as well as the focal length or beam spread of the instrument, is normally located in the lower left corner of the plate.

The color key explains what numbering and lettering system the designer is using for each brand and type of color medium. For example:

"R" Series = Roscolux
800 Series = Roscolene
500 Series = Cinemoid
100 and 200 Series = Lee
"G" Series = Geletran

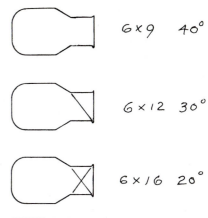

FIGURE 19–15
Instrument Types

Instrument Schedule and Hook-Up

Both these documents provide additional instrument information to an electrician, but each has a different purpose. The instrument schedule lists all instruments by location and instrument number and contains the following information in the following order:

1 Location and instrument number
2 Instrument type (specific)
3 Wattage/lamp designation
4 Color number
5 Use/focus area
6 Circuit
7 Dimmer/channel
8 Remarks

This schedule is simply a list of complete information about any given lighting instrument, some of which might not be included on the plot (Figure 19–16, page 486).

The hook-up lists instruments by dimmer number. The first column of this schedule should contain dimmer number, followed by circuit-number, location and instrument number, type, focus, and color (see Figure 19–24, page 499).

Both documents are seldom necessary; the designer's preference as well as specific production requirements will determine which one is best to use.

The Lighting Section

The center-line section is important to the lighting designer as a tool to help assure plot accuracy. An electrician need never see the section, but the designer will consult it for vertical slightlines, throw distances,

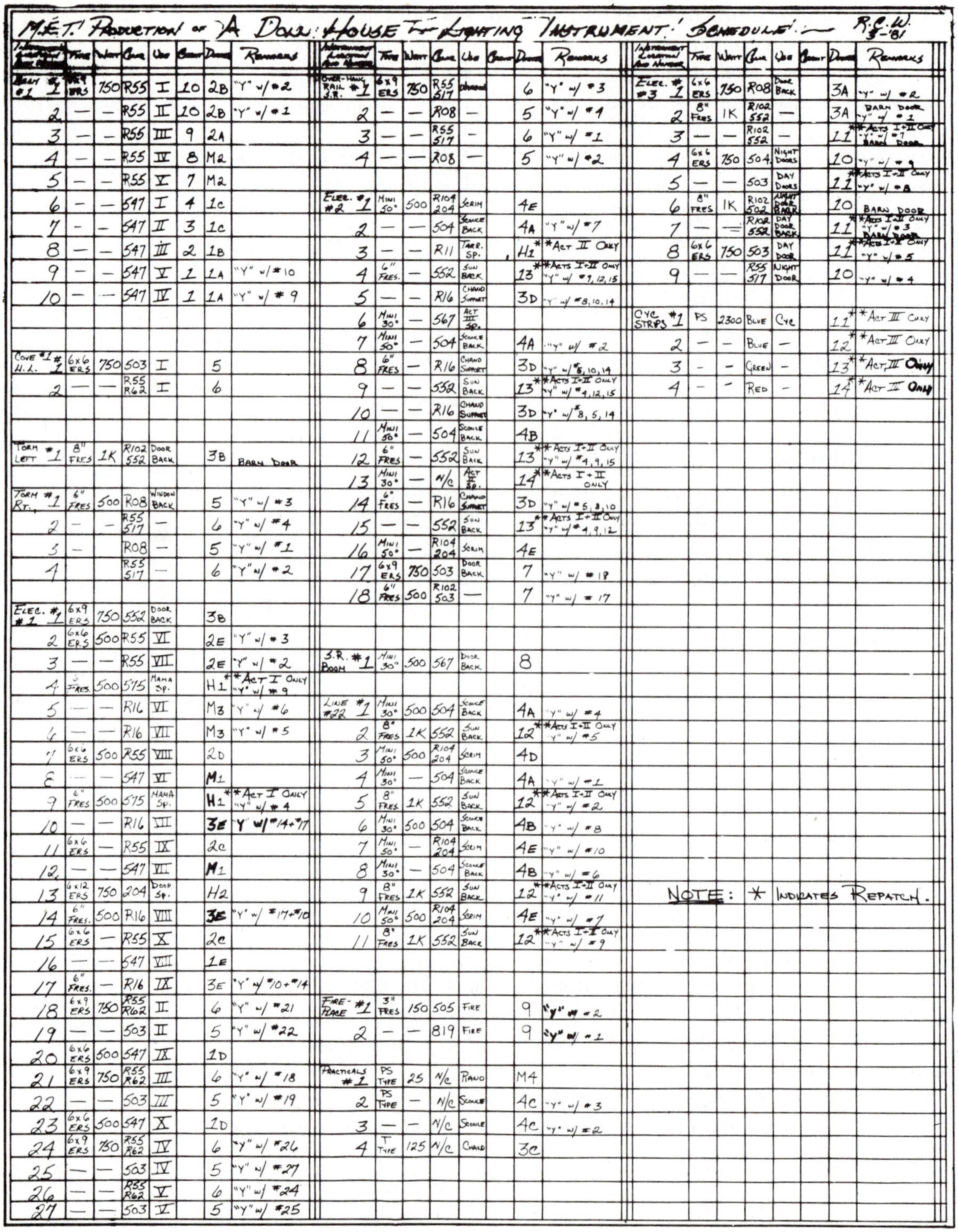

M.E.T. Production of "A Doll House" — Lighting Instrument Schedule — R.C.W. 5-'81

Panel 1

Instrument Location and Number	Type	Watt	Color	Use	Beam	Dimmer	Remarks
Box Beam #1 1	ERS	750	R55	I	10	2B	"Y" w/ #2
2	—	—	R55	II	10	2B	"Y" w/ #1
3	—	—	R55	III	9	2A	
4	—	—	R55	IV	8	M2	
5	—	—	R55	V	7	M2	
6	—	—	547	I	4	1C	
7	—	—	547	II	3	1C	
8	—	—	547	III	2	1B	
9	—	—	547	V	1	1A	"Y" w/ #10
10	—	—	547	IV	1	1A	"Y" w/ #9
Cove #1 H.L. 1	6x6 ERS	750	503	I	5		
2	—	—	R55 R62	I	6		
Torm #1 Left 1	8" Fres	1K	R102 552	Door Back	3B		Barn Door
Torm #1 Rt. 1	6" Fres	500	R08	Window Back	5		"Y" w/ #3
2	—	—	R55 517		6		"Y" w/ #4
3	—	—	R08	—	5		"Y" w/ #1
4	—	—	R55 517	—	6		"Y" w/ #2
Elec. #1 1	6x9 ERS	750	552	Door Back	3B		
2	6x6 ERS	500	R55	VI	2E		"Y" w/ #3
3	—	—	R55	VII	2E		"Y" w/ #2
4	3" Fres	500	575	Mama Sp.	H1		**Act I Only "Y" w/ #9
5	—	—	R16	VI	M3		"Y" w/ #6
6	—	—	R16	VII	M3		"Y" w/ #5
7	6x6 ERS	500	R55	VIII	2D		
8	—	—	547	VI	M1		
9	6" Fres	500	575	Mama Sp.	H1		**Act I Only "Y" w/ #4
10	—	—	R16	VII	3E		"Y" w/ #14 + #17
11	6x6 ERS	—	R55	IX	2C		
12	—	—	547	VII	M1		
13	6x6 ERS	750	204	Door Back	H2		
14	6" Fres	500	R16	VIII	3E		"Y" w/ #17 + #10
15	6x6 ERS	—	R55	X	2C		
16	—	—	547	VIII	1E		
17	6" Fres	—	R16	IX	3E		"Y" w/ #10 + #14
18	6x9 ERS	750	R55 R62	II	6		"Y" w/ #21
19	—	—	503	II	5		"Y" w/ #22
20	6x6 ERS	500	547	IX	1D		
21	6x9 ERS	750	R55 R62	III	6		"Y" w/ #18
22	—	—	503	III	5		"Y" w/ #19
23	6x6 ERS	500	547	X	1D		
24	6x9 ERS	750	R55 R62	IV	6		"Y" w/ #26
25	—	—	503	IV	5		"Y" w/ #27
26	—	—	R55 R62	V	6		"Y" w/ #24
27	—	—	503	V	5		"Y" w/ #25

Panel 2

Instrument Location and Number	Type	Watt	Color	Use	Beam	Dimmer	Remarks
Over-Head Rail S.R. #1 1	6x9 ERS	750	R55 517	phased	6		"Y" w/ #3
2	—	—	R08	—	5		"Y" w/ #4
3	—	—	R55 517	—	6		"Y" w/ #1
4	—	—	R08	—	5		"Y" w/ #2
Elec. #2 1	Mini 50°	500	R104 204	Scrim	4E		
2	—	—	504	Sconce Back	4A		
3	—	—	R11	Tarr. Sp.	H1		
4	6" Fres	—	552	Sun Back	13		"Y" w/ #9,12,15
5	—	—	R16	Chand Support	3D		"Y" w/ #8,10,14
6	Mini 30°	—	567	Act III Sp.			
7	Mini 50°	—	504	Sconce Back	4A		"Y" w/ #2
8	6" Fres	—	R16	Chand Support	3D		"Y" w/ #6,10,14
9	—	—	552	Sun Back	13		**Acts I+II Only "Y" w/ #4,12,15
10	—	—	R16	Chand Support	3D		"Y" #8,5,14
11	Mini 50°	—	504	Sconce Back	4B		
12	6" Fres	—	552	Sun Back	13		**Acts I+II Only "Y" w/ #4,9,15
13	Mini 30°	—	N/C	Act III Sp.	14		**Acts I+II Only
14	6" Fres	—	R16	Chand Support	3D		"Y" w/ #5,8,10
15	—	—	552	Sun Back	13		**Acts I+II Only "Y" w/ #4,9,12
16	Mini 50°	—	R104 204	Scrim	4E		
17	6x9 ERS	750	503	Door Back	7		"Y" w/ #18
18	6" Fres	500	R102 503		7		"Y" w/ #17
S.R. Boom #1 1	Mini 30°	500	567	Door Back	8		
Line #22 1	Mini 30°	500	504	Sconce Back	4A		"Y" w/ #4
2	8" Fres	1K	552	Sun Back	12		**Acts I+II Only "Y" w/ #5
3	Mini 50°	500	R104 204	Scrim	4D		
4	Mini 30°	—	504	Sconce Back	4A		"Y" w/ #1
5	8" Fres	1K	552	Sun Back	12		**Acts I+II Only "Y" w/ #2
6	Mini 30°	500	504	Sconce Back	4B		"Y" w/ #8
7	Mini 50°	—	R104 204	Scrim	4E		"Y" w/ #10
8	Mini 30°	—	504	Sconce Back	4B		"Y" w/ #6
9	8" Fres	1K	552	Sun Back	12		**Acts I+II Only "Y" w/ #7
10	Mini 50°	500	R104 204	Scrim	4E		"Y" w/ #7
11	8" Fres	1K	552	Sun Back	12		**Acts I+II Only "Y" w/ #9
Fire Place #1 1	3" Fres	150	505	Fire	9		"Y" w/ #2
2	—	—	819	Fire	9		"Y" w/ #1
Practicals #1 1	PS Type	25	N/C	Piano	M4		
2	PS Type	—	N/C	Sconce	4C		"Y" w/ #3
3	—	—	N/C	Sconce	4C		"Y" w/ #2
4	T Type	125	N/C	Chand	3C		

Panel 3

Instrument Location and Number	Type	Watt	Color	Use	Beam	Dimmer	Remarks
Elec. #3 1	6x6 ERS	750	R08	Door Back	3A		"Y" w/ #2
2	8" Fres	1K	R102 552	—	3A		Barn Door **Acts I+II Only "Y" w/ #1 Barn Door
3	—	—	R102 552	—	11		
4	6x6 ERS	750	504	Night Doors	10		"Y" w/ #9
5	—	—	503	Day Doors	11		**Acts I+II Only "Y" w/ #8
6	8" Fres	1K	R102 502	Night Day Back Door	10		Barn Door **Acts I+II Only "Y" w/ #3 Barn Door
7	—	—	R102 552	Day Door Back	11		**Acts I+II Only
8	6x6 ERS	750	503	Day Door	11		"Y" w/ #5
9	—	—	R55 517	Night Door	10		"Y" w/ #4
Cyc Strips #1 1	PS	2300	Blue	Cyc	11		*Act III Only
2	—	—	Blue	—	12		
3	—	—	Green	—	13		*Act III Only
4	—	—	Red	—	14		*Act III Only

NOTE: * Indicates Repatch.

FIGURE 19–16

The Instrument Schedule

The instrument schedule for *A Doll House* (Figure 19–12). Instruments are listed by position and number. Complete circuit information was added to the schedule during the put-in.

Designing the Lighting

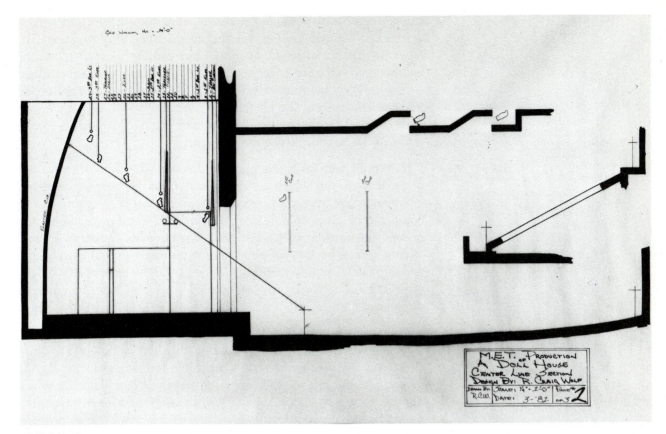

FIGURE 19–17

The Section

The center-line section for *A Doll House*. Note that the only masking is on lines number 2 and 13, forcing the up-stage electric pipes quite high.

acting levels above or below stage height, and accuracy of lighting angles (Figure 19–17).

The scene designer provides the lighting designer with a center-line sectional view of the stage that includes horizontal masking at trim height, critical audience sight points, as well as scenery placement. Occasionally various supplementary sectional views will be necessary; they can be easily and quickly drafted by the lighting designer.

Additional Paperwork

It should be fairly clear by now that the better prepared a lighting designer is before a production moves into the theatre, the easier the design will be realized. In fact, many professional designers would argue that preparation is as important as the design or artistic work. As a result, a variety of additional types of paperwork have been developed by designers in order to simplify the put-in and the execution of the design.

Batten Tapes. To expedite hanging and circuiting the electric pipes, the designer may wish to prepare batten tapes for each hanging position. These consist of rolled pieces of paper or cloth which have been premarked with center-line and specific instrument information. The tapes are simply attached to the batten and electricians follow the instructions on the tape. Information may include instrument number, circuit number, instrument type, color, and even focus. Tapes eliminate any measuring and chalking of the battens and, in combination with hanging cardboards, could eliminate the necessity of an electrician ever having to consult the light plot.

Hanging Cardboards. Hanging cardboards are pieces of stiff paper or cardboard onto which a single location and its respective instrumentation have been transferred from the master plot. A single cardboard can be given to an electrician during the put-in, allowing him or her the freedom of hanging and circuiting the position without having to refer back to the plot. Hanging cardboards will usually contain more detailed information than the plot and, like batten tapes, are especially useful for touring situations, where they can be reused a number of times.

The Cheat Sheet. The designer's cheat sheet (Figure 19–18) was developed as an aid in setting and adjusting lighting levels. The cheat sheet will list all dimmers, their function, and levels for any given preset. This information then allows the designer to find quickly which dimmer controls a specific instrument or set of instruments as well as its intensity. As mentioned earlier, board operators can record prewritten dimmer readings from the cheat sheet onto standard preset sheets or into a computer memory. In the latter case, the cheat sheets act as "hard copy" in the event of memory loss or board malfunction. Obviously these sheets must be kept up-to-date as levels are adjusted—a good task for an assistant.

The Magic Sheet. Another aid to the designer while setting levels, magic sheets are arranged to indicate which dimmers control a specific set-up or stage picture. These sheets may take a pictorial form similar to the color key shown in Figure 19–19, or they may simply be listings of dimmers involved in a set-up. For instance, one section of a magic sheet might indicate which dimmers control the high-side blues, while another section might show how the warm front lights are controlled.

The Color Key. The color key (not to be confused with the plot key of the same name) is a communication device for the designer. This representational drawing will indicate which instruments (and therefore colors) are playing for any given stage picture.

Figure 19–19 shows a typical lighting area with front light of R09 at a level of 80 percent, R55 at a level of 60 percent, and side light from stage right in R04 at 90 percent. This key initially was developed as an educational tool offering a student designer a quick, nonverbal means of communicating lighting intentions.

Designing the Lighting

Cue # || Preset # || Count:

Dim #	1	2	3	4	5	6	7*	8*	9	10	11	12
Use	S.L. ZONE 1	HI S.L. ZONE 2	SIDE C.S. ZONE 2	204 S.R. ZONE 2	S.L. ZONE 3	S.R. ZONE 3	204 SIDE ABOVE	B-B-O HOUSE BACK	S.R. ZONE 1	HI S.L. ZONE 2	SIDE C.S. ZONE 2	117 S.R. ZONE 2
Level												

Dim #	13	14*	15	16*	17	18	19	20	21	22*	23	24
Use	117 S.L. ZONE 3	117 SIDE ABOVE	117 ZONE 4	COUNCIL CHAMBER	BACK ZONE 1	WARM S.L. ZONE 2	C.S. ZONE 2	S.R. ZONE 2	ZONE 3	HERALD 3P.	BACK ZONE 1	COOL S.L. ZONE 2
Level												

Dim #	25	26	27	28*	29*	30*	31*	32*	33*	34*	35*	36*
Use	BACK C.S. ZONE 2	COOL S.R. ZONE 2	ZONE 3	TORCH S.L.	CH C.S.	→ S.R.	R55 S.L.	ABOVE S.R.	WARM S.L.	ABOVE S.R.	COOL S.L.	ABOVE S.R.
Level												

Dim #	37*	38	39	40	41*	42*	43*	44*	45	46	47	48
Use	✕	✕	✕	✕	GOBOS DS	→ US	WALL MAUVE	WASH BLUE	CYC. RED	TOP BLUE	→ GR.	AMB.
Level	✕	✕	✕	✕								

Micro - Q:

Dim #	1	2	3	4	5	6	7	8	9	10	11	12
Use	F.O.H. D.S.L.	H.R. D.S.C.	R55 D.S.R.	S.L.	C.S.	S.R.	U.S.L.	U.S.C.	U.S.R.	FAR U.S.	H.L. D.S.L.	WARM D.S.C.
Level												

Dim #	13	14	15	16	17	18	19	20	21	22	23	24
Use	F.O.H. D.S.R.	H.L. S.L.	WARM C.S.	S.R.	U.S.L.	U.S.C.	U.S.R.	FAR U.S.	F.O.H. D.S.L.	H.L. D.S.C.	COOL D.S.R.	S.L.
Level												

Dim #	25	26	27	28	29	30*	31*	32*
Use	F.O.H. C.S.	H.L. S.R.	COOL U.S.L.	U.S.C.	U.S.R.	TUNNEL S.L.	PIT S.R.	STEPS
Level								

FIGURE 19–18

The Designer's Cheat Sheet

This production of *Othello* used two dimmer boards: one with 48 dimmers and the second with 32 dimmers. A given lighting picture or preset is written on such a sheet, given to the board operator to transpose to running sheets, and later serves as reference for the designer in correcting levels. Lighting Design by R. Craig Wolf for the Virginia Shakespeare Festival.

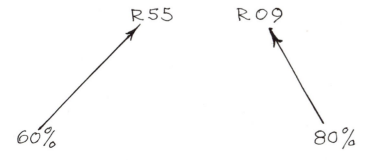

FIGURE 19–19

The Designer's Color Key

This particular color key indicates a stage-right side light source colored with R04 and running at 90 pecent of intensity, a front-of-house left source colored with R55 and running at 60 percent of intensity, and a front-of-house right source colored in R09 and running at 80 percent intensity. Color keys can be a simple method of indicating basic lighting intentions for a given lighting picture or preset.

REALIZING THE PLOT

The final step in lighting a production is, of course, realizing the plot. This process may be as short as two or three days or as long as two weeks and is always the most challenging time for the lighting designer. Let it be said one more time that any preparation completed before move-in will pay off tenfold while in the theatre.

Final Preparations and Put-In

Cues. Writing lighting cues is one of the most simple tasks for the lighting designer, although at first this might not seem to be so. The *rhythm* of a production will tell an observant designer where most of the cues belong. (The designer must be sure to attend several rehearsals and to concentrate on things other than blocking.) It is a good idea to note cue placement in the script during one of the final run-throughs before move-in. Cues can then be numbered and presets written. Cues should be numbered sequentially, with inserted cues having a letter suffix (Light Cue 12A) or decimal (Light Cue 12.1).

The cues and their placement, of course, must be given to the stage manager, who runs the show. This cue-writing session should take place at a sufficiently early date before the technical or first lighting rehearsal and ideally should include both the stage manager and the board operator. Set aside enough time for an uninterrupted discussion of the cues with both people so that they understand why a cue happens. Make sure that both know counts or cue times and, finally, make sure that your stage manager understands that the placement of some cues will most certainly change during the rehearsal process.

Cues should be called as follows:

"Warning Light Cue 12" (approximately 30 seconds before "go")
"Ready Light Cue 12" (approximately 15 seconds before "go")
"Light Cue 12 . . . Go"

The Put-in. The lighting designer should be present during the put-in, if for no other reason than to be available for questions. The lighting put-in should be carefully scheduled with the technical director in order to coordinate lighting and scenery, and step-by-step procedures should also be discussed with the head electrician. The designer should not take a major role in physically hanging the show. This is the crew's job and a designer's energy is best spent elsewhere.

Focus. Lighting focus takes concentration. If at all possible, electricians should have the stage to themselves during focus hours. Be prepared for the focus: be alert, have a dimmer list or cheat sheet with you, and work in a logical order. Front-of-house is often focused first. Learn to focus two electricians at once. Learn to focus with your back to the light, looking at your shadow. Learn to focus fast. And don't forget to give your crew periodic breaks.

Technical and Dress Rehearsals

The first time a show's director sees the product of the lighting designer's work will probably be at the technical or lighting rehearsal. This should *not*, however, be the first time the lighting designer sees his or her work. The ideal situation is to look at presets during the final run-through before the technical rehearsal, explaining to the cast and director that you will be adjusting a few levels and will most probably not be in sequence with the action on stage. This gives the designer a good chance to see the lighting on actors without the added pressure of a technical rehearsal.

The technical and dress period is most crucial to the lighting designer, for this is when the majority of design decisions are made. This is the time when the lighting designer is working the hardest. Accordingly, the designer *must* be fresh and alert—one can't see or think for very long with only four hours of sleep.

Technical rehearsals are infamous for being long and laborious affairs, hated by technicians as well as actors. If proper and thorough preparation has been done and if someone keeps things moving, the rehearsal can be relatively painless. Good judgment must be used in determining when to stop and fix something and when to keep going. Tactless people must be banned from technical rehearsals.

It is a good idea for the stage manager to call this rehearsal from the house rather than an isolated booth somewhere. He or she will be in better contact with the director, the designers, the technical staff, as well as the actors. Always make sure that headsets have been carefully checked out well before the technical rehearsal begins. Nothing is more frustrating (and, unfortunately, more common) than communications problems during a technical rehearsal.

The purpose of a technical rehearsal is to solve technical problems— *not* constantly to adjust light levels, and *certainly not* to write lighting presets. If presets are not complete before the technical rehearsal, the rehearsal should go on without lights. Remain objective, observe time deadlines and, above all, be sure that your operators and stage manager understand and record changes as they are made.

A production will normally have two or three dress rehearsals, with the first primarily devoted to costumes. Level changes have to be made during the dress rehearsal process, but the performance must not be stopped except for an exceptionally serious problem. Second and third dresses must never be stopped. The fewer changes made during dress rehearsals, the better your stage manager and operators will learn the show. Remember that the director's attention is divided among a great number of equally important things during this stage of a production. Never leave after a dress rehearsal without first talking to the director, the stage manager, and your operators.

FIGURE 19–20
The Lighting Laboratory
Shown is the Lighting Laboratory at Carnegie-Mellon University with a makeup area (below) adjacent to the lab.

THE LIGHTING LAB

Preceding chapters have discussed the importance of the lighting laboratory as a teaching tool. More and more institutions that are genuinely committed to training lighting designers are seeking and finding the space and equipment for such laboratory work. The light lab comes in many sizes and forms; most exist in found spaces that have been equipped by students and faculty with a limited budget. The available equipment is often ancient and may be less than useful in an actual production. However, the lab is also the place for experimentation with state-of-the-art instrumentation; many facilities select for purchase one or two new pieces of equipment each year to be used in the lab.

Designing the Lighting

Ideally the light lab will be on a human scale, with a grid somewhere between 12 and 15 feet high. It should have its own control system and circuitry, although neither need be elaborate. The lab shown in Figure 19–20 is a particularly intelligent arrangement, for make-up instruction which often requires stage lighting can take place in one area of the space. Lab exercises vary from reproduction of light in a painting to demonstrations of angle and quality of light.

An excellent example of the use of a large-scale model in the lighting lab is seen in Figure 19–21. Note the various uses of light angle for texture and composition.

LIGHTING FOR THE COMMERCIAL THEATRE

In the not-so-distant past we saw an amazing rebirth throughout the country of professional theatre, too long confined to New York

FIGURE 19–21
Using the Lighting Lab
In lieu of the training advantages of actual production lighting, a well-equipped lighting lab offers a simulated but parallel experience. The student lighting designer can reconstruct lighting angles and position of any stage—proscenium, arena, or thrust—and discover hands-on some of the compositional properties of light. In this exercise the scenic form purposely contains a variety of surfaces. Sweeping curves, sharp corners, openings, and texture lend interest. The photographs show some of the effects.

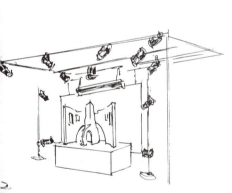

and a few other large centers. Now it is a rare city that does not have its repertory or stock theatre, run by professional producers and directors and employing professional actors and designers.

Nearly all of these regional theatres (often called LORT houses after the type of Equity contract issued the actors) run apprentice programs which seldom pay much but which offer exceptional experience and valuable professional contacts. Theatre Communications Group (T.C.G.) publishes a complete list of theatres and programs which is available by writing to T.C.G. More and more college graduates, and even college students, are working in these theatres, on full- or part-time bases. This section is intended to give such people a picture of lighting practices and limitations of the commercial theatre.

BROADWAY PRACTICES

Broadway, for better or worse, is the ultimate in commercial usages and restrictions. Many of these pertain as well to resident professional theatres in other parts of the country, with considerable and unpredictable variations among localities.

Equipment in a Broadway Theatre

Most people would be surprised to learn that no commercial theatre on what is commonly referred to as Broadway has any lighting equipment of its own beyond the few items here listed: There will be a dimmer for the house lights; there will be a company switch furnishing considerable power, to which a show's dimmers may be connected; there will be current at appropriate locations for the use of follow spots; and, a fairly recent addition, there will be wiring in conduit to the front of the balcony and to the box booms, vertical pipes erected on either side of the auditorium in the upper boxes closest to the stage. Occasionally there will be conduit to a second balcony, if one exists.

This means that everything else must come in with the show: all the instruments and their accessories, the dimmers and plugging boxes, cable sufficient to connect all instruments to the dimmers, booms for offstage instruments, asbestos cloth to protect flying scenery from lights hung above the stage, work lights, all special rigging devices, everything!

The Broadway Lighting Designer

Before being permitted to light a show on Broadway, the designer must become a member of the United Scenic Artists Union (U.S.A.). To be admitted to this organization, the applicant must pass a difficult examination given once a year in either New York or Chicago.

The lighting designer is hired, often at the suggestion of the director or the scene designer, by the producer of the play. Under the rules of United Scenic Artists he or she must receive a minimum fee, although established designers ask for and get a great deal more than this minimum. It is not uncommon for a well-known designer to receive, in addition to a straight fee, a royalty based on a percentage of the gross receipts.

Hiring Equipment and Electricians

Because all expenses related to the play must be approved by the producer or business manager, the light designer must work within the figures that they have in mind. All the equipment is rented, the usual contract calling for a down payment of 10 percent of its price for the first three-week period, a lower charge for the next three weeks, and a reduced rental for the balance of the run of the play. Some producers make a practice of asking for competitive bids from the few companies that are engaged in the rental of lighting equipment for the stage; others always work with the same company. Some accept recommendations of the lighting designer to deal with a certain firm.

These bids are based on an equipment list called a shop order which must be drafted by the lighting designer or assistant well before the production moves into the theatre. For this reason, the Broadway lighting designer must complete the plot several weeks earlier than is required of a designer working primarily with in-house equipment. The shop order must carefully specify every piece of equipment to be rented or purchased (Figure 19–22, page 496). This includes instruments, cable, mounting equipment, connectors, lamps, dimmer boards, color, and even tape and tie line.

Even more important than the equipment costs are the wages paid to the electricians who set up and run the show. In New York these people must be members of Local No. 1 of The International Alliance of Theatrical Stage Employees, commonly called the IA. IA electricians are paid a substantial hourly wage and prudent use of their time is imperative. The fact is that labor costs on Broadway have recently become so high that they are frequently a limiting factor of design artistry.

Some electricians are far better than others, and a good chief electrician can help the designer immeasurably. For this reason a designer well established in New York will probably have in mind someone with whom he or she works well and will recommend that the producer hire this person. But the beginner must ask around to locate the best person available.

The chief electrician estimates how many people will be required to run the show, based on the number of instruments and type of control used and the number and complexity of the cues. If the show has electrical sound effects, the sound person is also under the jurisdiction of the chief electrician.

CYRANO | Equipment List

A Richard Gregson - Apjac Production

Lighting - Gilbert V. Hemsley, Jr. 608-836-1197

Electrician - Joe Monaco 914-949-6587

Company Manager - Victor Samrock 212-751-1290

Load out to Toronto Feb. 15 or 16, 1973

Load in to Toronto Feb. 18, followed by a possible stand at the Colonial in Boston, and the Palace in New York.

Balcony Rail (This will be split between 2 Balconys in Toronto)

24 750w 8 x 12 Lekos CC and CF

16 750w 8 x 12 Lekos T and S, CC and CF

12 750w 8 x 16 Lekos CC and CF

6 500w 6 x 6 (Step Lens Wide Angle) CC and CF

4 L.S. Units (Will come from Minn.)

20 Twofers

2 Threefers

Rehearsal Worklites

Cables and Jumpers (CK with Royal Alex, Colonial, and Palace)

Box Boom Left

24 750w 6 x 12 Lekos (Would prefer 6 x 16"s) CF

Palace 12 Long Side Arms 2 T Joints Each (Same for Colonial ??)

Royal Alex Possible C Clamps Ck with House

12 Twofers

Cables and Jumpers, ck with house

FIGURE 19–22

The Shop Order

The first page of the equipment list for the Broadway production of *Cyrano de Bergerac,* prepared by Gilbert Hemsley, Jr., the lighting designer. Abbreviations used: "CC" = C-clamp, "CF" = color frame, "T" = template (or gobo), and "S" = shutters.

PLANNING THE LIGHTING

After reading and rereading the script, the lighting designer consults the playwright, the director, the scene and costume designers, and others. Sometimes a producer will hold meetings at which the lighting designer can exchange views with these co-workers, but on other occasions they must be sought out. The designer must study the color renderings of the scenic designer and visit the shop where the scenery is being built to note the painting. He or she will wish to see samples of fabrics to be used in the costumes, and will consider the make-up to be worn by the actors. Most important, the designer will discuss with the director the visual effects desired for each scene of the play and the nature of all changes and cues that affect the lighting. At all times the designer must remember that he or she is part of a team, each member of which is striving to make the production a success, and all of whom have opinions that merit respect and consideration.

Of course, right from the start the designer has attended rehearsals to see how the director is interpreting the script and the style of the final presentation. And toward the end of the rehearsal period the designer will want to have learned the movements and positions of the actors, the timing of the cues, and any variations in approach that the director is taking.

The lighting designer will visit the New York theatre in which the play is to open and inspect it as to mounting positions and their distances from the stage, any possible difficulties in placing instruments exactly where desired, and all physical aspects that could affect the lighting of the play.

As mentioned earlier, the shop order is due well before move-in (at least one week and, more normally, two or three), therefore the plot may have to be completed before the designer has had a chance to attend to everything mentioned above. Nonetheless, late rehearsals must be attended—for cueing if nothing else.

It is accepted practice in New York to draw one's plot in ½-inch scale (Figure 19–23). This probably means that the scaled distance from front-of-house positions to the stage will be inaccurate.

Pre-Move-in. One week before the rented lighting equipment is to move out of the contractor's shop, the chief electrician and first assistant must carefully inspect and test everything ordered, rejecting all items that are not in satisfactory condition. They must also frame the color media, label the bundles of cable, prepare any special effects, and otherwise organize matters as far as possible.

The lighting designer also visits the shop and checks over the colors to be sure there will be no surprises when in the theatre. The designer will also check with the electrician to make sure that wall brackets and chandeliers are properly wired, and with the scene shop to be certain that the scenery on which lighting fixtures are to hang has been adequately braced. Electrification of turntables and other electrical devices should be checked. Lens systems for projections must be correct. Nothing is left to chance; whatever is delivered to the theatre must be exactly what is required.

Several days before move-in, the designer's time will be devoted to writing preset levels and giving cue placement to the stage manager.

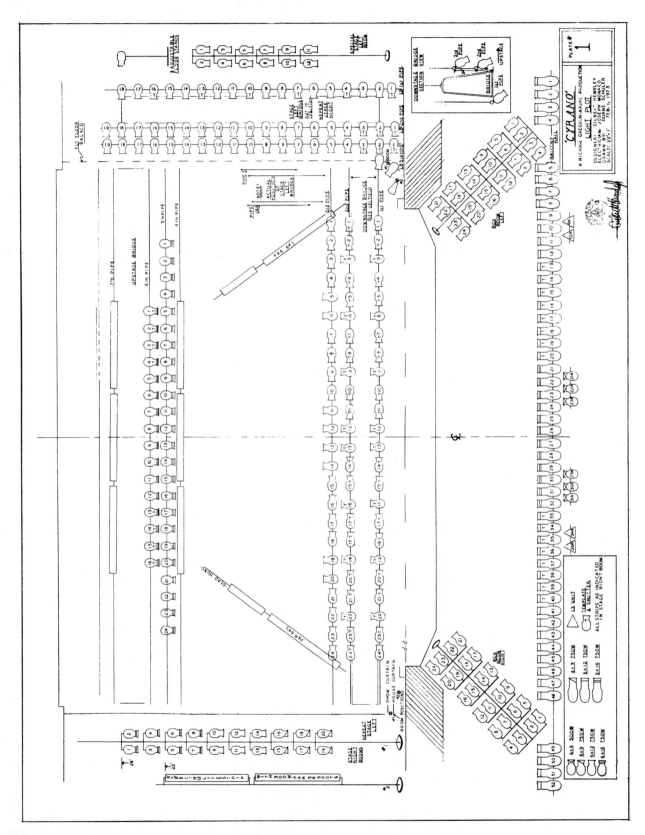

FIGURE 19–23

Professional Lighting Layout

Page 498: A lighting layout for the Broadway production of *Cyrano de Bergerac* by Gilbert Hemsley, Jr. Unlike most layouts, there is no floor plan of the setting. Because there are several arrangements of scenery it is difficult to show a composite of floor plans without causing confusion. In such cases the lighting designer frequently prepares a layout on transparent paper or plastic which is then placed over each floor plan in turn. In any event the layout is not a representational diagram but is a schematic working drawing for the lighting designer and crew.

CYRANO
BOARD #1

SWITCH	POSITION	TYPE	FOCUS	COLOR
1	Box Boom L 9·10·11·12	4·750w 6×12	L AREA 1	½ C.B.
2	Box Boom R 1·2·3·4	4·750w 6×12	R AREA 1	½ C.B.
3	Box Boom L 5·6·7·8	4·750w 6×12	L AREA 2	½ C.B.
4	Box Boom R 5·6·7·8	4·750w 6×12	R AREA 2	½ C.B
5	Box Boom L 1·2·3·4	4·750w 6×12	L AREA 3	½ C.B
6	Box Boom R 9·10·11·12	4·750w 6×12	R AREA 3	½ C.B.
7	#1 Boom L 16-18 #1 Boom R 4-6	2·750w 6×9 2·750w 6×16	AREA 1	½ C.B.
8	#1 Boom L 10-12 #1 Boom R 10-12	2·750w 6×12 2·750w 6×12	AREA 2	½ C.B
9	#1 Boom L 4-6 #1 Boom R 16-18	2·750w 6×16 2·750w 6×9	AREA 3	½ C.B.
10	#1 Boom L 15-17 #1 Boom R 3-5	2·750w 6×9 2·750w 6×16	AREA 4	½ C.B.
11	#1 Boom L 9-11 #1 Boom R 9-11	2·750w 6×12 2·750w 6×12	AREA 5	½ C.B.
12	#1 Boom L 3-5 #1 Boom R 15-17	2·750w 6×16 2·750w 6×9	AREA 6	½ C.B.
13 M 131 132 133 134	BAL. RAIL 21 22 31 32	4·750w 8×16	SPECIALS	½ C.B.
14	BAL. RAIL 21A 22A 23A 29A 30A 31A	6·500w 6×6	FRONT CURTAIN WASH	911

1 OF 20

FIGURE 19–24

General Hook-up

A portion of the hook-up for the Broadway production of *Cyrano de Bergerac*. This organizes the nearly three hundred instruments of the layout into a scheme of control by designating the hook-up of each instrument to a dimmer in one of the system's six switchboards, ten auxiliary preset boards, or five auto transformer boards used for group mastering. The schedule also indicates the hanging position and type of instrument, its focus and color.

Stage Lighting Practice

Setting up the Lighting

Move-in and Set-up. On move-in day all the rented equipment is delivered to the theatre. Because there is a vast amount of work to be done, and done fast, the chief electrician will have called for such additional hands as needed to get the instruments mounted and cabled. Under the electrician's direction, and following the designer's layout, this work proceeds while at the same time the scenery is being erected on the stage. Usually, to avoid conflict with the carpenters, the front-of-house lights are the first to be put in place, with the onstage equipment following. Great cooperation is necessary at this time between the two departments; it is at this stage that a competent electrician can prove of great value to a production.

Focusing and Setting Cues. By the time the lights are in reasonably good shape—hung and connected to the dimmers—the light designer, who has been observing the work and double-checking the position of the instruments, takes over. It is normal to start with the front-of-house spotlights, sometimes while the upstage equipment is still being hung. The light designer will not have the exclusive use of the stage, but must carry on the work of focusing despite all manner of confusion, possibly even before all the scenery is in place.

If a regular technical run-through is scheduled, the designer may rough in the dimmer readings and cues. But all too often these delicate operations must be done under the most frustrating conditions, sometimes even with the houselights and stage work lights ablaze! And it is important that all be finished quickly, so that the regular crew will not run into overtime and the extra hands hired for the set-up may be let go. The job must be done right the first time, for if it becomes necessary to send someone up a tall ladder at a later time, a ladder crew of four people must be hired for the minimum of half a day just to adjust one poorly placed instrument.

During rehearsals the lighting people continue their work, adjusting dimmer readings, sharpening cues, and taking copious notes for refocusing, rehanging, matting, masking, changing color media, and the like. The designer frequently has an assistant to help with the paperwork and to keep in touch with the stage manager, and perhaps with any follow-spot operators, by means of a telephone or a headset system.

In this manner adjustments are made right up to the moment when the curtain rises before an audience, and once the play has started the designer will continue to make notes during this and subsequent previews. All changes are passed on to the chief electrician and stage manager, the people who henceforth are in charge of running the show.

It must be emphasized that the lighting designer never goes back-

Designing the Lighting

stage during either rehearsal or performance, regardless of any temptation to do so. Instead notes are delivered after the final curtain.

According to union regulations, under no condition whatever may the light designer or an assistant handle any lighting equipment, but must request one of the electricians to do so. This applies to even such innocent actions as handing a wrench to its owner, or steadying a ladder on which an electrician is working.

After the Opening. It has long been a custom to open Broadway shows out of town, usually with a short run in one of the cities along the Atlantic seaboard such as New Haven, Boston, Philadelphia, Washington, and then to move it on to another city, polishing the play as it goes, before the official opening on Broadway. When these tryout runs are scheduled, the first of such openings pretty much follows the procedures that have been described above. Occasionally the lighting designer will stay with the show through all its wanderings to New York. More often he or she will leave it at its first stop, possibly dropping in later in another city, or, most likely, not seeing it again until New York. Meanwhile the chief electrician and the stage manager are responsible for the lighting.

Recently it has become popular not to venture a play out of New York at all, but to run only a series of preview performances in the theatre in which it is scheduled to open. The audience at such previews understands that the play is not yet in its final form but is undergoing continual revisions. Such revisions include the lighting, of course, thus giving the designer ample time to experiment and make changes, bringing concepts to perfection at comparative leisure.

But no matter how the play opens, it is advisable for the designer to drop in every once in a while during its run. Often things will start to slip a little from what had originally been set.

Going on the Road

If, after its Broadway run, a show takes to the road—or a national company is formed to troup about the country—it is necessary for the designer to work out a simplified plot. The road production will almost always carry less equipment. If the show is to play in schools, municipal auditoriums, or other than conventional theatres a simplified light plot is all the more essential.

Various techniques have been developed to make setting up and focusing as easy as possible. For one example, the original production may have used a great battery of beam projectors for back lighting the actors. For the road, large striplights burning high-wattage PAR lamps may be substituted; such units can be hung and focused in a fraction of the time.

Today when a show goes on the road its scenery, properties, costumes, and lighting equipment are always moved by truck. The lighting instruments frequently are left right on their pipes, and the whole unit is placed aboard the vehicle, where it is hung safely and securely until the next city is reached. More and more, instead of pipes, so-called tracks are used, to which instruments are hung and in which their cabling is enclosed. The use of either pipe or track permits many shortcuts in the remounting of instruments in the next theatre.

REGIONAL THEATRES

Many of the professional practices which apply to lighting design on Broadway are also standard for the country's regional theatres. However, accepted practice in the regional theatres will vary a great deal from theatre to theatre. Production schemes, from repertory to stock, will influence how a lighting designer approaches his or her work. Local union rules and regulations will differ; in-house equipment will probably exist, but will be radically different from house to house; and technical production practices will be unique to each situation.

Designing for Repertory

Traditional repertory production generally requires a daily change-over from show to show and may involve as few as two or as many as eight individual productions. The lighting designer will develop a repertory plot which acts as a basis for all shows and then add special instrumentation for each individual production. Repatching and some-times color changes may take place during changeovers, but extensive refocusing should be avoided in repertory situations. As might be expected, a repertory design will require much more equipment than normal, and often an individual show's demands must be compromised for the sake of the entire production scheme. The repertory experience is an extremely valuable one in the developmental process of any young lighting designer.

Designing for Stock

The vast majority of regional theatres will produce their shows in a stock arrangement, running each production continuously for a period of two to six weeks. (Summer stock productions may run only one week.) Such a scheme requires rapid changeovers from show to show and normally a new lighting design for each production. The stock designer must be able to work quickly and efficiently, remaining one step ahead of the production schedule at all times.

Those theatres which run a production for more than three weeks will most often job-in their lighting designers for each production, while those operations with shorter runs may very well employ a resident lighting designer. Either way, the lighting designer is always under a great deal of time pressure. Like repertory production, the stock experience is invaluable for the young lighting designer.

Regional Production

Some regional theatres will hire only designers who are United Scenic Artist members, while others pay no attention to requirements of union membership. There currently exist only two U.S.A. "locals": 829, the New York local with jurisdiction over Broadway and the East Coast; and 350, located in Chicago and having jurisdiction in the Midwest. Designing on the West Coast is through a reciprocal agreement with the IA.

Most cities have their own IA local. Rules and regulations will vary radically from local to local as will quality of workmanship. This fact is of particular concern to the regional designer, for he or she can only be sure of the quality of any local membership by previous experience or word-of-mouth. It is wise to carefully evaluate the potential work force in addition to local rule idiosyncrasies well before a production is mounted.

Stage-lighting rental houses have grown in numbers along with the spread of regional theatres across the country. Some of these local businesses will be surprisingly efficient and well-stocked, while others are woefully ill-equipped and lacking in knowledgeable personnel. The designer must anticipate the possibility of having to go to New York or some other major center for equipment needs, a situation which will surely affect budget and time considerations.

More important than commercial usage is the quite different matter of professional standards. No one should consider for a moment going into any level of commercial theatre unless he or she plans to devote total energy and ability to the routines and the problems that present themselves. It is no place for the casual enthusiast or the dilettante, nor for the easily discouraged, the supersensitive, or the noncooperative.

20

Lighting for the Proscenium Theatre

This and the following chapter will investigate lighting layouts for different types of production in a variety of spaces. Certainly the proscenium remains the most common type of performance space today. The designer will surely encounter a great variety of production styles within this space. We will consider four typical but quite different sorts of presentation: a realistic interior, a realistic exterior, a wing-and-border setting, and unit or simultaneous approaches.

The following examples have been greatly simplified for clarity and ease of presentation. The lighting layouts are deliberately designed to show the minimum number of instruments necessary to achieve acceptable lighting in each case.

Let us assume that the theatre we are using is of medium size. The stage will have a 30-foot proscenium opening. There will be ample provisions for hanging scenery and instruments above the stage. About 20 feet from the proscenium line will be a beam for mounting front spotlights.

THE REALISTIC INTERIOR

A realistic interior usually calls for some variation of the conventional box setting, either with or without a ceiling piece. As one might expect, the existence of a ceiling will have a great effect on lighting possibilities. The primary interest is within the walls of this set, while the backgrounds seen through windows and doors are of less importance. The lighting is often motivated by apparent sources; in practically all cases it is realistically plausible.

Figure 20–2 shows such a setting. On the stage-left wall is a door leading to some other room or passage. In the up-left corner a flight of stairs comes down into the room from off left. In the center of the upstage wall is an archway opening into a corridor with an entrance at the stage-left end.

FIGURE 20–1

Lighting Positions in the Proscenium Theatre

(1) Ceiling beams. (2) Box booms or house-slot position. (3) Balcony front. (4) Apron or footlight. (5) Teaser. (6) Tormentor boom. (7) Midstage backlight position. (8) Wing ladder. (9) Backdrop or cyclorama lights. (10) Cyclorama base or horizon lights. (11) Translucent drop backlight. (12) Follow spot.

FIGURE 20–2

Sketch of a Realistic Interior Setting

505

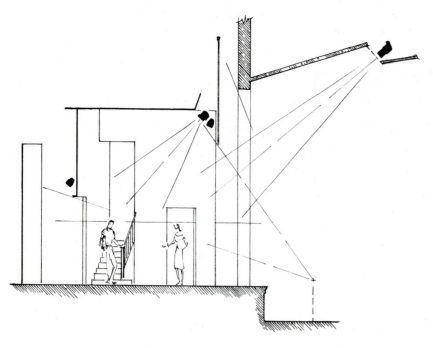

FIGURE 20–3
The Realistic Interior
This and the following lighting layouts are simplified to demonstrate the basic instrumentation for some typical proscenium-type productions. They are illustrations and should not be considered professional lighting layouts. For professional planning techniques see Chapter 19. A lighting layout, instrument schedule, and center-line sectional view are included.

NO.	INSTRUMENT	LOCATION	PURPOSE	LAMP	COLOR	REMARKS
1	6" ELLIPS'L-REF'R SPOTLIGHT	BEAM – L	AREA 2 L	750 T12	848	
2	" " " "	" "	" 1 L	"	848	FRAME OFF RETURN
3	" " " "	" "	" 3 L	"	848	
4	" " " "	BEAM – R	" 1 R	"	803	
5	" " " "	" "	" 3 R	"	803	FRAME OFF RETURN
6	" " " "	" "	" 2 R	"	803	
7	6" FRESNEL-LENS SPOTLIGHT	1ST PIPE – L	AREA 4 L	500 T20	848	MAT TOP
8	" " "	" – C	" 5 L	"	848	" "
9	6" ELLIPS'L-REF'R SPOTLIGHT	1ST PIPE – C	STAIR SPECIAL	750 T12	803	FRAME TO STAIR
10	" " " "	" "	ARCH SPECIAL	"	803	FRAME TO ARCH
11	6" FRESNEL-LENS SPOTLIGHT	1ST PIPE – R	AREA 5 R	500 T20	803	MAT TOP
12	" " " "	" "	" 4 R	"	803	" "
13	6" ELLIPS'L-REF'R SPOTLIGHT	STAND – L	STAIR BACKLIGHT	750 T12	810	
14	10" FLOOD LIGHT	SCENERY – L	DOOR BACKING	250 G30	810	HIGH ON SCENERY
15	" " "	FIRE PLACE	FIRE GLOW	100 A21	818	GANG WITH #24
16	16" BEAM PROJECTOR	R- STAGE WALL	SUNLIGHT	1000 G40	–	HIGH AS POSSIBLE
17	6" x 6'-0" STRIPLIGHT	1ST PIPE	X – RAYS	150 R40	RED	
18	" "			COLORED	BL. WHITE AMBER	
19	6" x 4'-6" "	FLOOR – R	SKY BACKING	"	RED, BLUE, AMBER	
20	6" x 6'-0" "	BEHIND ARCH	HALL	"	RED, BLUE WHITE, AMBER	
21	SPECIAL	FIREPLACE	FIRE EFFECT	2- 60A21	VARIED	GANG WITH #15
22	DESK LAMP	UL CORNER	LAMP	150 A23	–	SHIELD TOP & SIDE
23	WALL SCONCE	L OF ARCH	WALL FIXTURE	15 FC/V		GANG - CANDELABRA
24	" "	R OF ARCH	" "	"	–	SOCKET ADAPTERS

Designing the Lighting

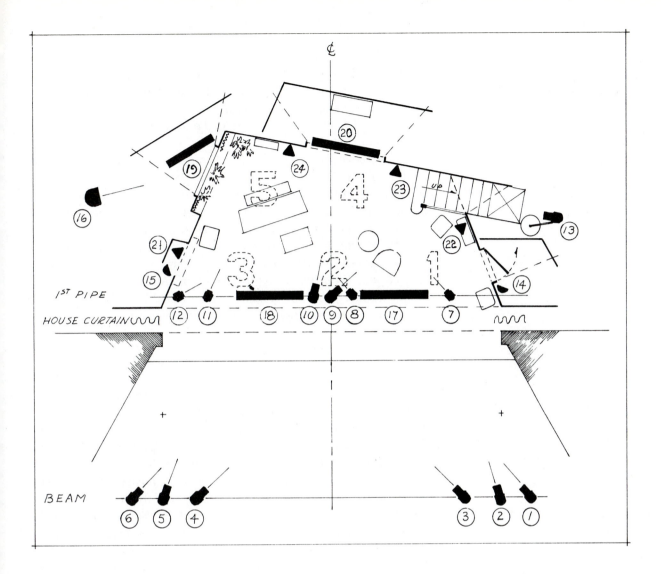

The stage-right wall contains a window and a fireplace. Through the window is seen a backing with painted sky and a scene of distant hills. This set has a ceiling piece which covers from the up-stage wall nearly to the first pipe position.

Two scenes are involved. In Act I bright sunlight streams in through the window. In Act II it is dark night outside and a fire is burning on the hearth.

Downstage Areas

In dividing the stage into acting areas, we find that the conventional three will be needed across the downstage zone, but only two will be required upstage. To cover areas 1, 2, 3, we mount 30° or 6 × 12 ellipsoidal reflector spotlights in our front beam position. We select the ERS over the Fresnel because the latter, though quite powerful, has such side spill that we would have light all over the proscenium wall. For a longer throw than the one we have assumed for this theatre, we would naturally use the 20°, 6-by-16 or 8-inch ERS with their narrower and more powerful beams. For a shorter throw we could use one of several instruments: the 40° ERS, a 6-by-9 ERS, or one of the variety of smaller instruments such as the Mini-Ellipse.

In choosing the mounting positions for these instruments we attempt to achieve the ideal 45-degree angle, but note that we must mount the Area 1L instrument (number 2) somewhat in from the end of the beam in order to reach the extreme downstage-left corner of the stage without being cut off by the proscenium. In like manner, the Area 3R instrument must come somewhat nearer the center.

Therefore, we have sacrificed to some extent the ideal angle, but this is a necessary compromise. The remaining four instruments can be placed just about where we prefer them. All six instruments are carefully framed so as not to spill distracting light on the face of the stage apron, on the overhead teaser, and, in the case of numbers two and five, on the proscenium.

Upstage Areas

To cover the upstage areas we will use 6-inch Fresnels mounted on the first pipe. Fresnels are picked for this location because the soft edge of their beams makes blending between the areas much easier, and no sharp, distracting beam patterns will appear on the walls of the set. Numbers 7, 8, and 12 can be focused at close to the 45-degree angle for their respective areas, but number 11, focused on Area 5R, must move in a little in order to keep spill light off the stage-right wall.

All five areas must be consistent in regard to colors. Because in both acts warm light (sunbeams and fireglow) seems to come from the right of the stage, we can use a warm filter in instruments 4, 5, 6, 11, and 12. The opposite side of the room would need a relatively cool color for contrast in instruments 1, 2, 3, 7, and 8. Roscolene No. 803 (Pale Gold) and No. 848 (Water Blue) make an excellent combination for such a situation without appearing too strong in either shade.

The Stairway

Of course, the stairway must not be overlooked. But rather than consider it another area, it is preferable to handle it as a special problem because of its different levels. To light it properly, yet avoid spilling, we use an ellipsoidal reflector spotlight in soft focus from the first pipe, framing its beam to the stairs themselves and only high enough to cover the actor moving up and down. This would be instrument 9 (a 6-by-9), and because its beam is substantially at the same angle as the other stage-right instruments, its color should agree with these: a No. 803. To light the stairway from the other side, and particularly to

Designing the Lighting

FIGURE 20–4
Lighting Instrument with Side-arm Mounted on a Boom

catch the face of an ascending actor another ellipsoidal spotlight (13) can be mounted on a boom (or from an overhead line) at the head of the stairs, about 8 feet offstage. The beam from this instrument may be presumed to come from a hall light at the head of the stairs, and a No. 810 (No Color Amber) filter could be used here for realism.

Booms. A brief word about floor stands or booms is necessary at this point. A boom normally consists of a heavy metal base into which screws a length of 1¼- or 1½-inch black pipe. Any length of pipe may be used, but booms of any great height must be tied off above for safety. A lighting instrument is then hung off the boom by using a cross-pipe or "side-arm" (Figure 20–4).

The boom can be represented on a light plot in one of two manners:

1   Drawing the pipe at scaled length and at an angle of 45 to 60 degrees directly out of its base. The various instruments are then shown in relationship to their boom pipe (Figure 20–5a). This is similar to an isometric view.
2   Showing the boom base and pipe in plan view, but without instrument specifications, with an additional elevation of the boom placed on the side of the drafting plate. The elevation will specify instrumentation (Figure 20–5b).

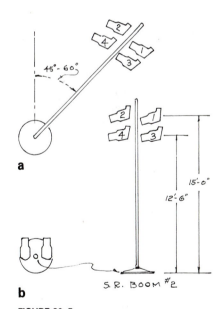

FIGURE 20–5
Representing a Boom on the Light Plot
(a) The isometric method shows the boom base in its actual position on stage. (b) The plan and elevation method is often desirable when space on the plan is tight.

Lighting for the Proscenium Theatre

509

The Archway

The acting area immediately beyond the archway is of utmost importance. Here the most vital entrances are made, and the actor must be well lighted as he or she prepares to come into the room. In fact, the director may even play brief but important scenes in just this location. To cover this area, instrument 10 (another 6-by-9) may be mounted in the center of the first pipe and framed to the opening of the archway.

Floodlights

Having listed the spotlights, we should next see what floodlights are desired. Two of the small, 10-inch variety are useful. Instrument 14 is placed behind the downstage-left door to throw illumination on the backing so this will not appear as a dark hole whenever the door is opened. This flood is placed at least 10 feet high on the scenery to throw its light downward as from a ceiling or wall bracket. A 250-watt G-30 lamp will give ample illumination, and a No. 810 filter will provide a color that resembles the warm light usually associated with such household fixtures. However, the choice of color will depend somewhat on the painted color of the masking flat behind the door.

Instrument 15 has a very different use: it is placed in the fireplace to throw a warm glow over all who approach it. It should not be too brilliant (and hence distracting), so a 100-watt A-21 is all that is necessary, with a No. 818 filter (orange), a more realistic color for fireglow than the traditional red.

Sunbeams

A large spotlight might be used for the strong beams of sunlight entering the window, but a beam projector is better because of the powerful punch of its parallel rays. No. 16 should be mounted well offstage, if possible even farther than our layout indicates. A producing group with ample equipment would use two or more instruments for this purpose. The height above the floor would depend on the hour of day as expressed by the script; a great height for near midday, a low, flat, angle for dawn or late afternoon. The color used would also depend on the time. Sunlight is often thought of as having a strong amber hue, but actually this is the case only in the late afternoon. For such a scene a No. 815 (Golden Amber) could be used. But noonday sun is much closer to white, and for such an effect it is probably wise to use no color medium at all.

X-rays

Borderlights have also been hung: two 6-foot strips on the first pipe, spaced slightly apart to allow certain spotlights to be mounted between them. A little more punch is needed for these "x-rays," so we have used 150-watt R-40 lamps in instruments 17 and 18, with the circuits being designated as red, blue-white, and amber. Considering that these lights are to blend and tone an interior, we need not bother with greens or very strong blues; the cheerful warmth of the amber will be useful in both our sunlit and firelit scenes.

Backing Strips

Instrument 19 is a 4½-foot striplight placed on the floor before the sky backing and focused on it. Considerable variation in color is desired here, so the 150-watt R-40 lamps would be in red, blue, and amber. The amber and blue mix will make a light blue daylight sky, while a rich night sky can be obtained by adding a small amount of red to the blue. If people in the rear of the auditorium can see this striplight through the low window, or if there are balcony spectators who would surely see it, the better technique would be to hang the instrument overhead and focus it down on the backing.

A 6-foot strip, instrument 20, is hung behind the header over the archway to light the passage and its back wall. Again the 150-watt Rs can be used, but these may well be amber, blue-white, and red lamps as a more useful combination for this interior corridor.

Note that different length strips are employed for these two backings because the area that can be seen by the audience varies: about 9 feet in one case, and 15 in the other. Such an analysis is always essential and is plotted carefully on the layout from the worst seat on each side of the auditorium (indicated by + on the plan) through the extreme limits of the openings to the backgrounds. For illustration purposes these sight lines are shown as dashed lines in the plan shown in Figure 20–3.

Specials

With the regular instruments cared for, we can turn to the specials. Instrument 21 is a fire effect: two 60-watt lamps hidden behind two or three logs. Their light will be seen through pieces of colored glass, or crumpled gel, to give the effect of glowing coals. Although this will be seen by only a small segment of the audience, it is a worthwhile device to give the fireplace a touch of realism and warmth.

In the corner between the wall and the stairs is another special, instrument 22, a conventional desk lamp with cord running offstage to connect with the regular stage cable. Because its shade has been made more dense by use of a brown-paper lining, a 150-watt lamp may be used to throw a strong downward light.

Finally, on the upstage wall are two sconces or wall brackets, instruments 23 and 24, one on either side of the arch. These have unshaded lamps, therefore ones of small wattage must be used to prevent glare uncomfortable to an audience. The 15FC/V lamp, a flame-shaped decorative style, is employed. Because these have candelabra-sized bases, adapters must be placed in the regular sockets of the sconces, unless these are already of the proper small size.

Control

Modest as our hypothetical layout is, it would still require no fewer than twenty dimmers to control the lights properly. There are twenty-four listed instruments, but the two sconces can be ganged, as can the fire glow and fire effect. On the other hand, the striplights each have three color circuits, each demanding its own control. The largest loads would be 1200 watts for each circuit of the borderlights.

If the control board could not furnish the necessary circuits, some ganging would have to be done. Great ingenuity is often displayed in doing this, but a truly artistic use of lights and color values could not be maintained with many less than twenty dimmers.

Losing the Ceiling

Figure 20–6 illustrates a lighting layout for the realistic interior with-

No	INSTRUMENT	LOCATION	PURPOSE	LAMP	COLOR	REMARKS
1	8" ELLIPS'L SPOTLIGHT	CEILING-L	AREA 2L	750 T12	R02	
2	8" " "	"	" 7L	" "	R02	
3	8" " "	"	" 3L	" "	R02	
4	8" " "	"	" 4L	" "	R02	
5	8" " "	"	SPECIAL	" "	R02	SOFA
6	8" " "	CEILING-R	AREA 1R	" "	R60	
7	8" " "	"	SPECIAL	" "	R60	SOFA
8	8" " "	"	AREA 2R	" "	R60	
9	8" " "	"	" 4R	" "	R60	
10	8" " "	"	" 3R	" "	R60	
11	6" ELLIPS'L SPOTLIGHT	1ST PIPE	AREA 9L	500 T12	R02	
12	6" FRESNEL SPOTLIGHT	"	" 5L	500 T20	R02	
13	6" " "	"	" 6L	" "	R02	
14	6" ELLIPS'L SPOTLIGHT	"	SPECIAL	500 T12	02	STAIR & LANDING
15	6" FRESNEL SPOTLIGHT	"	AREA 9L	500·T20	R02	
16	6" " "	"	" 7L	" "	R02	
17	6" " "	"	" 5R	" "	R60	
18	6" ELLIPS'L SPOTLIGHT	"	SPECIAL	500 T12	R02	UPPER LANDING
19	6" FRESNEL SPOTLIGHT	"	"	" "	R02	WINDOW SEAT
20	3½" ELLIPS'L SPOTLIGHT	"	"	300W TH-L	R60	FRAME ON TROPHY
21	6" FRESNEL SPOTLIGHT	"	AREA 6R	500 T20	R60	
22	6" ELLIPS'L SPOTLIGHT	"	SPECIAL	500 T12	R02	AREA 9-FRAME TO ARCH
23	6" FRESNEL SPOTLIGHT	"	"	500 T20	R02	WINDOW SEAT
24	6" " "	"	AREA 7R	" "	R60	
25	6" " "	"	" 9R	" "	R60	
26	8" FRESNEL SPOTLIGHT	2ND PIPE	7L BACK LT.	1000 G40	R09	MAT OFF SCENERY TOP
27	6" " "	"	STAIR-LEFT	500 T20	R02	" " " "
28	8" " "	"	2L BACK LT.	1000 G40	R02	
29	8" " "	"	1R " "	1000 G40	CLEAR	
30	6" " "	"	AREA 8L	500 T20	R02	
31	8" " "	"	3L BACK LT.	1000 G40	R09	
32	6" " "	"	STAIR RIGHT	500 T20	R60	
33	6" " "	"	AREA 8R	" "	R60	
34	8" " "	"	2R BACK LT.	1000 G40	CLEAR	
35	8" " "	"	4L " "	" "	R09	
36	3½" ELLIPS'L SPOTLIGHT	"	SPECIAL	300W TH-L	CLEAR	FRAME ON TROPHY
37	8" FRESNEL SPOTLIGHT	"	3R BACK LT.	1000 G40	CLEAR	
38	8" " "	"	4R "	1000 G40	CLEAR	
39	6" " "	14' BOOM #1	KITCHEN LT.	500 T20	"	
40	6" " "	16' " #2	HALL+UPPER	" "	R02	
41	6" " "	"	LANDING	" "	R02	
42	8" " "	SPOTLINE PIPE #2	STREET LTS.	1000 G40	R62	
43	8" " "	"	" "	" "	R62	
44	8" " "	"	" "	" "	R62	
45	SPECIAL	SPOTLINE PIPE #1	PORCH LIGHT	100 W	CLEAR	
46	"	"	" "	"	"	B.S. FIXTURE IN VIEW
47	14" ELLIPS'L R. FLOOD	"	WINDOW WASH	500 PS	R02	
48	9" " " "	HALL	WALL WASH	250 G30	R02	
49	SPECIAL	HALL	CEILING FIXTURE	3/40W	CLEAR	
50	"	S.R. WALL	WALL FIXTURE	2/40W	"	
51	"	STAIR	" "	2/40W	"	

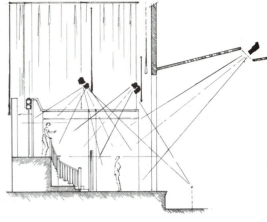

FIGURE 20–6

The Realistic Interior Without Ceiling

Present-day staging frequently omits the ceiling of an interior setting to facilitate the lighting. Shown are the instrument schedule, the sketch of the setting and a layout of lighting instruments, and a section.

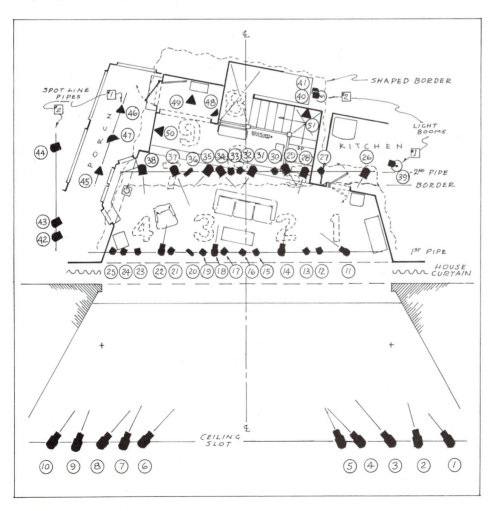

out a ceiling. Although losing the ceiling allows the designer a great deal more flexibility and variety, it may force trim heights up a good deal, depending upon masking. Additional high side lighting from stage right would be possible to support the bay windows. The color indicated is Roscolux.

REALISTIC EXTERIORS

The realistic exterior setting is one of the most difficult to light effectively because of the many maskings needed to prevent the audience from seeing into the wings or up into the hanging space. These maskings—flat surfaces painted to resemble natural objects—are never very convincing and tend to catch stray, unwanted beams of light.

An exterior setting almost always includes a large sky area or a painted scene in the background that needs special attention. Apparent motivation is necessary for all the lighting.

An Exterior Setting

Figure 20–7 (pages 516 and 517) shows a typical exterior setting including many of the features frequently encountered. On stage left three sets of woodwings, painted as tree clusters, serve to mask the wings on that side of the stage. On the right there is a cottage which masks that side. In connection with the downstage woodwings, leaf borders cross the stage to mask overhead. Across the back of the playing areas is a ground row, 3 feet high in its lowest portion and representing hills in the middle distance.

The backdrop consists of a translucency, the lower portion of which is painted with opaque media to represent rolling hills and woods; above this the translucency is painted with dye colors to permit the light to pass through from the rear for greater luminosity and depth.

There are two scenes involved. In the first scene brilliant sunshine pours in from stage left. In the second, moonlight floods the set from the same direction.

Area Spots

The front lights are placed substantially as they were for the realistic interior, but because the sunlight and moonlight make two different effects necessary, the stage-left instruments are double hung; that is, there are two instruments focused on each area from this side. One set works in the first scene, the other set in the second. Or they might be used together at different intensities.

The three upstage areas are handled the same way, but because the first leaf border will hang so low, the usual first pipe location cannot be used. Instead this pipe is moved behind the leaf border. Great care must still be taken to prevent stray beams from touching corners of the second cloth border. Although Fresnels are indicated, a 6-inch ERS would be a possible substitute from the first pipe in order to keep light off the border. Careful use of the section will help to determine exact instrument placement and trim height.

Double-Hung Spotlights

The stage-left instruments that will work when the sun is shining are called the left-warms and they have No. 808 (Medium Straw) filters to give the effect of warmth on that side of the stage. Opposite them, in the stage-right spotlights, we use No. 842 (Special Lavender), a medium gel that will appear quite cool opposite the warm No. 808. But in Scene Two the left instruments contain No. 856 (Light Blue) which is so very cool that the lavender actually seems warm in contrast. This use of a neutral filter on one side of the stage to work alternately against a warm and a cool on the other is a device that is often of extreme value when instruments or control circuits are not too abundant.

Instead of lavender, many people would use no color at all. While it is true that the so-called white light from an ungelled spotlight is actually a trifle on the warm side of the spectrum, if used opposite a definitely warm color, such as amber, it will appear quite cool. Of course, opposite a cool color, it will seem even warmer than before.

Because the space just beyond the fence would be frequently used, especially for entrances, we are considering it a seventh area, with instruments (numbers 19, 20, and 21) mounted behind the second border. To make sure that an actor leaving or entering at stage right is completely covered, we place an additional spotlight (22) off right. The sunlight and moonlight coming in from stage left (as explained below) will take care of that side of the stage.

Sunlight and Moonlight

For a completely realistic effect, a great many powerful instruments would probably be needed for the sunlight and moonlight. But to keep our example within proper bounds, we will use only four for each. Because the moonlight need not be as bright, we have used 8-inch Fresnels, which give a much smoother and broader beam. Numbers 23 and 24 would be placed behind the first woodwing with their focuses overlapping across the stage. The remaining Fresnels, 25 and 26, would be mounted one each behind the other two wings. No 853 (Middle Blue) would give quite a realistic appearance as moonbeams.

The powerful beam projectors with 1500-watt lamps will be necessary for sunlight, to cut through the general light on the stage. These have been mounted in the same manner as the Fresnels and a No. 805 (Light Straw) used with them to give them a bit more warmth than the natural light from these instruments. This light will still appear whiter than the stage-left area lights with their No. 808.

No.	INSTRUMENT	LOCATION	PURPOSE	LAMP	COLOR	REMARKS
1	6" ELLIPS'L-REF'R SPOTLIGHT	BEAM-L	AREA 2L-WARM	750T12	808	SOFT EDGE
2	" " " "	" "	" 2L-COOL	"	856	" "
3	" " " "	" "	" 1L-WARM	"	808	FRAME OFF TORM.
4	" " " "	" "	" 1L-COOL	"	856	" " "
5	" " " "	" "	" 3L-WARM	"	808	
6	" " " "	" "	" 3L-COOL	"	856	
7	" " " "	BEAM-R	" 1R·	"	842	
8	" " " "	" "	" 3R	"	842	FRAME OFF TORM.
9	" " " "	" "	" 2R	"	842	SOFT EDGE
10	6" FRESNEL-LENS SPOTLIGHT	1ST PIPE-L	" 4L WARM	500T20	808	
11	" " " "	" "	" 4L COOL	"	856	
12	" " " "	" "	" 5L WARM	"	808	
13	" " " "	" "	" 5L COOL	"	856	
14	" " " "	" "	" 6L WARM	"	808	
15	" " " "	" "	" 6L COOL	"	856	
16	" " " "	1ST PIPE-R	" 4R	"	842	
17	" " " "	" "	" 5R	"	842	
18	" " " "	" "	" 6R	"	842	
19	" " " "	2ND PIPE-L	" 7L WARM	"	808	
20	" " " "	" " "	" 7L COOL	"	856	
21	" " " "	2ND PIPE-R	" 7R	"	842	
22	" " " "	3RD PIPE-R	" 7 SPECIAL	"	842	MAT OFF DROP
23	8" FRESNEL-LENS SPOTLIGHT	1ST PIPE-L	MOONLIGHT	1000G40	853	FOCUS ON AREA 2,3
24	" " " "	" " "	"	"	853	" " " 1,2
25	" " " "	2ND PIPE-L	"	"	853	" " " 5
26	" " " "	3RD PIPE-L	"	"	853	" " " 7
27	10" FLOOD	SCENERY-R	DOOR BACKING	250G30	810	MOUNT HIGH ON SCENERY
28	16" BEAM PROJECTOR	1ST PIPE-L	SUN LIGHT	1500G40	805	FOCUS ON AREA 2,3
29	" " "	" "	"	"	805	" " " 1,2
30	" " "	2ND PIPE-L	"	"	805	" " " 5
31	" " "	3RD PIPE-L	"	"	805	" " " 7
32	6" X 6'-0" STRIPLIGHTS					FOCUS ON PAINTED
33	" "				AMBER	PORTION
34	" "	ON FLOOR	TRANSLUCENCY	300R40	BLUE	ROUNDELS
35	" "	BEHIND GROUND ROW	FRONT LIGHT	FLOOD	BL-GREEN	
36	" "					
37	6" X 4'-6" STRIPLIGHTS	4TH PIPE	TRANSLUCENCY	150 PAR38	861	
38	6" X 6'-0" "	BEHIND	BACKLIGHT	SPOT	819	3-COLOR CIRCUIT
39	" "	TRANSLUCENCY			854	FEED THROUGH
40	" "	VERY HIGH				FOCUS ON
41	" "					TRANSLUCENT
42	6" X 4'-6" STRIPLIGHTS					PORTION

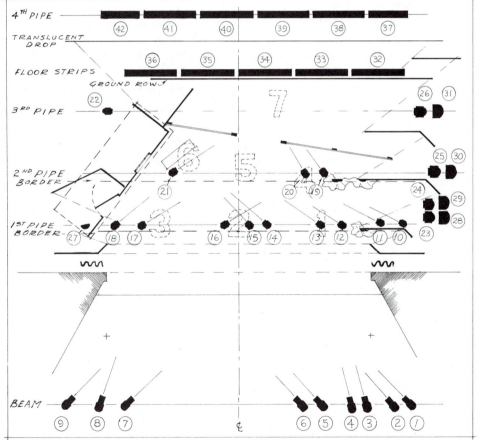

FIGURE 20–7

A Realistic Exterior Setting

(Opposite page) Instrument schedule. (This page) Sketch of setting and layout of lighting instruments.

On the stage with limited equipment it is possible to employ the same instrument for suns and moons, changing the color media between scenes, of course.

Translucent Backdrop

And finally we come to the background with a distant view painted opaquely at the bottom. This portion, of course, must be lighted from the front, and therefore five 6-foot lengths of striplights are placed on the floor, not too close, so that their various beams may have room to blend smoothly over the surface. They should be as close to the ground row as necessary to be hidden from the audience (this is especially important if there is a balcony). Because the light to be thrown on this portion is limited to the realistic daylight and nighttime colors, we may use amber, blue-green, and blue roundels over the 300-watt R-floods. Glass is essential here, for plastic would quickly burn out over these powerful lamps.

The upper portion of the backdrop is a true translucency, and therefore its light should come from behind. Four 6-foot lengths and two shorter lengths of strips with 150-watt PAR-spots are flown well above the highest visible part of the translucency and are focused down it to give it a sheet of light. Some form of backdrop might also be hung behind these, to reflect additional light through the translucency. This is a particularly effective device to furnish extra punch. As these strips are focused downwards, standard filters may be used safely. Quite a variation of color is needed for this sky, so the three circuits may well have No. 861 (Surprise Blue), No. 819 (Orange-Amber), and No. 854 (Steel Blue). By mixing the first and last, a daylight sky can be achieved; the 819 and 854 can give a sunset amber, while a touch of 819 added to the strong blue will provide a rich night sky. Many variations of these are possible.

Control

In a setting of this nature it is amazing how rapidly the dimmer requirements mount up. Certainly the twenty-two area spotlights each deserve individual control. The four moons could be ganged but would then require a dimmer of 4000-watt capacity. Similarly the suns could be controlled together, but would need a 6000-watt dimmer or two of 3000 watts each.

The translucency front strips make up as three 20-lamp color circuits of 6000 watts apiece. There are 22 lamps per color circuit in the rear strips, at 3300 watts each.

If the largest dimmers are 2000 watts, then the moons will require two, the suns four, translucency fronts nine, and rear six—a total of twenty-one dimmers!

On many boards this would necessitate ganging area spotlights, with the resulting loss of artistic control. Of course it may be necessary

Designing the Lighting

to fall back on awkward replugging between scenes, using the same dimmers for the moons in the second scene as were used for the suns in the first and the left area cools in place of the warms on the same group of controls.

WING-AND-BORDER SETTINGS

The wing-and-border setting presents problems very different from the realistic exterior and interior types. Here realism and plausibility are usually of little concern. Rather, the large expanses of flat scenery demand flat lighting, and against these brilliant backgrounds the actors must be picked out by powerful lighting directed on them. The use of follow spots for this purpose is fairly standard.

Setting for a Musical

Figure 20–8 (pages 520 and 521) shows a wing-and-border set for a typical musical. Because a traveler show curtain with appropriate design is hung immediately behind the house curtain, the house tormentors and teaser have been removed and their functions assumed by a show portal hung just upstage of the show curtain. The zone across the stage just above the portal is usually referred to as "In One." Its upstage boundary is marked by a second traveler, a second portal, and a drop beyond. In turn, some feet upstage of this group is yet another consisting of a second drop, a third portal, and then two more drops. Finally, beyond all is a sky-blue backing.

The several drops will not all be solid cloth; some will be cut out in part so that the audience sees through to other scenic elements beyond. The various drops will work with the curtains and portals in different combinations as the show progresses, while set pieces, furniture, and the like will be moved on and off stage for different scenes. Often special lighting is needed for such pieces.

The sketch shows the three portals, drop No. 2, representing a cutout of trees, and drop No. 4, a distant view.

Lighting the In-One Zone

In order to provide the punch of light on the actors required by this type of presentation, we have double hung all the area lighting spotlights. This means that in the beams there are twelve 6 × 12 ellipsoidal spotlights, two to a side on each of the three "In One" areas. Care must be taken to focus these spots far enough downstage on the apron to cover the probable movement of the players. In this style of production it is not uncommon for the actors to be brought clear down to the very edge of the stage.

With four instruments on each area, considerable variation in the colors is possible. Rather than simply use the same tints on the op-

No.	INSTRUMENT	LOCATION	PURPOSE	LAMP	COLOR	REMARKS
1	6" ELLIPS'L-REF'R SPOTLIGHT	BEAM - L	AREA 2L WARM	750 T 12	826	
2	" " " "	" "	" 2L COOL	"	850	
3	" " " "	" "	" 1L WARM	"	826	FRAME TO PORTAL
4	" " " "	" "	" 1L COOL	"	850	" " "
5	" " " "	" "	" 3L WARM	"	826	
6	" " " "	" "	" 3L COOL	"	850	
7	8 ELLIPS'L-REF'R SPOTLIGHT	BEAM - C	FOLLW SPOT	1000 T 12	CLEAR	
8	" " " "	" "	"	"	"	
9	6" ELLIPS'L-REF'R SPOTLIGHT	BEAM - R	AREA 1R WARM	750 T 12	802	
10	" " " "	" "	" 1R COOL	"	842	
11	" " " "	" "	" 3R WARM	"	802	FRAME OFF PORTAL
12	" " " "	" "	" 3R COOL	"	842	" " "
13	" " " "	" "	" 2R WARM	"	802	
14	" " " "	" "	" 2R COOL	"	842	
15	" " " "	1ST STAND - L	CROSS LIGHT	750 T 12	852	FOCUS ON AREA 2,3
16	" " " "	" "	" "	500 T 12	852	" " " 1,2
17	6" FRESNEL-LENS SPOTLIGHT	1ST PIPE - L	AREA 5L WARM	500 T 20	826	
18	" " " "	" "	5L COOL	"	850	
19	" " " "	" "	4L WARM	"	826	
20	" " " "	" "	4L COOL	"	850	
21	" " " "	" "	6L WARM	"	826	
22	" " " "	" "	6L COOL	"	850	
23	" " " "	1ST PIPE - R	4R WARM	"	802	
24	" " " "	" "	4R COOL	"	842	
25	" " " "	" "	6R WARM	"	802	
26	" " " "	" "	6R COOL	"	842	
27	" " " "	" "	5R WARM	"	802	
28	" " " "	" "	5R COOL	"	842	
29	6" ELLIPS'L-REF'R SPOTLIGHT	1ST STAND - R	CROSSLIGHT	750 T 12	810	FOCUS ON AREA 1,2
30	" " " "	" R	"	500 T 12	810	" " " 2,3
31	" " " "	2ND STAND - L	"	750 T 12	852	" " " 5,6
32	" " " "	" - L	"	500 T 12	852	" " " 4,5
33	" " " "	" - R	"	750 T 12	810	" " " 4,5
34	" " " "	" - R	"	500 T 12	810	" " " 5,6
35	" " " "	3RD STAND - L	"	750 T 12	852	FOCUS FAR
36	" " " "	" - L	"	500 T 12	852	" NEAR
37	" " " "	" - R	"	750 T 12	810	" FAR
38	" " " "	" - R	"	500 T 12	810	" NEAR
39	16" BEAM PROJECTOR	2ND PIPE - L	DOWNLIGHT	1000 G 40	802	FOCUS DOWNSTAGE
40	" " "	" - L	"	"	802	" "
41	" " "	" - R	"	"	802	" "
42	" " "	" - R	"	"	802	" "
43	6" x 6'-0" STRIPLIGHTS				R	
44	" "	APRON	FOOTLIGHTS	150 R 40	G ROUNDEL	3-COLOR CIRCUIT
45	" "			FLOOD	B	FEED THROUGH
46	" "				828	
47	" "	1ST PIPE	1ST BORDER	150 R 40	815	
48	" "			SPOT	858	
49	" "				828	
50	" "	3RD PIPE	2ND BORDER	150 R 40	815	
51	" "			SPOT	858	
52	" "				828	
53	" "	4TH PIPE	BACK DROP	300 R 40	863	
54	" "			SPOT	853	
55	" "				810	

Designing the Lighting

FIGURE 20–8

A Wing-and-Border Setting

(Opposite page) Instrument schedule. (This page) Sketch of setting and layout of lighting instruments.

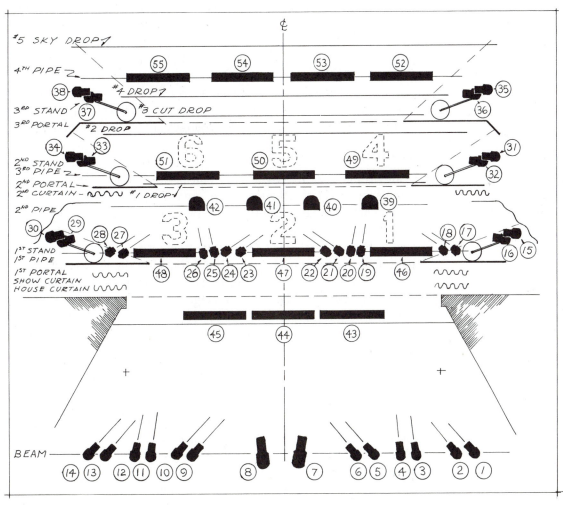

posite side of the stage, we prefer to put the flattering No. 826 (Flesh Pink) as the warm color on the left and No. 802 on the right. For most productions of this type, a generally romantic feeling is desired, so the cools should not be saturated. No. 850 is a deep enough blue to be used on the left, while the rather neutral No. 842 (Special Lavender) on the right will appear quite cool in comparison to the warm colors used with it.

Follow Spots

Frequently, it is desirable to have special instruments in the beams to illuminate the decorative show curtain. But to keep this layout on the modest side, we have forgone these and will let the footlights do the job. But a pair of 8-inch narrow-beam ellipsoidal spotlights, burning 1000-watt lamps and equipped with irises, are used as follow spots. We assume that operators may be stationed in the theatre's beam. In plants where this is not possible, some other location must be found (for example, balcony, box booms, or rear of balcony projection booth). Musicals without spotlights to accent the leading players on the brightly lighted stage lack a great deal of the theatrical glamor that goes with this sort of presentation. Most of the time these follow spots will be most effective with no color medium at all. If any is used, a No. 825 (No Color Pink) is appropriate. Of course, for occasional and particular purposes other and stronger colors may be used, including a very dense blue filter especially made for ultraviolet effects. With an operator in constant attendance, color changes are easily accomplished.

The In-Two Zone

Moving to the "In-Two" zone, that between the second and third portals, we light the three upstage areas by means of twelve 6-inch Fresnel spots hanging from the first pipe, although 6 × 9 ellipsoidals would also be a good choice. Their colors match the downstage area spotlights, as usual. These instruments must be carefully focused to pass under the second portal without touching the edges with a distracting glare. Many times a third set of spotlights is employed for the "In-Three" zone, but because our stage is not deep, and we are trying to be economical with instruments, we shall hope that the extra light is not needed this far upstage. Of course, viewing rehearsals would tell us for sure.

Side Lighting

Side lighting—lighting from the wings—has become a convention with the wing-and-border setting. It has three important aspects: its low angle from the side adds to the plasticity of the actor's appearance; it can add extra color effects; and it helps to tie together the zones across which it is focused. In each of our six side entrances we have provided two 6-inch ellipsoidal spotlights mounted on boom stands.

Designing the Lighting

The upper instrument is focused across the stage to catch both the center and the far acting areas, and, because of this long throw, it burns a 750-watt lamp and is the narrower beam 6 × 12. The lower one, a 6 × 9 mounted at least 10 feet above stage level, ties in the near and the center areas and uses the 500-watt lamp. Because we are not using strong colors for our regular area spotlights, in these side-lighting instruments we choose No. 852 (Smokey Blue) from the left and No. 810 (No Color Amber) from the right.

Down Lights

Another feature that is becoming almost a must for musicals are the downlights which we have placed over the "In-One" zone. These are hung quite high and just downstage of the traveler curtain and the second portal so that they tend to back-light the actors standing at the front of the zone. A No. 802 filter in these 16-inch beam projectors with their 1000-watt lamps will throw a flattering high light on the head and shoulders of the actors and set them out from the scenery. A second set of down lights over the "In-Two" zone might not be amiss, but our list of instruments is already startlingly long.

Footlights

Striplights have been used extensively to tie in the various portions of the stage, to give tonal washes over scenery and actors, and generally to provide illumination. The footlights consist of the regular three 6-foot lengths, in this case burning 150-watt R-40 lamps behind glass roundels in the primary colors. The unusually high wattage here is to provide a strong wash of light for the show curtain. Musicals and revues can use rather strong footlights to supplement the regular front lighting especially for chorus-line sequences, to throw illumination under large hats, to wash the company with special colors, and the like.

Border Lights

For the first and second borders, three 6-foot lengths each are used. Those on the first pipe must be placed well apart to leave room for area spotlights to be mounted between the lengths; on the third pipe less space is needed. But in both cases somewhat wider extension into the wings is necessary in order properly to wash the scenery hanging upstage of each set of strips. The 150-watt R-40 floods are used with colors approaching the secondaries: No. 828 (Follies Pink), No. 815 (Golden Amber), and No. 858 (Light Green Blue), a combination that should allow almost any tint desired to flood the stage.

The Backdrop

And for the background, the cloth or other surface painted to represent the sky, four lengths of strips have been hung as far downstage from the surface as other flown elements permit so that as smooth a wash as possible can be achieved. Here it is necessary to go to the 300-watt R-40 spots because a good punch will be needed. A dark night sky can be achieved by use of a No. 863 (Medium Blue), and if this is a bit too deep it can be lightened a little by mixing in No. 853 (Middle Blue). For a bright daylight sky we add No. 810 (No Color Amber).

Control

There are twenty-four area spotlights, all of which will be working at the same time in several scenes, so no replugging is possible in this production. Although it would be pleasant to have an individual dimmer assigned to each cross-lighting instrument, we can get along by ganging the pair at each location, thereby holding the dimmer requirements to six. The downlights, too, may well be ganged: on a 4000-watt dimmer, if one is available, if not, in pairs on two 2000-watt dimmers.

The footlights and first and second border will each require three 1800-watt circuits—nine all together. But the backdrop calls for three circuits of 4800 watts apiece. On boards with small capacity these loads must be split up in some manner, depending on what is available.

Obviously, individual control over the two follow spots is absolutely essential. The total and minimum demands for this layout, therefore, would be forty-three dimmers that can handle up to 2000 watts each, and three of far greater capacity. And this is a very modest plot for a musical play.

OTHER TYPES OF PROSCENIUM STAGING

Today, the types of presentation that fall within the categories of unit settings, simultaneous settings, or space staging have become increasingly popular. These forms of production generally have very little concern with realistic scenery. Often the scenic elements consist of an abstract arrangement of platforms and possibly a form or two of suggestive (but not very representational) shape. The background frequently will be a surrounding of black velour drapery but may also be an open cyclorama. In either case, lighting which separates the actor from his or her background is imperative.

The scenery may move to help establish various locales, or the lighting designer may be called upon exclusively to set a scene. If this is the case, careful planning as well as extensive communication with both the scene designer and director is of utmost importance. The lighting designer's approach to such a production will have a great deal to do with the number of scenes and their respective complexity. If the script only calls for a few locale changes, the designer may design each scene separately and then combine all into a unified plot. However, if the play has many scenes, the approach will most likely be one of full-stage area lighting with tight control and added special instrumentation when required.

Whether scenic forms are used or not, light plays a major role in the creation and composition of acting space. Movement of light will alter focus and must be considered early in the planning stages. High-angle distribution is often preferred in order to keep the area being lit as tight as possible, but care must be taken to avoid deep facial shadows that could prove disturbing.

The lighting designer must use creative instincts to their fullest potential in supporting the stage action within the limitations of equipment and control. As might be expected, this style of performance presents an exciting challenge to the lighting designer.

21

Lighting for Other Production Forms

So far we have discussed only the types of production presented on a conventional stage, where practically all action is separated from the audience by "the fourth wall." But other forms are rapidly gaining in popularity, forms in which the division between audience area and acting area is less obvious. These vary from a proscenium stage with action coming out into the auditorium on side stages, ramps, and steps to the complete arena form in which the audience surrounds the playing area on all four sides. Techniques useful for lighting in-the-round stages differ from those used for performances done on a proscenium stage.

ARENA PRODUCTION

The designer need not be bothered with lighting the scenery in a truly in-the-round production, for arena staging uses little scenery, and what does exist is adequately lighted by the same beams that strike nearby actors. However, this lack of scenery deprives the designer of valuable mounting positions for instruments, and, more important, eliminates a background. The actors must be lit from all sides, just as they must play to all sides.

Accuracy of Focus

With the spectators crowded closely—often too closely—about the playing areas, instruments that have hard-to-control beams are of little value. Floodlights are impossible. Striplights may be used discreetly and with side maskings to give an overall tonality of rather low intensity. Fresnel spots must be focused with particular accuracy and, in addition, a top hat or barn doors must be added to control the beam spill.

Functions of Arena Lighting

Visibility remains, of course, the primary function in arena-production lighting, and this means that the actors must be effectively lighted for all members of the surrounding audience. Composition takes the form of holding the spectators' attention to the acting areas and thus the lighting must have definition and great precision of form. Tight and specific area control is often required in the arena, adding another compositional requirement to the designer's list. Mood must be accomplished by means of intensity and color toning but both within limited ranges. In addition, the color, texture, and compositional makeup of the stage floor takes on greater visual importance in arena production because of audience viewing angle.

Mounting Positions

Because arena stages and the buildings surrounding them vary so greatly, it is difficult to suggest a typical lighting arrangement. An arena stage in the center of a large gymnasium floor, for example, would probably offer all sorts of lofty and convenient mounting places for overhead lighting instruments, while a formal hall with a plastered ceiling of no great height would present enormous, if not impossible, difficulties. However, let us assume a reasonable amount of overhead flexibility in our discussion of this form of presentation.

Arena Lighting Areas

It is convenient to divide the arena stage into a number of acting areas, each of which can be effectively covered by the beam of a spotlight mounted along a 45-degree angle. Just what type of spotlight this would be would depend on the mounting locations and their distances. If a good, long throw is possible, the 6 × 12 ellipsoidal spotlight with a 750-watt lamp would be fine; for much shorter throws, say of 15 to 20 feet, one of the wider-beam ellipsoidals would work very well.

Lighting for Other Production Forms   **527**

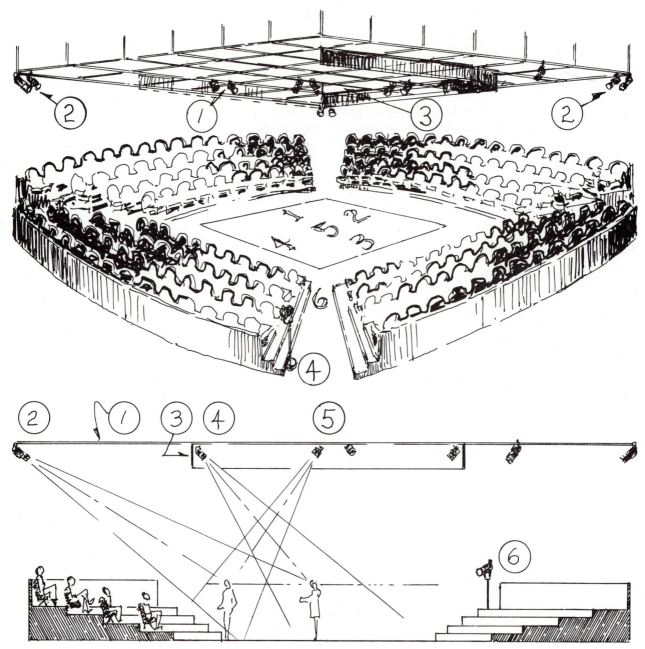

FIGURE 21–1

Arena Stage Lighting Positions

(Top) A perspective view of an arena stage showing a pipe grid over the audience and acting area. (1) The nearest frontal position behind the valance. (2) Extreme position on the outer edge of the grid. (3) Central position over the acting area for down lighting and back lighting. (4) Special position in the aisle for an occasional effect.

The acting areas are numbered from one to five. The number of areas is, of course, optional and would vary with the requirements of the production.

(Above) A cross section through the arena showing the various angles of distribution. (1) Pipe grid. (2) Outside position. (3) Valance. (4) Inner position behind valance. (5) Central position. (6) Special position in aisle.

On the proscenium stage each area must be covered by two spotlights, each ideally 45 degrees on the actor. In an arena, however, where the actor is seen from all sides, more instruments are necessary. There are two popular approaches to the solution. One is that three instruments per area be used, evenly spaced about the area and thus at 120 degrees from one another. The second approach is to use four spots on each area, putting them 90 degrees from each other and shooting along the diagonals of the space.

Color in the Arena

With either approach, the system of using one warm and one cool color on each area is no longer applicable. In the three-spotlight plan the third instrument is assigned a neutral color, such as Special Lavender—which, we have seen, appears cool opposite a warm filter and warm opposite a cool one. Light Flesh Pink is also a possibility for scenes that are basically warm and romantic. No color at all also can be quite effective.

The four-instrument system suggests two color variations. In the first, a warm and a cool are used on opposite sides, while the two intermediate instruments have a neutral medium. An alternate approach is to use two warms, each opposite the other, and two cools, also opposite each other. The latter will most often prove more satisfactory.

A word of warning about the choice of colors in arena productions: Because the directionality of the spotlights on each side of each area is so definite, colors show up much stronger on the actors than in a proscenium production, where there is far more mixing of different beams. Or perhaps this seems true to the audience because of its closeness to the action. In any event, the use of more saturated colors is rarely advisable.

Blending

The use of blending strips to give a tonality to the scene, much as first border strips are used on a proscenium stage, may be quite effective if properly handled. Two or three of the 6-foot lengths might be hung down the center line of the arena, or two strips might be placed along opposite sides and focused across the stage. Striplights, so used, must be provided with blinders (side maskings) that will prevent their beams from falling on the audience, particularly that portion of it seated on the opposite side of the stage.

Six-inch Fresnel down lights at flood focus will also provide good blending and color toning. Although Fresnels do not offer as much color flexibility as striplights, they allow for greater control. Finally, don't forget to use top hats.

Lighting for Other Production Forms

Unmasked Instruments

It would be fruitless in a temporary arena setup to attempt to hide the instruments from the audience. They can, of course, be hung and maintained in a neat manner, with wiring carefully tied off and the like. But a frank acceptance of the fact that the instruments are there for all to view is better than a lot of makeshift, dust-catching, and fire-prone draperies.

However, if a stage house has been designed especially for arena production, a false ceiling should be provided with openings through which the beams of light may be focused from instruments hung well above and out of sight. Catwalks must be installed so the electrician can reach all instruments with ease for maintenance, focusing, and color changes.

Blinding the Spectators

The most difficult problem in any form of arena production is to keep the beams of the area spotlights out of the eyes of spectators seated on the opposite side of the stage. As long as light persists in traveling in a straight line, and as long as directors wish to play their actors at the very edge of the arena stage, just so long will a compromise be necessary between a well-lighted actor and a half-blinded spectator.

To solve the problem, the angle of the instrument or instruments spilling into the audience can be raised, but this compromise only helps so much. If the first row of the audience can be raised higher than the stage level, or be set back from it, or both, the problem can be greatly eased. In any event, this is one of the greatest problems confronting the light designer in arena production.

Designing the Lighting for an Arena Production

Should the lighting designer attempt to create the same lighting picture for everyone in the arena audience? Experience has shown that such an approach is quite restrictive and leads to fairly bland lighting. Nonetheless, the designer should always be concerned about the quality of lighting from all viewing angles in an arena theatre.

Figures 21–1 through 21–3 illustrate our sample arena layout with properties in place on the stage floor. There are two boxes in which lighting instruments may be hung overhead. A layout and an instrument schedule for a suitable lighting design are also shown.

The designer has divided the stage into five areas, which have been numbered clockwise from one through four, with area five in the center. Dotted lines on the layout mark the approximate limits of these areas, although it is, of course, understood that actually they will overlap one another and their lights will blend smoothly. The instruments have been numbered systematically, from the top, clockwise around the stage, in the outer box first and then the inner.

No.	INSTRUMENT	PURPOSE	LAMP	COLOR	REMARKS
①	6" ELLIPS'L-REF'L SPOTLIGHT	AREA 1	500 T12	803	
2	" " "	" 2	"	803	
3	8" FRESNEL SPOTLIGHT	MOONLIGHT SPECIAL	1000 G40	856	FOCUS CENTER
4	6" ELLIPS'L-REF'L SPOTLIGHT	AREA 2	500 T12	848	
5	" " "	" 3	"	848	
6	" " "	DIVAN SPECIAL	750 T12	826	FRAME TO DIVAN
7	" " "	AREA 3	500 T12	805	
8	" " "	" 4	"	805	
9	" " "	" 4	"	842	
⑩	" " "	" 1	"	842	
11	40° MINI-ELLIPSE	" 4	500 W Q	803	MAT TOP
12	6" FRESNEL SPOTLIGHT	" 5	500 T20	803	TOP HAT
13	40° MINI-ELLIPSE	" 3	500 W Q	803	MAT TOP
⑭	" "	" 1	"	848	" "
15	6" FRESNEL SPOTLIGHT	" 5	500 T20	848	TOP HAT
16	40° MINI-ELLIPSE	" 4	500 W Q	848	MAT TOP
17	" "	" 2	"	805	" "
18	6" FRESNEL SPOTLIGHT	" 5	500 T20	805	TOP-HAT
19	4½" ELLIPS'L-REF'L SPOTLIGHT	CENTER ACCENT	500 T12	CLEAR	FOCUS CENTER
⑳	40° MINI-ELLIPSE	AREA 1	500 W Q	805	MAT TOP
21	" "	" 3	"	842	" "
22	" "	DIVAN SPECIAL #2	"	802	MAT TO DIVAN
23	6" FRESNEL SPOTLIGHT	AREA 5	500 T20	842	TOP HAT
24	40° MINI-ELLIPSE	" 2	500 W Q	842	MAT TOP
25	FIXTURE	TABLE LAMP #1	40 A	–	GANG WITH #26
26	"	" " #2	40 A	–	" " #25

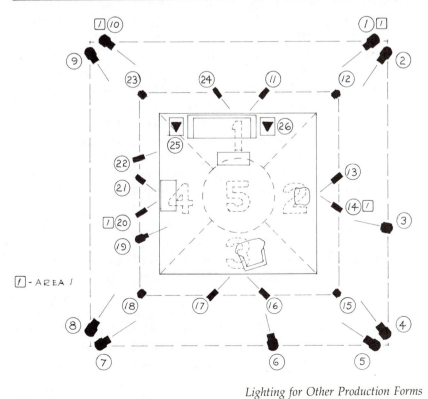

1 - AREA 1

FIGURE 21–2
An Arena-Production Setting
(Left) Layout of lighting instruments.
(Above) Instrument schedule.

Lighting for Other Production Forms

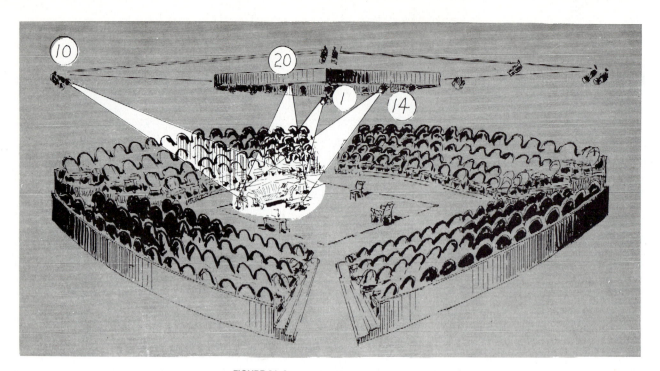

FIGURE 21–3

Arena Stage Lighting Layout

Coverage on one of the five acting areas. Note the four different angles. Note Area 1 in floor plan showing lighting layout, Figure 21–2.

From each corner of the outer box a pair of 6 × 12 ellipsoidal reflector spotlights is focused on the two closest areas, giving each of these two beams of light at approximately right angles to one another. From the inner box two 40° Mini-Ellipse spotlights are focused on each of the same areas. The ERS is used here because the upper portion of its beam can be effectively matted to prevent light from glaring into the eyes of spectators seated on the opposite side of the stage.

Area 5, in the center, is hit from the four corners of the inner box by 6-inch Fresnel spotlights. Here the danger of spill light annoying the audience is less marked than in the outer areas, but top hats are used on the instruments just the same. The typical soft-edged Fresnel-beam pattern is useful to blend this center light with the illumination on the adjacent areas.

The color system in Roscolene plastic is that of opposite warms and cools. The warm light, working diagonally out of the upper-right corner of the layout, is from a Roscolene No. 803 (Pale Gold) Filter. The identical color might have been employed also from the lower left, but the designer preferred to use a slightly different tint, Roscolene No. 805 (Light Straw). In like manner, the cools are not identical: from the lower right is a No. 848 (Water Blue), while opposite it is a No. 842 (Special Lavender). This is not an especially cool color, but it has been chosen here because we are assuming that this is a warm, pleasant

Designing the Lighting

type of play. Had it been a cold, stark drama, we might have selected a combination of No. 851 and No. 848 for the cools, while the versatile No. 842 might have been one of the warms, with perhaps no color at all in the opposite instruments.

A few specials have been provided. On the right side there is an 8-inch Fresnel with a No. 856 (Light Blue) gel to give the effect of moonbeams for a brief scene. Instrument 6 is focused carefully on the divan with a romantic No. 826 (Flesh Pink) for a tender moment. Toward the upper-left corner is another divan special with No. 802 (Bastard Amber) for a different scene. Also on the left, a wide-beamed ellipsoidal-reflector spotlight without color serves as an accent on the central area for some special action there. The two table lamps at either end of the divan are practical fixtures, meaning that they will be lit at some point in the production.

Control

Twenty-four dimmers would be necessary for this simple arena layout, assuming that we can repatch one of the specials. Arena and thrust lighting almost always require tighter and more individual control than proscenium production.

THRUST STAGE PRODUCTION

The Extended Apron

Chapter 2 discusses two forms of theatrical presentation that recently have become extremely popular: the extended apron and the thrust stage. The former is really a variation of regular proscenium production as far as lighting is concerned. Some additional spotlights in the beams, on the balcony front, in side slots in the auditorium walls, and on booms in side boxes can all be used on the extended stage. If the stage is not too deep, it may be back lighted from behind the proscenium, except, of course, when the curtain is closed. The use of striplights and floods is impractical. The only real problem presented is that of keeping the beam patterns from being too prominent on the walls of the auditorium and off the audience itself.

An Approach to Thrust Stage Lighting

Any theatre designed for a thrust stage should include provision for good mounting positions for the lighting instruments. The simplest manner of doing this is a grid of pipes or other mounting structure over the entire stage and extending over the audience as well in all directions as far from the edge of the stage as the height of the grid above the stage floor. There should be a great number of electrical outlets provided on this grid, unless it is the intention to string cables from backstage to the specific instruments. If the grid is not too high,

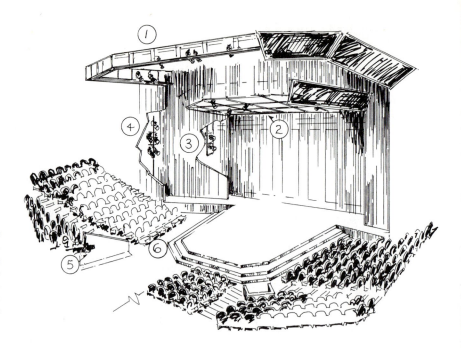

FIGURE 21–4

Thrust Stage Lighting Positions

A perspective view of a thrust stage showing its various lighting positions. The stage division into acting areas would vary with each production. (1) Outer valance position. (2) Second valance and gridiron over stage. (3) Wing ladder, side lighting. (4) Tormentor boom. (5) Vomitory rail. (6) Gutter.

it can be reached by ladders from below. But if it is over 14 feet above the floor, a network of catwalks, so numerous that an electrician can safely reach every inch of the grid from them, should be provided above the pipes.

Boxes or valances to hide the instruments are often provided, but because of the necessity to be able to hang spotlights on any portion of the grid, especially over the stage itself, these devices are not wholly effective. Therefore instruments should be mounted and cabled neatly and securely so as to be neither a distraction nor a danger. Those spectators in the side seats particularly will find that the lenses of instruments focused in their general direction will be in full view. But as long as top hats are used, this should not prove too great a distraction. Care must be taken to mask or frame off the upper part of the beams from such instruments to be sure they do not glare directly into the eyes of those seated facing them. Ellipsoidal reflector spotlights can use their internal framing shutters to good advantage; Fresnels should be provided with barn doors.

Often the arrangement of set pieces and properties will dictate how a thrust stage is best divided into acting areas, and each of these will require several instruments focused on it from several directions. Every actor on a thrust stage is seen from three sides at the same time. Top or back lighting is also essential to set the actor off from the background. Blending and toning are best accomplished by use of soft-beamed spotlights to throw color washes over large portions of the stage.

As with arena staging, strong colors are not desirable on the thrust stage, although we can become somewhat bolder because of the one closed side. Spots to hit the stage at the familiar 45-degree angle from the front might use very pale tints, while other instruments on the same area can take stronger shades of the same basic colors, with those coming in directly from the sides using quite deep tones. The down or back lighting is often not far from white light.

The stage floor becomes a major scenic element in most thrust houses because of the steep audience rake. As in the arena, lighting color, texture, and composition will read quite strongly on the floor.

Designing the Lighting

Figure 21–5 (pages 536–537) shows a sketch of a typical thrust stage with properties and a few scenic pieces set for a play. Also shown are a layout for lighting this production and schedule of the instruments to be used.

The stage divides itself into five natural areas: the upper platform and archway being 1; the central section as outlined by the carpet, 2; and the margin of the platform surrounding the carpet, 3, 4, and 5. The designer has sought to put five to seven instruments on each area, but the difficulty of focusing to cover an area properly without hitting the audience at the same time has limited this in some instances. The further to the side the instruments are mounted, the deeper the colors they use. For this layout Lee filters are employed.

Taking area 1 as an example, we find that it is covered from the front by two 6 × 12 ellipsoidal reflector spotlights, 32 and 36, mounted in the inner box. Two 8-inch ellipsoidals, 1 and 23, strike it from the booms placed in the ramp entrances on either side of the stage. Two more 6-inchers, 27 and 41, are on the ladders hung in the upstage entrances. One 6-inch ellipsoidal works as a back light from above the upstage archway. The colors, working from front to rear on the left side are Lee 117 (Steel Blue), 144 (No Color Blue), and 141 (Bright Blue). On the right side they are 152 (Pale Gold), 151 (Gold Tint), and a double 153 (Pale Salmon). The back light is clear. The other areas use these same colors for instruments working from the same angles.

A pair of 8-inch Fresnel spotlights strikes the entire set from dead ahead to give it a tonal wash that may be varied by dimming the warm and cool instruments to different readings. Two pairs of 6-inch Fresnels, on either side of the inner box, and two pairs of 6-inch ellipsoidals in the ramp entrances work with the others. For the cool wash a 119 (Dark Blue) is used, for the warm wash a 134 (Golden Amber).

A great many specials have been hung. The extreme up-left and up-right corners, which might almost be considered areas in themselves, are each covered by three spots from front and sides, plus a back light. The tunnel entrances through the audience section (called vomitory entrances), the entrances along the ramps left and right, and those at the extreme back, as well as the archway in the center of the backwall, are all lighted. The bench, the window seat, the sofa, and the steps

Lighting for Other Production Forms

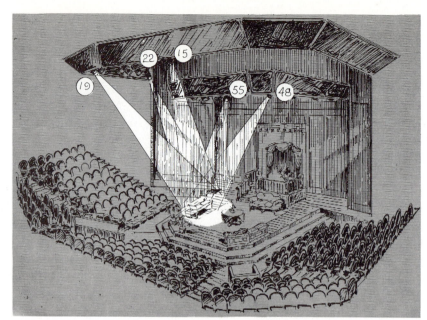

FIGURE 21–5

Thrust Stage Lighting Layout

(a) Isolated coverage of a single acting area, Area 4. Note the five different angles. (b) Floor plan showing lighting layout. Note Area 4. (c) Instrument schedule.

a

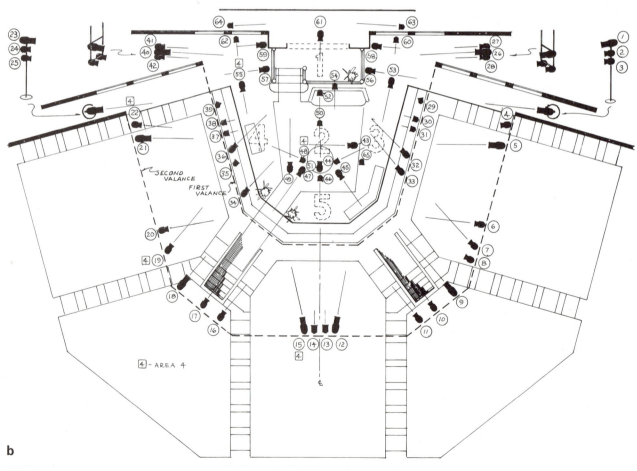

SECOND VALANCE

FIRST VALANCE

4 - AREA 4

b

Designing the Lighting

No.	INSTRUMENT	LOCATION	PURPOSE	LAMP	COLOR	REMARKS
1	8" ELLIPS'L REF'R SPOTLIGHT	LEFT BOOM	AREA 1	1000 T12	144	L. BOOM TOP
2	6" " " "	" "	WASH - WARM	750 T12	134	" MIDDLE SOFT EDGE
3	6" " " "	" "	" - COOL	750 T12	119	" BOTTOM " "
4	6" " " "	2ND. VALANCE - L	AREA 3	1000 T12	141	
5	8" " " "	" " "	" 2	"	141	
6	6" " " "	" " "	" 5	750 T12	141	
7	6" " " "	" " "	" 3	"	144	
8	6" " " "	" " "	WINDOW SEAT	750 T12	144	
9	8" " " "	" " "	AREA 2	1200 T12	117	
10	6" " " "	" " "	LEFT TUNNEL	750 T12	115	FRAME TO TUNNEL
11	6" " " "	" " "	AREA 5	750 T12	117	
12	8" " " "	2ND VALANCE - C	" 3	1000 T12	117	FRAME OFF AUDIENCE
13	8" FRESNEL-LENS SPOTLIGHT	" " "	WASH - COOL	1500 G40	119	BARN DOOR - OFF "
14	8" " " "	" " "	" - WARM	"	134	" " " "
15	8" ELLIPS'L REF'R SPOTLIGHT	" " "	AREA 4	1000 T12	152	FRAME OFF "
16	6" " " "	2ND VALANCE - R	" 5	750 T12	152	
17	6" " " "	" " "	RIGHT TUNNEL	750 T12	115	FRAME TO TUNNEL
18	8" " " "	" " "	AREA 2	1000 T2	152	
19	6" " " "	" " "	" 4	750 T12	151	
20	6" " " "	" " "	" 5	"	153(2)	
21	8" " " "	" " "	" 2	1000 T12	153(2)	
22	6" " " "	" " "	" 4	750 T12	153(2)	
23	8" " " "	RIGHT BOOM	" 1	1000 T12	151	R. BOOM - TOP
24	6" " " "	" "	WASH - WARM	750 T12	134	" MIDDLE - SOFT EDGE
25	6" " " "	" "	" - COOL	"	119	" BOTTOM " "
26	8" " " "	LEFT LADDER	U.R. CORNER	1000 T12	141	L. LADDER - TOP - FRAME SIDES
27	6" " " "	" "	AREA 1	750 T12	141	" BOTTOM " US
28	6" " " "	" "	U.L. CORNER	500 T12	141	" " " " "
29	6" FRESNEL-LENS SPOTLIGHT	1ST VALANCE - L	" "	500 T20	117	
30	6" " " "	" " "	WASH - COOL	"	119	BARN DOOR - OFF AUDIENCE
31	6" " " "	" " "	" - WARM	"	134	" " " "
32	6" ELLIPS'L REF'R SPOTLIGHT	" " "	AREA 1	750 T12	117	
33	6" " " "	" " "	SOFA	"	117	
34	6" " " "	1ST VALANCE R.	"	"	152	
35	6" FRESNEL-LENS SPOTLIGHT	" " "	BENCH	500 T20	152	
36	6" ELLIPS'L REF'R "	" " "	AREA 1	750 T12	152	FRAME BOTTOM
37	6" FRESNEL-LENS "	" " "	WASH - WARM	500 T20	134	BARN DOOR OFF AUDIENCE
38	6" " " "	" " "	" - COOL	"	119	" " " "
39	6" " " "	" " "	U.R. CORNER	"	152	
40	8" ELLIPS'L REF'R SPOTLIGHT	RIGHT LADDER	U.L. "	1000 T12	153(2)	R. LADDER - TOP FRAME SIDE
41	6" " " "	" "	AREA 1	750 T12	153(2)	" BOTTOM " US
42	6" " " "	" "	U.R. CORNER	"	153(2)	" " " US
43	6" " " "	GRID. OVER STAGE	BENCH	750 T12	117	SOFT E. FRAME OFF AUDIENCE
44	6" FRESNEL-LENS "	" " "	AREA 3	500 T20	CLEAR	BARNDOOR " "
45	6" ELLIPS'L REF'R "	" " "	LEFT TUNNEL	750 T12	102	FRAME TO TUNNEL
46	6" FRESNEL-LENS "	" " "	AREA 5	500 T20	CLEAR	BARN DOOR OFF AUDIENCE
47	6" ELLIPS'L REF'R "	" " "	RIGHT TUNNEL	750 T12	102	FRAME TO TUNNEL
48	6" FRESNEL-LENS "	" " "	AREA 4	500 T20	CLEAR	BARN DOOR OFF AUDIENCE
49	6" ELLIPS'L REF'R "	" " "	STEPS	750 T12	152	SOFT E. FRAME TO STEPS
50	6" FRESNEL-LENS "	" " "	AREA 2 DS	500 T20	CLEAR	
51	6" ELLIPS'L REF'R "	" " "	ARCHWAY	750 T12	102	FRAME TO ARCHWAY
52	6" FRESNEL-LENS "	" " "	AREA 2 US	500 T20	CLEAR	
53	6" ELLIPS'L REF'R "	" " "	AREA 3	750 T12	"	FRAME L AND TOP
54	6" FRESNEL LENS "	" " "	SOFA	500 T20	"	
55	6" ELLIPS'L REF'R "	" " "	AREA 4	750 T12	"	FRAME R AND TOP
56	6" " " "	" " "	LEFT RAMP	"	103	" OFF R. WALL
57	6" " " "	" " "	RIGHT "	"	103	" " L. "
58	6" " " "	" " "	UL ENTRANCE	"	103	" " R. "
59	6" " " "	" " "	UR "	"	103	" " L. "
60	6" FRESNEL-LENS "	" " "	UL CORNER	500 T20	CLEAR	
61	6" ELLIPS'L REF'R "	" " "	AREA 1	750 T12	"	SOFT EDGE
62	6" FRESNEL-LENS "	" " "	UR CORNER	500 T20	"	
63	6" " " "	" " "	HALL WAY - L	"	104	
64	6" " " "	" " "	" R	"	104	
65	6" " " "	" " "	WINDOW SEAT	"	CLEAR	BARN DOOR OFF AUDIENCE

leading up to Area 1 have appropriate coverage. Additional specials might be suggested, particularly as we see the development of the director's staging. Actors might, for example, be placed on the steps leading down from the platform, in which case, of course, suitable lighting would have to be provided.

The ellipsoidal reflector spotlights have been used a great deal in this layout because of the good control we have over their beams. When possible they are soft-edged by shifting the lenses to throw the gate out of focus, so as to cut down on sharp patterns and abrupt changes of intensity on the stage and actors. For the same reason Fresnel spotlights are used when their spill light will not be critical, and even then barn doors are suggested on many instruments.

Variations

Our sample lighting layout is designed for a rather light and charming piece of drama with a simple interior setting. Lighting angles are standard for good visibility and the colors are chosen for their pale tints. The arrangements of color (cool on one side and warm on the other) and angle are derived from proscenium lighting and provide good coverage. However, a two-sided color approach allows for very little variety or color interest and may not be desirable for a production with a number of scenes each demanding specific lighting.

With a minimum of five instruments on each acting area and a color arrangement as shown in Figure 21–6, the designer is provided with several more options.

1 The two warms can act as key light with the cools filling.
2 The two cools can act as key with the warms filling.
3 Any one instrument (except the back light neutral) can be lowered in intensity or dropped out completely, causing a color shift as well as compositional change.

If more than the minimum five instruments per area is possible, even greater variety of color and distribution can be achieved.

For more dramatic productions, the vertical angle of side light can be raised. The following occurs:

1 Higher angle distribution will cause sharper facial and body shadows.
2 Spill into side audience seating is more controllable.
3 Area control can be tighter.

Texture achieved by patterns or gobos can break up the sometimes flat and dull surface of the thrust stage, with high side often being a desirable angle.

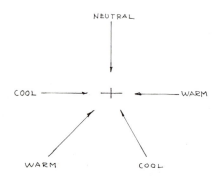

FIGURE 21–6
A Possible Color Key for the Thrust

Designing the Lighting

THE FLEXIBLE STAGE

Another form of performance space which should not go without mention is the increasingly popular "black box." This flexible space is primarily intended as an actor's performance space rather than a production facility, but lighting nonetheless is often required. Black box seating can be set up in any number of configurations that will, as a result, define the playing space. Common seating arrangements are:

1 One-sided, or full front—a proscenium-type orientation.
2 Two-sided, or corner staging.
3 Three-sided, or thrust.
4 Four-sided, or arena.
5 Aisle—with seats on two sides of a central aisle.

Lighting the Black Box

Lighting the flexible space is not very different from lighting one of the several theatre forms previously examined except that the lighting positions are generally closer to the stage. But lighting positions must also be flexible. A cross-pipe grid over the entire space is a fair solution to the problem of flexibility. Such a grid will allow lighting instruments to be hung in any position and focused in any direction. Another— and probably better—solution is the tension wire grid (Figure 21–7). One-eighth-inch wire rope is woven in all directions, forming a weight-bearing surface upon which an electrician can walk. Pipes supported from the ceiling are arranged to allow complete hanging flexibility with a minimum of time and effort. The lighting instruments shoot through the thin wire mesh as shown in the photograph. This grid is ideal for the flexible space as well as extremely useful in arena or over-thrust situations.

FIGURE 21–7

The Tension Wire Grid

A woven grid of aircraft cable under tension. Designed as a ceiling grid, it is weight-bearing and gives complete access to overhead lighting positions. (Left) View of a grid installation over the auditorium of a proscenium theatre. (Photo—Eiseman) (Right) Detail of grid and lighting position. Developed by George Izenour; manufactured by J. R. Clancy.

LIGHTING DANCE

The following discussion on lighting for the dance is based in part on the theories and techniques of Thomas Skelton, a leading practitioner in this field.

At first glance, dance, which is almost always performed in a wing-and-border setting on a proscenium stage, would seem to require the same sort of lighting as do other forms of production. But there is one most important difference: when we attend a play we are vitally interested in the face of the actor to tell us character, thoughts, and emotion. This is not true in dance, particularly ballet, in which the position and movement of the dancer's body tell us all. A knowledgeable lover of ballet will scarcely notice a dancer's face and will surely not concentrate on it. The primary concern is movement, which good dance lighting will reveal and emphasize.

To do this, the axis of the principal light should parallel the axis of the movement. Thus a ballerina spinning in a pirouette should have the light hitting straight down on her or straight up from below. The latter, which has been used for trick effects in modern dance routines, would probably not be appropriate for classical ballet. Although light from directly overhead tends to make the human body appear shortened, it is still the best way to accent the rapid turning of the dance.

Assume that a dancer faces the audience and raises her arm gracefully from her side to an angle of 45 degrees above her shoulder. This kind of movement is best accented by a light striking her armpit along the center line of the angle through which her arm was raised. A spotlight about 13 feet away at stage level would fulfill the requirement and would be hidden from the view of the audience if the dancer is close to the wings. If she is farther away, the ideal angle would no longer be possible, but this same location remains the best available position.

Of course it would be quite impractical to attempt to cover every single movement of a dance. A prodigious number of spotlights and an extremely complicated list of cues and light changes would be required. But provision can be made for some of the most significant moments and for more general lighting that will best suit the major movements of the work. The light designer must attend as many rehearsals as possible and take careful notes before sitting down at the drawing board. Fortunately, dances do fall into certain basic patterns of movement which can usually be covered successfully by one or more of the areas suggested in Figure 21–8.

Location of Instruments

The following are the more usual mounting positions for instruments (almost invariably spotlights).

Designing the Lighting

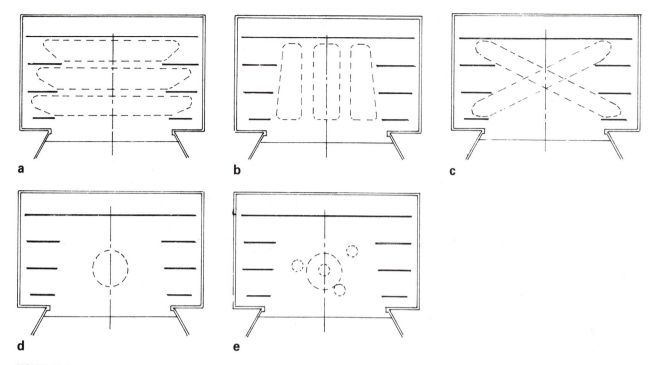

FIGURE 21–8

Lighting Areas for Dance

These coincide with the principal movements of the dancers on the stage. (a) *Cross-stage.* Dancers emerge from and disappear into the wings, dance across the stage, and work in lines that parallel the footlights. (b) *Up-and-down stage.* Dancers move toward the footlights and away again. In ballet the chorus frequently poses along the sides while the principals take center stage. (c) *Diagonal movement.* A most important aspect of modern dance. Dancers emerge from upstage wings and exit downstage on the opposite side, or vice versa. (d) *Center stage.* An obvious location for important dancing. The principal, or principals, or a small group, frequently work here in a circular pattern. (e) *Special Spots.* These may be any place on the stage (a few possibilities are indicated) in which a tight movement by the leading dancer is performed.

Low Front. For the low-front position, the lights might be mounted on a low balcony rail. Although light from this angle tends to wash out body form, a little is desirable for the sake of visibility and/or color washing.

Medium Front. These lights would be mounted on a second balcony or a beam position. Again, this does little for the body and accentuates the shadows of the dancers' costumes on their legs. This angle corresponds with the 45-degree visibility light common to theatrical presentation and can be used as such if necessary.

High-Front. Roughly at a 60-degree angle, high-front is much more useful for dramatic presentation than for dance. This angle casts serious costume shadows on the legs of an otherwise beautiful ballerina.

Low-Side. For the low-side position, light would come from the floor of the wings. Although an unnatural angle, it is flattering to dancers, for it tends to lift the body. Low-side lighting instruments are called

Lighting for Other Production Forms

"shin kickers" or "shin busters" for obvious reasons. They are normally clear or colored with very light tints, and their light can fairly effectively be cut off the floor surface in order to eliminate scallops from the beams.

Medium-Side. For the medium-side position, lights are mounted about 8 or 10 feet above the floor in the wings. This may be regarded as *the* basic dance-lighting angle. It throws a wash across the stage with little important shadowing. It may be desirable to mount one or two additional spotlights a few feet higher to carry across to the far side of the stage. In this case both long- and short-throw spots are focused so that the centers of their beams are parallel. Medium-side should not be confused with high-side, which is described below.

High-Side. Light in the high-side position comes from 15 to 20 feet high in the wings or from the ends of electric battens (such units are called "pipe ends"). If too high an angle is chosen, the light will tend to push the dancers down and make them seem squat. However, a 60-degree high-side can be very effective for a dramatic moment and is particularly useful in modern dance.

Straight-Back. In the straight-back position, light comes from above but also from behind the dancer. This is a very fine position, for it highlights the body in space, separating it from the background, and it does not cause one dancer to throw a shadow on the next one.

Diagonal-Back. Like the straight-back position, light comes from above and behind the dancer but from an angle to the side as well. Frequently this is more desirable than straight-back because more of the dancer's body is lighted.

Down-Light. In the down-light position, lights are mounted directly overhead, an effect that tends to push the body down. They are useful only for specialized moments.

Follow Spots. The follow spot may come from the house or from some on-stage location. This must be unobtrusive and should be used with a superior operator who can keep it so. Of course, in musical comedy dancing and the like, the blatant follow spots are all part of the show.

Booms

Low and medium side lighting require floor stands or booms as hanging positions. A dance concert or ballet will almost always call for a boom in each wing on both sides of the stage. This can total twelve booms for a large production. It is traditional to hang lighting instruments to the side of booms in the theatre, but for dance they

Designing the Lighting

should be mounted straight out from the boom pipes. In this way, the boom will take up as little wing space as possible, allowing more freedom for dancer entrances and exits (often leaps into the wings).

Booms must be clean and safe, with safety ties from the top of the pipe to the grid. Cable to booms will be neatest if run up the boom and onto an electric pipe for circuiting. However, many times floor pockets will have to be used. If this is the case, run the cable straight off-stage from the boom and then turn up- or down-stage to floor pocket locations. Cover the cable with carpeting and tape it securely.

Caution. Inexperienced dancers may try to use light booms as balance bars to warm up. Discourage this practice without being rude.

Color

For most ballet, strong colors are not desirable, but a basic tint certainly is. Pale lavender is frequently used, but for some ballets tradition may prescribe some other tint. Whatever color is selected becomes the neutral for the particular ballet. The other shades work in relation to it, and when blended together on the stage, approximate the neutral. Thus if lavender is the neutral, a violet next to it will appear quite warm and a light blue will appear cool, while the violet and blue together will mix to lavender.

An excellent effect is obtained by use of advancing and receding colors, which add apparent depth to the stage. The use of slightly cooler tints on the upstage dancers will make them appear farther away than they would seem otherwise. Likewise, warmer shades on the downstage dancers will bring them even farther forward. Care must be taken in using this technique, however. The tints must not be so far apart that the dancers visibly change color as they move through the zones.

The use of stronger colors for modern dance, especially in the side lights, is a common technique for expressing mood. Double hanging from the sides with a light tint or no color mixing into a more saturated color can offer the designer much variety.

Cueing and Other Considerations

Cue placement for a dramatic piece is often dictated by the rhythm of the work. This is even more true of dance. Movement nearly always corresponds to the music, and cueing should do the same. The cues for a ballet should be called by the stage manager from the score. The lighting designer should become extremely familiar with the music before beginning the design.

Dancers maintain balance by finding their "center." The lighting designer can help them by placing a "spotting light" or "centering light" in the auditorium. This should be a small 7½- or 15-watt red light located dead center at head height from the stage.

FIGURE 21–9

FIGURE 21–9

Sketch for *Giselle,* Act II

The scale and style of both modern and classical ballet provide unique lighting opportunities. Realistic illumination is of less importance than atmosphere and color. Even classical ballet is a theatrical extension of life into a highly stylized performance technique.

The Dance Plot

Figure 21–10 is a lighting layout designed by Pat Simmons for the second act of the classical ballet *Giselle.* The scene is a wooded bower sheltering Giselle's grave (Figure 21–9) and the color is basic moonlight blue that warms a little as dawn approaches at the end of the ballet.

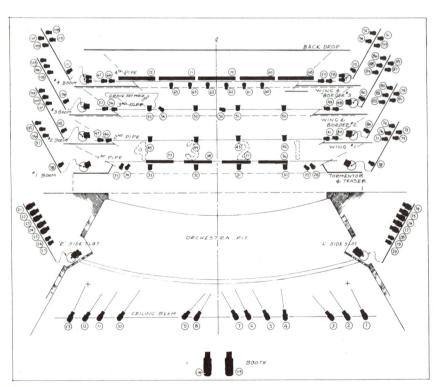

FIGURE 21–10

Lighting Layout for Ballet

(Left) Layout for *Giselle,* Act II. Note that only the down-one zone has been divided into conventional lighting areas. The balance of the plot is more dependent on side, down, and back lighting for effect. (Page 545) *The Instrument Schedule.* All color is Roscolux. (Layout courtesy of Pat Simmons, lighting designer, Pittsburgh Ballet Theatre).

The thirteen front-of-house sources are 8 × 10 ellipsoidals located in the ceiling beam and all colored in Roscolux No. R65 (Daylight Blue). Cross lights from auditorium side slots both left and right are a deeper shade of blue (No. R68—Sky Blue). Pipe-end instruments create a fairly high side light in the same blue used front-of-house, while Fresnel down lights covering the entire dance space are colored in No. R79 (Bright Blue). Six-by-twelve ERS back lights on the fourth pipe are colored in R64 (Light Steel Blue) and R51 (Surprise Pink). These colors, which are slightly less saturated than those examined so far, were chosen to punch through the other color and rim the dancers with light.

The design thus far uses a great deal of blue. But we have yet to look at the all-important side light. Both sides are again colored in R68 with the shin kickers in R64 for increased intensity. Additional side light is added stage left for the slow fade to dawn. These instruments are in R37 (Pale Rose Pink) and R18 (Flame). Two follow spots shoot from the rear-of-house booth. The follow spots will stay with the principals while the corps of dancers and scenery are bathed in blue moonlight.

No	INSTRUMENT	LOCATION	PURPOSE	LAMP	COLOR	REMARKS
1	8X12 ELLIPS'L SPOT	BEAM	AREA 1 DL	1000W QUARTZ	65	
2	"	"	" 2 DLC	" "	65	
3	"	"	" 3 DRC	" "	65	
4	"	"	SPECIAL	" "	CLEAR	QUEEN WILLIE AREA
5	"	"	AREA 3 DR	" "	65	
6	"	"	" 4 DR	" "	65	
7	"	"	" 4 DRC	" "	65	
8	"	"	" 1 DL	" "	65	
9	"	"	" 1 DLC	" "	65	
10	"	"	" 2 DLC	" "	65	
11	"	"	" 2 DL	" "	65	
12	"	"	" 3 DR	" "	65	
13	"	"	" 4 DR	" "	65	
14	8X10 ELLIPS'L SPOT	'L' SLOT	CROSS LT. DS	"	68	CUT OFF BACK DROP
15	"	"	"	"	68	
16	"	"	"	"	68	
17	"	"	"	"	68	
18	"	"	"	"	68	
19	6X14 ELLIPS'L SPOT	"	WASH DS	750W Q	79	CUTOFF ORCH PIT & DROP
20	"	"	"	"	79	
21	8X10 ELLIPS'L SPOT	'R' SLOT	CROSS LT. DS	1000W Q	68	CUT OFF BACK DROP
22	"	"	"	"	68	
23	"	"	"	"	68	
24	"	"	"	"	68	
25	"	"	"	"	68	
26	6X14 ELLIPS'L SPOT	"	WASH DS	750W Q	79	CUT OFF ORCH. PIT & DROP
27	"	"	"	"	79	
28	6X12 ELLIPS'L SPOT	1ST PIPE	PIPE END	750W	65	CUT OFF WINGS
29	"	"	"	"	65	
30	8" FRESNEL	"	DOWN LIGHT	1000W	79	MID-SPOT FOCUS
31	"	"	"	"	79	
32	"	"	"	"	79	
33	"	"	"	"	79	
34	6X12 ELLIPS'L SPOT	"	PIPE END	750W	65	CUT OFF WINGS
35	"	"	"	"	65	
36	6'X6'0 STRIP LIGHT	"	BORDER WASH	150W R-40	65	4-COLOR FEED THRU
37	"	"	"	"	79	
38	"	"	"	"	64	
39	"	"	"	"	20	
40	6X12 ELLIPS'L SPOT	2ND PIPE	PIPE END	750W	65	CUT OFF #2 WING
41	"	"	"	"	65	
42	8" FRESNEL	"	DOWN LIGHT	1000W	79	MID-SPOT FOCUS
43	"	"	"	"	79	
44	"	"	"	"	79	
45	"	"	"	"	79	
46	6X12 ELLIPS'L SPOT	"	PIPE END	750W	65	CUT OFF #2 WING
47	"	"	"	"	65	
48	"	"	3RD PIPE	"	65	CUT OFF #3 WING
49	"	"	"	"	65	
50	8" FRESNEL	"	DOWN LIGHT	1000W	79	MID-SPOT FOCUS
51	"	"	"	"	79	
52	6X9 ELLIPS'L SPOT	"	SPECIAL	750W	62	SOFT FOCUS-GRAVE
53	8" FRESNEL	"	DOWNLIGHT	1000W	79	MID-SPOT FOCUS
54	6X9 ELLIPS'L SPOT	"	SPECIAL	750W	62	SOFT FOCUS-GRAVE
55	8" FRESNEL	"	DOWNLIGHT	1000W	79	MID-SPOT FOCUS
56	6X12 ELLIPS'L SPOT	"	PIPE END	750W	65	CUT OFF #3 WING
57	"	"	"	"	65	

No	INSTRUMENT	LOCATION	PURPOSE	LAMP	COLOR	REMARKS
58	6X12 ELLIPS'L SPOT	4TH PIPE	PIPE END	750W	65	CUT OFF #4 WING
59	"	"	"	"	65	
60	6X12 ELLIPS'L SPOT	"	BACK LIGHT	750W	64	HARD FOCUS
61	"	"	"	"	51	
62	"	"	"	"	64	
63	"	"	"	"	51	
64	"	"	"	"	64	
65	"	"	"	"	51	
66	6X12 ELLIPS'L SPOT	"	PIPE END	"	64	
67	"	"	"	"	64	
68	8'X7'6' STRIP LIGHT	"	BACK DROP WASH	500W QUARTZ	79	4-COLOR FEED THRU
69	"	"	"	"	64	
70	"	"	"	"	20	
71	"	"	"	"	91	
72	"	"	"	"		
73	6X12 ELLIPS'L SPOT	#1 BOOM-L	CROSSLIGHT	750W	37	SHARP FOCUS-IN '1'
74	"	"	"	"	68	
75	"	"	"	"	37	
76	"	"	"	"	68	
77	6X9	"	"	"	68	
78	6X12 ELLIPS'L SPOT	"	SHIN KICKERS	"	64	CUT OFF HEAD
79	6X12 ELLIPS'L SPOT	#2 BOOM-L	CROSSLIGHT	"	37	SHARP FOCUS IN '2'
80	"	"	"	"	68	
81	"	"	"	"	37	
82	"	"	"	"	68	
83	6X9	"	"	"	68	
84	"	"	"	SHIN KICKER	"	64	SHARP FOCUS- OFF HEAD
85	6X12 ELLIPS'L SPOT	#3 BOOM-L	CROSS LIGHT	"	18	
86	"	"	"	"	68	
87	"	"	"	"	68	
88	"	"	"	"	37	
89	6X9	"	"	"	68	
90	"	"	"	SHIN KICKER	"	64	SHARP FOCUS OFF HEAD
91	6X12 ELLIPS'L SPOT	#4 BOOM-L	CROSSLIGHT	"	18	" " IN '4'
92	6X12	"	"	"	68	
93	6X9	"	"	"	37	
94	6X9	"	"	"	68	
95	6X12 ELLIPS'L SPOT	#1 BOOM-R	CROSSLIGHT	750W	68	SHARP FOCUS IN '1'
96	"	"	"	"	68	
97	6X9	"	"	"	68	
98	"	"	"	SHIN KICKER	"	64	SHARP FOCUS OFF HEAD
99	6X12 ELLIPS'L SPOT	#2 BOOM-R	CROSSLIGHT	"	68	" " IN '2'
100	"	"	"	"	68	
101	6X9	"	"	"	68	
102	"	"	"	SHIN KICKER	"	64	SHARP FOCUS OFF HEAD
103	6X12 ELLIPS'L SPOT	#3 BOOM-R	CROSSLIGHT	"	68	" " IN '3'
104	"	"	"	"	68	
105	6X9	"	"	"	68	
106	"	"	"	SHIN KICKER	"	64	SHARP FOCUS OFF HEAD
107	6X12 ELLIPS'L SPOT	#4 BOOM-R	CROSSLIGHT	"	68	" " IN '4'
108	"	"	"	"	68	
109	6X9	"	"	"	68	
110	"	"	"	"	68	
111	"	"	"	SHIN KICKER	"	64	SHARP FOCUS OFF HEAD
112	"	"	#4 BOOM-L	"	"	64	
113	'STRONG' XENON	BOOTH	FOLLOW SPOT			
114	"	"	"			

22

Scenic Projection, Practicals, and Special Effects

LIGHT AS SCENERY

Much has been said and written about the use of light in a supportive role to reveal the actor and illuminate the scene. Light, however, can become the basic element of a production. In recent years the use of light as scenery has reached an extreme height in popularity. Many reasons can be pointed out: (1) the increased use of theatre forms other than the proscenium stage, such as the thrust and arena stages where light is more obviously a major part of the total visual effect; (2) the impact of modern film and video techniques on live theatre as a stimulus for the use of film and multimedia experiments; (3) the tremendous advances in stage lighting technology assisted by the computer revolution; and (4) the more specific and complete training of designers in the use of lighting as a design element.

The consolidation of all these influences has led to a new attitude toward the use of light as a design element in all but the most conventional stage setting.

This new concept of lighting does not mean conventional illumination will disappear. Nor does it mean that scenery and the scene designer will cease to exist. It should also be apparent that flashy lighting does not fit every play or production and that the role of the lighting designer is routinely supportive more often than it is freely innovative.

Light begins to be a scenic element the moment an open source is present on the stage. Such motivating lights as realistic chandeliers and sconces generally bring elegance and high style to the scene. On the other hand, gaudy carousel lights or burlesque runway lights are frankly decorative and theatrical in their impact. Although motivating lights can make a strong visual contribution to the total design, they are a supporting element and normally not the basic scheme of production.

PROJECTED SCENERY

The most familiar and accepted application of light as scenery is through the use of projections. Projections and projected scenery (usually backgrounds) are not new to the theatre. They are as old as the "magic lantern," which entered the theatre in the 1860s, before the incandescent lamp. The early experiments with the projection of moving images, first as crude animations and then later as motion pictures, are well-known events in theatre history. The resurgence of projections in modern theatre is the result not only of improved equipment design but also of a change in attitude toward their use.

Paint versus Light. It is most important to realize that a projection is *light* and not *paint* and that there is a world of difference between the two media. Because color in light is more brilliant than in paint, and has a limited value scale by comparison, its use in a projection is more dramatic and eye-catching. For these reasons, when projections are used as background to substitute for painted scenery, the actor may have to fight for attention. This is not to say that projections do not work as background, for they can, either at controlled levels of intensity or in a highly dramatic situation. The director and designers soon learn that the most successful use of a projection is not as a substitute realistic background, but as a medium of its own, where it expresses itself best in abstract or thematic terms and almost becomes an additional actor.

The inexperienced designer may be tempted to consider projection as a means of saving either time or money. This reasoning is totally fallacious. Good projections require a great deal of effort and often more lead-time than standard theatrical scenery; they must never be considered a last-minute production detail. In addition, projection equipment is very expensive to buy and often difficult to rent.

Both paint and light, as individual mediums of expression, have their advantages and disadvantages. Thus, it is important to realize that one is *not* the substitute for the other. This is one of the places where everyone concerned, the director and the scene and lighting designers, must be in full agreement and completely knowledgeable, or misconceptions will develop that will adversely affect the end result.

FIGURE 22–1

Light as Scenery

(a) The exposed light sources are a part of the visual composition. *Stop the World, I Want to Get Off,* by Leslie Bricusse and Anthony Newley. Set Designer—James Hooks; Lighting Designer—Steve Ross. (b) A curtain of light. The shape of visible light rays turns light into substance and becomes the design form. An early use of high-intensity low-voltage light sources by Josef Svoboda, the Czechoslovak scenographer. Light rays are caught in a special aerosol spray of minute electrostatically charged oil-emulsion droplets capable of staying suspended in the air for a prolonged time. The hyperdense air catches the light and takes on a form of eerie solidity. A light column is the central portion of the design by Svoboda for Wagner's *Tristan und Isolde.* (c) Curtain or walls of light for Verdi's *I Vespri Siciliani (Sicilian Vespers).* (Photos reprinted from *The Scenography of Josef Svoboda* by permission of Wesleyan University Press. Copyright © 1971 by Jarka Burian.) [Continued on page 550]

a

Designing the Lighting

b ↑   c ↓

d

Projection Techniques

Reduced to its simplest elements, the projection process consists of a light source, the object or slide, the projected object or image, and the projection surface most commonly known as the screen, although it is possible to project the image onto almost any type of surface.

The image is projected by two different methods: lens projection or shadow projection. Though both images are shadows in essence, the term shadow projection is used to define all projections obtained without a lens.

The projection apparatus may be placed in front (downstage) of an opaque screen for a front projection, or at the rear (upstage) of a translucent screen for a rear projection. For a front projection the source is normally hidden from view of the audience. It must also be placed so that it has a clear throw onto the screen. In a rear-projection arrangement the problem of hiding the source is solved, although backstage space still has to be kept clear of the throw to the screen (Figure 22–2).

The Shadow Projector

Of the two methods of projection, shadow projection is the easiest to achieve. Because the process depends upon direct emanation from the light source, without lens, the image is not as sharp or intense as a comparable lens projection.

Designing the Lighting

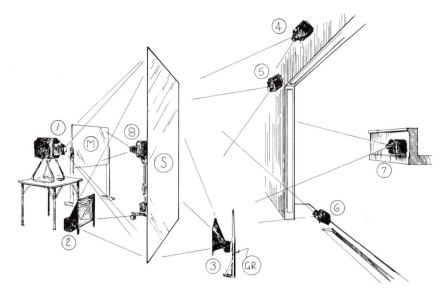

FIGURE 22–2
Screen and Projector Positions

The screen (S) is in the center of the stage. *Rear projections.* (1) Lens projector on platform to align with the center of the screen. (2) Linnebach projector on floor. *Front projections.* (3) Linnebach on floor masked by a groundrow. (4) Center teaser position. (5) High tormentor position. (6) Side apron position. (7) Balcony front. *Rear projection under limited space conditions.* (8) Lens projector angled upstage into a first surface mirror (M), which redirects the image onto the screen.

The Linnebach Projector. The basic instrument for straightline, shadow projection is the familiar device known as the Linnebach Projector (Figure 22–3a). It is a large, plain hood with a source of light—sometimes an arc but more often a high-wattage incandescent lamp—at the center of a system of diverging sides. The outer edge of the hood has a slot for holding the slide.

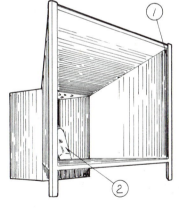

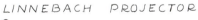

LINNEBACH PROJECTOR
a
b

FIGURE 22–3

(a) The Linnebach Projector. (1) Slide holder. (2) Concentrated-filament T-shaped lamp. (b) Low-voltage, high-intensity Linnebach. A small, specially built shadow projector using a small source for a sharp projection. (1) Section view showing the position and adjustment of light socket. (2) General Electric Quartzline lamp, FCS 24 volts. The lamp, though miniature, is about 250 watts. It was designed for use in photographic studios. Adapted for use on the stage, it requires a variable transformer to reduce voltage. (3) Slide.

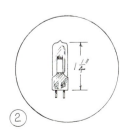

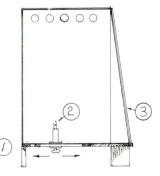

Scenic Projection, Practicals, and Special Effects

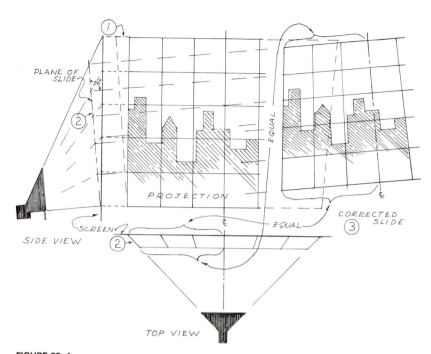

FIGURE 22–4

Correction of Distortion

The Linnebach projector is tilted backward to project the image high on the screen. The plane of the slide is no longer parallel to the screen, resulting in a distortion of all vertical lines in the image. The diagram shows the method of countering the distortion with a corrected slide. (1) Keystoning or distortion of the rectangle. (2) Reference line established in side view parallel to the plane of the slide. It is then located in the top view and vertical line plotted. (3) Corrected grid is constructed perpendicular to the plane of the slide and the verticals are plotted with information from the top view. The corrected slide is drawn into the new grid.

The slide of the Linnebach projector or any variation of shadow projector can be a simple cardboard cutout or painted glass. If the slide is kept parallel to the screen there is no distortion of the image on the screen. It is not always possible to place the instrument and the slide in this ideal relationship, hence the designer must be able to cope with distortion. Once the position of the instrument has been determined image distortion can be corrected by building in a counter distortion in the slide. Distortion on one plane is, of course, easier to correct than on two planes. Figure 22–4 diagrams the methods of correcting simple and complex distortions.

Figure 22–3b illustrates a Linnebach projector using a high-intensity, low-voltage lamp (ANSI Code = FCS). Low-voltage lamps are desirable for shadow projectors because of their reduced filament size. The smaller the lamp filament, the clearer and sharper the image.

The Cinebach Projector. Another variation of the Linnebach is the Cinebach projector, a homemade device that has proved extremely satisfactory for lighting the curved plaster cyclorama of a small stage. In its simplest form it is two D-shaped plywood panels, each about 20 inches wide, fastened about 24 inches apart to a plywood back piece. A sheet of acetate or of plastic color medium, clear or tinted, is tacked around the edges. On the bottom panel is a socket with a large-wattage lamp. Ventilation holes are drilled through both bottom and top panels, and frequently light baffles are built to shield these (see Figure 22–5).

Any sort of design may be painted on the plastic, just as on a conventional Linnebach slide. Because of the curved surface, this device is especially effective for lighting a curved surface and can be valuable even if no more than a plain blue wash is required for a sky. If the Cinebach (which gets its name from the use of Cinemoid as a slide material) is to be placed at the bottom of the curved cyclorama, the top panel may be built smaller than the bottom one to permit the light to spread upward more smoothly.

The Lens Projector

The second and more complex type of instrument for projecting an image is the lens projector. The light source in a lens projector is concentrated on the slide surface by a condensing lens system. The illuminated slide is then transmitted into an image as it passes through the objective-lens system. The size of the image on the screen is determined by the beam-spread capacity of the objective-lens system (focal length). There are adjustments within the system of lenses (lens train) to bring the image of the slide into sharp focus.

Lens projectors used for theatrical performance vary a great deal, and selection depends on the specific application desired. However, there are several guidelines to follow:

1. The longer the throw or the larger the image, the brighter the light source should be.
2. A large slide size will produce a clearer image than a small slide.
3. The larger the slide format, the more expensive and bulky the equipment.

Slide sizes vary from the convenient 35mm (1.346 × 0.902 inches) to the large continental size of 9 × 9 inches.

The Plano-Convex Effect Head. Figure 22–6 (page 554) is an illustration of what once was the lens projector workhorse of the theatre, the effect head. It is an assemblage on the front of a plano-convex spotlight and consists of a condensing lens, slide holder, and objective-lens system. The effect head is so named because it turns an ordinary working spotlight into a lighting instrument that produces effects beyond the spotlight's normal powers of illumination.

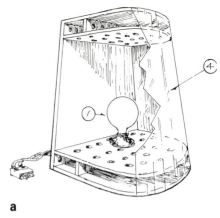

a

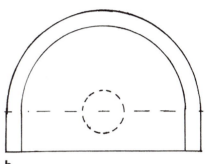

b

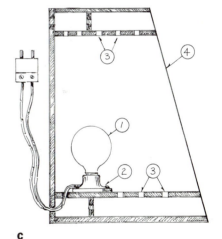

c

FIGURE 22–5

The Cinebach

(a) A pictorial representation. (b) Section. (c) Plan. (1) High wattage lamp. (2) Socket for lamp. (3) Ventilation holes. (4) Curved sheet of clear or colored plastic.

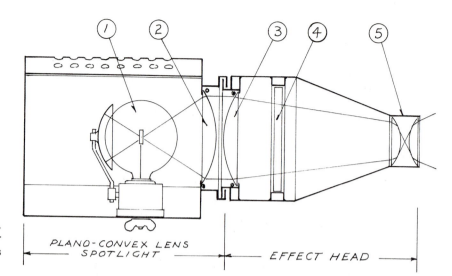

FIGURE 22–6

The Lens Projector

(1) G-shaped lamp. (2) Plano-convex lens. (3) Additional concentrating lens (or "Dutchman"). (4) Slide. (5) Objective-lens system.

PLANO-CONVEX LENS SPOTLIGHT

EFFECT HEAD

There is an additional piece of apparatus that can be applied to the effect head assembly. A drumlike device with a motor drive known as an effect machine can be mounted on the spotlight at the slide position. It provides moving effects such as water ripples, flames, snowflakes, and the like. These are expensive and the results are rather too obvious for the tastes of today's audience.

The "Scene Machine." The "Scene Machine" is a modern imitation of the plano-convex lighting instrument with an effect head (Figure 22–7). This scenic projector, distributed in the United States by The Great American Market, takes a 4 × 5-inch slide and is available with a high intensity 1200-watt or 2000-watt quartz lamp. The projector head (equivalent to the plano-convex spotlight) is sold separately from the slide carrier and objective-lens systems. Lenses are available in focal lengths of 4, 6, 8, 10, 12, and 16 inches. Optional equipment includes a spiral machine, disc machine (which acts as a remote-control slide changer), film machine, and other types of effect heads. Although fairly expensive, this is one of the few useful large-format scenic projectors available in the United States.

The Kodak Carousel Projector. Very few people in this country are unfamiliar with the Carousel projector. While the theatre has used this projector for years, it has only recently become the best choice of 35mm projectors because of its improved lamp. Keep in mind the following valuable bits of information about this lamp and the projector in general:

1   The standard lamp recommended by Kodak is the ELH (300 watt, 30-hour life). An acceptable substitute is the ENG (300 watt, 4-hour life). While the life of the ENG is only a fraction of that of the ELH, its light output is greatly increased. It is the ENG that enables the Carousel to be a viable scenic projection unit.

Designing the Lighting

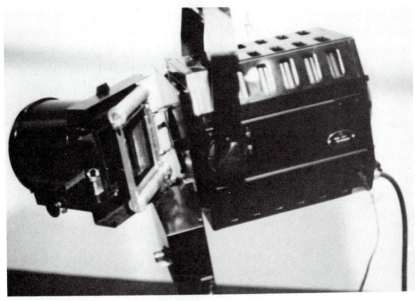

FIGURE 22–7
The "Scene Machine"
Shows film loop rollers. Manufactured by Ryudensha Co., Japan.

2 The Carousel as wired cannot be dimmed because of its fan and slide-changer motor, although Kodak manufactures a dissolve unit which will cross-fade two projectors. However, it is possible to add an external dimmer in-line with the projector's lamp without any sort of rewiring. A two-pin male plug (Radio Shack Cat. No. 274–342) fits into a pair of holes in the rear of the projector and interrupts power to the lamp. Power need only be directed through any remote dimmer of 300-watt or greater capacity. *Caution*: Power is supplied from the projector, through the dimmer, to the lamp—one may not connect the projector to a conventional stage circuit and dimmer without causing a short circuit.

Scenic Projection, Practicals, and Special Effects

3 While Kodak sells a large range of its own lenses, Buhl Optical Co. manufactures an even larger range of superior lenses. Focal lengths of Buhl lenses made to fit the Carousel projector begin at a very wide 1 inch and go to a narrow 9.5 inches. These lenses are available in varying speeds, with the faster lenses being best for scenic projection.

Kodak sells 25-foot extension cables for the projector's remote controller, allowing control over projectors hung over-stage or placed in the auditorium. One final thing to remember is that the Carousel operates on a gravity-feed principle for changing slides. This means that the projector cannot be tilted too much in any direction without danger of slides jamming.

Arc Projection. High-intensity arc lamps mounted in a scenic projector provide a great deal of intensity for long-throw applications. Several arc projectors for both film and slides are available to the theatrical designer, but all have the disadvantage of being impossible to dim (Figure 22–8).

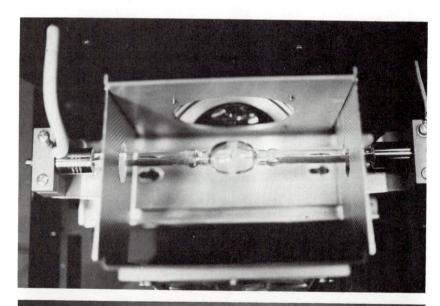

FIGURE 22–8

Short-Arc Lamp Slide Projector

The Metro-lite ME 100 produces a sharp, high-intensity image. (Top) HMI 2500-watt lamp. (Bottom) Projector with top removed showing position of lamp, color filter, slide holder, condensing lens and objective system (George Snell Associates).

556

The Overhead Projector. The most unusual instrument in the lens-projector category is the overhead projector. Its large slide deck (about 12 × 12 inches) is a translucent, horizontal surface with the light source underneath. The slide image, after passing through a vertically mounted objective-lens systems, is redirected by a mirror onto the screen (Figure 22–9).

The advantages of the overhead projector, which was originally designed to animate or illustrate the classroom lecture, are twofold: (1) The large area of the slide permits handpainted slides, allowing the photographic process to be omitted, thereby saving time and money, and (2) the horizontal position of the slide deck provides the opportunity to bring movement to the image. On-the-spot animation is possible by such actions as moving transparent film across the slide deck, agitating with an air jet a shallow transparent dish of colored dyes in oil or water, or blowing smoke across the deck. The movement of smoke across the deck can appear on the screen as a descending fog, rising smoke from a fire, or the engulfing black cloud of an approaching storm.

The overhead projector is not as efficient as a regular lens-projector, but because of its wide-angle objective system it can work close to the screen. It functions best with short-throw, small-image projections.

The overhead projector obviously requires an operator and therefore cannot be used in a remote position. It is best for rear projections, although it has been used for front projections from an extreme off-stage side position.

The Opaque Projector. There is another lens projector that has not been mentioned: the opaque projector. The slide, which is opaque, is reflected by mirrors into the objective-lens system and projected onto the screen. Because the slide is not transparent the image is not as bright; thus, the inefficiency of the instrument renders it impractical for stage use. Its chief use in the theatre is to facilitate the cartooning and painting of scenery. If a drawing bearing a grid of scaled squares is projected to match over a corresponding full-scale grid of a scenic element or drop, it can serve as a quick guide for drawing an enlargement of the original painting.

The Television Projector. The television or video projector is a complex and highly specialized piece of equipment that is capable of projecting a live televised image. It has been used as a dramatic extension of action on stage or of a scene occurring just offstage. Intimate business or emotions expressed by live actors can be supported by simultaneously enlarged television projection elsewhere on the stage.

Gobos. One form of lens projection that does not require any special apparatus other than a common ellipsoidal reflector spotlight is the gobo, also known as a cookie. The gobo is a sheet of highly heat-

FIGURE 22–9
Overhead Projector

Wide-angle overhead projector with a 10 x 10-inch transparent slide deck. The objective-lens system can be operated vertically, as shown, or swung into a horizontal position. The hinged shutters at the top protect the mirror, which is at a 45-degree angle to the slide surface (Buhl Optical).

Scenic Projection, Practicals, and Special Effects

557

a

b

c

resistant material from which some shape, pattern, or design has been cut. When placed at the gate of an ellipsoidal spot, this pattern is projected by the lens (or lenses) onto any appropriate surface.

Commercial equipment houses sell gobos in a variety of designs; some are fairly realistic, but most are simply pleasant patterns. These are frequently used in television, where the background is rarely in sharp focus, to give interest to an otherwise plain drop or wall.

Patterns may be home-designed and cut from heavy aluminum foil or the bottom of a cheap tin pie plate. Two especially useful effects are clouds, cut from foil, which may be wrinkled slightly to give out-of-focus soft edges, and stars, made by pricking tiny holes through a piece of tin kept carefully flat to make all edges sharp. Both are projected in a white light against a blue drop or cyclorama.

Regrettably, neither color nor fine detail can be used at the present because the only transparent material that will withstand the terrific heat at the gate of an ellipsoidal spot is a very expensive clear ceramic requiring special paints and a carefully controlled fixing process not available to the public.

d

e

FIGURE 22–10

Slide Projection Equipment

A few of the many slide and film projectors available for projected scenery. Separated into slide sizes and automatic slide-changing capabilities, they are: (a) Hi-Lite (Buhl Optical) 35mm carousel changer, 1200 watts (incandescent or quartz). A dependable changer, small, good in remote positions. The same projector, a modified Kodak Carousel, can be adapted to a Zenon package for a more brilliant source but less flexible dimming capabilities. (b) Pani 5000-watt scenic projector. Uses 180mm square slides; optional automatic slide magazine available—Strand Century. (c) 5000-watt 7 x 7-inch slide projector. Its one-for-one optics (1-foot coverage at a 1-foot distance) makes it good for wide-coverage rear projections. The 7 x 7-inch slide size is large enough to be hand-painted if desired as well as adaptable to a conventional 5 x 7-inch film size in Ektachrome color transparencies. (d) A 16mm 500-watt Baur film projector with an ECU-RP (Extreme Close Up Rear Projection) lens and a built-in mirror system; lens—Buhl Optical. (e) Film loop projector (moving projection) with speed control; Kliegl Bros. Film Machine (moving projection).

Designing the Lighting

The Mathematics of Projection

To eliminate trial-and-error methods of selecting lenses and placing projectors, the use of the following simple formulas should be understood:

> F = Focal length of lens.
>
> D = Projection throw distance.
>
> S = Slide size.
>
> I = Image size.

$$F = \frac{D \times S}{I}$$

$$D = \frac{F \times I}{S}$$

$$I = \frac{D \times S}{F}$$

Remember that all these distances must be expressed in the same units, usually inches. If the horizontal dimension of the slide is used, the horizontal dimension of the image will be obtained; if the vertical measurement of the image is needed, one must use the vertical measurement of the slide.

The Screen

Aside from the increased efficiency of projection equipment, the innovative exploitation of the screen or projection surface is perhaps the greatest contribution to the imaginative use of light as scenery. Projected scenery has graduated in a very short time from the large single-screen background to multiscreen compositions and to an infinite variety of sizes, shapes, and three-dimensional forms.

Under conditions where time and money are no obstacle the possibilities of the highly dramatic and imaginative use of projection is unlimited. The leader and prime innovator in the development of light as scenery is without a doubt the Czechoslovakian scenographer, Josef Svoboda. His inventive and artistic genius has unlocked traditional scenery and lighting practices and opened the doors to a less restricted attitude toward scene design and lighting.

Figure 22–11 (page 560) illustrates a few of the many screen arrangements and projector positions. They range from a single rear-projection screen, a mixture of both rear- and front-projection screens, multishapes and sizes to three-dimensional front-projection surfaces.

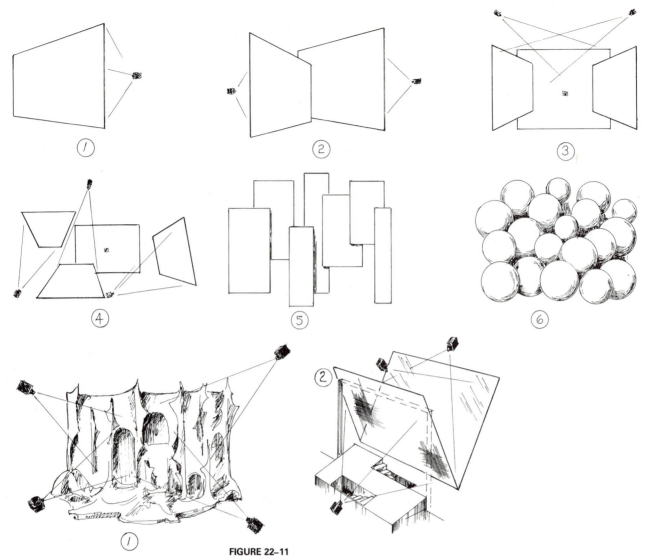

FIGURE 22–11

Projection Screen Arrangements

Rear projections. (1) Single screen. (2) Double rear-projection screen arrangement. (3) Two front-projection screens right and left, with rear-projection screen in center. (4) Multiscreen arrangement. (5) Three-dimensional surface made up of flat planes designed for a single projection. (6) A projection surface of balloons or Styrofoam spheres. (Bottom sketches) (1) Sculptural surface planned for many angles of projection. (2) Slanted surfaces. The downstage screen is scrim, providing the possibility of front, rear, and see-through projections.

Front Projection versus Rear Projection

The single screen, rear-projection technique has been used as background for dramatic productions for some time. The original location of the projector and screen was governed by the need of having an operator, as well as the reluctance to stop thinking of the screen as a painted drop. A rear-projection screen is translucent enough to diffuse the bright spot of the projector's source, yet transparent enough to

FIGURE 22–12
Multiscreen Technique
The use of many screens is best illustrated by the work of the originator, Josef Svoboda. Although the production of *The Journey* repeats the square screen, the technique can involve a variety of screen shapes and sizes, each with its individual slide projector. The screens are deliberately treated as projection surfaces and not as scenic background. The organic harmony or contrasting interplay of the several screens can fluctuate in scenic style from a documentary to a kind of surrealistic reality. (Photos reprinted from *The Scenography of Josef Svoboda* by permission of Wesleyan University Press. Copyright © 1971 by Jarka Burian.)

transmit the image. A professionally made rear-projection screen is constructed with the greatest density in the center to offset the hotspot of the projector source and is polarized to allow for equal distribution of the light. Because of the general high density of a rear-projection screen a lot of light is stopped; consequently a rear projection requires a higher intensity to equal a similar projection from the front.

Scenic Projection, Practicals, and Special Effects   **561**

Front projections have become more popular and practical for two reasons: the first, which has been mentioned frequently, is the change in attitude from thinking of projections as a substitute for painted scenery, and second, the great improvement in the efficiency and reliability of remote-control projection equipment.

Front projection does have the disadvantage of having to throw from a more extreme angle or a greater distance than does a rear projection because of the necessity of hiding the instrument from the view of the audience.

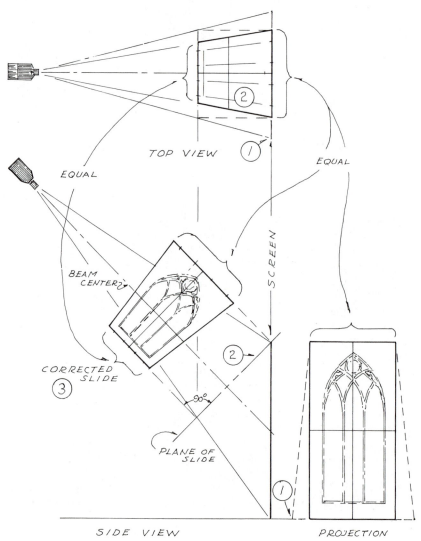

FIGURE 22–13

Distortion Correction for a Lens Projection

The projection position is perpendicular to the screen in top view but angled in the side view, resulting in a keystone distortion (1) of the image. Reference line (2) is constructed parallel to the plane of the slide. The counter distortion is plotted in the top view of the slide plane (2). The corrected slide (3) is drawn perpendicular to the reference plane with information from the top view.

Designing the Lighting

Distortion. The extreme angle of a front projection also causes distortion problems. They are not insurmountable but do necessitate extra drawing for the scene designer. If the slide is to be a photographed transparency, the designer has to make two designs. The first is the projection as it is to appear free of distortion, and the second shows the built-in counter distortion that is to be photographed and processed into a color transparency for the slide. If the slide is not too small or too detailed it can be painted directly on the slide glass using the same counter-distortion control. The correction process for one-plane distortion is diagramed in Figure 22–13. The corrected grid on the slide should, however, always be checked under actual conditions before painting or photographing any quantity of slides.

To demonstrate distortion-correction solutions for projections involving two-plane distortion, a small, mixed-media production of Elmer Rice's *The Adding Machine* is shown in Figure 22–14 (page 564). The steps taken to make the slides for a pair of sharply angled front-projection machines are depicted. The expressionistic style of the play allowed for the strong visual statement of projections as an extension of the actor. Larger productions, more screens, or different angles of projections would follow the same approach for distortion solutions.

Not all distortions need to be corrected. There are times when the distortions of an angled projection are accepted as part of the design, especially if the slide is abstract or nonobjective in style.

Projections and the Actor

The lighting of the actor in relation to a projected background is very tricky and varies with the direction of the projection, front or rear. Any projection suffers from reflected light on the front of the screen, which tends to wash out the intensity of colors and design in the image. Care must be taken to choose angles to light the actor that will not reflect off the floor onto the screen (Figure 22–15, page 566).

In addition to the control of distribution, bounce light can be minimized in other ways: (1) The reflective quality of the floor can be deadened with a cover of black or dark gray felt or carpeting; or (2) reflected light can be kept off the screen by hanging a seamless black scrim about a foot in front. It serves to absorb the reflected light but does not affect the quality of the image.

The reflected light problem can also be helped by the design and position of the screen or the image on the screen. If, for example, the screen or the image on the screen begins about 4 feet or more above the floor, it is less likely to suffer from bounce light. This elevation coupled with the directing technique of keeping actors away from the screen by maintaining a so-called neutral zone of about 4 feet makes it easier to light the actor and not lose the intensity of the projection.

Back lighting and side lighting are especially helpful in separating the actor from a projected background. Otherwise, it is difficult com-

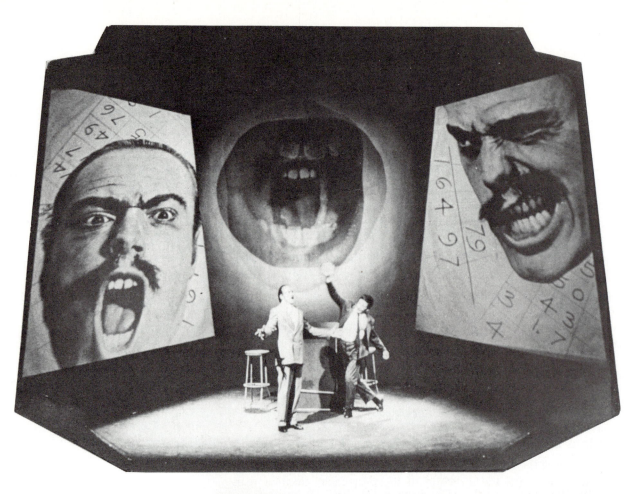

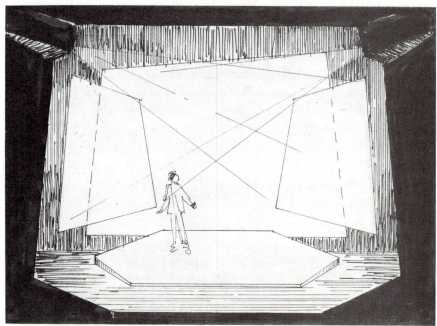

Designing the Lighting

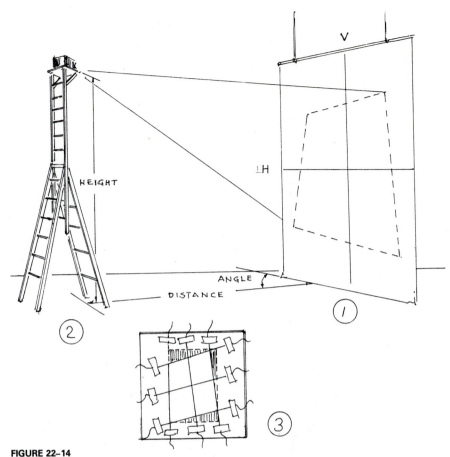

FIGURE 22–14

Projected Scenery

To illustrate the planning and execution of projected scenery, an all-projection production of Elmer Rice's expressionistic play *The Adding Machine* is illustrated. (Left, top) The pulsating images on the screen heighten the action in the scene. (Bottom) Sketch of the screen arrangement. Three screens were used, two small downstage front-projection screens backed by a large rear-projection screen. (Above) Sketch showing the method used to figure the counterdistortion of the front-projection slides caused by the steep angle of projection. (1) A temporary screen was hung at the site of the finished screen. The shape of the planned screen was drawn on the temporary surface with established horizontal (H) and vertical (V) center lines. (2) The right projector position at the top of the ladder duplicated the distance, height, and angle of the final mounting position in the upper stage right of the portal. (3) Taped threads on a clear 35mm slide were moved by trial and error until the projection of the threads matched the outline and cross lines on the screen. The projector was tilted slightly to bring one projected edge of the slide into alignment with the upstage edge of the screen.

positionally to balance the intensity of the background and the area lights without one or the other becoming dull.

The use of front projections allows greater creativity in the design of the screen. It may be three-dimensional or it may be pierced, to permit action behind or through the screen. In a more practical vein, the screen position can be farther upstage, thereby giving more space to the actor and providing for an occasional scenic element.

Scenic Projection, Practicals, and Special Effects

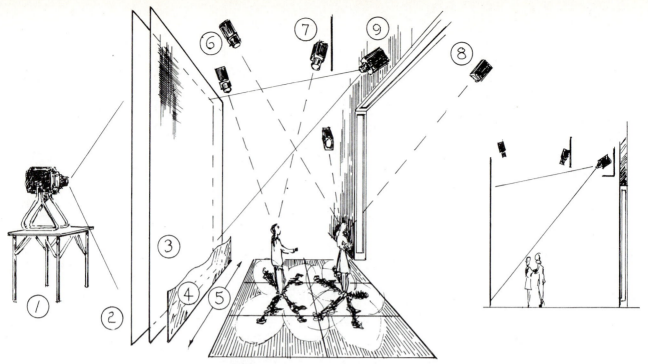

FIGURE 22–15

Projections and the Actor

The effective use of large-scale projections as a background requires special lighting techniques. To avoid undue spill of reflected light onto the screen, the acting-area lights are kept at a steep angle along with the obvious use of back and cross lighting to throw the actors' shadows away from the screen. (Left) Diagram of a rear-projection setup. (1) Rear-projection machine. (2) Rear-projection screen. (3) Black scrim drop hung in front of screen to absorb reflected light from the front. (4) Groundrow or screen frame to kill light reflected from the floor. (5) Unit area, called neutral zone, about 3 or 4 feet in front of screen. (6) Back light on actor to help define him against a projected background. Note top hat or funnel on the front of the spotlight to prevent a flare of light onto the screen. (7) Sharply angled upstage-area spotlights to keep light and shadows off screen. (8) Front-area ceiling spotlight. The normal angle is usually good. (9) Center teaser position for front projection. (Right) Front-projection setup. The lighting of the actor remains the same. The black scrim is removed to allow projections from the teaser position. Note the angle of front projection. It is planned to miss actors at the edge of the neutral zone.

Front projections can also frankly involve the actor as a projection surface or use the shadow that he or she casts as a part of the image. The imaginative mixture of light, projections, and performers is so successfully executed by Alwin T. Nikolais and his dancers that their performances are both a stimulating experience in the theatrical form of sight and sound and epitomize light as scenery (Figure 22–16).

Light as a Scheme of Production

In his productions of Wagner's *Tristan und Isolde* and Verdi's *I Vespri Siciliani* (*Sicilian Vespers*), Josef Svoboda uses light as a scheme of production (Figure 22–1). Another quite different but equally effective use of light and projection is shown in Figure 22–17 (pages 568–569). These illustrations and photographs are from the English National Opera's 1979 production of Britten's *The Turn of the Screw.*

Designing the Lighting

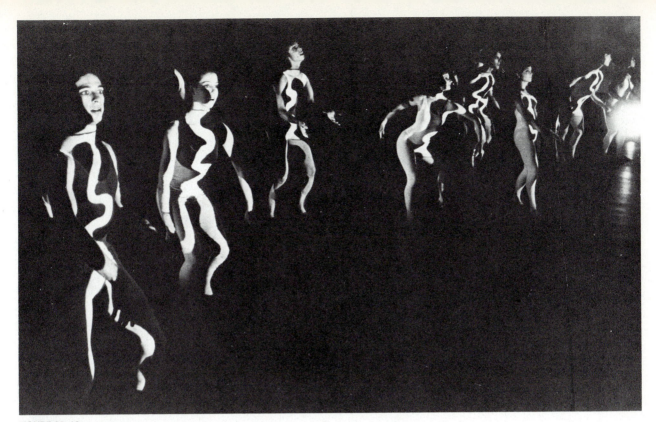

FIGURE 22–16
Projections on the Actor
The abstract form of the dance adapts easily to the unconventional use of projections on the actor or performer, thereby heightening theatricality and visual impact. *Scenario,* a production of the Nikolais Dance Theater (Photo—Oleaga).

The expanded metal screens shown in Figure 22–17a were reception surfaces for both front and rear projection. Kodak Carousel projectors and Pani 5000 watt projectors as well as Strand's Patt 752 projectors were all employed from front-of-house, stage-left and stage-right wings, and backstage. Note the extremely effective use of texture on the stage floor in Figure 22–17.

PRACTICALS

Practicals refer to on-stage working light sources such as lanterns, lamps, fireplaces, or candles. The wiring and maintenance of such units are the responsibility of the electrical department, and their use is sure to be a concern of the lighting designer. Playwrights or directors will call for practicals for any of several reasons:

1 The particular light given off by a practical will enhance the desired mood of a scene.
2 The use of a practical will indicate time of day, season, or even period.
3 Practicals help reinforce the reality of a scene or location.

Scenic Projection, Practicals, and Special Effects

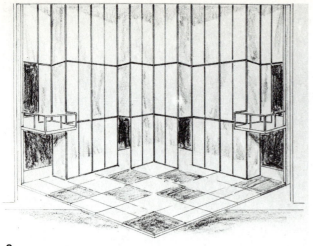

a

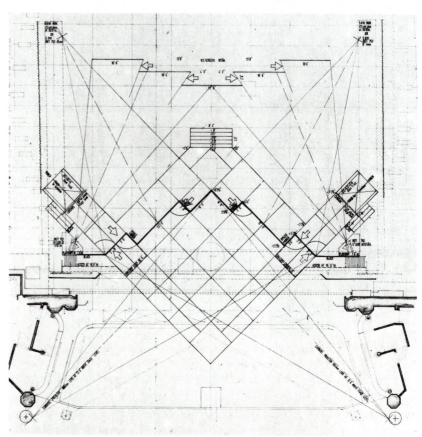

b

FIGURE 22–17

Light as a Scheme of Production

Bly, a gloomy Victorian country house, is the locale for the English National Opera's production of *The Turn of the Screw* by Benjamin Britten. The eerie mood of the opera lends itself to the extremely effective use of projected scenery as the action moves rapidly through fifteen variations. (a) Line drawing shows the arrangement of screens that form the basic setting. A third screen, upstage, occasionally adds

c

greater depth to the composition. The surface of the basic set is an expanded metal screen allowing projections from the front and rear as well as a clear view of the upstage screen when necessary. Walls perpendicular to the two major planes were covered with mylar mirror to reflect the image of the projection. (b) Floor plan shows relationship of screens and location of projectors. (c) Photographs of two of the many variations. Scene Designer—Patrick Robertson, Lighting Designer—David Hersey. Projections were by Mr. Robertson. (Photos—courtesy Noel Staunton, Technical Director, English National Opera, London Coliseum)

Scenic Projection, Practicals, and Special Effects

One rule to remember in dealing with practicals is that whenever possible they should be controlled by dimmers. Never allow an actor to switch on a major motivating practical and then expect your light board operator to support it on cue—it simply doesn't work.

Fire Effects

Open fires are rarely convincing on the stage. Yet play after play calls for them. If it is possible to design the setting so that the hearth is located in a side wall, reasonably good results can be attained by simply letting a flickering light move over the far corner of the fireplace. Even this must be kept at low intensity so as not to take attention from the actors.

All too often the demands of the script force the designer to put a fire in full view of the audience. If no flames are required, then a mere glow, through crumpled gelatin (orange and red), broken glass splashed with translucent orange paint, or the like, will suffice. If flames must be shown, then a glow on some form of rising smoke, or on thin streamers of chiffon or China silk, blown upward by a small fan, can be used. Another method of simulating fire from a fireplace is to use a slowly rotating drum covered with crumpled foil and painted in various fire colors. Lights mounted above the drum in the hearth and out of audience sight are then trained upon the turning cylinder. The designer can also go to the extremes of using a color organ or one of the several available flicker generators hooked up to various colored low-wattage lamps.

In every case, however, the designer is placed on the horns of this dilemma: whether to make the fire effects so realistic as to grab the attention of the audience or so phony as to arouse their ridicule. It must be stated emphatically that, on the whole, the less fire effect you can get away with, the more fortunate you and your production will be.

Flames. Torches are particularly difficult to simulate. Perhaps a flashlight hidden in the handle and focused on streamers of very light silk is as good a solution as any, but it is not very convincing, even when the torch is stationary and the silk can be blown upward by a hidden fan. Perhaps a smoke device can be incorporated and the flashlight trained on its fumes. If real flame is necessary, a can of Sterno is securely mounted in the top of the torch, but liquid fuel must never be used.

Oil-burning lanterns should never be used on the stage. To begin with, their use is strictly against all fire rules and insurance regulations. A real hazard is presented by their use, for in case of accident the stage will become flooded with blazing oil. Fortunately, oil lanterns conventionally have glass chimneys which can be realistically smoke-stained to hide a small lamp bulb placed inside.

If the lantern is never moved during the action, it can be connected to the regular stage wiring and dimmed up and down from the control board. Of course, actors, when pretending to adjust the wick, or touch a match to it, or whatever, must always be careful to mask this fakery by placing their bodies between the lantern and the audience until the process of dimming has been completed. If a lantern is to be carried about the stage a battery must be hidden within it and a silent switch provided for the actor to control.

Candles. Unlike oil lanterns, candles, which usually extinguish themselves when dropped, are permissible on most stages if properly handled. In some locations they must be encased in transparent mica shields. If you have any doubts about the legality of using candles on stage, consult the local authorities. In no case should candles be placed near draperies or other easily flammable materials, including human hair and frilly costumes.

Even if candles are allowed, however, they probably should be avoided, for their bright light and particularly their flickering at the smallest breath of air can be most distracting for the audience. Very effective faking of candles can be done by means of a small battery or pencil flashlight hidden in a white paper tube. A tiny lamp on the top, with a twist of colored gelatin about it gives a steady and quite convincing glow.

Lighting Fixtures

Chandeliers, wall sconces, table lamps, and similar household lighting fixtures generally offer no vast problems except for the wattage of the lamps actually used in them. Such fixtures should never be counted on to produce all the light that seems to emanate from them. Frequently they are in quite the wrong locations to light the faces of the actors playing near them, so additional illumination must be provided by spotlights especially mounted for the purpose, or the acting area lights may be varied to give the effects desired.

This is particularly true when the fixtures have bulbs visible to the audience, for these, if at all bright, will throw a most annoying (even blinding) glare. Such bare bulbs must always be of extremely low wattage, and even then may have to be dimmed still further. Obviously little light will emanate from such fixtures, so the extra instruments become doubly important.

But if the bulbs are shielded by shades, then the glare is hidden and extra large-wattage lamps may be used to give a more realistic effect on an already bright stage. Such shades must be quite opaque, of course, or brown paper linings can be put inside them. Often an additional baffle must be placed over the bulb to prevent an unsightly hot spot on the walls and ceiling of the setting.

SPECIAL EFFECTS

All uses of light that are not directly involved in lighting the actor or illuminating the scene may be grouped in the category of special effects. Examples include explosions, fires, ghosts, or psychedelic lighting. Working out special effects is almost always enjoyable but can take a great deal of time. They should not be left to the end as an afterthought.

Moon and Stars

Some day a playwright undoubtedly will call for a realistic sun on the stage! Until then we have quite enough trouble with the moon and stars that are so often required. If the background is in the form of a cloth drop or cyclorama, quite a realistic moon can be devised by cutting the desired shape—fully round or crescent—into a large sheet of thin material such as cardboard or plywood, which is pressed firmly against the back of the drop. A small spotlight is then focused on the cutout from the rear. If the background is not a cloth, then a projection from an effects machine or an ellipsoidal reflector spotlight with an iris or a gobo may be used from the front.

Stars can be quite effective, but are tricky to handle. The tiniest bulbs obtainable look like great blobs of light against a darkened sky. It is advisable to tape these over; a mere pin-prick will pass enough light. If a dark-blue gauze or scrim is hung a few feet in front of the sky drop, it will help cut down excessive brightness and also will hide the wiring to the star bulbs. When the cyclorama is a permanent one of plaster or wood, tiny holes are often drilled through it and clips provided on the back to hold the little lamps in place. Usually for such effects, strings of low-voltage lamps can be bought at any hobby shop together with an appropriate transformer. Even Christmas tree strings can be used.

Stars can be projected from the front but, unless they are done by the gobo technique, they are rarely convincing, for even the best slide equipment reproduces them as large and somewhat indistinct smudges of light. For unrealistic, stylized effects, both stars and moon can be projected by a Linnebach with good results.

Lightning

Lightning is a device in many plays. Fortunately, it is usually not necessary to show forks of light springing from the sky, but only the sudden, rapid, and irregular bursts of high illumination as seen through windows or coming from the wings. By striking and breaking the contacts rapidly, a carbon arc can be used to give excellent results for this purpose. In fact a so-called arc striker that makes this even easier to handle is available commercially.

Another method is to switch rapidly on and off a number of small sources. It is better to use a striplight with many white and daylight-blue lamps of low wattage than a single large source which would respond more slowly to the irregular, staccato timing of typical lightning. A special switch may be devised to make the closing and the opening of the circuit easier to control.

Large photoflash bulbs, although fairly expensive, create a wonderfully bright burst of light. They can be mounted in an old plano-convex housing (with or without lens) or a simple tin can to avoid unwanted spill. Some photoflood lamps have a quick response time and also deliver a good deal of intensity.

If the lightning flash has to be seen against the sky, a projection must be used. Because of the slow response of the high-wattage lamp, it is well to have the instrument already turned on and an operator stationed at it to reveal and conceal the beam of light by means of a cap or other masking device. And several different slides should be provided, rather than show the same shaped flash again and again. Scratches on black-painted slides can be drawn quite realistically for these.

Explosions and Flashes

To produce these offstage, in the wings, the same general techniques can be applied as were suggested for lightning flashes, with the addition of mechanically produced noises when required. But for the same effects on the stage, in view of the audience, a flash pot is necessary.

A good flash pot consists of a metal pan with a tight-fitting wire screen over it. The bottom is covered by a piece of asbestos board, to which two electric terminals are fastened (small brass screws will do very nicely) but they must be carefully insulated from the box itself or a short circuit will develop. The two terminals may be about 1 inch apart. They are connected respectively to the two wires of a circuit that also contains a switch. Between the two terminals a single, very thin strand of copper wire is strung, wound firmly around each screw and lying flat on the asbestos board. A small quantity of flash powder is poured over this wire, covering all portions of it. When the switch is closed, the thin wire will burn out, igniting the powder. After each use the wire and powder must be replaced.

A variation of the flash box uses a fuse of very low amperage set in an appropriate fuse clip or socket. The fuse is cut open—in the case of a plug fuse by prying out the isinglass window—with a cartridge fuse by cutting away part of the paper cover. Care is taken not to damage the fuse link. The resulting cavity is then filled with the flash powder. As with the flash box, the opened fuse and the powder must be renewed after each use.

Flash powder, when set off in this way, gives a good burst of light, but little smoke. If smoke is desired, some sal ammoniac powder may be mixed with the flash powder. In any case, the flash device must be well protected with a screen and should never be fired close to flammable materials or to people.

Caution. Flash pots are extremely dangerous. Serious injury can happen if they are misused. It is a good precaution to include a low-wattage warning lamp in-line with the flash pot cable and close to the box itself. The lamp burning will indicate that the box is "live" and dangerous.

And a most important warning: *very little powder should be used at one time—and it should never be tamped down,* but poured loosely into place.

A commercial flash pot system called "Pyro-Pack" is available and tends to be safer than the older flash boxes. A number of dramatic effects can be achieved by using this system.

Fog and Smoke Effects

Many devices are used to produce smoke on the stage, but none is completely satisfactory. Perhaps the best known is sal ammoniac powder, which after a few moments in a hot plate or in a heating cone will give off a good volume of white smoke. In ordinary quantities this is neither too odorous nor dangerous to breathe, but if allowed to become too dense, it can be very unpleasant. Cinnamon powder may be added to sweeten the smell for the actors. Sal ammoniac powder has disadvantages. It cannot be started suddenly, nor can it be stopped on cue. It is also extremely corrosive on the producing elements.

Titanium tetrachloride combines with the moisture present in the air to give off a thin smoke that rises well. By adding a little water to it, or dropping a pinch of the powder into water, an instant response is produced that can be very effective, though the fumes are dangerous if breathed in quantity.

Dry ice can be dropped into water for a small quantity of smoke, but this tends to fall instead of rise. Dry ice may be quite effective in a fog machine (a metal drum with a heating element to keep the water from freezing when the solid carbon dioxide is lowered into it). If the drum is provided with a cover, quite a flow of fog can be produced suddenly and directed around the stage by means of a hose (Figure 22–18).

Smoke bombs are very smelly, impossible to control, and leave a greasy coating on the scenery and costumes. Steam is clean, but requires special piping and produces a loud hissing that makes it impractical for quiet scenes.

One device for generating smoke seems to be superior to any of the others mentioned. It consists of a container which is filled with a special liquid in which a heating coil is submerged. A handle for easy carrying is provided, and a plunger to pump the smoke about the stage at the desired rate and intensity. This mist tends to rise, but a

Designing the Lighting

FIGURE 22–18

Fog Machine

Solid carbon dioxide or dry ice changes state from a solid to a vapor without becoming a liquid. The rapidity of the change is increased when dry ice is submerged in hot water. The result is an almost instantaneous cloud of dense fog. (Center left) Assembled fog machine. (Left) Top removed showing dry ice basket on end of the plunger. (Center right) View into the tank revealing electric heating element to heat water. (Bottom left) Loading basket with crushed dry ice. (Bottom right) The plunging of the dry ice in hot water produces a blanket of fog. (Pictures courtesy Richard Thompson)

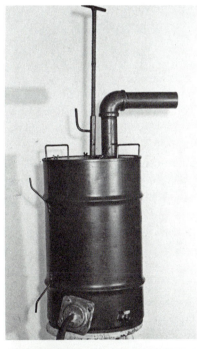

FIGURE 22–19

Portable Fog Machine

Small, lightweight tank vaporizes "fog juice" with electric heat. Fog is dense, white, and dissipates quickly. Basket can be attached to front of machine with dry ice to slow dissipation. Machine develops enough pressure to fill the stage very quickly. It can also be forced through PVC tube to remote parts of the stage. (Distributor—Mutual Hardware)

cage is provided that may be filled with dry ice and fastened over the nozzle of the container. When this is done, the fumes hug the floor. Plastic hose hidden about the stage has proved an easy way to make this mist appear wherever wanted. A second fluid may be used to help disperse the smoke, and several essences are available to scent it pleasantly. Their value is strictly a matter of individual taste. Actually, the fumes are not dreadfully unpleasant (Figure 22–19).

Controlling Smoke. Anyone using smoke of any nature on the stage is frequently faced with the problem of preventing it from flowing or blowing to where it is not wanted. Heavy fog that tends to hug the stage floor may easily spill over the footlights into the auditorium—a touch that is seldom appreciated by the audience.

The lighter-than-air smoke that rises is subject to the slightest breeze or draft. A ventilator at the top of the stage house may draw it swiftly upward, a cross-draft may set up eddies and swirls, while an exhaust fan that evacuates stale air from the auditorium can bring the smoke billowing into the house.

Ultraviolet Effects

One field in which it is impossible to surpass the carbon arc follow spot is in the use of ultraviolet effects. Because the output from this instrument is rich in these very short waves, a black-light filter that removes practically all the visible waves will still permit the ultraviolet ones to pass through in good quantity. Objects painted with a medium susceptible to such waves will glow under this stimulus and, if all other light is removed from the stage, weird and unworldly effects can be achieved.

Glossary

Arc Light A spotlight that has for its source an electric current arcing between two electrodes.

Amperage The rate of flow of an electric curent through a conductor. The capacity of an electrical conductor.

Angstrom A unit of length used to specify wavelengths of light.

ANSI American National Standards Institute. The ANSI Code is a three-letter code used to identify lamps.

Asbestos Fire-retardant curtain located at the proscenium opening.

Avista Change of scene or movement of scenery in full view of the audience.

Back Cloth English theatre expression for back drop.

Backstage Much the same as *offstage* but used generally in reference to stage workers and stage machinery rather than to actors.

Bag Line Pick-up or bull line on a sandbag to lift the weight of the bag while trimming or clewing a line-set.

Barn Doors A device consisting of two or four hinged metal flaps which is placed in front of a spotlight to reduce the beam spread in one or more directions.

Batten (1) Pipe batten. Horizontal pipe hung from a line-set of a flying system. (2) Wooden batten. Top and bottom of roll drop.

Beam Port A front-of-house lighting position located in the ceiling of the theatre.

Blackout The instantaneous killing of all stage lights.

Bleeding Brightly colored undercoat of paint showing a second coat.

Bloom Specular reflection from mirror or highly polished surface.

Boards Slang for stage.

Book Set a two-fold of scenery in an open-book position.

Boom or **Boomerang** A vertical pipe for mounting spotlights.

Bounce Reflected diffuse light off the floor or walls.

Box Booms Lighting booms located in front-of-house box-seat positions.

Break To fold or unfold scenery.

Breakaway Scenery or properties rigged to break on cue.

Breast Line Fixed line to wall or gridiron that drags or breasts a piece of hanging scenery into an excentric position. Also called a *drag line*.

Bridle Means of dividing the load of each liftline by spreading the pick-up points along the batten.

Bull Line Heavy four-stranded hemp rope used on a winch to lift uncounterweighted scenery.

Bumper (1) Low platform downstage of portal against which castered wagons bump. (2) Metal hoop fastened to a batten carrying lighting instruments to protect them from flying scenery and the scenery from hot instruments.

Bump-up Sudden movement of lights to a higher intensity.

Channel A lighting control path. *Channel* replaces the term *dimmer* in modern usage.

Circuit Established paths of electricity.

Clewing Several lines are held together by knots or clew for handling as a single line.

Company Switch A distribution panel with hook-up terminals to supply the power for a traveling company's switchboard. Usually three-wire 220 volts, 600 amps on a side.

Cross Fade To fade from one lighting set-up to another without going through a dimout.

Cue A visual or audible signal from the stage manager to execute a predetermined movement of lights or scenery.

Cyc Short for cyclorama.

Cyc Knuckle Hardware for attaching side arms of a cyc batten to a regular pipe batten.

Dark House No performance or inactive theatre.

Deck Stage floor.

Diffusion A plastic medium placed in the color holder of a spotlight to break up the light in a variety of ways.

Dim Change the intensity of a light, either brighter or less bright.

Dimmer Apparatus for altering the flow of electric current to cause a light to be more or less bright.

Dimmer-per-Circuit A system in which an individual dimmer is permanently assiged to each stage circuit.

Disappearance Trap Special counterweighted elevator trap used as a quick exit or disappearance by an actor.

Disconnect *see* Company switch.

Dolly A type of wagon.

Donkey Electric winch.

Douser Mechanical means of putting out a light.

Downstage The area nearest the footlights and curtain.

Draw Line Operating line of a traveler curtain rigging.

Dutchman (1) Condensing lens in a lens projector. (2) Scab or mending cleat. (3) Cloth strip covering a hinged joint.

Edge-up Framed scenery maneuver; raise a flat upright on its edge.

EMF Electromotive force or voltage.

End for End Reverse the position of an object.

ERF Stage jargon for ellipsoidal reflector floodlights.

ERS Stage jargon for ellipsoidal reflector spotlights.

Feel-up Take slack out of lift lines prior to setting the trim.

FEV Short for French Enamel Varnish.

Fill Light Wash or soft light that fills in the light on the face from the direction opposite the key light.

Flag Small piece of cloth inserted into the lay of the purchase line as a trim mark.

Flat In the commercial theatre, the stiffening of two or more hinged wings into a flat plane or wall.

Flipper Jog hinged to a single wing.

Floatdown Kitelike action when a flat is allowed to fall or float to the floor.

Flood Widespread focus on a spotlight. Also, short for floodlight.

Floodlight A lighting instrument that produces a broad spread of light. Often misapplied to other lighting apparatus.

Focus (1) The direction in which a lighting instrument is aimed. (2) Adjustment of the size or shape of a light beam.

FOH Front-of-house. Anything located on the audience side of the proscenium arch.

Follow Cue A cue timed to follow an original cue so quickly it does not warrant a separate cue number.

Follow Spot A high-intensity, long throw spotlight requiring an operator in order to follow action on stage.

Footcandle The measurement of illumination; the amount of light from one candle that will fall on a surface one foot from the candle.

Fresnel (correctly pronounced Fre' nel) A lens recognized by its concentric rings. The spotlight designed to use this lens.

Front Lighting Illumination on the stage from instruments placed in the auditorium.

Frost *see* Diffusion.

Funnel Also known as a top hat. A short metal cylinder placed in front of a spotlight to reduce the beam spread.

Gobo A metal cutout used with a spotlight to obtain a patterned beam.

Grand Drape Decorative first border in old proscenium-type theatres.

Greek-it Fake lettering that has no meaning; doubletalk.

Grip Stagehand.

Gripping Running scenery on the floor by stagehands or grips.

Halation Undesirable spreading of light from a spotlight. A halo of light around the beam.

Head Block Multigrooved pulley or multipulley sheave in a line-set.

Head Spot Very narrow beam from a spotlight focused on an actor's head. Also called *pin spot*.

Hook-up A lighting schedule which lists instruments by dimmer number.

House Curtain Main curtain of a proscenium theatre designed to tie in with the house decorations. Also called act curtain.

IA Short for IATSE—International Alliance of Theatrical Stage Employees. The stagehands' union.

In-one Foremost downstage acting position, traditionally in front of oleo.

Interconnect A flexible system allowing the electrical connection of any stage circuit with any dimmer. Also called patch panel.

Iris Mechanical means of closing the aperture of a spotlight.

Jack Framed brace to hold scenery upright.

Jackknife Pivoting wagon movement like the action of blades in a jackknife.

Jog Narrow-width wing.

Juice Commercial slang for electricity.

Jumper Cable connecting two or more lighting instruments.

Key Light Accent or highlight on actor's face, usually from the direction of the motivating light for the scene.

Keystoning Distortion of a projected image when the projector is oblique to the screen.

Klieglight A type of spotlight sold by Kleigl Bros. *Klieg* is often used as a synonym for any bright light.

Knife Steel guide for a tracked wagon.

Ladder Hanging ladderlike frame for mounting spotlights.

Lamp (1) Correctly, the name of what is often called a light bulb. (2) In the commercial theatre the term for any lighting instrument, particularly a spotlight.

Lead Cable from power supply.

Left Stage To the actor's left as he or she faces the audience.

Lekolite A type of spotlight sold by Century-Strand. *Leko* is often used as a generic term for any ellipsoidal reflector spotlight.

Light Leak Unwanted spill from an instrument or through scenery.

Line Set A group of from three to five lines using the same head block to lift a pipe batten or unit of scenery.

Lip A beveled three-ply strip attached so as to overhang the edge of a framed unit of scenery and thereby conceal the open crack of a joint with an adjacent unit.

Load Lamp or instrument.

Loft Block Individual pulley on the gridiron of a line set.

Lumen Intensity measurement of a source of light.

Make-up Put together a setting.

Mask Conceal from the audience, usually by scenic pieces or neutral hangings, any portion of the backstage area or equipment.

Mat Shutter or matting material over the face of a spotlight to change the shape of the beam.

Muling Block Pulley to change the horizontal direction of a moving line.

Offstage Out of sight of the audience. Away from the center of the stage.

Ohm An electrical measurement of resistance in a circuit.

Ohm's Law A statement of the relationship of current, electric potential, and resistance in a circuit. It may be expressed by the equation: $I = \dfrac{E}{R}$.

Oleo Traditionally the in-one backdrop. A decoratively painted ad-drop from vaudeville days.

Olivette Old stand floodlight.

On and Off Referring to scenery sitting parallel to the footlights.

Onstage In sight of the audience. Toward the center of the stage.

P and OP Promp and Opposite Promp. An English and old American method indicating the left and right side of the stage. *Promp* was the side of the prompter or stage manager.

PAR Short for parabolic aluminized reflector lamp.

PAR Head Slang for PAR 64 lighting instrument.

Patch Panel *see* Interconnect.

P-C Plano convex lens or lighting instrument.

Peek Expose the backstage or see past masking.

Picture The general composition of the setting as seen from the average sightline seat.

Pigtail Short length of lead cable.

Pin Spot *see* Head spot.

Plot Short for lighting plot.

Practical Descriptive of something that can be used by the actor, like a window sash that can actually be raised or a light that can be switched on and off.

Pre-set (1) A pre-arranged lighting set-up held in readiness for later use. (2) Preposition scenery that will be revealed later in the scene.

Prop Short for *property*. Also refers to anything not real or practical.

Purchase Line Flyman's operating line in a counterweight system.

Quartz-iodine Early name for what is now known as the tungsten-halogen lamp.

Raked Scenery or stage floor angled to the footlights.

Return Element of scenery that returns the downstage edge of the setting offstage to the right or left.

Right Stage To the actor's right as he or she faces the audience.

Roundel A glass color filter for lighting instruments.

RPF Short for Rigid Plastic Foam. Styrofoam.

RUF Short for Rigid (Poly)Urethane Foam.

Sandbag Counterweight for pin-and-rail flying system.

Scenography (In European theatre, **scenographie**) Literally, the graphics of scenery, drawing, and painting. In modern usage, combining the design of scenery, lighting, and costumes into a single visual concept.

Scoop Slang for ellipsoidal reflector floodlight.

Sharp Focus Narrow-beam focus of a spotlight.

Shoe (1) Special construction on the end of the toggle rail, the internal framing member of a flat. (2) Framed platform to encase the legs of furniture for protection on tour.

Shop Order A lighting rental equipment list for the purpose of bids.

Short Slang for short circuit, the term for the escape of electricity from its prescribed path.

Show Portal Framed teaser and tormentor designed especially for the show.

Shutter A beam-framing device located at the aperture of an ellipsoidal reflector spotlight.

Slash A diagonal beam of side

lighting on a stage drapery or window curtain creating an arbitrary pattern of light.

Snatch Block Pulley block with removable side to permit its insertion into rigging or tackle system without having to rethread all the line.

Snatching To hook and unhook a flown piece of scenery during the shift.

Spike Mark on floor to locate the working position of scenery or properties.

Spot Focus Narrow beam focus.

Spot Line A fixed line spotted on the gridiron directly over its working position.

Spotlight A lighting instrument with a lens that throws an intense light on a defined area. The term is often misapplied to other lighting instruments.

Spot Sheave The special placement of a loft sheave on the gridiron for an additional or single running line.

Stab Low trim or tie-off on the bottom rail of the pin-and-rail flying system.

Stage Left and **Stage Right** see Left stage and Right stage.

Stage Peg and Plug Bolt-threaded peg which fits into an inside threaded plug.

Stage Screw Screw-threaded peg.

Strike Take down a setting. Remove properties or lights.

Sunday Knot used to clew or hold several lines together.

Surround or **Shroud** Carry-off platforms that surround a turntable.

Switchboard Fixed or movable panel with switches, dimmers, and so forth to control the stage lights.

Tails Lines dropped from a batten to hang scenery several feet below the batten.

Teaser Top or horizontal member of the adjustable frame downstage of the setting.

Top Hat see Funnel.

Tormentor Side or vertical members of the adjustable frame downstage of the setting.

Traps System of openings through the stage floor.

Trick Line Small line used to trigger a breakaway or trick device.

Trim Mark designating the height of a line set. **High Trim** Height of a flown piece when in *out* position. **Low Trim** Height of flown piece when in an *in* (or working) position.

Tripping Raising a piece of soft scenery from the bottom as well as from the top.

Tungsten-Halogen An improved form of the incandescent filament lamp which contains a small quantity of a halogen gas in the bulb.

Up and Down Reference to scenery sitting perpendicular to the footlights.

Upstage On the stage but away from the audience.

USA United Scenic Artists. Theatrical union for scenic artists; scenery, costume, and lighting designers; and allied crafts.

Voltage The pressure behind electrical flow.

Wagon A platform on casters.

Wattage An electrical term for the rate of doing work.

Wash Low angle front-of-house lighting sources which illuminate in a general manner.

Wild Hinged portion of a setting that is free to move.

Wing In the commercial theatre the term *single wing* refers to the basic unit of framed scenery, commonly called a *flat* in the noncommercial theatre.

Wings Area offstage right and left, stemming from the era of wings and backdrops.

X-Rays Old expression designating the first row of border lights.

Zone A single stage-left to stage-right lighting area; most often used in dance lighting.

Additional Reading on Scene Design

The following books are recommended as additional reading to increase the reader's understanding of the philosophy and historical background of scene design as part of the art of theatre.

THE DESIGN CONCEPT

Appia, Adolphe. "*Adolphe Appia: A Gospel for Modern Stage.*" Theatre Arts Monthly, August 1932.
    Entire issue devoted to Appia's influence on present-day scene and lighting design.

Bay, Howard. *Stage Design.* New York: Drama Book 1978.

Brockett, Oscar G. *History of the Theatre.* Boston: Allyn & Bacon, 1977.

Brockett, Oscar G. *The Theatre: An Introduction,* 4th ed. New York: Holt, Rinehart and Winston, 1979.

Burian, Jarka. *The Scenography of Josef Svoboda.* Middletown, Conn.: Wesleyan University Press, 1971.

Cheney, Sheldon. *Stage Decoration.* New York: Blom, 1967.

Clay, James H., and Krempel, Daniel. *The Theatrical Image,* New York: McGraw-Hill, 1967.

Craig, Edward Gordon. *On the Art of the Theatre.* New York: Theatre Arts Books, 1956.

Craig, Edward Gordon. *Toward a New Theatre.* New York: Blom, 1968.

Fuerst, Walter R., and Hume, Samuel J. *Twentieth Century Stage Dec-*

oration; Vol. 1, text; Vol. 2, ill. New York: Dover, 1968.

Gascoigne, Bamber, *World Theatre.* Boston: Little, Brown, 1968.

Gassner, John. *Directions in Modern Theatre and Drama.* New York: Holt, Rinehart and Winston, 1965.

Gorelik, Mordeca. *New Theatres for Old.* New York: Samuel French. 1975.

Izenour, George. *Theatre Design.* New York: McGraw-Hill, 1979.

Jones, Robert E. *The Dramatic Imagination.* New York: Duell, Sloan & Pearce, 1941.

Kernodle, George R. *From Art to Theatre.* Chicago: University of Chicago Press, 1965.

Mielziner, Jo. *Designing for the Theatre.* New York: Atheneum, 1965.

Nicoll, Allardyce. *Theatre and Dramatic Theory.* London: Greenwood, 1962.

Oenslager, Donald M. *The Theatre of Donald Oenslager.* Middletown, Conn.: Wesleyan University Press, 1978.

Oenslager, Donald M. *Scenery, Then and Now.* New York: Russell & Russell, 1966.

Pierson, William H. J. F., and Davidson, Martha (editors). *Arts of the United States* (Stage Design section). New York: McGraw-Hill, 1960.

> A collection of color slides assembled by the University of Georgia under a grant by the Carnegie Corporation of New York. Contains an excellent essay by Donald Oenslager on U.S. scene design.

Simonson, Lee. *The Art of Scenic Design.* Westport: Greenwood, 1973.

Simonson, Lee. *The Stage is Set.* New York: Ayer, 1975.

Welker, David. *Theatrical Set Design.* Boston: Allyn & Bacon, 1979.

DESIGN APPLICATION

The following are recommended to broaden knowledge of the practicable application of design principles to modern theatre practices and related theatrical forms.

Bretz, Rudy. *Techniques of Television Production,* 2nd ed. New York: McGraw, 1962.

Garrick, David. *Art and Design of British Film* New York: Ayer, 1972.

Dean, Alexander and Carra, Lawrence. *Fundamentals of Play Directing,* 3d ed. New York: Holt, Rinehart and Winston, 1974.

Hainaux, René (ed.) *Stage Design Throughout the World Since 1960.* New York: Theatre Arts, 1972.

Hainaux, René (ed.) *Stage Design Throughout the World Since 1970.* New York: Theatre Arts, 1975.

Levin, Richard. *Television by Design.* London: Bodley Head, 1961.

Nagler, Alois. *Source Book in Theatre History.* New York: Dover, 1952.

Payne, Darwin R. *Materials and Crafts of the Scenographic Model.* Carbondale: Southern Illinois University Press, 1976.

Payne, Darwin R. *The Scenographic Imagination.* Carbondale: Southern Illinois University Press, 1981.

Southern, Richard. *Proscenium and Sightlines.* New York: Theatre Arts Books, 1964.

DRAWING AND PAINTING

The following books are recommended to the student scene designer to help develop his skill as a visual artist and draftsman.

Albers, Josef. *The Interaction of Color.* New Haven: Yale University Press, 1975.

Birren, Faber. *A Grammar of Color,* based on Munsell. New York: Van Nostrand Rienhold, 1969.

Chevreul, M. E. *The Principles of Harmony and Contrast of Colors.* New York: Reinhold, 1981.

Color Harmony Manual, Ostwald Theory of Color.

> Limited ed., expertly presented Chicago: Container Corporation of America, 1948.

Graves, Maitland. *The Art of Color and Design.* New York: McGraw-Hill, 1951.

Guptill, Arthur L. *Drawing in Pen and Ink.* New York: Reinhold, 1961.

Itten, Johannes. *The Art of Color.* New York: Van Nostrand Reinhold, 1973.

Jacobson, Egbert. *Basic Color: An Interpretation of the Ostwald Color System.* Chicago: Paul Theobald, 1952.

Jones, Tom Douglas. *The Art of Light and Color.* New York: Van Nostrand Reinhold, 1972.

Kepes, Gyorgy. *The Nature and the Art of Motion.* London: Studio, 1965.

Munsell Book of Color. Baltimore: Munsell Color Co., 1942.

Ostwald, Wilhelm. *The Color Primer.* New York: Van Nostrand Reinhold, 1969.

Parker, W. Oren. *Sceno-Graphic Techniques.* New York: Drama Book Publishers, 1964.

Patten, Lawton, and Rogness, Milton. *Architectural Drawing,* rev. ed. Dubuque, Iowa: William C. Brown, 1971.

Pope, Arthur. *The Language of Drawing and Painting.* Cambridge, Mass.: Harvard University Press, 1949.

FURNITURE AND DECORATIONS

The following are recommended as general reference material for designing furniture and decorating interiors.

Aronson, Joseph. *The Encyclopedia of Furniture,* 3rd ed. New York: Crown, 1968.

Gottshall, Franklin H., *How to Make Colonial Furniture.* New York: Macmillan, 1980.

Grant, Ian (editor). *Great Interiors.* London: Hamlyn, 1971.

Hardy, Kay. *Beauty Treatments for the Home.* New York: Funk & Wagnalls, 1945.

Hayward, Helena (editor). *World Furniture.* London: Hamlyn, 1971.

Joel, David. *The Adventure of British Furniture, 1851–1951.* London: Theodore Brun, 1953.

Jones, Bernard E. *The Complete Woodworker*. Berkeley, Calif: Ten Speed Press, 1980.

Meyer, Franz S. *Handbook of Ornament*. New York: Dover, 1957.

Otto, Celia J. *American Furniture of the Nineteenth Century*. New York: Viking Press, 1965.

Potter, Margaret and Alexander. *Houses*. London: John Murray, 1948.

Potter, Margaret and Alexander. *Interiors*. London: John Murray, 1957.

Praz, Mario. *An Illustrated History of Furnishing*. New York: Braziller, 1964.

Richter, G. M. *The Furniture of the Greeks, Etruscans and Romans*. London: Phaidon, 1966.

Strange, T. Arthur. *A Guide to Collectors: English Furniture and Decoration*. London: McCorquodale, 1903. In the rare book class, but still an excellent compilation and analysis of seventeenth- and eighteenth-century English and French furniture, interior styles.

Strange, T. Arthur. *Historical Guide to French Interiors*. London: McCorquodale, 1903.

Wilson, Jose, and Leaman Arthur. *Decorating Defined*. New York: Simon and Schuster, 1970. A dictionary of decoration and design.

Additional Reading on Technical Production

The following books are recommended as additional reading to give the reader a greater insight into scenery construction techniques and general shop practices.

SCENERY CONSTRUCTION

Bowman, Ned. *Handbook of Technical Practice for the Performing Arts.* Winkinsbury, Pa.: Scenographic Media, 1972.

Bryson, Nicholas L. *Thermoplastic Scenery for the Theatre.* New York: Drama Bookshop, 1970.

Burris-Meyer, Harold, and Cole, Edward C. *Scenery for the Theatre,* rev. ed. Boston: Little, Brown, 1972.

The Complete Woodworker. New York: David McKay Co., n.d.

Cornberg, Sol, and Gebauer, Emanuel L. *A Stage Crew Handbook.* rev. ed. New York: Harper & Row, 1957.

Daniels, George. *How to Use Hand and Power Tools.* New York: Van Nostrand Reinhold, 1978.

Dykes Lumber Company, *Moulding Catalog,* No. 49. Dykes Lumber Co., 137 West 24th Street, New York, N.Y., 10011, n.d.

Feirer, John, and Hutchings, Gilbert. *Carpentry and Building Construction.* New York: Scribner, 1981.

Haines, Ray E. *Carpentry and Woodworking.* Princeton, N.J.: Van Nostrand, 1945.

Krenov, James. *Worker in Wood.* New York: Van Nostrand Reinhold, 1981.

Parker, H., and Kidder, F. E. *Architect's and Builder's Handbook.* New York: Wiley, 1931.

Ramsey, Charles G., and Sleeper, Harold R. *Architectural Graphic Standards,* 7th ed. New York: Wiley, 1981.

Salaman, R. A. *Carpentry Tools.* New York: Scribner, 1976.

Taylor, Douglas C. *Metalworking for the Designer and Technician.* New York: Drama Book Publishers, 1974.

U.S. Department of Agriculture, Forest Products Laboratory. *The Wood Handbook.* Agriculture Handbook #72. Washington, D.C. U.S. Government Printing Office, 1935.

THE HANDLING OF SCENERY

The following provide a more specialized knowledge of the various methods of moving scenery, backstage organization, and rigging techniques.

Burris-Meyer, Harold, and Mallory, Vincent. *Sound in the Theatre.* N.Y.: Theatre Arts, 1979.

Gassner, John. *Producing the Play,* with *New Scene Technicians' Handbook* by Philip Barber. New York: Holt, Rinehart and Winston, 1953.

Gillette, A. S. *Stage Scenery.* New York: Harper & Row. 3rd ed. 1980.

How to Put Rope to Work. Plymouth Cordage Company, North Plymouth, Mass.

Irving, J., and Searl. *Knots, Ties and Splices.* New York: Routledge & Kegan Paul, 1978.

Kranich, Freidrich. *Buhnintechinik der Gegenwart,* Vol. I. Berlin: R. Oldenbourg, 1929.

Rose, A. *Stage Effects.* New York: Dutton, 1920.

Southern, Richard. *Changeable Scenery.* London: Faber & Faber, 1952.

Southern, Richard. *Stage Setting.* London: Faber & Faber, 1937.

PAINTING AND PROPERTIES

The following are recommended to expand skill in scene-painting techniques and the building of properties.

Ashworth, Bradford. *Notes on Scene Painting,* edited by Donald Oenslager. New Haven, Conn.: Whitlock's, 1952.

Kenton, Warren. *Stage Properties and How to Make Them.* New York: Drama Books 1978.

Motley. *Theatre Props.* New York: Drama Books, 1976.

Pecktal, Lynn. *Designing and Painting for the Theatre.* New York: Holt, Rinehart and Winston, 1975.

Polunin, Vladimir. *The Continental Method of Scene Painting.* Princeton, N.J.: Princeton Book, 1980.

Stern, Lawrence. *Stage Management.* Boston: Allyn & Bacon, 1974.

GENERAL

The following books are recommended as supplementary reading in the generalized area of scene design, technical production, and stage lighting.

Adix, Vern. *Theatre Scenecraft.* Cloverlot, Anchorage, Ky.: Children's Theatre Press, 1957.

Bellman, Willard F. *Scene Design, Stage Lighting, Sound, Costume and Makeup.* New York: Harper & Row, 1983.

Friederich, Williard J., and Fraser, John H. *Scenery Design for the Amateur Stage.* New York: Macmillan, 1950.

Selden, Samuel, and Rezzuto, Tom. *Essentials of Stage Scenery.* New York: Appleton-Century-Crofts, 1972.

Theatre Design and Technology. The official journal of the U.S. Institute of Theatre Technology, 330 West 42nd St., New York, N.Y. 10036.

Additional Reading on Stage Lighting

The following books are recommended as supplementary reading, either to broaden the reader's view of the field or to assist him in understanding knotty problems. They would form an invaluable nucleus for the private library of anyone genuinely interested in the field.

The general list contains books of broad approach to the whole stage-lighting picture, and offers material of value in several facets of theatre lighting. The Supplementary titles contain matter related to specific aspects, and also include a few periodicals that frequently carry articles of interest to the lighting designer for the stage.

GENERAL

Bellman, Willard F. *Lighting the Stage: Art and Practice*, 2nd ed. New York: Chandler, 1974.

Bentham, Frederick. *The Art of Stage Lighting*, 2nd ed. New York: Theatre Arts Books, 1976.

Covers the field well, but for the American reader the British terminology is sometimes confusing.

Fuchs, Theodore. *Stage Lighting*. Boston: Little, Brown, 1929.

Many portions are outdated today, but there is much pure gold still to be found in it.

Gassner, John. *Producing the Play*, rev. ed. New York: Holt, Rinehart and Winston, 1953.

Contains a capsule survey of the field by some of Broadway's most successful lighting practitioners.

Gillette, J. Michael. *Designing with Light*. Palo Alto; Mayfield, 1978.

Kook, Edward F. *Images in Light for*

the *Living Theatre*. New York: privately printed, 1963.

McCandless, Stanley. *A Method of Lighting the Stage*. 4th ed. New York: Theatre Arts Books, 1958.

Though it does not go into the more technical aspects, this is probably the most influential book ever published on the subject.

McCandless, Stanley. *A Syllabus of Stage Lighting*, 11th ed. New York: Drama Book Publishers, n.d.

A reference book and dictionary of all stage-lighting terms.

Pilbrow, Richard, *Stage Lighting*, rev. ed. New York: Drama Book Publishers, 1979.

An extremely fine design book, but does not cover lighting mechanics.

Rosenthal, Jean, and Wertenbaker, Lael. *The Magic of Light*. Boston: Little, Brown, 1972.

Rubin, Joel E., and Watson, Leland H. *Theatrical Lighting Practice*. New York: Theatre Arts Books, 1954.

A survey of the usual lighting practices of all types and levels of dramatic production.

Sellman, H. D. *Essentials of Stage Lighting*. New York: Appleton-Century-Crofts, 1972.

Warfel, William. *Handbook of Stage Lighting Graphics*. New York: Drama Book Publishers, 1974.

Williams, Rollo G. *The Technique of Stage Lighting*. London: Pitman, 1952.

Especially good on color. British terminology may confuse.

SUPPLEMENTARY

Bureau of Naval Personnel. *Basic Electricity*. New York: Dover Publications. Inc., 1962.

Clear and simple presentation of the fundamentals of electricity. The best available text.

Colortran, Burbank, Calif. Equipment catalogues.

General Electric Company. Cleveland. *Fundamentals of Light and Lighting*, 1956.

Excellent material on color, sources, and behavior of light.

General Electric Company. Cleveland. *Large Lamp Bulletin*.

Almost a textbook on sources. Excellent illustrations.

GTE Sylvania Lighting Handbook, 7th ed. Danvers, Mass.: GTE Sylvania Lighting Center, 1985.

Very good information on lamps and basic lighting considerations.

Illuminating Engineering Society, New York, *IES Lighting Handbook*.

Pertinent information on color, instruments, equipment, and use.

Kliegl Bros., New York. Equipment catalogues.

Strand Century Company, New York. Equipment catalogues.

Tabs.

This little magazine is brought out four times a year by Strand Electric and Engineering Co., Ltd., London and is available by writing to Rank Strand, P.O. Box 51, Great West Road, Brentford, Middlesex TW8 9HR, England.

Theatre Crafts.

Published nine times a year by Theatre Craft Associates, P.O. Box 630, Holmes, PA 19043.

Lighting Dimensions.

Published seven times a year by Lighting Dimensions Publishing, Inc., P.O. Box 471, South Laguna, CA 92677.

Index